Reprobates

By the same author

Donne: The Reformed Soul

Reprobates

The Cavaliers of the English Civil War

JOHN STUBBS

W. W. Norton and Company

New York • London

Copyright © 2011 by John Stubbs

First American Edition 2011

First published in Great Britain by Viking,
a publishing division of Penguin Books Ltd.

For information about special discounts for bulk
purchases, please contact W. W. Norton Special Sales at
specialsales@wwnorton.com or 800-233-4830

Manufacturing by Courier Westford
Production manager: Anna Oler

Library of Congress Cataloging-in-Publication Data

Stubbs, John, 1977–
Reprobates : the cavaliers of the English Civil War /
John Stubbs. — 1st American ed. 2011.
    p. cm.
Includes bibliographical references and index.
ISBN 978-0-393-06880-1 (hardcover)
1. Great Britain—History—Civil War, 1642–1649.
2. Great Britain—Courts and courtiers—History—17th century.
3. Great Britain—Intellectual life—17th century.
4. Great Britain—Civilization—17th century. I. Title.
DA415.S78 2011
942.06′2—dc22

                                        2011013849

W. W. Norton & Company, Inc.
500 Fifth Avenue, New York, N.Y. 10110
www.wwnorton.com

W. W. Norton & Company Ltd.
Castle House, 75/76 Wells Street, London W1T 3QT

1 2 3 4 5 6 7 8 9 0

For Katja, Lana and Martin

For the People are naturally not valiant, and not much cavalier.

– Sir John Suckling

Note on the Text

Superscribed numerals refer to notes at the end of the text, which are mainly bibliographical. Early modern spelling has been preserved except where it would no longer be intelligible to the general reader. Dates are given according to new style – i.e. following a calendar beginning on 1 January rather than on 25 March.

Contents

Introduction

1

In mid-March 1641, a military rider was dispatched to London from a defeated army in the north. Captain John Chudleigh bore a letter from a council of officers at York intended for their commander-in-chief, the Earl of Northumberland. 'Wee complayne as gentleman,' they wrote. They were owed pay, they were supporting their men out of their own pockets, and they were despised in the towns and villages where they were billeted. But it was more important to them that they be allowed to redeem their honour against the rebel Scottish army currently occupying the north-east of England. Their forces had been routed by the Scots at Newburn the summer before.

The capital Chudleigh entered on 21 March was on the verge of a coup d'état. The king was being plucked of his powers by Parliament: his two chief councillors faced a trial for their lives. Mobs regularly took to the streets demanding the head of 'Black Tom Tyrant' – Thomas Wentworth, Earl of Strafford, Lord Lieutenant of Ireland.

Given the urgency of his assignment, it was strange that Chudleigh did not immediately seek out Northumberland, who harboured grievances of his own from the worsening quarrel. For instead, on riding past the mews and into the rambling precincts of the palace of Whitehall, he shared the letter with the poet laureate, Sir William Davenant, a playwright and masque-maker with an amiable bearing and a ruined countenance.

Davenant was both troubled and excited by what he read. The officers' words were formal and restrained, but the depth of feeling behind them was obvious and sent a stronger message – this, he told Chudleigh, was a matter 'of greater consequence than he imagined'. He persuaded the captain to come and meet some friends.

Chudleigh may already have been acquainted with Sir John Suckling, infamous for his losses at the card table and the bowling green, and for his drubbing in a dispute over an heiress. Only a complete stranger to the court, meanwhile, would have been unfamiliar with Henry Jermyn, the queen's favourite. Davenant convened their meeting hastily, ushering in the courier to a back-room and urging him to share the contents of the letter once more. Chudleigh was willing, yet again, to do so.

Suckling and Davenant were brother officers and veterans of the two disastrous campaigns against the Scottish rebellion. Suckling and Jermyn were also long-standing associates, although a pair of figures less alike would be difficult to find. Suckling was a slight, 'light-timbered', almost boyishly built man; Jermyn, the court's most notorious philanderer, was louche and heavy-limbed, with the shoulders of a drayman and the backbone – said Andrew Marvell – of an elephant. Both, however, were equally coiffeured – Suckling with a well-brushed reddish mane – attired in rustling silks, and marked by an arrogant demeanour. Both also shared the burden of disgrace. Jermyn had returned not long before from banishment. He had been packed off to France after one of the queen's ladies-in-waiting became pregnant with his child.

The two courtiers agreed with Davenant. The letter meant more than the messenger could know; and could be made to mean more than its writers intended. With practised circumspection Jermyn asked Chudleigh if he might show the letter to the queen. At this point Chudleigh remembered himself. He refused to leave the paper with them before delivering it to Northumberland.[1]

Why should this meeting of minor personages matter, to the civil war which was to follow or to the longer course of English history? Davenant was the chief writer of royal entertainments. His contemporaries noted him chiefly by his all but destroyed nose, burnt off by a cure for syphilis. Suckling was a gambler and a showman. Jermyn was rumoured to be the queen's lover. Meanwhile Chudleigh had a walk-on, walk-off part in the conspiratorial drama. When he rode from London a week later, bearing notes for his comrades in the north, his significance in the larger story came to an end.

The hasty conference established in the minds of Suckling, Jermyn and Davenant that they might rely on the army to come south and take London for the king. They could set in motion a plot which, until that point, had seemed little more than fantasy. They were willing to use force against Parliament, to free the king's chief minister and regain control of the capital. Now it appeared that the military lay at their disposal. The impression they took from their interview with Chudleigh placed them, for the first time, in a state of civil war. It also brought about the creation of a faction and the coining of a byword for impractical heroics, dash, disdain and debauchery. When Davenant, Suckling and Jermyn met the dusty horseman on that early spring day in 1641, they were courtiers of varying influence in an embattled royal entourage. When they let Chudleigh go on his way, displeased at his reluctance to give up his missive but stirred by the sea-change it suggested, they merited the name their enemies would cast upon them in the streets: they were cavaliers.

The predicament of King Charles was truly dire; and he shouldered his share of the blame. In 1639 he had faced a rebellion from his subjects in Scotland. His campaign that year to crush the Scottish covenant ended in an anti-climax that his officers found humiliating. The next year he took up arms against the Scots again; and this time his forces were routed. In the meantime the situation in England had shifted against him. Mistakes in foreign policy touched old insecurities. Long-held grudges against his rule rose up at the worst possible moment. Yet he needed money for his war in the north, and for this he was obliged to summon a Parliament for the first time in eleven years. A strong party of critics in the House of Commons, directed by a set of dissatisfied peers, insisted on reparation for old wrongs before they would grant the king funds. He dismissed them disgustedly. Recalled, however, after his army's defeat in the summer of 1640, the Commons began forcing Charles to give up key powers and renounce much-hated ministers. The Archbishop of Canterbury was locked up in the Tower. Other councillors fled – one making for France in a rowboat.

Charles's dictator in Ireland, the Earl of Strafford, walked calmly into the lions' den. He too was imprisoned by order of Parliament, and was put on trial for his life in the spring of 1641, when Davenant, Suckling and other court-based conspirators began to think of taking action. As the year softened, their thoughts took shape in a climate of deepening chaos. A respite in the summer that year was then violently broken by the onset of rebellion in Ireland. Clashes broke out in the streets of

Westminster between demobbed officers defending the king and crowds of petitioners protesting on behalf of Parliament. 'And from those contestations,' recalled the chief royalist chronicler of the time, 'they who were looked upon as servants to the King being then called "*Cavaliers*," and the other of the rabble [were] contemned and despised under the names of "*Roundheads*".'[2]

These two camps afforded compelling caricatures. Everyone who knows anything about the civil wars which ensued in each of Charles's three kingdoms knows that those wars were fought between cavaliers and roundheads. In myth the cavaliers were elegant gentlemen, chivalrous if sometimes dissipated, while the roundheads were religious and social revolutionaries. Everyone can picture him, the cavalier, with his lovelocks, his broad hat, his mantle and bucket-topped boots, the basket-handled rapier at his side, a buskin covering his satin doublet. The roundhead, meanwhile, is a more prosaic character, his cropped hair suggesting that he served in peacetime as an apprentice, his clothes plain, his armour better made and more efficient, betokening the higher levels of equipage and organization which would eventually defeat King Charles. He despises luxury and mere show; he believes in and follows the Word of God, not the ornaments and vestments to be found in the king's Church.

In reality 'roundheads' and 'cavaliers' looked similar, depending on their rank. There were many officers in Parliament's army who dressed every bit as dandily as Suckling or Jermyn; and many in the king's service who frowned on such luxurious garments as effeminate and decadent. The enlisted men on both sides came from labouring or manufacturing backgrounds, and were equally likely to wear their hair short – because it made sense practically or because an indenture required it.

The king himself at times looked awkward among his glamorous courtiers, and for some that loomed large among his failings. 'It is fit for the Kinge to doe somethinge extraordinary,' Suckling told Jermyn, in a letter which shortly found its way to the press. Others saw strength in Charles's willingness to make concessions to Parliament, as they did in his characteristic reserve and reticence, his stiffness of manner and discomfort with levity. Who more than Charles, in fact, was so puritanical in his private and public worship? He spent hours before bed and on rising in prayer and meditation, and would insist on hearing part of the liturgy before eating – even on his hunting trips, no matter how late he came in or how hungry he and his servants were. He was scrupulous to a fault in attending daily chapel, and insisted that a great many of his nobles joined him. He was at best, then, an imperfect cavalier.

His one stroke of pure panache came early in adulthood when, on an impulse, he and the royal favourite Buckingham rode unattended all the way to Spain. He journeyed to Madrid to court the Spanish Infanta Maria in person; and the mission, for all its show of gallantry, was an unqualified disaster. The episode marked a turning point in Charles's life and in his politics, and a chapter will be devoted to it in due course. After another string of military catastrophes in the late 1620s, the young king became cautious in the extreme in his attitude to arms. He insisted on quiet and mannerly behaviour in his court. Through this, and through his handling of the crisis before the civil war, he gained an unwarranted reputation as a somewhat shambling, thin-blooded character. Yet while his icy reserve concealed the doubts inherent in a thoughtful, introverted personality, he never made a poor show in the saddle. 'He was a person, tho' born sickly, yet who came thro' temperance and exercise, to have as firm and strong a body, as most persons I ever knew, and throughout all the fatigues of the wars, or during his imprisonment, never sick.'[3]

The civil wars determined the future of Britain and Ireland. They opened the modern phase of a struggle to define where power lay – in the monarch or in Parliament, in the peerage or in the Commons – and to draw a line between Church and state. Within that ongoing story, the cavalier and the puritan are potent archetypes. The puritan upholds the work ethic and the will to give up pleasure, scourging the soul for its flaws. In the cavalier we have the individualist, more attuned to the passing moment and in greater touch with his desires. He too, though, is capable of self-sacrifice. He sets his life at a pin's fee, throws himself into the breach for a fleeting triumph or resounding gesture.

If the puritan is more dominant in recent times, present in the astonishing intellectual and physical achievements of the modern era – achieved at crushing human cost – the cavalier also surfaces at crucial moments. He is present erratically rather than constantly. We can glimpse him, for example, in Marlborough's campaigns, in a number of colonial last stands and, later still, among 'the few', the long-haired fighter pilots of 1940.

'Cavalier' came to denote the allegiances of half the English nation – and by extension of all those who supported the king in his three kingdoms. From the 1640s on, cavaliers were active across England, Scotland, Ireland and Wales; yet the word took its social, political and indeed literary associations from a particularly English social context, pertinent above all to the English civil war (which is to say, the English dimension of the armed conflict across the British and Irish islands). Yet the sense it carried at the beginning of the war was more specific still.

Thinking of the civil wartime cavaliers, it is probably the famous royalist generals who come to mind – Prince Rupert in particular, the Duke of Newcastle and Sir Ralph Hopton. The title 'cavalier' became a badge of partisan pride and the mark of a royalist gentleman; but it is important to remember that it started political life, in the early 1640s, as a term of abuse and reprobation. Militant supporters of Parliament were not thinking of a fine horseman or cavalry commander when they cornered a fashionable officer and branded him a cavalier. They were being ironic. Instead they saw a degenerate creature, bred up on Continental trifles and polluted with popery; a fraud and a boaster, a glossy, superficial type, forever gambling what he had borrowed, in perpetual debt to his tailor. The first 'cavaliers', in short, were men of the kind who met John Chudleigh on that day in early spring 1641: the disreputable likes of Suckling and syphilis-scarred Davenant – prodigals and playboys.

As it happened, these two particular cavaliers were also poets, or in slightly heightened parlance, 'makers'; and through their inventions we can follow the cultural creation of the civil-war cavalier. These were the foot soldiers of degeneracy, with their loose lifestyles, and their poetry celebrating those lifestyles. Writing of Suckling's part in the army plot of 1641, the historian John Adamson recently described him as a virtual parody of the stock cavalier figure.[4] Similarly, the works of the poet Thomas Carew, a mutual friend of Suckling and Davenant, were singled out in Parliament for their hideous influence on public morality.

In their interviews with Chudleigh, in a side chamber in Whitehall or a back-room in a Westminster tavern, it is easy to see these characters as the roundheads saw them: courtly parasites, conspirators against the king's godly subjects. Yet, as scholars have begun insisting over the past thirty years or so, there was more to them than that: many who were supposedly cavaliers were reserved, devout characters and in many cases shared the concerns raised by the king's opponents. This caveat applies even to Suckling and Davenant. That they were labelled cavaliers at all, as historians now stress, was both unfortunate and inaccurate. For that implies that a cavalier faction existed before the civil war: when it was the war, in fact, that changed the meaning of the word.[5]

Since we cannot cancel the term 'cavalier' in the record altogether, we should try to comprehend the depth and variety of qualities it actually denoted. The wits gathered in these pages can help us do just that. Through Davenant, Suckling and others, in a largely forgotten pocket of writers, we gain a view of both the complacencies and the anxieties of the age that made them, and of the world that was altered for ever by the civil wars.

A famous poem, commonly viewed as a cavalier anthem, urged maidens to 'Gather ye rosebuds while ye may,' and marry while time permitted. It is in fact an almost austere lyric, gaining pathos from its publication at a time when the number of young husbands available to 'the virgins' had been vastly and violently reduced. Our sense of this old standard should also change on closer acquaintance with its author. Robert Herrick, the 'cavalier' who wrote the poem, was an Anglican priest who avoided all personal exposure to war after travelling as a chaplain on a disastrous naval mission to the French coast in 1627. The thousands of Englishmen who died off La Rochelle, and the countless more who fought as mercenaries in the Continent's ongoing wars of religion, gave a limp to the cavalier swagger – and a plangency which is often missed in Herrick's deceptively simple verse.

A better symbol for our classical sense of the cavalier is the diverted songbird in a lesser-known poem by Davenant:

> The Lark now leaves his watry Nest
> And climbing, shakes his dewy Wings;
> He takes this window for the East;
> And to implore your Light, he Sings,
> Awake, awake, the morn will never rise
> Till she can dress her Beauty at your Eyes.[6]

This is a fitting hymn for 'cavalier poets' – altering course by pure instinct towards such beauty; they would, however, swerve once more to speak scornfully of the same attractions if their attentions were neglected or rebuffed. These poets were champions of youth and love, frank about their desires and distrustful of matrimony. But the same writers also thought and wrote intently on friendship and the role of art, on matters of religion and political philosophy. A close friend of Thomas Hobbes, Davenant came to see beauty and delight as socially constructive, a means of putting people in touch with their better natures.

One writer who comes to prominence in the following chapters would undoubtedly have protested at being put among such company. This is the statesman and historian Edward Hyde, eventually Earl of Clarendon and Lord Chancellor of England. He was indisputably a reluctant cavalier: although eventually the chief royalist chronicler of the mid-century's events, he entered the controversy between king and Parliament as a moderate, with deep reservations towards both parties. As his memoirs and majestic history of the age frequently remind us, he was an altogether more austere figure than the original 'gallant' cavaliers of Suckling and his ilk. Yet, as these works simultaneously indicate, he was never so very remote from their circles, however critically he viewed the Bacchanalia: his chief social gift, before greatness was thrust upon him, lay in his ability to mingle with all. Although a respectable married man for most of his life and thus no frequenter of disreputable places, he enjoyed social dinners and sociable drinking and was at times to be found at the gaming greens and tables on Piccadilly. In his post-war wandering and exile, even though troubled severely by gout, he was ever alive to the sometimes wearying magic of travel – enriching his autobiography with accounts of the characters, spectacles and incidents he came by. His crowning achievement, *The History of the Rebellion*, has all the tartness, cynicism and urbanity of lesser royalist wit, even though it takes those qualities to an unequalled level. He was no cavalier in the earlier senses of the word; but his testimony about the cavaliers is crucial. And, as portraits suggest, he too grew his hair down in lovelocks.

Writers such as Davenant and Suckling were important in literary terms, forming a bridge between their heroes Shakespeare and Jonson and the lighter literature of the Restoration. At street level they may have looked foppish, but on closer acquaintance many were thinkers, creators and moralists. And in a period that crushed a great many people – including the most powerful – into claustrophobic categories, they were broader souls, at once coarser and finer than most, more comfortable with irony than with absolutes. They give us something apart from the rhetoric of the age, with its high sectarian stakes, its disputes over the divine rights of kings or the priesthood of the individual soul. They direct us back to the passing moment, the transient plenty of life. They were not, of course, free of the standard xenophobia and misogyny of the time, nor of the class bias peculiar to their courtier lifestyle; indeed part of their historical value resides in their shameless expression of those preconceptions in their poetry, drama and correspondence. But their literary talent and psychological realism make them precious witnesses of an age in which extremism became the norm. This book tells the story of that time from their perspective, covering approximately the reigns of Charles I and II.

2

The making of the cavaliers involved more than the formation of an army or the manufacture of a social stereotype. Understanding it means learning about the variety of temperaments and attitudes which, rightly or wrongly, were tarred with the same war-paint in the early 1640s. Amending such brushwork involves drawing nicer distinctions: the portraiture of the court artist van Dyck, for example, does not embody a cavalier style, and his subjects were certainly not all cavaliers, but the painter himself did conform to the popular image of a fashionable cavalier gallant. Conversely, Thomas Carew, in life a reserved and consistently pacific person, was nevertheless taken to typify the cavalier attitude through his early reputation for promiscuity and his scandalous erotic 'raptures'. Restoring the complexity of such figures means following their experiences abroad and at home, the art they made and the literature they enjoyed; and it means taking the measure of the period in which their outlook was defined.

Perhaps the most surprising thing about the way the word itself was used is that, before 1642, 'cavalier' usually occurs in non-military contexts. The historian Kevin Sharpe, in his now classic study of *The Personal Rule of Charles I*, suggests that it referred most often to a 'gallant or a gay blade'; it was an epithet encompassing both the more and less reputable elements in the king's heterogeneous court.[7] Something in the very odour of the word suggested that these original cavaliers – fashionable, high-spirited and undoubtedly prone to duelling – were less comfortable in the field than at their urban recreations.

One of their favourite haunts is a good place to watch the flow and counter-currents of their time: the 'private' theatre of Blackfriars on the north side of the Thames. Once a hall belonging to a dissolved priory, the location affords a long view of English history.

The theatre is easily reached, a short walk past Shoemaker Row and the other lanes of merchants' houses when you turn off the straggling thoroughfare of Ludgate Hill down one of seemingly innumerable alleys. Alternatively, by river, it is a short pull from the waterside mansions of the Strand or Whitehall itself to a sometimes precarious wharf, where passage to the steps is hampered by many other boats and barges. By carriage, it is always difficult to get near to the front door, so busy are the streets that seem to narrow the closer one gets, complaints about the racket descending from the windows.

Long before it hosted tragedies and comic misunderstandings, Blackfriars was wholly accustomed to dramatic struggles. In the first half of the sixteenth century, in the days of Henry VIII's Great Matter, tranquillity could still be found in the orchards and gardens to the west of the priory buildings by London's great river. But the priory complex, at the south-west corner of the walled city, sat at the hub of the kingdom. A two-storey gallery across Fleet Ditch connected Blackfriars to Bridewell Palace, the main London residence of King Henry. To the north-east lay St Paul's, its legendary spire still intact, harpooning the clouds bringing lightning to strike it. At ground level, like the cathedral, Blackfriars was something of a thoroughfare for citizens, and those wishing to travel by river could wander down a lane from the top entrance, past the church and vast refectory, to the water gate and the traffic of the Thames. The intersecting cloisters themselves were no isolated conclave for the Dominican friars whose dark robes gave the priory its popular name. The friars, unlike monks, were bound by their vows to go out and seize hold of the world, not to retire from it. For centuries they had roamed London's streets and beyond in pairs, begging their bread and spreading the word. They had no fear of living beside royalty. Hundreds of years before, when Blackfriars was still relatively young and the Dominicans needed more space, they were permitted to change the very line of London's Roman walls.

The proximity of the palace and the court, since a fire in the royal apartments at Westminster, politicized the priory further: it became the regular venue for Parliament. There was, however, nothing in its past to equal the divisive affair of state fought out in the summer of 1528. Early in the morning of 21 June King Henry left Bridewell and was called into the priory's Parliament Chamber to challenge the legality of his marriage to Catherine of Aragón. This would open the way for him to marry his new love, Anne Boleyn. His councillors sat as judges behind a table covered with cloth of gold. For the first time in English history a monarch was summoned by his subjects to account for himself, when the call went out for 'Harry, King of England' to enter the chamber.

This was the 'Great Matter': Catherine's spirited defence, the predetermined verdict and the women of London's mass outrage at her abandonment formed the opening scenes of a drama that transformed the nation. To get his divorce, Henry renounced the jurisdiction of the pope and made himself head of the Church in England. The English Reformation began. Ten years after the trial, the black-robed Preaching Friars of London, familiar presences in the city since 1275, were dispossessed, as the monasteries across the kingdom were dissolved and their vast properties distributed among the new Protestant ascendancy. Having been tacked ever more closely to the royal palace, Blackfriars was now absorbed entirely, reconstituted, and split into smaller domiciles. Some of its green spaces provided private gardens. Many of its ancient fruit trees were felled and dragged away to make room for more building.

A whiff of controversy lingered over the precincts after Catherine's rough treatment, for towards the end of the sixteenth century, Blackfriars remained a subject for opprobrium, and a source of trouble to its neighbours. In 1576 a section of the old priory changed nature again, when one of the great chambers was leased to the master of the Chapel Royal choir for the boys to have their rehearsals ('For that it is meet that our Chapel Royal should be furnished with well-singing children from time to time'). This was closed, however, under protest from city officials, less than ten years later. Then at the end of the century, 'a collection of rooms, large and small, cellars and yards and including seven great upper rooms' was taken over by the theatrical entrepreneur James Burbage, who needed a new venue. The terms of the licence made it clear that this was to be a private auditorium, not a public establishment open to all. Disgruntled neighbours and critics were not convinced, but despite periodic rushes of plague that shut all public places down, this time the theatre's roots held. The smell of mutton-wax candles and oil from the cressets expunged any lingering odour of incense.

Local residents were quickly up in arms again, arguing that the theatre would become intolerable because of the 'vagrant and lewd persons' consorting there. The protests were sustained over the following decades, and the furthest they came to closing down Blackfriars was in 1619: 'for such is the unruliness of some of the resorters to that house . . . in those narrow and crooked streets, that many hurts have heretofore been done.'[8]

In truth, the indoor theatre attracted a more well-mannered – at least wealthier – clientele than the open-roofed round theatres on the other side of the river. It was, admittedly, no more a 'private' theatre than its competitors; but here one did not see the regular pitched battles that took place between 'gentlemen' spectators and apprentices in Southwark. Yet as the seventeenth century progressed it became associated nevertheless with a more aristocratic form of delinquency, a dilettante set of which Sir John Suckling was one of many champions. There was no remedy for what Davenant dubbed the 'gallant humour of the age': for this was:

> *London*, the Spheare of Light and harmony,
> Where still your Taverne Bush is green, and flourishing,
> Your Punke [prostitute] dancing in Purple,
> With Musick that would make a Hermit frisk
> Like a young Dancer on a Rope.[9]

Accordingly, one saw very few long-gowned guildsmen or aldermen in the audience. The actors' neighbours – hard-working merchants and shopkeepers – kept up their complaints at the danger, noise and inconvenience of the growing numbers of carriages congesting the narrow streets around the theatre on performance afternoons. The nearby feather merchants (or 'feathermen') were among the bitterest. Even among those with no specific ideological objections, there was a dislike of the bustle, of the volatility surrounding the playhouse and the frequent riotry of the theatregoers: 'sometimes all their streets cannot contain them,' remarked a stern order of 1619, 'that they endanger one the other, break down stalls, throw down men's goods from their shops . . . whereby many times quarrels and effusion of blood hath followed.'[10]

Drama sent people out full of possibilities, voices raised, re-running half-remembered dialogues with their companions, simply enlivened by a funny show, or aware of things they had not known about themselves before; and that, if the regular protests and petitions are to be believed, did not feel safe. A good sermon could leave one feeling shattered, awestruck, determined to reform, but nothing else in early modern London had the same effect as theatre. The playhouse did not urge one to mend one's ways, but implied that human ways were tragically or comically unmendable. This could not be borne by those campaigning, sincerely and tirelessly, for greater civic order.

To the City Fathers and much of the citizenry, the more refined environment Blackfriars claimed to offer was only a charade to cover up decadence. The patrons and practitioners of the stage, in a phrase heard from the 1590s to the 1640s, were only so many 'roaring boys' – debauched assailants on true Christian behaviour.

The enemies of theatre had to wait a long time for their moment. But it came in 1642, as England joined Scotland and Ireland in the descent into civil war. Having been suspended for more than a decade, Parliament had reacted to troubles in the north and across the Irish Sea by attempting to take control of his council and the army away from the king. When the English war broke, the city was left in the hands of theatre's opponents. The playhouses were sealed.

The King's Men, Shakespeare and Burbage's old company, was thus immediately disbanded. Most of the troupe became cavaliers, joining the king's army, 'and like good Men and true, Serv'd their Old Master, tho' in a different, yet more honourable, Capacity.' One can only imagine what the pioneer stalwarts would have felt. As he watched the Globe burn thirty years earlier, John Heminge, founding member of the company, broke down weeping, and was lightly mocked:

> Then with swolne eyes, druncken Flemminges,
> Distressed stood old stuttering Heminges.[11]

He could be forgiven for crying now. At Blackfriars, the carriages no longer clustered around the old priory site. If the locals had not been full of worry or partisan anger, they might have enjoyed the peace in the streets in the evenings.

The occasional play was managed during the war, and now there was much pity for the starving players who put them on. At the interval in the fighting in 1647, while the king lay in Parliamentary custody and the authorities were preoccupied with his future, companies began performing openly across the city. Rudimentary theatres stirred again to life at The Cockpit in Drury Lane, Salisbury Court near Fleet Street, The Fortune in Golding Lane. The Red Bull in Clerkenwell, the roughest venue of them all, kept going longer than any of them. Performances, however, were still officially forbidden on the brisk day in January 1649 when Charles Stuart – no longer addressed officially by royal title – put his head to the block outside the Banqueting Hall at Whitehall. The diminutive, long-haired and plainly dressed prisoner had given a memorable performance at his trial, and met his end with long-practised composure. The blow of the axe brought out one of the city's most memorable moments of communal empathy. The crowd let out a visceral collective groan, as spontaneous as the gasp any murder or deposition had raised in the 'wooden O' in Southwark, or below the beamed ceiling at Blackfriars. Yet for many, even most, in the great crowd that day outside the palace, satisfaction followed the purely instinctual lurch of the gut. Finally, there seemed to be a chance of completing the work begun, indirectly, by Catherine of Aragón's bitter trial at Blackfriars more than a hundred years before. In 1655, at the height of Cromwell's English Commonwealth, derelict for some time, the old buildings were pulled down.

By then, Davenant had narrowly avoided a traitor's death, after many close shaves during the war. His old companion Suckling had committed suicide in Paris many years earlier, before the civil war proper even began, distraught at his country's course and brought low by the collapse of his personal fortunes. Others of the old school, including Davenant, sought peace with Cromwell. By the 1650s the hey-day of such men during the peaceful years of Charles's reign had acquired a strong nostalgic glow. This was an aura Davenant sought to recover in his post-war work and which was also nourished by a score of other writers, notably his friend John Aubrey, the antiquary and author of *Brief Lives*. Later chapters of this book will consider how relics of that former age were recovered or manufactured, and how the next generation of wits sought to regain identity and consensus.

But what must follow first is an account of the experience these survivors and their successors sought to commemorate, and a search for aspects of it they preferred to forget. For a key ingredient in almost any cavalier story is the disappointment or defiance of a father's hopes. From King Charles downward, this was a generation which defined itself by failing to meet paternal expectations – the demands of both natural and symbolic fathers, authorities ranging from James I to the old poet Ben Jonson. To speak of how that happened, it is necessary to visit decades that were turbulent enough before civil war resulted.

1. Fathers and Sons

He seem'd the Heir to prosp'rous Parents toiles;
Gay as young Kings, that woo in forraign Courts;
Or Youthful Victors in their *Persian* spoiles;
He seem'd like Love and Musick made for sports.

But wore his clothing loose, and wildly cast,
As Princes high with Feasting, who to wine
Are seldom us'd: shew'd warm, and more unbrac't
Than Ravishers, oppos'd in their designe.

— Davenant, *Gondibert*, Book III, Canto vi

1

Leaving Hyde Park, expunge the cold bulk of Marble Arch. There is no
imperial stone, no Victorian cast iron, no post-modern steel; there are no
tinted panels of inscrutable glass. Place yourself at the landward fringe,
north-west, of an irregular riverside city. You have approached London
the wrong way, reversing the route taken by those under sentence of
death. Only in recent times have the parklands behind you, formerly
royal hunting grounds, been open to commoners. Here at Tyburn you
might be edified by the spectacle of a hanging, perhaps twenty felons at
one go, on the sturdy derrick. From the sparse, open field on which the
gallows stands it is a long, melancholy drag up to St Giles-in-the-Fields,
once the site of a hostel for lepers, and still a place attracting unfortu-
nates. This is the route of the rag-tag Calvary run that travels one-way in
the opposite direction. The wagons bearing felons from Newgate stop
here for the condemned to be given a last cup of ale.[1]

Beyond St Giles, however, nearing Holborn, the surroundings
brighten. 'On the high street have ye many fair houses built, and

lodgings for gentlemen and such-like,' writes the chronicler Stow.[2] The signs of the bush are thicker on the ground and the houses lean over you like prepossessing drunkards. Further down the broad thoroughfare, towards Holborn Hill, stand large, exclusive mansions. This is a district of lawyers, scriveners, students and servants of the law: on the corner of the road which takes you up to Hampstead, the gatehouse of Gray's Inn leads into lawns and courtyards. Just before this, to the right, Chancery Lane runs down to Fleet Street, the Middle Temple and the City. Behind the street front, the trees are still patchily bare around the traders, riders and japers in Lincoln's Inn Fields.

One day late in February 1613, in the study of his home among the 'divers fair houses and gardens' in Chancery Lane, an elderly man can be found writing a letter. The room may be somewhat spare, yet the collection of books is comprehensive. The letter on the writing table is despondent, and it surely deepens the gentleman's irreversible frown as he writes. He came to fatherhood at an advanced stage of life, twenty years ago, and has never quite recovered.

He has been cheated of something near £9,000, almost the sum of his estate, in an investment in land. One of his sons, Cromer, is dying of a lingering disease which costs the old man forty shillings a day in medical expenses. The eldest, Mathew, only 'runneth vp and downe after houndes and hawkes,' while the other, Thomas, is at the Middle Temple – 'but I feare studieth the law very little'. Many a dreary and sorrowful day has passed since his last letter (he is writing to his nephew, a man of consequence), and yet all this has still not, inexplicably, been enough to still the letter-writer's hand; God will not grant him release. The kingdom's grief oppresses him too. He has lived to see the death of 'our hopefull prynce', the never-to-be Henry IX, the previous year. But the Princess Elizabeth's marriage to Count Frederick of the Palatinate has entirely passed him by, shut up as he has been with sorrow during the masques and nuptial celebrations.

The gentleman is Sir Mathew Carew, a Master of Chancery, gowned and grey. At the Court of Equity he carries much authority and commands great respect for his knowledge of the Civil Law. Beyond his immediate professional circle in Westminster Hall, his word is honoured rather than followed. The news is spreading that he is likely to lose his last farthing.

The letter is looking for a favour, though even Sir Mathew himself is unsure exactly what form that boon might take. In any case, writing it has filled an hour and brought the solace of articulation; it is sealed and dispatched. It will take a good while to reach Venice, where Sir Mathew's nephew is ambassador, crossing the Channel and making the trip over-land to the Adriatic coast. Sir Mathew may well forget it, tightening his brows, permanently knit by age and care, in anxious calculations as the spring comes unnoticed outside his windows:

> Now that the winters gone, the earth hath lost
> Her snow-white robes, and now no more the frost
> Candies the grasse, or casts an ycie creame
> Vpon the silver Lake, or Chrystall streame:
> But the warme Sunne thawes the benummed Earth,
> And makes it tender, gives a sacred birth
> To the dead Swallow; wakes in hollow tree
> The drowzie Cuckow, and the Humble-bee.[3]

Sir Mathew is oblivious to waking swallows and candied grass: 'benumbed Earth' fills up his mind; a tract of land that has bereft him of his fortune; a smaller plot that will receive his tired body.

It was in fact only a little later in 1613 that Thomas Carew, Sir Mathew's middle son, arrived in Venice to wait on Sir Dudley Carleton, the English ambassador, as a secretary. Born in 1594 or 1595, Thomas was eighteen at the most when he reached the English residence. He was careful in his dress, and tall, if not quite with the heavy build ascribed to him in later life; a younger son, but a gentleman of the Inns of Court, with a confident, somewhat severe and critical manner. The usual route to Venice was across the Alps, through the Mont Cenis pass under the guidance of incredibly hardy '*Marrons*', over the staggering path once travelled by King Arthur in the company of a bear.

The Venice Carew reached was already the city so clear yet elusive in the mind's eye today – Piazza San Marco, Ponte dei Sospiri, Ponte Rialto, the horses treading air above St Mark's were all components of the scene. St Mark's itself, fronted with plates of pink marble, sliced from the same perfect block and thus symmetrical, looked much the same, as did the broad magnificence of the Grand Canal. There was the same seasonal bother of high water, requiring walkways to be placed above the flood, the same liquid beauty of the place in sunlight, the same ghostliness in winter cloud.

It would be two centuries before the cult of the sublime would seize on Venice as its holy city, but despite their suspicions of the supposed venality of the place, the luxury goods (which they nevertheless bought and prized), the cost of things and the gondoliers who robbed, kidnapped or knifed you, travellers of Carew's time were helpless before its wonders. His acquaintance and almost exact contemporary James Howell said that Venice well deserved its title of 'the maiden city', and not only because she was 'never defloured by any Enemy since she had a being':

I protest to you, at my first landing I was for some days ravished with the high Beauty of this Maid, with her lovely Countenance. I admired her magnificent Buildings, her marvellous Situation, her dainty smooth neat Streets, whereon you may walk most days in the year in a Silk Stocking and Sattin-Slippers, without soiling them.

London's bourses – Gresham's bustling Royal Exchange and more recently the New Exchange – paled by comparison. Early modern travellers took a more mercantile and strategic view than the later aesthetes. Venice was, as Howell put it, 'a City that all *Europe* is bound unto, for she is her greatest Rampart against that huge Eastern Tyrant the *Turk* by sea'.[4] There was a sense that its sway might be passing; but no city state could be so successful for so long without lulls, without enemies and without critics. To Francisco de Quevedo, the acrid master of Spanish satire, the Venetian empire was 'the very anus, the drain and sink of monarchies, both in war and peace', doing nothing more but help 'the Turks to vex the Christians, and the Christians to gall the Turks'.[5]

It was not necessary to go on the Italian tour to have one's fancy caught and subverted by foreign influences – papism being much more dangerous than prostitution. The potential power of Venice over the imagination was an example of why parents and guardians were keen that the influence of travel should be censored and directed. For an elegant summary of the expectations a father, a supporting uncle or an elder brother might have of a young Englishman touring the Continent, we can take the views of Sir Philip Sidney, poet, soldier, and the model courtier of the previous generation. In 1578 Sidney wrote a long letter of advice to his brother Robert, who was then abroad, in which he set out his ideas on what should be taken from travel, and how it should be taken. He makes it clear that Robert should not travel merely for the sake of travelling:

Your purpose is being a Gentleman borne, to furnish your selfe with the knowledge of such thinges, as maie be serviceable to your Countriee, and fitt for your calling which certainelie standes not in the chaunge of ayre, for the warmest sonne makes not a wise man.[6]

The young English traveller was expected to fortify his character from his journeying, not to pick up exotic habits or flashy accoutrements. In that spirit, Sir Mathew Carew was relying on Sir Dudley Carleton, a sober sort of man, to keep an eye on Thomas, and keep him free of 'disguisements'. He could be reassured that his son was presented to persons of the highest quality. In Florence that first year Thomas met the connoisseur and collector the Earl of Arundel, enjoying a tour of the northern Italian kingdoms after escorting Princess Elizabeth and her husband, Frederick, to the Palatinate.[7] Also in the earl's party was Inigo Jones, the royal surveyor and designer, gathering ideas and techniques for courtly spectacles.

Such flourishes, such acquaintances were all fine and well: yet there was no escaping the fact that travel was a finishing touch to the making of a gentleman. Almost sixty years earlier, Carew's father, Sir Mathew, had luxuriated in his time abroad during the papist reign of Queen Mary. Twelve years he devoted to the study of languages and jurisprudence at Louvain, Paris, Padua, Bologna and Siena. On his return to England he wandered as deep as he could into the mazes of the law, becoming Master of Chancery in 1576.[8] Yet for all the honour and respect accrued, his fortunes in 1613 suggested he had lost touch with the gentry's basic concern: maintaining and acquiring property.

The crisis in the Carew estates that year contrasted painfully with the shrewd marketeering of successful landed families. Sir John Suckling the elder, for example, an accomplished courtier and Parliament man holding lands across the south-east and up into Norfolk, closed a deal he had long coveted on the Suffolk manor and advowson of Barsham. The moated house which came with the deeds was a seat in the old style; the hall and stately rooms built about a quadrangle. A spiral staircase ascended a tower on the eastern side, a romancey touch once highly practical in wilder times. It carried the astounding value of £4,000. For the time being, Suckling was unsure what to do with the place: he had bought it not from any need but to avoid the pain of losing its future returns. 'It is now mine,' he told his brother; 'and I trust that the name of the Sucklings shall inheritt and possess it, when I am dead and rotten.'[9] Thomas Carew seemed all but oblivious to such concerns; and in this respect he typified a neglect which many besides his father would observe in the coming generation.

On arriving back in England late in 1614, Carleton retained young Carew's services for his next posting, to The Hague, the following spring. He also gave solid practical and financial assistance to the family. Sir Mathew was ailing, and had been obliged to mortgage the property on Chancery Lane to a younger, more prosperous relative. Carleton responded by helping with a large loan, which freed his uncle of this burden. In addition Sir Mathew was heartened by Sir Dudley's 'good likeng of my sons service'. His greatest wish amidst his troubles was that 'Thomas must not [be] lauishe' while he wrestled with his debts. Of all Sir Dudley's gifts and acts of assistance, it was his moral guardianship of Thomas for which Sir Mathew was most grateful.

The venerable Master of Chancery therefore had a shock, in August 1616, when Thomas turned up at his door without warning. 'It was strange to me,' he immediately wrote to Carleton, 'to see my sonne Thomas appeer before me in my little parlour.' Carleton had apparently sent Thomas home to seek employment with a rather distant relative, and to apply for a post with the Earl of Arundel. Quite abruptly, it seemed, Thomas's former patron wanted him off his hands. Sir Mathew was alarmed, 'for I fear that if he be not narrowly loked vnto, and called from his wandering distractions, he wil soone overthrowe himself.' Thomas, he realized, was something of a free spirit. 'I doubt [fear] more of his idleness and lewd courses here, then I shold doe there.' His letter suggested that he had shown insufficient gratitude for Carleton's munifi-cence. But he closed saying that his eldest son, Mathew, having broken his promise many times, had finally left a greyhound at the Carletons' house in town as a gift for the ambassador.[10]

Sir Mathew questioned Thomas sternly and thoroughly as to what might have lowered Sir Dudley's regard for him. Aside from the pastoral considerations, Thomas's presence back in London increased the financial strain on his father. But Thomas, preoccupied with his 'wandering distractions', responded blankly to interrogation. He followed Carleton's instruction to seek a place with another patron, but got nowhere. In good faith, he kept his old master informed of his attempts; but as the first lord to whom he applied told him, 'my languages & whateuer seruiceable partes I had would rust in his seruice for want of vse.'[11] He had been trained for foreign service, and anything else was a waste of his talents.

Thomas saw his predicament as lying with no fault or action of his own. He seems to have believed that Carleton was merely concerned that he make further connections at home in England. A certain narcissism, something certainly beyond self-confidence, is detectable in his letters to Sir Dudley. He had not quite mastered the arts of supplication that his station required. He mentioned having had to 'prostitute' himself by asking for employment, and said that he would not feel 'disparaged' if a patron gave him his due and accepted him. He was a gentleman, and a gentleman deluxe, polished up in Italy: there was no need, as he saw it, to accept lower offers. Addressing Sir Dudley as his *primum mobile*, he fished for an invitation back to the Continent.

It was not offered. In the autumn of 1616, after weeks of circumspection, Sir Dudley revealed why he had sent Thomas away. The protégé had made highly offensive remarks about Lady Carleton in a private written exercise which had fallen into Sir Dudley's hands. He had also written disparagingly about the ambassador's horses. Like the diplomat he was, Sir Dudley had taken the insult to his wife, house and stable on the chin, and for the family's sake restrained any impulse to ruin his young relative; but his honour could not allow the secretary to remain with him.

Sir Mathew's reaction to this bombshell was vividly relayed to Sir Dudley by the messenger who had taken his letter in person to Chancery Lane. Watching the 'good old gent' read, he observed that when the old man 'came to that part, which did make knowne his sonnes foule offence, he burst out into these words (Gods boddy) and no sooner had he ended your Letter, but Mr Carew came into his studdy, whom presently he reviled before me, & told him, he had vtterly ouerthrowne his fortune'.

Thomas had no idea what his father was talking about. Sir Mathew thrust Carleton's letter into his hands, pointing a choppy finger at the passage which made the matter perfectly plain. Thomas skimmed through the paper (which has not, unfortunately, survived), and his response was revealing. The offence, he said coolly, 'was in no way worthy of blame' – he could hardly credit that Sir Dudley should be so upset, since what he had written was merely 'a thing done by him, not in dishonor of your Lordship or my Lady nor intended euer to be divulged, but only (as his owne words were) for his priuate ends and direction'. So that, then, made his comments perfectly innocent. In fact, Carleton could reasonably infer that Thomas felt it was he who had been wronged, by the intrusion into his personal papers. While Thomas stood unrepentant, Sir Mathew was devastated, and ordered him to write immediately 'an humble and submissiue letter' to his patron. Thomas said he would, the messenger reported, but Sir Dudley had yet to receive it. There is little sign that it was ever sent.[12]

Sir Mathew persisted in pleading for Sir Dudley to take Thomas back; though he did so by repeatedly stating his complete agreement with Sir Dudley's course of action. Thomas, he said, had 'irrecuperablye lost your lordships and my ladyes fauours'. Sir Mathew himself was entirely on their side. 'I am now so far deiected from any expectance of goodnes in hym, that he and I be now irreconciliable.' He was 'stupefied' that Thomas could have thought such things, let alone set them down, *although*, he trailed as an afterthought, 'I doe not think that his hart was in any ways drawen from eyther of you bothe how so euer he would set his pen a work.' He was a father betrayed by an ingrate; yet Sir Mathew's standard position in such transactions with his nephew – that of the victim – failed to melt Sir Dudley's resolve.

As for Thomas, he still felt he had right on his side. The affair revealed self-assurance steelier than mere blitheness, an attitude that would find its way into his writing. He was his own authority; he went by his own standards. What his father dismissed as 'wandering distractions' and 'lewd courses' were for him a serious business, conducted, regardless of others, for his 'priuate ends and direction'. When Sir Mathew asked him what he had been thinking, writing libels about his employers and bene-factors, he replied without hesitation that 'he doth for his owne instruction and for the direction of his own actions, set down in notes how he shold govern hym[selfe].'[13]

He did not let the matter hold him back. A few weeks after Sir Dud-ley's fateful letter reached the Carew household, in November 1616, Thomas attended on a Knight of the Bath at the investiture of Prince Charles as Prince of Wales. One of Sir Dudley's friends, apparently ignorant of the scandal, reported that 'our gallants flaunt it out in their greatest bravery at the prince's creation, which was performed on Mon-day at Whitehall, with all solemnitie . . . Tom Carew and Phil Lytton, as I hear, were squires of high degree for cost and bravery.'[14]

Despite the fine trimmings, the ceremony and festivities for Charles were on the whole rather glum. The memory of the dead prince, his brother Henry, held like a screen of cloud above the river as a flotilla of boats, however impressive, bore Charles towards Whitehall. There was a pageant on water, and another awaiting him outside the palace. Yet his mother absented herself from the occasion altogether, and when the ceremony took place behind closed doors the following day the bishop accidentally prayed for Henry rather than Charles. A more notable benchmark was made in January when George Villiers, Viscount of Buckingham, was elevated to an earldom.

At home in Chancery Lane, Sir Mathew remained desolate, sending regular apologies to his nephew for his son's 'idle writeng'. In 1617 he reported that 'Ever since his departure from your lordship he hathe lin-gered heere with me, myspending his tyme, and now lieth sick with me of a new disease com in amongest us, by the which I pray God that he may be chastised to amend his lyfe here or els to take hym awaye to his mercye.' Thomas's misspent time, the call for chastisement and his illness are taken to be connected, the 'new disease' probably being the first of a collection of venereal illnesses which was to consign him to an early grave. In March 1618, Sir Mathew was mortified when Lady Carleton did not call at his house on a visit to England, and may have regretted confid-ing Thomas's infection to her and her husband. 'Al the proiectes that haue bene made for hym haue failed,' was his verdict on his ailing son. Complaining about his offspring to the last, he died in August 1618.[15]

The following May, Thomas Carew travelled to Paris as an attendant to the English ambassador, Sir Edward Herbert. Carew was one in a train of a hundred which embarked on the day King James's Danish consort, Queen Anne, was finally buried, her funeral having been delayed by a shortage of funds.

Paris would normally have been the perfect place for Carew to work on the careless disdain required of the courtier, had it not been for the political tensions afflicting the embassy. Anglo-French relations had been more than faintly strained over the previous decade, since the French married their young king, Louis XIII, to 'Anne of Austria' (the Infanta Anna of Spain), thus depriving King James of the first Spanish mate he had intended for his own heir. Now central Europe was in open war over the kingdom of Bohemia. James's son-in-law, the Elector Frederick IV of the Palatine, had accepted the Bohemian crown, having been goaded by his wife, Elizabeth, for dithering – and presently lost everything to Spanish and Holy Roman forces, the armies of militant Catholicism. Herbert and his excellent wits had come to Paris to discourage the French king from entering the war on the side of his fellow Catholics, promoting the search instead for a peaceful solution. But Louis's ministers were perfectly aware that James was simultaneously – albeit, in fact, with increasing reluctance – sending money and messengers to German Protestant courts in the hope they might lend Frederick support in the field.

Writing letters for the ambassador, brushing shoulders with courtiers in the Louvre, Carew could devote all the energy he pleased to his exercise. His fellow traveller James Howell had much the same interests and aspirations but much poorer connections. While Carew enjoyed lodgings at Sir Edward Herbert's rented mansion in the Faubourg St-Germain, on Rue Tournon, Howell found a room near the fortress of the Bastille. Yet he wished, he insisted, to be further away from the places where the English usually resorted, 'for I would get on to a little Language as soon as I could.'

Howell was stunned by Paris, 'this huge Magazine of Men'. He was always caught up in the drama of wherever he was, until new sights and sounds became habitual; and then he moved on. He was for the time being 'well contented with this wandering course of life'. In doing so he became one of the period's finest travel-writers, tingeing direct impressions with little theories of his own on why things should be so, drawing on a rudimentary training in medicine and natural philosophy.

Paris was the largest of the European capitals, and by reputation the grandest. Howell was fascinated with the dirt and danger of the city. 'There's never a Night passes but some Robbing or Murder is committed in this Town,' he reported. The area around Pont Neuf was especially one to avoid late at night, as he discovered wandering back one time through the warm small hours of May 'in some jovial Company abroad'. The group was attacked by a crew of 'Night-Rogues' with blades drawn. Several passes were exchanged, and Howell himself received two or three thrusts into his cloak. They were fortunate to be rescued by a municipal *chevalier du guet*, employed to keep the peace, who had the measure of their assailants. The company walked on. The assault, and the news the same week of an English secretary gulled and 'unmantled' at the same place, made Howell miss the 'excellent nocturnal Government of our City of *London*, where one may pass and repass securely all hours of the Night, if he gives good word to the Watch'.[16]

In Sir Edward Herbert's service, it is likely that Carew's wandering distractions received more encouragement than they had from Carleton. The purpose of the special embassy was a mission of peace, a task for which Herbert's qualifications were dubious. He was rightly regarded as one of the most dangerous men of his time, on one occasion fighting off a team of assassins with little more than the hilt of his sword, having broken the blade on the first pass. A married man, he saw civilized adultery as an activity his status in life demanded of him. A fearsome soldier, he had seen action across Europe. A poet, he was the friend of Donne and one of the most notoriously obscure conceit-makers of the day. He took Carew on as one of his 'principal gentlemen', and remembered him in his memoirs as 'that excellent wit'. The errant secretary had at last found acceptance among his own kind.

2

The early career of Thomas Carew illustrates for us the formation of a privileged literary gentleman, an 'idle' writer. The hard-working vagrant James Howell, ever ingratiating, ever on the lookout for a patron and a niche, is more typical of London's struggling hacks. In rare instances, however, one finds a writer who combines Carew's self-assurance with Howell's humbler status.

William Davenant arrived in London during the summer of 1622. He was sixteen years old, the second of an Oxford tavern-keeper's four sons. He had been to an excellent grammar school, the Merchant Taylors', and received private tuition, but was tired of study.[17] A later portrait suggested a soft charm, a pleasant pudginess to a subsequently damaged face, and gave him surprisingly sensitive dark round eyes. His late father had wanted him to learn a trade, and had bequeathed enough to provide for an apprenticeship, but William had other plans.

Shortly after turning up in town he ordered himself a splendid silk suit.[18] He had no means, and possibly no intention, of paying for the outfit, but it helped him achieve his first goal. Before long, he became a servant to one of the court's great ladies, the Duchess of Richmond. Family connections assisted him: the duchess's first husband had been one of the city's leading merchant vintners, a warden and master of his company and an alderman. Davenant had relatives in the same trade on both the maternal and paternal side, who had also been servants in the earlier Jacobean court. By chance, the duchess (then Frances Howard), Davenant's mother and aunt had been patients at the same time to the well-known London physician Simon Forman: all three in the 1590s had gone to the doctor with worries about pregnancy, and it seems reasonable, as Mary Edmond suggests, that they grew acquainted through their visits, if not before.[19] So the way for what looks like a big step or an extremely lucky break for a young out-of-towner was in fact smoothed by a set of slight but important social contacts. Davenant got his foot in at court, and with his fine new coat could look the part.

One anecdote from his period in the duchess's train throws light not only on Davenant's inquisitive personality but on some of the presumptions of his time. He quickly won the trust of his new mistress. Davenant's duchess took only the rarest of panaceas, and many years later, after the rebellion, Davenant recalled how she would send him to fetch for her a drug made from the pulverized horn of a unicorn.

The virtues held in a shaving of 'unicorn' were all but innumerable. Apothecaries expressed their confidence and pride in it by making a unicorn's head the standard image on the signs above their doors. While restoring depleted sexual energies, a dose of horn helped one 'resist an Injury from an unsound Bedfellow'. It was held the best antidote for poisons of all kinds, and was also thought to repel any viper or venomous insect. With a turn of wit which still, decades afterwards, seemed worthy of remark, Davenant once put a sample to the test. On returning from his supplier, he poured the precious dust out in a ring. He then took a spider he had caught, and put it in the circle. If this was real unicorn, or if real unicorn really worked, the spider should have shrivelled up on contact. Instead the creature crossed the line carelessly, wandering back and forth until scuttering away.[20]

The experiment was not in truth original to Davenant. The tragedian John Webster – who was drawn to such things – mentioned it as a standard test for verifying unicorn. Indeed, given Davenant's passion for the playhouse, Webster's lines on the subject may well have given the younger man his idea. Other common procedures included submerging a length of unbroken horn and checking for bubbles or calefaction, or seeing if a pinch revived a pigeon fed with arsenic. A noted French scholar recommended scorpions.[21]

The test might be taken as a portent of a later, more scientific age. Yet John Aubrey, who recorded the story, was clear that Davenant's researches sought to gratify a youthfully sadistic instinct rather than increase human knowledge. The spider was a fly to a wanton boy, whose 'expected success' was to see it choke and burn on the duchess's medicine. This was an expectation disappointed when the little beast went 'over, through and through, unconcerned'. What might seem to us to resemble empirical research was in its moment more a private circus show, a miniature version of the cruel and often freakish displays to be found every day on Lincoln's Inn Fields or at Smithfield.

Privy to the secrets of a duchess's closet, Davenant's early career illustrates the surprising social mobility that was possible in a culture so stratified as that of the seventeenth century. The secret, his writing suggests, was London itself: Davenant's metropolis teems with possibilities requiring nothing more than a touch of curiosity. A chance meeting can lead to love or fortune, or to comic disaster. A sense of this latent fluidity, despite the strict hierarchies, is present in his later description of the city – in the voice of a Parisian visitor – as an architectural mish-mash, a miscellany of dwellings:

Here stands one that aimes to be a Palace, and next it, another that professes to be a Hovel. Here a Giant, there a Dwarf, here slender, there broad, and all most admirably different in their faces as well as in height and bulk.[22]

The proximity of palaces to hovels, the cross-currents possible between buildings with their competing designs, suggests how a selective movement between spheres could take place – so long as one respected social rank at every step.

Davenant borrowed from his contacts the pinions he needed to catch a social thermal. It was still, of course, very easy to plummet. Not long after entering employment he married, which complicated his plans. He had no way back to an apprenticeship now, since the master of a trade would only accept him single and chaste. His great patroness was also unlikely to smile on a match made without her blessing. Certainly, his wife could not stay in the duchess's great city home, Ely House, up in Holborn, a neighbourhood where leaks from the underground streams 'were hard to be stopped in every house'.[23] Davenant could lay claim to one narrow nook, along with the other pages, up in the attic or even down in the leaky basement.

But he had set his sights on greater things than pricey clothing or a place in a noblewoman's household. He aspired to be a writer: and his role model was a professional theatre man who had died quietly in a country town in 1616, and whose works had recently been given monumental form in an impressive folio.

Early in the summer of 1604, the company of actors known as the King's Men rolled up in Oxford. The actors were reasonably sure of a warm reception. On the road they reverted to the venues which they and their forebears had used before the age of the purpose-built theatre, performing their repertoire in a courtyard of one of the city's larger inns or taverns. In October the following year they were back, on the same or a similar stage, to play for the mayor. A few months later, on 3 March 1606, the company's leading script-writer, William Shakespeare, stood as godfather in the church of St Martin's in Carfax, the blunt-towered Anglo-Saxon church in the middle of the city. The baby's parents owned a public house a few hundred yards away, which in later times was called The Crown, and where in those days, it was said, the playwright generally stopped off on the ride between London and Stratford-upon-Avon. Standing with the theatre man at the sandstone font was Jane Davenant, renowned as a great beauty, and her husband, John, a mild but serious man in his early forties, 'a very grave and discreet citizen'.[24]

Shakespeare held massive symbolic importance for Davenant throughout his life. Though he was barely ten when the playwright died, Davenant's brother remembered how 'Mr W. Shakespeare has given him [William] a hundred kisses.' Much later, when he grew 'pleasant over a glass of wine', Davenant often suggested he was more than Shakespeare's godson.[25]

As Davenant was growing up on the Cornmarket in Oxford, not far away, Robert Burton was writing *The Anatomy of Melancholy*, his colossal, comic and polymathic attempt to chart human emotions, and by mapping them, master them. The *Anatomy* was a book of all books, a summation of the theories of the mind and its labyrinthine oddities which had been produced to that date. The fatal missing step in Davenant's artistic development was that he failed to see that his godfather, intuitively rather than systematically, had pursued a similar project to Burton's. Shakespeare's vast body of work held the transcripts of a lifetime's experimentation with emotion in the controlled conditions of theatre. Davenant caught the sound and fury; but the introspection and analysis of motive evaded him. He lacked nothing in boldness, however, and had penned his first two tragedies by the time he was barely twenty.

Many years later, making use of his time in exile in Paris after the civil war, Davenant would disown 'those hasty digestions of thought which were published in my youth'. But while some wrote or claimed to write from 'officiousness of conscience', he never hid the fact that it was 'the desire of Fame made me a writer.'[26]

From Holborn, the focus of fame for Davenant lay to the south, in the theatre at Blackfriars. He was an avid watcher of Webster, Ford and Massinger, who all added strains of torture to his mottled tragedies. He felt the allure of the playhouse that his future friend Suckling would describe offhandedly:

> The sweat of learned *Johnsons* brain,
> And gentle *Shakespears* easier strain,
> A hackney-coach conveys you to,
> In spite of all that rain can do:
> And for your eighteen-pence you sit
> The Lord and Judge of all fresh wit.[27]

Davenant fell for the mixture of bustle and glamour that was a cut above the rougher theatre business on the opposite side of the river.

Yet looking in the opposite direction, toward Holborn Hill from the bank of the Thames, all that was visible to the principal public poet of the day was a river of sewage, the Fleet, streaming below the shelves of towers and houses through a neighbourhood of tanneries. Skinned cats in the water yowled to be relieved of their remaining lives. 'The sinks ran grease, and hair of measled hogs,/ The heads, houghs, entrails, and the hides of dogs.' But the detritus, the poet argued grimly, should have reassured those who saw or smelt it floating by: at least it wasn't being put on plates in taverns. 'For to say truth, what scullion is so nasty/ To put the skins and offal in a pasty?'[28]

This was the canyon of filth through which Ben Jonson sent two hopeful 'wights' in a long, turbid poem called 'On the Famous Voyage'. The poem was Jonson's contribution to the genre of the mock-epic, and in it he questioned the way literature could lend mythic grandeur to realms of excrement. The Fleet, in this treatment, was as much a way of thinking as a real river; and it was one in which Jonson was particularly keen to give his students and competitors a thorough ducking.

3

Only Lord Francis Bacon, from his more refined sphere as Viscount St Albans and Lord Chancellor, could challenge him as the most imposing literary presence in the capital. The unofficial laureate, Jonson was in his fifties now, and still the self-appointed champion of the high literary arts. There was no greater enemy of 'idle writing'. There was no escaping his influence nor, frequently, his heavy-breathed presence – a 'tun of man', twenty stone in weight, pale from writing through the nights after sweating off the poisons of his noontide drinking. In the early 1620s Jonson was at his social zenith; or rather, at the unnameable point before a failure to rise beyond an apparent peak becomes a measure of decline. He was an establishment. Younger poets styled themselves his sons. Almost annually he still wrote the Twelfth Night masque, the principal spectacle in the court's year. He was expected to receive a knighthood for artistic merit – rather than, as was more usual, having to pay for the honour. His name was also on the select list submitted to the king of suitable founding members for an 'English Academy'.

He was also a physically frightening person, and not simply because of the permanent bulging glare that came from his having one eye lower and larger than the other. There was a brawny core not far below the surface of the bulk he acquired as he aged. He was a man of great stamina and occasionally explosive strength. In his leather coachman's coat, with its slits cut in the armpits to allow easier perspiration, he cut a fiercely antithetic figure to the well-groomed, well-built courtier-versifiers he saw as being beneath the name of poet. One had to be careful where one stood with Jonson: it was all too easy to step outside the narrow spotlight in which he defined those worthy of companionship into shadows crowded with those below his contempt. He was especially scornful of social froth, of dandification, of pretence:

> Would you believe, when you this monsieur see,
> That his whole body should speak French, not he?
> That so much scarf of France, and hat, and feather,
> And shoe, and tie, and garter should come hither,
> And land on one, whose face durst never be
> Toward the sea, farther than halfway tree?[29]

Such accessories, presumably, were redeemed somewhat by the person of a cultivated 'monsieur' such as Carew, with his perfect French and Venetian Italian, and years of Continental travel in his portfolio. It was the fake for which the poet reserved his mightiest derision. Regardless of others, Jonson was wholly assured that his character and work were entirely free of superficial elements; and by his own definition, he was right.

He was immensely proud, for example, of his military record. On service in the Low Countries thirty years before he had killed an enemy in a display of single combat before both the warring camps and returned to barracks in true Achillean fashion, with his man's armour and weapons, the spoils of victory. Jonson was in no way ashamed, either, of the trade by which he had lived when writing failed to pay. His stepfather was a bricklayer, and Jonson had grown up doing honest hard labour, paying his dues to the guild well into the years of his greatest fame.[30]

His most popular and still enduring works, the comedies from the 1590s and early 1600s, including *Every Man in His Humour*, and the peerless satires *Volpone* and *The Alchemist*, typify the unsparing observation we take as Jonsonian. Compassion, intimacy, vulnerability, the contradictions of desire, are not among the attributes and experiences he dramatizes. His plays are parades of vice, streams of unerringly realized flaws fresh off the street. The builder of houses was a demolisher of human pretensions. So much so that it is all too easy to forget that when he turned his hand to the lyric, Jonson's craft became that of the watchmaker or diamond-cutter, or rather, one working with elementary verbal particles:

> Do but consider this small dust
> Here running in the glass,
> By atoms moved;
> Could you believe, that this,
> The body was
>   Of one that loved?

That the voice of the haranguing couplet-maker and fine-glass lyricist belonged to the same writer was nevertheless unmistakeable. Whether sifting the lover's dust or ridiculing the false French 'monsieur', Jonson put an equal pressure on his hypothetical listeners to accept the view of the subject he presents (the *erotema*, the rhetorical question-form used in both poems, 'would/could you believe?', is characteristically vehement). But the subtlety and variety of means by which the pressure is applied can be missed.

Easily overlooked, too, is just how much of Jonson's oeuvre consists of the most exclusive and, by its very nature, pretentious literary art form of all time: the masque. Or, strictly speaking, the speeches performed by professional actors that preceded and justified the occasion of the masque, in which aristocratic (and frequently royal) dancers descended from the stage and took their partners from the audience. The most genteel of genres, the masque was also the field of Jonson's bitterest artistic feud.

Inigo Jones, the designer and engineer whom Carew encountered in Italy, on tour with the Earl of Arundel, was like Jonson a driven, self-made man, with a towering confidence in his ability to extend his skills to any task. A year younger than Jonson, virtually nothing is known of Jones until he was thirty. Jointly commissioned on an almost yearly basis from 1605 on, their creative collaboration was essential to producing the royal entertainment. Between them, the pair virtually invented modern English theatre, making scenery dramatically integral to performance for the first time. But although the partnership lasted almost three decades, it was not long before Jonson and Jones could hardly abide one another.

Beside the clash of large, complex and creative egos, in artistic terms the enmity arising from their work together was brutally simple: Jonson aggressively and hurtfully asserted the greater importance of the words, and Jones, more quietly, subtly and in the end with more success, held fast to the primacy of the spectacle. Together they made oceans, mountains and forests rise and fall before the watching court, wildernesses vanish into dazzling palladia, deities burst from clouds. Yet Jonson, with some reason, felt that he alone was responsible for the plots and arguments supporting those sequences of special effects, the moral progressions those scene changes represented. The masque came to consist of two parts: the antimasque, in which a state of disorder or a force of evil was shown and confronted, and the masque proper, in which the stage was cleared of those lesser agents for the noble dancers to appear. Jones, felt Jonson, merely provided the pictures. As such, he termed his script the 'soul' of the masque, and Jones's physical imagery the 'body': while privately accepting the power of the plastic arts, he nevertheless insisted that 'of the two, the pen is more noble than the pencil. For that can speak to the understanding; the other, but to the sense.'[31]

He did not give his fellow writers an easy time either. Leading voices – Drayton, Dekker, Fletcher, Chapman, Daniel – all felt the sting of a swipe at their accomplishments. There was, however, in most cases a firm argument supporting the assault. Jonson famously declared that Shakespeare 'lacked art', but also distinguished him with his most developed and well-argued positive criticism. While in person a vocational contrarian, in his theory and practice of the art of writing Jonson argued strenuously against waywardness, idiosyncrasy for its own sake. He was a stringent advocate of the Horatian virtues of aptness, clarity and balance needed for expression to seem natural. 'But now nothing is good that is natural: right and natural language seems to have the least wit in it; that which is writhed and tortured, is counted the more exquisite.'[32]

By the 1620s, such verbal projectiles homed in on a target east of the taverns of Westminster and court galleries of Whitehall, at a 'fayre old house' south of St Paul's where the Dean of the Cathedral, John Donne, had his residence. Where Jonson embodied the force of tradition in poetry, Donne was an innovator, in his style and choice of subjects. From early on, Donne was more attracted by modish international trends such as the European fashion for *concepto* ('conceit').[33] Donne's poetic figures frequently go straight to the least straightforward, least tangible point of comparison or relation between the ideas and things he aligns. He was also prone to taking conceits further than they seemed at first able to bear. The idea that men were like clocks, for example, was commonplace. But Donne takes it onward, and gives human afflictions to a mechanism:

> Whose *hand* gets shaking palsies, and whose *string*
> (His sinews) slackens, and whose *Soule*, the spring,
> Expires, or languishes, whose pulse, the *flye*
> Either beates not, or beates unevenly,
> Whose voice, the *Bell*, doth rattle, or grow dumbe,
> Or idle, as men which to their last hours come.[34]

He then invests the concept with deeper moral consequence. In early adulthood, men are like pocket-watches, when their errors and failings influence only the few who consult them; but some become 'great clocks' later on in public life, when much greater numbers are guided or misled by them. 'Mismotions' in the works of the latter have much graver consequences than the former running a few minutes fast or late. There is no such extravagance of thought or expression in Jonson.

Those who knew Donne, lean, elegant, eloquent, to be seen consulting now and then the fashionable timepiece he carried with him habitually, were aware of how seriously he took his public responsibilities.[35] Jonson, an old acquaintance, noted how 'now, since he was made doctor, [Donne] repenteth highly, and seeketh to destroy all his poems.' But he was sceptical of Donne's former motives, in competing for example with Carew's master, Sir Edward Herbert, 'in obscureness' – in an elegy written for Prince Henry.[36] Jonson feared in any case that 'Donne himself, for not being understood, would perish.'[37]

Jonson and Donne thus set contrary examples for up-and-coming poets. Whereas Donne's writing would always be more striking (repellently so, to many, over many subsequent decades), the grandeur and harmony of Jonson's designs could take longer to appreciate. As one of his younger friends put it, Jonson's 'natural advantages were, judgment to order and govern fancy, rather than excess of fancy'.[38] Excess of fancy was in fact precisely the vice Jonson sought to check in his contemporaries. To the assertion that Shakespeare had never blotted a line, he famously rejoined that he should have blotted out a thousand. Jonson still praised Shakespeare – with deep sincerity – as 'Soul of the age!/ The applause, delight, the wonder of our stage!' But the quality he most admired in his 'beloved' fellow bard was diligence. Shakespeare knew that the poet:

> Who casts to write a living line, must sweat,
>   . . . and strike the second heat
> Upon the muses anvil.[39]

Sir John Suckling, picking up from this on the 'sweat of learned *Johnsons* brain', would observe the same earnestness in Carew: 'His Muse was hard bound, and th'issue of's brain/ Was seldom brought forth but with trouble and pain.' But the likes of Carew were insufficient to change Jonson's general verdict on his age: 'Now things daily fall; wits grow downward, and eloquence grows backward.'[40]

4

A few years before, this judgement had been delivered in the lengthiest and most detailed form that would be preserved for posterity, at a fireside far to the north of the poet's usual habitat. Jonson's ancestry was Scottish. His paternal family, the Johnstons or Johnstouns, had been formidable borderland brigands, and in the summer of 1618 the twenty-stone man of letters took his 'rocky face' and 'mountain belly', on foot, all the way up the Great Northern Road to the land of his forebears. He styled himself 'The Poet', but when Jonson arrived in Edinburgh he was greeted as a 'gildbrother' in his stepfather's profession, that of builder.[41] Late in the year, Jonson stayed three weeks with the poet William Drummond, hiking up the rocky outcrop to Drummond's home at Hawthornden Castle, a steep-sided lair a few miles south of Edinburgh overlooking the choppy passage of the River North Esk through a canyon beneath. It was there that Drummond, as different in appearance as could be to his gruff and hairy titanic guest – a wiry, light-haired man, high-browed and straight-nosed, clean-shaven, with a restrained, sardonic smile – was assembling a huge and immensely varied library; and where, sitting together among the books, the two shared one of the most celebrated exchanges in the history of English literature.

Drummond's notes on his 'Conversations' with Jonson, a summary of numerous, lengthy and wandering talks, give the impression that Jonson did little else but spout bile at the names of other writers, past and present. It was Drummond who recorded Jonson's view that Shakespeare 'lacked art', that Donne deserved hanging for the liberties he took with metre and would soon be forgotten anyway because he was too obscure; that his old theatrical mates were rogues and cheats. Petrarch's sonnets, said Jonson, reminded him of the bed on which the sadist Procrustes laid his victims, to stretch or squash them to the height he desired: 'some who were too short were racked, others too long cut short.' The Roman poet Lucan was 'taken in parts excellent, altogether nought'. Drummond's own verses were good, Jonson told him, 'save that they smelled too much of the schools'.[42]

That such remarks seem blunt and poorly argued is, as Ian Donaldson tells us, largely because they are taken from a rough private document that does not set out to record the detail of the discussions from which they arose. A charge of two-facedness is harder to answer, since Jonson was speaking of authors and others whom he had complimented, sincerely and measuredly, as in his elegy for Shakespeare, in other places. But Jonson was not addressing the public: he was bantering with a literary friend. Although Drummond obviously concentrated on setting down Jonson's opinions for future reference, his own are also enlightening, since they strongly suggest that he gave as good as Jonson in the debates, replying to the broadsword with the rapier, returning artillery blasts with often pinpoint sniper fire. Jonson's comments on Continental literature, for example, from Petrarch to Ronsard, were all 'to no purpose for he neither doth understand French or Italian'. Or as Drummond tartly remarked, Jonson had his degrees from Oxford and Cambridge – the 'two most equal sisters' he praised unctuously in the preface to *Volpone* – 'by their favour, not his study'.

At the end of January, Jonson left Leith, a huge swathed figure wearing boots which, he told Drummond, had lasted him all the way from Darlington, and 'which he minded to take back that far again'. Drummond completed his minutes on their conversations with an acerbic character sketch:

He is a great lover and praiser of himself, a contemner and scorner of others, given rather to lose a friend than a jest, jealous of every word and action of those about him (especially after drink, which is one of the elements in which he liveth), a dissembler [i.e. a concealer] of ill parts which reign in him, a bragger of some good that he wanteth.

It would do Drummond credit if he had been man enough to say all this to Jonson in person. There is every reason, however, to believe that he did: and no doubt whatsoever that Jonson was ready and able to take it, indeed expected nothing else. It was a sharp blow that could noticeably dint an ego as vast and weathered as Jonson's, but, as Drummond concluded, he took a critical retort to heart when it had truth behind it, being 'passionately kind and angry, careless either to gain or keep, vindictive, but, if he be well answered, at himself'.[43]

On his return, Jonson should have continued his steady ascent. He resumed his annual masque-writing duties by royal appointment, and his eminence in London's literary world, though not uncontested, was immoveable. He was a social landmark. He retained the friendship of a number of extraordinarily talented and in time influential 'persons of honour'. These included Sir Kenelm Digby, 'the most accomplished cavalier of his time', in Aubrey's view: traveller, diplomat, poet, philosopher, linguist, and the long-tortured lover and husband of Venetia Stanley, who endured his jealousies with patient languor. Ruddy-faced, balding, his stoutness disguising muscularity, Sir Kenelm could lift a seated man by the legs of his chair: he had the thick-limbed build of the Digby men which was in time to prove ominous for Carew's younger friend Suckling. In contrast to Digby although united by admiration for Jonson was his lean friend John Selden, the great jurist and scholar, defender of the subject's 'ancient liberties', whose researches had already upset the Stuart order by showing that the Church had no historical or legal foundation for extracting tithes.

Yet at a time when honour counted for all, Jonson went unrewarded, still penning dramas for a living at his old steady rate and leaning heavily on his annual pension as laureate of £100 from the Crown – a sufficient but far from extravagant sum. It was uncertain whether he had won the argument with Inigo Jones. 'I am too fat to envy him. He too lean/ To be worth envy,' Jonson would huff.[44] But the invective was matched by regular feats of engineering from his collaborator and adversary; and it was not altogether clear that Jonson's accomplished prose and verse was seen as indispensable. Even King James, a steady admirer of the poet, was wont to complain that the writing bored him and to cry out for more dancing. The dispute would drag on for another decade.

'Ill fortune never crushed that man, whom good fortune deceived not,' said Jonson.[45] He vulcanized his magnanimity by defining himself against his inferiors. Following a spell of perceived neglect in 1623, he wrote an epistle 'answering to One that Asked to be Sealed of the Tribe of Ben'. The 'tribe' was a semi-formal group of his admirers and imitators, writers and wits of Thomas Carew's generation who gathered around their chief at an appointed tavern – frequently, it is said, The Mermaid on Bread Street. Jonson had nothing but disdain, however, for mere acolytes, 'those that merely talk, and never think,/ That live in the wild anarchy of drink'.[46] He would accept only the best of free-thinkers as his tribesmen and symbolic sons.

It was a precautionary stance against disappointment. The English Academy, with Jonson as one of its foremost lights, never materialized; nor did the rumoured knighthood. Like his contemporary Edward Alleyn, once Christopher Marlowe's leading man, the original Faust and Tamburlaine, now Master of the Bears at Paris Garden, a mighty philanthropist and a cultural citizen of similar stature to Jonson, a title was beyond him; as was a secure posting in the court. Jonson would have scorned the idea of following the meteoric trajectory of Francis Bacon, whom he admired immensely and who rose to great political power. Yet the very serious reflections on how to advise a prince, in the notes collected as *Discoveries*, suggest he fancied himself a royal counsellor. As it was, formally at least, his wisdom was confined to the ambiguous political messages of his masques, dramas and poems.

When they came to perform at court, thespians took on the dignity of royal servants. Outside that context, however, players were widely perceived as delinquents. No one from that background could ever achieve full respectability, and Jonson was an exceptionally volatile case. He had in many senses two identities as man and writer. The one he assumed from the time he began writing masques was that of loyal servant to the monarch, the laureate who left even in his private notes an imperative to obey one's prince unquestioningly. Yet the other, earlier and enduring face of Jonson was that of one of literature's great indignant spirits, cynical about power and those who held it – including himself and his own considerable influence. He was a genie of chaos, often compelled to serve the 'wild anarchy of drink' he despised. In 1612 he travelled as tutor to Walter Ralegh the younger on what became a riotous tour of France and the Netherlands. It was not, Jonson remarked acidly to Drummond, *his* fault:

This youth, being knavishly inclined, among other pastimes (as the setting of favours of damsels on a codpiece [in a parody of knights carrying their ladies' scarves or trinkets on their lances]), caused him to be drunken, and dead drunk, so that he knew not where he was, thereafter laid him on a car, which he made to be drawn by pioneers through the streets, at every corner showing his governor stretched out, and telling them, that was a more lively image of the crucifix than any they had.[47]

Young Ralegh's mother enjoyed the tale of Ben's torment exceedingly. His father in his day, she said, had also been 'knavishly inclined'. Ralegh the elder, explorer and man for all seasons, was less amused by history repeating itself. This was the sort of incident Jonson had been hired to prevent.

Jacobean London had a long memory. It knew, for example, how Jonson had blinded in one eye another of his students, in a fit of corrective rage. He had not been knighted: but anyway, was it not Jonson who mocked how King James sold out honours, in *Eastward Ho*? He had only just escaped, back then, from having his ears and nostrils slit. Further, further back, in the time of Queen Elizabeth, London could remember how he and his crew had been thrown in gaol for their scandalous 'lewd matters' on stage, and interrogated by the sadist Topcliffe. It knew of his fistfights with his collaborators, how he disarmed and pistol-whipped John Marston with Marston's own gun. It knew of his unhappy marriage, how he was 'given to venery' when younger. And those who saw at close quarters his thumb raised to approve or anoint or twisted down to condemn would have seen an *F* imprinted on it, the brand of a convicted felon.

In the autumn of 1598 an argument with a fellow actor, Gabriel Spencer, led to a duel in the fields beyond Shoreditch. It was only a year since the pair had been in gaol together. Spencer managed to wound Jonson in the arm, but there was no matching him for strength. Although his blade was ten inches shorter than the other man's, Jonson overwhelmed and killed him, and was indicted for manslaughter. Even twenty-five years later, London knew that Jonson had only been saved from the cart-ride to Tyburn by the grace of an archaic law that saved anyone who could recite a passage from Psalm 51. The text in question was known as the 'neck-verse': 'Have mercy upon me, O God, according to thy lovingkindness: according unto the multitude of thy tender mercies blot out my transgressions.'

Most damagingly of all, however, it was also known that Jonson soon afterwards had become a Catholic, and had stood up for papists in following years. In 1605, a month before the planned attack on Parliament, he had shared an incriminating supper with several of the gunpowder plotters in a house on the Strand.

He damned them all, every slandering mouth among them, looked all in the eye, and respected only those who could stand up to his gaze. He was unashamed:

> Live to that point I will, for which I am man,
> And dwell as in my centre, as I can,
> Still looking to, and ever loving heaven;
> With reverence using all the gifts thence given.[48]

Yet however frequently Jonson's writing looked to the empyrean, its starting point was always the visceral, and its founding wisdom the principle that nobody can run far from their innards, or from the contents of others': and that our mortal remains end, at best, as manure. He wrote in praise of his monarch, but as the emperor Tiberius remarks in Jonson's satirical tragedy, *Sejanus*, 'Our empire, ensigns, axes, rods, and state/ Take not away our human nature from us.'[49] Human nature and humanity are thin words in Jonson. They are veils. He gives a stronger impression of the mutual meatiness of brain and bowel, the universal basics to which even the greatest can be reduced – as when his Roman magnate, Sejanus, is dismembered by the mob: 'Now torn and scattered, as he needs no grave . . . So he lies nowhere, and yet often buried.'[50]

Little more could be left of the most powerful, in other words, than of the roasted cats or flayed hogs whose remnants thickened the River Fleet. Jonson leaves the sense that when he looked about the town he dominated, he saw it as he described it in his 'Famous Voyage' up the Fleet some years before, bespattered with offal, beshitten. That poem formed the end of Jonson's *Epigrams*, which he declared were the 'ripest of my studies'. Enjoying this position, the 'Voyage' is thus in a sense the ripest of the ripest, though it is in fact a study of the past-ripe, the fetid and the decomposing. It envisages all animals, human or otherwise, as muck-sprayers, coating the environment in their egestions. The pools and rivers they made formed Jonson's basic soup of reality. For all the silk suits they might put on their backs, this was the substance to which history would reduce his various sons and all the finery of their age.

During the 1620s poets were emerging in London who looked to the pleasant and delicious elements in life. By the time Jonson's sun was just starting to set, for example, Thomas Carew had been recognized as 'a person of a pleasant and facetious wit' who had 'made many poems, (especially in the amorous way,) which for the sharpness of the fancy, and the elegancy of the language in which that fancy was spread, were at least equal, if not superior to any of that time'.[51] And whereas Jonson had battled every inch of the way, ultimately to disappointment and never a great distance from poverty, Carew was gliding. While Jonson was at one point 'almost at the gallows', Carew continued smoothly in quite the opposite direction from Tyburn, and had shown how such progress could be made in a manner that would have astounded old Sir Mathew. He now had a secure network of patrons, including Buckingham's brother, the Earl of Anglesey, and would in time be made a royal intimate, a Gentleman of the Royal Bedchamber. He kept a house for his assignations on King's Street, but otherwise spent little time there, preferring a temporary berth in one of his great friends' town or country homes.

However high they rose, minds that were great and free would always take Fortune's gifts lightly. A keen test of this maxim was provided by the case of Francis Bacon, the essayist, natural philosopher and Lord Chancellor. Bacon was scapegoated by King James on charges of corruption in 1620 and smeared with abuse for his alleged homosexuality. Yet Thomas Carew, and a few others like him, seemed not to be aiming at the heights at all. They were not interested in serving or furthering Poetry, merely receiving her favours. They apparently devoted themselves to the very vanities which Jonson saw as the worst waste of time:

What a deal of cold business doth a man misspend the better part of life in! In scattering compliments, tendering visits, gathering and venting news, following feasts and plays, making a little winter-love in a dark corner.[52]

The shade of Sir Mathew Carew could only agree.

2. The Quixotic Prince

In *Spaine* hee [the Englishman abroad] must bee much more carefull of his diet, abstemious from fruit, more reserved and cautelous in his Discours, but entertaine none at all touching *Religion*, unlesse it be with *Silence*; a punctuall repaire of visits, extraordinary humble in his comportment; for the *Spaniards*, of all other, love to be respected at their own homes, and cannot abide an insolent cariage in a Stranger.

— James Howell, *Instructions for Forreine Travell* (1642)

1

In 1622, James Howell's official business in Madrid was to lobby for the return of a richly laden English vessel the Spanish had impounded in Sardinia. He had quickly settled back into Spanish life, having visited the country a few years earlier, and was happy to escape a steady but frustrating position running a glass factory at home. There, as he complained, 'I was at a dead stand in the course of my fortunes.'[1] Born in 1594 or '95, he was in his late twenties, and an avowed 'son' of Jonson. The time had come to find a steady course. Despite remarkable powers of application, especially in learning languages, Howell had great need of external stimulation and excitement, a busy background, and was particularly sensitive to its currents when he found it. He was open to all refinements and delights from abroad, quickly absorbent of foreign custom. He tended to suffer 'a deep Fit of melancholy' when he felt his life stagnating, whether in Wales or in Venice, and when the influence of Saturn 'cast his black Influence o'er all my Intellectuals, methought I felt my heart as a lump of dough, and heavy as lead within my breast'.[2] He often claimed that letters from those close to him dispersed the fit of depression, since they to some extent transported him. The offer of a job from two friends, merchants in the Turkey Company, came in the nick of time.

His task of daily 'agitation' at the Spanish court, which was based in the old Arabic citadel overlooking Madrid, left him many hours to indulge his chief intellectual passion. Howell was a scriptomaniac, a compulsive transmitter of news and describer of the world about him to a wide circle of friends and acquaintances. Though now neglected outside scholarly circles, he was admired throughout the eighteenth and nineteenth centuries as one of the finest English travel-writers and social observers. Words were basic nutrients to him, and writing, he maintained, excelled speech – much as he adored a good talk:

The *Tongue*, and the *Pen*, are both of them Interpreters of the Mind; but I hold the Pen to be the more faithful of the two: The *Tongue in udo posita*, being seated in a moist slippery Place, may fail and faulter in her sudden extemporal Expressions; but the Pen having a greater advantage of Premeditation, is not so subject to error, and leaves things behind it upon firm and authentic record.[3]

Howell in fact had a distinctly flexible sense of authenticity. From a prison cell decades after his golden spell of voyages, he wrote his autobiography in epistolary form. The result was his *Familiar Letters*, a firm favourite for a further two centuries and a book to which Thackeray gave a permanent place at his bedside. Howell's method, it seems, was to recast and improve upon his original correspondence, remodelling the letters he could recover in the light of hindsight. A great many were clearly the product of memory and invention. Yet if they were fiction, they were fiction in the root Latin sense of something formed and fashioned, not made up from scratch. With an easy conscience, Howell put his memoir and reflections on the age in a continuous present tense. To this working practice, posterity owes the best account of one of the more eccentric episodes in seventeenth-century history.

Late in March 1623, just over a year after Howell arrived in the city, Madrid was gripped by 'dark rumours in every corner' concerning the arrival of a royal English rider, alone but for a single travelling companion and two weary attendants. Initially, 'among the vulgar', the 'great man of England' was said to be the king himself; but this was quickly dismissed by those who knew that James I, though a keen hunter in his day, was ague-ridden and failing. It was in fact his son and heir, Prince Charles. He had come in person to woo the Infanta Maria.

In the commercial community Howell dealt with in his daily professional life, the idea of a royal marriage sealing the peace between England and Spain had been supported for some time. It would eliminate precisely the sort of complication that had brought Howell to Spain in the first place. The nobility and gentry he lobbied on his sorties to the court, however, were much more circumspect: 'So that in this point,' he commented, 'the pulse of *Spain* beats quite contrary to that of England, where the People are averse to this Match, and the Nobility with most part of the Gentry inclinable.'[4] Howell himself was strongly in favour of the match, and admired its most prominent though also wariest advocate, Lord Digby, Earl of Bristol, the ambassador. Digby was on the point of sealing an agreement, Howell reported, 'and there wanted nothing to consummate all Things, when, to the wonderment of the World, the Prince and the Marquis of *Buckingham* arriv'd.'[5] The hardworking diplomat Digby was secretly appalled: the incipient agreement was immediately written off.

The next morning, Buckingham went early to the palace for a private audience with the king, who sent his leading courtier, Count Olivares, back to the ambassador's house. There Olivares knelt before Prince Charles, kissed his hands and hugged his legs, and reported the king's delight at his presence in Madrid. The next day, the king and his family took a coach ride beyond the precincts of the palace, in sight of the admirer. The Infanta wore a blue ribbon on her arm so that Charles could distinguish her from her ladies-in-waiting.

The impromptu plan was actually the brainchild of Buckingham. A match between Prince Charles and the Infanta had long been mooted, and was much desired by King James. It was 1623: a vast war was unfolding on the Continent, and James's daughter Elizabeth had been driven from her seat, the Palatinate, in central Europe. Her troops had been defeated by Habsburgian imperial forces. She and her husband, Frederick – whom she had rashly urged to confront the emperor – were driven from Prague when their army was routed at White Mountain. Simultaneously, a Spanish army had invaded the Palatinate. Amid the debris of personal effects the royal couple left behind, their enemies found Frederick's George Cross, the insignia of the Order of the Garter. It would be interesting to know if Prince Charles could have heard that such a precious item had been discarded even in the hastiest escape. His own Garter medal was one of his most treasured possessions, kept with him until just before the end – carefully placed in safe hands a short time before he stepped out on to the scaffold.

James had hoped that by marrying his son to a daughter of Spain he could win the lost territory back for his daughter and foolhardy son-in-law without more needless blood being spilt. But the Spanish, with their master of procrastination in London, Count Gondomar, were drawing matters out. It had still not been agreed whether Charles would be allowed even to set eyes upon the Infanta. In frustration, Buckingham hit upon the notion of cutting through the pedantry altogether and travelling directly and quite unofficially to Spain, where Charles could force his attentions on the sequestered maiden.

King James took much convincing; more, in fact, than his son and favourite could supply. His head was always turned by 'fine looks and fine clothes' – his confidence and delight in Buckingham was based at first on little else – but when it came to matters of war and peace, he was never convinced by panache. He thoroughly disliked the idea of letting his heir set off unprotected. Charles's arrival in Spain would also immediately cancel years of diplomatic toil: the Spaniards, with this new development, would insist on starting again from scratch. England had an able and experienced ambassador in Bristol, but he would be brought to heel by Buckingham, who was quite unqualified for the complex negotiations that followed.

James loved Buckingham, and knew his favourite's enemies would be only too delighted to rend limb from limb when the plan went amiss. The king warned that he would not be able to protect him in that instance. The people, and certain sections of the nobility, were set against the match with Spain, which could only bring with it full legal toleration of the hated Catholic faith in England. Suspicion of the old enemy still ran deep, and it was felt in some shires that a state of war between the two countries was essential to the natural balance of things. In the bookshops around St Paul's one frequently found pamphlets such as 'The Spanish Pilgrime . . . Shewing how necessary and important it is, for the Protestant Kings, Princes and Potentates of Europe, to Make warre vpon the King of Spaines owne Countrey: Also where, and by what meanes, his Dominions may be invaded and easily ruinated'.[6] The threat could not be ignored, it was persistently argued – 'we are in regard of the feare of Spanish greatnesse hereafter, which undoubtedly he will attain unto by the innumerable masses of his Indian treasures, which are the nerves and sinews of all martiall intendments.' The same author made a great deal, too, of the imperial Spaniard's unChristian brutality to his slaves. The tale was told of how, of all people, even Sir Francis Drake had been shocked when, watering at a Spanish possession in the Caribbean:

He found an old *Negro,* tyed in a chain of 20 yards long, which had been condemned by the justice of the place; for that sometimes being oppressed with too much labour, the poor old man would runne into the woods, and absent himselfe from his Majesties work, his sentence was, that he should be whipped, with whips, till he was all raw and bloody; and afterwards being tyed in a chain to be eaten with flies, which poore soule hee realeased from that miserable death, and took away with him. And therefore oh *Turke,* oh Scithians, and Tartarians, rejoyce yee all.[7]

The records of English traders and explorers did not provide so strong a contrast with such examples as the writer preferred to think. Yet that was overlooked in the call for a holy war. People were enduringly nervous about Spain. In London, the Spanish ambassador, Count Gondomar, was known by sight to everyone, and everyone was troubled by his influence on the king. His spell was hard to resist, though, when you met him. He 'cast out his Baite not onely for men, but if he found an *Atalanta,* whose tongue went nimbler than her feet, he would cast out his golden Balls to catch them also'. There was a story of one woman who rudely opened her mouth at him, in a cross between a yawn and a silent shriek, every time he rode past her window in his carriage. This disconcerted Gondomar. But he eventually won her over too, with a stream of gifts.[8]

King James's success in holding the country back from testing the nerves and sinews of Spain in a direct wrestling match is one of the most underrated achievements of royal diplomacy, as his son's careful evasion of full involvement in the Thirty Years' War would also be. Armada memories of 1588 blazed golden: but the wiser also remembered that England had only been spared from invasion by a great deal of luck. James's was an older man's policy; he was happy to let the prevarication drag on if it meant the absence of war – a war not only against Spain but against the Holy Roman Empire itself. Buckingham and Charles had embraced the notion of the Spanish match more aggressively and thus more clumsily, suggesting alternative means of achieving its end. In doing so they failed to see that the means *were* the ends.

Yet now James had foolishly promised to let Buckingham and the prince have their way before they even told him the substantial detail of their scheme, inadvertently putting them in a position where they could accuse him of going back on his word. Weak from argument, in the end he agreed, and called in one of the two courtiers who would attend them.

'"Cottington, here is Baby Charles and Stenny," [or 'Steenie', in a more customary spelling] (an appellation he always used of and toward the duke,) "who have a great mind to go by post into Spain to fetch the Infanta and will have but two more for their company, and have chosen you for one; what think you of the journey?"'

Sir Francis Cottington broke down trembling, and later claimed he was quite unable to speak. When pressed to give his opinion, he could only echo the king's own thoughts, saying that the measure would wreck all the work that had already been done towards the match and having the prince in their clutches would give the Spanish every advantage they needed to make 'new overtures'. Buckingham resented Cottington for this speech for many years afterwards. Yet when Buckingham decided to make an enemy, he would frequently at least inform the party concerned, allowing his victims to put their affairs in order. When the mission in Spain finally ended, as fruitlessly as expected, he let Cottington know in person that he meant to destroy him. But for the time being he satisfied himself with flying into a rage, for which the king strongly rebuked him. 'Nay, by God, Stenny, you are very much to blame to use him so. He answered me directly to the question I asked him, and very honestly and wisely: and you know he says no more than I told you before he was called in.'[9]

Eventually the old king was won over, largely from fatigue. Buckingham taunted him for disliking the plan only because he had failed to think of it first. But in principle King James remained opposed to it to the end, and 'never forgave the duke of Buckingham, but retained as sharp a memory of it as his memory could contain'.[10]

2

George Villiers, the future Duke of Buckingham, had staggered the king from first sight. He had been planted at a hunting party almost ten years before, and was then used by a faction of the court to distract James from a rival infatuation. He proved as cunning as he was handsome. Villiers was both adopted son and beloved to the monarch. Charles, by poignant contrast, had always struggled for real recognition or affection from his father. The prince was short, painfully earnest in his affections and in his desire to do well, and afflicted with a stammer that reinforced his natural introversion. His strict conscience had been tenderized further by the sermons of his chapel's mainly Calvinist ministers.

A much more expansive person than Charles would have had trouble diverting the king's love from Villiers. When James was indisposed, it was Buckingham who stepped in to placate and cheer him. 'Why don't they dance? What did you make me come here for?' cried James on Twelfth Night, 1618, at the performance of a masque he found crushingly dull: 'Devil take all of you, dance!' Before any of the other courtiers had the wit or opportunity to do anything, Buckingham stepped up and 'danced a number of high and very tiny capers with such grace and lightness that he made everyone love him, and also managed to calm the rage of his angry lord'.[11]

In the course of 1619, James sat down with his court favourite to dictate some words of advice for his son and heir. His counsel took the form of a meditation on the Gospel of St Matthew. 'One day reading privatly to myselfe the passion of CHRIST,' James recalled, 'I lighted vpon that part, where the Gouernors Souldiers mocked our *Sauiour*, with putting the ornaments of a King vpon him.' Familiar as the passage was, the king was newly moved, so that 'my head hammered vpon it diuers times after.' Nearing the end of his reign, and his life, James now saw kingship as a burden, even a curse, rather than a blessing. The mockery of Jesus said it all: the robes of a king brought only trouble and scorn. His precious young Buckingham was eager to act as amanuensis,

James told Charles in his preface, 'that hee might doe you some peece of seruice thereby'. A cynical observer might have remarked that Buckingham was also concerned with sustaining his pre-eminence after the succession, which could not now be many years away. The meditation and commentary, in any case, had a practical goal: 'this is but a short preparatiue for a Kings Inauguration,' James told his son, 'and a little forewarning of his great and heauie burthen.'[12]

The meditation was James's second work setting out fatherly advice to an heir. His first was written almost ten years before, when he acceded to the English throne of Elizabeth I in 1603. *Basilikon Doron* was written not for Charles, however, whom in those days he appears, on the whole, to have ignored, but for his more robust elder son, Henry, whose early death in 1612 left the nation numb with grief and Charles next in line of succession. The earlier work set out the famous Stuart doctrine of the divine right of kings, a doctrine the Welsh and English Tudors had also fostered, but without pushing it too forcibly on a loyal but sceptical nation. James neatly summarized the argument in a prefatory sonnet:

> God giues not Kings the stile of *Gods* in vaine,
> For on his Throne his Scepter doe they swey:
> And as their subiects ought them to obey,
> So Kings should feare and serue their God againe.[13]

The chain of command was clear enough. Subjects needed to fear and obey their king, and there was nothing they could or should do to oppose him, since the sovereign was there – for better or worse – by God's volition. It was sufficient for kings, meanwhile, to look out for the wrath of God.

It is a matter of speculation how closely the young Charles absorbed these works themselves. Together, nevertheless, their philosophy fixed the attitude he took to his own position in the universe. He saw his role as king as a greatness thrust on him by the Almighty. It was not, as some thought, a great gift of birth, but a massive weight on his very existence. Furthermore, it was a role he could never flinch from fulfilling, and one he could never allow to be compromised or subverted. This was the code he lived and died by. Politically, it fastened the monarchy in place. Personally, for Charles himself it must have gone some way to explaining the cosmically unfair chain of events that pressed absolute power upon him.

In early adulthood it seemed that he would have at least one subject with whom he could share the burden – Villiers, the object of the king's affections. Buckingham's charm soon dispelled their initial rivalry. By the time they slipped away on horseback to Spain, escorted only by Cottingham and one other rider, Endymion Porter, the two were fast friends. Buckingham carried with him a letter from James which elevated him to a dukedom: he was the first to be created such in many years. His new title augmented his negotiating power, and ruled out any ambiguity as to his status which may have existed in Spain. It also reinforced his standing there as the peer closest in rank and in affection to the prince.

Few in the English court knew and understood so well as Porter what awaited them. He was part Castilian by blood and had been brought up in the court of Count Olivares. Porter's maternal grandmother was a Spanish noblewoman, Doña Juana de Figueroa, whose family took their name from a medieval hero credited with saving a hundred local maidens from being given as tribute to the Moorish overlords. On breaking his spear, the horseman tore a sturdy branch from a fig tree to carry on thrashing the infidels, and was in time named after this improvised weapon.[14]

Few either had given so much personally as Porter to the cause of the Spanish match. In 1622 he had broken a shoulder and narrowly escaped death in shipwreck – with his brother at the helm – when sailing as an unofficial envoy to reopen the possibility of the marriage. His servant had been crushed below the hull.

Then came the journey itself with the prince. Haste and secrecy, Buckingham insisted, were essential to the enterprise. He and Charles set out from the royal palace at Theobalds with false beards and aliases, travelling as John and Tom Smith, but their disguise was compromised by Buckingham tipping the Gravesend ferryman with a purse of gold. Weighing the bag in his hand as the pair rode on, the ferryman decided he must inform the magistrates, for this was surely a pair of duellists on their way to fight in France. The alarm being raised, the group was promptly pursued all the way to Dover. There they met Porter, who had at that stage yet to be briefed on what exactly was afoot.

There followed a short, pleasant holiday in Paris, where Charles and

Buckingham were quickly recognized; but after that respite came real adventure. They reached Madrid in just thirteen days, riding 750 miles, at one point over a pass in the Pyrenees only2 feet wide, and then down the 'terribly stony' backbone of Spain, lodging by night in bereft villages which 'the devil himself doth inhabit, if he dwelleth on earth'.

But if all that counted was winning over the 'commonalty' of the *Madrileños*, no more than this feat was required. 'The People here do mightily magnify the Gallantry of the Journey, and cry out that he deserv'd to have the Infanta thrown into his Arms the first night he came.'[15] Howell, who had crossed the Channel with Endymion's brother Thomas, a friend to whom he wrote often, knew the journey and its hazards well. He described the country acutely yet resentfully, remembering in particular the 'monstrous abruptness of the way' down through the Pyrenees.[16] A Welshman by birth, Howell disliked the starkness and the sheerness of the landscape, with its 'uncouth huge monstrous Excrescences of Nature . . . nothing but craggy stones', the peaks 'blanched over all the Year long with snows'. He wrote not unsympathetically of the villagers in the valleys whose throats were inflamed with goitre from having nothing to drink besides snow-water.[17] He preferred humanity in larger clumps. He had found Barcelona, for example, 'a proud wealthy City', and had come to know it well on his earlier trip. In doing so, however, he had also been forced to explore the eastern mountains and coastline of Spain, and had words of warning and advice for any who took the same route.

'These Parts of the Pyrenees that border on the *Mediterranean* are never without Thieves by Land (called *Bandoleros*) and Pirates on the Sea-side, which lie sculking in the hollows of the Rocks.' Travellers were frequently kidnapped and sold as slaves in Turkey. The safest way to travel, Howell advised, was to disguise oneself as a pilgrim and join the great numbers of the faithful on their way to pray to the shrine of the Lady of Montserrat at the 'stupendous Monastery, built on the top of a huge Land-Rock, whither it is impossible to go up, or come down by a direct way, but a Path is cut out full of Windings and Turnings'. The shrine itself held an image of the Virgin Mary all 'Sunburnt and tanned' from her flight into Egypt. Protestant stalwarts of the kind Howell accounted himself were not above posing as papists for their own protection.[18]

Howell could report that the prince 'hath been entertain'd with all the magnificence that possibly could be devised'.[19] Charles and Buckingham were given a vast apartment up in the royal palace above the city, the ancient Moorish Alcázar, claimed by the house of Castille after the Reconquest. They were also treated to the spectacle of a bullfight, which Howell, with the unperturbed interest in blood sports common to the time, explained to his correspondents in detail. 'It hath happen'd often-times,' he wrote calmly, 'that a Bull hath taken up two men upon his horns with their guts dangling about them; the horsemen run with lances and swords, the foot with goads.' For this reason, priests were stationed about the bullring. The pope, typically, had betrayed himself as spoilsport as well as antichrist by declaring the bullfight illegal and ungodly: 'yet it will not be left, the Nation hath taken such an habitual delight in it.'[20]

One sphere of clerical activity it was much more difficult to resist, or even escape, was that of the Inquisition, a nightmare shadow at the back of the English imagination. Among those interrogated and imprisoned, 'There are few,' Howell testified, when asked for an account of the frightening society's methods, 'do scape the Rack, or the *San-benito*, which is a strait yellow Coat without Sleeves, having the pourtrait of the Devil painted up and down in black.' The process of investigation into heresy began with an unheralded knock at the suspect's door, at any hour of day or night. The pockets, closets and barns of any thought to be 'brangling and pendulous' in their Catholic faith were instantly open to the inquisitors' sergeant, or 'familiar', as those officers were known. Judgement was passed behind closed doors, and the broken convict then passed over to the civil authorities for sentencing, since churchmen were forbidden to stain their hands with blood.[21]

Despite all his enemies would aver against him in coming decades, Charles was never tempted to emulate the methods of the Inquisition; but he admired the intense singularity of the Christian faith in Spain, and the inflexible system of hierarchy by which the Spanish court operated. He was impressed by the formality, the levels of decorum rising pyramidically in stringency and elaboration to the person of the king himself. It was the attention to detail, up on the hill above Madrid, that most impressed. When a royal sat to eat, the table was covered 'with a carpet, vpon which a Cloath is layd, and vpon this a Leather Carpet, and also a Cloath vpon that'. Each dish would be brought in by a procession of '3 corporals of the Spanish Guards, Germans & Burgundians: then 2 sergeants at Armes in maces of silver and gilt, engraved with the arms of Castilla and Leon', and so on, until the food was presented by a further series of servers. Silence, when the joint or morsel was shown, was taken to mean assent.

In other regions of life, every little routine action of the monarch or a member of the family set off a regimentalized chain reaction through the entire palace. The same could almost be said of the English court, too, yet the Spanish had greater rigour, placed greater weight in the merest particular, against far greater climactic odds. For an entirely casual sortie in the royal coach, 'the Drummes beate and Trumpets sound to give notice to the Nobility and Gentry at Court, to be ready with their attendance.' No event could be anything other than a state occasion.[22] It was, however, exactly this ceremonial rigidity that killed any hope of quick progress in Charles's courtship of the Infanta. He and Buckingham had tunnelled under the fortifications of Spanish diplomatic procedure, but they could not break through the barriers, visible and virtual, of the court itself. Merely being granted a sight of the Infanta was seen by the hosts as a major concession. Yet the longer the rituals went on of the retinues meeting each day or so, and sitting in baking silence, the dimmer any chances of regaining the Palatinate became. It had been all but impossible to broach the subject, since the prince's descent on the city had dashed to pieces the results of all previous discussion. 'He that deals with this Nation must have a great deal of phlegm,' as Howell later put it.[23]

Howell's pen left the clearest image of the Infanta herself: 'she is a very comely Lady, rather of a Flemish complexion than *Spanish*, fair-hair'd, and carrieth a most pure mixture of red and white in her Face: She is full and big-lipp'd; which is held a Beauty rather than a Blemish, or any Excess, in the Austrian family.' The twenty-year-old king had the same Habsburgian colouring, as did his youngest brother, Don Hernando, 'who, tho' a Youth of twelve, yet he is Cardinal and Archbishop of *Toledo*; which, in regard it hath the Chancellorship of *Castile* annexed to it, is the greatest spiritual Dignity in Christendom after the Papacy'. The people's favourite was the middle brother, Don Carlos, who was 'black-hair'd and of a Spanish hue'. Although he lacked any position within the state save that, unofficially, of acting as King Philip's constant companion, it was clearly Carlos the people had in mind when they sighed, 'O when shall we have a King again of our own Colour!' (As the contemporaneous author of *The Present Estate of Spayne* also noted, 'Nothing is more fearefull to them than the terror of the Inquisition, and nothing almost more desired by them then a king of a blacke complexion.')[24]

The English gentlemen squared up to their Spanish counterparts suspiciously, nervously, and with fascination. Disquietingly, there was much to admire, in dress and in deed. 'They are curiously apparelled in black' – as English gallants sometimes were: one thinks of John Donne's iconic portrait 'taken in shadows' – 'and their chiefest delights for recreation and pleasure are feates of Armes and Horses for service [dressage].' Even in a positive description such as Howell's, the Spaniards' refinements seemed more than a touch effete and narcissistic. 'They are stately in carriage, and much addicted to painting and perfuming of themselves.' It was their restraint, however, which proved most overpowering to the more choleric English gallants. Montaigne observed that the French and the Spanish were congenitally slow in reacting to intimidation or threat: they would not be discomposed until they were in the midst of a danger or eye to eye with an assailant.[25] Beyond that point, an unbelievable emotionalism exploded. According to Howell, the cavaliers of Madrid drank little wine and disliked duelling, 'but often vse priuate quarrelling in the streets, and are much giuen to suddaine desperate stabbing'.

Yet in the palace, such outbursts were not to be expected on the Spanish side. Their control of the baroqueries of negotiation was absolute. In a test of nerves, on Spanish soil, there could be only one winner.[26]

3

The spring grew beyond the height of an English summer, and as it did, the patience of the accumulating English delegation began to fail. Some years before, on a trip to Valencia (which had, he declared, 'the strongest Silks, the sweetest Wines, the excellentest Almonds, the best Oils, and beautiful'st Females of all *Spain*'), Howell had wondered how it was the same sun shining on all regions of the globe, since its effects were so different: 'those Rays that do but warm you in *England*, do half roast us here; those Beams that irradiate only, and gild your Honeysuckle Fields, do scorch and parch this chinky gaping Soil, and so put too many Wrinkles upon the Face of our common Mother the Earth.'[27] He was neither the first nor last red-faced Briton abroad to pant for a wet summer day.

Among those most frustrated was Prince Charles himself. Howell believed that he had not only taken his political business deeply to heart but had also really fallen for the Infanta Maria. On his visits to court, when the couple sat – some distance apart – before the public gaze, the English on one side, the Infanta with her parents, Don Carlos and the 'little cardinal' on the other, the letter-writer claimed to detect signs of genuine desire. 'I have seen the Prince have his Eyes immoveably fix'd upon the *Infanta* half an hour together in a thoughtful speculative posture, which sure would needs be tedious, unless affection did sweeten it.' He had seen him wait for an hour in a coach on the street to catch a glimpse of her when she left the palace in her carriage. About two months after reaching Madrid, the prince decided to break the deadlock.

It was reported that the Infanta rose at dawn to gather May-dew in the palace grounds, making her way to a little summer house. This was where, early one morning, Charles planned to catch her, and force a private interview. Yet instead she remained within a private orchard, obliging the prince to climb the inner garden wall, and make the drop – 'a great height' – to the lawn below. Endymion Porter, his attendant, translator and accomplice for the day, a dozen years his senior, followed, landed sorely, and had just gathered his senses when they were shaken loose once more by a young woman shrieking in horror. The Infanta Maria had spotted the prince making his way towards her through the garden. Her ladies-in-waiting quickly added their voices in alarm, bringing back something of the characteristic reserve the prince had fought down in order to take this impetuous step. His way was blocked by the Infanta's guardian, an old nobleman, who fell on his knees before him. When Charles's attendant caught up, rustling and panting in his ruff and doublet, he explained that the gentleman was begging the prince to retire – he would pay with his head if the Infanta were caught with the prince. Round-faced, pale-skinned Doña Maria was already long gone, back inside the shadows of the Alcázar, its walls and turrets beginning to dazzle in the morning light.

They left the orchard, abashed, and the day broadened into yet another of fruitless ceremony, the round broken only by strident protest from the Spanish at the prince's breach of protocol. Endymion Porter returned wearily to the quarters their hosts had set aside for them. They were accommodated in the Moorish palace above the city, flat nothing to the east beyond the walls, the Guadarrama mountains behind to the west. Charles and Buckingham were treated well, but their attendants – who grew considerably in number as the year went on – were given less comfortable lodging. The rooms were 'so nasty and illfavourably kept that a farmer in England would be ashamed of such another', said one of Endymion's younger colleagues on the mission.[28]

It was domestic strife that weighed more heavily on Porter. For months now he had been writing to his wife, Olive, that he would soon be coming home, and for months he had had to calm her suspicions and soothe her disappointments. Troubling reports that reached her had to be quashed many weeks after the event. It was extraordinary, too, how rumour travelled. 'As I hope for mercy at God's hands I neither kissed nor touched any woman since I left you, and for the innkeeper's daughter at Boulogne, I was so far from kissing her, that as I hope to be saved I cannot remember that I saw any such woman. No, Olive, I am not a dissembler.' She could not, at least, rebuke him for failing to write. From his first nights in Madrid he had sat late with a candle. 'Although I have so much employment here that I have scarce time to dress myself, yet if I should not watch and lose my sleep to write to thee, I were unworthy of such a wife and could not deserve the smallest part of thy inestimable love to me.'[29] The ink would blur before his tired eyes as he blew it dry with a sprinkling of cold ash, the letter would be sealed – sometimes with a ring or another trifle, sometimes bound up in a parcel with a pouch of sovereigns, or a bag of pennies for Olive to use as counters at cards – and be dispatched as another delayed instalment of love. Endymion relied a lot, over the years, on such deliveries to service his marriage. At home in the Cotswolds, Olive prompted him tartly to maintain the supply.

Endymion was perfectly acquainted with the crust of formality the Spanish built up within the Alcázar to seal out the poverty in the streets of Madrid, the discontent within its more prosperous quarters, and was unbothered by it. His private and official letters reveal none of the exasperation his friend the Earl of Carlisle expressed, for example, on having to kneel before the Infanta for more than an hour, while she sat 'as the image of the Virgin Mary', without a murmur or a nod of acknowledgement. He also saw how genuinely charmed the court and the Spanish public had been by the manner of the prince's arrival.

Knowing Olivares well since boyhood, Endymion could not fail to see how the count out-manoeuvred Buckingham. Like so many in the English court, he owed the duke everything – his houses, his monopolies, even his wife, Buckingham's niece, Olivia Boteler – but he was not blind. Perhaps most embarrassingly of all, Prince Charles himself continued his impromptu attempts to break through the impasse. At a strictly scripted meeting with the Infanta before the court, he outraged her by departing from the agreed declaration by stammering out an improvised speech of his own. Doña Maria turned and left the burnished chamber without a word. She had been appalled from the beginning at the very idea of wedding a Protestant infidel. 'What a comfortable bedfellow you will have,' her confessor supposedly told her when the prince had first arrived. 'He who lies by your side, and who will be the father of your children, is certain to go to hell.'[30]

What Porter did not understand so well was the battered and impoverished society against which all the grave dignity and infinitesimally exact laws of the court were mustered in denial. The country was 'drained and discommodated' by its wars in Europe:[31] the gold shipped from the Indies was not enriching the country but merely plating its aristocracy. Howell's letters are silent as to the gentlemanly beggars and swindlers of Spanish satire, enemies of the daylight that exposed their clothes' straying thread. He was not among those waking from lice-ridden beds to assemble the twelve patches of a single shirt. Yet they seem real enough; the arch-satirist Quevedo, present in Madrid throughout the prince's stay, suggests that the capital would have been a ghostly city without them.[32] They are the literary symbols of a wider effort to maintain appearances.

These different realities were reflected in the Spanish literature Howell now read deeply and widely. The poets of the golden age of Spanish wit displayed the full potential of conceit which Donne tried bringing into English, and outdid Jonson with their ear for common speech. The scholar Arthur Terry, commending 'the power of artifice' those writers demonstrated, notes an extraordinary ability to 'combine the popular and the sophisticated in a single poem'.[33] Spanish poets pierced the highest realms of Neoplatonic vision, exploited their *palabras cultas* ('cultured words') to the full; yet they could not exclude a savage, ragged panoply of life. Quevedo, who had the misfortune to be lame and extremely short-sighted, and held a bitter view of human nature, harpooned the predators of those depths unerringly. Yet satire is frequently a means for the writer of restraining – or concealing – a buried sentimentality; and Quevedo, for all his superlative harshness, was no exception. Locked in the *Epístola satírica y censoria*, written for his patron Olivares, was a heartfelt wish to bring back a Spain of true wonder which was largely, though not entirely, of his own imagining.

Once, while Porter, Prince Charles and Buckingham, peeping through the curtains of their 'private' coach, were observing the Infanta passing through the streets with her parents in an open carriage, Porter was alarmed at how 'the searching vulgar', the pressing, nameless crowds, closed in on and surrounded them, so that they could not move on. 'The King's guard was forced to beat them from it and make way through the multitude,' he told Olive. 'They all cried, "God bless him,"' he was happy to add, 'and showed as much affection generally as ever was seen among people, only they took it ill he showed not himself to them in a more public manner.'[34] Charles, as he would for the rest of his life, took kindlier to more elegant attentions. The wits of the Spanish court, still 'much taken with our Prince, and the bravery of his journey, and his discrete comportment since', were busy composing encomia for him, celebrating his love for the Infanta. Howell fed a number of translations to his readers in England:

> Grateful's to me the fire, the wound, the chain,
> By which *Love* burns, *Love* binds, and giveth pain;
> But for to quench this fire, these bonds to lose,
> These wounds to heal, I would not could I choose:
> Strange sickness, where the wounds, the bonds, the fire
> That burns, that bind, that hurt, I must desire –[35]

He was eager for his readers' opinion on the verses; and some might have been tempted to observe an allusion to syphilis in the Latin hexastich Howell rendered competently enough here. It approaches the sort of thing covered by the harsh 'decree against poets' Quevedo once suggested might be necessary.[36]

Outside and below the palace, Madrid continued to blaze and go brown. Howell reported that the English now had 'a flourishing Court' of their own in place, although they continued to denounce their lodgings as sties: the Earls of Carlisle, Rochfort, Holland, Denbigh 'and divers others' had assembled, along with the comptroller of the prince's household and large numbers of other gentlemen.[37]

Here in Madrid such men were *caballeros*, cavaliers; a standard term in Romance languages for gentlemen with the right to bear arms. Historically the modern cavalier had his origins among the twelfth-century *caballeros villanos*, as a 'commoner knight' granted certain feudal freedoms.[38] Symbolically, though, the word still conjured up the medieval ideal of the beautiful life, the existence of a knight in arms, a vision of decorum and chivalry. Yet in England and in the English language the cavalier attracted suspicion, not only as of something foreign, imported and possibly effeminate, but also a dangerous and antisocial character. When Jonson's solid citizenry see 'a gallant, a *cavaliero*', he seems to them 'right hangman cut' – ready made for the gallows.[39]

Behind the palace walls, the Alcázar grounds were green, fed by underwater springs the Moors had tapped seven hundred years before. The pre-nuptial talks, meanwhile, kept catching on snag after snag. A special dispensation was needed from the pope to permit the devout Infanta to marry the heretic prince. Shortly after it came, compromised with many conditions and subclauses the English could never accept, the pope died – and his successor insisted that all discussions must go back, once again, to the very beginning. All such delays, Buckingham in particular realized, suited Olivares's intentions perfectly. As Madrid entered the dog days, tempers snapped and the process began to unravel. One of the prince's young pages collapsed with heat stroke. A short while before the boy died and was buried beneath a fig tree in the ambassador's garden, a Catholic priest tried going in to murmur absolution. Spotting him, one of the Englishmen[40] stopped the cleric on the stairs and punched him in the face.

For his part, King James's bottom line was that the marriage could only go ahead if 'the surrendry of the Palatinate' took place simultaneously, returning his daughter to her throne. When these terms were finally put to him so bluntly, the young Spanish king could only protest that ''Twas none of his to give; 'tis true, he had a few Towns there, but he held them as Commissioner only for the [Holy Roman] Emperor, and he could not command an Emperor.' With this, 'all was dash'd in pieces, and that frame which was rearing so many years [a match between Spanish and British royalty] was ruin'd in a moment.'[41]

By late August, Prince Charles could stay no longer. An English fleet was at sea to collect him. The dignity of the escort fell somewhat flat when Charles fell into the sea and had to be rescued by one of his followers. Back in Madrid, Howell reported, 'There are many here shrink in their shoulders, and are very sensible of his departure, and the Lady *Infanta* resents it more than any.' She had a mass offered daily in her chapel for the prince to have a safe journey. His persistence, in the view of some observers at least, had gone some way to winning her appreciation, if nothing else. 'The *Spaniards* themselves confess there was never Princess so bravely woo'd.'[42]

On the flagship making for England, the Duke of Buckingham seethed: he had lost all patience with the Spanish, and with his own ambassador, Lord Digby. On saying farewell the duke had promised Count Olivares that he would have his revenge. Whether or not Endymion Porter translated his exact words has not been recorded, but the count could presumably read the body language. Buckingham was also determined to see the complete ruination of Digby, whom he despised for less tangible reasons. Yet when the prince eventually reached London, the whole city – indeed the whole country – was waiting for him with celebratory bonfires and fanfares, so great was the relief that the unholy alliance had failed. From Spain one could forget the hatred the match inspired in countless English hearts. The loathing of the old enemy and their Church went too deep: when a secret chapel near St Paul's collapsed in November 1623, the disaster prompted Alexander Gill to gloat in verse over the Catholics crushed to death beneath the roof. When the prince and his favourite returned, some beat drums, waved torches crazily and danced about the pyres; some made their opinion clear in subtler and longer lasting form. In thanksgiving for the prince returning a bachelor, Lord Camfield built Groombridge church in Kent according to a strictly non-cruciform plan, conspicuously suppressing any hint of papist design.[43] The opposition, socialized and elaborated to different degrees, was equally implacable, and would shortly dictate a sharp turn in policy.

4

Time was also passing in the larger world. That summer Madrid was shaken by news from the east of the assassination of Sultan Osman, the Grand Turk, 'a violent hater of Christians, in the flower of his years, in the heat and height of his courage'. He was killed by a mere foot soldier, Howell learned; although his murder might have taken any number of forms in the days and weeks just before, since the Ottoman empire was incensed with him for a poor campaign against the Polish.

Osman had blamed the failure on his Janissaries, accusing them of being more eager to return to their wives than wage honest war. Having lost the love of his army, he then outraged the clergy by melting down sacred silver and gold for an offering he was purporting to make on pilgrimage to Mecca. He did not get the chance to set out. A junta came to his palace and demanded he drop his plans to go abroad and dismiss his 'ill Counselors' – a phrase that became one of the standard revolutionary formulas of the age, far to the west. The party of nobles had the sultan's grand vizier dismembered on the spot, while Osman himself fled for cover to an outhouse in the gardens. By the time he was found and clapped in irons, the rebels had decided to bring Osman's simpleminded uncle, Mustapha, out of imprisonment and to install him as temporary sultan. A new grand vizier was on his way to supervise the strangulation of Osman in prison when 'a robust boisterous Rogue' beat him to the task, knocking the sultan down with a battle axe.

In a long account of the coup, savouring the detail and the supposed differences between the Turkish civilization and his own, Howell wrote of how 'this Tragedy makes me give over wondering at any thing that ever I heard or read, to shew the lubricity of *mundan* Greatness, as also the fury of the Vulgar, which, like an impetuous Torrent, gathers strength by degrees as it meets with divers Dams, and being come to the height, cannot stop itself.'[44] The production of Osman's uncle Mustapha from prison reminded him of how the future Queen Elizabeth was also brought uncertainly from captivity in 1558. His correspondent, Sir James Crofts, might have objected to the comparison, but further, future parallels would offer themselves.

Alert and alive to the course of distant news that reached the despondency of Madrid, Howell was in his letters still preoccupied above all with immediate events, which they narrate and comment on with unparalleled fluency and liveliness. For a few months, the tight bulb of political activity over the Alcázar had contained the future of English history, and to an extent that of the Continent as well. Reflecting on the outcome – 'dash'd all in pieces' – Howell's busy pen led him to meditate on how the tiniest of events could overturn long processes. He compared 'the civil actions of men . . . with the natural production of man', and lost himself for many lines in a protracted description of conception and gestation. 'To make man, there are many acts must precede; first a meeting and copulation of the Sexes, then Conception, which requires a well-disposed Womb to retain the prolifical seed . . .' He wrote with care and some pride in his knowledge of natural science – his physician in London was William Harvey, the demonstrator of the blood's circulation. Returning to the matter at hand, he went on, 'And as the *Embryo* in the Womb is wrapp'd in three membranes or tunicles, so this great business, you know better than I, was involv'd in many difficulties, and died so entangled before it could break through them.'[45]

Howell soon enough returned to England, not much more successfully than Prince Charles. He sailed aboard a ship that was carrying a set of jewels which Charles had given the Infanta, and which the Spanish were very decently returning. In London he found his own 'vital Spirits' fighting again for survival, and decided to place his hopes upon some form of employment with Buckingham, by now the greatest power in the land. By this time Buckingham had turned heel on his hosts in Madrid, and was urging Parliament to fund a war with Spain – largely to relieve his feelings. Howell, a Hispanophile and an unflagging supporter of the Spanish match, decided to write the duke a letter of advice:

My Lord, you are a great Prince, and all Eyes are upon your Actions; this makes you more subject to envy, which like the Sun-beams beats always upon Rising-grounds. I know your Grace hath many sage and solid Heads about you; yet I trust it will prove no offence, if out of the late relation I have to your Grace by the recommendation of such noble Personages, I put in also my *Mite*.[46]

Howell's customary voice only peeped through in that last word, his speck of timely counsel. He thought it best, however, to keep his thoughts on foreign policy to himself. His main suggestion was that the duke should give him a job in the Admiralty.

He was disappointed; the duke, he was told, had learned that Howell was too '*Digbyfied*', too much a friend of Buckingham's rival in Spain, the Earl of Bristol. Which was the truth, though Howell still denied it, with little pity for the adept destruction of his hopes and fortunes Lord Digby was then experiencing at Buckingham's hands. Briefly, it had seemed that England and Scotland had a *caballero* as their future king, raising the hopes of internationalists such as Howell. But the patriots in London and further afield had their way; and so, Howell told his father, in the phrase he always used, 'I was now the fourth time at a dead stand in the course of my Fortune.'[47]

3. The End of Steenie

The people . . . will much resent it, that in businesses wherein
the wealth, peace and reputation of a Kingdome is interessed,
Kings should adventure for the gaining of a little, to put
themselves in hazard of losing much.

– Juan de Santa Maria, *Christian Policie* (translated 1632)

1

The ships that suffered their way out into the Channel on a stiff day late
in June 1627 made a less than convincing display. 'Such a rotten, miserable fleet set out to sea no men ever saw,' was one verdict that woke
many echoes. 'Our enemies seeing it may scoff at our nation.'[1] This was
hardly the navy's fault: Parliament had refused the mission a penny in
funds. Buckingham was relying instead on a deeply unpopular Forced
Loan, imposed directly by the Crown. Yet a full easterly wind saw them
out from Stokes Bay, and it was hard to deny the power of that sight,
the silent magnitude of the sails in the main, whatever flaws an expert
eye might have found. The plan was to relieve the community of Protestants at the French port of La Rochelle, which was besieged by the
forces of Cardinal Richelieu.

However shabby in appearance as a whole, the fleet still included
some of the country's most affluent and fashionable younger gentlemen
and nobles. Among these 'voluntaries' was John Suckling, fresh out of
Cambridge and newly enrolled at the Middle Temple. Very recently his
father had died, and as the eldest son Suckling was to inherit all the family's 'Mannors, Messuages, houses, Landes, Tenaments & heridaments
across Suffolk, Lincoln & Middlesex', along with a sprinkling of other
lucrative properties. The full legacy, however, would only be his when
Suckling reached the age of twenty-five: in 1627 he was eighteen, and

thus planned to spend the interim acquiring some experience of war and travel. On 18 May he and three other cadets went to enlist in Lord Mountjoy's company at Southampton, 'mounted vpon sufficient horses'. They were to bear 'their armes according to the discipline and practise of Carebins a Cheval' – cavaliers.[2]

Even favourable commentators put the blame for what ensued firmly on the English expedition's general, Buckingham, the Lord High Admiral. 'Wanting judgement in himself, he was facile to follow other men that had less than himself,' was the verdict of Sir John Oglander, former deputy-governor of Portsmouth, who was well acquainted with the navy's preparations. Yet for Oglander, Buckingham was also 'one of the handsomest men in the whole world . . . of a kind, liberal and free nature'.[3]

A chaplain aboard Buckingham's flagship agreed with this view. Robert Herrick, who had been a slightly unlikely priest for four years by then, was much more at home among his books or with book-loving company in town than he was at sea or in the field, but his duty as well as his welfare lay here at the Great Duke's side.

The expedition began inauspiciously, when the fleet was distracted by some Dunkirk pirates in the Channel and gave chase for five days; thus giving the forces occupying the environs of La Rochelle, and the close-lying Île de Ré, still more time to prepare than Richelieu's agents had already provided. From his house and gardens on the Isle of Wight, laid out in the noble yet intimate Elizabethan style, like many other engaged subjects John Oglander was perfectly clear in his own mind as to what went wrong and where the mistakes were made. His contacts back at Portsmouth kept him precisely informed, and he recorded his views at some length in his commonplace book.

La Rochelle was a prospering town with strong sea defences and long, airy arcaded boulevards, freshened by the huge seaboard skies. The populace harboured fierce memories still of the previous century's religious civil wars, which reinforced a partisan identity: however much the marble suggested an Atlantic Venice, or a lost Dalmatian city, the prosperity of La Rochelle was built on Protestant trade. James Howell was upset by the manners of the people when he visited in 1620. 'I do not find them so gentle and debonair to Strangers, nor so hospitable as the rest of *France*.' He put the inhospitality down to republican leanings.[4] The Rochelais bided their time, it seemed, in judging a venture. When the Duke of Rohan made an ill-advised and opportunistic stand against Richelieu, the Huguenot burghers of the town waited to see if it marked the beginning of a true national crusade against the cardinal and his *dévots*. But they would still bear the brunt of Richelieu's reprisals.

La Rochelle was besieged on its landward side; and later, in 1625, the year that Rohan charged and fired ships that had been allocated to blockade the city, Buckingham was duped into lending Richelieu the vessels he needed to wipe out the Huguenots' fleet. At home, Buckingham had thus appeared the friend of Catholic tyrants yet again, putting honest Protestants to fire and sword. In truth he had merely honoured the terms of England's new alliance with France (and the Dutch Republic) against Spain. So now, two years later, he was sailing to right matters. He would rescue La Rochelle, and trigger a rebellion across France against Richelieu. The Rochelais, wary enough of the trouble their own volatile champion, Rohan, had brought them, were not especially eager for Buckingham's assistance.

Île de Ré is a low-lying, swift-looking, wind-rushed island, oddly serpentine, the shape of something wriggling away from the mainland. Its garrison, blockading La Rochelle, was stationed on the slanting northern side of the island, in the Fort of St Martin, a small but impregnable citadel. Its thick, sloping walls were set out, as the art of fortification dictated, in the shape of a star, thus increasing both the number of surfaces the enemy had to bombard, and the fire to which he was exposed between its points.

With plenty of forewarning, the garrison's commanding officer, Toiras, prepared for a long siege, and evacuated the women and children in the last of his ships. On a strong northerly wind, the huge if dowdy English invasion force rose over the horizon, and drew in to the island. It took several attempts, and several clashes, to find a viable disembarking point, a protruding stretch of coast accessible on either side that the ships from their berths could easily support with enfilade fire. As the army landed, Toiras dispatched a fierce greeting to welcome them, but seeing the odds were hopeless in the open, left the remainder of the island to the invaders and shut fast the doors of St Martin.

So far so good: 'Our first Invasion was magnanimous and brave,' was James Howell's estimate. The number of French dead, no doubt exaggerated, was put at two hundred, and from a cosy niche in London Howell chortled at the story that, when English despoilers were 'rifling the bodies of the *French* Gentlemen . . . they found that many of them had their Mistresses' Favours ty'd about their genitories.'[5]

On landing on Ré, leading 'those brave chevaliers, such spirits as France could not equal', Buckingham decided to dig in for a siege.[6] The odds, certainly, seemed overwhelming. Yet Toiras elegantly declined the terms 'Bouqingam' offered, and sent a confident letter to King Louis, via a messenger forced to swim for his life, that he would hold both the fort and the island. The two generals continued the most courteous and genial of correspondences. When Toiras requested that three injured gentlemen be allowed safe passage to the mainland, Buckingham sent a ship to carry them, past the entire English fleet, in a cabin finely hung and furnished, with musicians to soothe their distress. Toiras sent gifts in thanks, vases of chypre and flasks of orange-water.

If ever a Dumas-style plot could be proven in which Buckingham disabled his own army in order to honour a secret pact with Richelieu, then the course of events would corroborate it perfectly; but no other explanation than bad luck and less than inspired leadership, rather than duplicity or even outright incompetence, has so far come to light. With chaplains such as Herrick and his friend John Weekes, meanwhile, more given to classical allusion and wordplay in sermons than militant exhortation, Buckingham and his officers may have lacked divine inspiration.

They waited to attack any of the strategic positions until their under-fed, under-equipped and under-motivated men were 'most sick and dead'. This was the point the English had reached by 6 November, when Buckingham decided to launch a frontal assault. The attack was bravely rebuffed by a garrison also at the point of breaking; two days later Buckingham sent word to Toiras that he intended to withdraw. But he was not allowed to leave with either the remains of his reputation or his famishing army intact.

French reinforcements on the mainland were now at the point of deployment, and the English found themselves exposed. Transfixed as in a dream, weighed down by the inertia of exhausted numbers, they neither retreated coherently nor rallied for a full engagement, 'until so many French had landed they were forced to retire'. A wretched showing then turned into an outright military catastrophe. As the

French encroached from sea and land, Buckingham led a messy with-drawal from the position his engineers had in fact managed to fortify reasonably well to another, completely exposed, minor atoll, 'being a small salt island'. Split apart and lost, in many cases unarmed, the English soldiers had to scramble for their honour and their lives in the island's crumbling gulleys, moving as best they could in the general direction of their helpless ships. One officer, Colonel Gray, was sucked into a salt pit, 'and being ready to be drown'd, he cry'd out, *Cent mille escus pour ma rançon*; *A hundred thousand Crowns for my ransom.*' He was quickly rescued by French fortune hunters, who were disappointed to learn their catch 'was not worth a hundred thousand pence'.[7]

The majority falling into French hands were not so lucky. A massacre ensued: 'some 20 Colours – such a loss as France never before could brag they got of the English'. It was a shocking reversal, and the carnage only slowed with the early fall of November darkness, pitiless and cold, when 'the French, with their pikes, did at their pleasure now kill those men (lying in the water and mudde) whose eies before they durst scarse behold.'[8] Many of the deaths, however, were due to organizational fail-ure on the part of the duke and his officers. From the relative safety of the flagship, Herrick could only watch as hundreds of retreating Eng-lish infantrymen were trodden down by their own cavalry, which had been placed in the rear instead of the van. 'I may truly say our own horse killed as many as the enemy,' wrote Oglander. Among these cav-alrymen were inexperienced debutants such as Suckling, no doubt unnerved, their accoutrements as 'Carebins a Cheval' disordered or abandoned in the rush to safety. The colours struck and terms accepted, the wounded lay a long time aboard the English ships until the winds allowed them to begin the voyage back, on 17 November. Only three thousand of Buckingham's eight thousand-strong army returned from the Île de Ré. The mission was described as England's 'shamefulest overthrow' since the loss of Normandy, or 'since England was England', as one commentator put it.[9]

Yet unlike his counterparts in London, at least the duke's chaplain, Robert Herrick, had the clearing of the bloodstained beaches, the burn-ing of the horses' carcasses, and his hurried and exhausted prayers for the dead to occupy his mind on the winter crossing home, and distract him for a while from fears about his living.

Saint-Martin-de-Ré is now a busy seaside town, the restaurants in the harbour full of cyclists and hikers, the houses where Lord Toiras's men were billeted painted white, with roughly matching green shutters on the windows. The air on the island still has a saline virtue. Outside the old fortress walls, however, the surfaces have a stark look about them, as if scrubbed very forcibly clean. The island later became the point of departure for convicts on their way to Devil's Island.

2

A few attempts, however, were naturally made to cast the episode in a positive, even a glorious light. Edward, Lord Herbert of Cherbury, was indignant at the crowing which reached his ears from France. The valour of Buckingham's men had surely earned a share of the laurels. 'It will perpetually renowne you,' he addressed the French (in Latin) from his desk, 'that you affected a safe rather than a doubtfull victory . . . besides that great slaughter you made of our men and taking away of our Collours, may be reported among the cheefest Trophees and spoiles you have ever gotten.' But he declared that the fine show the English had made in the early skirmishes, their occupation of the island for three months, their repulsion of any attempt at dislodging them, were equally worth honouring. It surely counted for something, too, that 'we offered to fight with you, both by sea and land, so many times.' And if the justice of that was denied, well then – 'our victories were masculine, glorious, and due to our virtue; . . . yours was only opportune, obnoxious, and momentary.'[10]

Yet Parliament and the public thought otherwise. The martial sensibilities of the nation had been gravely wounded. It was not so much the scale as the manner of the defeat, the ineptitude, the wasting of time and provisions, the apparent loss of nerve in sitting still so long. Had Buckingham's bold plan worked – or even had it come asunder on the ramparts of St Martin, and not in the survivors' miserable crawl through the 'nooks and windinges of the ditches' towards refuge – he would have been immortalized. Instead, on his return, unrepentant but disheartened, Buckingham found himself in real political danger, and with him, necessarily, the entire structure of patronage and administration he had built up over a decade of unassailable influence. If Buckingham fell, his dependants would soon fall with him, and topple much further down past him.

There would always be creatures and clients, there would always be enemies, but since Steenie could never tolerate an equal he had few sure friends on whom to rely. The slightest sign of autonomy, meanwhile, among his minions, made their removal necessary. His former ally (and Suckling's uncle) the Earl of Middlesex, as an example, had considered marrying a relative of Buckingham's enemy the Earl of Southampton while Charles and the duke were courting the Infanta in Madrid. Thus when they returned, Middlesex was fed to Parliament's wolves in 1624.

He was a major loss to Buckingham's camp. He had risen from middle-class origins to the peerage and the post of Lord Treasurer. A merchant by trade, and a hugely successful one, Middlesex had always opposed a costly and futile war with Spain or France. He disliked expensive embassies too, but supported the diplomacy for the Spanish match as a sensible move for trade and security. When Buckingham made his about-turn towards Spain in favour of war, Middlesex was left isolated. Irregularities were found in his book-keeping; he was impeached, and withdrew from politics for the remainder of his days, sustained by his vast private fortune. Another possible competitor and critic was thus eliminated: but also a competent ally for the Buckingham cabal. Besides the dry accountant's eye he brought to the business of government, which did much to improve the royal finances during his spell in office, Middlesex was privy to every shady practice in the tight community of London's merchants. Although disparaged by hereditary nobles as a shopkeeper, and disliked by former fellow traders as a turncoat, by his position and past history Middlesex briefly held a unique power over both species of English magnate – the high-born and the self-made. In earlier Jacobean parliaments he had also proven himself a shrewd political operator.

These assets were lost to Buckingham when he decided Middlesex was possibly too intelligent for his own good. Toppling a court figure of Middlesex's stature, moreover, necessarily created resentment lower down the chain of political being. The Earl of Middlesex's nephew John Suckling, for example, was financially secure to the point of utter complacency; but he looked upon his uncle as a mentor, and although he volunteered for Buckingham's excursion to Ré – that being simply the done thing – his early writings reveal a marked ambivalence towards the duke. A sweet and simple early poem about Judgement Day remarks how, at the 'last *Trompe*', the young man could rely on no political favours to buy off the Almighty:

> And now noe summes of gold, noe bribes (alasse)
> Could mee reprieve, Sentence must straight waie passe.
> Great Frends could nothing doe, noe lustfull Peere,
> Noe smooth-fac'd *Buckingham*, was *Favourite* here.

The very absence of a Buckingham, however, in a nicely understated paradox, ensures that the celestial court can reach a fair and generous verdict. All the persona of Suckling's young poem need do is resort to the formula of repentance that had guaranteed salvation for countless generations of Christians until the Reformation:

> But yet methoughts it was too much to dy,
> To die a while, much lesse eternally:
> And therefore straight I did my Sinnes unmaske
> And in *Christ's* name, a *Pardon* there did aske
> Which *God* then granted; and *God* grant hee may
> Make this my dreame prove true i'th'latter day.[11]

There is a great deal of confidence in this closing prayer. Suckling's notebook of school-day verse opens the gate to a kingdom a long way from the political tensions of Buckingham's court, the angst hanging over London's Calvinist merchants and puritan apprentices. He would always describe himself – wryly, for sure – as trying to be a 'good Protestant', but emotionally he lay closer to the Catholic certainties of an earlier century, an undivided England, when France and not Spain was the enemy to be feared.

Suckling's mother, Martha Cranfield, was the sister of Lionel, later Earl of Middlesex, and it was from her, guessed Aubrey in his brief life of the poet, that Suckling inherited his wit. This was a quality, at least, to which her tombstone paid tribute: Martha died in 1613, when Suckling was four. His maternal relatives connected Suckling to the edginess of city trade and urban wit, the nervous preoccupation with finding a new angle on things: Cranfield was a patron of the Mermaid Tavern's literary circle and a friend of John Donne. Suckling's father, however, Sir John the elder, the substantial landowner, merchant and politician, 'was but a dull fellow'. He had no more poetry to his credit than a few lines which most declared execrable.[12]

In the Sucklings and the Cranfields the young poet combined two of the dominant, if not always entirely compatible, seams in the English gentry; the one, nouveau riche and cosmopolitan, the other rooted and by outlook rural. The clan had moreover followed the course which Sir John Oglander swore was essential for the English gentry. Writing in his own blood, as he did for all his most earnest entries, he declared that country gentlemen could not stay in the country. Following the plough would keep them honest, but they must get themselves to town, learn to be merchants, lawyers or sailors.[13]

Suckling as yet remained a Middlesex boy, close to the city, but not of it. The dominant impressions in his earliest manuscripts are of immemorial country sports and practices occasioned by feast days in the ancient Christian calendar, and images of rural pedlars and games of barley break would linger on well into his adult writing. Puritan 'plough-day writs' are deprecated in spirited defences of the 'god of sports' and Christmas holidays. Herod's massacre of the innocents is lamented in conventional terms, but death, let alone damnation, was not to be contemplated.

This world of minor but upwardly mobile gentry was essentially that in which George Villiers, Duke of Buckingham, was formed, and those who looked on its comforts too fondly were prey to nostalgia. Many in England were weighed down by the memory of times they were convinced were better. 'Now Peace and Law have beggared us all,' complained Oglander of King James's rule, which ended in 1625. Born in 1586, for Oglander the reign of Queen Elizabeth was the golden age. Money was more evenly distributed, the markets thrived and tenants were happy. England was at war with Spain rather than with her partners and customers in France, and the Dutch were kept in their place.[14]

That whole distant period was gilded with delight. In the summer of 1596, Oglander recalled, when he was just a boy of ten, the Captain of the Isle of Wight threw a farewell banquet in the forest of Parkhurst, where the trees spread and interlocked so thickly that a good climber could make his way right across the woods from bough to bough. The captain, Sir George Carew, was leaving Wight to take up the post of Lord Chamberlain at Elizabeth's court, and he made sure the feast was a lavish occasion. There was a play performed in the woods by young people from the island, the militia paraded, and artillery fire sounded at every toast. As a special touch, a local man was sent up into the branches of 'My Lady's Oak', with the task of pouring sweet water to run down the grooves in the bole when grace was said, to give the impression that the tree was blessing the feast with its sap. Unfortunately, this stage assistant fell asleep, and when the prayer was said no water flowed. Behind the scenes, someone thrust a pike up through the branches. The sleeper woke with a start, and, so Oglander guessed, must have dropped his basin in shock and pain. For instead of dripping down gently, the water fell in one splash, drenching everyone beneath.[15]

This was recognizably the bucolic world that a privileged child of the gentry such as Suckling had never had to leave, and which the Reverend Robert Herrick, though a city-dweller by birth, came to celebrate:

> There's not a budding Boy, or Girle, this day,
> But is got up, and gone to bring in May.
> A deale of Youth, ere this, is come
> Back, and with *White-thorn* laden home.
> Some have dispatcht their Cakes and Creame,
> Before that we have left to dreame:
> And some have wept, and woo'd, and plighted Troth,
> And chose their Priest, ere we can cast off Sloth.[16]

Ben Jonson had this kind of writing in mind when he wrote, 'It hath blood and juice, when the words are proper and apt, their sound sweet, and the phrase neat and picked.'[17] Yet Oglander's well-fed air, the aura of a vintage memory taken up from the cellar, is absent here. For Herrick was not recalling the past but writing a fiction about a moment in the vanishing present. His idyll had not passed but *was* passing, had not yet been fully tasted, and would live insufficiently in depressed, middle-aged memory. Casting off sloth was thus of the greatest importance:

Get up, sweet Slug-a-bed, and see
The Dew-besprangling Herbe and Tree.
Each Flower has wept, and bowed toward the East,
Above an houre since; yet you not drest,
Nay! Not so much as out of bed?[18]

Time and again in his festive verse, apparently so happy, he presses the young to enjoy their moment. The tone of these poems, though, is always complicated by the constituency of the imagined listeners. There are those for whom Herrick's urgency has immediate relevance – the boys and girls out Maying; and there are those for whom it is already too late. It is never quite clear whether Herrick's own poetic speaker belongs to those who cast off sloth in time or those who failed to do so. In the poem quoted above, 'Corinna's Going a Maying', the poet takes on the voice of one dragging his love from her bed to enjoy the pursuits he lingers over so delectably – the cakes and ale, the cream, the 'dew-besprangling' forms of early morning. But he (and she) significantly are not among the young people already out collecting dew and, before the day is out, plighting their troth. They are already missing out. The poem instead creates a sense of what it is *like* to be one of those boys and girls, out, by sheer instinct, in the first dewy sun. The simple jolliness of the poem is not so simple at all. Participating in the idyll is not so much a matter of going to a certain place, performing a certain ritual or getting up at a certain time as attaining a certain state of mind, one in which pleasures can be felt – and one to which the boys and girls of 'Corinna' might really not be necessary. Herrick's depth as a poet lies in his striving for the superficial, his avoidance of over-witty complexity. His blood and juice, his neat and picked phrasing, have a sense of something missed rather than a sentimental longing for something enjoyed, since they summon up ideas of pleasures not (or not *quite*) partaken of.

Herrick personally had less happy memories of the late Elizabethan era that was so precious in memory to Oglander and others. He was still a baby when his father was killed by a fall. Master Nicholas Herrick was a goldsmith, the father of seven surviving children, who lived with his family in an ample townhouse in Cheapside. The Herricks came from solid mercantile, middle-class stock: Nicholas's family was from Leicestershire, where his grandfather John had served as the county town's mayor. His wife, Julian, was the daughter of another London tradesman. The couple had been married for ten years when in November 1592 Nicholas drew up his will, describing himself as being 'of perfect memorye in sowle, but sicke in bodye'. Two days later he died in the street below an upper-storey window of their house on Goldsmith's Row.

The question, as the gravedigger and amateur jurist in *Hamlet* would have it, was whether Nicholas had gone to the water or whether the water had come to him. This was not merely a question of emotional importance to a bereaved family coming to terms with his death. Proven suicides were not only denied full burial rites but immediately forfeited their estates to the High Almoner, at that time the Lord Bishop of Bristol, one Dr Fletcher. If Fletcher felt that Master Nicholas had taken his own life, the Herrick family stood to be disinherited.

Robert was only fifteen months old, and thus had no conscious memories of the confusion and upset in the troubled household. In the event, the High Almoner agreed to a single payment of £220. He has often been criticized for his avarice; but considering that Nicholas Herrick's estate turned out to be worth more than £3,000, the family did well to satisfy the bishop with the sum he accepted. Evidently the case of suicide could not be proven beyond doubt, and it was conceivable to the coroner as well as to some charitably minded neighbours and acquaintances that the goldsmith might simply have leaned too far out of his upstairs window, to converse with someone living opposite in the narrow street of close-packed, forward-tilting houses. He might have had a drop too much to drink. Yet the fact that a payment was necessary at all suggests that there were compelling reasons to think that poor Master Herrick had died by his own hand. Certainly the manner of his burial reflects this ambiguity: Robert, by then a priest in Devon, was in his mid-thirties before he discovered the exact place of Nicholas's grave:

> That for seven lusters I did never come
> To do the rites to thy religious tomb;
> That neither hair was cut, or true tears shed
> By me, o'er thee, as justments to the dead,
> Forgive, forgive me; since I did not know
> Whether thy bones had here their rest or no.

The likelihood is that, being 'sick in bodye', with a terminal disease for which sixteenth-century medicine could offer no relief in its final stages, Nicholas Herrick accelerated his own demise. If so, he was escaping physical pain rather than a state of spiritual desperation, and it may have been this which inclined Bishop Fletcher to clemency in his judgement of the case.[19]

At that time, the verdict made little difference to Robert in practical terms. He was soon separated from his mother too, who placed him in the care of his rich uncle William, another goldsmith. While Sir William – knighted for lending money to the Exchequer – brought up his own sons to be gentlemen, he expected his nephew to follow his trade. Yet Herrick tired of gold, and five years into his apprenticeship, implored his uncle to let him study. From Cambridge, he later penned elaborate complimentary letters to Sir William begging for money that in fact was owed him anyway from his father's inheritance. On leaving university, Herrick had moved back to London, where the attempt to live by his pen appears to have failed. He did, however, win the patronage of Endymion Porter, Charles and Buckingham's travelling companion, translator, ambassador and purchaser of art, who evidently encouraged him to take orders, and was well placed to secure him his position as chaplain to the duke.

Quite what Herrick made of Buckingham's decision to lead the mission to La Rochelle in person, thus obliging his chaplain to be present, we shall never know. Certainly the expedition is the one known adventure in this retiring man's life, and the poetry itself, undateable as it is on the whole, suggests a person of wholly peaceable impulses. Herrick has often been dismissed as nothing but a cheery poet, and thus an insubstantial one, since the merriness allowed to poets is in general strictly rationed. No poetry in English, it is true, takes as much simple pleasure in itself as Herrick's, and we shall return to its delightedness later. Yet the book he eventually published, miraculously, in 1648, *Hesperides*, is also full of faintly disgruntled farewells, valedictions to a life he enjoyed more. One gathers that, had a fellowship come up, he would quite happily have stayed in Cambridge; then, had it been possible to pursue his literary career without leaving the tavern life he was compelled to surrender, he might also have foregone his vocation in the Church. *Hesperides* is full of imaginary joys, yet the evenings remembered with

Ben Jonson and his 'tribe' seem not to belong to that category, so specific is Herrick about 'those *Lyrick* Feasts,/ Made at the *Sun*, / The *Dog*,
the Triple *Tunne*' (all the names of pubs).[20] Hence perhaps the peculiar
dab-handedness of his writing, the concern not to let a word go
unheeded or to waste; and the overall emphasis he places on seizing the
day, enjoying the pleasures of the present while they last, as expressed
most famously of all in 'To the Virgins, to Make Much of Time':

> Gather ye Rosebuds while ye may,
>   Old Time is still a flying:
> And this same flower that smiles to day,
>   To morrow will be dying.[21]

This comes as close as anything to capturing the life-philosophy of
Herrick's master. Buckingham was all for living in the present, and for
making much of time. He refused to be mortified by his disgrace when
the fleet creaked raggedly back from France to port, or to bow to the
growing calls for his banishment or his head. Yet his defeat on the Île de
Ré was not forgotten, even when Buckingham himself was fading into
history. There were still residues of its taint in the profound sense of
national self-dissatisfaction that surfaced so vehemently after the second
Bishops' War in 1640. Yet in the short term, although opposition to his
rule only grew, Buckingham still commanded sensational loyalty among
his followers, from the king downwards.

Herrick remained entirely the Great Duke's creature. 'Never my
book's perfection did appear/ Till I had got the name of Villiers here,'
he said proudly in an epigram for his patron, the 'high and noble *prince*',
Buckingham (italics mine).[22] Whatever his private thoughts about Villiers' character, Herrick's public view was that those in power had to be
obeyed without question, since they were there by God's will:

> Good Princes must be pray'd for; for the bad
> They must be borne with, and in rev'rence had.
> Do they first pill [fleece] thee, next pluck off thy skin?
> Good children kiss the rods that punish sin.
> Touch not the tyrant; let the gods alone
> To strike him dead that but usurps a throne.[23]

This was a meditation provoked by later events, but Charles and Buckingham could not have agreed more. Herrick was saying that people should not unseat even princes who seemed tyrannical. He was also saying, however, that they should leave it to the gods to kill off those who *did* usurp a throne. That is, even a rebel should be obeyed once he was in power. This was a lesson in how to keep one's skin unplucked, if not unfleeced. It was also, obviously, a note-perfect redaction of the Stuart view of kingship, one that Herrick reiterated without hesitation. ''Twixt Kings and Subjects ther's this mighty odds,/ Subjects are taught by *Men*; Kings by the *Gods*.'[24] Yet Herrick leaves open the question of just *how* God (or the gods, if you will) would give the tyrant king his comeuppance. He does not turn to the thought that tyrants will get their just deserts in hell, but mentions them being struck dead on earth. The agents of divine will are left to history to provide. There is thus the sense that Herrick is merely advising moderate, peaceable, essentially law-abiding people like himself, the sort who keep the basic threads of society together no matter how odious the government of the day, not to get involved in rebellion when it happens. When he published the fruits of a lifetime of poetry, twenty years after the island landing, he had this to say about royal favourites accruing too much power:

> That Princes may possesse a surer seat,
> 'Tis fit they make no One of them too great.[25]

Over many decades, he would develop a poetics of civic passivity, urging his readers to abstain from destructive movements and to pursue fleeting pleasures; to foster the private causes of their future melancholy.

3

There was a story that one of King Charles's officers of the wardrobe at Windsor Castle was visited by a ghost early in the spring of 1628. Nicholas Towse, a steady, middle-aged gentleman of middling rank reputed 'for honesty and discretion', was woken in bed one night by the ghost of Buckingham's father. Sir George Villiers, dead for more than twenty years, had been a Leicestershire magnate in sheep farming, and Towse recognized the apparition immediately, since he had gone to school in the parish where Sir George had lived. The 'venerable aspect', the very suit of clothes on the figure, was that of the knight in his prime. He had come with a warning for his son: Towse must go to the duke and urge him to do more to please the people. If he failed, the ghost announced, Buckingham's days were numbered.

Towse's reputation for good sense may have rested latterly on his refusal, when he woke up the next day, to treat the incident as anything more than a dream. Yet not long passed before the ghost disturbed his dreams again, and this time treated Towse a little more sternly than before. Why, asked the shade of Sir George, had he not passed on the message? Towse, insensible with fear, sputtered his apologies; yet when he woke up the next morning he was able, though less assuredly, to dismiss the visitation again as a nightmare. But in his next appearance Sir George apparently deployed some of the firmer techniques that roaming spirits reserve for getting their way with the living, blasting Towse's bed curtains 'with a terrible countenance, and bitterly reproaching him for not performing what he had promised to do'. This time, not wishing to lose more years of his life than those the haunting had cost him already, Towse cast aside his self-respect and went to London to pass on the warning to the duke. As the ghost flamed and loured at him, however, Towse did have the presence of mind to ask how he would get Buckingham to take his words seriously. Impressed by this point, Sir George shared with him 'two or three particulars' that Towse was never to reveal to anyone else but which would give the duke no choice but to believe him.[26]

Towse had protested that it was too difficult to gain an audience with Buckingham. Certainly, for the average person going to town in the hope of getting a word with the land's most powerful subject, the ghost's commission meant joining the crowds streaming down from Charing Cross, past the old tilting yard, to the gateway that marked the entry to a further thoroughfare leading by the riverside palace of Whitehall down to Westminster, and hoping to persuade a porter at the lodge that he had valid business at court: even then his hopes lay with catching a glimpse of the duke in the presence chamber, on his way in or out of the grounds, or paying a series of courtiers to pass on his request.

By this time – 1628 – Buckingham did not go anywhere without armed guard. His father's ghost was sending good advice: word of the public's hatred for Buckingham had even reached the afterlife. But although the duke had certainly accumulated his great wealth, and an all but unrivalled collection of art, by corrupt means, he was hardly unique in doing so. The same charge could be levelled at a score of the great nobles. It also seems that Buckingham lavished much more on patronage and great building works than he was able to extort from the sale of honours in his gift. Much of the best in art and literature of the day could not have been accomplished without his corruption.

His unpopularity resulted instead from envy at the unrivalled scope of the power he enjoyed, and from a sequence of political and military disasters for which he was almost universally held responsible. The first cause of resentment was undoubtedly real. 'All preferments in Church and state were given by him; all his kindred and friends promoted to the degree in honour, or riches, or offices as he thought fit, and all his enemies and enviers discountenanced, and kept at that distance from the court as he appointed.'[27] Yet even on this score, it seems that whenever the king opposed his choice for an appointment or promotion, Steenie did not have his way. As for the second charge of culpability, Buckingham may simply have been cursed by bad luck, and by the misfortune of having to pit his wits against the foremost politician of the age, Cardinal Richelieu.

Catastrophe came thick and fast after something of a honeymoon with the political nation in the winter of 1623–4. On their return from Madrid, Charles and Buckingham were convinced that diplomacy and marriage were equally useless when it came to the Spanish: they now proposed military action as the only way of crippling Spain's support for the imperial campaign against the Protestants of Europe – and thus regaining the lost Palatinate. Buckingham therefore persuaded Charles to create an alliance with France, and reinforce it by marrying King Louis XIII's young sister, Henrietta Maria. Buckingham again went in person to conduct the pre-nuptial discussions, though compromised the negotiations and enraged the king by attempting to seduce the queen, Anne of Austria.

Buckingham was disappointed in his hopes for the alliance with France; and also let down by a lack of support at home. The Parliament

that met in 1624, still exultant that the Spanish match had failed, had
warmly approved of warring with Spain, or so it seemed. King James
watched with some dismay Buckingham and his son playing to the gallery in Parliament, enjoying massive public favour in the anti-Spanish
turn their policy had taken. In Clarendon's dramatic reconstruction, the
king cried, 'By God, Stenny, you are a fool, and will shortly repent this
folly, and will find that in this fit of popularity you are making a rod
with which you will be scourged yourself.' Turning to the prince, he
warned him that he 'would live to have his bellyful of Parliaments'.[28]
Yet James, 'in the spring following, after a short indisposition by the
gout, fell into a quartan ague, which, meeting many humours in a fat,
unwieldy body of fifty-eight years old, in four or five fits carried him
out of the world'.[29]

In his last hours, it was said, James had something urgent to tell
Charles, and struggled to lift himself on his pillow – 'but his spirits were
so spent, that he had not strength to make his words audible'. On
27 March 1625 Charles was proclaimed king at Whitehall 'in a sad shower
of Rain'.[30]

The late king was swiftly proved right. For when Buckingham asked
a session of Parliament at Oxford – the capital then was in the grip of
one of the worst epidemics of plague it had ever seen – to fund an attack
on Spain at sea, he did not win their confidence. Public faith had already
been shaken in 1624 by the fate of an expedition to the Palatinate under
the command of a mercenary, Count Mansfeld. Kept too long aboard
their transports while James hesitated and the French pulled out their
support, the force of ten thousand infantry was riddled with lethal
infection before a shot could be fired. Buckingham was convinced a
naval mission, however, would prove a masterstroke against the
Habsburgs' dominance in Europe. Yet the later in the year the fleet set
out, the less chance it had of succeeding, either by intercepting the
Spanish galleons lumbering back from the Indies, or in having the weather required to conduct any meaningful strike on the Atlantic seaboard.
As it happened, the fleet of 1625 – supplemented by ships from the
Dutch United Provinces – was delayed until October, saved by a private
loan from the City of London. When the force fell inexpertly on Cadiz,
after much argument as to where was the best place to strike, large numbers of the troops were diverted from taking the harbour by the pleasures

to be had inland. They broke open the 'Fryars' Caves and other Cellars of sweet Wines, where many hundreds of them being surprised, and found dead-drunk, the *Spaniards* came and tore off their Ears and Noses, and pluck'd out their Eyes'.[31] In fact, many of those captured were treated humanely; certainly the prisoners ransomed by the Spanish had an easier passage home than their comrades who made it back aboard, since the fleet had almost no provisions for the return leg of the voyage. The crews were skeletal, literally and metaphorically, when they reached the south coast.

The following year Parliament tried impeaching Buckingham. Again, in purely strategic terms, his critics in the Commons and the Lords should have shared the blame with him. The war with Spain could not be prosecuted without proper funding, which the king now decided to obtain by means of a Forced Loan compelling those capable of contributing to the war effort to do so. Despite the attempted prosecution, Buckingham, who among his other high posts of state was Lord High Admiral, had actually not done a bad job of reforming the navy in peacetime. He had cut the costs of the service, raised the ordinary sailors' pay and at the same time increased the number of seaworthy ships. But the strain of conducting a sea war, as opposed to policing the rampant piracy on the home coasts, exposed the navy's limitations pitifully. Buckingham's nadir came in the autumn of 1627 when, the alliance with France in tatters, he personally led the ill-starred mission to relieve La Rochelle.

So if no subject had ever possessed so much power, few had been so widely despised as the Duke of Buckingham. A request from a stranger to speak with him was one to attract suspicion. Fortunately, Nicholas Towse, carrying a paternal direction from beyond the grave, was on good terms with Sir Ralph Freeman, the Master of Requests, and managed to convince him that he had 'somewhat extraordinary' to tell the duke. Towse was told to report across the river at five the following morning, at the Lambeth jetty, where Buckingham would land and meet his horses to join the king on an early hunt. There Buckingham promised he would listen to Towse for as long as was necessary.

The interview at the riverbank lasted an hour, beyond earshot of the servants standing with the horses and Sir Ralph, who nevertheless watched all that passed intently. He saw Buckingham respond vehemently to what Towse said, and lash out angry and astonished at the moment that Towse passed on the secrets the ghost had given him to verify the story; details which Buckingham swore, as Towse related afterwards, could only have come from the devil. Only one other person alive besides the duke – and now Towse – knew of those 'particulars'.

A story of blackmail, of hallucination, or a piece of mere make-believe may lie behind this little anecdote, one of a great number produced to corroborate the year's later turn of events. It features in Clarendon's history, and is one of the few instances where he indulges himself in the sort of good old-fashioned ghost story so beloved of more relaxed historians such as Izaak Walton and John Aubrey. With concern for his own credibility, Clarendon places immense stress on Towse's soundness of mind.

The tale ends with an angry conference behind closed doors between the duke and his mother, the Dowager Countess of Buckingham. His father had married her, a penniless gentleman's daughter, for love alone; a Catholic, regarded by some as a sorceress, it had been rumoured that she had murdered the late king with poison in the plasters she applied to his stomach shortly before he died. The morning he spoke with Towse on Lambeth Bridge, Buckingham went through with his hunting trip as planned, but was abstracted and pensive throughout, and on his return to Whitehall stalked Hamlet-like to his mother's apartment in the palace. When he emerged, after an argument that echoed through the building, he 'appeared full of trouble with a mixture of anger; a countenance that was never before observed in him in any encounters with her'.[32]

George Villiers, the Great Duke, was among the most vilified of a long list of colossi who divided the English people through the seventeenth century. Yet perhaps all he really wanted was to stop being Steenie, the purported catamite of an old king with a weakness for handsome young men. King James had nicknamed Buckingham after St Stephen, who was said to have had the face of an angel. In the view of the leading modern scholar and biographer of the duke, Buckingham wanted to be more than that, as he had shown by taking charge of the navy back in 1619.[33] He tried showing that he could hold near-supreme public power by merit as well as charm, good looks and ruthlessness.

When Charles called his third Parliament in March 1628, another move began against his favourite, culminating in a Remonstrance urging him to dismiss Buckingham altogether from his presence. Parliament now offered subsidies, but only in return for the king accepting a Petition of Right in which the liberties of English subjects would be given quasi-constitutional status. Yet the anger against Buckingham within the House of Commons paled beside the public rage beyond Westminster. In June, Buckingham's astrologer, John Lambe, popularly known as 'the duke's devil', was seized by a mob and butchered in the street. The crowds were known to chant:

> Let Charles and George do what they can
> The Duke shall die like Doctor Lambe.[34]

That August, while he was inspecting the fleet for another attack on La Rochelle, a horde of hungry, unpaid sailors rushed the duke. One climbed up into his carriage. He oversaw the execution of the attacker personally, and ordered a troop of horse to charge the mob with swords drawn. Yet he also protested that no one had ever done so much for the navy, or so much for ordinary sailors. Early on 23 August, a discontented lieutenant, convinced he was doing God's will, stabbed Buckingham amid a crowd of officers at his headquarters in Portsmouth. The assassin, John Felton, was sure 'that if he had but cut his finger, the duke would have died of it'. According to Oglander, the duke's surgeons bore out this conviction: had they been asked to guide Felton's hand, they could not have chosen a more fatal place than that the knife entered by chance.

Reports invariably set Felton down as a man vengeful and deranged, driven by an unhinged mind and a grudge towards his victim. A synonym of 'crazed' almost always collocates with 'assassin'; yet every assassination has an objective and makes a statement, and this one was no different. From the moment he was apprehended by Buckingham's guards Felton entered a rhetorical tussle to fix the meaning of his action. He had not 'undone us all', as one staff officer claimed, but remade the nation. Two notes he carried with him, sewn into his clothes – written in the event of his being killed in the act – made his point at greater length. But he needed the person of Buckingham in order to drive it home. And he succeeded: for many months the English gentry and aristocracy were seized with fears of general insurrection and popular revolt. Senior courtiers and churchmen and other beneficiaries of Buckingham's patronage walked in fear.

The assassination brought out a thousand commonplaces on fortune's wheel and the dangers of eminence. Barely a week before, Oglander had watched dukes and earls bare their heads before the duke and wait on him. It was the age of ruling favourites, but Europe had surely never seen a subject so powerful. So passes all the glory of the world, Oglander reflected – for in a matter of days the duke lay gored on the floor of an inn, a stark warning to all who might wish to emulate him, and indeed all who owed their status to the pleasures of the monarch.[35]

4

It is difficult to say exactly when the reign of King Charles I properly began, and when it technically ended. Those loyal to him would always insist that his rule ceased only with the axe that fell on 30 January 1649, but in practical terms it was cut short some years before, when his forces were defeated in the first civil war. Some might even put his loss of effective power still further back, perhaps even as early as the spring of 1642, by which time Parliament had all but made him a puppet of committee rule. Equally, the real beginning of the reign is difficult to place, since for so long after coming to the throne in 1625 Charles was – or was seen to be – so wholly under the influence of the duke. The two slept together the night after Charles's coronation, radiating the message from the privy chamber through the court that their friendship was unbreakable. Charles's new queen, Henrietta Maria, had no choice but to wait in line. Buckingham was even unafraid to chide her roughly, on one occasion, when she argued with his mother.

So the day when Charles first felt the full weight of the crown on his temples could well have been the one in August 1628 when the message was brought to him that Steenie was dead.[36] Charles was in chapel when the news was whispered to him, listening to a sermon. Characteristically, he made no show of emotion, and did not move until the service had ended. Then he shut himself in his chamber, and did not emerge for days. He was alone with a restless nation deeply at odds with his rule: alone, too, with a wife who hated her new home and could hardly stand the sight of him. The shift in royal policy which took England to war with her country hardly nourished the relationship.

Charles's letters show the depth of the confidence he placed in Buckingham, to the point of following his guidance in marital affairs. 'You know what patience I have had with the unkind usages of my wife,' he once wrote. Buckingham, apparently very happy with his own spouse – even though the marriage was decided by political and financial concerns – had advised the young king to try being nice to her. 'I am sure you have erred in your opinion,' was Charles's response: 'for I find daily worse and worse effects of ill offices done between us, my kind usages having no power to mend anything.'[37] When Charles decided on the drastic measure of banishing her extended entourage back to France, he needed Buckingham's approval, though he insisted he had made up his mind. 'I pray you send me word with what speed you may, whether you like this course or not, for I shall put nothing of this in execution until I hear from you . . . but I am resolute.'[38] To the end of his life, Charles would never place a strong trust in anyone he knew to have disliked or spoken badly of the duke: except, that is, his wife.

The marriage did not begin well. First of all, the couple were taken to separate churches for a wedding that took place by proxy in Paris and Whitehall. Not long afterwards, Henrietta Maria gained the reputation of a sturdy traveller, but the rough crossing to Dover both reinforced and expressed her mood. A Catholic, she had been married off to a heretic. Charles accepted that she had reason to be unhappy and bewildered ('knowing her to be but young . . . and coming to a strange country') but was still hurt by the treatment he received. Henrietta's first request was that he should bear her inexperience in mind at all times, and should not on any account lose his temper with her. He agreed, asking that she would deal with him accordingly. In a tart letter to Buckingham he insisted she certainly did not grant him equal treatment. In addition, Henrietta brought with her a huge train of followers: besides the public outcry at the seeming hordes of wealthy foreign papists now infesting the city, Charles soon found himself beset with her attendants' machinations, convinced that their 'ill crafty counsels' were only feeding her aversion. When he sent a group of councillors to revive the services and customs of his late mother's household, she demanded 'leave to order her house as she list herself'. He was staggered by such open denunciation;

along with 'many little neglects I will not take the pains to set down', she would not spend time with him, would speak with him only through a servant, and took as little trouble as she could with learning English. He was sure her mother was poisoning her mind still more against him.

One of his trustiest servants, had he been allowed to share a confidence or look the king in the eye, might have told him such things were all part of marriage. An unfinished argument still hung over Endymion Porter, the veteran of the Spanish negotiations, when he took the road to Dover to meet the queen. He was stung by a message his wife, Olive, had sent after him; and responded with the mixture of wounded magnanimity and devotion which seemed to serve him well over the years. 'I did not think to have received such a swaggering letter from you, but I see you can do anything now, for time hath worn out the kindest part of your love . . . I will preserve mine whilst I have breath, nor shall age nor time make me forget my Olive.'[39]

James Howell, still angling for employment, was impressed by the reception that met the queen and hoped she was pleased with it: 'there were a goodly train of choice Ladies attended her coming upon the Bowling-green on *Barham* Downs upon the way, who divided themselves into two rows, and they appear'd like so many Constellations; but methought the Country Ladies out-shined the Courtiers.' However threatened and resentful she felt, Henrietta quickly won admirers. Howell waxed lyrical:

for we have now a most noble new Queen of England, who in true Beauty is beyond the long-woo'd *Infanta*; for she was of a fading flaxen-hair, big-lipp'd, and somewhat heavy-eyed; but this Daughter of *France*, this youngest Branch of *Bourbon* . . . is of a more lovely and lasting Complexion, a dark brown; she hath Eyes that sparkle like Stars; and for her Physiognomy, she may be said to be a Mirror of Perfection.[40]

Queen Henrietta soon enchanted many more than Howell, but her religion was always bound to be a problem. 'If it please God to bless this marriage, and he grant me the favour to give me progeny,' she reassured her old confessor in 1625, 'I will not choose any but Catholics to nurse and educate the children who shall be born.'[41]

Frank attention was paid to when and where the king first 'bedded with' Henrietta. Endymion was by this time making up with Olive. 'This last night the King and the Queen did lie together here at Canterburie, long may they do so, and have as many children as we are like to have . . . I have sent you this little ruby ring which I would have you wear for my sake.'[42] One of the Porters' sons had recently died. There was loneliness, guilt and some acrimony in the marriage. This was the kind of gradual reconciliatory recovery, with dignity preserved on both sides, which Charles apparently found very difficult at first but which the loss of Buckingham forced him to undertake alone.

When Buckingham was knifed down in August 1628 the outburst of shock and delight raised by his death distracted public attention from the murder soon afterwards of another whom, for many, deserved greater sorrow. Fulke Greville, Baron Brooke of Beauchamps Court, a poet and formerly a councillor to King James, died in a manner not out of place in one of the brutal closet tragedies his young servant, William Davenant, had begun sending to the King's Men. Greville had spent his interrupted final years collecting and touching up earlier compositions and committing to paper his last thoughts on the fallibility of humankind. He was placid, that is, melancholy and concentrated to the last. The savage death he met in the autumn of 1628 did not really belong to him.

Davenant had entered Brooke's service towards the end of 1624. The Duke of Richmond had died, obliging his widow to reduce her train and move out of the mansion in Holborn. Her young page was among those she had to let go. The loss of place came at a sticky moment in Davenant's affairs. He faced arrest and legal action for non-payment of debts, and the birth of his first son, William, had made the need for further advancement all the more pressing. But he took the setback with the sanguine and positive approach that brought him good fortune through what proved to be a long life. Just when he seemed hemmed in, much like the spider in his trial of the duchess's medicine, he would trot unconcernedly through a boundary which should have destroyed him. When the Duchess of Richmond dismissed him, not long passed before he was employed by her neighbour Lord Brooke. Typically, in celebration he ordered up 'cloth lace and other necessaries' from the same tailor who had recently taken him to court – a sign of no hard feelings on either side.[43]

Davenant's new master was a Knight of the Bath and for a time had had responsibilities in the Treasury, joining the long, slow campaign to bring Jacobean finances under control. James was a lavish spender, and Greville's part in the struggle against excess sat uneasily with his own expenditure. Financially independent himself, he had put £10,000 into restoring his home at Warwick Castle. Yet Greville is chiefly remembered as one defined by another's absence. For almost three decades he had mourned and preserved the memory of Sir Philip Sidney. He was a prolific and accomplished poet and thinker in his own right, the author of a well-regarded sonnet sequence, *Caelica*, but his commemorations of Sidney stood out from the rest of his work. Sidney, in Ben Jonson's memory 'no pleasant man in countenance, his face being spoiled with pimples', had gone to his death on military service, fighting the Spanish in the Netherlands in 1586, and tall, grave, wide-browed and long-jawed Greville, who remained a bachelor all his life, had missed him sorely but stoically ever since.[44]

Greville claimed to write only for those 'that are weather-beaten in the sea of this World'. Some years earlier he had burnt the only copy of his version of the tragedy of *Antony and Cleopatra*, worried that the 'irregular passions' he had unusually let loose in it might pervert the young. When Davenant came to work for him, Greville was busy revising his works, bracing and tightening the rhythms and reasoning of poems written a lifetime before. In Davenant's view he spoiled what airiness they had 'with too much judgment and refining'.[45]

It is unclear whether he shared the early drafts of his own efforts with Greville. The young servant had no reservations about the extreme emotions the elder poet felt obliged to excise from his works. Davenant, in one of his first efforts for the stage, decided to let loose every imaginable ferocity, and the result was *The Tragedy of Albovine, King of the Lombards*. Albovine, the self-styled 'broome of heauen' (in an absurd echo of Marlowe's Tamburlaine, 'the Scourge of God') is betrothed to Rhodolinda, the daughter of one of his many conquered enemies, and courts her with a drink served in her father's hollowed skull. Rhodolinda then goes to the play's villain, Hermegild, for help. Hermegild obliges her by brutally murdering Albovine. But Rhodolinda suffers an appalling end herself when one Paradine, avenging Albovine, bites off her lips in a deceitful clinch before stabbing her.

Greville had been sick during the winter of 1627–8. In February he drew up his will, leaving his title and estate to a younger cousin, Robert

Greville. At the end of the month he called his retainers up to his study to witness the testament. Many had served him for decades: one of his valets, Ralph Haywood, was as old as his lord. Evidently Greville intended to outlive them all, because he made no provision for any of them, provoking still more surprise than hurt. Nobody could understand this sudden attack of meanness in the old man. Yet while the rancour grew below stairs at Brooke House, Greville's attention was elsewhere. For him the will had been a routine piece of business, a late precaution. The final revisions to his manuscripts filled the front of his mind. A few months later, when he learned that his attendants were upset, he softened, and arranged for small annuities to the stalwarts of his household. One name, however, was missing from the codicil.

One of Ralph Haywood's nicely defined and jealously defended duties was to wait on Greville at the lavatory. His role involved helping him unbutton and untie the elaborate Elizabethan costume that hindered the old man in getting to the chamber pot. He had contained his grief at being overlooked in Greville's will all through the spring and summer, all through the commotion of the abortive French campaign and Buckingham's assassination. One early autumn morning as he helped Greville with his morning toilet, Haywood began to remonstrate about the will. His chain of thought broken, and his time of ease ruined, Greville rebuked him sharply. Outside, they could be heard arguing. Yet it was a familiar domestic, almost marital exchange, during which both servant and master kept to their accustomed routine. On leaving the commode Greville raised his arms for Haywood to lace up his points, the old-fashioned cords which fastened his hose to his doublet. Haywood stabbed him in the stomach.

Greville was gasping on the floor when other attendants burst in, and urged them not to pursue the assassin. Otherwise the room was empty; but an adjoining one was locked. When the door was forced, they found Haywood slumped over his own blade, having killed himself with a cleaner thrust than the one he gave his master. It took Greville almost a month to die; like his beloved Sidney, of gangrene. He was buried in Warwick Castle, beneath a tombstone he had had made long before: 'Folk Grevill – Servant to Queene Elizabeth – Conceller to King James – Frend to Sir Philip Sidney. Trophaeum Peccati.'

Greville's death marked the end of an era, the end of a period of mourning: it also left William Davenant adrift once more. With this, Davenant's means of supporting his wife and little son were heavily cut, since his writing had yet to bear dividends. While a competent exercise in its genre, the old-fashioned scarlet tragedy Davenant had had performed at Blackfriars, *The Cruel Brother*, had failed to take the town by storm. With Greville's help, however, Davenant had begun to gain the affection and esteem of other supporters, including, most importantly, his friend and country neighbour Endymion Porter. If lacking the aloofness of Thomas Carew, with whom he seems by this time to have grown acquainted, Davenant had also established himself as a recognizable presence about town – where he thrived on his companionable qualities. Having made friends with a serious and ascetic young lawyer, Edward Hyde, he made himself at home in Hyde's lodgings in the Middle Temple. His wife and son meanwhile were deposited with relatives – or, at least for a while, with his tailor, John Urswick, whom he still owed a small fortune for his expensive suits.

'Hate London, as to live there, without thou hast a vocation that calleth thee to it.' This was Sir John Oglander's advice, penned in blood, to his descendants. 'Dice and whores,' he added, 'are the instrumental causes that bring many to beggary.'[46] He had the agreement of Edward Hyde in the Middle Temple. Hyde was doing his best to keep to civilized company, but in the wake of the military failures of the mid to late 1620s, the city was rougher than ever: 'the town was full of soldiers, and of young gentlemen who intended to be soldiers, or as like them as they could; great license used of all kinds, in clothes, in diet, in gaming.' Hyde himself had to tread carefully, since, being a sociable and convivial man, he ran the risk of being 'thought a person of more license than in truth he was'.[47]

The habitual excesses in dress, drink and gambling were presumably harder to maintain in the impoverished aftermath of the French campaign. Yet the critics of such company were fully aware of the fascination it held. Awash with *reformados*, disbanded officers forced to serve as ordinary soldiers, 'your decayed, ruinous, worm-eaten gentlemen of the round', London buzzed with their yarns. There were those as well who were sorry not to have been aboard on the missions to France and Spain.[48] Among these was Edward Hyde's room-mate. Davenant had missed the expedition to Ré in order to oversee the production of *The Cruel Brother*, and was inspired to assist Buckingham's cause. As the *reformados* called for their back pay, better leadership, and vengeance against France, the Privy Council received a bizarre offer to blow up the arsenal at Dunkirk, from 'Mr Dauenant, Lodging in ye middle temple with Mr Hide'. Davenant claimed that he had a friend, 'who is now Officiall in the Magazin', who could get him inside. 'I have knowledge of a small Engine [an explosive device],' he promised, 'that will inforce a usefull fire . . . I shall performe this service, though with the losse of my life.'[49]

This wild offer may have been one of the early warning signs that caused Hyde to look somewhat sceptically and condescendingly on Davenant, and to draw a veil over the acquaintance in his memoirs. Hyde was a few years too late to see the 'young Turk' Oliver Cromwell terrorizing the tavern-keepers around Lincoln's Inn ('Here comes young Cromwell, shut up your doors!')[50] yet many years later he recalled that 'there was never an age, in which, in so short a time, so many young gentlemen, who had not experience in the world, or some good tutelary angel to protect them, were insensibly and suddenly overwhelmed in that sea of wine, and women, and quarrels, and gaming, which almost overspread the whole kingdom.'[51]

Sir John Oglander was bitter about the contagion of vice which had spread to his own, normally quiet outpost. During the wars with France and Spain, a regiment of Scottish soldiers had been billeted in towns across the Isle of Wight. The island's scant resources had been stretched, with the shortage of corn, the peace disturbed, and maidens corrupted; there had been 'murders, rapes, robberies, burglaries, getting of bastards and almost the undoing of the whole Island'. The soldiers themselves had not been paid, nor the islanders recompensed for the cost of their billeting. Oglander did not like the Scots, though he respected them as soldiers: 'a people base and proud' was his verdict on them. Without prior warning, on 1 September 1628, King Charles visited the island. Oglander was forced to throw together a reception party as best he could, sending his wife and daughters ahead to Ryde to greet the king. He had known Charles since the king was a very young man, and had not been long in his company before mentioning the island's grievances. He was touched by Charles's response: the king was always at his best when company and circumstances allowed him to be sincere. Taking Oglander's hand, he asked him to thank the entire island in his name for their patient treatment of the Scottish soldiery. It was only two days later that the Scots took ship and the islanders were freed from occupation. There had been nothing like it since the Vikings, said Oglander.[52]

Nevertheless, the following January he and a delegation of Wight's leading gentry made the journey, Oglander reluctantly, to the capital of 'dice and whores'. Their purpose was to present a petition asking for the redress of lasting concerns. They still needed payment for the soldiers' keep. More pressingly, with Britain still at war with France, they were worried about the state of the island's defences – since Wight would be at the front line in any invasion. The southerly wind was so strong it blasted them across the Solent to Portsmouth in just half an hour with only half the foresail spread. It was proving a wretched winter; not frosty, but so wet that no landowners could inspect their grounds without a new stream appearing, and no animal find a dry bed. At least the gentlemen of Wight were mollified by their reception at court. They were promised payment and new fortifications the moment funds became available. Concern was expressed, however, at the rumour they had moved their families to the mainland.

From the evidence of Oglander and the community he writes about, there was very little slavish loyalty to be found beyond the court's direct clientele. He was – and history would put him to the test – a king's man through and through; but that was because he saw the Crown as being entirely functional. It existed to keep the balance, provide redress, permit endeavour, preserve the inherited good. He has been labelled a royalist; but in the 1620s and '30s would still have recognized no meaning in that term. He was unafraid to criticize Crown policies, since his duty as a subject required him to do so. As a member of the Commons in 1626–7 Oglander voted against the royal demand for a Forced Loan. Although he was not one of the seventy-six gentle and noblemen who refused to pay, he clearly sympathized with the celebrated 'five knights' who sought – and were denied – a writ of habeas corpus for imprisonment without charge. The king's command was, in the end, sacred to Oglander: yet on one occasion he disobeyed a command to send corn to the mainland when Wight's supplies were insufficient. Now he had no qualms refusing to keep his wife and daughters in danger on the island.

Their home at Nunwell, on its eastern side, overlooked a broad haven where thirty sail of ships could berth. They would be among the very first to greet the French navy as it poured in from the Channel. They were often startled in their nightshirts by false alarms.

Respectful yet querulous suits of this kind were part of the king's servants' daily routine. Yet in 1629 it did feel that the complaints were coming thicker and faster than ever. In 1628 a stormy Parliament had forced a Petition of Right upon King Charles, pressing him to define the rights of his subjects – to declare, once and for all, that the 'good old law called Magna Carta' still held. In doing so, they implicitly urged him to define the limits of his own prerogative, which he had already used to imprison a number of his more difficult subjects without trial. Traditionally, in accepting such a petition the king tacitly acknowledged he had done wrong, and offered redress, and Charles was in no way willing to make this concession. The 1628 Commons responded by drafting their Remonstrance against Buckingham.

In the early months of 1629, as Oglander returned home to find the earth too swamped to sow wheat, Parliament regrouped to pursue grievances over almost every conceivable area of policy. There was anger at abuses of power, favouritism, popery in the Church, the disastrous wars, and renewed insistence that Charles endorse the Petition of Right. He agreed to, but with provisos of his own, which spurred Parliament to continue refusing to give him funds. This included the profits of the tax on Tunnage and Poundage, which every monarch since Edward IV had received all but automatically, as a 'gift' of the people. On 2 March, the Speaker of the House of Commons was told to adjourn the session, but was physically prevented from standing to do so. Two burly MPs, Denzil Holles and Benjamin Valentine, held him down, and a fight ensued. Outside, Black Rod, the king's envoy, hammered at the doors with his staff, but the Commons would not leave till they had resolved not to give the king a penny, and declared any in favour of doing so a 'capital enemy'.

There was no Buckingham now to impeach; and Charles was shocked that such rancour still lasted. In the proclamation he issued after Parliament dissolved, the king accepted, surprisingly, that the duke had been a 'wall of separation between us and our people', an obstruction, implicitly, as well as a necessary buffer. 'But now he is dead, no alteration was found amongst those envenomed spirits which troubled then the blessed harmony between us and our subjects.'[53] He made it plain that he would rule for a time without calling a Parliament.

Oglander was glad to be out of London as quickly as he could. The town was as edgy as ever, with the country still technically at war, the tumult of Parliament still felt. There were signs, however, that a shift had taken place. Among the smaller of these was the departure of one, a former servant of the duke's, who was sorrier than Oglander to leave London behind. He was, nevertheless, one of the luckier among Buckingham's vast former entourage.

In September 1629 Robert Herrick was presented to a living at Dean Prior in Devon, probably through Endymion Porter's intercession. It was, though a stroke of material good fortune, an effective order of banishment, dispossession from the world, made all the worse by bereavement the following year. Waiting for the paperwork to be completed and the vicarage in Devon to become available, Robert Herrick seems to have been living in Westminster with the family of his brother William and his wife, Elizabeth. William, a year younger than Robert, had been 'the staffe, the prop, the shelt'ring wall/ Whereon my vine did crawl'.[54] In November he fell ill and died:

> Life of my life, take not so soone thy flight,
> But stay the time till we have bade Good night.
> Thou hast both Wind and Tide with thee; Thy way
> As soone dispatcht is by the Night, as Day.
> Let us not then so rudely henceforth goe
> Till we have wept, kist, sigh't, shook hands, or so.[55]

That 'or so' is perhaps the true stress-point of Herrick's touching elegy. It seems a throwaway phrase, pushed in merely for the sake of rhyme; a wobble, a momentary loss of care by the craftsman. But it is also the master's touch required to give that impression of distractedness in despair, a mark of accomplishment, in fact, disguising itself as neglect. In Jonsonian poetics the effect often lies in the things one does not notice, rather than in complex or ostentatious phrasing. The achievement of Herrick's art is both cloaked and revealed at such moments.

The following year, as the court continued finding its shape in the post-duke era, Herrick packed a wagon of belongings and set out for Devon, on the old road past Salisbury Plain and down through Yeovil, with his brother's widow and two of her children. His loss of London was William Davenant's gain. The older poet left a gap in the entourage of a major court personality with whom Davenant was already acquainted – the wealthy aesthete Endymion Porter. The great collector of poems, paintings and people now promoted Davenant as his town laureate, sponsoring his writing and his idling at the Middle Temple. Accordingly Davenant would lay all the riches he could gather in verse at Porter's impeccably shod feet:.

> Wise Love, that sought a noble choyce,
> To tune my Harp, and raise my voyce,
>   Forbids my pinnace rest
> Till I had cured weak Hope again
> By safely anchoring within
>   Endymion's breast.[56]

Deaths and departures, minute daily changes not recognized as change: at the sign of The Dog on King Street, one of Westminster's best taverns (much later a favourite of Pepys's), the landlord passed away. George German was the largest man in England, unable at the last to get to his feet. Oglander knew him from his visits, and heard that his entrails in post mortem were found to be the size of an ox's, the fat on his belly eleven inches deep, and seven inches on his breast.[57] The town would not be the same, nor the 'lyrick feasts' of Herrick and his friends at The Dog.

A short way up the road, beyond the gatehouse leading through to Whitehall and the royal mews (the present Trafalgar Square), alterations had also been noticed in the palace household. The king and queen for some time now had been on better terms. A gentleman of the bedchamber, Thomas Carew, observed 'such a degree of kindness as he would imagine him [Charles] a wooer again and her gladder to receive his caresses than he to make them'. Charles was growing more 'galan', more cavalier-like, by the day, solemnizing Henrietta's birthday with a display of his own horsemanship. There seemed no danger now of another Buckingham rising to power. The king, claimed Carew, had 'so wholly made over all his affections to his wife that he dare say that they are out of danger of any other favourite'.[58] Or, as Carew's friend Davenant put it allusively, and more tartly, in a play that seems not to have got past the royal censor, the depth of affection was genuinely surprising:

> 'The King is now in love.'
> 'With whom?'
> 'With the Queen.'
> 'In love with his own Wife! That's held incest in Court.'[59]

There had been changes, too, in the way the court itself was run. King Charles had imported some of the stiffer gentilities he had seen years earlier in Spain. His personal reservedness and attention to decorum had only strengthened as he mourned his father. As his reign went on, he began imposing this sobriety more systematically on the court.

King James was notoriously fastidious in avoiding contact with the wider public, but had been free with a select and often hard-drinking inner entourage. That changed for good as Charles began implementing and updating neglected old ordinances on behaviour in and about the royal household. At the palace gate, the porters and Knight Marshal saw to it that 'no ragged boys or unseemly persons' found their way into the grounds. Entry could only be permitted if one's name was on the day-list. Among the palace staff and even the courtiers, any 'notorious drunkard, swearer, railer or quarreller' was to be thrown out with as little fuss as possible by the marshal of the household. It was impossible to police as stringently as Charles might have wished the great straggling compound of Whitehall, no singular building but a collection of interlocking courtyards, galleries and originally separate mansions, with a thoroughfare running through it to the site of the old tilting ground and the mews beyond; but there was no mistaking the new order he imposed on all those close to his own person, in the privy chamber and the royal bedchamber. There was to be no more relaxing in state chambers, as they liked, for the nobles, over a quiet drink or game of cards – they were to be at their stations and on call as the detail of their posts demanded. An ambassador could no longer come in and take a seat at the royal supper table but had to content himself with the company of an official. In imitation of the high ceremony shown to the monarch in Spain at mealtimes, a minutely choreographed ritual took place whenever the king and queen sat down to eat. And the higher one happened to be, the tighter the demands. Members of the most elite fraternity, the Order of the Garter, newly restyled along the lines of the Habsburg Order of the Golden Fleece, were to wear their splendid badges, bearing the Cross of St George, at all times, and exemplify the noblest standards of chivalry, piety and propriety.[60]

The court, in other words, was building up a dam against 'the sea of wine, and women, and quarrels, and gaming' in which the wits had splashed about in the late 1620s. From top to bottom, the king required his servants to sharpen their conduct, all with reference and reverence to the divine appointment he held. The new era of personal rule made the court more than ever the chief font of reward and redress, and in fact merely brought back some of the old Tudor customs which had slackened over the past thirty years. But the reforms made the monarch and the highest officers even harder than before to reach, and the conditions still more stifling when a suitor finally did get through to them. Simultaneously, Charles shouldered an enormous workload of business and hospitality: even the queen, on her birthday, asked if they could have one meal without the presence of strange faces.

By now the nation was at peace. In January 1629 Endymion Porter was washed up from his latest mission to Spain. He had been back in Madrid, suffering the extremes of August and the endless prevarications of Castilian diplomacy, when he heard of Buckingham's death in 1628. It had been one of the wettest Julys in memory when he left England the previous year, in the suspicious company of an Irish Dominican friar, his purported business being to acquire in Italy some further pictures for the king's collection. His real errand was to open the way for peace with Spain, thus freeing the navy's limited energies to concentrate on the war with France.

He was devastated by the assassination of the duke, which left his own fortunes more than slightly uncertain. It was December 1628 when he finally hoped to extricate himself from the discussions with Count Olivares and escape the howling cold that had descended on the plateaux around the palace in Madrid. 'Good sweet Olive,' he wrote before leaving Spain, 'make much of yourself that by seeing you I may receive a remedy for the hurt that grief hath caused in me.'[61]

It was another terrible crossing. When the Spanish ship carrying him back rolled on to the rocks of Burton, Dorset, the locals picked their way down and stripped the vessel bare, along with all aboard. Endymion and his companions stood shivering on the harbour as the villagers carried off the booty on their backs. No leniency was shown to shipwrecked foreigners, especially Spaniards. Endymion protested that he was a servant of the king, and these gentlemen – the perplexed Spaniards in their underwear – were his guests. The king's council had to send a man down from the city to sort the business out. He found the mariners and passengers famished and close to hypothermia. New clothes were ordered for Porter, his companions and the Spanish crew, a new telescope for the captain. Then Porter and his colleagues were coached up to London to give an account of themselves. It was not long afterwards, in April 1629, that a peace was also concluded with France. The king dropped his cavalier pretensions as defender of the Huguenots.

However reviled by the Commons, Steenie was mourned. Even Queen Henrietta had warmed to him by the end. He had given her a much-loved addition to her retinue, though her new servant was barely two feet tall. She first laid eyes on Jeffrey Hudson at a banquet held in her honour by the duke, when he burst out of a pie and greeted her. He was a peace offering, and she immediately gave him a place in her household. In 1630, when travelling to give birth under the care of her old governess, 'Mamie', she took her dwarf with her. Davenant wrote a poem in honour of the journey, a mock-epic he called 'Jeffreidos'. In this Jeffrey was captured by Spanish pirates and interrogated for state secrets. On reaching dry land he fought a long battle with a dragon-sized turkey. The poem also expressed great concern about her womb: two years before, her first child had died within two days. But the queen was by now a hardy traveller, and on returning with her baby within four months she was writing to Mamie, 'I think he would send you his compliments, he is so fat and so tall . . . I will send you his portrait as soon as he is a little fairer, for at present he is so dark I am ashamed of him.'[62]

Whatever the baby Charles looked like, the kingdom had an heir. No more Buckinghams. The realm, so it appeared, was safe.

4. Dancing to the Drum

O happy Art! And wise epitome
Of bearing arms! Most civil Soldiery!

– Jonson, 'A Speech according to Horace', *Underwoods*

1

In the 1580s Philip Sidney and Fulke Greville had repeatedly asked the queen to be given commissions in the wars abroad, and Elizabeth had constantly refused from fear for their safety. This was so at least until Sidney implored her to let him accompany his uncle, the Earl of Leicester, on a tour of duty in the Low Countries. She relented, but Greville stayed behind; and for forty years the image of his friend's fate remained with him. 'Thus they go on,' he saw them in memory, 'every man in the head of his own Troop; and the weather being misty, fell unawares upon the enemie, who had made a strong stand to receive them, near to the very walls of *Zutphen*.' Stretchered from the front line with a wound in the thigh that no one could prevent from mortifying, Sidney called for a drink of water: 'but as he was putting the bottle to his mouth, he saw a poor Souldier carried along, who had eaten his last at the same Feast, gastly casting up his eyes at the bottle. Which Sir *Philip* perceiving,' so Greville had been informed, 'took it from his head, before he drank, and delivered it to the poor man, with these words, *Thy necessity is greater than mine.*'[1]

Sidney haunted Greville for decades, and stood out as an icon of chivalry. His example of militant action against the papist threat from Europe inspired and troubled the gallants of successive generations; all the more given the humiliations suffered in the 1620s. No English or Scottish army was ever officially sent to relieve the beleaguered Protestants of central Europe, or to help Princess Elizabeth and Count

Frederick (the 'Palsgrave') regain the Palatinate or Bohemia. King James did, however, allow individuals to recruit and sponsor bands of volunteers to fight as private soldiers of conscience, and the custom continued under Charles. Ben Jonson urged a sound-hearted countryman to answer the call:

> Wake, friend, from forth thy lethargy: the drum
> Beats brave, and loud in Europe, and bids come
> All that dare rouse: or are not loth to quit
> Their vicious ease, and be o'erwhelmed with it.[2]

The drumbeat pummelled countless consciences, all the more fiercely as the anti-imperial party fared terribly after Prague and then Heidelberg, 'entred with extreme cruelties', fell to the Catholic League. The image of Sir Gerrard Herbert at the doomed defence of the latter stayed woundingly fresh. 'Almost all the defenders forsook their stations,' wrote John Donne, who had travelled on a peace mission to Austria in 1619. 'Only Sir *Ger.* Herbert maintained his nobly, to the repulsing of the enemy three times, but having ease in the other parts, 800 fresh men were put upon his quarter, and after he had broke 4 pikes, and done very well, he was shot dead in the place.'[3] Throughout the 1620s the European war spread from central to northern Germany, and blew into life once more in the Low Countries with the expiry of a truce between the Dutch United Provinces and the Spanish-controlled Netherlands. Scandinavia entered the fray; armies of enormous size and savagery lumbered across the Continent. By the end of the decade the forces of Ferdinand II's empire, supported but yet distinct from the Catholic League maintained chiefly by Spain, had claimed the upper hand, albeit one with bruised and broken fingers.

By the time Charles I determined on 'personal rule' in England, the drum beating for volunteers had never sounded so strongly. Even after the drubbings Englishmen had suffered at sea in recent years, experience of the battlefield was thought to be no bad thing in itself, notwithstanding the cause. The trained bands of militia in the shires were in a wretched state, and something of a national joke. Demobbed soldiers were to be met with in virtually any European city, but they could hardly be blamed for the sea of wine and promiscuity that, so Edward Hyde claimed, swamped London at this time. The riotous types Hyde had in mind were most likely the sons of rich men merely sampling the profession of arms; they were men such as John Suckling, who in 1629, aged twenty, joined a regiment led and funded by Lord Wimbledon against the Spanish in the Netherlands. For Suckling and his like 'vicious ease' and voluntary service were not the mutual exclusives Ben Jonson, Hyde's much-admired friend, imagined. In the same poem quoted above, Jonson wrote furiously of the sexual opportunism of the gentry and more decadent aristocracy:

> How much did Stallion spend
> To have his court-bred filly there commend
> His lace and starch? And fall upon her back
> In admiration, stretched upon the rack
> Of lust, to his rich suit and title, Lord?
> Aye, that's a charm and half![4]

But the military colours of the same young lord were just as likely to charm as his lace suit and starched linen. These men too answered the drum; possibly to Jonson's even greater disgust, the 'Stallions' of the 1620s were for the most part men with a literary education, many being poetasters of a kind he particularly despised. And they agreed wholeheartedly with his Horatian edicts on the improving nature of martial life. Without considering the experience of such volunteers in the European wars, one cannot claim a proper acquaintance with the ranks of opposing swordsmen who assembled in 1642. Through his travels and ordeals during an important period for the Protestant cause in Europe, the young John Suckling is an articulate and ironic witness to these campaigns. The sufferings of his friend Davenant at home, meanwhile, yielded a painfully vivid account of a perennial health risk to stallions and mares in court and camp alike.

2

It was April 1629 when the company Suckling had joined set out from The Hague on the spring campaign, to join the Prince of Orange in his siege of Den Bosch. The scene of this action was the ancient settlement of Bois-le-Duc, modern-day 's-Hertogenbosch, or 'the Busse', as the English called it at the time. A cathedral city in the south of modern Holland, with a deep, gorge-like channel running through its medieval centre, Den Bosch was the capital of North Brabant, one of many tightly walled strongholds that had to be prised loose from Spanish control. Through Hieronymus Bosch, the city's most famous native, it had sheltered the birth of the most disquieting – if often wittiest – chimeras in European art. As the endless war continued, it remained near the heart of the Continent's nightmares.

Henry Hexham, a tough veteran and a captain in the regiment, was impressed by the forces of the Orange free-staters surrounding the city. 'It was admirable to see the vigillancie and carefulnes of the Prince; for there was not a patch of ground, by which the enemie might have relieved the Town.'[5] Hexham was moved by military spectacle in general, approvingly noting his men setting up camp with a Virgilian motif – 'as so many Bees to their hives, so each souldier brings something to the making up of his hutt' – and refreshed to camp out under the 'canopy of heaven'.[6] Hexham left a professional soldier's account of the slow tightening of the ring around Den Bosch, which was more a matter of patient engineering than martial valiance. The River Dommel was diverted and dammed to irrigate the camp, and ground was gained by 'windings and turnings', as the besieging army extended its construction of 'gardes, batteries, traverses and blinds'.[7] The water supply to the city itself was in the meantime cut off, by the 'admirable stratagem' of '34 mathematicall milles', turned by horses.[8]

The operation was undermined, early in the summer, by the loss to the east of Wesel, the German city located at the meeting of the River Lippe with the Rhine. It should have come as little surprise; until recently the city had been in Spanish hands since 1614. Their victory, however, raised the prospect of the Spanish now relieving Den Bosch, leaving as it did the Dutch army vulnerable to an attack from the rear. It meant in any case that at least some of the army's energies must be taken off the business of the siege. Hexham said that all the soldiers 'hung downe their heads like bulrushes' on learning the news, for which the unfortunate messenger bearing it was beaten and threatened with hanging.[9] As so often in the campaign, military intelligence was garnished with outraged piety. The Protestant civilians of Wesel, the Dutch were informed, had been herded together and locked up in the great church of St Weillibord, with the Spaniards offering to release them if they converted.

This moral surrender proved unnecessary, as the battle for Wesel turned out to be one of the more minor episodes of inhumanity in the war's long catalogue of spectacular and futile reversals; for 'the Lord heard the sobs & prayers of his afflicted Servants in this Towne, and sent them a sudden deliverance in an unexpected time.' The Spaniards had evidently been unable to seal the town's defences: in August the Dutch managed to oust them for good. Hexham relived the thrill that had alleviated long months of digging, mining and watching in a passage of excitement descending into incoherence:

downe goes the bridge the horse which stood before the port enters, the trumpets sound *tantara*, they scowre the streets, and drawes vp in bataile into the market place de coup en pied, with their pistols in their hands, The Spaniards fled out of the Towne to the Sconces, our foote follows the horse, besets the wall, and possesses all their guards, breakes downe their bridge, which lay ouer the Rhyne, and which draue downe the streame towards Rees, & sets fire on some sloopes and punts, which were on the other side of the water.

'The brunt being over,' he concluded, 'the soldiers fell a plundering.' The Protestants were released from their confinement in the church. It did not trouble their rescuers that the sacred building had been used as a prison, since it now served its old purpose well as a gaol for imperial officers. 'O Lord I cannot call to minde this thy glorious work,' reflected Hexham, 'but I must render thankes unto thee, and sing forth thy prayses with the rest of thy people.'[10]

One night back at Den Bosch, the army celebrated the capture of Wesel with a series of great volleys, every soldier in the camp burning a faggot attached to the tip of his pike. The eerie stadium of flame surrounding the city made nervous viewing for the imperial soldiers stationed on its battlements. The August evenings started drawing in, and the drudgery of siege wore on. Suckling, mentioned in Hexham's account as one of the voluntaries who 'bore armes and trayled pikes', may even have packed his kit and gone home by the time the pressure told, after a random offensive, one day early in September. The final straw was applied by Dutch engineers laying explosives at the foot of the city wall: a gap was blown, and the army trickled forward to exploit the leak. Imperial soldiers stoutly defended the breach; but their pikes were broken by carronade fire from outside. The besiegers poured through, and Hexham recalled the terrible alarm that seized the town, 'so that the bells rang, the women and children cryed, the Burger and the popish priests by flockes ran to the Governor'. After a four-month encampment, the action resolved itself quickly: the street-fighting was swift, only moderately bloody, and surprisingly decisive. Hexham could not help admitting that a climax was wanting. He and his men expected a bout of looting – to have 'ransackt their bags, and meted out veluets, and satins by the pikes length' – but instead the commanders reached a 'composition'.[11] The soldiers put away their frustration for future relief.

Suckling was one of those given honourable mention at the end of Hexham's account, which does not however specify whether he was still present at the town's capture. By October 1629 he was back in England, and was soon recruited for another tour of duty in Lord Wimbledon's regiment. It may be that business called him back – in February he would turn twenty-one – or the luxury of a rest at home and a burst of high spirits in town; or, quite possibly, his licence to leave England had expired. Another was issued to him on 22 October, permitting him to rejoin his comrades in Utrecht.[12]

The first hint we get of Suckling's attitude and response to his travels comes in the first of his surviving letters, written at the end of October to his cousin and, it seems, beloved of the time, Mary Cranfield. He was writing from Gravesend, awaiting departure; he was unable, he claimed, to do justice to the melancholy he felt upon leaving her. His valediction also carried a (faintly jocular) echo of Hamlet's dejected sense of the world as a prison – 'a goodly one, in which there are many confines, wards, and dungeons'. He thus allotted writer and reader their respective roles.[13] Suckling is the Renaissance man, scholar, courtier and soldier setting forth; but Mary Cranfield may not have been content to be cast as Ophelia. His later letters suggest she was not only too shrewd but knew him too well to take his rhetoric uncritically. The gallantry of this one needs to be read alongside the bits of doggerel he was also composing at the time:

There is a thing which in the Light
Is seldom us'd, but in the Night
It serves the Maiden Female crew,
The Ladies and the Good-wives too:
They use to take it in their hand,
And then it will uprightly stand . . .

(He was writing about a candle.)

And to a hole they it apply,
Where by its good will it would die:
It spends, goes out, and still within
It leaves its moisture thick and thin.[14]

'Your Ladyship is too wise to suppose to your self impossibilities,' he would in time tell Mary, 'and therefore cannot think of such a thing, as of making me absolutely good.'[15]

Thus after a rocky return crossing in October 1629, we find Suckling reporting that 'the winde is as women are, for the most parte bad!' Life in the lands he sailed to *was*, as it turned out, like that in a prison, and a less than goodly one. In a letter from Leiden in November, he wrote that Holland was hungry, penny-pinched, and depressed with war. There was 'not a man here but would doe that which *Judas* did, for halfe the money' – if, that is, as he commented in another letter a few months later, there had been anyone in the country 'to furnish out the 30 peices of silver'. His disapproval of supposed avarice may in fact shelter a touch of envy: as one who never took money very seriously, Suckling was inclined to ridicule those who did, but in his journey through United Province territory he would, had he cared to look, have been able to observe the germination of a vast economic empire. James Howell, on a trip to the region ten years earlier, had been struck by the 'slow nature of the Inhabitants', but his sharper, less affluent eye had noticed how that made the Dutch and the Flemish 'patient and constant', combining invention with limitless industry:

They have all a *Genius* inclin'd to Commerce, very intentive and witty in Manufactures, witness the Art of *Printing, Painting,* and *Colouring in Glass*;

those curious Quadrants, Chimes, and Dials, those kind of *Waggons* which are used up and down Christendom, were first used by them.[16]

Suckling was more inclined to comment on manners and appearances:

Since my coming a shoare, I finde, that the people of this Cuntry, are a kinde of Infidells, not believing in scripture . . . And sure their auncestors when they begott them thought on nothing but Munkeys, and Bores, and Asses and such like ill favor'd creatures; for their Phisonomyes are soe wide from the rules of proportion, that I should spoyle my prose to let in the description of them. In a word, they are almost as bad as those of *Leicestershire*.[17]

The irreverence in his letters comes at times close to contempt, although Thomas Clayton, one of the chief authorities on Suckling's life and work, has said that broadsides such as the above are 'not to be taken as derision in earnest: in these epistolary characters, the national stereotypes are *données* of the satirical genre.'[18] Always referring to himself as a 'good Protestant', Suckling was critical of hypocrisy and hysteria in both Reformed and Roman Catholic communities. He had the chance to observe both. His regiment was disbanded early in the winter to conserve scanty funds: with no official military designation, he could now travel in Spanish-controlled regions of the Low Countries, and over the next few months continued sending word home in the same vein as above. Writing from Brussels in May he conceded that certain elements of a papist country did have their charm, since the Roman sacrament of confession offered the sinner a reliable insurance policy. Catholicism was ideal for young men: all sins from drunkenness to incest could be speedily absolved the next morning. A mumbled '*Ave Maria*' was the going rate for each successful seduction.[19]

Ben Jonson, rumoured to be a Roman Catholic convert, had outlined with characteristic vehemence the alternatives of honourable service and 'vicious ease' as a choice of virtue as opposed to venery. Back in London a Juvenalian eye could observe with practised despair:

> Man's whole good fixed
> In bravery, or gluttony, or coin,
> All which he makes the servants of the groin.[20]

By 'the wars', in contrast, Jonson means not only the specific conflict in the Low Countries but an almost generic option of military service. The wars are a worthwhile last resort as a means of escaping turpitude at home. 'It is a sweet and decorous thing to die for one's country,' wrote Horace – and a relief, adds Jonson, when that country is sinking into an urban chasm of vice. The pious narrative of an honest if at times ungrammatical field historian such as Hexham supports that conceit: from his campaign notes one would think that the depravities Jonson writes of never crossed an honest soldier's mind. Suckling's letters from Belgium, however, give a disillusioned commentary on that construction. They can be read with Jonson's 'Epistle to a Friend, to Persuade Him to the Wars', as a sardonic but melancholy continuation in prose: the types that disgust Jonson, servants of groin and coin, are to be found in all places. Suckling gives the impression that there is no 'clean' war to run away to; the same sordid fight to survive, on the other hand, is everywhere. Hamlet's idea of the world as a prison never seems far from his thoughts – and there is little to do but laugh in the cell where you find yourself.

Suckling wrote bawdily to make a smart acquaintance smile. But he sent more sombre political commentary to his favourite uncle, the Earl of Middlesex. Whereas in the United Provinces he had found that the economic difficulties were confined to the 'public purse', as the Prince of Orange stretched his resources in the push against the imperials, in Brussels there were signs of deeper 'private' poverty, even below the knotty pinnacle of the Hôtel de Ville, where the headquarters of the city's infamously wealthy guilds sat in permanent conference. The Lower Town of Brussels did not then present quite the same spectacle of opulence it did a century later – and does to this day. The baroque guild halls of the current Grand' Place only replaced the humbler wooden terraces which Suckling saw after a bombardment by the French in 1695. The city ached with the effort of war. John of Nassau had recently ridden forth to scrape together an army in Germany; meanwhile, veterans from the previous years' campaigns drifted destitute. Suckling was moved by captains unashamed to beg and the desperate insolence of ordinary soldiers. His more usual whimsy took over when he remarked that their superstitious faith and love of the Infanta made them ready to forego their pay.

Above, in the palace on Coudenberg, throughout the Spanish Netherlands, indeed across the Holy Roman Empire, the troops' princes were doing little to foster this affection, set more on punishing their officers than trying to improve the terrible conditions in which their subjects and soldiers were living. At Antwerp it had now emerged that the former governor of Wesel was to be put to death, with the confiscation of all his estates, for losing the city the summer before. Some railed against him, some pardoned him; most felt pity. Suckling sensed defeat in the air.[21]

3

While Suckling was touring the Low Countries, William Davenant was learning and demonstrating the dangers of service to the groin. He had taken what Suckling metaphorically described as a journey to France and contracted syphilis, *morbus Gallicus*, 'the French disease', from a 'handsome black wench', after an encounter in a little cul-de-sac near the site of the present Downing Street. The close had an aptly grim name, Axe Yard. The record is hazy as to whether the place was his or hers, or merely a location convenient for both. It is also unknown where Davenant's wife and child were living at the time. According to John Aubrey, the dark-haired or dark-complexioned woman provided the rueful inspiration for a temptress encountered in Davenant's uncompleted epic, *Gondibert*. She stops two of his heroes in their tracks on their way through town:

> For a black Beauty did her pride display
> Through a large Window, and in Jewels shon,
> As if to please the World, weeping for day,
> Night had put all her Starry Jewels on.

The verse is somewhat shaky (note the slightly clumsy repetition of 'jewels'), but the two men's responses to this apparition, by the name of 'Black Dalga', neatly observed. One, immediately overcome with a strong weakness, 'Hung down his Head, but yet did lift his Eyes/ As if hee fain would see a little more'; while his companion 'did like a blushless

Statue stare' – not stonily immune, but openly mesmerized, and 'ready to cry out, that he was took! [i.e. ensnared]'. From what is known of him, the latter's reaction bears the greater resemblance to Davenant's.[22]

The incident highlights the rapacious activity Jonson condemned so readily in younger men. It also shows up the attitudes they held to their sexual partners. Reading Davenant for one of the youngsters in the poem, and his 'black wench' for Black Dalga, who 'with black Eyes does Sinners draw/ And with her voice holds fast repenting Men', the party to blame for the poet's seduction and subsequent infection in Westminster is more than obvious.[23] The female is guilty for her own attractiveness, or what Davenant calls in *Gondibert* 'a wicked Woman's prosp'rous Art', calculated down to the 'seeming modesty' with which Dalga closes her window to leave the two youths tantalized in the street below.[24] However, leaving aside Davenant's alleged efforts to rationalize and revise his experiences of solicited sex, the figure of this woman in his biography carries more than a hint of further literary embellishment. It looks like another part of his effort to make his life run like that of his godfather, another subliminal suggestion to Aubrey that if he was not Shakespeare's natural son he was at any rate his symbolic heir. Shakespeare had his dark lady; Davenant was entrapped by his 'handsome black wench'. The resulting allusion is unfortunate, if a counterpoint between the lady of the sonnets and 'Black Dalga' was not intended in jest.

Davenant's early readers already had evidence that he wished to fashion a strong literary persona. When his tragedy of *Albovine* was published in 1629 he altered his surname on the cover to D'Avenant, trailing the idea that his lineage descended from Lombardy, where many of his fictions would be set, and not from a family of London merchants with an older branch in Essex. Contemporaries spotted his attempt to mystify his origins, and celebrated it maliciously:

> As severall Cities made their claim
> Of *Homers* birth to have the fame;
> So after ages will not want
> Towns claiming to be *Avenant*:
> Great doubt there is where now it lies,
> Whether in *Lombard* or the *Skies*.[25]

This was standard fare for the time. The men in this milieu were wits; and wit, like honour, placed certain demands upon them. If a joke was there for the taking, it was wrong to let it pass, or leave it to someone else. As Count Baldassare Castiglione declared in *The Book of the Courtier* – an old book in an old translation but still a standard guide to good conduct – wit was more than a literary talent: it was a faculty, an often vital tool and a medium of social exchange. And as Castiglione also recognized, battles of wit were a form of sublimated duelling, in which the best points came from using your adversary's own words against him:

among other merry sayings [forms of speech], they have a verie good grace, that arise when a man at the nipping talke of his fellow, taketh the verie same words in the selfe same sense, and returneth them backe againe, pricking him with his owne weapon.[26]

Wit was strongly allied to masculinity, since 'a wit' was invariably male (or a woman dressed or acting or speaking like a man). Banter was like swordplay, and a man's wit was like his blade; and so, predictably and rather tediously, it was also like his penis.

Despite the sallies he invited, Davenant alias D'Avenant had nevertheless been making some progress as a writer. His early works show him reflecting the tastes and expectations of different audiences. *Albovine*, which went unperformed but made it into print, and *The Cruel Brother*, which was performed without notable success, are studies in scarlet tragedy; in each the blood has barely time to clot before more is spilt. A dark seam of misogyny runs through both. The eponymous cruel brother of the latter play is Foreste, a zealot of the cult of male honour, who first suspects his wife ('my she-goat!') of adultery, and then murders his sister for allowing their ruler, the lecherous Duke of Sienna, to rape her. What is rape, he asks, tying her to a chair: 'If compulsion doth insist until/ Enforcement breed delight, we cannot say/ The female suffers.'[27] He fetches a basin and dismisses her last pleas:

> Thy veins are cut. Here
> In this bason bleed; till dryness make them curl
> Like lutestrings in the fire.[28]

The theatre of revenge was filled with actions of furious and mis-guided blindness, but Davenant took the unusual step of presenting a revenger with no moral basis, one with whom the audience could not at all sympathize; one whose supposed virtues are more psychopathic than the vices of the duke he wishes to eliminate. Revenge for Davenant becomes the act of a fanatic, punishing the innocent for the crimes of their corrupt governors.

Davenant's early tragedies also contained elements of social criticism. The implicitly pederastic relationship between the duke and his favour-ite the count in *The Cruel Brother* had more than a faint savour of the closeness of both Stuart kings to Buckingham; there were sardonic comments too on bones of contention of the 1620s, monopolies and bribery, the status of the law, and the lot of unpaid, neglected soldiers broken by fruitless campaigning. Davenant frequently invoked the commonplace of the metropolis as a centre of vice and decadence. The veteran Grimold in *Albovine* complains how 'this luxurious City hath made me so rotten, I dare not walk in the wind, lest I be blown in pieces.'[29] The idea was familiar, but it had peculiar force in the climate of 1628–9 – one possible reason that *Albovine* was denied a licence for performance – and a strong personal resonance after Davenant fell ill, and almost physically apart, in 1630.

Given the limited success of his tragedies, Davenant began applying his gifts as a versifier in the pursuit of patronage. The dramatic representation of tyrants did not necessarily portray England's current rulers, but served as a corrective and a warning to their darker tendencies. So although he was ungenerous to governors as a rule in the theatre, Davenant felt able to tell the Duchess of Buckingham, obeying convention in one of two con-solatory poems he addressed to her, that the nation shared her grief:

> For gone is now the Pilot of the State,
> The Courts bright Star, the Clergies Advocate,
> The Poets highest Theame, the Lovers flame,
> And Souldiers Glory, mighty *Buckingham*.[30]

At New Year, 1630, Davenant was praising Charles as 'th'example, and the law,/ By whom the good are taught, not kept in awe'; a little later in the year he was pooh-poohing scaremongers who claimed that the suspension of Parliament would unhinge the state. In the latter poem, directed against a prophet of doom whose brains had 'curdled in his skull', Davenant's voice took on a new, harsher, confrontational tone. 'Canst thou believe, who dost a storm foretell,/ That it will come because thy passions swell?' His poem urged instead reconciliation between a 'fearless Parliament' and an honourable monarch, invoking the magical but still widely accepted principle that 'When Thrones are rich, the People richer grow;/ As Rivers gain by Seas to which they flow.'[31]

Davenant and Carew were presently able to compare notes, had they wished, on their ailments. Suckling dismissed Davenant's syphilis as a 'mischance'. It was not the infection itself, it seems, which proved disfiguring and almost fatal, but his first attempt to have it treated. A dose of mercury was the customary prescription, to be administered in a number of ways. One common method of applying the cure was absorbing its vapour through a steam bath. This would bring out the purgative 'quicksilver sweat' which Donne's poem 'The Apparition' had sardonically observed in a mistress. Sometimes too a sample that had been 'coagulated with time' was taken more directly, burnt in a little spirits of wine. Given the harm it inflicted, Davenant, shuddering and burning in his room, must have tried inhaling the fumes like an olbas oil cure for catarrh, with an extra measure or so to do the job properly. The results were horrific, as medical writers had been warning for many years: 'malignant accidents' of mercury included 'ulcerations in the mouth and gums, tongue & throte, with continuall fluxe of flegmatic matter day and night running'.[32] Davenant's nose, eyes and mouth bled; and at one point on lifting his face from his hands he found them cupping the remains of his septum.

After the wizening effects of the syphilis, and the toxic damage inflicted by the quicksilver, it was surprising that he ever picked up a pen again. But Davenant's first poems after the initial danger of his illness had passed are remarkable both for their good humour and their honesty about how frightening the experience had been. His first act of writing, in the immediate pain and confusion, appears to have been a note calling for help from his friends and patrons at court. Rather than the quick-fix quack he had consulted at first, he needed an excellent doctor as soon as possible. It was Endymion Porter who came to his rescue, by sending the queen's own physician to dress the poet's sores, quite possibly with Henrietta Maria's knowledge and consent.

Thomas Cademan was a wealthy and privileged Roman Catholic, enjoying not only the queen's protection but also a number of lucrative monopolies awarded by the king, including one for the manufacture of vinegar.[33] Recusants lived much more freely under the early Stuarts than they had in the reign of Elizabeth, but even then non-conforming physicians were granted a special degree of unofficial toleration on the basis of their skills. John Donne's stepfather, the late John Symynges, had for example sustained a wide and profitable practice even at the height of the Elizabethan terror. Dr Cademan belonged to the same tradition of professionals, whose faith had allowed them access to some of the older Continental medical schools in Roman Catholic lands that were off limits to conforming English Protestants. Davenant certainly had nothing but praise for Cademan's knowledge, lack of pedantry and 'ready heart': as soon as he could, he wrote with lavish thanks, 'For setting now my condemn'd body free,/ From that no God, but Devil *Mercurie*'. In place of quicksilver, Cademan supplied him with benign medicines more fit for 'Eastern Queens that teeme' (that is, constitutionally delicate, while regularly bearing children) than a rough, and possibly now sterile poetaster.

Davenant's poem to Cademan bears witness, nevertheless, to a terrible course of treatment. He had spent an unspecified period of time with his head sown into a medicated hood to protect his ruined palate, unable to speak or swallow except with the greatest discomfort. He later wrote eloquently of the isolation sickness enforces, cutting the patient off from the normal divisions of time. To Cademan, however, he described the ordeal in strangely newsy, contemporaneous, if still hallucinogenic terms. Imagining those who lacked the doctor's expert care and Porter's financial generosity, his sympathies travelled, as his plays suggest they often did, to demobbed and wounded servicemen. His helplessness raised the spectres of some of those who had suffered most in the naval debacles of the previous decade. The doctor had saved him from being dumped, like a sick sailor, on the charity of some unspeakable Admiralty hospital, where his remains would be recycled into rope, his 'revolted teeth' threaded on a fake pearl necklace. Such places were a common sight in the south-coast cities of the 1620s, the inmates put ashore and 'suffered to perish, for want of being looked unto, their toes and feet rotting from their bodies, and so smelling that none are able to come into the room where they are'.[34]

Davenant drew on a wide and varied xenophobic vocabulary. When he ate, he still grimaced like a Jew being forced to eat non-kosher food; he could only indicate his wishes by making signs, spitting and foaming as he did so like a 'Turks poyson'd Mute'. But Cademan had prevented his swollen face from resembling the 'Saracen's Head' as commonly painted on tavern signs.[35] (When defeated westerners returned from fighting the Fatimids, as John Selden scornfully explained, 'they pictur'd them with huge big terrible faces . . . when in truth they were like other men, but this they did to save their owne credits.')[36]

Each 'stanza' of the poem begins with a big 'For', the syntax promising a subsequent clause to deliver an oratorical reward:

> For thy Victorious cares, thy ready heart;
> Thy so small tyranny to so much Art;
> For visits made to my disease
> And me (Alas) not to my Fees.

Yet the prize does not turn up. Instead the poem runs through a 'litany' of the good Cademan has done Davenant and the ills from which he has saved him, while repeatedly deferring the expression of thanks it keeps leading the reader to expect. That is, it catalogues the debts but keeps on failing to pay the bills.

Davenant connected his suffering, and a feared loss of masculinity, to a loss of nationhood, and a loss of his proper religion. Stifled in his shroud, he was like a silenced puritan minister. Each of his symptoms meanwhile took the form of one in a stock list of enemies of the Protestant English, from the Saracen to the Jew. Syphilis would always be a disease of foreigners. For Davenant it was one of infidels. The 'Devil *Mercury*' sires a brood of heathen adversaries, Muslims and Jews for the most part. Davenant's ailments, in short, had nothing to do with him personally; he remained a sound Englishman at heart, just one under occupation, enduring a drawn-out 'Concealment of my Mothertongue'. It is worth noting – though not, of course, surprising – how a figure usually found in this roster of orthodox bigotry, the Roman Catholic, is conspicuously absent.

Cademan had thus in effect ransomed him from the Ottoman galley of venereal disease. Davenant could never repay him, quite literally; he apologized for not being able to pay his expenses. As Mary Edmond points out, the poem offers another gift than the long-expected, long-put-off 'thank you'.[37] This non-payment is the poem's running joke. Davenant ended instead, more inventively, by hoping that every spring would bring a 'Ripe Plenty of Diseases' to the rich, to swell Cademan's coffers, and 'Health to the poor' – to save the doctor from having to treat the likes of Davenant out of pity.

A friend of Davenant had his cloak stolen by his manservant, and Davenant wrote to commiserate from his place of confinement. He was sorry, he said, 'my sick Joynts cannot accompany/ Thy Hue-on-cry.' His old midnight conferences with parish constables – accosting him for raucous behaviour and nocturnal wandering – were 'silenc'd long since'. But he vowed to find the thief by the force of wit alone. His little fiction was broken by a rap at the door:

> But hark! who knocks; good truth my Muse is staid,
> By an Apothecaries Bill unpaid;
> Whose length, not strange-nam'd Drugs, makes her afraid.[38]

He was not as unprotected against such expenses as the lines suggest. In one of his verse epistles to Endymion Porter, he claimed rather optimistically that 'nought justly payes' a doctor's art but 'praise'. The same approach did not seem to work on the chemist, but he could seemingly rely on Porter. Davenant had, though, learned his lessons. His model from now on would be Endymion, who had taught the world how courtship could 'subdue the minde, and not the man betray'. Whether or not Davenant was referring to Olivia Porter or the mistresses Endymion constantly denied having to his wife is left an open question. In the same poem, as physical wholeness and a return to 'midnight parlies' began to seem distantly possible, Davenant promised that if he was ever again able:

> To wash our Fleet-street Altars with new Wine,
> I will (since 'tis to thee a Sacrifice)
> Take care, that plenty swell not into vice,
> Lest by a fiery surfeit I be led
> Once more to grow devout in a strange bed.[39]

William Davenant could depend on considerable charity from powerful friends, on their sympathy for his disfigurement, and as William
D'Avenant was sustained by some admiration for his literary industry –
but probably not from Madame D'Avenant, and not from the ruthless
society of wits to which he hoped to return:

> Thus *Will*, intending *D'Avenant* to grace
> Has made a Notch in's name like that in's face.[40]

Of the lines, notches and wormholes Davenant's mistress endured, or
those he perhaps unwittingly transmitted to other unfortunate partners,
nothing more is known.

4

There is some doubt as to when exactly Suckling made Davenant's
acquaintance: he did not, significantly, contribute laudatory verses to
Davenant's early publications. This may have been due to his frequent
absence abroad during the late 1620s and early 1630s. Davenant's illness
almost certainly prevented Suckling becoming at this time the 'intimate
friend' he was a few years later.[41] It is also likely to have marked something of a watershed in Davenant's social life, estranging him from
Edward Hyde, his old room-mate at the Middle Temple, and others
averse to washing Fleet Street's altars with wine. Some time would
therefore pass before they would set out together into the town; yet by
or soon after September 1630, when Suckling was knighted at Theobalds
despite the difference in their fortunes they belonged to a common
milieu, sharing at least one friend in Thomas Carew.

Between their expectations and separate social standing, however,
there was a large gap. Davenant's prospects, despite the support he
received, were not entirely favourable; while Suckling's background
and family connections put him on an equal footing with some of
Whitehall's most influential courtiers. He was able to follow at close
hand the permutations of an ongoing division in the court. There were
those who supported closer alliances with Spain, and those who urged
direct military action against the Habsburgs. Both wanted to recover

the Palatinate (and if possible the crown of Bohemia) for King Charles's nephews, though the parties had differing long-term agendas. Some favoured pacification of Spain and Austria as the best policy for British interests; others saw Protestant war as the only safe (and moral) course of action. ''Tis true, *Faction* there is,' Suckling told his Uncle Middlesex in the autumn of 1631; 'but 'tis as true, that it is as winds are, to clear, and keep places free from corruption.'[42]

The situation in Europe had been complicated – and energized – by the emergence of a new Protestant hero. Despite the deadlock in the Low Countries, by 1630 much of modern northern Germany lay under the de facto control of Ferdinand II, the Holy Roman Emperor. Ferdinand had decided against magnanimity in victory, despite the warnings of his general, Wallenstein: he had imposed a crushing Edict of Restitution on the region's Protestant nobles. By this he restored to Catholic control all lands that had taken on Protestant loyalties since the Treaty of Passau in 1552. In doing so, he tore up what remained of the fragile détente that had eased the first explosion of post-Reformation war. Christian IV of Denmark, who had intervened to support the Northern Protestants in 1625, had also been defeated. Indeed, soon abandoned by his putative allies in France and England, by 1627 he had been driven right back over his own borders by one of Wallenstein's most startling and decisive counter-offensives. It was only Wallenstein's intervention, tempering Ferdinand's inclination to deprive Christian of Jutland and exact gigantic reparations, that saved Denmark from a thoroughly degrading settlement in the Treaty of Lübeck in 1629.

Accompanying the Earl of Leicester on a special embassy in 1632, James Howell found the Danish court still in belligerent and bibulous form, King Christian drinking thirty-five toasts with the earl (each of which required the draining of the glass) and then going to hunt at daybreak, but their taste for the campaign had gone. Instead, Howell noted, 'The King begins to fill his Chests apace, which were so emptied in his late Marches to *Germany*.'[43] With the Danes eliminated, the way was clear for Christian's chief Baltic rival, Gustavus Adolphus II of Sweden, to enter the contest. Gustavus had already sent unofficial support to embattled fellow Protestants in northern German territories; now, having strung together a loose but firm network of alliances in Pomerania, Mecklenburg, Hesse-Kassel and Brunswick, and concluded a crucial treaty with the French in January 1631, he was ready for a direct attack on Ferdinand's imperial armies. His case was made the stronger by the massacre carried out at Magdeburg in May, the worst of the whole war, by the army of the Count of Tilly. This alienated support for Ferdinand within the empire itself: two vital players, the princes of Brandenburg and Saxony, discarding their legal obligations as electors of the emperor, declared their support for Gustavus. With the diplomatic and moral advantage, Gustavus cornered Tilly's army near Leipzig in September, slaughtering twenty thousand out of thirty-five thousand tired, hungry and unpaid troops of the Catholic League at Breitenfeld. In England, Suckling alluded flippantly to the battle in once more bidding Mary Cranfield adieu: 'He never knew you, that will not think the losse of your Company greater than the Imperialists can at this time the losse of all their Companies.'[44]

These appalling events, with the English claim on the Palatinate (and Bohemia) in mind, left King Charles in a delicate position. Gustavus demanded both military and financial aid and a formal alliance: yet the question remained, which side to back? If the English supported Gustavus and he lost, they could not expect concessions from the imperials; nor could they from Gustavus, if they refused to send arms and money and he still won. To date Charles's solution had been to allow a Scottish noble, the Marquis of Hamilton, to take a private force of six thousand soldiers from England and Scotland to support the Swedes, thereby making no definite commitment to either side but sending mixed signals to both. The mission was a mess: Hamilton's men had landed at the wrong place, and in ensuing weeks been reduced by disease to a few companies of foot. Hamilton then sulked at being made subordinate to one of Gustavus's commanders. The atrocities at Breitenfeld, however, presented a moment of truth – at which Charles again evaded a clear decision by sending an embassy to Gustavus to 'enter into a league . . . upon emergent occasions'. The delegation was headed by Sir Henry Vane, who was said personally to oppose any close formal alliance with Sweden. Suckling was chosen as one of the party.

For his supposed betrayal of the royal cause a decade later, Edward Hyde damned Vane as an opportunistic mediocrity bent on nothing more than enrichment. 'He was of very ordinary parts by nature, and he had not cultivated them at all by art; for he was illiterate. But being of a stirring and boisterous disposition, very industrious and very bold, he still wrought [himself] into some employment.' Vane had been a creature of King James's two great favourites, first of Somerset then of Buckingham, and thus grew 'acquainted with the vicissitudes of Court'. Vane however misjudged the moment when Charles and Buckingham pursued vengeance on Madrid in the mid-1620s by continuing to support the Spanish match, which brought him 'severe mortification'.[45] On a return to favour after Buckingham's death he was given a series of thankless diplomatic tasks, the first of which in 1629 was to explain to the republican Dutch why England sought peace with France and Spain. He was by then, again slightly late in the day, a vigorous defender of assertive military action by the English Crown, urging Charles in dispatches to redeem his honour by putting ships to sea. Charles kept on sending Vane as special envoy to The Hague, entrusting him with dirty and delicate work. The king had neglected paying his sister's rent, and in a fiery interview in 1630 Frederick waved Charles's letters in Vane's face, remonstrated furiously, and burst into tears.

Vane was thus the natural candidate for the German assignment in 1631, being neither a 'Spaniard' of the currently dominant faction at court, nor an out-and-out interventionist like his main and much more dignified rival, the diplomat and explorer Sir Thomas Roe. Why Suckling should have been so eager to be one of his attendants comes through in a couple of the letters he sent to Middlesex that autumn and winter. His uncle, though one of the major politicians of the previous two decades, was remaining aloof in country retirement; and to some it appeared that he was either sulking or waiting for the right opportunity. Suckling, for his part, as he told the earl, hated to 'consider that great soul of yours, like a Spider, working all inwards, and sending forth nothing, but like the Cloister'd Schoolmens Divinity, threads fine and unprofitable'. From Europe Suckling urged Middlesex that 'while all the world is thus in action, pardon me (my Lord) if I must hope your Lordshipp will not long be idle . . . The Christian world never more needing able men than at present.'[46] To some extent these are the courtesies due to an elder statesman from a younger relative, but Suckling felt the call of active public life; and his letters show him caught up in the excitement, confusion and distress of one of the century's most extraordinary campaigns.

It took quite some time for Vane and his men to catch up with

Gustavus. They sailed from Yarmouth on 20 September to Hamburg, buffeted on arrival by the surging atmosphere created by the victory at Breitenfeld, in which almost all the news Suckling relayed giddily to his uncle was inaccurate. Howell was in the city later in the year accompanying Leicester on his embassy to Denmark. Hamburg, then a protectorate of Denmark, was 'a huge wealthy place'. Looking at the people in the region, 'observing well their Physiognomies, their Complexions and Gait, I thought verily I was in *England*, for they resemble the *English* more than either *Welsh* or *Scot*.'[47] For a moment one might even think this European war had reached England.

No one could know for sure where the Swedes were or where they would strike next; only that Gustavus was, as Suckling said, 'entring still farther into *Germanye* and at this time being in the very heart of it'. On 11 October the English left Hamburg to look for Gustavus, their only guide a widening scatter-pattern of resounding military successes. The king was in fact settling his army down for the winter at Würzburg, having captured with a dazzling assault the imperial fortress, arsenal and treasury of Marienberg on the opposite bank of the Main. So much loot had awaited the troops there that ordinary soldiers could be seen, using their drums as card tables, gambling for three hundred ducats a hand.

In pursuit of the Swede the party had a hard and vagarious winter ride through what Suckling called 'the ruines of countryes'.[48] They spent the best part of a month out in the angst and disorientation of the war zone. Parties of horse and foot crossed and re-crossed their wandering path down a series of trails that went dead. Troubled on the way through a string of torn-up towns by imperial patrols, whose sergeants demanded to see their diplomatic passports, they were offered safe passage through Holy Roman territory but kept wherever possible to the regions under the de facto control of the Swedish king, seeking his armies in Bamberg, Braunschweig and Erfut. Apologizing to a friend for his failure to write, Suckling excused himself by saying, 'We have ever since been upon a March, and the places we are come to, have afforded rather blood than Inke: and of all things, Sheets have been the hardest to come by, specially those of paper.'[49] It was 5 November, three weeks after they left Hamburg, when a troop led by the Swedish Field Marshal Gustavus Horn rode out to meet the English horsemen at the gates of Würzburg.

Gustavus Adolphus had ruled Sweden since 1611, succeeding his father at the age of seventeen. Towering, pale-haired, blue-eyed, he was a man of indomitable energy and courage, relishing the hunt and the foray into battle, where he always plunged into the thick of the fight. He had proved his mettle and his political nerve by declaring war on Poland in 1625, to end a dynastic argument which had rattled on for decades. At home in the court, Gustavus was a person of equal extroversion, combined with perfect refinement in dancing, cavorting and charming. He was in many respects the perfect prince and cavalier. With his thick limbs, huge chest and jaw, his physical presence recalled to English minds the figure of Henry VIII, and suggested what the lost Stuart king, Charles's brother Prince Henry, might have been. Those who grew better acquainted with him, however, bore the brunt of an excitable nature which bordered at moments on instability. His loyal and long-serving chancellor possessed exemplary patience, and needed it. Gustavus had a slightly manic turn of humour, mimicking and mocking some notables (such as Hamilton) who took themselves too seriously. An explosive temper fuelled his battle-fury, but could also leave him insensate in the council chamber. Yet he would repent of it afterwards; after many heated interviews he told Vane sadly 'that he would give all he had to be Master of his Passions; but that when he begins to be moved, he hath something rises in his Brain, that makes him forget what he saith or doth'.[50]

Vane had little time to speak with Gustavus in person. Two days after the English rolled up at Würzburg, bespattered and broken-booted, the king marched off with thirteen thousand of his men, leaving his field marshal behind with seven thousand. Gustavus's army moved in columns along both banks of the Rhine, its supplies and artillery carried on barges in the river between them. It was rumoured that Tilly, despite his heavy defeat at Breitenfeld, still had an army of a hundred thousand in the field, and that Wallenstein had taken Prague; but Gustavus's confidence alone, along with his eye for opportunity and seemingly unerring judgement of the moment, made him unbeatable. Nine days later, just as he had boasted, Gustavus entered Frankfurt am Main. Wearily, the English mustered themselves to join him.

Before they left, Suckling attended a dinner held by the Marquis of Hamilton, the Scotsman who had taken an army of volunteers to

Germany earlier in the year and was now preparing to besiege the town of Magdeburg at the head of nearly eight thousand men: of which, however, most were supplied by Gustavus, 'for his owne are al dead of the plage', saving a thousand or so survivors. Despite the misfortune of his expedition, Suckling found Hamilton in ebullient form, since he claimed 'the king esteems much of him.' When Suckling himself, inspired, expressed a wish that some opportunity might arise for him to do the marquis some service, Hamilton was very pleased to tell him about his mission to Magdeburg, implicitly inviting the young courtier to join it. Perhaps he was bound to follow Vane; yet in any case Suckling let the chance pass silently.[51]

While expressing his eagerness for a life of action, Suckling did not think much of sleeping out rough, as he was presently obliged to once more. Sheets of paper or of bedlinen were again hard to come by as the embassy followed the freezing track to Frankfurt, having the 'misery of lying in straw foure nights together' and their nerves juddered by 'continuall Alarums' in each place they visited. On their arrival, they found that Gustavus had installed only 'a slight garrison' of six hundred men to hold the city. At the end of November, Suckling found the space and composure to write another newsletter to his uncle. Gustavus meanwhile was shortly on the road again, now setting his sights on Mainz, taking which both he and Suckling (joking of how 'so great a statesman am I grown on the suddain') thought would be a harder task than his earlier haul of German cities had presented. In the event the king made a diversion to Heidelberg, which Tilly had left unprotected.

This 'sudden change' sent a thrill through all opponents of Vienna and Madrid: Heidelberg, the centre of Reformation learning, was the capital of the Palatinate. Suckling and all the other delegates left at Frankfurt had no doubt the city would rise on behalf of Gustavus against its current custodian, Maximilian of Bavaria.

Although the English were technically neutral (and insisted on being treated as such by the imperial platoons they met on the roads), Suckling's letters leave no doubt as to whom he and others in the delegation were supporting. The troops of the Holy Roman Emperor and the Catholic League were 'the Enemy'; their friends were the embroiled German Protestants. Where Gustavus stood with regard to the English, however, had yet to be decided. Meanwhile the inhabitants of the

Palatinate and Bohemia were becoming impatient, Suckling reported, 'and would faine see their prince [Frederick] in armes; the receavd opinion that 6000 men would now recover all, makes them storme at the Palsgraves backwardness, and they have much adoe to forebeare the state of *England*, in which they think the fault to be of his not coming up [i.e. coming forth, to muster an army].'[52]

In military and political reality, Frederick was even less than a pawn. There was nothing he could do without a powerful backer, and to all the major players he scarcely seemed worth manipulating. His brother-in-law in England had declined to assume this role, and as for the Swedish strongman who had swept in to rescue the Protestants of Germany, Gustavus was unsure if shouldering Frederick's burden made practical sense as yet. His mind was clear nevertheless as to who should pay the bill: that was a family affair. In the tense and increasingly heated conferences he granted Vane over the winter and into the spring of 1632, he insisted that the cost for Charles of any alliance would be to send him regiments and pay him subsidies, while protecting Sweden at sea from any naval assault launched by the Spanish. Gustavus in the meantime should be left to prosecute the war as he saw fit, with the reclamation of Frederick's lands as a long-term objective. He also demanded a free hand in making the subsequent peace. For any immediate all-out strike on Bohemia and the Palatinate, his demands went up drastically and, as he probably knew, impossibly. The figures mentioned included twelve thousand men, recruited and maintained by the English Crown, along with £25,000 a month. But time was running out for England; by very early in 1632 it seemed as if Gustavus would be able to settle the future shape of the region entirely as he wished.

Having taken Mainz with ease, as it turned out, Gustavus had made his base there for the winter. It was February 1632 when Frederick nervously presented himself there in state, supported by a Dutch bank loan. With Heidelberg already under Gustavus's control, Frederick could do little else but hold out his hand; he could claim none of the credit for the city's rescue, only assert his legal rights and hope for Gustavus's charity. As always, Gustavus was the very model of honour and cordiality, treating Frederick with every formal courtesy due to a prince. Yet Frederick was not a party to the real negotiations over Heidelberg's future. Vane, quite behind Frederick's back, was still trying to keep an

English stake in the dispute alive; even as his masters in London began recoiling from the whole affair. From France, Richelieu told Gustavus that restoring the Palatine region to Frederick, when Sweden had conquered it, was not a sound option: his 'feebleness and frivolity', the cardinal judged, made him apt only 'to lose it or misuse it'.[53] As might be expected, Richelieu had cut to the heart of the question – given Frederick's record, given the likelihood of a counter-attack by the Habsburgs, could he truly be relied upon to retain all that Gustavus had won back?

Such questions tantalized Suckling; all a public man should want, as he had chided Middlesex, was proximity to the court chambers in which they were debated. '*Germany* hath no whit altered me,' he claimed.[54] But the campaign itself was wearing, from the nights to be spent without warning in fields, haylofts or on horseback, to the perpetual agitation in the strongholds where they billeted. He chaffed meanwhile with unvented libido. He had been sorry when a friend on the mission, one John Gifford, was sent home bearing dispatches. Suckling wrote to him with cordial envy in December: 'you are now beyond all our fears, and have nothing to take heed on your self, but fair Ladies. A pretty point of security, and such a one as all *Germany* cannot afford.' The 'northern beauties' Suckling encountered here and there failed, by contrast, to 'kindle a spark'. 'There is nothing either fair or good in this part of the world; and I cannot name the thing can give me any content, but the thought that you enjoy enough otherwhere.'[55]

While Gustavus established his winter headquarters at Mainz, Vane and his retinue remained in Frankfurt, where they negotiated via the Swedish chancellor, Oxenstierna. Frederick only grew gloomier, as it now appeared that Gustavus wished to bind him into a semi-feudal allegiance, acknowledging the Swede as his overlord. To certain observers it seemed that Gustavus had a new structure in mind for the region to replace the old subordinations of the empire he was dismantling. His hand continued to strengthen. Early in March he took Nuremberg, entering the city in massive triumph. On 5 April he claimed perhaps his greatest scalp when the Swedes defeated the Catholic League army in another huge battle, this time at Rain, by the Danube, and their general Tilly was mortally wounded in the engagement.

By this time, to his relief, Suckling was already on his way home.

Vane had decided he must speak more with Gustavus in person, and for greater mobility to keep with him only a skeleton staff. Suckling was thus sent to London bearing letters and the order to deliver a verbal report to King Charles of the latest developments. Having departed on 31 March or early on 1 April, and stopping to collect further dispatches from the English ambassador at Metz, he drew up breathless in London on 10 April, bursting with news of the European drama: if England was to sign an advantageous pact with Gustavus, a speedy decision was more essential than ever. It was late in the day, and too late; and he was deflated to find the court did not share the embassy's sense of urgency. 'The fault at first I layd upon the night and my owne bad eys, but the next day made it cleare and plaine.' Returning as instructed to Whitehall the following morning, he was received by the Lord Treasurer, Richard Weston, who, Suckling reported in a flap, 'both to the bearer and the news seemd alike indifferent! Somethinge coole if not cold!' But this, Suckling jibed, was merely 'perchance his garb'. After a further wait, he was taken through to the privy chamber to see Charles, and hoped to gain a private interview, but 'the bedchamber men were most of them there' – including, possibly, Suckling's friend Thomas Carew – 'and the King spoke lowd.' Charles tepidly welcomed the news of Protestant gains, but Suckling realized that his report was 'somethinge too much *Sweden* and monarchy'. Suffering what looks like a lapse of interest in the whole affair, Suckling left it almost a fortnight before writing a packed and in tone rather frantic letter to his ambassador. In this he gave his view that support for Vane's mission had been cut off at the root. The 'Spanish-imperial' faction at court had taken control of the agenda, a shift of power confirmed by Weston's promotion to chief secretary to the king in June. Suckling could in fact sum up the international situation with great perspicuity:

. . . the King of Swede knows too well, that *England* satisfyed in the demands of the Palatinate, and things at a full point concerning that particular, this crowne [i.e. England] will no longer make court to him, and after it hee must expect no great matters from hence. Besides, *France* which in show pretends to goe along with us, really perchance intends nothing less, since there is nothing but that of the Palatinate, that can keepe *Spain* and us from tying a more strict knot together, and nothing but that has kept us so long asunder.[56]

Three days after Suckling sent this letter, Gustavus Adolphus entered Munich in huge pomp for what amounted to his apotheosis. The king of Sweden was in effect the ruler of almost all Germany. At his side for the triumph, poignantly as it transpired, was Frederick the Palsgrave, the one-time king of Bohemia. It was a moment of optimistic unity which by September would decompose into shrill indignation on Frederick's part and wounded benevolence on Gustavus's. In fact, Gustavus's success had taken him to a very lonely altitude, with the larger diplomatic triad of Britain, France and Spain ready to leave him to his fate at the first moment he failed. The truth was that, regardless of denomination, Europe's great powers did not want another militant emperor on their hands: 'if his Majesty of *Swede* make larger progresses and bee more fortunate,' as Suckling summed it up, 'wee shall feare him as too great.' A colder reasoning power was at work than the sheer heroic force, epitomizing the cavalier ideal, which Gustavus continued to display. In the field Gustavus had critics even among his admirers; even the Marquis of Hamilton, who owed the king whatever remained of his martial dignity, complained of his 'excessif ambision and intolerable pryd'.[57]

Closer to home, Suckling was only mistaken in thinking that Vane's position had been seriously compromised by the embassy. He advised his chief to return home with all speed. The warning was unnecessary. It actually suited Charles's longer-term purposes to have an ambassador who seemed committed to a deal with Sweden, since that was all the more convincing, but who in private shared his reservations. Vane was in due course amply rewarded for his exertions. That reward, however, would come a long time after the Swedish epitome of arms was separated from his troops in heavy autumn fog near Leipzig, where he was later found despoiled, riddled with bullets, in a heap of naked corpses.

5

The shockwaves sent out by the fall of Gustavus at the battle of Lützen rumbled across the Continent, around the Baltic and the German Ocean, and over the Channel, catching the ship that was carrying James Howell back to London. Howell was well satisfied by the part he had played in

Leicester's embassy, during which he was given the task of delivering a speech in Latin to the Danish king. 'My good brother, I am safely return'd from *Germany*, thanks be to God,' he wrote late in 1632, grieved that 'the news which we heard at Sea by a *Dutch* Skipper, about the midst of our Voyage from *Hamburgh*, proves too true.' Howell had no doubt that the impact of the loss of Gustavus would be enormous, but unlike the many elegists driven to genuine despair gave a measured assessment of the king himself:

Questionless this *Gustavus* (whose Anagram is *Augustus*) was a great Captain, and a gallant man, and had he surviv'd that last victory, he would have put the Emperor to such a plunge, that some think he would hardly have been able to have made head against him to any purpose again. Yet his [Gustavus's] own Allies confess, that none knew the bottom of his designs.[58]

Howell, like many, was irked by Gustavus's 'harshness to our ambassadors, and the rigid terms he would have tied the Prince *Palsgrave* to'. Had Gustavus lived, the Thirty Years' War might only have been a fifteen years' war; had Charles entered a formal alliance with him, he would have won some easy popularity at home and deprived his opponents in 1642 of one of their hardest grudges. As it was, the Emperor Ferdinand 'made head' once more against his other enemies.

Back in London, where Howell gratefully re-established himself towards the end of November 1632, sending out accounts of his Latin oration and impressions of Denmark and the north of Germany, Sir John Suckling's fervour for public life had abated and he had altered his views on the importance of 'faction' in court affairs. The death of Gustavus at Lützen – even, all the more unbearably, at yet another moment of victory – was shattering to the militant Protestant cause; but also, less tangibly, hugely dispiriting to the admirers and followers of the direct, chivalrous approach the king had embodied. Sweden had been out-manoeuvred in the council chamber rather than outfought in the field. It is an irony that so many in the pro-Spanish element at the English court would belong to the side branded 'cavaliers' in the British and Irish civil wars, since their cold political realism in the early thirties had very little of the cavalier about it. It was a strong sense of irony, in fact, which saved Suckling from the excesses of grief for the fallen hero to be seen in other quarters. He had seen a little too much of statecraft to take the cause, or the blow it suffered in losing Gustavus, to heart. He did not however emulate his uncle Middlesex, still in political exile, by withdrawing spider-like to a high corner and 'working all inwards': as we shall see, by the autumn of 1632 he was consoling himself with other distractions.

On the ground at Lützen, Gustavus had simply slipped out of position: 'in a sudden Fog that fell, the Cavalry on both sides being engag'd, he was kill'd in the midst of the Troops, and none knows who kill'd him, whether one of his own men, or the enemy; but finding himself mortally hurt, he told *Saxen Waymar* (Weimar), *Cousin, I pray look to the Troops, for I think I have enough.*'[59] As a thousand commonplaces could confirm, life was brief and precarious, even for the mighty.

During Suckling's long winter in Germany, Davenant had continued recovering from his infections and his mercury burns. He had retreated to the country, leading to a rumour that he had in fact died – a common assumption when a regular face went missing from town, to which Davenant responded with a verse letter '*sent with Mellons*'.[60] Dealing with such gossip became something of a motif in the epistolary literature of the period: 'Before this instant I did not believe *Warwickshire* the other world, or that *Milcot* walks had been the blessed shade,' wrote Suckling once to Mary Cranfield, on returning from her to court after a longer than expected absence. 'At my arrival here I am saluted by all as risen from the dead . . . This (Madam) may seem strange unto you now, who know the Company I was in; and certainly if at that time I had departed this transitory World, it had been a way they had never thought on.'[61]

Davenant, however, really had tottered on his heels at the edge of the world. One of the plays by his godfather which most influenced him in subsequent years was *Measure for Measure*: indeed after the Restoration he adapted the comedy for a remake called *The Law against Lovers*, the original then being deemed too harsh and its language too obscure. Significantly, in his scene-for-scene rewriting of Shakespeare's script, he omitted the duke's austere lecture on preparing oneself for death, enjoining Claudio to 'Reason thus with life:/ If I do lose thee, I do lose a thing/ That none but fools would keep' (3.1.7–8). But he did try offering his own version of Claudio's great protest against resignation, his chilling meditation on what dying might really involve – 'Ay, but to *die* . . . To lie in cold obstruction, and to rot' (3.1.122). He was drawn to the voice that clung to life, not the one that reasoned with it: he could never treat the question of death theoretically again, after the labyrinthine solitudes of illness he described to Endymion Porter:

> And when my long forgotten Eies, and Mind,
> Awak'd, I thought to see the Sun declin'd
> Through age, to' th' influence of a Star, and Men
> So small, that they might live in Wombes agen.

Instead of the pale, attenuated world he expected to see beyond the blinds, he was staggered by the power of the impressions it made once more in him, and by his own magnitude, over-estimating his abilities like all positive convalescents, but in resounding fashion: he felt like a Titan of the first age:

> . . . my strength's so giantly, that were
> The great Hill-lifters once more toyling here,
> They'd choose me out, for active Back, for Bone,
> To heave at *Paelion* first, and heave alone.

Having been like truth lost in the delirium of error, he told Endymion, 'Now by the softness of thy noble care,/ Reason and Light, my lov'd Companions are.'[62] Reason and Light: it is notable that the grotesque executions, the experiments with pain, vanish from Davenant's future dramas.

Amid the furore that surrounded the death of Gustavus in November 1632, Davenant was preoccupied with troubles of his own. His tailor sued him for outstanding fees, including, bizarrely, monies owed him for accommodating and maintaining Davenant's young family. The poet had evidently used the old tactic of stalling a creditor by requesting yet more goods, as he had some years before when he stifled a previous request for payment for a suit of clothes by ordering one for his brother Robert, who was visiting him from Oxford at the time. But the £9 due to Urswick 'for meate and drinck & apparel making for the Complainants wife' may tell another story. It is possible that Davenant's wife, Mary, had left him to go and live with Urswick, and the tailor was now rubbing salt in the wound by charging him for her expenses. Speculation surrounds the case, which went unresolved; halted either by Davenant's influential friends or a counter-action he launched in the dreaded halls of Chancery.

As Urswick complained, Davenant seems to have been glad for any opportunity to 'obscure himself' and get out of town.[63] The soot and smell of sea-coal smoke, newly harsh to his damaged nose and throat, became his standard image for the physical atmosphere of the city. A verse-letter surely referring to this time (and if not, to one of Urswick's earlier actions against him) mentions his relief at escaping London for Worcestershire, leaving 'ill Plays, sour Wines/ Fierce Serjeants and the plague' behind him, along with a barbarous tailor.[64] In another he claimed that if Porter had not awoken in him the desire for poetic fame, he would never have asked for anything more than a life of drowsy village comforts.[65] He had, in other words, recovered well; but he would be a walking illustration for the rest of his days of the lifestyle commonly deplored as cavalier.

6

One of the most famous and widely circulated poems to mourn Gustavus Adolphus was addressed to Thomas Carew. The poet was Aurelian Townshend, like Carew a child of the late Elizabethan era, and who, again like Carew, had served the volatile diplomat Sir Edward Herbert on one of his earlier missions to France. Herbert commended Townshend's great aptitude in modern languages, and his usefulness in carrying challenges to Frenchmen with whom the ambassador found it necessary to duel. He was disappointed, however, that Townshend (along with a number of other servants) had done nothing to aid him at a tricky moment during a boar hunt.[66] The poet had subsequently settled into a modest existence at the wings of the court, entering the limelight briefly in 1632 for two masques he composed for the king and queen, *Albion's*

Triumph and *Tempe Restored*. Unwillingly, he claimed, being as 'loath to be brought upon the Stage as an unhansom man is to see himselfe in a great Glasse'; he may also have wished to avoid the wrath of Jonson, whose place he took for the commission.[67] Literary scholars have occasionally wondered why Townshend's star should have faded so abruptly after the success of these two masques. Part of the answer may lie with his elegiac outburst for the fallen king of Sweden.

His poem begins by praising Tom Carew's person and his wit, 'that chooses to be sweete/ Rather then sharpe, therefore in Lirique feete/ Steales to thy mistresse'. Recently, says Townshend, Carew's cast of lovers had been busy lamenting the passing of 'deuine *Donne*' – Donne the deity of wit and, more literally, Donne the divine, the late patriarch of St Paul's. But now their tears must be diverted to register another, still greater loss:

> So when the windes from euery corner bring
> The too true nuse of the dead conquering king,
> Lett our land['s] waters meeting by consent
> The showres descending from the Firmament,
> Make a new flood; one whose teare-swelling face
> Clos'd in an arke of fatall Cyprisse, place
> Gustauus bodie, wound about with bayes.

In extravagant but conventional terms Townshend continues by describing the funeral fit for Gustavus, and at one or two points comes close in his frustration and upset to saying something controversial:

> Prinses ambitious of renoune shall still
> Strive for his spures to help them vp the hill.
> His gloryus gauntlets shall vnquestiond lye,
> Till hands are found fit for a monarchie.

Townshend clearly implies that all of Europe – with which the Protestant English are unusually united in a poetic and political community of grief – waits for a ruler to emerge who is worthy (as Gustavus was) of kingship. A quiet interrogative cough can be heard in the silence when these lines are put on pause and placed back in the context of the situation at court observed by Suckling in the early 1630s: notwithstanding the fact that staunch affection for Gustavus was hardly welcome at that time in royal servants, the courtiers reading these lines were entitled to ask of the poet, 'And what about Charles's hands? Are *they* "fit for a monarchie"?' Apart from a few incidental verses, Townshend was not invited to make any further contributions to royal performances, and by the early 1640s was described as a 'poore & pocky Poett' living on his own meagre resources in the Barbican.[68]

The finer poem Carew wrote in response to Townshend in 1633 takes as its cue the idea that his friend had invited him to compose an ode in honour of Gustavus. Subsequent readers have always taken this to be the case; but at no point in Townshend's poem is such a request really issued. Instead he suggests that Carew, like everyone else, will be left wordless by the disaster.[69]

Carew's answer to Townshend's poem nevertheless takes it that an invitation has been made. In response he advises Townshend, and the poem's wider readership, that an elegy of the kind desired is impossible and imprudent. He is certainly not the man to produce such a poem: he is a creature of comfort:

> Alas! how may
> My Lyrique feet, that of the smooth soft way
> Of Love, and Beautie, onely know the tread,
> In dancing paces celebrate the dead
> Victorious King, or his Majesticke Hearse
> Prophane with th'humble touch of their low verse?

He goes on to echo Townshend's closing assertion that no verse could be equal to the task of elegizing Gustavus, and very delicately and diplomatically consigns the dead king to history. Instead his advice to Townshend and other writers listening, is that they should confine themselves to the kind of artificial pastoral in which 'criticism and compliment' of the regime was acceptable.[70] Furthermore, enjoying England's current state of peace was a matter of propriety as much as straightforward relaxation. Carew issued an infamous summary of the moment that to some has always appeared to deny the real zeitgeist:

Tourneyes, Masques, Theaters, better become
Our *Halcyon* dayes; what though the German Drum
Bellow for freedome and revenge, the noyse
Concernes not us, nor should divert our joyes;
Nor ought the thunder of their Carabins
Drowne the sweet Ayres of our tun'd Violins . . .[71]

The lines stirred memories of Ovid's *Metamorphoses*: some may also have been familiar with canonic passages in Plutarch and Montaigne. The halcyon was the mystical kingfisher who built and tended her nest on the sea during a winter period of miraculous calm. With the mention of 'Tourneyes' (tournaments), readers were for a moment back in the world to which Gustavus has been dispatched, that of Romance, the realm of the Sun Knight. With the progression to masques and theatres they rejoined the urbane environment of the Stuart court.

To many later readers Carew unwittingly spelled out the cause of King Charles's fall: if this preference for the primrose path of dalliance summed up the cavalier attitude, then the catastrophe to come was no surprise. More recently some have asked whether Carew was not merely telling the truth sincerely as it appeared: to many throughout the land, the contrast between Europe's disarray and England's peace and relative prosperity was proof that the 'halcyon days' were a reality.

Yet in the context of Carew's own social circle, calling 1632 a halcyon time is an expression more of hope than fact. The poem is written in the public knowledge of the British soldiers going overseas – like the six thousand taken by Hamilton of which only an estimated six hundred returned; and in the private awareness brought by access to the inner workings of the court, and an acquaintance with such jaded witnesses to events abroad as Sir John Suckling. There are more personal resonances still which should not be drowned out by the bellowing drum, and which lend pathos to the literary topos Carew's poem ultimately invokes, namely the Horatian command to seize the day, to make a life while you have the chance. The blighted profile of Carew's friend Davenant, by this time seizing, if not halcyonic calm, then at least some respite from long sickness, is not altogether absent from the pacifist aura of this poem.

In the opening exchanges of the new play Davenant was working on, one of his sprightly city creatures asks a veteran of the wars, 'Hast thou danc'd to the drum?' – and goes on to question the point of doing so:

> Wherefore shouldst thou bleed for him,
> Whose Money, Wine, nor Wench, thou ne'er hast us'd?
> Or why destroy some poor Root-eating Souldier,
> Who never gave thee the lye, deny'd to pledge
> The health of thy poor Mistress, nor return'd
> Thy Tooth-pick ragged, which he borrowed whole?[72]

There were other wars being fought, other hazards being run, than those overseas; other drumbeats luring people to dance to their destruction. Carew himself had been coping with the consequences of syphilis for more than a decade, though unlike Davenant (if Townshend's compliments are to be trusted) without the loss of his looks. Yet as Suckling commented nastily, Carew was prone to relapses:

> Troth, *Tom*. I must confess I much admire
> Thy water should find passage through the fire:
> For fire and water never could agree,
> These now by nature have some sympathie:
> Sure then his way he forces; for all know
> The French ne'r grants a passage to his foe.[73]

The language used for the pox, the Gallic disease, draws on the language of contemporary battlefields. 'Hast thou danc'd to the drum?' There was no way of not dancing. By ignoring the call of one beat abroad you fell under the spell of another at home, the pulse of your own desires. The only course was to live; gather rosebuds; make a nest while the water was calm.

5. Backslidings

That there is somewhat in us which ought to be hated, bare
reason will convince us; and yet there is no religion but the
Christian which enjoins us to hate ourselves; wherefore no other
religion ought to be entertained by those who know and confess
themselves to be worthy of nothing but hatred.

– Pascal, *Thoughts on Religion*, trans. Basil Kennett (1704)

1

Even among his brethren, Archibald Johnston was exceptional in the
pains he suffered discovering the Lord's true will. He was born in Edinburgh in 1611, and became a gifted student of law. A sense of vocation for
the priesthood, however, still disturbed his peace. Often crying aloud on
the Lord, he waited through whole days of prayer for the surge of spirit
he could take as assurance. Wit, for Johnston, had he recognized even the
validity of the word, consisted in applying the principles and symbolism
of the appropriate passages from scripture to the havoc of the fallen
world, spotting the punishing discrepancies and (occasionally) the frail
concurrences between his actions and the commands of God.

Very frequently the answer came unprompted, from a word he
lighted on upon opening a book, or a phrase that surprised him in a sermon. And on three occasions in his life he was gifted with 'extraordinar
motions' that made his course clear. The first came during an arduous
childhood of illness and unceasing application; the next during a period
of study and worship in France, on graduating from Glasgow. The last,
leaving the coming decades void of divine intimation, touched him on
his return to Edinburgh a few months later, at the age of twenty-one.

Shortly afterwards, he was presented with his first real decision,
whether or not to marry. His parents, devout Presbyterians, his father a

well-to-do merchant, devised the match. The young woman came from another godly family, being the daughter of an eminent advocate. Johnston himself resisted at first. Jean Stewart was not yet fourteen years old. He had heard that she was 'haistie and kankard, and that her face was spoiled by the poks'.[1] At their first meeting, one early autumn morning in church, his spirits rose on mistaking another woman, Maggie Wondrame, as his intended – until he remembered the disfigurement. Johnston fought to conform to God's providence and the counsel of his friends.

Yet when Jean's aunt remembered that her niece's features were like 'rae collops for greating' – like strips of deer-flesh – that morning when she first met Johnston at communion, she did not mean to be unkind. The Stewarts were not giving their child away lightly. Jean was well loved for her warmth, wit and piety. Noting her uncle's habit of lying in a little later on Sunday mornings, she once quipped, 'Lord eimie, fra ye ryse al the week soone for to winne gold, I think ye sould ryse far sooner on Sunday to winne Gods word.'[2]

One of Johnston's sisters considered Jean 'bot ane weak, silly, seakly creature'. But it was while he was praying at home with this sister that he first felt assured that God would not punish him in his marriage, since his soul had just been cleansed at the communion. On emerging from the room he went and told his mother 'as the Lord lives he wil blisse me visibly and shortly in my mariage, and I trou this woman shal be my wyfe.'[3] A few days later he went to pay his first visit as suitor. Proposing to Jean, he asked her not to tell him ay or nay yet, but to ask God on her knees whether the marriage would further his glory, and to beg him to hinder it if it were not. During their conference by a window in the hall he found his heart warming to her, and hers to him. It was a strange sensation. When he came back to hear her answer, one or two less earnest family members jested she was growing devout, by which he knew that she had done as he asked. He was glad when she accepted him kindly. Both families, and even 'indifferent persons hearing of it, thought it the fittest match that ever was in Edimbrugh.'[4]

But Johnston still had to prepare. Every day after the engagement, morning and evening, he poured out his heart to the Lord. His future wife's age no longer troubled him: it would make directing her heart to God all the more easy. The signs also suggested a blessing. It pleased him that he had first decided to propose after receiving communion, that Jean and he had first met after a communion, and that the wedding would take place not long after another. Early that October, exactly a fortnight before the wedding day, all the godly of Edinburgh humbled themselves with a fast.

The Scots did things differently. There were still fastnesses of Catholicism, notably in the Highlands; but the Scottish Reformation had been conducted much more thoroughly than its counterpart in England, under the harsh tuition and militant direction of John Knox. In England there were puritans, a heterogeneous array of religious radicals who looked towards Geneva for guidance and inspiration; but these were, almost by their very nature, groups at the fringes. The high standards they demanded in public life had been usefully appropriated by the later Elizabethan and Jacobean regime, but English puritanism still lay outside the orthodox. In Scotland it was otherwise. The Presbyterian Kirk had a developed and strictly ordered hierarchy which sat uneasily with the echelons of bishops and ministers King James superimposed, quite artificially, upon it. In every parish, 'it is governed by pastors, elders and deacons,' as a contemporary visitor from England explained. The elders and deacons had specific communal responsibilities, the former providing for the poor, the latter taking notice of 'all fornications, adulteries, thefts, drunkards, swearers, blasphemers, slanderers, extortioners, and all other scandalous offences'. All guilty parties were shamed publicly by sitting for prescribed lengths of time on 'a stool of repentance'.[5] This seat would normally be set in a prominent place in every church, normally on top of a platform or pillar. On Sabbath the rules were especially severe. Anyone found loitering in the streets during servicetime was taken to the Tollbooth. Supporting the community and enforcing law and order, the Kirk in practical terms made any other internal authority potentially redundant.

The Johnstons, industrious, prospering burghers, were exemplary Presbyterians. Yet Archibald's devoutness to each particle of doctrine was extraordinary. His mentors, including blind Archibald Scaldee, a scintillating preacher, were probably wise in discouraging him from the priesthood: he was simply too delicate, even too conscientious. At least the law put him at some emotional distance from his work, despite the endless parade of sin it necessarily brought.

In town he lived with his mother and sisters in a property the family held in The Meadows, the wide parklands to the south of the old city, in view of the castle, which before the Reformation had been part of a nunnery. On the Sunday before the wedding he went out to one of the old outlying barns at two in the morning and cried to the Lord until six, begging him to bless his wedding as a token of forgiveness. Wednesday, after he had risen at two again, brought his ongoing prayer to a climax. For wedding gifts he called on Christ as his elder brother to send his graces, God the Father his blessing, the Holy Spirit his consolations. Recalling all that they had given him already, he wept violently.

The nuptial celebrations only reminded Johnston that all was 'bot vanitie and vexation'. When they were alone afterwards, he and Jean prayed together. He thanked the Lord heartily for keeping his body free from 'outward pollution of lust' – to which he had often been tempted – until that hour. Climbing up into bed, he promised God too that he preferred the sight of his face to all 'carnal contentments'.

The next morning he and Jean made a pact. Archibald promised never to 'gloume nor glunche' at her in front of other people, if she would obey him in any 'campaign' they made together. This was also the first of many times he questioned Jean in bed on her catechism, she answering so perfectly that he kissed her, blessed God and rejoiced in his heart 'to seie sutch ane young creatur to knou God', quite 'ravisched', as he put it, with her responses. And this became their pattern through most winter mornings. Archibald would expound from the Greek gospel, and then Jean by herself would continue memorizing the psalms – sometimes learning two in one day. On Sundays Archibald would take down Gerhard's *Week Work of Meditations and Prayers* and the couple would read it together. One morning as he left for communion, he sank to his knees on seeing how moved she was by a prayer he gave, then called her back upstairs and knelt with her, 'forced to blisse God for thos present tears and softnes of heart he had given to us both'. Against his expectations, he came to be delighted with his wife. 'O saule,' he later told himself, 'hir bludered faice seimed then most beautiful to thee.'[6]

The summer had just come and they had been married less than eight months when one Sunday early in June Jean complained that her belly hurt. Johnston recalled that he had just read her a sermon by the English puritan divine, William Pemble. For the twenty days before she had kept a period of intense private meditation. In the evening she took a medicine Archibald brought her, but by the following night was crying out in pain. Alarmed, Johnston set out immediately to fetch one of the city's best doctors. When he and the physician returned, Jean begged him to pray at her bedside, and through the short remaining hours of darkness he recommended her to the Lord, 'yet fearing nothing'. She suffered through the day, with one brief improvement, and died very early the next, 12 June.

What cavaliers grieve for as misfortune, puritans interpret as the judgement of God on their souls. Jean was buried swiftly and unceremoniously, in the sparse Presbyterian manner, and her husband disintegrated. 'O saule,' he rebuked himself, 'remember thy carnal securite and impenitency, thy backslidings, the breaking of thy voues, thy unthankfulnes for and abuse of the blessing.' The death scene itself had consumed his very soul with the terror of God. As Jean slipped further away, he had already collapsed in his study, pleading to know what he had done to deserve the loss he saw coming. He was roused by hearing Jean crying out for him, her 'dear burd'. 'Quhen thou set in the bed beyond hir and sau dead sueat on hir, O Lord, thou knoueth only then if my saule was not then in the gall of bitternes.'[7]

2

On the same day in midsummer that Jean Johnston lay dying in Edinburgh, a large group of masters and lairds awaited their king at a small castle near Scotland's south-east border. Back in the capital, Archibald Johnston was one of the few in his milieu who was distracted from the occasion, since this was the most important public event the country had seen in quite some time, possibly since the last king, James VI of Scotland, had journeyed south thirty years previously, to succeed the queen the English still missed, his cousin Elizabeth. Charles I of England, Wales, Scotland and Ireland was paying his first visit as monarch to his northern kingdom. It was, in actual fact, his first visit since infancy, and for many in Scotland it was long overdue. Charles had inherited the throne in 1625, and it was only now, on 15 June 1633, that he arrived in his homeland to be crowned.

If many took the long absence as a slight, it was also fair to say that business had detained him, and Charles was nothing if not a conscientious ruler. Too conscientious by half for some, who wished that he would stay out of matters that others could handle more aptly. His efforts to reach Scotland had been thwarted by war, by the assassination of Buckingham, the negotiations for peace, and much strife with the House of Commons. Since 1629 Charles had been ruling without Parliament, and he had made it known that he intended to keep doing so. More recently he had been preoccupied, too, with putting his own stamp on the English court. The ordering principle of his restructuring was deference, and strictly observed distance, to his royal person; an idea at odds with the practice of his father – a rougher, wilier and more lyrical character – or indeed of any previous sovereign of Scotland.

On the Scottish side, precisely through long absence and, as some would see it, neglect, there was still some ignorance as to just how much the rules had changed. The Scottish nobles, the masters and the baronial lairds were accustomed from the example of their fathers and their fathers' fathers to a more direct exchange of views and favours with their monarch, whom they regarded as their chief, a 'first among equals', and not, as Charles (and even James) would have preferred to be seen, one quite apart and in fact appointed to his place by God.

The nobility and gentry waiting to receive the king at the border, at Dunbar and at Edinburgh had done their best to learn some of the English court's ways and cater to Charles's rarefied tastes, but they still looked forward to the visit as an opportunity to coax some much belated assurances and concessions from the royal master. At the top of the list was a concern to protect the rites of the Scottish Kirk; yet beneath that a powerful number were still anxious and angry about an Act of Revocation made by Charles some seven years before. There was a tradition of new Scottish monarchs reclaiming and re-bestowing property distributed during their minority, but Charles had gone further, arguably well beyond what his legal right allowed, and had reapportioned lands taken from the Church during Scotland's Reformation in the 1540s. The beneficiaries of this Revocation had, of course, been favourites of the king, who spent much more time in London than they did on their estates far to the north. A delegation that had gone to appeal the Revocation had been baffled by the young king refusing to let them sit, hand on knee, in open debate with him as tradition permitted but insisting that they kneel when they wished to speak. And when this new manner of conducting business had sunk in they had been bitterly offended.

So it was eight years after becoming king that Charles and his retinue first crossed the high stone bridge at Dunglass into East Lothian, having taken the Great Northern Road from London. This, for all practical purposes the main and solitary route, followed a fine edge along the fraught eastern coastline. From Newcastle and then through Berwickshire it ran by eroding clifftops and tenacious fishing towns. In one of these, Cockburnspath, the tall, slim, blunt-headed Mercat Cross, a lonely and ironic stela in the centre of the village, marked the first step on the historical path to union in the borderlands. Charles's ancestor, James IV, had the cross carved and set up in the marketplace in 1503, when he married Margaret, the sister of Henry VIII of England, to whom he presented the surrounding glens and well-used military passes as a dowry. The prospected peace lasted just ten years, and James IV met his fate at the Battle of Flodden.

The precise point at which England passed over into Scotland was still open to dispute. The last major settlement south of the border was Berwick, the old fortress town, an island of English sovereignty. In the minds of some, nevertheless, the fine lines were clear: 'though it be seated in Scotland, yet it is England,' wrote one English traveller of the time. The country was not defined as Scottish, he continued, for several miles further north, though even this spot was a moving target. The land itself did not welcome political definition. Beyond Berwick, a place of much poverty, inland from the northern road swept 'the largest and vastest moors' the English journeyer had ever seen, 'now dry, whereupon (in most parts) is neither sheep, beast, nor horse', and where the few inhabitants relied on turf for their fires.[8]

This was the road's least miry time of year and Charles and his court could have made good progress in their cortege of stately paced carriages, wagons and riders. But they took their time, as they had since leaving London over a month before, until they reached the stream and bridge at Dunglass. There was no longer an English garrison at Berwick, but the bridge was a sign of the still-recent join between the two countries. Before James and the Stuarts moved to England, the burn which ran eastwards to the North Sea coast had to be forded on the beach itself, where petrified roots protruded from the crumbling cliffs above the shingle.

At Dunglass a reception party was waiting, and there, for an indiscernible instant, the king shed the apparatus of his royal court and was briefly just a small, dark-eyed man with fox-coloured hair, a stiff, awkward bearing and a stammer. Charles Stuart's early mentors had considered cutting the cords of his tongue to cure him of this evil: it caused him no problem, however, in switching easily to his native Scots as he received the lairds' welcome.[9] This was the point at which the servants of his English household gave way to their Scottish counterparts. Apologists were later keen to stress how smoothly the transfer passed, but any handing over of authority brought with it a memory of the friction that went with the competition for places at court. One of the gentlemen of the king's privy chamber, Thomas Carew, had been the cause of the 'regret of the whole Scotch nation' when he was appointed in place of a candidate certain Scottish lords preferred.[10] Carew had been given the privileged and important post of Sewer-in-Ordinary, and with it intimate contact with Charles: his job was to taste dishes for the king and place them in front of him.

Such coups, which entirely changed the standing of a courtier, and the triumph and resentment they brought, flavoured the discrete exchange of offices which took place at Dunglass. Certainly Carew was not an impassionate man. It had been a long road, too, to this current respectability, since he was expelled from Venice for insulting the ambassador's wife. But all afterwards agreed that whatever tensions might have strained the summer air at the first encounter, they were left unexpressed.

Many of the English had and felt much in common with the godly customs of their Scottish fellow subjects. But among the English gentry there was long-standing condescension and scorn towards the northern people. 'First, for the country, I must confess it is good for those who possess it, and too bad for others, to be at the charge to conquer it,' began one of the most contemptuous descriptions of the land. 'The air might be wholesome but for the stinking people that inhabit it; the ground might be fruitful had they the wit to manure it.'[11] Such comments were not directed to the 'nobler sort' who met the retinue that day in June, 'brave, well-bred men, and [note] well reformed', but even

English visitors who found much to admire in Scotland criticized a tendency towards 'sluttishness and nastiness'.[12] In doing so they forgot the tumult of deprivation and roaring beggary their steeds and carriages had clattered past on leaving London.

On the way up the long northern road from the southern capital, with several protracted digressions to call on notable subjects, there had been several sparkling examples of how the king liked and expected to be entertained, and by whom. When announcing his intention to set out for Scotland, Charles bid the nobility of England to accompany him and to feast him with all the splendour they could when he came to their gates. Most of them were vying for greater honour. After a delay for several nights at his own lodge at Theobalds in Hertfordshire, a lavish feast was given for Charles in Lincolnshire by the Earl of Essex. Passing through the shades of Sherwood, the retinue was then accommodated by the Earl of Arundel at Worksop Manor. Arundel was later caricatured as 'a man supercilious and proud . . . willing to be thought a scholar, and to understand the most mysterious parts of antiquity, because he made a wonderful and costly purchase of excellent statues whilst he was in Italy . . . whereas in truth he was only able to buy them, never to understand them'. Nevertheless the king approved of the state the earl kept: Arundel's 'expenses were without any measure, and always exceeded very much his revenue'.[13]

During the short stay at Worksop, the king and court visited Welbeck House, 'a noble yet melancholy seat, environed with woods', where a banquet and theatrical spectacle had been prepared for them by the Earl of Newcastle. Newcastle sought higher office and status – as the court's star at the art of dressage, he had his eye on the position of Master of the Royal Horse – and hoped that his efforts at Welbeck would win the king's favour. He was disappointed. One greedy courtier reported in his journal that the standing buffet after dinner had alone cost £700, but the show for the king passed without much note being taken of it. *The King's Entertainment at Welbeck* was one of the last efforts by Ben Jonson, technically the poet laureate, to regain something of his former sway. The year before, Jonson had written sadly to Newcastle, describing himself as 'now like an old bankrupt in wit'.[14] The earl, who was fond of the poet, gave Jonson the commission to entertain the king. He did not consider that a show of friendship to Jonson was unlikely to achieve much for either, given the royal support Inigo Jones currently enjoyed.

The performance combined local Sherwood references, some rather lame jokes, a pantomime of quintain in allusion to the Earl of Newcastle's celebrated horsemanship. The king, though 'royally feasted' at Welbeck and seemingly well pleased with the occasion, did not offer his host any distinct advancement as reward for his hospitality, which had set the earl back some £5,000.[15] In the outer court of Welbeck after the performance, the assembly witnessed the marriage of 'an exceeding tall wench and a very low Dwarf' in the May evening.

The journey northwards continued. Towards the shelving, sandy sea line at Dunbar, the travellers could observe heaps of grass, seaweed and driftwood salvaged from the tide for fuel. The cliffs and nearby lands teemed with wild geese, cormorants and guillemots, and their noise could be heard for miles. The carriages moved on towards Edinburgh, stopping another night at Seaton House, 'a dainty seat placed upon the sea', to admire the gardens and orchards, of 'apple trees, walnut-trees, sycamore . . . and other kinds of wood which prosper well', in spite of the bitter sea air.[16] The approach to Edinburgh led them past the expanses of salt-plains at Sheildes, and the labourers' 'poor houses', and then within sight, and within range, of the city's high castle, a fortress in itself 'of no great receipt, but mighty strength'.

The Scots made every effort to entertain the king on the scale to which he was accustomed. At his formal entry into Edinburgh, the aldermen of the city, along with the members of his Scottish council, were awaiting him in their black velvet robes of office. A basin and purses of gold were presented; long speeches made. A company of the town's militia rode by, uniformed in white satin doublets 'with hatts, fedders, scarffes, buds and the rest correspondent'. As the king was brought along Edinburgh's great high street, 'the glory and the beauty of this city', with its 'fair, spacious and capacious walk', he was treated to a series of open-air, masque-like spectacles. Approaching the Tollbooth, the customary home of the Scottish Parliament, a turreted, irregularly shaped mansion situated before the huge and overpowering Kirk of St Giles, he was treated to a genealogical vision of the kings of Scotland, 'delicately paynted'. A masquer dressed as Bacchus toasted him heartily at the Market Cross, the edifice overflowing with wine for the occasion, and a little further on a scene of Parnassus had been built, rich with gold and greenery, 'where nyne prettie boys, representing the nine nymphs or muses, was nymph-like clad'. There were more speeches.[17]

The scripts for these pageants came predominantly from the pen of William Drummond of Hawthornden, Ben Jonson's friend and intellectual sparring partner, who was in attendance for the ceremony. He was a sallower character by this time, troubled with the stone, never quite the same physically after a dose of pleurisy which nearly killed him more than a decade before. Nor was he quite the same emotionally after witnessing Scotland's great famine of 1623. Scores of people had died of hunger in the streets along which King Charles and his followers now paraded. Drummond's writing had taken on a leaner, edgier quality since Jonson's visit, in his collection of largely religious poems, *Flowers of Sion*. Yet with a mistress and three children to solace his days, he persisted in his 'sweet solitary life' in his rocky fort above the River North Esk.

The rest of the visit continued in similar fashion to the grand opening. The coronation itself was, naturally, a high state occasion. In his furred robes the king went on horseback from the gates of Holyrood at the head of the high street; on his right hand rode the Duke of Lennox, on his left the Marquess of Hamilton. The Earl of Buchan carried the sword, at the head of the procession, and the Earl of Rothes bore the sceptre. The lords and the rest of the nobles followed, clad in scarlet, their horses 'furnished with rich saddles and foot mantles', and rode through the streets before returning for the crowning itself in Holyrood Chapel. To the English it was just a pity that the progress through the capital's magnificent broad thoroughfare should be marred by the fronts of the high, solidly constructed and otherwise very fine stone houses lining the way, covered up shabbily as they were with wooden boards.

The ceremony itself was controversial, although the cries of '*Vivat!*' and the throwing to the crowds of silver coins, minted especially for the day, proceeded without a hitch. The bishops conducting the service, it was noted, wore ornate white linen vestments, with lace sleeves decorated with loops of gold, over the ordinary black habits of a Scottish minister; an altar table bearing golden candlesticks, unheard of in Presbyterian services, had been set up, and a rich tapestry hung behind it 'wherein the crucifix was curiously wrought'. As the presiding bishops passed it by, they genuflected. All of which, to the Archbishop of

Glasgow, who had added nothing to his ordinary plain habit for the occasion, not to mention the ranks of Presbyterian elders assembled in the church, suggested nothing less than the 'inbringing of poperie'. The Presbyterians redressed the balance with sermons that lengthened the service by hours.

Afterwards, Charles's stamina failed him. As Edinburgh warmed up for a night of bonfires and festivities, he took his new crown back to Holyrood and had a quiet private dinner. Much business lay ahead, not least the holding of a Scottish Parliament, in the Tollbooth and the ancillary chambers of St Giles. The lairds and masters were itching to air long-stifled grudges. When the time came, Charles denied earldoms to Lords Loudoun and Lindsey for their obstreperousness; forced through a new tax, the 'two in ten'; and turned a stony face from the protests of the Earl of Rothes against the bill asserting the royal prerogative. The same bill declared the king's royal power to dictate the vestments of judges and clergymen. After the vote, in furious scenes, Rothes demanded a recount, forcing Charles to lose his composure. It had to be remembered that Rothes bore a grudge for losing his tobacco monopoly, and for losing land claimed back under the Revocation eight years before. Tiresome, yet a part, as Charles knew from his English parliaments, of political life, and not to be dwelt on too gloomily since, for the most part, he and those close to him were well satisfied with their reception, even if they were fairly eager to be off.

Critics of Charles would accuse him of not knowing his history or the legal traditions of his kingdoms well enough. It could rather be said that he was only too aware of political precedent, in particular the experiences of his predecessors north of the border – of how James III, for example, had completely lost control to Parliament a hundred and fifty years before, and had to lay a siege to rescue his kidnapped brother, Albany. Ever since disputes had first been played out in the open, centuries before, on the Moothill at Scone, the meeting of a Parliament had been a wrestling match for power. Charles was far from alone among contemporary monarchs in taking steps to place himself well above all that: the trend across the Habsburg-dominated Continent was a movement towards absolutism. There is no saying whether each step he took in that direction – the dictating of what a priest of the Church should wear during divine service, for example – formed part of any conscious strategy: unlike King James, Charles did not write tracts. But the direction in policy was there if one looked for it.

In Scotland, though, there was the unpredictable climate of an emotionally separate world. His loyal councillors and aldermen had spared no cost in entertaining him, as lavishly, they felt confident, as he could ever expect in the south; but there was still some missing smoothness of invention, something stilted about their pageants – the nagging indication that it grated. Still, they flung themselves wholeheartedly into the task of hospitality. On Monday 24 June, after another 'sumptuous banquet', the provost, baileys and councillors themselves, holding hands, went dancing down the high street, 'with all sort of musick, trumpeters and drums'. Yet there was a touch of grit in Charles's compliments. 'It is said his majestie commended our Scottish entertainment and brave behaviour; albeit some lords grudged with him, as ye shall hear, which bred much sorrow.'[18]

3

As the king and his retinue left Scotland at the end of July, Archibald Johnston was still reaping a whirlwind of grief and desperation. In addition to the emotional emergency, the Lord had been pleased to give him 'a secret unknouen torment' in his belly that would afflict him in times of stress for the rest of his days. The symptoms suggested an ulcer; but also, in the beginning, sympathy pains for the abdominal spasms that had killed Jean.

The shock of his loss had unhinged him. 'Oh the suddainte of it confounds me yet,' he wrote years later. Moreover he took Jean's death as proof of his 'bygon abominations' and impending damnation. He had just begun foreseeing the pattern his future happiness would take when it was completely destroyed. Bereavement left him confounded by the 'unsupportable wrath of God, and the impossibilite to think quhou to leave in the world'. At first he could not believe that it was his 'old Comforter', the Lord, who was now drowning his soul in bitterness, filling it with gall and wormwood.

He prostrated himself in his old barn, prayed with his sisters, fixated his entire nervous system on every word at the kirk. Marking dates and times precisely, he recorded every turn his spirits took. His notes show how his feelings took on a pattern of swift, violent swings between comfort and despair. He called to mind how his marriage had rescued him from the sin of temptation. But thinking on God's 'Fatherly indulgence' in giving him Jean only made his 'hot displeasure and indignation' all the more plain.[19] A comforting word in a psalm put him in sight of heaven again. A note of chastisement reduced him to dust. Scripture spoke his feelings perfectly:

> I am lyk a pelican of the wilderness:
> I am lyk ane oule of the desart:
> I watche, and am as a sparrou alone upon the house top . . .
> for thou hast lifted me up, and cast me doune.[20]

Sometimes on the swing between reassurance and desolation he dropped back into simple sorrow. Praying one day in his sister's chamber he remembered that this was the room where he first felt God bless his marriage. He broke Jean's 'woupe', her wedding ring, in two by trying to fit it on his finger. The gold must have been very soft. Inside it was engraved 'ane freind to the end', and it broke exactly at the word 'end'. A big crow frightened him with an omen when it flapped over him. He dreamed of death and while asleep often desired it.

But his hours awake were prone to constant terror of what was in store for him when he died. He set his inward sights on 'delyvery', some confirmation that he was one of those whom God had chosen to save. This was the sign he was waiting for; 'and God hauing put thes thoughts in thy head, hou instantly, yea with som secret hope, thou cryed, "Nou come, Lord Jesus, come, Lord Jesus; my saule longeth for thee." '[21]

As the weeks passed, he slowly reached one precarious point of security in his meditations. He continued falling back through the abyss and rising giddily on the occasional thermals, but he found a way of reconciling God's previous favour with what seemed his present displeasure. This was to rationalize the death of Jean by taking it to be the most recent and generous in a long succession of divine gifts. Telling over the Lord's benevolences, Johnston began including 'this hinmost accident of thy lyfe by taking thy wyfe away, for therby admirably he had moved thee to repentance, he had untied thy affections from the world'.[22] This, at last, suggested that he was not predestined for the torments of Satan. His marriage to Jean had been a blessing, but her death a greater one.

In these ruptures and recoveries Johnston was one of many thousands in Europe living at that time under the influence of the teachings of Jean Calvin and his followers. In Calvin's interpretation of the bible, as it was generally understood, there were those whom God had marked out in advance as his elect, predestined to join him in heaven no matter what they did on earth. Some also maintained that God had determined others as reprobates, bound quite as irretrievably for hell, although on this point there was less agreement. It was thought possible for some to carry within themselves the knowledge that they were among the elect, and that this might be confirmed by a spiritual sign. This was the intimation of 'secret hope' Johnston implored the Lord to send. But until assurance came, even the godly could not be excluded from the number of the reprobate. God's will in fact was such that even the dissolute and undeserving – or dilettantes such as King Charles's attendant masque-makers – might be given a place in heaven while wholly devout Christian burghers were sent to the flames.

Calvinism appealed to worshippers already willing to consider themselves intrinsically worthless and polluted by original sin. Its implications were stark and unpitying for most, while granting joys of unequalled intensity to those who could come to regard themselves as members of the elect. Many, including those wholly possessed by it, tried resisting its conclusions. Sometimes in his long grief, Archibald Johnston of Wariston fought the shade of Calvin, as on the day when 'on my knees half desperate I put God in memorie and read unto him his auine promise, or Chrysts auine speatch [John 3.14] "And as Moses lifted up the serpent in the wildernes evin so must" (yea nou was) "the son of man be lifted up; that quhosoever beleaveth in him sould not perisch, bot haive lyfe everlasting."'

Some later puritans, John Milton among them, hoped and even trusted they could redeem themselves by their works – a notion previously attributed to the errors of Catholicism. In this they were influenced by the Dutch theologian Jacobus Arminius, at whose door many of Charles I's and Archbishop Laud's innovations in worship were laid. But Calvin and the more dominant Reformed Tradition he inspired offered no such way out. There was only helplessness and human evil, and the hope of assurance from God purely on the basis of divine mercy. The good might go to the flames; those who seemed pure evil, on earth, ascend to paradise. It was a stark and unforgiving creed, however much some preachers sought to describe it as a 'comfortable doctrine'.[23]

Johnston's thoughts and prayers during his long mourning followed well-trodden circles. Jean dying seemed wholly irreconcilable with the Lord's former kindness. But rather than entertain the idea that God, if God was truly responsible, had acted unfairly or even vehemently towards him, Johnston preferred to draw the conclusion that it was he who must have been wicked to deserve such a calamity. He saw his own abominations in contrast to the Lord's 'superincomprehensible goodness'.[24] This rationalization was wholly in keeping with a conclusion accepted, albeit in clashing forms, across Christian Europe.

While opposing the Christianity of Protest, the Catholic Church had not been immune from reforming energies. One outgrowth of its 'Counter-Reformation' was the creed that developed from the writings of Cornelius Jansen, a Netherlandian scholar and Bishop of Ypres. In considering the doctrine of original sin – the blotch left on humanity by Adam and Eve in the garden of Eden – the Jansenist Blaise Pascal asked, 'For what can be more repugnant to the rules of our miserable justice than to doom to eternal ruin an infant without will or choice for an offence which shows so little probability of affecting him, as to have been committed six thousand years before his existence in the world?'[25] God seemed unjust; but this for Pascal and most others only proved that God had hidden his reasons for allowing this state of affairs more profoundly than mere human intellect could reach. The 'knot' in which the benign truth was tied hung well beyond mortal grasp.

'I was ever in ane fear to doe evil,' Johnston wrote: 'fo by doolful experience I may knou the sliperie sliderines of my affections.'[26] Whatever he suffered, he had not only brought on himself: it was his just deserts. The same went for everyone, including the monarch, well pleased with his month's work, enjoying the journey back south.

4

Court functionaries had a new system for ensuring that only those with invitations could enter the Banqueting House. On the evening of Shrove Tuesday, 1634, members of the Inns of Court attending the royal masque in Whitehall filed past 'a turning Chair', at which their tickets were inspected. The king had graciously invited the 'Templers' to his masque for Henrietta Maria in return for the spectacular entertainment they had held in his honour earlier in the year.[27] This, as we shall see, had in turn been offered as apology and redress for an outrage committed in print by a member of the Inns.

On getting through the makeshift turnstile, the audience took their seats in echelons around the royal state, the canopied platform which bore seats for Charles and Henrietta. More distinguished spectators arrived, more ceremoniously, from more privileged entrances. The nobler the person, the closer to the royal couple he or she was placed. None presented their back to the king or the queen, who entered last of all, with great ceremony.

Framing the stage set up for the occasion, a proscenium arch was densely decorated with 'foliage growing out of leaves and huskes'. No inch, in imitation of the universe itself, was allowed to go free of emblematic detail. In the centre, on the very top, was the motif of a crown. In the middle was a compartment containing 'harpies with wings and Lions clawes, and their hinder parts converted into leaves and branches'. These were positioned around a frontispiece, itself 'wrought with scrowles and masque heads of Children', and bearing the inscription '*COELUM BRITANNICUM*' – the British heaven.

The pilasters of the arch were no less elaborate. The supports were twin trunks creating a majestic bower. Yet the symmetry within and between the overgrowths was unmissable. At the base of each sat two naked boys, 'in their natural colours', each pair supporting a golden vase. On each vase were figured two young women, robed, arm in arm, figures of royal glory and gentleness on one side, and of nobility and fecundity on the other. These maids supported the two most significant details in the ensemble: the imprese of the king and queen, he symbolized by a lion wearing a crown, she by an arrangement of lilies signifying, among other things, her French lineage. 'All this Ornament was heightned with Gold, and for the Invention and various composition, was the newest and most gracious that hath been done in this place.'

'These shows are nothing else but pictures with light and motion,' claimed their author, Inigo Jones, mischievously, provocatively and victoriously.[28] Although he was unlikely to have been present in person at Whitehall in 1634, the offended shadow of Ben Jonson still slunk in the margins at any royal masque. It appeared that his words had been bettered by Jones's images and machines, and his services at court were no longer required. He had received his last commission in 1631, and while he still in theory received his pension from the king, would not regain his old pre-eminence.

One of his retrospective strategies was magnanimity. Why should he lower himself, Jonson asked, to compete with Jones or reply to his acolytes? 'The Lybian lion hunts no butterflies,' he snorted, majestically echoing the baited poets of old. He told the literati to go and scrawl their tittle-tattle on the walls outside the pubs. 'Thy forehead is too narrow for my brand,' was his scorching last word on that subject.[29] Yet the lion was ailing, physically and creatively. Jonson, now in his sixties, had suffered a stroke in 1628. This had only stopped him briefly – he barely ceased writing at all, and by 1630 one reads of him still holding his old sway among his tavern-mates, generously feasting his friends (and many of his detractors) and spending freely what means he had. His old hunger for work was undiminished: but the call for it, and the faith in its vitality, was no longer there. Away from the court, in the realm of the public theatre, it was widely believed that he had lost his inspiration. For the moment, on Shrovetide 1634, he was forgotten.

Beneath the gorgeous arch, the curtain suddenly rose. It revealed a backdrop, in perspective, depicting a fallen ancient city – 'old Arches, old Palaces, decayed walls, parts of Temples, Theaters, Basilica's and Therme, with heaps of broken Columnes, Bases, Coronices and Statues'. Represented here was Britain's Roman heritage, the basis on which future monuments would be set, and at the same time the shattered glory the current age was destined to restore.[30]

The spectators let their eyes wander through the ruins. Then in an instant their reverie was broken by a burst of music and the swift arrival of a chariot in which the sole passenger wore a coat of flame, a mantle of silver and gold, and a feathered wreath on his head. The bonnet of his carriage bore a cockerel, 'in action of crowing', and when the strange figure dismounted, a pair of wings could be seen to have grown from the heels of his slippers. The focus in a royal masque was always split, between the action on stage and the observing monarch, but here was an entry to claim complete attention. The apparition then brought all views in the hall to a point of single concentration by pacing to the royal seats, set as ever at the perfect point of vantage (and of maximum illusion). The king and queen's response was watched for keenly.[31]

The impressive character introduced himself as Mercury, the messenger of the gods. He had arrived, he continued, to tell Charles and Henrietta that Jupiter in Elysium had been chastened by their example of pure love on earth. The great god had thus resolved to lay aside his 'wild lusts', and his spouse, Juno, her 'raging jealousies', and to reform heaven on the model of the English court. 'When in the Chrystall myrrour of your reigne/ He viewed himselfe, he found his loathsome staine.' Accordingly, he had purged the empyreal realm of its 'loose Strumpets' and unrepentant deities. This had left room in the heavens for new tenants to be stellified. The first of these would of course be Charles and Henrietta and their 'noble traine, of either sex'.[32] A few places, however, still remained to be allotted, and much of the subsequent spectacle would be devoted to determining their occupants.

The dominant contemporary allusion in Mercury's opening speech presented little difficulty to those watching. He was referring to the new creed of pure 'Platonic' love the queen now sought to cultivate in her subjects at court. Her ideals had been treated to their most elaborate celebration only a couple of months before, in a performance combining (most unusually) elements of masque with drama. Walter Montagu's *The Shepheard's Paradise* was a pastoral pageant depicting the triumph of reason over the passions in love. It had lasted all day, and the queen had danced in it herself.

It was the start of a new fashion of social ideas. Later in 1634, James Howell sent a brief report on its progress to his friend Philip Warwick in Paris:

The Court affords little news at present, but that there is a Love call'd Platonick Love, which much sways there of late; it is a Love abstracted from all corporeal gross Impressions and sensual Appetite, but consists in Contemplations and Ideas of the Mind, not in any carnal Fruition. This Love sets the Wits of the Town on work; and they say there will be a Mask shortly of it, whereof Her Majesty and her Maids of Honour will be part.[33]

The wish for a love free from slavery to corporeal appetites suggests a puritan desire, of the kind on which Jean and Archibald Johnston, 'dear burds', touchingly founded their marriage. But the new trend could hardly have been couched in a more different setting. The new masque Howell mentioned was to be Davenant's *Temple of Love*, to be produced the following year. As he openly admitted, Davenant found it difficult getting to grips with the Neoplatonic theme the queen required him to address. The cult of 'Platonick Love' puzzled and preoccupied him, as it did many other court poets for several years to come. In a splendid riff of fantasy in his play *The Platonic Lovers*, one of Davenant's characters insists that Plato himself has been grossly misrepresented, citing the philosopher's passionate affair with 'a plump brown wench'.[34]

A satirist was hardly needed to point out the discrepancy between what was said and what was done at court. In 1634 memories were still fresh of a major indiscretion committed by Henry Jermyn, a favourite of the queen's. Jermyn had made Henrietta's lady-in-waiting Eleanor Villiers pregnant, and Charles had had them both confined to the Tower for a spell. One of Villiers' male relatives, who felt his family's honour touched by the affair, insisted that 'the injury was of that nature, that the young lord thought of nothing but repairing it in his own way' – that is, by calling Jermyn out to the fields. He was incarcerated as much for his own protection as for punishment, since Charles was still 'satisfied that there was a promise of marriage in the case'. The Villiers clan called on a young but well-respected lawyer to manage their side of the dispute, and in doing so introduced Davenant's sometime fellow lodger, Edward Hyde, 'into another way of conversation than he had formerly been accustomed to'. He successfully calmed the Villiers' cavaliers but failed to bring about the desired match. Hyde thought that the case not only tarred the reputation of the king's household, but also that the scandal prompted a new interest from women in public affairs. On the latter point he was long behind the times; but the incident did notch the start of one of the century's most prominent court careers – his own.[35]

When Jermyn refused to marry Villiers (who had other offers in any case) Charles banished the philanderer from court. The episode highlighted the incongruity between Neoplatonic theory and the realities of life; but it also showed that the king and queen were nevertheless in earnest, offering their own newly happy marriage as a model. It was the incongruity, after all, which made the theory necessary.

Yet there was something strange in asking Thomas Carew to write a masque advancing the theory and set out the idea of a chaste heaven. It was odd to hear his Mercury say that he was no longer Jove's pander, and that he had *not* come:

> as of old, to whisper amorous tales
> Of wanton love, into the glowing eare
> Of some choice beauty in this numerous traine;
> Those dayes are fled, the rebell flame is quenched
> In heavenly brests.[36]

Odd, because Carew's best-known poem to that date imagined a very different, unrestrained version of paradise. In 'A Rapture', a long erotic extravaganza written as much as a decade earlier, Carew's speaker bid his mistress ('Celia', the name meaning 'heavenly one') sail with him to 'Love's Elyzium'. Casting decorum to the winds, 'A Rapture' renounced and revised the sexual traumas of received mythology. Its alterations are frequently disturbing. Lucrece, the model of Renaissance feminine virtue (raped by Tarquin, she killed herself on informing her husband of the outrage), is shown training 'her plyant body in the act of love' to satisfy her assailant:

> To quench the burning Ravisher, she hurles
> Her limbes into a thousand winding curles.

Daphne and Apollo are united. Penelope abandons her two-decade wait for Ulysses to sport with her suitors. From more recent times, Laura rests in Petrarch's 'learned arms'. With these examples and many more, Carew's persona urges his beloved to see that 'lust, modest, chaste, or shame/ Are vaine and empty words.'[37] To one point of view, 'A Rapture' showed just why Platonic love was necessary as a social restraint; to another, it made plain that it could never last.

Intriguingly, 'A Rapture' was distinctly masque-like in its language and structure. The lovers, it is said, shall 'cut the flitting air', as Inigo Jones's costumed courtiers were wont to on wire-lifted devices. They recline amid the sort of shimmering setting that Jones was expert at rendering – a bower of 'trembling leaves', for example, stirred by gentle blasts from the west wind.[38] A boat journey between the legs of the Colossus of Rhodes would admittedly have presented a challenge; yet one of Carew's subtler touches in 'A Rapture' is to suggest that the two basic mechanical principles – of turning and sliding surfaces – underpinning Jones's sceneries could be used to any moral purpose. Carew's poem develops its setting as if by a textual *scena ductilis*, the sliding shutter-system that in Jones's mature work revealed wonder upon wonder; only here the scene shifts progressively to further levels of abandon.

In 1640 a member of the House of Commons would declare that such literature could only end in the 'disgrace of Religion . . . to the increase of all Vice'.[39] To those who knew Carew's earlier work, there was a distinct risk of *Coelum Britannicum* seeming more than a little ridiculous, although both his poem and his masque were really just concerned with the same problem: how could sexual desire be detached from low social conduct? The masque, quite conventionally, suggested Platonic love and chastity. The 'Rapture' urged instead a lifting of the taboos surrounding concupiscence. Both merely tested different strategies for ridding the heavens, and by association the governing order, of 'wild lusts' and 'raging jealousies'.

At this stage of the masque, those who knew Carew might have begun thinking that he had lost his edge. Yet the rebel flame was not quite quenched, and the more radical side of his imagination was shortly unloosed upon the stage.

5

Mercury had just finished saying how the 'British stars' would illumine the 'lower globe' when his precedence on stage was jostled by the arrival of his counter-spirit, Momus, striding in superciliously, regardless of proprieties. His costume emphasized his general spikiness: 'attired in a long, darkish Robe all wrought over with poniards, Serpents tongues, eyes and eares, his beard and haire party coloured [dyed to various shades], and upon his head a wreath stucke with Feathers, and a Porcupine in the forepart'. Momus, the god of mockery, represented the elements of Mercury the masque proper excised, the attributes of 'Hermes, the cheater' (in Jonson's phrase); his associations with thievery, deceit and trickery, the unpredictable and the volatile – in short, the mercurial. Yet as the audience was fully aware, this was the antimasque, the phase of the performance in which the forces of disorder were released, to be mastered in the dancing of the masque proper.

As 'The Supreme Theomastix' ('scourge of God'), and by his vituperative idiom, Momus more than faintly recalled and ridiculed one very recent unruly agent in particular. In 1633 one William Prynne, a young lawyer with 'the countenance of a witch', had asked, rhetorically and voluminously:

How many Novices and Youngsters have been corrupted, debauched, and led away captive by the Divel, by their owne outrageous lusts, by Panders, Players, Bawdes, Adulteresses, Whores and other lewd companions, who had continued studious, civill, hopeful, towardly and ingenious, had they not resorted unto Stage-playes, the originall causes of their dolefull ruine?[40]

Prynne's thousand-page *Histriomastix, The Players Scourge or Actors Tragedie* was the frenzied masterpiece of puritan protest against the stage – against virtually any form of open performance. The book requires at least a week of day-long reading, though its main point, buttressed by incessant, lengthy and obsessively detailed quotations from scripture and theology, is abundantly clear from the outset. Prynne denounced theatre; but, more generally, he denounced everything about the age as being nothing more than theatre, and being decadent for that. A typical argument runs as follows: theatre displays the vices, thus infecting those listening and watching. Vice attracts the most sordid elements, and so any innocent person wandering into a theatre will immediately be seized on by pimps and prostitutes. As for those sinfully inclined already, 'will not then the premeditated voluntary delightfull beholding of an unchaste adulterous Play, much more contaminate a voluptuous, carnall, graceless Play-haunter, who lies rotting in the stink of his most beastly lusts?'[41]

There had been many attacks on theatre over the years. It would be wrong to identify this view of theatre as a typically 'puritan' view: many 'puritans' (John Milton being a famous example) realized that the stage, even the masque, was a superb medium for spiritual instruction. In drama the show of human 'vice' was likely to make people better understand themselves; the fates the vices met with on stage would cause audiences to think twice before emulating them. So Prynne's monumental work of cultural abrasion could have been left to sink away peacefully, had he not tried scourging royalty. 'It hath always been a most infamous thing for Kings, and Emperors to act Playes or Masques either in private or publike; or to sing, or dance upon a stage or theatre; or to delight in Playes and Actors.'[42] Charles, the dancing king and patron of dramatists, was thus guilty on all counts. Yet the worst of Prynne's comments, it was felt, were clearly directed at Henrietta Maria.

For the core problem *Histriomastix* has with the world as Prynne found it is the very existence of women. Women, the book insists at every available point, do nothing but excite otherwise 'hopefull' (promising) males to think and act sinfully. It is worth sampling the fervour with which Prynne insisted this was so: 'For if he who without these provocations [i.e. of seeing women acting on stage] seeth a woman, is yet notwithstanding drawne sometimes to lust after her, and commits adultery only by lusting; he who not only seeth, but likewise earnestly beholds a naked lascivious woman with his whole minde, how is he not a thousand times made the captive of lust?'[43] This was why it was equally corrupting if – as was then entirely the case in public theatre – men dressed up as women and performed female roles: that not only demeaned the men themselves, but the very idea of the women they represented was enough to trigger mental acts of adultery. For this reason, too, Prynne absolutely opposed any 'effeminacy' in male attire or behaviour in any context whatsoever. In his book he lingered obsessively over the physical features he most despised. Female hair especially became a running hate-motif. 'Is it a seemly thing, that a woman pray unto God uncovered? Doth not nature it selfe teach you, that if a man have long haire, it is a shame unto him?' A woman's hair was only a 'glory' as a form of natural covering (when she wasn't praying).[44]

Histriomastix is a colossally unendable piece of writing, insane in its reasoning, astonishing in its stamina, hurling verbiage and citation from an abyss of loathing. From this distance it is clear that it is haunted by the great enemy of the age – 'passion', the demon of men from Gustavus Adolphus down; the force of emotions beyond the control of reason. Again, trying to unmake one's emotional being, or at least stifle any possible stimuli of an outlawed feeling, cannot be classified as an exclusively 'puritan' social strategy. Even Suckling by times employed the topos of male complaint against the seemingly irrational side of life: 'The *Sea's* my mind, which calm would be/ Were it from winds (my passions) free.'[45]

To many of the 'modern love lock wearers' so thoroughly reviled by Prynne, his book was undoubtedly a strange piece of madness: to a few in Thomas Carew's circle, to some of his readers at any rate, *Histriomastix* may have given new force to the argument of 'A Rapture'. The best way to avoid the sort of corruption Prynne feared, Carew was saying, was to stop treating its perceived causes as corrupt. Once desire was seen as natural, it stopped being a passion that could be subverted to impure or harmful ends – to men killing one another, for example, out of sexual rivalry. It made more sense to end taboos – to fling them aside with 'A Rapture's' gusto – than to enforce them; though, admittedly, Carew only said so to the relatively elite readership with access to a manuscript of his poem.

Prynne's insult to the queen could not be left unpunished. He was tried and, as if in the very masochistic climax his book was calling for all along, had his ears clipped at the pillory. He was then imprisoned. The episode was of course only the first in many, many more public appearances by William Prynne. His burning pen never rested. Aubrey pictures him for us writing away, a peaked quilt cap protecting his eyes from the glare of the candle, a servant bringing him some bread and ale every few hours to sustain him, with the rusty sword of his forefathers, magistrates of Bath, stored reverently in his chambers. He was a misogynist and a rebel, though not, as a recent biographical article points out, a Calvinist or a representative puritan in other respects.[46] He was no religious radical: it was rather the lost, imagined cleanliness of the early, post-Reformation Tudor Church that he sought to recover. His aims were not, in fact, so very different to King Charles's; it was the means they saw of achieving them, the form the ends would take, that were so deeply at odds.

The truth was that the king's strategies were expansive, frequently liberal and complex. Early in 1634 Charles had been brought into an argument over William Davenant's latest play. During his illness and recovery Davenant evidently realized that his real strengths lay not with unlikely tragedies in far-flung locations but in observation of the life-forms closer to hand. 'The Wits', which he presented for inspection to Sir Henry Herbert, the Master of the Revels, late in 1633, was Davenant's first full-length comedy, incorporating the flair for humour glimpsed intermittently in his earlier revenge plays. Herbert found the piece profane, and declined to license it for performance. On hearing this, suspecting a 'cruel faction' was at work against his friend, Endymion

Porter asked the king to arbitrate. Taking the matter with his usual seriousness, Charles jarred the censor's nerves by summoning Herbert for
a private conversation on 9 January and instructing him to bring the
script. 'This morning,' Herbert noted in his records, 'the kinge was
pleased to call me into his withdrawing chamber to the window, wher
he went over all that I had croste in Davenants play-booke.' Charles
decided that the phrases Herbert had deleted as profane should be
considered 'asseverations' rather than prohibited 'oaths', although he
retained some of Herbert's 'reformation' (the word has pietistic over-
tones). 'This was done,' Herbert recorded, making a note of his enemy,
'upon a complaint of Mr. Endymion Porters.' His rather pinched entry
went on to accept Charles's verdict on the supposed 'asseverations': 'to
which I doe humbly submit as my masters judgment', but he set down
haughtily his own 'opinion and submission', which was unchanged. Just
under three weeks later the play was performed at court.[47]

Unfortunately, and rather unfairly, the king emerges here in the puritan eye as a champion of obscenity: words with sacred meanings and
usages could not be used as casual oaths. Thus any swearing by 'faith' or
Christ's 'death' or 'light' was outlawed, propriety outweighing dramatic
realism. In fact Charles dealt very evenly and properly with all dispu-
tants, as Herbert's records show. The king refused to take a personal
copy of Davenant's play from Porter, insisting he be given the text his
Master of the Revels had edited. He ordered Davenant to go and receive
his 'play-booke' back from Herbert with every due courtesy.

To a puritan campaigner such formalities might simply cloak an alliance with the forces of profanity, yet Charles was notoriously delicate
on matters of decorum in public speech. Women were barred by royal
proclamation from attending the trial of the Earl of Castlehaven for
sodomy and rape, on pain of forfeiting any claim to modesty. Only one
incident is on record of the king making an awkward attempt at bawdi-
ness, when he suggested the Countess of Leicester was looking rather
underweight from having too much sex.[48] His handling of the dispute
over 'The Wits', as with his discernment when it came to art, shows a
greater maturity and relaxedness. As his critics suspected, this too may
have indicated the influence of Henrietta Maria, mellowing or corrupting, depending on the point of view.

The play itself was the best thing Davenant ever wrote, though

Herbert airily dismissed the success it enjoyed at Blackfriars and the royal court. 'It had a various fate on the stage, and at court, though the kinge commended the language, but dislikt the plott and characters.'[49] Yet the debate had never been about the plot, which gave spectators much to enjoy in the form of two gullible country 'wits' being tricked, robbed, locked up in a chest, arrested and generally riled.

To the intense discomfort of the legal community, Prynne, a practising member of Lincoln's Inn, had dedicated *Histriomastix* to his brother lawyers. Sources at Whitehall intimated that an act of collective atonement would be well received. Appropriately, almost cruelly, this took the form of a masque in honour of Charles and Henrietta Maria early in 1634. The Inns lavished the gigantic sum of £21,000 on the performance, which took place largely in the open, as a show of loyalty and redress to the king and queen before the whole of London. Kevin Sharpe observes that the occasion felt more like a Tudor procession than a Caroline masque.[50] Beginning at Ely House, Davenant's former home and a symbolically aristocratic address in Holborn, hundreds of masquers, musicians, riders and charioteers, with crowds lining the torch-lit streets, progressed down Chancery Lane towards Whitehall. As they arrived, watching from a balcony the king sent word that the whole cortege should make a final lap of honour around the royal tilting yard, so that he could have a second view of the fabulous display. At the palace the audience was filtered of its less select constituents, and the antimasque and masque itself were played, to general delight and in particular to the great pleasure of the king. The palace warmly commended the show, entitled *The Triumph of Peace*, a collaboration between the master-designer, Inigo Jones, and James Shirley, a jobbing playwright, with the backing of the Inns' 'brave cavallata'.[51] Thanks were offered in the form of a reciprocal invitation, to leading members of the Inns, to Carew's *Coelum Britannicum* a fortnight later.

6

When Mercury, having rebuked him for his 'rude scurrilous chat', asked for the latest news from heaven, he pulled Momus up short.[52] 'Heaven!' he replied. 'Heaven is no longer the place it was.' It had become, he said, a fearful, litigious place, plastered with too many rules. In a wonderful passage, one of the period's greatest solos of satirical prose, Momus describes some of the innovations, which of course denote parallel stringencies in the country at large, and in the Caroline court. Tedious new orders, he said, had been introduced to Jove's presence chamber. 'Injunctions are gone out to the Nectar Brewers, for the purging of the heavenly Beverage of a narcotic weed which hath rendred the Idæes confus'd in the Divine Intellects' (Charles had forbidden the sale of tobacco in public houses). Celestial courtiers had been disgruntled by the command to spend a fixed quota of time on their estates, 'for the restoring of decayed housekeeping', a direct echo of a Caroline edict. Bacchus had ordered the taverns to close at ten sharp. 'Ganimede is forbidden the bedchamber' – a risky observation on the absence of any successor to Buckingham as absolute favourite – and all tomfoolery in the precincts of the palace is frowned upon severely.

'In briefe, the whole state of the Hierarchy suffers a state of total reformation.' Very cleverly, though, Carew had Momus juxtapose irritating and intrusive measures – prohibitions of acts such as Vulcan's 'driving in a plate of Iron into one of the Sunnes Chariot-wheeles and frost-nailing his horses' – with changes which could only be commended and admired. '*Venus* hath confest all her adulteries' and, possibly in reference to the huge improvement in the royals' marital relations over the previous nine years, Momus also pointed out how:

Iupiter too beginnes to learne to lead his owne wife, I left him practising in the milky way; and there is no doubt of an universall obedience, where the Lawgiver himselfe in his owne person observes his decrees so punctually.

Only a person such as Charles was capable of such fastidious observance, some in the hall were entitled to reflect. Yet Momus's moderate joshing of the king, the master Carew waited on regularly as one of his closest servants, was tempered by the highest compliment, sketching as it did a monarch ruling by example. The greatest of the gods now had the motto 'Carlomaria' engraved above the door of his bedchamber. The disapproval of a god like Momus, a force of mockery and misrule, is of course a strong indicator that Jupiter's new regime must be making progress in moralizing the state. Yet that did not impede the delivery of a critical message to the king, advising him in some respects to learn some levity.[53]

As Momus and Mercury held their debate, the scene changed – the ruined city had given way to 'a Spheare, with Starres placed in their severall Images', this borne by 'a huge naked Figure (onely a peece of Drapery hanging over his thigh) kneeling', which everyone in the hall could recognize as Atlas.[54] The remainder of the antimasque was taken up with a process of purgation: the task now facing both deities on stage was to clear the heavenly sphere on the giant's shoulders of all monstrosities and vices, so that the British virtues could be stellified. Shortly, Momus took his leave, and the antimasque shimmered to its close; Atlas with his stellar burden disappeared, and a new mountainous landscape took shape before the court, with a smooth, quiet clicking of sliding screens. A 'more grave' antimasque was danced 'of Picts, the naturall inhabitants of this Isle, antient Scots and Irish', at which a hill rose, little by little, from the wilderness, with figures representing the kingdoms of England, Scotland and Ireland, richly robed, seated upon it. Above these 'sate a young man in a white embroidered robe . . . holding in his hand a Cornucopia fill'd with corne and fruits', the embodiment of the 'genius' of the three kingdoms.[55] Dance, song and music now predominated, in a stately succession of allegorical wonders, levered and wound into place by Jones's crew backstage. Hatches opened caves and apertures for the masquers to emerge from, 'a troope of young Lords and Noblemens sonnes bearing Torches of Virgin-Wax . . . apparelled after the old British fashion in white Coats, embroidered with silver, girt, and full gathered'; and with that dance past, a vast, almost hallucinatory cloud descended, collected the genius of the kingdoms and carried him upwards, triggering, at the very instant it disappeared into the heavens, the sudden swift subsidence of the mountain below, a 'great cause of admiration'. Through it all, the young man and the three kingdoms sang as the dancers moved gracefully on the stage below. And now the king himself was dancing:

> Here are shapes form'd fit for heaven,
> These move gracefully and even.[56]

And still the scene kept shifting, changing to a palace garden, where the masquers and their ladies danced the revels, 'which continued a great part of the night'.[57] Hours later, the performance had still not finished. With the revels over, the king sitting beside the queen once more, a wind blew from one side, and a great cloud filled the middle level of the sky below the proscenium arch. Two further clouds split away from it, each bearing an allegorical group, on one side Religion, Truth and Wisdom, on the other Concord, Government and Reputation. Then the great cloud split, and Eternity sailed out of the rift on a globe, dressed in a cloak of light blue, 'wrought all over with Stars of gold'. In the air about Eternity hovered a host of fifteen stars, each signifying British heroes, with another, larger than the rest, standing for Charles. And in the distance, on the horizon, Windsor Castle could be seen, 'the famous seat of the most honourable order of the Garter'.[58] After more lyrics, more dancing, the final view was of nothing but a serene sky, a consummated blankness perfectly expressing the court's satiety with sheer marvels. 'It was the noblest masque of my time to this day,' said Sir Henry Herbert, 'the best poetrye, best scenes and best habitts.'[59] The queen singled out the costumes for particular praise.

It was fantasy, but in the same way that the rooftop of Chambord is fantasy. It was fantasy, that is, made concrete, and it was the manifestation that counted. That was the point of the technology of the masque. The masque was not a monarch's daydream but an absolutist saying, 'I can do this': at the royal command, an engineer with Jones's vision and abilities could bring the imaginary into being. Elements of criticism, even subversion, slipped into the performance, but the fact that the censor approved them if anything reinforced the confidence of the overall show. They were subsumed in the whole the way moments of private fun in Gothic masonry are engrossed into a cathedral's structure.

Quite understandably, there were those who wished the king would spend his money on more practical things. The Exchequer had been skirting complete financial ruin for the past thirty years. When one of the Lord Deputy of Ireland's agents in London heard how much the Inns of Court were spending on *The Triumph of Peace*, he asked why could they not simply give the Crown the money, or use the energy they were expending on the masque to raising some revenue. 'For it gives me no Satisfaction, who am but a poor looker on, to see a Rich Commonwealth, a Rich People, and the Crown poor. God direct them to remedy this quickly.'[60] Yet for the king the 'illusion of power' was worth the impoverishment – the royal argument rested on reasoning not the need.

7

In some accounts of his reign, Charles himself emerges as a puritan *manqué*, a ruler tragically captured by Babylonic darkness, and also by the haughty Catholic beauty to whom he became 'a most uxorious husband'. The former court, that of King James, had for the poet Lucy Hutchinson been ruled by vice, with light entertainment distracting the minions from signs of growing resistance in the country: 'to keep the people in their deplorable security till vengeance overtook them, they were entertained with masks, stage plays and ruder sports. Then began murder, incest, adultery, drunkenness, swearing, fornication and all sort of ribaldry.'[61] Hutchinson was much less than fair to James, famous for his love of learned sermons and, although tending to lose patience and temper when a performance lasted too long, fond of rhetorically complex theatre. She was mistaken too in suggesting that the masque was ousted by Charles, when the young king's lavish taste in the visual arts only made it a still more extravagant genre. His efforts to reform the gentry also met with questionable success, as a *rodomontado* in the autumn of 1634 made only too clear.

'*Rodomontado*': referring to a display of bragging or showing off, and frequently identifying the boaster with the boast, the word was plucked straight out of Jonsonian satire. George Garrard, writing to the Lord Deputy of Ireland, briskly sketched out the circumstances. A fortune-hunter had courted a young heiress for purely mercenary purposes. The king himself had approved the suit, and instructed the woman's father to let it proceed. There was nothing unusual about that; but the father had learned that the suitor, having already sold huge portions of his patrimony, needed the marriage only to liquidate his debts. He then dispatched the man he preferred for his daughter to make the trouble-maker sign a paper disavowing any further interest in her. This statement was dictated, it was said, by the lady herself.

Her name was Ann Willoughby, daughter of Sir Henry and, so

Garrard was informed, the 'heir to a Thousand a year'. The man she and her father favoured was one of the country's most formidable men, belonging to a family of physical, intellectual and financial heavy-weights. His name was John Digby, remembered years afterwards as 'a proper person of great strength, and courage answerable, and admitted to be the best swordsman of his time'. Riding post haste to London with the document in his pocket and three other horsemen as seconds and witnesses, he met his rival's coach at Nottingham Bridge, on the way to Sir Henry's country seat at Risley. Dismounting and taking a sound cudgel in hand, Digby confronted the enemy there and then. The other party, by contrast with Digby, was 'but a slight timberd man, and of middling stature'.[62] His name was 'Sir *John Sutling* . . . famous for nothing before but that he was a great Gamester'. It was also known, however, that a powerful friend of Suckling's had 'got the King to write for him to Sir *Henry Willoughby*, by which means he hoped to get her'. King Charles had in fact ordered the family to give Suckling access to Ann.[63] She in turn had given in under this pressure, and signed a note accepting the proposal of marriage.

The encounter between Digby and Suckling on the Midlands carriageway was short and bloody. Digby asked Suckling what he was doing, and demanded that he sign the disavowal; Suckling only replied that he was on the king's business. This seemed an unwisely smug allusion to the royal approval he had won for his courtship. Suckling, said Digby, had given out that Ann had accepted him: was this true? Suckling would not answer. Wasting no more time, Digby set about beating him. The club he had brought was little more than a handful of splinters by the time Suckling's companion and pander, Philip Willoughby, Ann's brother, reached the fray. Suckling clearly knew his match. Bleeding through his tatters, he took the beating, as London's reputation-makers noted solemnly, without once 'offering to draw his sword'.

Willoughby, 'a proper Gentleman, a man held stout', evidently managed to get Digby off his friend. But when Digby then demanded that he publicly renounce any notion of his sister marrying the slight-timbered, timber-pounded wretch lying at his feet, Willoughby refused. He was, as Garrard acknowledged, a man of 'a very fair Reputation'. Thus Digby punched him 'three or four times' in the face and stalked off the eight miles back to Risley, leaving the two schemers in the dirt.

This was late October 1634. After failing to draw or issue a challenge, whatever respect Suckling might have won through service abroad collapsed to nothing. While he lay clouding all over with bruises, his rivals were mobilizing the court against him. John Digby's brother Sir Kenelm, a more influential person, went to wait on the king at Hampton Court, assuring all that 'every Particle of this Business' bore out the very worst reports. Meeting Ann and Sir Henry Willoughby there, he asked her what he had been thinking of, associating with 'such baffled Fellows'. Opinion solidified irrevocably against the bedraggled Suckling. Adventurer, soldier, man of letters and science, Sir Kenelm Digby was even more formidable than his brother, moreover matching force with refinement. 'Give me leave to congratulate your happy return from the *Levant*,' Howell had greeted him after a spectacular expedition; 'and the great honour you have acquir'd by your gallant comportment in *Algier* . . . by bearing up so bravely against the *Venetian* Fleet in the Bay of *Scanderoon*, and making the *Pantaloni* to know themselves and *You* better.'[64]

A match for anything in Islam or Christendom, Sir Kenelm had little to fear from his brother's wiry adversary. He sent no reply to a shrill two-line note Suckling wrote in mid-November. In this Suckling advised him not to be so 'large' in his talk, while claiming that *he* had had the better of the fight with his brother. Doing, Suckling huffed outrageously, became a man better than talking.[65] For the time being, wrote Garrard on 10 November, '*Sutling* and *Philip Willoughby* are both in *London*, but they stir not.'

The elder Digby left the next engagement to a time of Suckling's choosing. For on 18 November, the *actus secundus* of the struggle took place. John Digby was on his way in or out of the theatre at Blackfriars, in the tight little network of lanes off Fleet Street, when he was ambushed. Suckling jumped out with a party of swordsmen. It seems unlikely that there were as many as the sixteen mentioned by some witnesses, since Digby beat them all off, killing one of his attackers in the process. Suckling could do nothing but show him his heels; and, on being arrested, spend a dampening week in prison until his allies could extricate him from the legal consequences of the assault. A less protected individual would have found himself at the end of a rope. Suckling was seen being hurried away in his coach on 25 November.[66]

While Garrard knew Suckling only as a gambler, Davenant later remembered that Suckling returned from Europe in 1632 'an extraordinarily accomplished gentleman, [and] grew famous for his ready sparkling wit which was envied'.[67] By common standards, the Willoughby affair should have put Suckling beyond the pale of respectable society. The conduct Suckling displayed was of the kind most enemies of the king's party in the civil wars associated with 'cavaliers'. Yet a double standard was in force, nevertheless. Enemies of degeneracy frowned on random violence; but they still expected better of a man. Suckling's outlaw conduct stirred great disapproval, but at the same time his failure to act as a proper cavalier invited ridicule and reprehension. He had let the affront go unchallenged, and sought revenge through common assault rather than honourable single combat. However much statesmen deplored the custom of duelling, still rife, it was popularly upheld as the right way of settling a dispute:

> By *Laws* of learned *Duellists*
> They that are bruis'd with *wood*, or *fists*,
> And think one beating may for once
> Suffice, are *Cowards* and *Pultroons*:
> But if they dare engage t'a second,
> They'r *stout* and *gallant* fellows reckon'd.[68]

The words, uttered by one of the most popular comic creations of the century, could almost have been written with Suckling in mind. Thirty years later the incident was still remembered: ''twas strange to see the envie and ill nature of people to trample, and scoffe at, and deject one in disgrace,' said Aubrey, reflecting a softer attitude; 'inhumane as well as un-christian.'[69]

So far as his suit was concerned, Suckling's chief sin lay not in discounting the feelings of his intended bride, but in trying to cheat the system through which she was to be obtained. In the case of Suckling and Ann Willoughby, King Charles had declared himself perfectly satisfied with the arrangements as he understood them, directing her father to approve the match on the unusually sensitive condition that 'his daughter's affection could be gained' for Suckling's suit.[70] Sir Henry later informed the king that Ann was resolute against accepting Suckling; but the deciding factor was not so much her inability to 'affect him' as the results of inquiries Willoughby made into the particulars of Suckling's estate.[71]

Suckling needed Ann Willoughby for her money and her land. Garrard drastically underestimated the size of her assets. Sir Henry Willoughby had no sons: as the eldest of his surviving daughters, she stood to inherit everything he had, along with the considerable properties of her mother. We can rule out Suckling falling prey to Cupid. A mortal aversion to fidelity (or any real intimacy with women) streaks every page of his writing. Indeed the theme brought out his best artistry as a poet, as in the conventional but superbly structured argument of 'Loves Sanctuary'. In this his 'wild unruly heart' is tamed by 'one pair of Eyes' but in typical fashion is still vulnerable to an arrow of love from the next.[72] It is the flare of first attraction that matters; a hatred for the humbug of marital custom comes across strongly. He seems to have been perfectly serious in arguing 'Against Fruition':

> Urge not 'tis necessary, alas! we know
> The homeliest thing which mankind does is so;
> The World is of a vast extent we see,
> And must be peopled; Children then must be;
> So must bread too; but since there are enough
> Born to the drudgery, what need we plough?[73]

Suckling had begun courting Willoughby in the autumn of 1633, after building up huge debts from disasters in bowls and cards. He had sold large portions of his patrimony a year before he could even inherit it, borrowed huge sums from a wool merchant on the promise of repaying twice as much, and then rashly and flashily lent a fellow gambler £2,600 in the summer of 1634.[74] Had sound finances been discovered, even Suckling's 'secret practises', corrupting servants in the Willoughby household, would surely not have brought Sir Henry to support Ann's personal preferences against the king's approval. As it was, while sparing Suckling from further repercussions, the king did not argue with the figures. The matter was referred to Suckling's old master Sir Henry

Vane, now Comptroller of the Royal Household, and quietly dropped when the Willoughbys proved adamant.

Apart from alpha-feelings for a disputed female, there was another ingredient to John Digby's rage. The really maddening thing about Suckling was that he appeared not to take the quarrel seriously. The more one tried crushing him, the more badinage he came out with. Destroyed at Nottingham Bridge and then at Blackfriars, he still claimed it was he who had 'switched' Digby. His deportment bears out the impressions that Davenant, slightly starstruck, confided to John Aubrey, for 'he was (Sir William said) the bull that was baited. He was incomparably ready at reparteeing, and his wit most sparkling when most set upon and provoked.'[75] Among his poems are lyrics to a rival inviting a sense of brotherhood in their common purpose.

However he grieved at the eventual beating, Suckling took the courtship lightly. Ann Willoughby's finances were as good as any, and he meant to have control of them. A letter apparently to her shows him jinking with wit, protesting sincerity in flippant terms. He jokes with the Calvinist doctrine that Willoughby herself is quite likely to have taken as gospel. 'I am not so ill a Protestant as to beleeve in merit [Calvinists believing deeds were irrelevant to salvation], yet if you please to give answer under your owne hand, such as I shall for ever rely upon.' He barely restrains from a leer and a twirl of the moustache: 'if I have not deserv'd it [her answer] already, it is not impossible but I may.' An answer in the end was forced rather than given, as Suckling made use of his connections at court.[76] At the same time a cruel mangling of old affections was taking place behind the scenes. In exchange for his sister, Philip Willoughby evidently wished to be better acquainted with Suckling's old flame, Mary Cranfield. A note from Suckling's sister Martha chided her for not welcoming his attentions.[77] By then whatever feeling existed between Mary and Suckling had gone cold: a new confidante would emerge a year or so later.

A feminine take on what poets of the day invariably call 'the sport' of sexual and reproductive life is hard to find before the Restoration. One searches hard for the woman's point of view in the Willoughby affair, the fright of having one's future determined by a fight at the roadside, or in a chamber of old men at Whitehall. The 'paper of writing' Ann Willoughby dictated for Suckling to sign is lost from the records of the case, perhaps balled up in the fist of John Digby as he left his enemy on that autumn day in Nottinghamshire, or dropped by him on to Suckling's semi-conscious form. Yet despite the vast scholarly recovery of much writing by women from unpublished sources, the other side of the larger story is difficult to find even in the works of those women whose literary efforts were encouraged or, at least, tolerated.

Lucy Hutchinson, née Apsley, only fourteen at the time of the Suckling scandal, thought it high praise that her future husband recognized her as more than a 'she-wit'. He admired the masculine quality of her writing, its 'rationality'. Reading her *Memoirs* of Hutchinson's life, that measure of approval sticks in the mind as one takes in her tendency to belittle the few women of her age who possessed some real political power. She notably contrasts the 'haughty spirit' of Henrietta Maria with Queen Elizabeth, whose reign was a success only because of her 'submission to her masculine and wise counsellors'. No irony seems intended as she castigates King Charles for not standing up to his wife: 'wherever male princes are so effeminate to suffer women of foreign birth and different religions to intermeddle with the affairs of state, it is always found to produce sad desolations.'[78]

If a defence of 'she-wit' is not to be found in Hutchinson, there is little point looking for it in Suckling, however much he claimed to enjoy the company of women such as his cousin. The poet Lucy Hay, for example, Countess of Carlisle, was much admired by other members of his set, including Thomas Carew; but Suckling brushed her off to his cronies as 'your sorry Lady Muse',[79] and conscripted Carew's persona into an unpleasant verse dialogue in which he imagined undressing her. Where others beheld a goddess walking in the garden at Hampton Court, Suckling saw merely another woman there for the taking, and eager for it, he liked to think:

> Troth in her face I could descry
> No danger, no divinity.
> But since the pillars were so good
> On which the lovely fountain stood,
> Being once come so near, I think
> I should have ventur'd hard to drink.

> What ever fool like me had been
> If I'd not done as well as seen?
> There to be lost why should I doubt,
> Where fools with ease go in and out?[80]

Suckling can look up the rich lady's skirt, admire her thighs and 'parts more dear', but cannot know her, cannot give her a vocal or truly subjective part in his poem, and has no wish to. The testosterone levels are much vaunted, but the men are oddly monosexual creatures, and gaze on the woman as a curiosity, a being belonging to an alien species.

Another dialogue between Suckling and Carew over a woman took the form of an exchange of letters. They debated the question of whether Carew should marry a wealthy widow. Unsurprisingly Suckling advised his friend against the move:

'Tis not *love* (Tom) that doth the mischief, but *constancy* . . . Dost thou know what *marriage* is? 'Tis *curing* of *Love* the *dearest way*, or waking a *losing Gamester* out of a *winning dream*: and after a long expectation of a strange *banquet*, a presentation of a *homely meal*. Alas!

After all this, to marry a *Widow*, a kind of *chew'd-meat*! What a fantastical stomack hast thou, that cannot eat of a dish til another man hath cut of it?

Carew could have pointed out that it was Suckling rather than he who had been cured of mercenary courtships 'the dearest way'. As it was, he rebutted Suckling's arguments on less than idealistic grounds: 'there goes more charge to the keeping of a *Stable full* of *horses*, than *one* onely *Steed* . . . when, be the errand what it will, this *one Steed* shall serve your turn as well as twenty more.'[81]

These letters savour more of a rhetorical exercise on a set theme than a real episode in Carew's life. No record exists, at least, of his marriage or engagement to the widow. The situation served as an occasion for casually misogynistic set pieces. Rejecting Suckling's point about 'chew'd meat', Carew replied that he preferred an experienced sexual partner who knew, as he put it, how to chew. But a key skill in debating was arguing '*ut utramque partem*', from either point of view: and elsewhere Carew said he liked his women younger:

Give me a wench about thirteen,
Already voted to the Queene
Of lust and lovers, whose soft haire,
Fann'd with the breath of gentle aire
O'er spreads her shoulders like a tent,
And is her vaile and ornament:
Whose tender touch, will make the blood
Wild in the aged, and the good.[82]

In those 'sweet embraces I/ May melt myself to lust, and die'. Carew made the point often enough for it to stand as his motto: dismissing the 'worldling' for his love of money, the husband for his pleasure in wife and children, 'This is true blisse, and I confesse,/ There is no other happinesse.'[83]

Traditionally, we might call such writings 'cavalier', and oppose them to the supposedly puritan attitudes espoused by William Prynne towards women. But Prynne and Suckling are essentially the same in their view of the opposite sex: both are sensible of the same charms, both similarly oblivious to women as people. To both, females are little more than walking temptations. The real difference between these writers lies in their attitude to the sensations and fantasies provoked in the male. Suckling and Carew permit the wishes Prynne prohibits, yet at root the thoughts of cavalier and puritan are identical.

8

Even without the pride forfeited at Nottingham Bridge and Blackfriars, and the henchman's life lost at the latter, as a 'famous gamester' Suckling had no place in decent company for the civic-minded puritan. Yet gambling, as later during the Restoration, was a tolerated vice. The otherwise prudish Edward Hyde, for example, had nothing to say against the 'fair house for entertainment and gaming' which stood on Piccadilly, with 'handsome gravel walks for shade, and where were an upper and a lower bowling-green, whither very many of the nobility and gentry of the best quality resorted, both for exercise and conversation'.[84]

There among this quality Suckling was frequently to be found; it was there, so the story went, that his sisters once tried stopping him from playing, 'for fear he should lose all their dowries'. 'He was the greatest gallant of his time,' declared Aubrey, 'and the greatest gamester, both for bowling and cards.' No shopkeeper of the day would let him away with sixpence, since one day he was good for purchases of £200, while the next he could be worth 'less than nothing'. Davenant remembered how Suckling would practise alone with a pack spread out on his bed, 'and there studied how the best way of managing his cards should be'.[85]

For this diligence and concentration Suckling is credited with inventing a card game of his own, cribbage. Forty years after Suckling's heyday, gambling was recognized as a compulsive and consuming pastime. As the author of *The Compleat Gambler* put it, in terms which recall the way some also spoke of love, 'Gambling is an enchanting witchery, gotten betwixt idleness and avarice: an itching disease, that makes some scratch the head, whilst others, as if they were bitten by a Tarantula, are laughing themselves to death.'[86]

Despite his losses and the prosecutions for debt which ensued, Suckling was undeterred. After a short spell of reclusion after his beating, he returned to the green and the table in 1635, winning almost £2,000 in a game of ninepins played at Tunbridge Wells in early September. He took care not to become the threadbare sort of person identified as an archetypal gamester in the century's principal manual on the subject. 'Amongst his other shipwracks, he hath happily lost shame,' wrote Charles Cotton of this epitome. 'No man puts his brain to more use than he; for his life is a daily invention, and each meal a new stratagem, and like a flie [he] will boldly sup at every mans cup.'[87] By contrast, as Davenant recalled, Suckling made a point of displaying all the opulence he could muster. 'Sir William (who was his intimate friend, and loved him entirely) would say that Sir John, when he was at his lowest ebb in gaming, I mean when unfortunate, would make himselfe most glorious in apparel, and said that he had then best luck when he was most gallant, and his spirits were highest.'[88]

Accordingly, Suckling was soon rumoured to be pursuing another wealthy bride, 'and had spent on her, and in treating her, some thousand of pounds'. This woman could not have been, as Aubrey claims, the Countess of Middlesex (she being his aunt), but at any rate she could not forego riling him for his 'late received baffle' at a splendid party in Surrey. Sensing blood, other ladies joined the attack, and Suckling slunk to the outskirts of the entertainment. He had great cause to be thankful to his hostess, Lady Moray:

Seeing Sir John out of countenance, for whose worth she always had a respect: 'Well,' said she, 'I am a merry wench, and will never forget an old friend in disgrace, so come sit down by me, Sir John' (said she), and seated him on her right hand, and countenanced him. This raysed Sir John's dejected spirits that he threw his reparties about the table with so much sparklingness and gentleness of wit, to the admiration of them all.[89]

Haw-haws burst out all round; but years would pass before Suckling put himself in the way of opponents more formidable than the rightly derogatory mistress from which Lady Moray rescued him here. The rudimentary mace of Sir John Digby, broken to a 'handful' on his flimsy shoulders, still cast its shadow over him. Davenant and others remembered him as having 'slight strength, brisk round eye, reddish-faced and red nose (ill liver), his head not very big, his hair a kind of sand colour', a description that makes it easier to imagine him discharging his shrill *rodomontado* around town.

Suckling rolled on regardless of the months, the years and the legal actions, gloating over his wins and brazening out his losses, re-emerging after the bad nights in another shining suit of clothes, putting on another show of still greater gallantry. Such was his devotion to profligacy, however, that he kept a surprisingly modest home in the city. With his properties in town sold or mortgaged, he took lodgings in the house of a tailor, William Sharowe, in Fleet Street.[90] It surely simplified matters, owing the same person for rent as well as clothes.

He seemed as careless for his immortal soul as he did about his debts. He appeared to live, in fact, as if there were no afterlife, no damnation. But if, as the Calvinists claimed, God had already made up his mind on the elect, what did a little pleasure matter?[91] Suckling worked on dissoluteness as a puritan might concentrate on mortifying the spirit. His existence was an ongoing confession of triviality, of the emptiness of a being which God could value as he pleased. He lived as one who knew he was among the reprobates – socially and theologically. 'Today, for instance he might be worth £200,' Aubrey heard, 'the next day he might not be worth half so much, or perhaps be sometimes *minus nihilo*.'[92] So, perhaps, the condition of his soul was in similar flux; and if not, if all was decided already, he was free to pour himself away.

One can almost hear Wentworth, Lord Deputy of Ireland, sniff with disdain on reading of the Suckling–Digby affair. He learned of it in the dispatch from his regular agent and correspondent in London, George Garrard, in November 1634.

Wentworth typified the very opposite traits to those of a Suckling. He was 'a man of deep policy, stern resolution and ambitious zeal to keep up the glory of his own greatness'.[93] In the 1628 Parliament he was seen as a radical, instrumental in drafting the Petition of Right defending the liberties of free subjects against the king; yet in 1629 he emerged as more of a conciliator, resisting the escalation of the quarrel. Rather than buying him off with an appointment, and while still hesitating to take him into confidence, Charles had seen his potential as an enforcer.

The head of one of northern England's leading families, a member of every Parliament since 1614, this indefatigable Yorkshireman took up residence at Dublin Castle in July 1633 and assumed dictatorial powers over Ireland in the king's name. He quickly began rationalizing the province's finances, claiming overdue or formerly overlooked revenues for the Crown from the disparate ascendancy of new and old colonists. He was not long in embarking on a course of stiff measures which antagonized the whole island: whether in battling the Irish coast's pirates, continuing the long-standing persecution of the native Roman Catholics, riling the Scots planters of Ulster, bringing upstart nobles to heel, claiming lands for the Crown or weeding out dissident clergy-men, Wentworth's approach was inflexible and his measures invariably confrontational. Condemning the state of the army from his first day in office, he was on occasion to be seen in his suit of black armour, crested with a black plume of feathers, training his troops in person in the hills beyond Dublin.

Quick-minded, with a will of marble, serious in the extreme, Went-worth despised profanity and lewdness only slightly less than he did laziness or a failure to pay his office the respect it was owed. He made the king new enemies and alienated those who should have been his friends with equal certainty. 'Let us then in the name of God go cheerfully and boldly,' he told his friend and ally Archbishop Laud, in words which came to represent an entire theory of government: 'if others do not their parts I am confident the honour shall be ours and the shame theirs, and thus you have my Thorough and Thorough.'[94]

There was considerable doubt nevertheless as to whether Lord Thorough, as he was soon known, pursued his iron purities in the name of God, the king, or himself. From this distance it is uncertain too whether Suckling's rashness in quarrels was any more self-destructive than Wentworth's.

6. Blind Mouths

Beloved, there are some things in which all Religions agree; The worship of God, the holinesse of Life . . . Men and brethren, I am a Papist, that is, I will fast and pray as much as any Papist . . . Men and brethren, I am a Puritan, that is, I will endeavour to be pure, as my Father in heaven is pure, as far as any Puritan.

– John Donne, sermon preached 25 January 1630

1

The dog days had settled on London when they set out on a pleasure trip across Wiltshire; the company being Suckling, Davenant and a mutual friend, one Jack Young, whose only lasting mark in English letters was a memorial for the dead poet laureate. Young was ambling through Westminster Abbey as the masons were covering the grave of Ben Jonson, who died earlier that August 1637, and gave one of them eighteen pence to carve the following letters in a square of blue marble:

O RARE BENN JOHNSON

It was an ambivalent epitaph, typical of a wit. Depending on how much space you made out between the 'O' and the 'R', it was not an admiring expostulation ('Oh, rare Ben Jonson') but a plea for the passerby's prayers (the Latin imperative *orare*), with a nod to Jonson's Catholicism. The poet had been ailing for some time, his stock at court dwindling even faster than before. But he had grown accustomed to physical weakness, after his first stroke almost a decade earlier, and to living on the borderline of actual poverty. He would sell his books to make up the difference, buying them back when fortune and patronage allowed. Yet it was impossible now for him to sink into obscurity. He was a fixture in London's cultural cityscape, as much as Blackfriars, Paris Garden or St Paul's, the dilapidated cathedral which reminded the antiquary Thomas Fuller of someone indeed rather like Jonson in his declining years, a heavy man impeded, 'one struck with the dead palsy on one side'.[1]

Yet his belligerent egoism was undiminished to the end. Slighted by his royal master, he neither asked for pity, nor needed it. A few years earlier, Howell was among the many present at one of Jonson's 'solemn suppers' for his literary sons and brethren, and enjoyed 'good company, excellent cheer, choice wines, and jovial welcome'. Only one thing grated, 'which almost spoil'd the relish of the rest'; and that was when 'B. [Jonson] began to engross all the discourse, to vapour extremely of himself, and, by villifying others, to magnify his own *Muse*.' Seated beside him, Carew whispered in Howell's ear that for all the learning Ben had 'barrell'd up', he had still not learned that self-praise was 'an ill-favour'd solecism'. For his part Howell was reminded of the graceless hostess who spoilt the entertainment at another excellent party. When a roast capon was served, instead of spooning wine over the meat she took some in her mouth and spat on the bird. 'Be a man's breath ever so sweet, yet it makes one's praise stink, if he makes his own mouth the conduit-pipe for it.'[2] Appropriately, Jonson's funeral at Westminster Abbey was a considerable affair, with almost all the gentles and nobles still in town at that punishing time – mid-August – joining the procession.

Now Whitehall and Westminster were still. The law courts were closed. A comic poem by Davenant from the mid-1630s captures the mood of a typical day during the long vacation, beginning with a gambler sneaking out of town at the crack of dawn to avoid a request for rent. It is still cool: he is wrapped in a coarse woollen cloak. A little later, ladies of Cheapside excitedly walk to the dairies of Islington, at that time a village to the north of the city. A little later still, their husbands set out in the same direction, to hunt ducks in the ponds beyond Islington Green. Prostitutes on Turnbull Street, hungry while business is slack, tout for trade from the few stray gallants, clerks and galloon-trimmed servants. On the river, a jobless actor seeks work as a ferryman, and his boat lies still all afternoon. A barge bearing dung drifts by; traffic is sparse. In the City proper, the few remaining officials relax. Aldermen

gamble lightly, for tiny stakes: a piece of mutton, a chicken. In Westminster Hall, the sergeant-at-arms has no prisoner to grasp by the
shoulder and take from the dock. In the vast nave of St Paul's, the proc-
tor has no bawds or idlers to disperse. He sets out with his friend, a
sleek, well-fed attorney, for a little archery practice in Finsbury Fields.
London rests like a ship in harbour. The passengers have disembarked,
the crew have only light duties. Another group of whey-faced apprentices hire gasping steeds and leave to visit country relatives. The last of
the town wits, seeing there is no one left to borrow from, accept their
lot and join the scattered exodus: 'Our Mules are come! Dissolve the
Club!' There is little to be had now, in any case, by way of entertainment. The puppets nod in their boxes. Morocco, the Scotsman Banks's
performing horse, is led away for the summer. London's acrobats and
showpeople are also deserting the greens and open spaces:

> Now Vaulter good, and dancing Lass
> On Rope, and Man that cryes hey pass,
> And Tumbler young that needs but stoop,
> Lay head to heel to creep through Hoope . . .
> All these on hoof now trudge from Town,
> To cheat poor Turnip-eating Clown.[3]

On reflection, mid-summer was the proper time for Jonson to die,
when the life of the city which inspired and tormented him dipped also,
this year with something like respect. It was shortly after his interment
that Suckling, Davenant and Young set out on their journey into Wiltshire, in search of rustic turnip-eaters. They travelled along the old
Bath road, following the route of the present A4, but through unspoilt
country.

Wiltshire had a special place in the minds and hearts of the mid-
century antiquaries who looked back with affection on the world of
England before the civil war, in particular John Aubrey, who preserved
Davenant's memories of this particular excursion. This was the county
where one found Salisbury Cathedral, the best tobacco-pipes in all
England (manufactured at Amesbury) and the marvel of knot-grass,
growing up to fifteen feet in length under winter marshes and yielding
'both hay and provender, the joint-like knots whereof will fat swine'.

And as a whole, this low breezy land was unequalled, as Thomas Fuller asserted:

I have heard a wise man say that an ox left to himself would, of all England, choose to live in the north, a sheep in the south part hereof, and a man in the middle betwixt both, as partaking of the pleasure of the plain, and the wealth of the deep country.[4]

Davenant's party was headed, ultimately, for Bath, with a spirit of impulse governing it along the way. According to Aubrey, Suckling travelled 'like a young prince for all manner of equipage and convenience, and Sir W Davenant told me that he had a cart of books carried down'. The story brought on one of Aubrey's nostalgic reveries: ''Twas as pleasant a journey as ever men had; in the height of a long peace and luxury, and in the venison season.'

The mention of Suckling's regal conveyance suggests that rather than hiring a postmasters' horse at threepence a mile, he travelled by private coach. This mark of status was no guarantee of comfort, nevertheless, let alone luxury. No wonder Suckling had to have his books sent after him. Travellers then sat in the boot, that being the term for the leather-covered chassis, which could accommodate two persons at best, with precious little in the way of mudguards or cover from lateral blasts of rain. Being coached, remarks one historian of transport, was synonymous with being jolted violently about.[5] Still the passengers travelling in state were better off than the driver, who made do with a padded cross-bar for his seat above the carriage pole.

Yet whether horse-drawn or on horseback, Davenant's recollections suggest the weather spared them the worst discomforts of the unpaved, unreliable road, or that the trio was able simply to disregard them. Transmitted through Aubrey, their appetite for the outing, the exercise and wayside exploits comes through infectiously. The chief anecdote arising from the trip shows to excellent effect Aubrey's skill with scene-setting and compressed narration − not so much of brief lives as full lives in brief:

The second night they lay at Marlborough, and walking on the delicate fine downes at the backside of the town, whilest supper was making ready, the maids were drying of cloathes on the bushes. Jack Young had espied a very pretty young girl, and had got her consent for an assignation, which was about midnight.

Davenant and Suckling, meanwhile, on the other side of a hedge, overheard Young's conversation, and 'resolved to frustrate his design'. Returning to the inn for supper, after which it was their custom to play cards into the night, they informed their hostess that Young was prone to walking in his sleep and harming himself and those he met as he did so. When Young began feigning tiredness, in order to retire early and so make his rendezvous, one of his friends warned the landlady, 'Observe this poor gentleman how he yawnes, now is his mad fit coming upon him. We beseech you that you make fast his doors, and get somebody to watch and look to him, for about midnight he will fall to be most out-ragious.' The landlady, concerned, assigned an ostler to the post:

Jack Young slept not, but was ready to goe out as the clock struck to the hour of appointment, and then goeing to open the door he was disappointed, knocks, bounces, stampes, calls, 'Tapster! Chamberlain! Ostler!' swears and curses dreadfully; nobody would come to him. Sir John and W. Davenant were expectant all this time and ready to dye with laughter.

Young was evidently able to kick down the door, but on crashing onwards down the stairs encountered the servant who had been keep-ing watch. Young, like Suckling, was not best suited to a direct sparring match:

The ostler, a huge lusty fellow, fell upon him, and held him, and cryed, 'Good sir, take God in your mind, you shall not goe out to destroy yourself.' J. Young struggled and strived, insomuch that at last he was quite spent and dispirited, and faine to go to bed to rest himself.

The next morning the landlady kindly brought up Young a warm tonic to calm his spirits, expressing her sympathy for the 'heavy fit' he had suffered during the night. Young, sitting up on his pillows, 'thought the woman had been mad', and 'being exceedingly vexed' flung the pot-ful of medicine in her face.

Little pity has been spared for the unfortunate innkeeper, blinking with shock and hurt at this outrage, in accounts of the incident from Aubrey's on; yet even to a contemporary, the comedy of Jack Young's unsown oats goes sour at this point. The fraternity of city men out in the country compares unfavourably to the landlady's humane naivety, or the good-natured ostler sitting up till all hours and telling Young simply, 'Take God in your mind.' Suckling and Davenant both had their country refuges, but they were far from sympathetic to provincial attitudes. A metropolitan condescension flavours much of Davenant's work in particular, as with his heroine's scorn for 'Country Madams' in 'The Wits':

> Poor humble wretches, they still frisk and dance,
> In narrow Parlers, to a single Fiddle,
> Which squeaks forth tunes, like a departing Pig.[6]

Davenant's contempt was not directed at the countryside itself so much as its inhabitants. He was a keen supporter of the company which travelled to the Cotswolds, most summers, to take part in the English Olympics. These were the games organized by 'Captain' Robert Dover, a noted worthy of the county, a lawyer by training who had long ceased practising, since he 'preferred resolving disputes to pursuing cases'. Dover was commemorated as 'an old English gentleman, bred all of the olden time'. Being 'full of activity, and of a generous, free, and public spirit', many years before, he had asked King James's permission to hold sports 'on Cotswolds Hill in Gloucestershire'. The place selected was not far from Endymion Porter's country home, and Porter, 'a person also of a most generous spirit', passed on to Dover some cast-offs from the king's own wardrobe, 'with a hat and feather and ruff, purposely to grace him and consequently the solemnity'. The games attracted the gentry from all over the south of England and featured:

Men playing at cudgels, wrestling, leaping, pitching the bar, throwing the iron hammer, handling the pyke, leaping over the heads of men kneeling, standing upon their hands, &c. Also the dancing of women, men hunting and coursing the hare with hounds and grey-hounds, &c.

Yearly, a mock-siege would take place of a castle 'built of boards on a hillock', with guns firing blanks over the heads of the raiders and clouds of smoke billowing over the onlookers. Almost everywhere one looked one met 'the picture of the great director Capt. Dover on horseback, riding from place to place'.[7]

Dover epitomized simpler, nobler bygones. William Davenant was one of those who had been asked to contribute to a volume in the honour of the 'yearly preserver' of the games. Weary from litigious struggles with his tailor, he chose to celebrate Dover's change of vocation from the law to the field. He addressed London's advocates, those 'whose hollow Teeth are stuffed with others bread': contrasting their vice with Dover's virtue, he warned them of their children's future:

> Ere you a Yeare are dead, your Sonnes shall watch
> And rore all Night with Ale, in house of Thatch.[8]

Davenant himself had not in his time been so averse to roaring all night; nor, forgetting his prostration on the back of a wagon, his drunken fistfights and regrets at dawn, had Ben Jonson, who composed an almost mournful reflection on Dover and his Olympiad. For Jonson, the games recalled 'the glories of our blessed James', under whose rule they had first been permitted, and with those glories a happier, more prosperous time for the weakening poet himself. Seeing through the nostalgia, however, Jonson observed the civic function performed by the festivals of exercise, pageantry, dancing and feasting:

> How they advance true love, and neighbourhood,
> And do both Church, and commonwealth the good,
> In spite of hypocrites, who are the worst
> Of subjects; let such envy, till they burst.[9]

And burst they would, those 'hypocrites', at least in the version of the civil wars that was accepted for three centuries. There was in this interpretation a radical mass nearing critical mass, waiting semi-consciously for the right occasion to detonate a 'puritan revolution'. When it came, Dover's Cotswold Games were among the trappings of 'Old England' finally swept away. The English Olympics continued each year 'till the rascally rebellion was begun by the Presbyterians, which gave a stop to their proceedings, and spoiled all that was generous or ingenious elsewhere'.[10]

Something about games had indeed always riled the stringent groups who acquired the label 'puritan'. 'Precise people', as they were also known, had campaigned rigorously for King James to declare sports and games illegal on the Sabbath as being unholy, even though they were an age-old diversion. Such 'frolicks', involving as they did displays of strength and physical charm by a community's younger people, always carried a sexual overtone.

Back in 1617, James had deemed it necessary to discipline puritans in Lancashire for their 'prohibiting and unlawful punishing' of those who played games on Sundays. So a royal declaration known popularly as 'the Book of Sports' was issued in which leaping, vaulting, archery, bowling, along with other 'harmless' – and timeless – recreations such as Whitsun ales, Morris dances and the 'setting up of May-poles' were formally approved. Sports and games were legitimized but puritan dissent in no way subdued. Precisians would burst into people's homes if they heard music, to see that the Sabbath was observed, breaking instruments and assaulting dancers. By the early 1630s, in Somerset, the vigilantism against merriment reached such a pitch that King Charles felt moved to reissue the Book of Sports in 1633 with a preface of his own.[11]

Dover's games were not Sabbath sports; yet they had an equally questionable flavour, with the captain's silken costume, the 'virgin dances' he encouraged and other suspect flourishes. For the time being, Davenant was perceptive in seeing another cause behind the Olympics' gradual demise. The greater immediate threat to the Cotswold Games, and other 'generous and ingenious' events, lay not with sour puritan 'hypocrites' but with gentlemen's sons who had no interest in the honest rural sport of the shires; urban hedonists, that is, like his companions Suckling and Young.

They continued their late-summer jaunt, and rode on through a prewar England, with none of their certainties questioned:

That night they went to Bronham House, Sir Edward Baynton's (then a noble seat, since burnt in the civill wars), where they were nobly entertained severall dayes. From thence, they went to West Kington, to Parson Davenant's, Sir William's eldest brother, where they stayed a week – mirth, witt, and good cheer flowing.

Blissfully absent from this account, 'in the height of a long peace and luxury', despite the glimpse in the text of that burnt-out ruin at Bronham, are problems which began to bite deeper, across the land, from that summer on.[12]

2

For now, as much as in the seventeenth century, it all depends on how you read the signs of unrest – and whether, to begin with, you accept they constitute such signs at all. By the time of Suckling's summer excursion, King Charles had funded his government without Parliament for more than seven years. To do so he had introduced a number of enduringly unpopular measures to raise revenues. By rights they should have appealed to England's sense of antiquity, since rather than being the 'innovations' as which they were attacked, most were strictly revivals of old fines and dues. A charge was pressed, for example, on all landowners whose property was worth more than £40 a year who had not been knighted. This statute dated from the time when every gentleman whose estate met a prescribed value was obliged to take on a knighthood to serve the king in war, or else make an equivalent financial contribution. Moribund forest laws, again belonging to a former age, punished proprietors who had enclosed or encroached upon lands which were found once to have been royal woodland. The most resented fiscal reform was the notorious levy of 'ship money'. Historically, the coastal shires had long been obliged to provide ships for the navy, for their own defence, and the first writ for ship money in 1634 had faithfully accorded with this precedent. In subsequent years, however, the writs departed from tradition by extending the levy to the inland counties. This would relieve the Exchequer altogether of the cost of the navy and balance the budget, if one excluded the long-standing national debt. But constitutionalists from Westminster to the West Country contended that the king himself could only take such action with the approval of Parliament.

Alongside those grievances, and a general charge of acting unconstitutionally by not summoning Parliament, Charles was harassed too by local grudges, from those of soap-makers in Bristol to the eel-men bereft by the draining of the Norfolk fens. Further still to the north, his subjects in Edinburgh were in open uproar against his attempt to impose a new prayer book on the Scottish Kirk. His government was by no means in crisis, and indeed Charles hardly seemed alarmed at all by the disturbances, but he took his summer retreat to the palace at Oatlands with some gratitude early in August 1637, delighted by the long-awaited delivery of his effigy in marble, carved by Bernini.[13]

The king did not attend Ben Jonson's funeral, but the argument as to who should take the laureate's place caught up with him. In October, George Garrard sent Lord Wentworth in Dublin a copy of a 'Ballad made of the Wits, sung to the King when he was in the *New Forest*'.[14] This ballad, often simply called 'The Wits', was a lyrical fiction of Suckling's also known as 'A Sessions of the Poets'. In it the foremost wits of the land – or those, by Suckling's wry reckoning, who would style themselves as such – gather in town to plead their claim to the laureateship. The 'Sessions' was thus a contest, judged by Apollo himself, over who should be proclaimed the poet of the age. The ballad looks as if it was written while Jonson was still alive. If he was not, it treated him as very much present in spirit, since the old laureate speaks up immediately when the company is assembled. Suckling's character sketch captured the attitude of those outside the patriarch of letters' 'tribe'; affectionate, but unfazed by his pretensions. Jonson insists that he should win the laurels, since his plays and poems constituted *Works* – which in real life he had collected together in a grand folio edition. In Suckling's sessions, he takes the jibing which ensues with extremely bad grace.[15]

Each pretender in turn has his (and, in one case, her) credentials considered and rejected. Thomas Carew, the next after 'good old Ben', is passed over on the grounds that 'His muse was hard bound'; the assembly agreeing with Apollo that a 'Laureats Muse should be easie and free'.[16] Davenant's suit is also presently declined for nothing more than his personal appearance. References to his afflicted countenance had not died down in the five or six years since his mishap with mercury, even among intimate friends such as Suckling:

> Surely the Company would have been content,
> If they could have found any Precedent;
> But in all their Records either in Verse or Prose,
> There was not one Laureat without a nose.[17]

The fact that court correspondents such as Garrard were distributing manuscripts of the 'Sessions' indicates that the long ballad brought the king's cautious smile to his face when it was sung for him at his lodge in the New Forest. Its sung quality is the key to its vitality: the setting has not survived but the slightly slapdash text is clearly better suited for performance than the page, with more formal improvisation than regularity.[18] It was the kind of work to titillate prominent egos with its treatment of recognizable figures from literary London – and to stir up questions over who was mentioned and who excluded. Suckling assembled friends and enemies alike for his Sessions. Present, for example, was Sir Kenelm Digby, the brother of Suckling's nemesis, and Thomas May, '*Lucans* translator', a writer with republican leanings and a robust dislike for Davenant and his set. Toby Mathew, recusant and court leech, had also managed to sneak in ('Pox on't! How came he here?' the poem mutters).[19]

Along with Digby, meanwhile, are other members of the most dignified intellectual circle in the country – the loose society of philosophically minded characters gathered and encouraged by Lucius Cary, Viscount Falkland. 'My lord lived much at Tew,' Aubrey recounted, 'which is a pleasant seat, and about 12 miles from Oxford; his lordship was acquainted with the best wits of that university, and his house was like a Colledge, full of learned men.'[20] Cary's 'most intimate and beloved favourite', William Chillingworth, an advocate of religious reconciliation with Rome, is also a member of Suckling's Sessions, but is kept from coming too close to Apollo: as Davenant told Aubrey, Chillingworth was disliked for his 'treachery' to a friend, a schoolmaster at St Paul's, with whom he used 'to nibble at state matters' in weekly conversations – even if the friend in question was only Alexander Gill.

Gill was an antagonist of Ben Jonson, and the poet who celebrated the collapse of a secret chapel on a Catholic congregation in 1623. When drinking together in the cellar of Trinity College, Oxford, a short time after the murder of Buckingham, Gill denounced Kings James and Charles as 'the old fool and the young one', and Chillingworth informed on him to his godfather, William Laud, then Bishop of London. Gill was eventually spared the punishment to which he was originally sentenced, though he showed little clemency to his unfortunate pupils. Like his father, whom he succeeded as headmaster of Paul's, Gill was famously given to 'whipping fits'. One such frenzy resulted in the governors of the school dismissing him for good.[21]

The links between Suckling and Falkland are in some ways surprising. Lucius Cary was praised, especially by Edward Hyde, as one of the most generous and gentle souls of the day. He is the only figure in Suckling's poem to be spared satirical comment. Suckling notes that Cary has been neglecting his muse, and his chances of winning the god's favour, through his preoccupations with divinity; and then adds:

> Though to say the truth (and *Apollo* did know it)
> He might have been both his Priest and his Poet.[22]

A vast distance normally divides Suckling the dissolute gamester and Cary the priest of Apollo in chronicles of the 1630s; but 'A Sessions' suggests mutual respect and even intimacy. Cary was remembered as England's first Socinian, that is, in the parlance of the time, a free-thinker in matters of religion, given to doubting the eternity of Christ or the reality of the Holy Trinity. He may have played some part in fostering Suckling's interest in heterodoxy, which he expressed openly for the first time that summer of 1637. For some, such interest in itself was equal to delinquency. 'I am not ignorant that the fear of *Socianisme* at this time,' wrote Suckling, 'renders every man that offers to give an account of Religion by Reason, suspected to have none at all.'[23] Cary's conduct, respected in the eyes of virtually all, placed him above such charges, and his name has rarely been heard in the same breath as Suckling's. Yet as Aubrey has it, Cary too 'in his youth was very wild, and also mischievous, as being apt to stab and do bloody mischiefs'.[24]

At the end of 'A Sessions of the Poets' none of those present are

awarded the laurel. To the amazement of all, Apollo gives his crown to
a wealthy London alderman who appears at random, assessing it 'the
best signe/ Of good store of wit to have good store of coyn'.[25] The conclusion is thus a barely veiled comment that, while the usual kind of wit
is in abundance in the kingdom, the variety that can raise hard capital is
in precious poor supply. Shocked and offended, the poets brighten at
the thought of asking their new laureate for a loan – although even that
hope is quickly dashed. Suckling's poem was later credited by Dr Johnson as creating a satirical sub-genre of its own; sessions of scribblers and
lovers abounded in English verse for another two centuries. But in it
Suckling is preoccupied with the present moment. Politically, he suggests that free debate was possible even without a Parliament; at the same
time he could be interpreted as hinting to the king, through the medium
of a comic song, that his subjects needed opportunity and a forum for
debate. If not inspired by Jonson's demise, meanwhile, its material
proved timely. To the group described in his poem, the laureate's death
was most likely the great event of the summer, displacing earlier news
which proved more consequential: the first hearings, for example, back
in May, of the trial of John Hampden for non-payment of ship money;
or the punishment of three inveterate puritan libellers in a manner
which dismayed temperate opinion.

On 30 June, William Prynne, Henry Burton and John Bastwick,
respectively a lawyer, a doctor and a clergyman, were whipped and led
to the pillory for mutilation. All three were venomous critics of the
regime and in particular of the state of the English Church. Prynne we
have encountered already through his epic-length onslaught on the theatre, *Histriomastix*; the lopping of his ears had not discouraged him from
his fight. Burton and Bastwick, meanwhile, if lacking the scope and
duration of Prynne's attacks in their polemic, almost equalled him in
excoriating bitterness. After a trial in which they were, to be fair, shown
due process – by the standards of the time – they were determined not
to miss their day of public exposure. Crowds packed Smithfield, some
to ogle and jeer, others to lend moral support. As the three prisoners
approached their pillories, Burton did not fail to see a comparison with
the three crosses on the hill of Calvary, inviting but not answering the
question as to which of them was Christ, and which two the pair of
thieves. Once locked to his post by the stocks, each man began reviling

the authority of his punishers. Burton, an elderly man, passed out when the executioner, ignoring the physician's directions and cutting down to the bone of the skull, sliced off his ears; but Prynne, surrendering the stumps left to him from his earlier ear-clipping, kept on preaching, even delivering a Latin epigram on the letters seared into his face.

S.L., his countenance now read: Seditious Libeller. One of the lords judging the three had wanted their noses slit as well, but had been out-voted. At Smithfield, the onlookers who had come to crow found the laughter sticking in their throats. Most present, whatever they thought of the prisoners' ideas, were moved by their fortitude throughout the ordeal. A zealous number of supporters at the front of the crowd, eager for keepsakes and relics, rushed forward to dip their handkerchiefs in the blood congealing around the pillories. And when the trio was eventually unfastened, and taken to separate prisons at distant points in the kingdom, they found themselves feted by crowds on their way. Prynne in particular was shown great hospitality on his summer journey north under armed guard.

It was customary to remit such punishment: Alexander Gill had been sentenced to lose an ear for denouncing the 'royal fools' and toasting Felton, but had been spared. After the mutilation of Prynne, Burton and Bastwick, the authorities looked and felt sheepish. The show of brutality, against three individuals who could easily have been dismissed as eccentrics, hardly enhanced royal dignity. It was a degrading event for all concerned. The Archbishop of Canterbury's chaplain reflected that entirely moderate people were troubled; and in Dublin, Viscount Wentworth observed that when a prince's punishments no longer instilled respect, the greater part of his authority was lost.[26]

3

Their stay at Parson Davenant's, in West Kington near Chippenham, marked the quiet stage of the journey. William Davenant's brother Robert had been the scholar of the Oxford tavern-keeper's family, cherished by an uncle who rose to be Bishop of Salisbury, in whose diocese he served. Robert Davenant was spoken of as a humourless man, but certain events in his life and the company he kept suggest he could relax when the occasion suited.[27] He could also succumb by times to his brother's influence. On a trip to visit Davenant in London he had once ordered a fine suit of clothes from Davenant's tailor – and the habitual victim of his spendthrift nature – John Urswick, for which (by Urswick's account) he never paid.[28] Equally, he had no qualms about taking Young, Suckling and Davenant into his home for a week on their rambling tour.

Hunting aside, at West Kington the three friends relaxed from their pursuits of the flesh. Young was chastened, in any case, by the firm handling of the ostler of Marlborough; and Davenant's brush with the clap had taught him to be careful. Although standing troths and marital arrangements were clearly no obstacle to 'assignations' on the road, Suckling's correspondence in the second half of the 1630s celebrates a deeper attachment, to a woman he calls 'Aglaura'. Surviving manuscripts show them to have been real, dispatched letters; and when published they still named the addressee directly at moments as his 'dear Mary'. Suckling's modern editors have put forward Mary Bulkeley of Baron Hill in Anglesey as the most likely recipient of these letters. Yet Suckling had numerous admirers who vied for the title of Aglaura, including the sister of his old flame Mary Cranfield, Frances, Countess of Dorset, who in later years 'took a very odd pride in boasting of her familiarities with Sir John'.[29] Yet the letters are written to a Mary not a Frances, although Suckling was clearly partial not only to Mary Bulkeley but to her sister Anne. He addressed the sisters as recluses from the unsavoury, gossip-ridden court and its circular rumouring of 'what old Loves are decay'd, or what new ones sprung up . . . Whether this Lady be too discreet, or that Cavalier not secret enough; [these] are things that concern not the inhabitants of Anglesey at all.'[30] There is little point debating how genuine his passion for Aglaura may have been: it was as real as the language in which Suckling addressed her and altered accordingly. By times he was the cynic, by times he liked to play the Petrarchan, enlightened and reformed by the sight of his beloved.

Her remoteness in this case, though, lay not so much with near-divinity as in Suckling's frequent absence from the foot of her pedestal. His habitual candour with the women he wrote to rested on the expectation that they tolerate and even nurture his acknowledged vices. Yet the letters to Aglaura are different. They are models of a sincere, rather than a witty style. '(Dear *Mary*),' reads one, 'I was ever yours since I had first the honour to know you, and consequently so little my self since I had the opportunity to part with you.'[31] In others, in spite of excuses for separation which may have been all too convenient, he plays the part of one heady and confused, disarmed:

My Dear Dear, Think I have kist your Letter to nothing, and now know not what to answer. Or that now I am answering, I am kissing you to nothing, and know not how to go on! For you must pardon, I must hate all I send you here, because it expresses nothing in respect of what it leaves behind with me. And oh! Why should I write then? Why should I not come my self? Those Tyrants, businesse, honour, and necessity, what have they to do with you and I?[32]

This is quite unlike the louche Suckling his friends knew and loved, who received his letters in bed, surrounded by his playing cards. Yet this, it seems, is what he meant when he once described himself to Thomas Carew as overflowing with love. The letter quoted below may well date from Suckling's visit to Bath at the end of August 1637. Carew, it seems, was staying with a distant country cousin:

Know then, Dear *Carew*, that at Eleven last night, flowing as much with Love as thou hast ebbed, thy Letter found me out. I read, considered, and admired, and did conclude at last, that *Horsley* Air did excel the Waters of the *Bath*; just so much as Love is a more noble disease then the Pox.[33]

If there were moments in his exchanges with Carew where he sounded too suave, too arch even for his worldly friend, so there were others in his letters to Aglaura where he strained credibility too far. 'When I receive your lines (my Dear Princesse) and find there expressions of a Passion . . . Then do I glory that my Virgin-Love has staid for such an object to fixe upon, and think how good the Stars were to me that kept me from quenching those flames (Youth or wild Love furnished me withal) in common and ordinary Waters.'[34]

Anglesey must indeed have been secluded for Mary Bulkeley to have taken that at face value. Indeed the earliest of his surviving letters to Bulkeley showed more of Suckling as he usually appeared, a social and sexual pragmatist. Along with his general comments on the liaisons of courtesans and cavaliers, he tut-tuts at the indiscretion of the Bulkeleys' cousin, Countess Katherine Villiers, the widow of the Duke of Buckingham. She had upset the king by marrying one of Suckling's old opponents at cards and ninepins, the Viscount Dunluce, with the loss of royal favour and with it many of her houses and 'most of her friends'.[35] Charles felt that he should have been consulted on the match, and possibly that the memory of his old favourite should have been kept pure by Lady Villiers remaining single. 'It is none of the least discourtesies money hath done us Mortals,' Suckling once told his cousin Martha, 'the making things easie in themselves, and natural, difficult: Yong and handsome people would have come together without half this trouble, if that had never been.'[36] While assisting his female relatives to the matches on which their subsistence depended, he advised his male friends and readers to avoid marriage wherever possible and refrain from 'fruition'.

His stay at Parson Davenant's in Wiltshire in August 1637 encouraged reflections of another kind. It was at the parlour table in the house in West Kington, the parson claimed, that Suckling wrote his *Account of Religion by Reason* in five or six days. This was Suckling's one recorded foray into theology, and the finished treatise was dispatched to its dedicatee, the Earl of Dorset, on 2 September.[37]

In a few days, and a dozen or so pages, he set out to establish the truth of the Christian religion through common sense. Deducing the existence of a deity from nature and reason, rather than from scripture, was a controversial but long-established exercise, the exemplar being Montaigne's 'Apology for Raymond Sebond'. In this tradition, Suckling went back to first principles. With his initial point, admittedly, he made something of a leap, since the existence of a god at all he took as self-evident. 'That there should be a great Disposer and Orderer of things, wise Rewarder and Punisher of good and evil, hath appeared so equitable to men, that by instinct they have concluded it necessary.'[38] With that out of the way, in a few paragraphs, he organized history into three ages of knowledge ('the *Unknown*, the *Fabulous*, and the *Historical*') and surveyed the richness of the pre-Christian past, examining 'the opinion of good wits, that the particular Religion of Christians has added little to the general Religion of the World'. The life of humanity from the first murk of time had been a process of divine realization. 'And to say truth, a great part of our Religion, either directly or indirectly hath been professed by Heathens.'[39] This, he quickly insisted, he took as confirming Christianity rather than casting doubt on its sole claim to the truth.

In his dedicatory epistle to the Earl of Dorset, long a patron of alternative thinking, and indeed of a political sub-faction at court, Suckling observed how his 'discourse' had 'frighted the Lady into a cold sweat, and which had like to have made me an *Atheist* at Court, and your Lordship no very good Christian'. Suckling dismissed such fears. He continued with the excellences Christianity had added and perfected in the religion of the world. Heaven, for example, had never seemed so worth trying for in any other creed, and the torments of the damned so important to avoid. He derogated the heathens for the 'gentle' punishments they had been able to imagine, nothing 'but the rolling of a stone, filling of a sieve with water, sitting before Banquets and not daring to touch them'.[40] The tortures awaiting Muslims and Jews were also insipid compared to the Christian faith's deterrents.

He denounced 'sensual' religions which treated 'temporal blessings' – 'the renewing of youth, high Feasts, a woman with great eyes, and drest up with a little more fancie' – as their greatest reward.[41] He could not, however, accept the emphasis so many religions placed on mortal suffering. Puritans were thus as mistaken as Jews and Muslims in missing the Christian God's concern that we enjoy the bounty of the creation: 'the strangest, though the most Epidemical disease of all Religions, has been an imagination men have had, that the imposing painful and difficult things upon themselves, was the best way to appease the Deity, grossly thinking the chief service and delight of the Creator to consist in the tortures and suffering of the Creature.'[42]

Presently he came to the points of Christian doctrine 'which so trouble the curious wits': these he listed as the incarnation of Christ, his passion and resurrection, and the mystery of the Trinity. Suckling had no trouble confirming the first three by the lights of his great reasoning. The resurrection of Jesus was manifestly possible, 'it being with easie Reason imagined, that he which can make a body [i.e. God], can lay it down, and take it up again.' A more pressing intellectual problem lay with the form we would take on reaching heaven: 'for since in our estate

we promise our selves hereafter, there will be no need of Food, Copulation or Excrement, to what purpose should we have a mouth, belly, or
lesse comely parts?' He found a happy solution. 'To this I should answer,
that as the body is partner in good or ill doing, so it is but just it should
share in the rewards or punishments hereafter.'[43]

By submitting religion to reason, Suckling really meant to assess how
readily and credibly the contents of scripture could be imagined. It was
a trial by wit. 'Reason' here was satisfied by the standard of proof
required by the dialectic reasoning in which Suckling had received some
instruction; that is, of probability, not certainty. He was seeing whether
the claims of faith could be pictured plausibly, and if they could, he
accepted them. God's body dying and coming back to life, for instance,
was 'easie' to imagine, if one had already taken on board the fact that
God made that body to begin with – and why not, since men found it
'necessary' that someone had made everything? Suckling's sticking
point was with the idea of the Holy Trinity, the three-in-one, God the
Father, the Son, and the Holy Spirit. He neither rejected nor affirmed
this idea, merely observing the 'poverty and narrownesse' of the words
available to treat of it.[44]

Leaving the comparison of one religion to another, he ended by side-
stepping the question of which particular denomination should be
followed. There were quite enough people bickering over this already,
he decided, 'perchance to the prejudice of Religion it self'. With no
other faith to contest it – conveniently forgetting the Turks to the east –
Christianity 'hath been forced to admit of Civil wars, and suffer under
its own excellency'.[45] In England, late in the summer of 1637, that could
still be taken as a metaphor; but not for much longer.

4

On a spring tide that August, a young Cambridge academic set sail from
Chester to visit his family in Ireland. Edward King, a fellow of Christ's
College, was travelling to support and console his brother and sisters
after the death of their father in January. As the time which elapsed
between then and King's journey might suggest, the crossing was not a
matter of routine: ships taking to the Irish Sea were regularly endangered

and often lost to storm and piracy. So the month before his departure, as both a precaution and perhaps a private charm against shipwreck or capture, King drew up his will, directing his executor in the event of his death to claim whatever he would of his books, burn his private papers and pay off his surprisingly extravagant debts.

Over the water, Viscount Wentworth's rule as Lord Deputy was proving financially fruitful but politically harmful. He had continued disgruntling more or less every faction on the island, from Roman Catholics of varying origin to the Presbyterians in Ulster. To the king's disapproval he had gruffly summoned an Irish Parliament in 1634, and all but challenged its members to defy his demands at their own risk. When they proved obstreperous, they were disbanded, King Charles commenting that parliaments 'are of the nature of cats, they ever grow curst with age'.[46] Yet Wentworth believed in cracking eggs, and skulls if necessary, when omelettes needed making. He claimed to care little about offending either his own officials or his backers in England. He lifted the tax burden on new colonists, for example, but took the collection of taxes into his own hands. In doing so he aggrieved the former tax-collectors, but did nothing to win the loyalty of recent planters, mostly Presbyterian, who despised his religious reforms. He sought out every penny of outstanding rent on every scrap of land leased by the Crown. In 1637, he was just beginning an especially bitter campaign for overdue compensation from the City of London. His critics across the three kingdoms noted that Wentworth did not neglect to maintain his own state, buying property, building stables and houses, and feasting lavishly in Dublin.

Edward King did not have the chance to make his mind up on the Irish situation. His ship struck a rock off the coast of Anglesey, and quickly sank. His body was never recovered. He was in his late twenties, and while records at Christ's suggest he was never an overly industrious teacher – he did not need the fees for his living – he was regarded as a scholar of great promise. Back in Cambridge, his friends gathered verses in his honour, commemorating his learning with a show of their own, praising King in Greek and Latin. Others expressed their loss more directly through the vernacular.[47]

A memorial volume, *Justa Edouardo King*, was brought out in 1638. By far the most famous of the poems it contains, one which preserved not only the book but also the memory of Edward King himself in literary history, was an anonymous piece entitled 'Lycidas', by a thirty-year-old scholar little known at this time as a poet. John Milton had withdrawn from Cambridge three years earlier to embark on a rigorous and exhausting course of personal study in the country at Horton. There he refined his sense of intellectual purpose, his political and spiritual opposition to the reign of King Charles, and kept his physical urges in check with exercise and 'frugal diet'. It is uncertain how well Milton knew Edward King, or how affectionate his feelings for him really were. 'Lycidas', Milton's elegy, is more a lament on the state of the nation as an expression of personal grief. Milton used the poem as an opportunity to rebuke the prevailing religious culture of the time, a culture shaped largely by the 'High' Church policies of the Archbishop of Canterbury, William Laud. For Milton and others of a radical and puritanical persuasion, Laud and the rest of the king's bishops had brought the nation's soul to stew again in 'popish' decadence.

There was the widespread blight of absenteeism, ministers holding several benefices while living in none, and the negligence and corruption that induced. Among those actually serving the parishes were a great many simple-minded, sometimes scarcely literate clerics. There were country parsons who ogled the local women and took a pot of ale too many, straightforward hypocrites like Nicholas Gamen, curate of Lamyatt, who preached against drunkenness but was frequently so drunk himself that he could not lift his leg over the saddle when mounting his horse.[48] The senior bishops had long since recognized the need to invigorate the Church's finances and improve the overall quality of the ministry, both morally and intellectually. Laud, nicknamed 'little Hocus Pocus' for his stature and the energy he gave his work, made the latter project one of his foremost concerns. Such drives to lift standards are rarely popular with existing staff, however; and they can rarely go far enough to satisfy their most zealous supporters.

England's shepherds were sightless, incapable of providing the guidance their flock desperately needed:

> Blind mouthes! that scarce themselves know how to hold
> A Sheep-hook, or have learned aught else the least
> That to the faithful Herdman's art belongs![49]

'Lycidas' also contains a veiled meditation on Milton's own vexed sense of vocation. He had originally been expected to take orders, but could not submit himself to ordination in a fallen Church. Yet King's premature death cautioned against burying oneself too deeply in the library. Milton's poem ends, quietly, beautifully, with a new beginning, as the 'uncouth swain' who has sung the elegy departs:

> And now the Sun had stretched out all the hills,
> And now was dropt into the Western bay;
> At last he rose, and twitched his Mantle blue:
> Tomorrow to fresh Woods, and pastures new.[50]

Prophetic or not, the lines mark a moment of change in Milton's life. Shortly after submitting 'Lycidas' for publication, he embarked for Italy.

We catch such vivid glimpses in subsequent decades of Milton the polemicist, the image-breaker, the servant of the republic and, in his apotheosis, Milton the epic poet, that his earlier, less assured self can be lost to time. Yet by 1638 Milton was already a formidable scholar, already *'molto erudita'*, and a supremely subtle and versatile writer. He was not yet the voice of freedom or the justifier of God's ways to men. He was not yet the experienced traveller, pronouncing his Latin like a European, the acquaintance of Galileo and the learned elders of Florence, who at the outset of the war strode naively from London into Oxfordshire to begin a disastrous courtship. But he was already the author of *Comus*, as it will always informally be known, *A Masque Presented at Ludlow Castle*, in the eponymous villain of which he created a striking prototype for his later creation, Satan.

When we think of Milton in retirement, we think of Milton in hiding, blind and vilified, during the early years of the Restoration, bringing the prelapsarian world of his epic into being. He is austere, monumental – the hero of English republicanism – yet also more than brilliant, more than erudite. We see him in his house among his books and musical instruments, swinging in his customized chair, taking his walks with a helper holding his elbow. A deluxe atlas, specially ordered, lies close to hand; on his desk is a tortoiseshell writing case and tobacco box. This Milton of the early 1660s is already past the hurt of his first mistaken marriage, if not the distrust of women it confirmed in him.[51] His task-maker's eye is surely content; he has nothing to prove. He is visited by his muse before dawn, and she gives him new lines for his epic. Then he waits in bed to dictate them to his secretary, who comes each morning to 'milk' him, as he puts it – with one of his rare and somewhat unsettling flashes of humour.[52]

It needs bearing in mind that the earlier time he spent in seclusion at Horton, twenty years before, was no less anxious, and this being Milton, perhaps even more so, since in his own eyes he had not yet proved his worth or found his purpose. He was an almost exact contemporary of Suckling and Davenant but was in all likelihood wholly unknown to them in 1637 – and no doubt averse to making their acquaintance, however much a friend they may have shared in Henry Lawes, the composer of the music for *Comus*. Milton himself was all but certainly absent from the performance of his masque at Ludlow in September 1634: Suckling, had he not been caught up in his vendetta with Digby and the Willoughbys, might conceivably have been among the audience. *Comus* was commissioned for the inauguration of John Egerton, Second Earl of Bridgewater, as Lord President of Wales. Suckling and Bridgewater were well acquainted and latterly, it seems, enemies in verse. If lines parodying a well-known Suckling lyric are indeed his, Bridgewater took a dim view of the disgraced cavalier:

> Why so fierce and grim, proud railer?
> > Prithee, why so grim?
> Thou didst look as pale or paler,
> When thou wast fooled like him.
> > Prithee, why so grim?[53]

The masque at Ludlow had not been an elaborately technical production of the kind engineered by Inigo Jones. Indeed Suckling wrote a fine description of the sort of old-fashioned entertainment to be expected in provincial houses:

> Expect not here a curious River fine,
> Our wits are short of that: alas the time!
> The neat refined language of the Court

We know not; if we did, our Country sport
Must not be too ambitious: 'tis for Kings,
Not for their Subjects, to have such rare things.[54]

Comus was innovative in its poetry and ideology rather than its engineering; it argued the case for what David Norbrook has called a 'Reformation' of the masque, breaking the monarchistic monopoly on the art form.[55] Milton cared neither for the court's neat refinements nor adapted his language for the simpler demands of country sport. *Comus* had been an exercise, a welcome break from his programme of reading. He did not see it opening an avenue to a future career, and was never tempted to break into the circle of writers congregating at court.

The challenge he laid down was not only artistic but nakedly political.[56] The passage in 'Lycidas' given above targets a specific breed of indolent priest. The lines are spoken by '*Comus*, reverend sire', a personification of the River Cam and by extension of the university. Clad in 'his mantle hairy, and his bonnet sedge', footing slow, this academic deity castigates the blind mouths for their 'lean and flashy songs': these pastors sing because that is something shepherds do, but the line draws attention to the kind of songs they sing, which 'grate on their scrannel pipes of wretched straw'.

There were comparatively few ex-university men in the Church who were not at least occasional poets. Dr Brian Duppa, formerly vice-chancellor of Oxford and the editor of the 1638 volume of elegies for Jonson, was exceptional in the 'comeliness of his presence, the gentleness of his carriage', but a typical churchman in having a number of Jonsonian verses to his name.[57] He was tutor, also, to the Prince of Wales and the young Duke of Buckingham. Such polished gentlemen of God, with patrons praising their manners and wit more than their religious purity, could not but appear to some as little more than lapsed cavaliers. The barb Milton directs at the blind mouths' grating songs thus looks very much like an attack not only on the illiterate but on the writing to which numerous leading clergymen were or had been inclined, from the late John Donne to his friends Henry King, John Earle and Richard Corbet, not to mention Milton's imminent adversary Joseph Hall; all of whom rose to episcopal rank.

The problem was that a Church had to exist in the world. It was thus a practical recourse for poor scholars and younger sons as a means of making a living. To the highest in its ranks, it was a route to wealth and power. In that respect, to puritan critiques, the blindest mouths of all were the bishops; the age-old paragons of avarice and complacency. It didn't matter that, with a few notable exceptions, the bishops were mostly purists of a fashion themselves, enforcers of new measures to maintain and restore the Church, renovating buildings, railing in communion tables – frequently, to keep out the dogs which wandered freely during service – and disciplining congregants for unruly behaviour. It didn't matter either that Archbishop Laud, for all his faults – his tendency to vindictiveness, to acting on the paranoia which left him at the mercy of frequent terrible dreams – was by no means blind politically. He foresaw the opposition the king's determination to regulate the Church would provoke, and directed his fellow bishops to proceed carefully and diplomatically.

But, as the idealists among the godly would find out soon enough, there was no way of extracting the Church from the world. Robert Herrick, by now settled in his distant Devon parish for the best part of a decade, was the perfect example of a highly lettered, university-educated minister, manifestly qualified for religious orders yet too much given to poetic amusements. By one Victorian editor's judgement, 'we should be wrong in imagining him as a "blind mouth".'[58] In his favour it was said that he used to throw the notes to his elegant sermons at members of the congregation when they nodded off or grumbled from the pews. Learnedness, however, was no guarantee against the blindness brought on by vanity, pride or outright delinquency. Herrick could not in all honesty be wholly exempted from the indictment in 'Lycidas' of pastors who 'creep and intrude, and climb into the fold' for nothing but their 'bellies' sake'. Taking the cloth, as it was for so many, had been a pragmatic move, and it had not, as Herrick frequently complained, turned out so well for him.

Despite continued contacts with the court, where several of his poems were 'sung' to the king, Herrick still missed London. Writing in a cottage he shared with a trusty housekeeper named Prudence and a pet pig, the only good thing he could say of his 'loathèd Devonshire' was that it had made him concentrate on his poetry. Yet it was an old, idealized rural life that gave him the most material for invention. When he

eventually published his lay poems, he told his readers at the outset what
to expect:

> I sing of *Brookes*, of *Blossomes*, *Birds* and *Bowers*:
> Of *April*, *May*, of *June*, and *July*-Flowers.
> I sing of *May-poles*, *Hock-carts*, *Wassails*, *Wakes*,
> Of *Bride-grooms*, *Brides* and of their *Bridall-cakes*;
> I write of *Youth*, of *Love*, and have Accesse
> By these, to sing of cleanly-*Wantonnesse*.[59]

The 'argument' listed, in short, prime targets of rural puritan reformers in their sometimes violent campaign against Sunday sports and other
customs. As for 'cleanly wantonness', had Herrick's poetry fallen into
the hands of John Milton or Alexander Gill (who were sympathetically
acquainted), the contents would have confirmed their worst estimates
of the religious establishment. Here was the former creature of Buckingham setting out his debased thoughts in verse: Herrick never married,
indeed celebrated his bachelorhood, and indulged in sometimes florid
fantasies. He seemed all too willing 'to sport with Amaryllis in the
shade', as another famous line from 'Lycidas' had it, although there was
a poignancy to his readiness. The sportive dreams eventually published
in Herrick's *Hesperides* are testimonies to suspended or diverted desire,
made as their author slips past his prime:

> Young I was, but now am old,
> But I am not yet grown cold;
> I can play, and I can twine
> 'Bout a Virgin like a Vine:
> In her lap too I can lye
> Melting, and in her fancie die.[60]

Herrick only published his poems at a point when he had nothing left
to lose, after the collapse of the king's cause in 1647. He printed his
Noble Numbers, religious meditations, in the same volume; but their
proximity to lusty bucolics and often very dark epigrams strengthened
the overall sense that a lyric of spiritual devotion was nothing more
than another empty exercise.

If Herrick were spared Milton's epithet, then presumably George Herbert, his fellow poet-priest and slightly older contemporary, was wholly immune from the charge. Herbert, who died in 1633, was one of the treasures of the English Church in its later adversities. Academically brilliant, personally modest, temperate and sensitive, he was not only a model priest, but wrote the book on how to be one. *A Priest to His Temple* (known also as *The Country Parson*) became an Anglican classic. Herbert held a number of benefices, but never high or lucrative office. Instead he oversaw and raised funds for such projects as restoring a disused and near-ruined church at Leighton Bromswold in Huntingdonshire, and supporting the community of prayer at Little Gidding that inspired T. S. Eliot's eponymous 'quartet'. He seems to have held off from ordination until a moment when he could make his commitment emotionally complete, and experience it to the full. He settled in the Salisbury parish of Bemerton, walking twice-weekly for musical evenings at the cathedral, leading an exemplary plain existence with his wife Jane (née Danvers) until his death from a long, degenerative condition, probably tubercular, aged forty. The hagiography set up by his first biographers does not quite fit either Herbert or his work, however. He had a lighter, truer touch, balancing faith with quiet bewilderment. His poetry gently undercuts the claims to saintliness and sapience soon made on his behalf. To put it simply, he had his doubts:

> I reade, and sigh, and wish I were a tree;
> > For sure then I should grow
> To fruit or shade.[61]

Herbert provided a template of one using his office to meet civic obligations and find a path through life. His 'little book', printed posthumously as *The Temple* in 1633, should have appealed strongly to those within the Church who wished to re-found it on principles of early Christian simplicity. It definitely enchanted a later puritan spirit, one tempered by Methodism and liberalism, and driven by a belief in the power of works – and of *experience* – rather than predestination. It drew pure pastoral from Samuel Gardiner, the great liberal authority on the period:

Among the simple peasants of the Wiltshire valley such teaching was not without its reward. The ploughman stopped in his daily toil and murmured a few words of prayer as he heard Herbert's bell sending forth its summons to common worship. From Herbert, and from such as Herbert, Laud had nothing to fear. To them it was a pleasure to be under authority, and to be bidden to submit to rules out of which their submissive minds might draw some hidden sweetness.[62]

Yet although celebrated for its 'plain' style, there is little in Herbert's book for 'simple peasants'. Herbert does not treat authority as something to be blindly followed or ignored; nor privilege as so insubstantial that it can be thrown aside heedlessly. Herbert's aristocratic background and his intellectual excellence had given him the option of an illustrious career in either state or Church. As University Orator at Cambridge he gave speeches for kings and ambassadors. He could not and did not deny the power of mortal rewards. He argued rather that simplicity of life was the hardest thing of all to achieve. For him, puritanism was more than a little naive. It meant nothing, not to be tempted: it meant nothing to give up or condemn gratifications of which you were ignorant:

> I know the wayes of Honour, what maintains
> The quick returns of courtesie and wit:
> In vies of favours whether partie gains,
> When glorie swells the heart, and moldeth it
> To all expressions both of hand and eye,
> Which on the world a true-love knot may tie,
> And bear the bundle, whereso'ere it goes:
> How many drammes of spirit there must be
> To sell my life unto my friends or foes:
> Yet I love thee.[63]

You could only reach the pearl, the kingdom of God, through a labyrinth of worldly distractions, much as Herbert reaches the simple last line of his stanza via 'expressions both of hand and eye', which only prove gradually to be debilitating. Herbert did not have self-righteous scorn for the cavalier conduct of Suckling and his like. His critique of life instead has more sympathy for those entangled by and dependent on 'the quick returns of courtesy and wit'.

For Herbert the spirit defines itself in a medium of resistance. It also needed channels for devotion. One could not worship in a void. As Gardiner put it, this time more plausibly:

To Herbert the outward forms of church worship, the repeated prayer, the pealing organ, the painted window, were loved and reverenced as teaching the struggling soul to offer up its own wandering fantasy and to restrain itself within the limits appointed by external authority. That which was to sink into his heart must first pass through the eye or ear. Even the pavement of a church could be made to read a lesson to him who stepped upon it.[64]

But there Gardiner touched upon the attribute which made even Herbert a 'blind mouth' from the perspective of those classed together as puritans. To simplify a startling range of clashing doctrines, the protests against ceremony, against ornament and against music had at their core a charge of idolatry. God did not dwell in painted glass or hymns, any more than he did in the communion host or wine. These were the accessories of papism, and thus their enforcement could be legitimately opposed. Yet the variety and idiosyncrasy of the protests, which now makes it difficult and precarious to speak of 'puritans' as a homogeneous body, at the time made it nigh on impossible to satisfy all of them. John Milton, for example, though a puritan, had no protest to make against music; indeed he later defended it. The divisions between reformed persuasions were minute but crucial. Zwinglians believed that the Eucharist merely commemorated the Lord's last supper, while Calvinists believed in God's spiritual presence at the rite. The idea of Christ's *real* presence in the blood and wine, however, took one back not only to Luther but also Catholicism and the domain of the beast. Politically and civically, nevertheless, it was deemed essential to engineer a Church in which these forces of belief could be contained, and unifying them, Archbishop Laud accepted, would be a long process.

In his determination to do so, however, King Charles himself was blind. He had been dazzled, years before, by the fabulous ceremony he witnessed in court and in chapel at Madrid. His personal art collection broadcast the grandeur of his place in the scheme of the world, and it was only fitting that the Church of England be given its due in magnificent churches with aptly ornamented interiors, its services conducted with proper ceremony, and punctuated with decorous music, despite the expense of realizing this dream. The major restoration project in London was the work carried out on St Paul's, with a new Corinthian portico by Inigo Jones taking slow but splendid if slightly incongruous shape at the cathedral's western end.

There was another, circumstantial form of blindness rife in the land: a failure to see the potential for revolt. This was nowhere more evident than in Scotland, where the senior clergy were ordered to bring their services into line with practice in England. Kneeling during service, the installation of tables at the east end of the church and the hearing of confession were enjoined. The aim was to harmonize the liturgy across Britain, and in Scotland these commands from London were immediately resented. They revived, and newly justified, endemic suspicion of the Stuart episcopacy. No bishops, no king: the bishops, as King James had said quite plainly, were political entities supporting monarchical power, and Charles had continued raising their importance in the state. The canons issued in 1634 had provided fresh food for the grudges nurtured by the Earl of Rothes and other magnates wounded by their treatment at the start of Charles's reign.

Yet the king proceeded, directing his bishops in Scotland to compose a standard prayer book on the model of that used in the English Church. Although accused at his eventual trial of overseeing the project, Archbishop Laud insisted he played no part in writing the prayer book, and indeed his correspondence suggests that he advised his colleagues in Scotland to use delicacy and discretion. This they did, but still with lamentable consequences. The taint of association was indelible: the presbyters smelt the influence of Laud. The phrasing of the prayer book was altered, potentially offensive terms (such as 'priest') were removed, but to the Kirk this only further suggested cynical doctoring, the concealment of dishonest motives.

For Archibald Johnston, now an attorney with a successful Edinburgh practice, remarried, and leading a slightly more stable internal life, the new prayer book was nothing less than 'the image of the beast'. When the book was first presented to a synod of the Kirk at the end of May 1637, he noted with pleasure that 'som gaive ane testimoni to the treuth.' Meanwhile his own zeal had been noticed. A few days later he was visited in his chambers by two of the leading dissenters, David Dickson and John Livingstone, who asked for his advice on what the legal consequences might be of opposing the prayer book.

Two months later, on 23 July, 'that blak doolful Sunday to the Kirk and Kingdome of Scotland', when the Bishop of Edinburgh tried reading from the book at St Giles, the congregation was primed to go berserk. Women at the back of the great church began shrieking, and there was then such 'mourning, rayling, stoolcasting, as the lyk was never seien in Scotland'. Seats were thrown, the bishop narrowly escaped being mobbed, and his carriage was stoned as he made his escape. The dean, Johnston reported, 'was forced to caige himself in the steeple'. This uproar, he observed with sardonic relish, 'in al historie wil be remarqued as the faire, plausible and peaceable wealcome the service book receaved in Scotland'.[65] The mouths of the bishops might be blind, but their eyes would soon be opened.

7. The Court and the Covenant

In Courts and Palaces he also Reigns
And in luxurious Cities, where the noyse
Of riot ascends above thir loftiest Towrs,
And injury and outrage: And when Night
Darkens the Streets, then wander forth the Sons
Of BELIAL, flown with insolence and wine.

— *Paradise Lost*, I

1

Sir Anthony van Dyck set up his London residence and studio in a riverside house in Blackfriars. The king and queen adored him. Charles, admittedly, had been slightly upset that van Dyck had painted his little children in their baby clothes, but for some time nevertheless the artist was accommodated at royal expense; and what the royal couple patronized, their court then coveted. By the late 1630s, van Dyck's work was in such demand that a special technique was needed for saving time in the studio. A session with his subjects would last an hour. The artist would sketch the whole composition in chalk, painting only the head – or heads, in the case of his much-desired group studies – from life, leaving assistants to colour in the figures using substitute models. The production-line approach did not quite satisfy Viscount Wentworth, for one, who insisted the painter saw to the finer details of his portraits personally, yet the end results never displeased: only Archbishop Laud dismissed the splendid portraits – including his own, which he did not commission – as 'vanity shows'.[1]

As such, virtually an entire ruling clique was captured in the idiom of a single artist. We see the dominant personalities of the early Stuart court through van Dyck's perceptive hand, stately yet at ease, relaxing in their finery, the crushes and folds in the fabrics exquisitely observed. Despite the air of privacy, they are rarely introverted, abstracted. They are figures on show, conscious of the viewer's gaze, and usually placed subtly above it.

A full-length portrait cost £50 or £60, a half-length £30, and a head-and-shoulders study £20.[2] Suckling, who sat for van Dyck probably in 1638, requested a full-length study. The studio was only a stroll or short carriage trip from his own room on Fleet Street, and it is likely the poet and artist knew each other well socially. Van Dyck was a close friend of Endymion Porter, with whom he painted himself in a unique double portrait. William Cavendish, Marquis of Newcastle, thought his pictures 'Nature & not Arte'. He had equal praise for the blessings of van Dyck's company and the sweetness of his conversation.[3] An Italian dignitary lodging in St James's Palace was not only breathless with admiration for the great equestrian portrait set up there of the king – his posture in the saddle effortlessly straight, the power of the steed self-evident yet mildly restrained – but full of esteem for the painter himself, 'the Chevalier Van Dyck'.[4]

Van Dyck's lifestyle was in harmony with Suckling's: flamboyant, expansive and spendthrift. Born in 1599, he was in his late thirties when he painted Suckling, thoroughly established in society and the art trade. He began his extended visits to London in the early 1620s, and from 1635 on was based there almost exclusively. He made a significant and lively addition to the culture of clubs and societies, the 'playgrounds for cultured men' into which social life outside the court often devolved. In keeping with it, he founded an English branch of the semi-secretive artists' guild, the *Campagna di San Luca*, 'the St Luke's Club', whose members, the Virtuosi, would meet at the Rose Tavern in Fleet Street.[5]

Van Dyck wore the finest clothes – and habitually a gold chain and feathered hat – and kept a large train of servants. He was a small man, somewhat tense in manner. In self-portraits he showed himself as dishevelled, or looking almost sternly back at the viewer over his shoulder, surprised or disturbed, with a peculiar mixture of self-satisfaction and untraceable agitation in his even, thin and rather handsome features. To Suckling he was the epitome of the enabled, industrious cavalier: active, fashionable yet autonomous. When the poet protested against his uncle Lord Middlesex's retirement, he summoned an image of van Dyck:

considering Middlesex's reclusion, 'I cannot but think it as odd a thing, as if I should see *Van Dike* with all his fine colours and Pensills about him, his Frame, and right Light, and every thing in order, and yet his hands tyed behind him.'[6] Certainly van Dyck worked like one afraid of losing his hands. He was the thrall of his own gifts. Others were struck by how he frequently burst beyond the focus and composure Suckling describes in his studio arrangement, in the enormous energy and appetite he displayed for his art: more than one observer found him frantic to the point of apparent dementia. Others had cause to complain of a vicious turn to his tongue. Almost everyone admiring and paying for his pictures looked away from the signs of a man working himself to death. His health collapsed in 1641, and he died soon afterwards.

He painted Suckling at a time when a symmetry between their destinies began to emerge. Both were bound for self-destruction. Suckling too was entering a period of hyperactivity; less directed, less systematic, but just as profligate with his resources.

Van Dyck was not a flatterer, as some have claimed, but neither was he a warts-and-all portraitist. He made subtle corrections to the sitter in his treatment of Suckling. There is, of course, no sign of the alcoholic complexion Aubrey records – the ringed eyes, the faintly rhinitic nose. Instead the poet gleams, from his blond-brown locks flowing at shoulder-length to the sheen of his metallic blue doublet, his cloak of lurid scarlet scalloped at the edges and fastened on his breast with a golden brooch. Even his boots, with bronze studs on the instep and the shin fastening down the bucket-style tops seem sprinkled with glittering dust. The rich hues of his outfit are set off by the white of his collar and shirtsleeves, and the snow on distant mountains, catching the light of a setting sun.

A portrait can be set forth as a snapshot in paint of a moment, or as the functional imprint, passport-style, of basic physiognomy. Van Dyck's pictures of Caroline gentry and nobles compress everything the subjects wished to see about themselves into the stilled drama of a single image. The division between natural, relaxed posture and artificial pose collapses. They ride, they sit in gently wild landscapes as if in their drawing rooms; their hands pat static yet still strokably real lordly pets. They are not staring blankly, as their forebears did in family portraits, square-set on the canvas, framed by murky oak panels. We do not see only what they looked like, or evidence of their wealth and status, we see what it meant to be them. Van Dyck gave extra depth to their eyes, a touch to suggest that all the external grandeur merely reflects an inner nobility. Of Peter Lely, the German artist who arrived in England during the war, hungry to take van Dyck's vacant place as chief court artist, Richard Lovelace remarked, 'None but my *Lilly* [Lely] ever drew a Minde.'[7] It was a compliment to which van Dyck had the prior and stronger right. As the Marquis of Newcastle did, it is possible to lose the sense of the paintings as physical objects, to see them as 'Nature & not Arte' and to enter into their serene and unthinkingly privileged fiction. In their presence one never thinks of them being knocked out by the dozen in van Dyck's furiously busy Blackfriars studio, or being loaded into wagons like prisoners and carted off to be hung.

2

Suckling stands alone in his portrait, sheltered by a rocky outcrop and leaning on a boulder, on which he rests a copy of a Shakespeare folio, open at *Hamlet*. In normal circumstances the weighty volume would be tortuously balanced, needing him to shift a knee to stop it slipping to the grass, and leaving him with the torn corner of the page he is in the act of turning. But in van Dyck's world, objects obey the requirements of style. The book, despite its obvious mass, has no weight, and at this moment Suckling has forgotten that he is holding it at all. He is steadily gazing, somewhat coldly, at something to his right, beyond his eremitic nook. On a boulder to Suckling's left a motto is inscribed in capitals: *NE TE QUÆSIVERAS EXTRA* ('Do not seek yourself beyond yourself').[8]

Yet the soigné gent who looks so purposefully outwards, declining to return our gaze, has clearly already sought and found himself within and is ready to move on. Despite his symbolic isolation, he does not forget outer things, or fail to project his energy. Unthinkingly, he follows the advice he gave once to his sequestered uncle the Earl of Middlesex, the fallen politician. In his warning to Middlesex that the mind could become lost, trammelled up like a spider in its own cobwebs, Suckling echoed a paragraph written by another ruined lord, whose fall was still more spectacular than Middlesex's. In *The Advancement of Learning*, Francis Bacon wrote of how:

The wit and mind of man, if it work upon matter, which is the contemplation of the creatures of God, worketh according to the stuff, and is limited thereby; but if it work upon itself, as the spider worketh his web, then it is endless, and brings forth cobwebs of learning, admirable for the fineness of thread and work, but of no substance or profit.[9]

Behind Bacon's phrasing was an adage of Erasmus's, with further antecedents still: the idea was rooted deep, in other words, in the intellectual culture of the northern European Renaissance. The passage encourages the reader to look upon the world experimentally and empirically, to emerge from the mazes of artificial (and chiefly Aristotelian) learning. In his letter to Middlesex, Suckling takes Bacon's words as a commonplace and applies them beyond the intellectual context, to the field of more general endeavour. In his portrait, that stance is reinforced by his choice of reading: it is Shakespeare he has taken into his seclusion, a text based on 'nature', no dusty work of abstract philosophy.

The figure in van Dyck's painting of Suckling is presented as a success in these terms. He is a pre-war cavalier, like the 'Chevalier Van Dyck' himself, 'a gallant or gay blade', the predominant meaning of the term in the 1630s, according to the historian Kevin Sharpe, but like van Dyck he is also something more than that.[10] Former ignominies are of course non-existent: there is no trace of the baffled knight crouching on a Midlands road waiting for the blows to stop falling, or the cad avoiding a fair fight by hiring a mob to beat up his rival. The figure shimmering here is the author of a play that is the talk of the town, the realm of fashion to which his impractical garments properly belong.

Already, the previous summer, when Suckling was proving religion by the light of reason, his former commander, Lord Conway, asked Garrard the court gossip to procure a copy of the script. Garrard, who had recounted Suckling's disgrace with such pert relish four years earlier, responded with greater familiarity than he dared show his patron, Lord Deputy Wentworth. 'How doe you think I should gett Sir John Sutlins playbook? 'Tis none of mine. He is going to marry young

Mrs. Whymen, a handsome wench, You have more Use of her then of Playbookes, or bookes.'[11] Nothing came of Suckling's rumoured marriage, but seven months later, in February 1638, *Aglaura* was produced at Blackfriars, 'with much Applause', as Garrard noted in his report to Wentworth. As ever, Garrard was attentive to expense. '*Sutlin's* Play cost three or four hundred Pounds setting out, eight or ten suits of new Cloaths he gave the players; an unheard of Prodigality.'[12]

Suckling had been experimenting with drama for some time. He abandoned his first surviving effort for the stage, *The Sad One*, but found his form in *Aglaura*, naming his heroine after his muse. During the same period he also wrote a tragic-comedy, *The Goblins*, a free adaptation of Shakespeare's *Tempest*, but it was *Aglaura* that he chose to produce first. Davenant had abandoned high-flown tragedy in the early 1630s, but Suckling evidently felt the genre needed him. The scene is Sicily, after a civil war. The king is perched uncertainly on his throne. The murder of a father awaits vengeance. Numerous courtiers crave power. The king's son is in love with Aglaura, and she with him, but the king desires her too, and means to have her. The principal revenger is sleeping with the queen, but she is in love with another – who happens to be one of his enemies. All is ready for much confusion and multiple killings, through simple stabbings and ingenious poisoned boxes.

As theatre, the piece's repartee and asides are stronger than its main action or set-piece speeches. Richard Flecknoe, a roaming courtly entertainer, later observed that *Aglaura* was 'full of fine flowers, but they seemed rather stuck than growing there'. Those flowers carry for all that a true scent of the sort of exchanges made at court – or the sort of exchanges courtiers liked to think they made.[13] In a big early hunting scene, the hunters' 'whooping and bellowing' is vibrantly put across. There is nice wit when one lord is thrown from his steed:

'. . . the ground was as hard, as if it had been pav'd with Platonicke Ladies hearts, and this unconscionable fellow askes whether I have no hurt; where's my horse?'
'Making love to the next mare, I thinke.'[14]

There are also suggestive glimpses of how gentlemen of leisure saw their lives and passed their time. It would be worth knowing if the following lines were censored when Henrietta Maria watched the play:

''Tis early yet; let's goe on the Queens side and foole a little; I love to warme my selfe before I go to bed, it does beget handsome and sprightly thoughts, and makes our dreames halfe solid pleasures.'

'Agreed: agreed.'[15]

Like a grandee planning a new chateau or pleasure-garden, Suckling put great energy and care into structuring and laying out the world of his fiction, down to the secret passage, in the rambling Romantic palace, by which Aglaura's lover is to escape:

> Here in these lodgings is a little doore,
> That leads unto another; that againe,
> Unto a vault, that has his passage under
> The little river, opening into the wood;
> From thence 'tis but some few minutes easie journey
> Unto a Servants house of mine (who for his faith
> And honestie, hereafter must
> Look big in Storie); there you are safe however. [16]

Yet the one truly remarkable thing about the play is its inbuilt comment on the provisional nature of genre itself. *Aglaura*, albeit not with total success, is both a hybrid and a quantum work of literature, existing in two alternative states. In its first version, performed at Blackfriars, the drama ends tragically, when Aglaura accidentally stilettos her lover the prince, mistaking him for his lecherous father, and then herself dies of shock and grief. In the second, performed before the king and queen in the Cockpit Theatre on 3 April 1638, it ends happily, relatively speaking, thanks to an alternative fifth act, in which major characters undergo psychic transformation instead of bloody deaths:

> 'Tis strange perchance (you'll thinke) that shee that di'de
> At Christmas, should at Easter be a Bride:
> But 'tis a privilege the Poets have
> To take the long-since dead out of the grave.[17]

As a whole, the piece seemed to be asking for the preservation of a fantasy: that no outcome is irrevocable, nothing that a little rewriting, or a little extra expense, cannot redress. It is surprising, when you consider the manner in which he manipulates his heroine, to recall the ladies who later competed for the title of Suckling's real-life Aglaura. Notwithstanding the attraction of being the lady yearned for, fought over and died for, she and the feelings connected with her are manifestly artificial. Less than a character, she is a construct, a property, to be used in one sort of play and then another.

As Garrard observed, *Aglaura* was sumptuously produced. 'When his *Aglaura* was acted he brought all the clothes himself,' John Aubrey noted, 'which were very rich; no tinsel, all the lace pure gold and silver, which cost him . . . I have now forgotten. He had some scenes [scenery] to it, which in those days were only used at masques.'[18] Suckling was being more than extravagant. There was a touch of audacity, bordering on impropriety, to his showmanship. He had brought to the theatre trappings normally found only in the most regal productions. The rocky backdrop in van Dyck's portrait of Suckling has reminded some scholars of sketches which Inigo Jones is often thought to have made for *Aglaura*. If so, Suckling had certainly magnified the dignity of his drama, but had implicitly diluted the theatre of majesty.

He could be judged by his own remarks. In September 1630, Lord Middlesex had running water installed in his grand house at Wiston. Middlesex's engineer, Sir John Lawrence, drew the water from a neighbouring stream into the mansion's 'brew-house', 'where it runs bravely into the furnace, and there is a brewing made with that water'. Lawrence then piped it into Wiston's stables, 'into a leaden troughe by the stable dore, for the horses to drink of the pure fountayne'.[19] It was the type of innovation so often brought in across the kingdom by the Caroline gentry and nobility, often to the dismay of neighbours and local communities. There is little mention in the records of the folk of Wiston deprived of their stream. Yet to celebrate the feat of technology, Suckling not only wrote Lawrence a commendatory poem ('And is the Water Come?') but also, it would seem, a simple masque taking the river as its central feature. Suckling's script is lost, but his prologue survived. In it, as we saw in the last chapter, he warned his audience not to expect the sort of show one saw at court: ''tis for Kings,/ Not for their Subjects, to have such rare things.'[20]

In the early months of 1638 Suckling broke his own word on that matter. In his letter to Wentworth about *Aglaura*, Garrard describes Suckling, confusingly, as one of the 'King's Servants', a 'Privy-Chamber man'. If the record is correct, he was getting slightly ahead of Suckling's actual progress at court. It is true that Suckling was made a Gentleman of the Privy Chamber Extraordinary at the end of 1638, on 20 November; but he clearly saw himself as being sufficiently elevated already to appropriate some royal stage devices. That he was able to do so without rebuke suggests he stood high enough in royal favour, and is another sign that, despite appearances, the king had a sense of humour. But the impression created was odd. The affects of majesty were spreading downwards. Simultaneously, the least salubrious of gentlemen appeared to be crawling ever upwards. Suckling's gambling, his womanizing, his alleged cowardice, were not forgotten by all.

The liberty taken with the staging of *Aglaura* looks especially strange given the king and queen's simultaneous decision to treat one another to a masque again. The royal masque had fallen out of custom for the previous three years, while a new performance space was constructed, and also possibly to let the acrimony of Jonson's feud with Jones die down. A long-term partner was needed to write the speeches and songs for Jones's technical miracles. The choice, when it was made, would effectively settle the question of who would succeed Ben Jonson as laureate. For some time the royals had commissioned a different poet for each masque, but that made successful collaboration more than slightly dependent on luck. Thomas Carew's text appears to have been too accomplished for Jones to have offered him a permanent partnership – had Carew even been interested in so much work. A strong candidate was Thomas May, glimpsed in Suckling's 'Sessions', whom King Charles once defended as '*his* poet'; but May's credentials were suspect. His translation of Lucan, made during the 1620s, had more than a whiff of anti-monarchism to it (ideas which resurfaced at the outset of the civil war). Instead, Davenant was asked to write both masques in 1638. He celebrated by having his portrait made too, although by a lesser artist than van Dyck, the English painter John Greenhill. While the original painting has not survived, copies (such as the frontispiece to Davenant's folio of *Works*) show the poet wearing laurels, with dark, shoulder-length hair. He has a heavy, roundish face, and the artist has been kinder to his nose than the wits ever were. It looks blurred, smudged on his face, rather than wholly destroyed.

The masques could no longer be performed in Inigo Jones's beautiful white Banqueting House. The celebrated and long-awaited series of paintings by Rubens, depicting the Stuart version of the Stuart monarchy, could not be put at risk of damage from theatricals, either from candle smoke or the heaving about of flats and machinery. The precious canvasses had lain a great time in storage while the Crown sought the thousands required to pay the artist, plus a weighty gold chain as a special gift. Rubens had been a darling of English art collectors for many years. 'I cannot subscribe your denial of being a Prince,' wrote Ambassador Carleton, Carew's old master, to Rubens in a charming yet typical exchange of letters in 1618, 'because I esteem you the Prince of Painters and of Gentlemen, and to that end I kiss your hands.'[21] The delay in shipping the precious Banqueting House canvasses had grievously embarrassed the English agents commissioned with handling them. Their French and Spanish counterparts laughed malignly at the poverty of King Charles. No possibility could therefore be allowed of the huge political dream those pictures captured coming to harm.

So instead Charles had built a temporary venue beside the Banqueting House. He was contemplating a vast new palace on Castilian scale, designed of course by Jones, in which a permanent structure would presumably have been incorporated. As it was, 'the greate new MASKING ROOME ATT WHITEHALL' had a more rustic feel to it. Inside, paradoxically, it must have seemed closer to the kind of rural mansion at which the truly 'rare things' of masque were normally not to be seen. Standing closer to the river, it was a 'room of timber', more than a hundred feet long and almost sixty wide, slightly larger than the Banqueting House itself, with rough brick outer walls and a roof of pantiles supported by twelve massive buttresses of fir. Timbers of fir also framed the chamber's twenty windows. The new masquing hall was a cross between a palace gallery, a hunting lodge and an Anglo-Saxon hall of old.

The Christmas masque, presented by the king, was called *Britannia Triumphans*. Set in the distant past, the great King Britanocles, 'the glory of the western world' (i.e. Charles, who took the role), is clearing the seas of pirates and bringing peace and enlightenment to his ancient kingdom:

So well *Britanocles* o're seas doth Raigne,
Reducing what was wild before,
That fairest sea-Nymphs leave the troubled maine,
And haste to visit him on the shore.[22]

An opening view of contemporary London is succeeded by the scene of a 'horrid hell', a cave where Merlin the magician summons the demonic (and occasionally comic) minions of antimasque. The segue is more than faintly controversial. The initial prospect of London could be taken as indicating that what was to follow would be an allegory of the current state of the realm, as the subsequent references to piracy and coastal policing duly confirm. Yet the masque-makers give the impression that Caroline London is represented, more specifically, by the image which immediately succeeds it of Merlin's horrid den. In due course, though, the motley crew of rebels, bandits and menials vanishes; a shining palace rises into view, and the masque proper begins. Invoked by Fame, flanked by fourteen lords, Charles makes his entrance as Britanocles, dancing to a chorus of poets.

3

Britannia Triumphans gives its own version of political reality, but does not blot it out. The campaign against pirates alludes to Charles's highly unpopular levy of 'ship money'. The masque sets out to justify the policy symbolically, concluding with the sight of a huge fleet calmly entering a haven. The choice of theme was a risky one. Instead of praising the lasting peace, Jones and Davenant hit upon the topic in which even the staunchest sycophants found the king blameworthy. This was regardless of the fact that ship money as a means of raising funds was expedient and efficient: it was channelled directly into the navy, relieving coastal regions of sole responsibility for funding defence. Its unpopularity even at court may have had a lot to do with the fact that, while constitutionally dubious, it was not exacted corruptly. Justices of the Peace collected the levy and handed it over to their county's sheriff, who then passed it directly to the Admiralty, with little loss on the way. At first the levy of ship money was blamed on the man credited with thinking of it, Charles's Attorney General William Noy. When Noy died in 1635, James Howell had interpreted his physical condition at death as a judgement on his character. 'Master Attorney-General *Noy*, is lately dead, nor could Tunbridge Waters do him any good: though he had good *matter* in his brain, he had, it seems, ill *materials* in his *body*; for his heart was shrivelled like a leather penny-purse when he was dissected, nor were his lungs sound.'[23] Good intellect, in other words, yet a rotten heart. Two, three years on, however, ship money was still being charged, was more widely detested than ever; and it could only be identified with the king and his closest councillors.

Further trouble was stirred when one landowner led a group of non-payers in mounting a direct challenge to the tax. John Hampden of Great Missenden refused to pay the twenty shillings due on his property in Buckinghamshire. He chose Oliver St John, legal adviser to the Providence Company, to represent him in the Exchequer Court. St John until then had been little known but was deeply read in constitutional law and made a powerful case. He argued that if the king could raise taxes as he wished, without recourse to Parliament, he then had de facto rights over all his subjects' assets. Ship money was required to protect the state from imminent peril; but where did the danger lie? England, as the king so often boasted, was enjoying a long peace. The precedents St John cited and the statutes he drew on troubled the judges who heard the case during Michaelmas 1637: his arguments, followed intently by a public almost bewitched by their interest in litigious matters, stirred questions about the liberties of subjects, the extent of their duty to obey their king, and of the monarch's prerogative over the law. The judges began issuing their verdicts in February 1638. In the end they decided against Hampden by a narrow majority. That narrowness, in truth, reflected their professional integrity, rather than a moral victory for the dissenting cause. The writs issued to Hampden for payment proved technically flawed, leaving five of the twelve no choice but to find in his favour. In principle, almost all of them approved the king's feudal right to raise revenue independently when the defence of the realm was at stake. More precisely, it had been shown that ship money was not a tax by the king on his subjects, but a service, the provision of a ship or a payment in lieu.[24] Yet a much blunter phrase from the trial would stick in the memory. 'Rex is lex,' ruled Justice Sir Robert Berkeley on 10 February: the king *is* the law, 'a living, a speaking, an acting law'.[25]

That was something of a shame, since the tenacity and complexity of legal reasoning in the case was generally admired, even by those upset by the verdict, as being 'full of rare and excellent learning'.[26] Good argument in law required fine wit, and it was no accident that most of the city's scribblers, full time or amateur, were alumni of the Inns of Court or legal autodidacts.

On reflection, one of the century's most noted thinkers came to consider these arguments beside the point. A scholar, translator, natural philosopher and geometrician, servant and client of both the 'Newcastle' and 'Devonshire' branches of the wealthy and influential Cavendish family, Thomas Hobbes of Malmesbury at that time had yet to discover the 'civil science' by which he made his name. But in collecting money in Derbyshire for the Forced Loan of 1627, he had already seen that the available methods of filling the Exchequer were inadequate when Parliament knotted its purse-strings. In his post-war masterwork, *Leviathan*, Hobbes analysed the source of the problem. Citing the 'late small revenue of the Crown' and alluding to the resultant acrimony, he argued that it was futile to protest when the sovereign ordered the coffers to be replenished. One of his more hair-raising points, so far as the protesters of the 1630s were concerned, was that a sovereign had absolute rights over private treasure as circumstance and the public need dictated. It was unwise to think of allocating a certain fund or amount of property to the sovereign: Hobbes observed that sovereigns would always overspend, and their expenditure would always be driven up by war or calamity. In a passage which obliviously bypasses our contemporary preoccupation with the public and private realms of economic life, he further claimed that:

Common-wealths can endure no Diet: for seeing their expence is not limited by their own appetite, but by externall Accidents, and the appetites of their neighbours, the Publique Riches cannot be limited by other limits, than those which the emergent occasions shall require.

In the Hobbesian analysis, the king's opponents over ship money, like Sir John Eliot and their other champions in the wild parliaments of the late 1620s, were mistaking the nature of their 'covenant' with the sovereign. They had, it was true, absolute rights over person and property with respect to one another. As sovereign, it was their king's duty to safeguard those rights. Indeed as soon as he failed to do so, in *Leviathan*'s tough political thesis, his subjects were free to dispense with him. But with respect to the sovereign himself, what was theirs, was Leviathan's: the question – no small one, admittedly – was how the share each offered up was to be determined proportionately. Yet when subjects began stipulating to their sovereign that 'so much is yours; make what you can of it', fencing off private capital from control of the sovereign and state, they began dealing with him not as their sovereign but simply as a more powerful subject, one among equals. And with that, as Hobbes deduced from the sorry tale of the 1640s, they moved towards 'the dissolution of Government, and to the condition of meere Nature, and War'.[27]

The idea is one of the lesser known and less predictable permutations of his famous argument; but that argument frequently did take both him and his readers in surprising directions. Hobbes thought it right, for example, that the sovereign monitor the goods merchants brought into the Commonwealth and forbid the import of useless or immoral junk – 'such things, as pleasing mens appetites, be nevertheless noxious, or at least unprofitable to them.'[28] His eye here would seem to be on the frivolous toys and pursuits on which characters such as Suckling wasted their income.

The progress of the ship money trial, and the anxiety surrounding it, did not disturb the course of the year's productions. Queen Henrietta's masque for Charles, *Luminalia*, featured some of Inigo Jones's most exquisite scenic effects. The argument of the masque was based upon a contest between darkness and light, with Henrietta herself appearing as a personification of Day, effacing the agents of Night with which the performance opens. 'Where is the sun?' debate Aurora and Hesperus, as Hecat dominates the stage in an owl-drawn chariot. Moonlit discussion then gives way to a burst of sheer radiance when the queen is presented, in the midst of a group of ladies dressed in splendour. The masque ends with a dance of sprites on a blazing cloud.

Luminalia: the masque encapsulated the queen's court's artistic preoccupation with the luminous, the iridescent. Henrietta Maria's effect on the imagination was stronger than reality, Davenant claimed. Only she could make London bearable. In one of his most elaborate compliments for the queen, published the year *Luminalia* was staged, he took his town to task for walking in 'mists of Sea-coale smoake' and poisoning the 'ever teeming Wives' who lived there. But when the queen was in residence, the sun came out, and buds unfolded their 'chary' leaves. He criticized London for relying on Henrietta Maria in this way, and thus failing in its duty to be beautiful.[29] Where would they all be without her?

The strategy of lauding a superior through the comedy of bossing about an imaginary inferior (and thus appearing as a puckish sort of poetic foreman in the process) was one Davenant used quite often. He drew on it, for example, in hustling various fairy-like beings to fetch fitting new-year gifts for Olivia Porter, wife of Endymion:

> Goe! Hunt the whiter Ermine! and present
> His wealthy skin, as this dayes Tribute sent
> To my *Endimions* Love; though she be farre
> More gently smooth, more soft than Ermines are!
> Goe! climbe that Rock! and when thou there hast found
> A Starre, contracted in a Diamond,
> Give it *Endimions* Love; whose glorious Eyes
> Darken the Starry Jewells of the Skies![30]

With so many bright eyes dazzling the skies above England, light pollution must have been a problem even in those days. Yet on this form it is easy to see how Davenant recommended himself as laureate, in return for the few 'twigs of bay' the informal post afforded, taking his task with comic seriousness. The two poems mentioned here are taken from a collection he published in his hectically creative year of 1638, one of the decade's finest and latterly most neglected books of poetry.

4

The readers of *Madagascar, With Other Poems* could follow the ordeals of their author from his syphilitic scare through to his rise as poetic doyen, calmly and courteously addressing Caroline grandees. The book's dedication was split between two close patrons, one being Davenant's old 'preserver' Endymion Porter, who was pressed to contribute some lines for the prefatory pages. Rather ably, Porter protested incapacity:

> If hee did know, but with what pains I make
> A Verse, hee'ld pittie then my wretched case;
> For at the birth of each, I twist my Face
> As if I drew a Tooth; I blot, and write,
> Then look as pale as some that goe to fight.[31]

Porter was strictly an occasional poet, but was more competent a maker than he has generally been credited as being: his other notable effort was an elegy which joined the group at the front of Donne's collected poems.

The co-dedicatee of Davenant's collection was a courtier with a chequered past. Flamboyant, artful Henry Jermyn, in his early thirties and the prime of life, had only returned from banishment in France in 1636. He was a bilingual Francophile – his father was governor of Jersey – and had been close to the queen since being appointed to her household in 1627. It was Henrietta Maria's patient pressure on her husband which brought Jermyn back from exile; and it was their intimacy, some thought, that had helped her come to terms with her English home. He was reputed the 'stallion' of the court, a heavy-set charmer. In future decades, after the ordeals of war, when he was 'full of soup and gold', Andrew Marvell pictured him heavy and concupiscent, 'with draymans shoulders, butchers mien/ Member'd like Mules, with Elephantine chine'.[32] Before his bulk went to fat, he deported it seductively; even afterwards, as Marvell said scathingly, he remained the 'pattern' of what was meant at court by elegance.

The story was told of a night in the palace when Thomas Carew was lighting the king's way to Henrietta Maria's bedroom. Leading the way, in the shadows of the chamber Carew saw Jermyn fumbling with the queen, 'his arm round her neck', and made a swift political decision in no less time than the instant it took to fake a stumble and extinguish his lamp. The king, benighted behind him, saw nothing. Jermyn slipped away through an adjoining door. 'Carew never told the King, and the King never knew it,' a gossipy old cove reported in his notebook. 'The Queen heaped favours on Carew.' As many have noted since, the source is unreliable: on the same page of the manuscript, the writer notes that 'Milton, the poet, died a Papist.'[33] Carew's favours also came mainly from King Charles, in whose household he served. Yet the anecdote illustrates how the queen's relationship with Jermyn was perceived.

Along with Porter, Jermyn features in a number of poems in *Madagascar*, styled heroically as 'Arigo' by Davenant. *Madagascar* itself was a diverse collection, holding songs, urban satire, as well as graceful panegyric verse of the kind sampled above. There was variety to be found within individual pieces as well as between them. In his elegant homage to Davenant, Carew mused on the propriety of the mixture of genres to be found in the book's title poem:

> What though Romances lye
> Thus blended with more faithfull Historie?
> Wee, of th'adulterate mixture not complaine,
> But thence more characters of Vertue gaine;
> More pregnant Patterns of transcendent worth
> Than barren and insipid Truth brings forth.[34]

Typically, Carew made a fairly conventional point and then took it to its extreme. It was one that had troubled students of eloquence since antiquity. They did not recognize a split between 'fiction' and 'non-fiction'. They saw different kinds of writing, rather, as fulfilling separate formal and moral requirements, and different kinds of reasoning as meeting different standards of proof. Thus, as Carew asked, was it acceptable to write of real events in a manner suitable for 'romance'? As it turned out, Davenant had placed actual living figures in what proved to be a fiction.

His poem 'Madagascar' reminded its readers in 1638 of a visit paid two years before by England's current European talisman. Prince Rupert, younger son of the late Palsgrave, the exiled elector Frederick, was to be the most volatile and inspired commander of the royalist forces in the 1640s, modelling his cavalry manoeuvres on those of Gustavus Adolphus. Yet in 1636, when visiting England with his more sullen, introverted elder brother, Charles Louis, still technically heir to the family's lost title in the Palatinate, Rupert was already the future hope of the anti-imperial cause at court. Manifestly, great things were awaiting him, notwithstanding the unpropitious start he and his brother made to their English visit. When the king's ships gave a volley to salute their flotilla off Dover, a stray cannonball nicked the Palsgrave's flagship and killed four of his servants.[35]

A superb horseman and cadet, a keen student of war, nearly six foot tall and only seventeen years old, Rupert was a prodigy: not only a soldier and athlete but also an accomplished musician since childhood, a mathematician of great talent and a scholar who had impressed the dons on a visit to Oxford. Charles Louis, a year his senior, was reasonably content to slink and quietly canvass support in palace alcoves, but Rupert was hungry to prove himself. His mother, the king's sister Elizabeth, had a secure place in the English public's affection. Few would begrudge her the annual pension of £20,000 Charles paid her, and most called foul in the years when he could not supply it. The old national craving for heroes was as strong as ever, and in Rupert people recognized one 'of a rare condition, full of spirit and action . . . whatever he wills, he wills vehemently'.[36]

A project was clearly required to direct and sharpen his energies. He responded with typical readiness when English prospectors suggested he lead a mission to claim Madagascar for the Crown. Thomas Howard, Earl of Arundel, was to be the patron of the expedition; the court's hardiest traveller, Endymion Porter, was to be Rupert's chief attendant.

Rupert's father Frederick had died a sorry man in 1632. One of fourteen children, Rupert had been left largely to his own devices growing up, almost overlooked on account of the continent of violence surrounding his family in its refuge at The Hague. In the narrow escape from Spanish forces at Prague in 1620, the infant Rupert was very nearly forgotten. By 1636, his widowed mother found more solace in her pet dogs and monkeys than in her children, but while keeping her son at a distance surveilled his movements closely. She worried that Queen Henrietta would turn him and his brother Catholic. Accepting that he would either be the saviour or the martyr of the family cause, she was not prepared to waste him. 'I am sure you know the Romance some would put into Ruperts head of Conquering Madagascar,' she wrote to one of her confidants, 'when he shall Don Quixotte-like conquer that famous island, but in ernest seek to put such windmills out of his head.'[37] She wrote to Rupert herself to put an end to the matter.

The idea provoked much interest, however, since it was thought that whichever nation held Madagascar could thereby control all of India: the plan, such as it was, jogged Davenant's imagination, not so much as an endeavour as an outing. The result was a poem of four hundred lines, evidently presented earlier but not printed until 1638.

By 1638 the Madagascar scheme had been shelved, but to the poet sending his soul forth from its 'narrow mansion', overseas to the southern hemisphere, it retained all its charm, providing an occasion for compliment, mock-heroic narration and a revealing reflection on the origins of imperialism. Floating to a point 'betweene the Southern *Tropick* and the *Line*' and alighting on a crystal rock, the poet sees Prince Rupert landing with a troop of 'advent'rous Youth'. All are possessed of 'one lib'rall mind', which the indigenous people of Madagascar recognize at first sight. Enchanted by Rupert's transmission of his mother's beauty, they hang up their bows on the surrounding olive trees, and bow to Rupert's majesty.[38]

The pleasantries are then disturbed by the beating of a drum and the arrival of a Spanish fleet to challenge English dominion. Davenant devotes a page to describing the conquistadors, who quickly land and crowd the shore with a huge army. Whereas Rupert's force is represented as an embassy or even an investigative expedition bearing goodwill and opportunity for the indigenous people, in number and manner the Spaniards have a locust-like, industrious aggression, blotting out the landscape they have set about devouring. They seek to make their imperial rule as universal across the globe as sunlight:

> For they believe their Monarch hath subdu'd
> Already such a spacious latitude,
> That sure, the good old Planet's bus'nesse is
> Of late, only to visit what is his.[39]

The armies face one another, in Homeric fashion, on the beach, with the bully of the case ripe for a fall.

The scene triggers the memory of a younger Davenant, the tragedian whose nationalism was more plainspoken, supporting wholeheartedly Buckingham's wars against France and Spain, and offering his services for a mission to blow up the citadel at Calais. Yet however easily anti-Hispanic sentiment may have vented from English pens, the fictional episode on the Madagascan beach could never have been officially condoned in the pacific climate of the early 1630s. Yet since 1635, when the war in Germany was quelled by the Peace of Prague, foreign policy had followed another direction.

The Peace ended the conflict between Emperor Ferdinand and his chief German opponent, John George of Saxony, who laid down his arms in return for Ferdinand rescinding the Edict of Restitution. No provision was made, however, for restoring the Palatinate to Charles Louis. An incestuous match between the emperor's daughter and her uncle the Duke of Bavaria, the possessor of the Palatinate in the new status quo, cut Count Frederick's sons out of succession. It was the renewed despair this prompted that brought the brothers Charles Louis and Rupert to England calling for aid, late in 1635. Spain, which had played a part in brokering the treaty, could no longer be trusted: King Charles had been considering a maritime treaty with the Spanish, but negotiations fell through. In the meantime, moreover, England had once more begun to appear significant, potentially at least, as a military power. The country's new fleet grew further, as ship money was extended to the inland regions of the kingdom. The Spanish, as so often before, made deceptive bids for closer ties with England, and suggested fanciful plans for recovering the lost lands of Princess Elizabeth's children. France and the Dutch Republic, meanwhile, were much more genuine in their pursuit of a naval alliance. Cardinal Richelieu's long-standing policy of undermining Spanish and Austrian hegemony had resulted in direct intervention, cutting off Spanish supply lines in Italy and then, late in 1634, sending men to cross the Rhine. By early 1635 it was a French army occupying the Palatinate, with a formal declaration of war against Spain in May.

Against this mutable international background, Davenant's 'Madagascar' is an illustration in negative of British failure to act, and also the sheer difficulty of doing otherwise. It is about a mission never pursued, and a confrontation which never took place. Almost any move in Europe seemed a wrong one: despite the grudge against Spain, too close an entente with the French, who were building up influence in both Germany and the Low Countries, also seemed out of the question. Complete withdrawal was no option either, rationally or emotionally: French and

Dutch ships scratched the paintwork of English pride by treating the seas, and occasionally the south coast itself, as their own. The Madagascar expedition, and Davenant's cordial poem about it, reflect an otherwise barely stated desire for a clear horizon, an escape from the congestion. In his poem, Davenant was moved to meditate on the shortage of room.

Firstly, to decide the contest, each army sends two champions to a duel. 'Endymion' (Porter) and 'Arigo' (Jermyn) comprise the unlikely duo Davenant selects for the English cause. When this fails (despite their valour) to resolve matters, battle is joined. Amid the fury, Davenant tells Rupert, 'I saw thy Uncles anger in thy brow.'[40] Charles's symbolic presence is invoked and felt throughout: at sea, Rupert bears the trident of Britanocles, which transforms into a sceptre the moment he touches dry land.

As the battle continues, the poet is lost in thought for a time, contemplating the nature of colonial enterprise itself. He is candid about its motives and surprisingly tepid in his support for them. He traces the problem to the shrinking size of the world relative to its growing population. In this, the most interesting passage of the poem, Davenant writes of how Adam could never have anticipated the most compelling argument for death: the shortage of habitable space on earth. In Adam's day, Eden was nothing but a '*Privie-garden*'; now it would be deemed a 'spacious Country'. To the first man, islands in the sea were nothing but hills in his moat:

> Parts and divisions were computed small,
> When rated by his measure that had all.[41]

By now, of course, that had changed: 'each Couple is become a Throng,' and as people ran out of space and resources, they sought more beyond the seas. Davenant recognizes that the rights and claims of colonists are wholly arbitrary. Yet the prevailing argument, he says, is necessity:

> Not that Man's nature is averse from peace;
> But all are wisely jealous of increase:
> For Eaters grow so fast, that wee must drive

> Our friends away to keepe our selves alive:
> And Warr would be lesse needful, if to die
> Had bin as pleasant as to multiplie.[42]

This is Davenant's view of paradise lost. There is no sense, however, that Davenant *prefers* the prelapsarian state of Adam above the exciting turbulence of his own time, despite the disadvantages. Eden is merely vacant, spacious, and thus boring; socially dead. The scar of original sin does not twinge strongly in Davenant. The problem for the present is one of human numbers.

His reasoning better describes the condition of a post-modern world nearing economic and environmental exhaustion than the still quite sparsely populated state of seventeenth-century Europe. The Continental congestion was political – too many states aspired to pre-eminence. This is not to say that there were not arguments prompted from basic want: but the proto-imperialists were not driven by concern for houseless heads and unfed sides. The real need lay with power. Only an overfed, over-abundant economy could hold up against its European rivals. Notwithstanding the economic facts of declining wages and inconstant supplies of corn, the interest in potential colonies such as Madagascar lay more with an insatiable English appetite for luxury imported goods and materials; the sort of gorgeous materials and accessories to be seen so vividly, in fact, adorning the land's great and good in van Dyck's portraits. Those senior court figures might have been the role models, but the demand for such fabrics and other precious things was far from confined to them. The lower-middle-class crowds thronging the arcades and pressing at the windows of London's New Exchange attested to that. Even the labouring poor were prepared to work longer, as wages fell or fluctuated, for small domestic luxuries – smarter clothes, better kitchenware, more furniture.[43]

Thus Davenant's 'Madagascar' is not overly concerned with assessing the farmland, water supply, or sites for habitation. Instead of reasoning the need, he looks for sources of lucrative trade. The poem is plump with observations of colonial swag; from pearls too heavy for flimsy divers to lift, to 'black suds' of ambergris washing up on the beach; from diamonds that would eclipse a sultan's treasury, to the wares of silkworms – always James I's favourite natural manufacturers.

The 'silken litel Weavers' of Madagascar excel by far those of the Middle East:

> The Persian worme (whose weary sommer toyles
> So long hath beene the rustling Courtiers spoyles)
> Compared to these, lives ever lazily.

The eye of Davenant's poem bears comparison with that of Comus, the villain of Milton's masque at Ludlow Castle. Comus famously sees his environment as pure resource, existing to be exploited, and asks his captive lady why else 'did Nature pour her bounties forth':

> And set to work millions of spinning Worms,
> That in their green shops weave the smooth-hair'd silk
> To deck her Sons . . . ?[44]

It is instructive that while Milton's descriptive energy concentrates on the silkworms themselves, and the natural texture of the 'smooth-haired silk', Davenant transfers his attention to the 'sons' for whom the end product is destined, 'the rustling Courtiers'. Yet whereas Davenant sees a world at capacity, struggling to provide for everyone, Comus thinks the earth would be 'cumber'd' and Nature 'strangled with her waste fertility' should humans stop reaping, slaughtering and mining her wealth.[45] Davenant's argument, despite its realist modesty, is the more disingenuous, and the more harmful in its implications. In Comus's over-abundant world, where rocks would buckle with the weight of gems, and herds would 'over-multitude their lords', expansionist tendencies are redundant; there is no need to fight over bounty lying everywhere. On Davenant's diminishing earth, colonial expeditions are vital to the survival of the species.

There was another way of viewing the situation, put forward stoutly by the Lady prisoner, in rebuttal to Comus, chastising the courtiers in the audience at Ludlow and the subsequent course of British history:

> If every just man that now pines with want
> Had but a moderate and beseeming share
> Of that which lewdly-pamper'd Luxury

> Now heaps upon som few with vast excess,
> Nature's full blessings would be well-dispensed
> In unsuperfluous even proportion.[46]

Nothing much could be further from necessity than an English colony in Madagascar or other similarly exotic locations; yet Davenant would prove to be among the majority for several centuries in believing there was no choice.

The poet's thoughts on Adam and the earth come in a day-dream parenthesis. He asks his prince's forgiveness for losing sight, for a moment, of the carnage on the shore, where the streams are running red with Spanish blood and Rupert is 'as weary growne to kill, as they to die'.[47] With the day won, Davenant concludes his poem with a radiant vision of the riches Rupert has secured for Britain, and adorns him with laurels. In return, he asks only for 'a little sprig of Bay,/ To weare in Greece on *Homers* holy day'.[48]

Two years after the fantasy was dropped, his friends observed that Davenant had thus achieved in verse what their masters had failed to make reality. 'When I behold, by warrant from thy Pen,' wrote Carew generously, 'a Prince rigging our Fleets, arming our Men . . . [I] thinke thy Poem may/ Impose upon Posteritie.' Suckling was cheekier:

> What mighty Princes Poets are! those things
> The great ones stick at, and our very Kings
> Lay downe, they venter on; and with great ease,
> Discover, conquer, what, and where they please.

He only asked that Will on his next return, 'fraught with laurel', should 'bring the Gold with thee too'.[49]

The first readers of *Madagascar* were shortly depressed by another disparity between the worlds of history and romance. By the close of 1638 the inspiration for Davenant's imperial rhapsody was being held fast prisoner. Trusting too much to valour and fortune, Rupert and his brother landed a small force on the German coast near Bremen. They were trapped by imperial troops on the River Weser near Vlotho, and while Charles Louis managed to slip away, Rupert was captured, and transported to the fortress at Linz on the Danube.

5

Suckling praised Davenant as the heir of Donne, writing 'so neere him, in's owne way'. But Davenant had little of Donne's intricate introspection, his layered textuality, although his learning has been underrated. His work, especially his songs, aimed at plainness, clearness, a line that recommended itself to a melody. Among the lyrics not published in *Madagascar* but probably belonging to this period is one of Davenant's finest miniatures, 'The Lark Now Leaves his Watry Nest', which was set by William Lawes. The simplicity of this aubade is in its way as remarkable as any Donnean triumph of paradox. It has narrative and argument, and a touch of magic in the little shake the lark gives his 'dewy wings' before ascent, only to be diverted by the light of a lady opening her curtains, the lady the poem addresses:

> Awake, awake, the Morn will never rise,
> Till she can dress her Beauty at your Eies.[50]

Davenant brought the same bright energy to any subject, any register. In his play *News from Plymouth*, as Douglas Bush observed many years ago, he seems to have parodied his own dawn-song:

> O Thou that sleep'st like *Pigg* in Straw,
> Thou *Lady* dear, arise;
> Open (to keep the *Sun* in awe)
> Thy pretty pinking eyes:
> And having stretcht each Leg and Arme,
> Put on your cleane white Smock.[51]

Captain Topsail's ode for Lady Loveright, heard by audiences in the summer of 1635, belonged to Blackfriars or the Cockpit, while the context for the songs of Davenant and his friends, or the lyrics sent up at intervals to Endymion Porter by Robert Herrick, is likely to have been informal music evenings in the homes of courtiers and royal servants, of the sort which Lucy Hutchinson describes her husband attending in the mid- to late 1630s. John Hutchinson, although a puritan, had no aversion to soirees which in only a few years' time could be misrepresented in memory as 'cavalier' gatherings. Like many of the men assembling on such occasions, regardless of their religious convictions, he sported 'lovelocks': his future wife, Lucy, admired his fine head of fashionably long hair.

Hutchinson frequented the house of John Coleman in Richmond, 'where he found a great deal of good young company'. Coleman, like the Lawes brothers, composed music for the royal court, and:

the King's musicians often met at his house to practise new airs and prepare them for the King; and divers of the gentlemen and ladies that were affected with music, came thither to hear; others that were not, took that pretence to entertain themselves with the company. Mr Hutchinson was soon courted into their acquaintance and invited to their houses, where he was nobly treated, with all the attractive arts that young women and their parents use to procure them lovers.[52]

It was at Coleman's house one day that Hutchinson came across a sonnet by his future wife 'which had been lately set' and which he found pleasingly masculine.[53] There is no masking just how pleasant, youthful and relaxedly creative were the setting and milieu in which he was moving. The king's musicians travelled for a rehearsal session; the table and chairs were pushed back to make room. Men and women alike called on houses where music could be heard, new people encountered. A song on a page caught a composer's ear, suggesting a refrain – of the kind so often to be found, without attribution, sketched in countless notebooks sitting now in manuscript stacks.

Other lines were made to fit familiar melodies. Some of the most popular Caroline songs to be set and disseminated in both ways came from the pen of Suckling. One, perhaps his most popular of all, gives us a view of court society in the person of an outsider coming across a great feast in the middle of London:

> I tell thee *Dick*, where I have been,
> Where I the rarest things have seen,
>   Oh things beyond compare!

Such sights again cannot be found
In any part of English ground
Be it at Wake, or Fair.[54]

'I Tell Thee *Dick*' is a generic ballad formula, and the speaker is a 'rustic', a farmer bringing his wares to sell in the city. For the sake of convention, let us call him Tom.[55] Tom is passing the mansions at the end of the Strand – 'At *Charing-Crosse*, hard by the way/ Where we (thou know'st) do sell our Hay' – when he is captivated by a mass rustle of finery from courtiers descending for a wedding. His eye picks out the groom:

Among the rest, one Pest'lent fine,
(His beard no bigger though then thine)
Walkt on before the rest:
Our Landlord looks like nothing to him:
The King, (God blesse him) 'twould undo him,
Should he go still so drest.[56]

This is the one moment in the poem – which stretches into twenty-two stanzas – at which there is even the slightest sense that something could go amiss in the world Tom describes. The young lord is decked out more splendidly than the narrator can imagine the king himself dressing. He hits uncomfortably close to the truth. Just briefly, we catch sight of the real state of the Exchequer, which gave Charles a smaller income in real terms than a good number of the great peers; too small a stock of capital, perhaps, to support the absolute monarchy he had tried to create.

If Suckling ignored the Toms and Dicks in England who were not dizzied by finery and festivities but who actively and often violently upset the Whitsun-ales and sports on the green, he paid no attention whatsoever in his ballad to their brethren in the forgotten kingdom of Scotland. As Suckling and Davenant devoted themselves to entertaining the court, in Scotland the protest against the new prayer book gained in momentum, scale and organization. Public oblivion in England to the Scottish situation was caused largely by the king's policy of confining all discussion of it to his closest councillors. It helped that there was little in the way of fervent appetite for news from the north to suppress in the south. 'And the truth is,' thought Edward Hyde long afterwards:

there was so little curiosity either in the Court or the country to know any thing of Scotland, or what was done there, that when the whole nation was solicitous to know what passed weekly in Germany and Poland and all other parts of Europe, no man ever inquired what was doing in Scotland, nor had that kingdom a place or mention in one page of any gazette, so little the world heard or thought of that people.[57]

Clarendon's statement obviously suggests that Scotland and the Scots lay outside the 'world', and sure enough one of the king's councillors did actually suggest blocking the troublesome nation out of it for ever. Once the Scots had been crushed by military force, Sir William Monson proposed that a new fortified wall be built from Glasgow to Stirling, and the rest of the country written off. The plan was far-fetched, but its premise was also optimistic. Monson assumed that holding Edinburgh would be a simple matter. Wentworth, taking the 'thorough' view of what needed doing, advocated the systematic anglicization of Scotland once an invasion had taken place.[58]

That it became necessary to entertain serious thoughts of such measures, from the summer of 1638, bore testimony to the strength and extension of the opposition Charles faced. He had been presented with mass protest in support of a revolutionary document, the famous Presbyterian 'Covenant', which rejected harmonization between the English and Scottish Churches and effectively set out new conditions for the union of the Crowns. In the late autumn of 1638, an assembly in Glasgow gave radical reforms to Church and state the force of law. Meanwhile, Scotland was mobilizing for war. Troops were raised and trained, and arms ordered from Europe. A chain of beacons was installed to warn Edinburgh of an invasion. The Covenanters outpaced Charles in every kind of preparation, hopelessly overriding the tactics of the king's chief representative, the Marquis of Hamilton. Prime recruits, zealous mercenaries, Scottish officers who had been fighting for the Calvinist cause for almost two decades, were recalled from their Dutch and Swedish regiments. Sir James Lumbden, a veteran of the German wars, recognized 'the authority placed by God and Nature over me' in the order to come home, 'which I cannot disobey as a cavalier who loves his honour'.[59] By early 1639, it looked as if the question would only be settled by a clash of cavaliers – the king's *and* the Covenant's.

It had been a turbulent couple of years for the legal mind responsible for much of the detail in the rebel cause. To his family's dismay, Archibald Johnston's earlier agonies were opened once more, with renewed force, when he was first asked for help in opposing the bishops and their liturgy. God seemed to be wondering, he thought, 'Quhat if I put upon thee this difficult piece of service now in hand?' Johnston protested his unworthiness and incapacity to play a leading part in the holy struggle.[60] Yet this time he at last felt that the way he had to take was clear. Throughout the autumn of 1637 and the winter that followed, he put more and more of his time at the disposal of the opposition's team of lawyers. He was instrumental in refining a formal petition against the prayer book. At the same time, the old 'secret torment' of his abdominal pains returned. Late in December 1637, King Charles gave his response to the enemies of the prayer book: any further public dissent would be considered treason. At this Johnston drafted another strident 'protestation' for the Presbyterians, and stood at the Market Cross in Edinburgh to read it to the crowd himself.

His practice was already suffering, not only through his fervour alienating potential clients, but also from the neglect of present business. He gave the opposition all his services for free. His brother-in-law accused him of wilful madness, throwing away 'profit, credit, ease, respect, payment of debt' – not to mention putting his life and property in danger. Johnston's reply to such arguments was 'I haive bein ever wel payed be my God.'[61]

The protesters' case against the king rested with the Covenant or Confession of Faith of 1580, in which King James had settled the constitution of the Kirk, outlawing all papist regressions. By now Johnston knew the Confession intimately. In the early months of 1638, he therefore became instrumental in preparing the Kirk's strongest and, as it turned out, most explosive document defying the new order. This was a new National Covenant, renewing the old Confession, summarizing the acts of Scottish Parliament barring the very practices King Charles had sought to introduce, and supplementing the 1580 text 'as the corruptiones of this tyme required'. On Wednesday 28 February 1638, the Covenant was presented at Greyfriars Church in Edinburgh for the endorsement of barons and noblemen. In the days and weeks that followed, it was then opened up for the whole Scottish nation to sign. Thousands upon thousands of names were immediately mustered. The text itself was obscure to most. What counted more was the act of testimony before God. In the church of Currie, where Johnston usually worshipped, he observed how the congregation was wholly silent – 'no motion' – when the minister finished explaining the detail of the Covenant. But when he bid them stand and lift their hands and hearts to God, 'in the twinkling of ane eye thair fell sutch ane extraordinarie influence of Gods Sprit upon the whol congregation, melting thair frozen hearts, waltering thair dry cheeks, chainging thair verry countenances'. The minister was 'suffocat almost with his auin tears, and astonisched at the motion of the whol people, sat doune in the pulpit in ane amazement'.[62]

A crucial revolutionary detail spotted by some was that, unlike its predecessor of 1580, this appeared to be not only a covenant between the people and God, but a covenant between each member of the covenant and all other signatories: that is, a document which, given the force of law, was something verging on the constitution of a religious state. In London, the king began to think of war. He sent a commissioner, the Marquis of Hamilton, to negotiate with the Covenanters, who by the summer had the clear majority of the Scottish people – with some coercion, admittedly, of tenants by their lords – on their side. The Covenanters now pushed for a national assembly to be held in which the matter would be settled, taking care to exclude the Scottish bishops from joining it.

In the last week of October, a month before the opening of the assembly, in which not only the long-forsaken prayer book but episcopacy itself was declared illegal in Scotland, Johnston brought a destitute visionary into his home to enlighten his family. Margaret Mitchel, soon famous as a 'shee prophetess', raved for hours on what the Lord had planned for Scotland, spouting predictions of the parts to be played by, among others, the reticent Earl of Argyll. Johnston was mesmerized.

Alone one evening a few days later, recalling Margaret's words, he cast aside his book and walked about his house at Wariston, attempting to follow her path in meditation. He tried bringing to mind the whole world, the entire cosmos, the heavens and every creature beneath, and then to encircle in his thoughts the God who had made it all, still preserving and ruling every atom. 'In every thought I plumbed ane unsearchable deep.' He thought of God's infinite wisdom in ordaining the fall of man, his infinite love in allowing an elect to be saved; and then, as so often before, when Johnston viewed his own soul and his 'damnable deservings to be ane reprobat', his spirit broke – 'my body quaiked and trembled al for feare, with ane cold shuddering through al my body especyaly at the roots of my haire.'

Then as if from above there came an 'intimation of reconciliation'. An astounding sensation of bliss filled Johnston's body. His shivering passed, and he stayed up a long time, hoping this was a blessing.[63]

8. Northern Discoveries

Certes our Authors are to blame,
For to make some well-sounding name
A Pattern fit for modern Knights,
To copy out in Frays and Fights,
(Like those that a whole street do raze,
To build a Palace in the place.)
They never care how many others
They kill, without regard of mothers,
Or wives, or children, so they can
Make up some fierce, dead-doing man.

– Samuel Butler, *Hudibras* (1.2)

1

The end was nigh: Lady Eleanor Douglas, née Touchet, and formerly
Davies, had been warning so for years. For the south also had its seers,
and this one, a gentlewoman in her late forties, had been living with
the heavy gift of prophecy since 1625, when a voice from heaven told
her that the world would end in nineteen and a half years' time. One
night at dinner the following December she broke down weeping at an
intimation that her husband, the aged and obese poet and lawyer Sir
John Davies, would soon die – as he did, just three days later. Despite a
ready appetite for millenarian promptings, the court had always been
uncertain what to make of Lady Eleanor. Her ecstasies, trances and
ciphered disclosures were close enough to witchcraft for a poorer, less
protected woman to find herself in flames. The queen had consulted her
during her first pregnancy; but Lady Eleanor lost many friends for
defending her brother in one of the darkest trials of the age. In 1631,
Mervin Touchet, Earl of Castlehaven, was convicted of sodomy and of

arranging the spectacle of a servant raping his wife, the countess. The evidence against him was so graphically dreadful that King Charles prohibited all women from hearing it. Though Castlehaven was put to death, his sister maintained his innocence for many years. Later in the 1630s, after she warned Archbishop Laud of the divine judgement in store for him, the authorities decided that Lady Eleanor was a menace.

Her first vision, back in 1625, had cast her in the role of the 'meek Virgin' in the apocalypse due in 1644. Her destiny as a medium was never in doubt, but her meekness became increasingly more symbolic than actual. Having been imprisoned, and after separating from her subsequent husband – a soldier, Sir Archibald Douglas, who was stricken by a disease of the mind Lady Eleanor claimed to have foreseen – she began acting on her convictions. In 1635 she disturbed a service in Lichfield Cathedral, claiming the bishop's throne and then pouring tar over the altar, declaring its ornaments and purple hangings abominable. As the king gathered his army against the Scots in early 1639, Lady Eleanor wondered whether the moment of the Second Coming had been brought forward. She recorded further prophecies in her cell in the Tower of London, using the hours of liberty granted to a prisoner of her status to take her visions on to the streets. The city, she warned, would lie in ruins by Easter.

The speeches of Lady Eleanor, and others who shared her convictions, if not her gift, were starting to spread from the pockets of fervour in which they originated. There was a sharp division between the states of mind to be found in the kingdom; between those who saw the Covenant and its repercussions as a severe case of feudal disobedience, and those to whom events in Scotland seemed like the living confirmation of scripture. January 1639 found Suckling and Carew in town as usual, adding expert touches to a play a friend had requested they revise. A revival of Jonson's classic, *The Alchemist*, had delighted audiences at Blackfriars. Mentioning their stage-work in a letter from Bedfordshire, a mutual acquaintance only feared that 'all the gallants should go for soldiers, and the ladies should want servants to accompany them.'[1]

Suckling had reacted with contempt to the 'Scottish business'. He viewed the matter of religion as nothing more than an excuse for stirring trouble. The previous year, as the crisis worsened, he had found time to sketch a satirical 'exchange' of letters between a London alderman and a Scottish lord. Both of his characters write as onlookers, both trying to define and get to grips with the quarrel. The Scot denies the charge of rebellion, although "True it is, that in case the King will not do what we would have him, we have provided Arms.' In any case, the alderman has heard the revolt spoken of as no more than 'a Boil broken out in the Breech of the Kingdom, and that when it is ripe, it will heal of it self'. The fictitious letters reflect not only the uncertainty of the moment, but also the lack of information available – even, perhaps, to a courtier as well placed as Suckling. He had his alderman claim that 'while one part of the Town is in whisper, and serious, the other part smiles.'[2] By January that smile was looking rather forced, especially the closer one got to the king himself.

A formidable army of Scots, commanded by Alexander Leslie, an accomplished veteran of the European wars, had been raised and was eyeing the chief cities of the kingdom with justified confidence. Already, within Scotland, those falling in with the Covenant and those opposing it saw in the prospect of combat an occasion to settle old territorial and tribal arguments. In response, south of Berwickshire, the king's call for English volunteers was issued on 26 January, and within three days Suckling had 'engaged to himself to bring upon his own purse 100 horse to the rendezvous'. Yet by the end of February, although he was praised as 'the exactest and forwardest man in this service', an official noted he had 'as yet given his men nothing but colours for their hats, and as I am informed will give them nothing more'.[3]

The kit Suckling eventually provided for his men made them the most fantastic troop in the entire army. The impression is hard to resist that he treated the exercise as another of his pieces of personal theatre. His men brought a gasp of amazement, as Davenant told Aubrey many years later, wherever they rode. They were '100 very handsome proper young men, whom he clad in white doubletts and scarlett breeches, and scarlet coates, hatts, and . . . feathers, well horsed, and armed'.[4] Notably, the mention of practical equipment – mounts and weaponry – comes at the very end of Aubrey's description, incidental in comparison to the matter of uniform. Yet in the event it is clear that Suckling did not stint on armour or munitions, since his correspondence of the following year reveals him doing his utmost to sell it off – at a moment when its need was in fact greater than ever. It was said he spent as much as £12,000 on the venture, a truly colossal sum: yet the smaller figure this exaggerates – perhaps a third or even a quarter of the alleged amount – would still have been huge. He was lavish indeed. Yet contemporary cavalry manuals made it emphatically clear that horsemen would need more than feathers in their hats in order to be effective. Each must be provided with:

a close casket or head-peece, gorget, brest-plate, pistol proffer, and packet to make it carbine-proofe. Poulderons, and Vambraces, Gauntlets, Taffets, Cassets and Garderons, to arme him fitly downe to the knee before, and so loe as the calves behind[;] with a Buffe Coate under his armes, a good sword stiffe and sharpe pointed, two good fire-locks, Pistols, in houlsters at the Saddle, with a good Poleaxe, [and finally] a good strong horse fifteen handfuls high, his Saddle and Bitt must be strong and usefull.[5]

The list of technical requirements was endless, as were the hard-won practical tips. 'Let not the neck of your spurs be overlong,' advised the writer quoted above, an 'honest plain-dealing cavalier', so as not to catch them on the stirrup of a man beside you while riding in formation.[6] Suckling was experienced enough a horseman to know such a thing, and that a horse must not only be trained to manoeuvre but also slowly and gently accustomed to the sound of gunpowder exploding; but the organizational ability and attention to detail required of him was enormous. Besides his limited taste of siege warfare and his ordeals as a diplomatic courier, his greatest advantage may well have lain with the skills he had acquired as a director and stage manager over the previous year. Yet the professional literature not only stressed how important it was for the leader of a troop to have a sound practical education in soldiering, it imposed moral specifications on his character. 'Gaming he must detest,' stipulated one writer, ominously for Suckling. 'In stead of costly apparel, let him delight in good armes and horses . . . He must be continent and sober, not given to luxurie or drunkennesse, but always be a good example to his soldiers.'[7]

Yet the handbooks published by seasoned military men in the 1630s and '40s did not belong to the same era in which Suckling still, despite all he had seen in Europe, believed he and his men existed. These proper young men were voluntaries of the old Elizabethan order, with Suckling casting himself in the part of lead swashbuckler, in the manner of the lamented Second Earl of Essex; and they were locked on a collision course with the strategic and technological realities of seventeenth-century warfare. The costumes of these cavalrymen bear an unsettling resemblance to the garb which several among their no doubt aristocratic number may already have worn as attendant lords and spirits in a royal masque. Implicit in Suckling's arrangement of his men, and in the letters he wrote from the north a little later, is an expectation that the ugly deviants of the Scottish antimasque would be dispelled by a breath of wind, or some stage device, by a *deus ex machina* shifting the scenery of nature.

The wit who came up with the verses 'Upon Sir John Suckling's Hundred Horse', a ballad which entered circulation very soon after the army of 1639 set off, feared that Suckling's dream might be sorely broken. Too many of his men were the sort to be scared by a tailor demanding payment, let alone a Scot fighting for his homeland. Meanwhile the memory remained gleefully fresh of Suckling's disaster and dishonour in his ambush on John Digby five years before:

> I tell thee *Jack* thou'st given the King,
> So rare a present as no thing
>   Would welcomer have been;
> A hundred horse, beshrew my heart!
> It was a Noble, Gallant part,
>   The like will scarce be seen . . .
>
> But yet methinks I see thee charge,
> Thy selfe with freedome to enlarge,
>   'Gainst foes that make a salley;
> Courage brave heart, courage brave *John*,
> I wish thou gost more bravely on,
>   Than in *Black-Friers* Alley.[8]

2

Peter Heylyn, a shrewd cleric and controversialist of extensive intellectual gifts, declared the army moving northwards to be 'the best for quality of the persons, completeness of arms, number of serviceable horse and necessary provision of all sorts that ever waited on a King of England to a war with Scotland'.[9] But this was the judgement of the chaplain of the Order of St George, favourably inclined by his loyalty to the king and unproven moreover as a connoisseur of arms. Others more directly involved in the business of mustering men, trying to arm, train and prevent them deserting, or paying off beggars and criminals to take their places, took a harder view of the force they could offer the king. After decades of peace – discounting the occasional scare – on English soil, the arsenals of the inland county militias yielded pikes warped and rotting with damp, tarnished swords and obsolete muskets. Weapons ordered from the Netherlands, with high expectations of Dutch craftsmanship and at great strain on the Exchequer, turned out to be little better. Some of the bandoliers when they arrived were found to be made of nothing more than brown paper.

The country at large had in any case lost touch with the ways of war. Horses and provisions were hard to come by. The sudden movement of troops on the highways was a shock to the system, and many in charge had no direct knowledge of the current technologies and tactics of warfare. One aristocrat turned out two long-encrusted full suits of armour which he was sure, with a little elbow grease, could be made to do good service once again. The navy, commanded by a nobleman who confessed openly his ignorance of sailing, was poorly victualled and manned – even many of the officers were 'no ways able to endure the sea'.[10] To make matters worse, the high command was bitterly divided. King Charles had appointed the Earl of Arundel as his commander-in-chief, with the Earl of Essex as his second. But he had placed one of the queen's favourites, the Earl of Holland, in charge of the cavalry, tangling the chain of command and, worse, giving Arundel cause to focus on his wounded honour rather than the preparations for war.

There was widespread dismay at the general level of military training. Old soldiers had been complaining for decades that practising 'posture' once every five or six years left the militia in no fit state to fight – 'Whose the fault is I know not,' muttered one back in 1635, 'only I pray God that it may be amended, lest shame and infamy be the least evils which our carelesse security may bring upon us.'[11] Of those who had kept in shape, and sought service overseas, a substantial number had greater sympathy than enmity for their rebellious yet godly northern neighbours.

Still, Suckling and his urbane friends – for Carew, Davenant and other wits had all volunteered as a matter of course – did not consider themselves out of their element. Bearing arms for the king was integral to their identity as royal servants, indeed as gentlemen. Just as the wits fancied themselves poets and scholars, with the contemplative life as their model, so they also considered themselves soldiers: it was all encapsulated in the Continental gentleman's title of 'cavalier'. This is not to say there was a 'cavalier court' of proto-partisans and roistering good fellows ready to defend the king before civil war was even thought of in England. We should not, that is, read the meaning the word 'cavalier' acquired in the 1640s back into its earlier usage.[12] Yet behind the common sobriquet for a well-dressed gallant remained the almost unconscious metaphor of mastery and agency in the title of a knight and horseman. Now the king's gentlemen had to give fresh proof that it was more than a metaphor. The man who lived up to the image was one whose wit and mind was oriented to the world and augmented by it. The more fields in which he proved his competence, and the greater those fields were, the higher he stood. He was, for Robert Herrick, the figure of a horseman who could ride the earth and the sea:

> Give me that man, that dares bestride
> The active Sea-horse, & with pride,
> Through that huge field of waters ride,
> Who, with his looks too, can appease
> The ruffling winds and raging seas.
> This a virtuous man can doe,
> Saile against Rocks, and split them too;
> Aye! And a world of Pikes pass through![13]

Herrick published these words at a time when the idea of a cavalier needed some defence and rehabilitation. His poem sets out the ideal which the Duke of Buckingham, Gustavus Adolphus, and countless more fleetingly famous heroes of the German wars had tried to fulfil; and which King Charles, to his credit, largely abstained from pursuing for more than ten years. It was a template which Sir John Suckling, in his various endeavours, had also strived to match.

Stacked against this effort was the popular perception of the sort of men in Suckling's troops. Later, the supporters of Parliament did not intend the label 'cavalier' to be taken as a compliment. It clearly signified one who fell short of the mark of a true *chevalier*; a petulant, disdainful, violent-minded dandy.

Yet the nobler roots of the word still held: and the medieval sense of a life in arms as the beautiful life still had great power. It gained an added dash of ancient integrity from the now standard humanist upbringing, instilled through the apophthegms Englishmen memorized as grammar-school boys, and was upheld by virtually any modern author whose pages they venerated. Montaigne, one of the period's great explorers of interior, emotional existence, but first and foremost a Gascon, found his ideal existence only on the march:

No profession or occupation is more pleasing then the military . . . The company and dayly conversation [concourse] of so many noble, young and active men, cannot but bee well-pleasing to you: the dayly and ordinary sight of so divers tragicall spectacles: the liberty and uncontrolled freedome of that artelesse and unaffected conversation, masculine and ceremonilesse maner of life: the hourely variety of a thousand ever changing and differing actions: the couragious and mind stirring harmony of warlike musicke, which at once entertaineth with delight and enflameth with longing, both your eares and your eyes: the imminent and matchless honour of that exercise . . . As a voluntary Souldier, or adventurous Knight, you enter the lists, the bands or particular hazards, according as your selfe judge of their successes or importance: and you see when your life may therein be excusably employed.[14]

The doctrine would wear rather thin for Thomas Carew, whose health was uncertain, and for more than a few others in the course of the campaign, but it explained a vital feature of the fully accomplished gentleman. There were professional soldiers, but they had by no means any monopoly on war. This was not yet the exclusive age of the specialist, but that of the aficionado.

As such, the commander-in-chief, Arundel, was a noted aesthete, art collector and patron of exploratory endeavours, but with no obvious qualifications as a soldier. Meanwhile, the abler man for the job, the Earl of Essex, a proven commander, was not only wasted but also lost, in the long term, by the king. The earl's 'rough proud nature' was in time further wounded by Charles's neglecting to grant the small boons that would have acknowledged and rewarded his service in the 1639 campaign. Sir Edward Hyde, the later Lord Clarendon, felt that simply granting Essex the care of the forest of Needwood, for example, conveniently vacated by the death of the previous incumbent, would have protected him from the subsequent rebellious 'impressions' which led to him becoming a Parliamentary general.

Behind the idyll presented by Montaigne and lesser writers of a 'masculine and ceremonilesse maner of life', a campaign was another setting for the court; an opportunity for bettering one's interests and evening scores, while earning the favour of a patron or even the monarch himself. Yet when it came to civil war, as opposed to a short tour of duty at a foreign siege or (better still) a few weeks of manoeuvring and tourneying, all were immediately alive to the horrors of conflict. In foreign lands, the experience of war was a robe of honour; in one's own, against one's own people, it was a poisoned shirt, and the wearer could only tear off his skin with the garment. As the English set their mission against the Scots in motion, this feeling found blunt expression in Suckling's latest work for the stage:

> Warre in our owne is like to too much heate
> Within, it makes the body sicke; when in
> Another Countrey, 'tis but exercise;
> Conveighs that heat abroad, and gives it health.[15]

Hanging over the expedition of 1639 was the uncertainty as to whether Englishmen were going to fight a war in their own country, or another with whom they shared a ruler. The Stuarts had made much of the idea of Britain, and indeed of a 'British heaven' encompassing all three of Charles's kingdoms. Yet Suckling for one was representative of those who suppressed their weak affinities with the north and concentrated on the foreignness of the enemy.

As procedure dictated, the ranks of horsemen spaced out on their marches by day, and drew closer together by darkness. The king reached York on 31 March. On 17 April, he reviewed troops camping out at Selby, some twelve miles away, including Suckling's men in their scarlet coats. Charles said he was well pleased, but it was not until the end of May that the army was brought together in the vicinity of Berwick to the north, by which time the Covenanters had taken Edinburgh and Aberdeen with virtually no resistance, and seemed ready to pour over the border.

Suckling's view of the confrontation had meanwhile developed. Admittedly the scale of the situation was still hard to judge, even from his proximity to the crisis in the far north of England. Far from his soft southern territory, he had already said he personally would be willing to cede Cumberland to the rebels 'for quietness sake . . . because it is so barren'.[16] The unbroken expanses of moorland seemed lunar to him in their emptiness. Writing a letter for general distribution but addressed to 'a gentleman in Norfolk', he resumed his comic vein – perhaps in persona once more – but less complacently:

The truth is, we here consider the Scottish affairs much after the rate that Mortals do the Moon: the simpler think it no bigger then a Bushel, and some (too wise) imagine it a vast World, with strange things undiscovered in it; two ill ways certainly of casting it up, since the first would make us too secure, the other too fearful.

Seeking the just mean, he still dismissed the religious cause of the Covenant leadership, political and military, as hypocrisy, distinguishing General Leslie in particular as one 'who because he could not live well here, took up a trade of killing men abroad, and is now return'd for Christs sake to kill men at home'. But he also recognized failings on Charles's part, albeit with arrogance towards the enemy. 'If you will have my opinion, I think their quarrel is, that which they may have to the Sun: He does not warm and visit them, as much as others.' The contemptuous metaphor makes royal negligence part of the fixed scheme of things – for how could the sun bring itself nearer to those regions which feel abandoned by it? – yet the writer condescends to understand how the inhabitants must feel. Carew concurred, writing shortly afterwards of the 'everlasting winter' in the 'wild north', a landscape of 'sterill Fearne, Thistles, and Brambles'.[17] Suckling could scarcely acknowledge the Scots as human at all. 'The great and wise Husbandman [that is to say, God] hath placed the Beasts in the Out-fields,' he judged, 'and they would break hedges to come into the Garden.'[18] His remarks invited, but firmly avoided, the question of how well the garden had been tended.

Notwithstanding the 'company and dayly conversation' of so many noble active men, young and otherwise, the sight of Berwick was enough to subdue martial spirits. In times past, England had always maintained a garrison at the border there: but that had been disbanded by King James, as both a gesture of unity between the kingdoms and a convenient cost-cutting measure. The 'fair, stately' bridge the old king had built across the Tweed, a wonder of the realm for its fifteen arches and its cost of a reputed £17,000, now stood as an emptily magnificent symbol of that projected union.

Travellers had always seen the potential for Berwick in the river and the estuary, 'abounding with all things necessary for food, yea with many dainties, as salmons and all kinds of shellfish'.[19] Yet remoteness, its immemorial function as the first line of defence and the silting of the haven from which it looked out, 'narrow, shallow, barred', had killed off hopes of trade in the town and given it the indelible bleakness of the outpost. Passing through in 1636, the future Parliamentarian Sir William Brereton was duly impressed by the old fortifications, 'double walled . . . the inner walls of invincible strength'; but noted 'only one little pink of about forty tons' and 'some few fishing-boats' in the harbour. With so little commercial life, he found Berwick 'a very poor town, many indigent persons and beggars within'. Its deprivation, as well as the danger of its location, made it a place of provisional allegiances and potential fifth columnists, unlikely to warm to southern officers who complained of the region's 'barrenness' but willing to milk them of their cash in overpriced billets. One officer reaching quarters in a nearby village described finding 'no other accommodation than a dark and rainy night . . . not a lock of hay nor peck of oats, and little shelter for horse or man'.[20]

The bulk of Charles's army, including Suckling's contingent, pitched up at the Birks, three miles to the west of Berwick itself. Davenant, who had been appointed a pay-master, had found pasture for the horses under his care at Goswick, six miles down the coast from the city.[21] The laureate celebrated his friend's more extravagant efforts after the war, but his own work in finding and organizing men, munitions and horses was clearly also considerable.

Despite the energy and invention Davenant devoted to his task, he was not focused exclusively on the great military project. He was evidently irked at circumstances taking him from London, where he hoped to open a little private theatre of his own, preferably near the hub of things in Fleet Street. In the spring, Endymion Porter, also caught up in the flow of larger events, instructed one of his factors in London to lobby for a licence for Davenant to adapt a suitable building. In the poet's absence, and with his powerful friends absorbed in the war against the Covenant, 'cruel and envious' enemies at court managed to block the scheme. No doubt prominent among them was Sir Henry Herbert, Master of the Revels. Thomas May was another old opponent. Yet the idea would preoccupy Davenant for many years to come.

With Suckling it was otherwise. The expense to which he went in equipping his troops, the energy he invested in his anti-Covenant letters and the surprising depth of his disgust for their cause, suggests that his mind was set firmly on the enemy mustering a few miles to the north. His devotion to the king's mission, and his hopes for distinction in its service, might be placed in a narrative of self-reaffirmation. Nowhere is it reliably indicated how sorely he remembered past embarrassments, yet Aubrey's anecdote of the party held by Lady Moray suggests how Suckling could be put 'out of countenance' by remarks about his 'late received baffle'.[22] The evidence more generally points to a desire for the limelight at almost any personal cost.

Since his drubbing at the hands of John Digby five years before, Suckling had done much to restore his reputation, at least in the eyes of those who would let him restore it, notably both the king and queen. He stormed the heights of fashion with his success at court with *Aglaura*. His approval and patronage were sought by other writers, and his opinions and revisions requested on the works many sent him. Appointment to the king's bedchamber confirmed his social rehabilitation, while his zeal and generosity on the king's behalf made him surely one of the most prominent 'voluntary knights' in the entire expedition. These achievements, dignities and expenses could always be written off by the cynical as mere vanities; but a solid act of heroism against the old enemy would surely quieten such chatter, possibly for good:

> Sir *John* got on a bonny browne Beast,
>   To *Scotland* for to ride a,
> A brave Buffe Coat upon his back,
>   A short sword by his side a,
> Alas young man, we *Sucklings* can
>   Pull down the Scottish pride a.[23]

3

The mustering of the king's army, one of the largest ever mobilized in England to that date, was no small accomplishment at such short notice. Yet the outlook for it was unpromising. Divisions in the royal council, some more than faintly treasonous, had widened during the king's stay at York. His hard-pressed representative in Scotland – now Duke of Hamilton – tangled in intrigues, was only surprised by how the situation managed to worsen. 'Your Ma*j*estties affaires ar in ane desperatt condition,' he wrote in May. 'The inraged people heir runes in to the height of Rebellion and walkes with a blind obedience, as by ther traitorous leaders they ar commanded.' Writing back, as always in his fluent Scots, Charles had offered a number of palliatives, and amnesty in return for a cessation of the revolt; but the Presbyterians stood firmly by their Covenant, which now appeared nothing other than the basis for a new Scottish state. While diehards on Charles's side, Suckling prominent among them, had fixed their sights on settling the quarrel by force, Hamilton was dismayed by the thought of such an offensive. 'Give me leaue humbly to say that a present rencounter is to be shunned, for, whilst they ar in this madness, I know not what the euent of a battle may proue.'[24] The only hope, he thought, lay with turning the Covenant leaders against one another; but the prospect of that seemed small.

The opposing armies were slowly moving closer together, and as the year began to warm, the desire for action grew stronger. On the English side, some troopers shot holes in the roofs of their tents to relieve their feelings, and regretted it when the next downpour cooled them off. 'I should judge it dawning towards earnest,' Suckling wrote of the stand-off at the beginning of June, possibly on the very day that the two commanders in the field, Arundel and Holland, took advance parties over the border to read a proclamation at Duns, some half-dozen miles inside Scotland. This called on the Scots to strike camp or face the consequences, and tempted them to show their hand. The bulk of the cavalry remained on the other side of the river, where Suckling waggishly told his correspondent, 'You may now imagine us walking up and down the banks of *Tweed* like the Tower-Lyons in their Cages, leaving the people to think what we would do if we were let loose.' Historical and literary precedents came to mind. This was where, he said, 'my Friend Mr. *William Shakespear*' – he thought of him as such – had Henry Hotspur fall out with his fellow rebels and move towards his ruin. Suckling only hoped a politician's trick would not deprive his comrades of the chance to put down this latest revolt. The horizon was crushingly still:

The Enemy is not much visible, (It may be it is the fault of the Climate, which brings Men as slowly forwards as Plants.) But it gives us fears that the Men of Peace will draw all this to a dumb shew, and so destroy a handsom opportunity which was now offered, of producing matter for future Chronicle.[25]

Suckling's desire to be both a part of that chronicle and the first bard to recount it come across strongly in the letter. He concluded by saying, 'These are but Conjectures, Sir,' yet within days, perhaps hours of writing, events finally began to take definite form. The conflict later aggrandized as the First Bishops' War moved towards its crisis in a moment of profound, ambiguous and unsettling anti-climax with which Suckling's name would forever be associated.

> I would advise thee take a course,
> That thou maist mount the swiftest horse,
>   Of all the troop thou givest:
> That when the battailes once begun,
> Thou swiftly then away maist run,
>   And show us that thou livest.[26]

In response to the challenge laid down at Duns, the Scottish army moved to Kelso, a small town perhaps twenty miles upriver from Berwick. On 3 June, the English shifted to meet them, crossing the Tweed, at last, with Holland at the head of 1,600 cavalry, in which Suckling's troop was firmly embedded. Yet the infantry supporting them – three thousand men less eager for the fray – soon lagged behind. In Suckling's version of events, which he gave in writing to the Earl of Middlesex a few days later, the horse pushed on, leaving the foot to catch up. Searching the ground ahead with their telescopes, the cavalry lighted on a modest-seeming body of enemy lancers under the command of Lord Carr – which despite their best run managed to elude them.

The ground they were advancing across sloped upwards, and presently Holland's force reached the height overlooking the Scots positions outside Kelso. Both horses and men were short of breath from the heat of the day and their exertions bearing arms, and in the pause they took at their vantage point, the army below were able to organize and advance. It seems then that a collective gulp went around the English cavalry. The number they faced was not, as their spy-glasses had initially suggested, 'contemptible'. A trumpeter was sent down the hill, to register a protest that the Scots had failed to respect the distance of ten miles behind their bank of the Tweed which Charles had ordered they keep. Down on the shady side of the pass, the Scots retorted that the English had done likewise. And then Lord Holland's order to charge died quietly on his lips. A dust cloud, claimed Suckling, had risen below, and on clearing it revealed an army greater in number than both of those which had faced one another a few minutes before, emerging from a fold in the valley. Eight thousand men now looked up at Suckling, he guessed: what a few moments earlier promised an uneven but still finely balanced encounter now looked like certain destruction, for the English foot were still hours behind. Intriguingly, Suckling presented a strikingly similar 'cloud of dust and men' to the eponymous hero of his last drama, *Brennoralt*, in the play's opening scene. It is impossible to say whether the real event influenced his writing, or whether his theatrical vision projected itself on to the scene at Kelso: but the outcome was less stirring in reality.[27]

A brisk retreat in any case, as Suckling readily conceded, was now the only option; but with such odds even that was far from guaranteed success. Suckling heard later that they were spared only because the elders of the Covenanters' army refused to open hostilities, having turned out only to defend their homes. He credited Lord Loudoun, later vilified by Clarendon as one of the subtlest miscreants in the Covenant camp, with the final decision. Most of those in English arms were not fanatics, the Scots judged, but 'cavaleirs' who were merely following their king. The English owed their peaceful retreat, Suckling reckoned, to that dignified restraint; and he admitted, grudgingly, the civility of the message. Although they were generally regarded as a disgrace, in Suckling's view, the events at Kelso actually show the Renaissance ideal of honourable warfare – the ideal which brought a glow to Montaigne's stoic heart – still holding true; but to the advantage of the Scots rather than the English.

By the time the story reached London, the 'quiet' withdrawal had been blown up into a panic-stricken volte face and a terrified rush back through the borderlands to the safety of the English lines – with Suckling, no less, at the head of the retreating cavalcade, he having squirmed to the rear of his company. Back in Scotland, frustrated and dismayed, searching for scapegoats, many of the cavalrymen blamed their scouts. They should have been warned, it was said, that the size of the enemy in the field so greatly exceeded their own.

Certainly the consensus of expert opinion in the science of cavalry placed great importance in the choice of scouts. If fighting in one's own territory, local men were crucial; if not, then persuading or bribing local men to switch sides equally so. But the military literature also insisted that, even when reconnaissance failed or proved faulty, even when the odds seemed against him, a good cavalry colonel still had options. Moreover, even when the range of strictly rational strategic possibilities was not available, the veterans said that much was to be gained from simply holding one's nerve. 'If you meet the enemie near his own quarter, and farre from yours' – exactly the situation presenting itself at Kelso – 'you must resolve with a generous courage to go and charge him; it being often seen that valiant revolutions are seconded with good luck.' For in the fray itself, 'there remaineth onely now, that every one (according to his office, rank, and abilitie) strive for honour and victory; propounding to himself the goodness of the cause, and authority of the Prince, the virtue of the souldiers, the honour of the conquest, and the disgrace and damage of the defeat.'[28]

When inequality of numbers really left no hope, the command should go out for every man to save himself, and to disband in all directions so as to prevent a charge. The Scots' terms made this unnecessary, but Suckling confessed that the complete about-turn did the horsemen little credit; especially since, when the mists rose from the riverbanks the following day, the Scottish army could be seen in plain view of the English camp. Suckling was happy to report that at least King Charles was not unnerved, pointing out airily that if General Leslie was now just four miles from him, he was only four miles from Leslie. The cavalry was ordered into readiness again, but Suckling leaves little doubt that they were not fit to fight. Their horses were wrecks in sinew and nerve – 'much harassed' – from their trial and the hard run back to camp, and the continual alarums and emergencies which kept sweeping over them. The horsemen too were equally destroyed, many sick with dysentery and chest colds, which Suckling attributed to drinking water from the river and marshes. At this point a note familiar from his letters from Europe eight years earlier creeps back into his writing: the air of heroic dispatch wilts, and it suddenly becomes transparent that he is speaking to his favourite uncle, who rests in a large, warm, safe house some four hundred miles away; that he is exhausted, bedraggled, mired and thoroughly wretched. He has had almost no sleep for a week – he is writing on 6 June – and if his body were to sue his mind for the suffering its decisions had brought, there is no payment it could make in its usual currency of clever thoughts or witticisms.[29]

Yet a few days later Suckling's epistolary style regained its habitual swagger and hauteur. 'At this instant it is grown a Calm greater than the Storm,' he complained once more to Middlesex, 'and if you will believe the Soldier, worse: Good Arms and Horses are already cheap, and there is nothing risen in value but a *Scotchman*.' The Scots across the river had asked for nothing more than that the king hear their complaints. Negotiations for a peace were already in progress. Forgetting the magnanimity which had allowed him and his men to make their escape a few days earlier, Suckling now felt that the rebels were getting off lightly. It was true that the huge English army had never been put to the test; but it was possible, too, to overlook its inferiority to the well-prepared enemy. 'Some (and not unreasonably) perchance will imagine that this may invite good Subjects to be ill,' wrote Suckling. He overestimated the king's bargaining position; but he reflected a wider view among the cavalry, bristling at its own dishonour, in which esteem for Charles had fallen. Majesty itself, so crucial, it was now manifest, to Suckling's outlook on life, had been given a bitter purgative. If the rebels won more concessions – and agreeing to treat, for Suckling, was already a concession – then 'posterity must tell this miracle, That there went an Army from the South, of which there was not one man lost, nor any man taken prisoner but the King.'[30]

Disgruntlement in camp worsened in the days leading up to the Pacification of Berwick, which was concluded on 18 June. A cessation was agreed to hostilities, but although both sides renewed their courtesies, each read further bellicose intent in the other. Archibald Johnston was one of the Covenanters' chief negotiators, and the only one to confront the king directly, accusing him of bad faith. He voiced the suspicion held by all: while agreeing that another assembly should be summoned, the king had resolved to fight a more effective campaign the following year, to bring the Covenanters properly to heel. Although some took Charles at his word, in the main the Scots saw that it was too late to reconcile their differences with London through discussion. When the assembly met later in the summer, they would use it to press home their political advantage. But the war was at least suspended for the moment, and the keys to Edinburgh Castle were returned to the king's representative.

Suckling had no insider's knowledge to offer on the agreement – 'I am no first Favourite to any Lord of Secrets at this time,' he insisted – but judged that 'the same Necessity which made them [the Covenanters] thus wise for Peace, will make them as desperate for War.' There had been no outcome, in short: and there was nothing for it but to grow a year older and poorer until a return to the north next spring.

He was diverted by Davenant, resourceful as ever in unpromising circumstances, and currently testing out communications with carrier pigeons. Before the campaign, Davenant had already made use of trained birds in the theatre, and now the war effort had petered out, he had reclaimed his cages from the Berwickshire loft or outhouse he had commandeered to store them, and 'now employs them all,' recorded Suckling, 'for the Queens use'. Since one of the basic methods of the pigeon trainer is using the hen essentially as bait to entice her mate home, this little glimpse of Davenant's service in 1639 adds a pleasurable iota to his poetic fascination with the instincts of birds in pursuit of their spouses and distracted by beauty. He was evidently adept with what Izaak Walton called 'birds of political use'.[31] Feathered if not tarred, as his friend cooed and coddled his valuable pets, Suckling nevertheless declined to send his letter via one of 'Mr. *Davenants* Barbary-Pigeons'; in case, with a weak witticism betraying his gall, the recipient should take this as a sign that the barbarians had prevailed.[32]

4

News of the war, the 'pacification' and the ignominy of both swept south. The Covenanters in particular managed a very clever publicity campaign, appealing for support to the godly – and the Christian community as a whole – in England, stressing the common Protestant cause, stoking up old fears of popery, and insisting they had no aggressive designs on the neighbouring kingdom. Rumours that the king was considering whether to use an army of Catholics from Ireland against them supported their arguments. Those standing for the king, meanwhile, were angry with the officers who had failed to uphold his rights, while wits on all sides made hay with the fall pride had taken. After the flamboyant show he had put on with his redcoats, Suckling offered an easy target.

> When he came to the Camp, he was in a damp [a cold sweat]
>   To see the *Scots* in sight a,
> And all his brave Troops like so many droops,
>   To fight they had no heart a.
> And when the Allarme called all to arme,
>   Sir *John* he went to shite a.[33]

Sir John had certainly made a 'Northern Discoverie', as the song termed it. This was a phrase usually applied to the goal sought in heroic efforts to navigate the 'Northwest Passage' since the late fifteenth century.[34] But Suckling, ran the poem, had discovered something much closer to home; something the balladeer claimed that everyone but he had known all along – that he was a coward, a mere 'carpet knight': one given his title kneeling indoors, in time of peace, not one who earned it in the field.

The hand usually suspected of penning these verses belonged to John Mennes (or 'Mince', as he signed himself), a poet of a minor order and minor ambitions, and a naval commander of great ability and experience.[35] Ten years older than his alleged target, Mennes was a veteran of Caribbean sea-battles, renowned for cancelling a sniper up in an enemy's topsail; formerly captain of the king's ships *Seahorse*, *Vanguard* and *The Red Lion* (among other vessels); and recently a vice-admiral of the Channel fleet. He had a broad set of friends in London and the court, and a penchant for buggery in times of need, but a general preference for straightforward relations with the women of Bury St Edmunds.[36] He was 'markt as a true-wit', had developed tastes in painting, and was the friend of Rubens and van Dyck (who painted him). He had been prominent since the early 1620s in one or more of London's proto-Masonic societies, the members of which made oaths by thrusting their daggers into bottles of wine and identified themselves by special beads and ribbons on their clothing.[37] In his person and his connections he was, in other words, a formidable adversary; and if there are shades of a rougher, bluffer John Digby to his character, it should be pointed out that he too was an admirer of Suckling's 'Aglaura', Mary Bulkeley.

The degree of genuine hostility in the ballads and the level of hurt they inflicted are nevertheless uncertain. Since Mennes and Suckling were probably acquaintances, and possibly comrades during the second Scottish campaign, it is hard to gauge how much the 'Hundred Horse' constitutes real contempt, a slur campaign or a warning shot across a rival's bow, or whether it is mere joshing. Mennes' portfolio indicates that he had more direct methods of aggressing those he truly disliked. His authorship, despite his proven skill with burlesque elsewhere, is also speculative. What the ballad does indicate powerfully is an attitude of punitive incredulity towards Suckling's intentions and military qualifications.

Against or even oblivious of such detractors, Suckling had robust ideas of the image he wished his peers to hold of him. He created an alter-ego for the stage, in the hero of *Brennoralt*, his final theatrical romance. Evidently written in the course of 1639–40, it is unlikely that he lived to see the piece performed. But it contains his fullest expression of what he wished to be: Brennoralt, a 'disaffected colonel', is a soldier's soldier and a wit's wit, caught up in an ugly borderland conflict: unhappy and stoic in love, haughty, encrusted with cynicism yet loyal and honourable to a fault, he must go against his direct martial instincts for the sake of his country and his lady. The passions are as rampant in his being as the forces of revolt and deceit are in his land, but he defies them to break his integrity:

> Poore *Brennoralt!*
> Thou art the Martyr of a thousand tyrants:
> Love, Honour and Ambition raigne by turnes,
> And shew their power upon thee.
> BRENNORALT: Why, let them; I'm still *Brennoralt*: Ev'n Kings
> Themselves, are by their servants ruled sometimes.[38]

The opening of the play finds him languid, in Achillean fashion; only an unbeatable foe can stir his interest ('The danger now grows worthy of our swords').[39] Yet in the course of the action he must pose as a politician, and deliver harsh advice on how rebels should be handled. He reserves the right, however, to voice his opinions and offer free counsel without being counted a conspirator:

> Do'st thinke cause I am angry
> With the King and State sometimes,
> I am fallen out with virtue, and my selfe?[40]

Contemporaries immediately smelt that Suckling identified himself with his last protagonist. Soon after the play was first distributed or performed, Richard Brome countered the image of Suckling as Brennoralt with the image of him as Sir Fernando in *The Court Beggar*, a fop, gamester and poetling less fortunate in his brush with the Scottish army. Brome took a sceptical view of Suckling's sincerity in the cause of king and country: the knight's huge outlay on his hundred horses looked like a lavish bet, on which he expected a worthwhile return when the Scots were finally defeated and the spoils divided. Taken prisoner, Sir Fernando challenges his captors to a game of cribbage – the game that Suckling reputedly invented – muttering, 'And though I lose all, I have yet a project/ That at the end o' th' war . . . / Shall fetch all in agen.'[41]

Suckling remained in the retinue of the Earl of Holland during the summer of 1639, puzzling over the progress of yet another national disaster. The agreement with the Scots had begun dissolving before the ink on the treaty could dry: the Covenanters were making further demands, while Charles did not dream of honouring those he had already in theory accepted. But while for many years Scotland had been the blind spot of policy as the court concentrated on foreign affairs, now the reverse was true. The diplomatic situation in Europe began to evade Charles's grasp, and in August he made a costly error of judgement. He had persisted in playing his potential allies (and enemies) off against one another, but in the summer agreed to provide a Spanish fleet bearing ten thousand troops for use against the French and Dutch with a naval escort through the Channel. On 8 September, as they passed through British waters, the Spanish ships were attacked by a Dutch squadron which drove them to take refuge in Dover. At this point, Charles saw a chance for further profit and advantage. Since his deal with Madrid had made no mention of an English port harbouring so many Spanish ships and troops, he recognized no obligation to protect them from the Dutch fleet now waiting for them in the Channel. Simultaneously he invited a counter-bid for his co-operation from France or the Netherlands. The ambassadors began new rounds of furious talks; Charles sat back and let them come courting.

He miscalculated. To a nation already nervous enough, with rebellion to the north and growing signs of puritan unrest in the old English trouble spots, Charles's crafty game looked like weakness if not negligence. There were limits to the stresses the populace could absorb. For as Suckling warned in *Brennoralt*:

> Dread Sir,
> The Common People are much like the Sea,
> That suffers things to fall and sinke unto
> The bottome in a Calme, which in a Storme
> Stird and inraged, it lifts, and does keep up.[42]

A Spanish fleet bearing enough men to capture London moored in the chief port of the realm, while other foreign powers viewed the southern English coast as an imminent theatre of operations. The Dutch admiral, Tromp, did not wait for the politicians to complete their discussions but simply attacked. Suckling, like everyone else, followed the ensuing duel with fear and mortification. Writing to his uncle on 30 September, he reported the rumour that the 'Hollander' had seventy-three to the 'Spaniard's' fifty-six ships, but with equivalence of tonnage making the fight too close to call. The outcome in any case was more or less irrelevant so far as English pride, let alone the integrity of national borders, was concerned.

In London, Suckling sent the Earl of Holland's hearty commendations to his uncle. He was also engaged in buying horses for Middlesex – including some belonging to Davenant's old saviour, the queen's physician Dr Cademan. Suckling's recent expenditure had perhaps made him appear something of an authority in the trade.[43]

Meanwhile he was oppressed by more than the national crisis. He mentioned his intention of riding to Anglesey, where it seemed that his 'Aglaura', Mary Bulkeley, was about to marry another man. He had written in his usual florid manner earlier in the summer, evidently to calm her on a point of some anxiety. It is possible that Bulkeley, quite reasonably, was expecting her carpet knight to propose. He tried soothing her with a tried and tested conceit. 'Since the inferiour Orbes move but by the first, without all question desires and hopes in me are to be govern'd still by you, as they by it. What mean these fears then? Dear Princesse.'[44] But the princess had found, been found by or been sold off to another suitor, and when he set out to visit '*Mistress* Bulkeley' in the west, Suckling hoped for nothing more than to 'kiss her hands'.[45] In a further, terser note, which the modern editor of his correspondence suggests was written after the couple's last meeting, Suckling admits that he left the house at Baron Hill somewhat brusquely. 'Abruptnesse is an eloquence in parting, when Spinning out of time, is but the weaving of new sorrow.'

In one last letter to Bulkeley, Suckling lamented but accepted the separation of their destinies. He still held that marrying was 'a last remedy, and (to say truth) worse than the disease'.[46] He claimed, nevertheless, 'There was a time too, when all was handsome in my heart; for you were there (Dear Princess) and filled the place alone.'[47] It is impossible to know how sincerely or seriously these words were meant, or whether they formed merely the concluding part of a cordial society game, one further piece of role-playing. Still, it is hard not to wonder what Mary

Bulkeley might have expected of Suckling; and what she looked for instead from her prospective spouse. After the ciphered but terribly public flattery of Suckling's letters and stage productions, it was surely hard for the play to end in such 'abruptnesse'. It is just conceivable that her friend and admirer John Mennes gave his opinion of the matter, and went some way to avenging her, in the ballads tentatively attributed to his name.

In any case, whether relieved or truly distraught, or experiencing a mixture of feigned and felt emotion, it seems that Suckling returned to London a lonelier man in October 1639, around the time when the naval emergency was dramatically resolved. The Hollander crushed the Spaniard off the Downs on 11 October, running some ships ashore and sinking others, leaving the survivors to scurry for their lives across distinctly hostile territory.

'A jolly glasse and right Company' was the cure Suckling prescribed for disappointments of the heart – and in all likelihood for disgraces of the nation as well;[48] but his course of treatment was distracted or at least delayed by further personal problems, this time in the form of a family crisis. His middle-aged Devonian brother-in-law, Sir George Southcot, committed suicide. Suckling had been instrumental in the marital transaction four years earlier, and had later criticized Sir George for his meanness and general curmudgeonliness. Sir George was evidently a saturnine character; while his younger wife, Martha, now thirty-four, had something of her brother's mercurial streak. A letter survives from the year of their wedding, in which Southcot glumly complains to the Earl of Middlesex (as the family patriarch) of Martha throwing parties for all and sundry, and neglecting those he called her 'special friends' and family. He utterly rejected, he said, the company she insisted on keeping. Suckling jibed that it would be easier to get a drink from a devil than his poor sister's husband; but although Middlesex also commented on Southcot's miserly tendencies, Sir George appealed to the principle of thrift, which had, he said, characterized the earl's management of King James's finances.[49] Four years later, he took his own life.

Suckling put down his thoughts in a letter to Martha, who remarried not long afterwards. He told her not to worry or feel responsible for Southcot's death, or guilty for the relief it clearly brought. Suckling also advised her not to ask too much about the details. 'I would not have you so much as enquire whether it were with his garters or his Cloak-bag strings,' he told her. 'Curiosity here would be as vain, as if a Cuckold should enquire whether it were upon the couch or a Bed, and whether the Cavalier pull'd off his Spurrs first or not.'

Conveniently forgetting that he was largely responsible for arranging the match in the first place, Suckling's advice to Lady Martha was that she should neither feel the loss too closely nor blame herself. 'If instead of putting off handsomely the chain of Matrimony [by offering, presumably, a divorce] he hath rudely broke it, 'tis at his own charge, nor should it cost you a tear.' He then considered the problem of how, if she could follow his counsel and not subside into 'counterfeit sorrow', she could prevent the socially requisite display of grief from seeming wholly artificial.

The state of the realm, Suckling said, deserved greater concern. He was aware his verdict on Sir George's suicide seemed harsh; but 'I assure you Christianity highly governs me in the minute in which I do not wish with all my heart that all the discontents in his Majesties three Kingdoms would find out this very way of satisfying themselves and the world.'[50] This abruptly serious note is surprising in one who was generally perceived as the archetypal fallen cavalier, a lightweight in word and deed, the very pattern of the scoundrel who does not even pause to remove his spurs.

Self-slaughter had never been further from the minds of the king's enemies in Scotland, nor from those of an increasingly coherent puritan movement in England. Some could sense at last their moment coming. The new assembly convened in Edinburgh had been an unqualified disaster for the Crown, not only banning episcopacy but declaring it in breach of God's Word – effectively repudiating the Stuart programme of the previous forty years. In England, open preparations for war were again in hand. Some were still living in denial: Lord Arundel, for example, made a move to revive the scheme to colonize Madagascar, going so far as to rig and victual half a dozen ships with the king's full approval, even though the mission's proposed commander, Prince Rupert, was still a prisoner-of-war in Austria.[51] But the fortifications at Berwick, Hull and Carlisle were being renewed; more arms and munitions had been ordered from Europe. Viscount Wentworth had been recalled from Ireland to lend some steel to the king's council. He saw the invasion and conquest of Scotland, with the subsequent installation of an English governor (modelled on his own lieutenancy of Ireland), as the only viable course.

Suckling's *Brennoralt*, along with his other writings from this time, are important for expressing the militant loyalist attitude to the political situation, while also considering the position of the enemy. He was in no doubt at all that the religious arguments of the puritan rebels were nothing more than subterfuge; genuinely held by some, no doubt, but engendered and manipulated by the leadership. But he gives dramatic air to the opinion that the Scots were not – however deceived and misled – rebelling over nothing. Those who have been driven to violent means, argues one councillor in the play, 'have first been violent by necessity'.[52] Implicitly, *Brennoralt* criticizes the delay by Charles and his advisers in taking the Covenant threat seriously. Suckling himself had also failed in this respect until his experience in June 1639, but Brennoralt is clear that 'harsh curbs' are necessary. If, when the nation's honour:

> Hangs in dispute, we should not draw our Swords,
> Why were we ever taught to weare 'em, Sir?[53]

5

Ever in search of 'halcion calmeness', Thomas Carew was in less bullish spirits than his friend. In a celebrated verse epistle he reported having had a woeful time during the long and wet spring campaign. He then retreated to the Earl of Kent's house at Wrest Park:

> Where I no more with raging stormes opprest,
> Weare the cold nights out by the banks of Tweed,
> On the bleak Mountains, where fierce tempests breed,
> And everlasting winter dwells.[54]

Undoubtedly he stressed his shivering misery in order to accentuate the 'temperate ayre' he found at Wrest, the park's pregnant earth all steeped in balmy dew, and indoors a model of social order and mutual

respect. The mansion house itself was devoid of all pretentious ornaments and pointless appendages:

> The Lord and Lady of this place delight
> Rather to be in act, than seeme in sight;
> In stead of Statues to adorne their wall
> They throng with living men, their merry Hall,
> Where at large Tables fill'd with wholesome meates
> The servant, Tennant, and kind neighbour eates.[55]

As many of Carew's first readers were well aware, however, the de
Greys had a more esoteric domestic regime than his poem explicitly
let on, one in key with Carew's own liberated proclivities. For some
considerable time the Countess, Elizabeth de Grey (née Talbot, a granddaughter of the famous Bess of Hardwick), had been the companion of
the jurist John Selden. Lord de Grey had been one of Selden's earliest
and consistently most generous patrons, support which marked out his
own political openness. Selden, a tall, loping man with 'a sharp oval
face', had long ago established his credentials as a free-thinker. He was a
member of Suckling's 'Sessions of the Poets', but would be a firm if
withdrawn supporter of the Parliamentary cause during the 1640s.

The earl and countess's townhouse, Whitefriars, conveniently
adjoined the Inner Temple, where Selden had his lodgings. Aubrey
heard the countess described as an 'ingeniose woman and loving men',
and it was common knowledge that she 'would let him [Selden] lye
with her, and her husband knew it'.[56] When the old earl died in 1639 and
an ancient clerical relative succeeded to the title, Selden and Lady de
Grey confirmed their long-standing private arrangement.

Carew's verse letter from Wrest Park is addressed to his friend 'G.N.',
possibly one Gilbert North, a comrade from the Bishops' War and at the
time of writing, Carew believed, on a hunting trip elsewhere in the
country.[57] At the end he draws out the contrast between their activities:

> Thus I enjoy my selfe, and taste the fruit
> Of this blest Peace, whilst toyl'd in the pursuit
> Of Bucks, and Stags, th'embleme of warre, you strive
> To keep the memory of our Armes alive.[58]

The imagery of plenty in the poem follows classical eulogies of aristo-cratic homes, with a particularly distinguished modern precedent in Ben Jonson's ode to Penshurst Place, the seat of the Sidney family. An import-ant conventional element in such panegyric is that the doors of the house are open and the fire is lit for all those seeking shelter and charity on their way. Thus the cordial atmosphere to be found in Carew's earlier mansion poem, 'To Saxham', where the 'weary Pilgrim' is ever welcome, is strong at Wrest.[59] In keeping with the Jonsonian model, Carew also celebrates Wrest's simplicity. There are no fancy foreign imports, structural or hor-ticultural, to be found at Wrest, no useless adornments. But where he parts company with the master is in insisting on the isolation of the estate from the rest of the realm: as Michael P. Parker argued, while Jonson placed Penshurst in the heart of the political hierarchy, Carew sought to cut Wrest off from that larger system, and presented the place instead as a sanctuary from public life.[60] Within the estate, there is peace; outside there is only discord, un-Wrest. Yet he was still speaking to the outside world, to fellow soldiers and courtiers such as his hunting friend 'Ghib'. In firmly treating the Scottish war as a 'memory' and in praising the art-istic and moral virtues of economy, Carew discouraged readers from contemplating sallies abroad or another costly venture against the Scots – a war that might risk the way of life his poem extols. He subtly urged Charles, or those who could influence him, to stick to the 'temperate' policies which had served the country well for a decade.

An army was mustering to the north, and the Crown had no real source of funds to finance the war to stop it. Charles had in fact accepted that no horn of plenty was currently at his disposal. Grudgingly, after a decade of personal rule, he bowed at last to the need to summon Parlia-ment to raise funds for the war. Wentworth assured him he would take the same firm hand to Westminster that he had shown in subduing the assembly in Ireland. In the meantime, through the winter between the Scottish wars, the court kept up old customs. Davenant and Jones com-bined to put their very best into a new masque for the king and queen, the latter declaring it Jones's finest effort. There was no question now of who was the senior partner in such productions; but the title-page of the published transcript did allow that 'both' poet and designer decided upon the subject-matter.

Performed in January and February 1640, *Salmacida Spolia*, 'The Spoils of Salmacis' (Salmacis in Greek myth being a fountain whose waters had a calming effect on rebels), proved to be the final Caroline adventure in that most luxurious of theatrical genres. Earlier masques, back in the days of Jonson and King James, had been obliged to put a positive gloss on failures and disappointments, but no state of affairs in forty years had concealed its silver lining so effectively as the current Scottish situation. Yet the tempestuous forces of Discord were dispelled in the customary fashion, the queen's dwarf Jeffrey did a dance in an antimasque, and Henrietta Maria herself, pregnant again, descended to the stage in another breathtaking cloud; but the recognition of the need for the wise king's virtues of patience and endurance in 'adverse times' lent a newly sombre air to the performance.[61] Critical messages could always be delivered in the form of compliment, yet political realism, in the world of court entertainment, was all but equivalent to despondency. Though the masque marked the technical summit of Inigo Jones's art, it warned the audience against raising their expectations too high in the year ahead.

In general, from Carew in the country to Davenant in town, the king's poets were urging caution, hearts shrunken by the northern wind. The land was louder than ever with puritan rhetoric, and opposition to ship money was steadfast. In February 1640, shortly after the masque was performed, a party of Covenanters travelled to London for further negotiations. They were led by Lord Loudoun, the saviour of the English cavalry at Kelso. On their way they distributed 'An Information to All Good Christians within the Kingdom of England', first published the summer before, in which they reassured their English brethren of their peaceful intent. They claimed merely to oppose the 'plot' to impose popery on their reformed religion and state, and asked leave to continue following their own beliefs and customs. Countless English Protestants could see the justice of that request, and the clerks of Westminster could well be impressed by the conscientious, lawyerly men who made the trip down to what they saw as the lair of neo-popery, the home of episcopacy, the heart of darkness. Largely the work of Archibald Johnston, and blending his confessional sincerity with a characteristic legal sharpness, the 'Information' had been burnt at the scaffold – which only served to give it further publicity. Meanwhile the negotiations in February, while proving fruitless, allowed the Covenant preachers to win more listeners, more sympathy.

It took a politician of Thomas Wentworth's self-certainty to believe that calling Parliament, after all this time, was the way for the king to achieve his ends. But a substantial number were of his mind. Suckling for one evidently felt that a show of confidence would go a long way. Charles's subjects would measure the monarch by his manner: if he put on an air of sure majesty, he could not fail to win the public trust – and fear. This may sound very much like the gambler advocating a bluff, and one is reminded of the way Suckling used to deal with heavy setbacks: after a loss at cards or bowls, the next day he would appear in more dazzling and costly attire than ever before. Yet Suckling trusted to his methods. In a New Year message to Charles, his prayer was that the very elements which seemed to threaten the king's position could be turned to support it:

> May all the discords in Your State
> (Like those in Musick we create)
> Be govern'd at so wise a rate,
> That what would of it self sound harsh, or fright,
> May be so temper'd that it may delight.[62]

Suckling never wrote a royal masque, but had he done so, this could have been its biggest number. Events were expected to follow the classic Jonsonian plot of harmony emerging from disorder. And if they did not? That was a problem for another day. The tactic of a gambler with a faith in the divine right of majesty was not to flinch, for a moment, from the certainty that they would.

In March, Wentworth returned to Ireland to raise an army for use against the Scots. The king ordered the lieutenant of Edinburgh Castle to fire on the town below at the first sign of trouble. And in Sudbury, the mayor showed what he thought of the royal will by shutting up a tax-collector in a cage, and leaving him to the mercy of locals armed with rocks, mud-pies and rotting vegetables.

6

As spring forced the country back into active service, the early months of 1640 saw another huge force being raised, not without lethargy and protest, for the invasion of Scotland. How the army would be fed, equipped and paid was an open question to which the king and his councillors hoped that Parliament would supply a ready answer. The election of the House of Commons was a major work of mobilization in itself at the best of times. Now, with old grudges to be settled and the honour of the Crown at stake, both the king's enemies and his most steadfast servants went to extra lengths to secure a controlling interest in the chamber. A radical nucleus had already formed around John Pym, an old Parliamentary hand who became the leader and organizer of members with long-standing grudges against the Caroline regime. The leading opponents of ship money, Hampden and St John, were also quickly prominent.

Although John Suckling's place technically lay in the north, at the head of his troops, he clearly felt that he could do more for his master by staying where he was and voicing his opinions in the House. He had already made it plain that he would not be putting up another £12,000 to pay and equip his men. On 14 March, he even went so far as to begin selling off the store of armour and firearms he had built up the previous year, with various patrons and old friends agreeing in the end to take them off his hands.[63] The Suckling finances had been stretched too thin to repeat the previous year's performance.

But he may also have harboured real political ambitions. Suckling had still been in his minority when the last Parliament was held: barring the ultimate goal of a place at the board of the Privy Council, this was perhaps the one remaining venue for a courtier he had yet to sample. Suckling was thus determined to take his seat in Westminster by whatever means were possible, and there were strong signs of gamesmanship in the course which eventually brought about his election, two weeks after the Parliament opened on 13 April. He failed to win in Yarmouth, which his family friend the Earl of Dorset initially tried reserving for him, but was then returned for Bramber, in Sussex, with the help of a little skulduggery. A protest was floated in the Lords that 'undue means' had brought about the victory at Bramber. Suckling was accused of going there personally – perhaps with another troupe of former comrades, such as that he had deployed less successfully against John Digby – and physically intimidating the 'better sort of Burgesses', who shied away from even attending the election.[64] Such stories were no more uncommon in 1640 than they had been in Parliamentary elections for centuries, but subtler methods than Suckling's were in evidence. The defeat of Edward Nicholas, for example, one of the king's key men, was brought about by gently wafting abroad the rumour that he was a Catholic.

No formal party system existed in those days: the English House of Commons was technically a council chamber, in which advice was supposed to be delivered by consensus. For one young lawyer, who soon established himself as one of the leading moderate authorities in the 1640 Commons, this ancient constituency held true – and was worth fighting for. Edward Hyde sincerely believed that the assembly which gathered in April 1640 was still dominated by a sensible and fair-minded majority with no revolutionary agenda whatsoever. He also believed that the balance to be found in the debating chamber represented the equilibrium which still existed in the country at large. There were, however, as Hyde accepted, after eleven years without a Parliament, wrongs to be redressed. In his opening speech he too had complaints at injustice of the kind with which the city bristled. The servant of an earl had refused to pay a waterman his proper fare. Spotting the livery of a swan on the upstart's arm, the waterman told him to 'be gone with his goose': and for the insult found himself in deep trouble with the Earl Marshal's court. Another man Hyde mentioned, a tailor, had gone to the lodgings of a fashionable gentleman who owed him money for clothes. His debtor assaulted him, and tried throwing the tradesman into the street. During the struggle, the tailor protested that he was as good a man as the other: and for calling into question the miscreant's nobility – and superiority – he too was roughly handled by a court which, in Hyde's informed opinion, had no foundation for its sentences in law. These and countless similar abuses needed righting before the country could go on enjoying the unprecedented peace and prosperity, and 'the greatest measure of felicity that it had ever known'.[65]

Hyde recalled many an appreciative chortle in the course of his address. At the time he was unaware of the harder views taken by a sizeable number of his listeners on opposing sides. The camp of Pym, Hampden and St John had its sights on reform that went much further than the minor ombudsman-work Hyde's examples would require.

But Hyde was right in pointing out that the House and its old-timers – the members who had sat in the last years of Elizabeth –

had their own customs, their own institutional biorhythms. They left their inns, their townhouses, their lodgings in the Inns of Court or the rooms provided them by benevolent relatives or patrons, for business to begin at eight o'clock. They would then rise for lunch at twelve, devoting the afternoon to committee work and personal preparation for the next day's debate. The session itself could only be set in motion by lengthy writs and rural wrangling, followed by slow processions and an easy-paced speech by the Lord Keeper on the day of opening. Nothing of great moment was ever attempted, Hyde pointed out, in the first fortnight of a Parliament. As Suckling's rough work in Sussex bore testimony, there were always objections about results to be heard, committees to be composed, and countless other 'ceremonies and preparations' to be observed, along with a regrettable proportion of random and unforeseen business to be dealt with from the world outside Westminster Hall.

The greater bulk of the House, inherently irritable but always willing to be pleased by favour and appreciation from above, was therefore offended by the haste and rudeness with which the king and court approached it. There was the imminence of war with Scotland and the need of funds to pursue the campaign: but wasn't the state of affairs with Spain and Holland, the recent contempt shown for English waters, of equal if not greater moment? Yet the king needed money, quickly, and his overture was simply to demand it. In retrospect, Hyde fully understood the urgency. Yet a Parliamentary grant of subsidies, however quickly it was promised, would take months to arrive in the Exchequer. Delay being unavoidable, it was all the wiser that the king adhere to protocol and hopefully swell the final figure. Instead, nervousness determined the royal tactics. The House of Peers agreed to press ahead with a vote on financing the king; but this immediately provoked outrage in the lower chamber. Since time immemorial, subsidies had always been a freely offered gift from the Commons to the Crown, initiated by the House itself. Now it seemed that every 'ancient right and privilege' — so many returned to the House's collective memory — had gone by the board. The king seemed to have forgotten that an interval of eleven years had passed: this was like inviting a long-absent, long-unseen brother to stay and then pressing him for a loan the moment he stepped through the door. Edward Hyde, only a little over thirty but already a close friend of the great and good and a respected respecter of procedure, watched spirits in the Commons tighten and fray. The spring debates became a dialogue of the deaf: a mismade fugue of unanswered complaints and counter-demands.

Satisfied with preparations in Ireland, Wentworth soon returned from Dublin, snapping at every obstacle. Entering middle age, and physically compromised by gout and kidney stones, in mind and word he was more resolute than ever. His authority in Ireland seemed unassailable, reinforced by promotion from Lord Deputy to Lord Lieutenant. Yet, indestructible as he seemed, more ruthless even than Buckingham, and with an army of at least eight thousand mustering in his fiefdom, his days were numbered. That winter, the viscount had been raised to an earldom, and took 'Strafford' as his title, after a district in his old Yorkshire heartland. At the same time he insisted on a viscountcy for his son, and chose the title 'Raby'. To the court the affront this constituted was immediately clear. Wentworth was already notorious for eliminating real and potential opponents in Ireland: now he was marking his turf in Whitehall, while pursuing an old family feud to boot. For Raby Castle was the country seat of Sir Henry Vane, Suckling's former chief of staff on the frustrating embassy to Gustavus, and now one of the king's chief secretaries, but more to the point an ancient enemy of Wentworth. The sheer wit it took to devise and carry off such a pinpoint stroke of malice was astonishing: there was an admiration buried even in the anger directed now at Strafford, father of Raby. As Hyde later had it, echoing Sulla, if no man exceeded Wentworth in helping his friends, none either could excel him in hurting his enemies.[66]

Squabbles of such pettiness — but of great magnitude in consequence — preoccupied the court while the Scots prepared for war and the officials of the Providence Company, the puritan-dominated body of which Pym was the secretary, prepared to force their will on the Crown. At the end of April, the first shots in Edinburgh were fired, by the royal garrison; simultaneously, in London, the clash over the grant of subsidies and the redress of grievances came close to breaking point. Suddenly, and perhaps duplicitously, certainly without the king's permission, Secretary Vane offered to abolish ship money if the House supplied the money the Crown had requested. Whether the offer was a gamble or sabotage, Pym's men tried pressing home their newly won advantage, but only prompted Charles to dissolve the Parliament, in alarm and outrage, on 5 May.

This was also the day on which the Earl of Strafford sealed his fate, at the agitated council meeting before the dissolution. Strafford was still sure he could bring the Commons to heel; yet, with no choice but to accept the king's decision, he told Charles – or apparently told him, at any rate – that even without English money, 'You have an army in Ireland you may employ here to reduce this kingdom.' Sir Henry Vane, scribbling, entered the sentence in his hazardously ambiguous notes of the meeting. When the papers were discovered by his son, at a conveniently delicate stage in Strafford's subsequent trial, the question of *which* kingdom exactly the earl was speaking of remained perilously open. It seemed reasonable to assume, the topic of the meeting then being the war against the Covenant, that Strafford meant his Irish troops were ready to subdue the Scots. But it took little nimbleness of mind to take 'this kingdom' as referring, potentially at least, to England: and there lay a doubt too great to leave with mere grammarians.

For the moment, however, the war in the north, with or without funds to fight it, called all those who cared. Suckling's old commander, Lord Conway, who had been named General of the Horse for this new 'Bishops' War', had been pressing him for some time to report for duty. Conway was reputed to be very much a man in Suckling's mould, 'voluptuous' in his meat, drink and pleasures of the flesh, but who could entertain the respect of graver, wiser characters, and who still found time and energy for diligence in an appointed enterprise. Like Suckling, he was well read, and could appear as learned as he liked when it suited him.[67] Conway was in the north from early April, doing what he could with the men and arms available, and nagging Suckling and other tardy captains to join him in Newcastle. In a letter to his general written a month or two later, Suckling expressed astonishment that Conway, like God himself, could still spare a thought for such lowly creatures when he had the care of all heaven and earth to think of. He excused himself on the grounds of falling sick at the very moment he put his foot in the stirrup.[68]

In London, the streets, always volatile in May, were turning dangerous. A day or so before the king dissolved Parliament, Edward Hyde paid an anxious visit to his kind if sometimes cantankerous friend the Archbishop of Canterbury. At Lambeth Palace he found Laud in his habitually distant mood, prone to tetchiness at interruption but on that day especially 'sad, and full of thoughts'. Since early on in their acquaintance, Hyde had tried showing Laud how his manner and tone of voice often brought adverse responses when he had never intended offence: Laud, missing the point, had promised his young friend that he would reform his heart but could not answer for his tongue, which too often had a mind of its own. Now Hyde pleaded with him to see that that mistakenly given hurt had reached its peak, and that the king must hold his faith with the Parliament, where the 'number disaffected to the church or state was very small'. Laud listened, simply murmured that the king would most likely dissolve the Parliament in any case, and the two continued their stroll through the palace's blooming garden.[69]

Hyde's confidence in the majority of the Commons did not apply to the people at large. It was not long after his interview with Laud that a mob tried storming Lambeth Palace, forcing the archbishop to retreat to Whitehall for his safety. In response, there was a convocation of clergy to insist on a universal oath of loyalty being sworn to the Church's 'Archbishops, Bishops, deans and archdeacons, &c', a paper instantly dubbed the Et Cetera Oath by puritan wits exultant with fresh fuel for outrage. The head of the sailor who tried prising open the front door of the palace was spiked on London Bridge as a customary warning to others. The man who urged on the crowd by beating a drum was tortured at length. Charles, shaken, ordered preparations to continue for the war.

7

Like Suckling, Davenant also took himself northwards; but this time Thomas Carew would not be following the king. He was buried in London, on 23 March, before the 'Short' Parliament even opened, his funeral taking place at St Dunstan-in-the-West, a church at which Donne had often preached and Felton, Buckingham's assassin, regularly worshipped. The funeral was decent rather than lavish, costing 48 shillings, as befitted one of the king's principal servants, a 'bedchamber man'. Although the cause of his death was not specified, it can be reasonably attributed to his ordeals in the borderlands the year before, despite his recuperation at Wrest, straining too greatly the syphilitic knots which had afflicted his body for years. Carew was perfectly open about his preference for a bed of roses above the rigours of horseback or the ferns, brambles and thistles he complained of by the Tweed. As a young man, Edward Hyde had counted Carew among the older wits he most admired and sought as his companions, but had notably drawn back from too close a confidence with him. Carew was barely forty-five when he died, and there was some dispute as to whether he had ever moderated the lifestyle attributed to him, no doubt unfairly in part, on account of poems written 'in the amorous way'.

Hyde thought that he had, and that his true 'glory' lay in the manner of his passing, in that 'after fifty years of life, spent with less severity or exactness than it ought to have been, he died with the greatest remorse for that license, and with the greatest manifestation of Christianity, that his best friends could desire.'[70] This epitaph has always seemed at variance with a more detailed account of his last day offered by Izaak Walton, the biographer of Donne and Herbert. As Walton had it, Carew sought absolution on his deathbed from an old friend and teacher, John Hales, a prominent and respected figure in London society. In his 'Sessions of the Poets', Suckling pictured him sitting somewhat apart, smiling gravely to see the company in 'such a coil' over the contest for the laurels.[71] A serious scholar, Hales had been a fellow at Merton when Carew was an undergraduate there, and was remembered and admired for his edition of St Chrysostom. If he was somewhat removed from Carew's early exploits, he was a witness at close hand of his greatest indiscretion, for the acquaintance continued when Hales joined Carew on Sir Dudley Carleton's embassy to The Hague, travelling as the mission's chaplain. Any part he played in the scandal of Carew's libel against Lady Carleton and the ambassador's horses was unknown, but over time the younger man clearly regarded him as a friend and a counsellor. Like Carew, Hales had no overweening ambition in his chosen world, refusing every preferment except for a position at Eton which, he said, gave him '£50 more a year than he could spend'. He would come to London perhaps once a year. Hyde also valued Hales's friendship, long after he distanced himself from Carew's, and his account of the churchman's character does much to explain a continuing sympathy between Hales and the promiscuous courtier. Like Carew, Hales was a liberated thinker who declared he would renounce the Church of England the next day, 'if it obliged him to believe that any other Christians should be damned'. He went so far as to say that 'nobody would conclude another man to be damned, who did not wish him so.'[72]

On an earlier occasion when he thought his end was near, Carew had asked Hales to hear and absolve him of his sins, to which Hales agreed on the promise of amendment, as Walton put it. But on recovering, Walton went on, Carew 'fell to his old company and into a more visable Scandalus life', and Hales said nothing more. However, in the early months of 1640, when Carew truly was close to his last gasp, and sought Hales's absolution once again, his old minister refused to give it: unimpressed, in a view that Walton clearly shared, with the repentance being shown. Thus an unreformed philanderer met with his just deserts, in this life and the next. In Walton's account Hales offered the dying man his prayers but not the sacrament he craved, and is supported for doing so. Yet this pitiless treatment sits wrongly with the detailed picture drawn of him by Hyde, who was a much sterner and shrewder judge of character than Walton's sentimental view of life could ever let him be. In Hyde's description Hales was 'of a very open and pleasant conversation . . . pleased with the resort of his friends to him', strict on himself, but to others 'so charitable as to their opinions, that he thought that other men were more in fault for their carriage towards them, than the men themselves who erred'. This defender of reprobates does not fit the image of the unforgiving visitant with whom Walton sides. He evidently held reservations, as Carew did, about the entire doctrine of damnation.

What is missing, unsurprisingly enough, from the story of the death of Thomas Carew, is Carew's own side of that story. We do not hear how earnestly he craved the sacrament of absolution as compared with the other spiritual comforts Hales's company brought to his bedside. Certainly it is hard to see Hales denying the rite to an old friend begging for its solace; more likely that he thought it inessential to Carew's vision of his afterlife, a vision of a breadth he shared.

Carew's work could be said to lay out a narrative of failed conversion. He produced English versions of the psalms, but it is impossible to tell

whether those fell into a certain period of his life, and whether that came
towards its end, or whether he worked on them occasionally or even
during the heat of his numerous affairs. The truth about Carew was that
he saw nothing in life as intrinsically unholy: he did not believe in sin so
much as in lapses of spirit or taste. He admired Donne, for example, for
things that Donne himself was much less willing to pardon by the time
Carew heard him in the pulpit. In his elegy for the older poet, a piece
which is sometimes – unfairly – thought of as Carew's best poem, he
praised Donne for banishing 'the lazie seeds/ Of servile imitation' from
his work. But as his modern editor points out, Carew was content to
keep sowing those seeds in his own, and to retain 'the goodly exil'd
traine/ Of gods and goddesses' which Donne had sent into banishment.[73]
Carew liked those pagan presences; their lifestyle suited him. But for
Carew as for many contemporaries, despite Donne's own best efforts, the
preacher melded with the poet of erotic satire. It was that in fact which
gave him his unique credibility in Carew's eyes. Donne's achievement
rested with his treatment of every aspect of life as a source of spiritual
experience, deploying a rhetorical power on reader and listener that was
capable of realizing anything. It was a power, Carew appreciated, that
could not only be misused but could seem evil even when it was not:

> the flame
> Of thy brave Soule, that shot such heat and light,
> As burnt our earth, and made our darknesse bright,
> Committed holy Rapes upon our Will,
> Did through the eye the melting heart distill;
> And the deepe knowledge of darke truths so teach,
> As sense might judge, what phansie could not reach.[74]

The truth, Carew argued via the example of Donne, could seem dark
to the unenlightened; it took a writer of Donne's courage to work the
illumination required for his 'deepe knowledge' to be instilled and understood. If this elegy were to be taken as Carew's manifesto for poetry, the
greatest criticism of his work would be to point out his failure to follow
Donne's lead, especially after the explosion of iconoclastic potential
shown by 'A Rapture'. Carew could retort that he applied Donne's teaching in life rather than letters, discovering through the senses 'what phansie

could not reach'. 'A Rapture' had taken him to the boundary of what he could pass back into poetic language.

Those who survived and remembered Carew were nevertheless anxious that he repent, and Walton's story of him begging Hales for absolution reflects that demand; as, more colourfully, did an anonymous long poem published in 1645. In a mock debate which bears the stamp of Suckling's 'Sessions', Carew is appointed to a jury, along with other 'men of worth,/ If wit may passe for worth'.[75] Their task is to serve justice upon a number of libellous broadsides, but the action is delayed by a mini-trial of Carew himself, attacked by the prisoner for polluting the Thespian fountain with 'foule conceits' and 'thoughts uncleane'. Given the chance to speak by Apollo, Carew – or his ghost – decides that the best form of defence is apology, and voices his regret for the lines that slipped from his pen, including what he now denounces as the 'foule extasie' of his Rapture, written 'in wisdomes nonage, and unriper yeares', and 'which since with teares/ I laboured to expunge'.[76] In life Carew never repented for such ecstasy, though in a poem commending a friend, George Sandys, for his translation of the psalms, he did express a sense of unease in sanctified spaces:

> I presse not to the Quire, nor dare I greet
> The holy place with my unhallowed feet;
> My unwasht Muse, polutes not things Divine,
> Nor mingles her prophaner notes with thine.

Despite his privileged place at court, Carew thus pictured himself far to the rear of the cathedral, among the dissidents refusing to bow or kneel at the name of Jesus who so angered Archbishop Laud and the other high reformers. Carew modifies that note of humility, however, towards the end of the poem, when it emerges that he simply prefers his muse unwashed. His spirit might seem to taint the nave, but that is implicitly due more to the fact that the Church cannot contain or comprehend him. He announces a search for the immortal on his own terms:

> Perhaps my restless soule, ty'rde with persuit
> Of mortall beauty, seeking without fruit
> Contentment there, which hath not, when enjoy'd,

Quencht all her thirst, nor satisfied, though cloy'd;
Weary of her vaine search below, Above
In the first Faire may find th'immortall Love.[77]

And that is where we should take our last glimpse of Carew, still at loose in the spheres above, as his friends dragged themselves and their kit through the early summer heat towards Newcastle.

In many counties they passed through, paying for their billets out of their own pocket, public order was on the point of collapse. Violence inspired by the May riots in the capital was now rife in patches across the country. Disorderly conscripts were the culprits, for the most part; men levied in distant shires and then hustled upcountry, often with no means of getting their bread. Following the example of London's sailors and apprentices, they saw papists and the king's own churchmen to blame for the plight of the nation, and vented their anger on altar rails and effigies in foreign, suspect parishes – and often living victims. These unwilling recruits distrusted their commanders and sympathized with the Scots' defence of their homeland. They resented being pressed to fight a war the king would now be paying for, so rumours from Westminster informed them, with Spanish money or donations from his northern papist gentry. In Somerset, always a volatile shire, a young Catholic officer was murdered; in Berkshire, another was beaten, stoned and dragged unconscious through the streets of Faringdon by soldiers on the march from Dorset. Clergymen who followed the archbishop's line, and treated the Et Cetera Oath with too much reverence, sensibly feared for their safety.

This year Suckling sent no crowing dispatches from Northumbria to friends in Whitehall or his relations' neighbours in Norfolk. Yet the reports his general gave the king's council had a great deal of the confidence and condescension of Suckling's satirical letters in 1639. From his headquarters in Newcastle, Lord Conway assured Charles, Strafford and Laud of his intelligence that the Covenanters were under-equipped and their leadership divided – by a rift between Lords Argyll and Montrose. There could hardly have been a greater variance between Conway's upbeat memos to the council in July and the defining images of the brief and utterly decisive advance by the Scots: a force of twenty thousand marching through Northumbria, singing psalms as they went; the Earl of Montrose, the most lyrical commander of the seventeenth century, leading the way across the brimming Tweed, chest-deep in water; and the vast Scottish camp confronting Conway's scouts on the far side of the Tyne, camped in tents made from three thousand sets of Edinburghers' bedsheets. However worldly some of the lairds' ulterior motives may have been, in uniting their old tribal interests with the religious question, this was an army of united purpose and community. The contrast could not have been sharper with the force Conway stationed, in a fluster, on the banks of the Tyne at Newburn Ford, made up of malnourished working men on foot who had no quarrel with the enemy, and peppering gentlemen on horseback, stirred but also addled by the memory of Kelso.

It almost seemed a mockery that the first party sent by the Scottish general Leslie across the ford on 20 August consisted of a group of Edinburgh lawyers, who pushed on bravely despite a fierce barrage from English artillery. When the Scots foot reached the shore, the infantry they encountered promptly deserted their trenches. As darkness gathered, Leslie had all the time and quiet he needed to feed his men in dribs and drabs across the water. The cavalry engagements on the open ground beyond the river unfairly put the last nail in Suckling's reputation at home. The English horse in fact made a brave attempt to dislodge the Scottish musketeers from the breastworks their own troops had recently vacated; driven back by a Scottish charge with Leslie himself at the fore, they regrouped and surged again – and were crushed.

Sir John Suckling's final discovery in the north, despite the satirists' subsequent version of events, was that he really was a cavalier. Far from leading the retreat for which the comic ballads blamed him, the Scottish sources show that he was there in the heat of that counter-attack, and was unseated in the course of it. Despite his sale of weaponry and equestrian gear a few months before, he had evidently held on to at least some of his splendid steeds from the first war of 1639, because they made rich trophies for Scottish officers who won the day. An account collected by the Scottish chronicler Spalding speaks of the Covenanters 'doubling there resolutioun and courage, did . . . also put Schir Johne Suckling bak with his horss troups, being the prime of all England (which ar oppositis)'. By this the reporter scornfully suggested it was oxymoronic to speak of Suckling and his men as the enemy's crack troops; but simultaneously admits they were the best the English had, and that it took a strong fight to quell them. At their retreat, the Scots 'took sum of his [Suckling's] horssis, whereof one (being most excelent) was presentit to our Generall'. Others their captors were allowed to keep, 'to encourage everie brave gentilman to adventour'.[78] Another wag later wrote a jeering letter of thanks to Suckling in Leslie's name; though by the time it was published Suckling was dead.

None of Davenant's pigeons were needed to carry the news. The deserters took it themselves back to Newcastle, which immediately had to be evacuated. The city had decent stocks of food, and surprising numbers of muskets and cannon, but – to general disbelief – no ammunition to put in them. Tyneside was in any case unable to stand a siege. The English had refortified Berwick, believing that traditional first port of call would take the main assault. But the Scots had thrown away the history book; they simply bypassed the border fort and, scarcely able to believe the ease of it, helped themselves instead to England's chief supplier of sea-coal, thus putting the southern kingdom at their mercy for the approaching winter. Neither furious notes from Strafford, winded by a savage burst of gout, nor the presence of King Charles, who arrived at York the day Newcastle fell, could make any difference.

Thirty years later, the former wartime chancellor of both Charles I and his son remembered Newburn Ford as the scene of the worst retreat and greatest disgrace in the history of English arms, and vilified Lord Conway for not 'doing anything like a commander', despite the actual loss of only a handful of men – many of whom, as the year before at Kelso, were soon revising events in their minds and eager to redeem themselves.[79] At the time, Edward Hyde saw that the disaster made the king's position weak indeed. Although the participants were spared the carnage seen on the Île de Ré, or the debauchery and butchery at Cadiz, Newburn encapsulated twenty years of English military ignominy.

Suckling had to take his share of the blame for the defeat, and he was seized on gleefully by old sparring partners as a figurehead for the whole army's inadequacies. Instead of the smart modern swordsman, the wit and wonder he aspired to be, he was converted by lyric and broadsheet into one of the oldest caricatures of the seventeenth-century stage – the silly English knight, the Andrew Aguecheek, the braggart exposed as a coward. But Newburn at least showed him giving everything to the attempt: at the close of *Brennoralt*, when the 'strange and intricate' events of a war reach their end, 'back to my private life I will return,' vows Suckling's protagonist and alter ego. That option was closing for Suckling himself – he had lost his last excellent horse, and had nothing put away for his retirement.[80]

9. Plots and Prodigals

He shows himself most Poet, that most feigns:
To find out vertues strangely hid in me,
Aye, there's the art and learned Poetrie.

– Suckling, 'An Answer to Some Verses Made in His Praise'

1

Yorkshire was among the affable Thomas Fuller's favourite counties, one of several he proclaimed the best in all England for certain things. It could, he said, challenge any territory of similar size in all Europe for its fish, fowl, forest and pasture. He called it a 'solid square of continent' in its own right: 'though other counties have more of the warm sun, this hath as much as any of God's temporal blessings.'[1]

Yet this was not the case in the autumn of 1640, and it pained the Earl of Strafford, a Yorkshireman, hugely. He saw the army regrouping shamefacedly around the River Ouse as a disgrace to the Roman capital. It even emerged that the single English hero to catch the light since the catastrophe at Newburn, one John Smith, was a papist. His glory in repelling a Scottish advance party crossing the Tees was thus short-lived. It merely provided further evidence to puritan propagandists that the army was riddled with popery. Closer to headquarters, moreover, Strafford's countrymen had signally failed to rise up against the invading Scots. Won over instead by Covenant literature and spontaneous sympathy for the Scottish cause, York's vocal burghers put their energy into urging the king to call another Parliament.

A chronic state of outrage had overtaken Strafford since the miserable capitulation in August. He was entrusted by Charles with getting the army back in shape – a hopeless commission, since all in the council knew the Crown had been bankrupted by the campaign. The troops were restless to be home, and large numbers did not wait to be dismissed. The force, depleted immediately by mass desertion at Newcastle, was still dissolving. Officers were impatient to return to their estates or their lives in London, with an eye too on standing for the Parliament everyone now expected.

A substantial residue, however, did not wish to leave, fixing their sights instead on a rematch against the Scots. The word was that Leslie's army had been as surprised by their success at Newcastle as the English were shocked. Suckling's eagerness for the fight is not a matter of record, but he was one of those who seemed determined to remain. Besides their defence of the king's honour, the cost of living in the north was less than it was down south. 'What it lacketh of London in bigness and beauty of buildings, it hath in cheapness and plenty of provisions,' reads Fuller's entry on York in *The Worthies of England*, and by this stage Suckling had to mind every penny.[2] His gaming debts were as heavy as ever. When a tailor arrived all the way from London to see him, and stayed in York ten days, Suckling was nowhere to be found.

At this time the king summoned at York a 'Council of Peers', rather than a full Parliament in London. Tactically, the decision was both poor and puzzling, although on emotional grounds the king's reasons were fairly apparent. An assembly of the peers would presumably treat him more sympathetically than a sitting of the Commons. But the council could only appear a stroke of elitism to the country at large, and suggest nothing other than skulduggery, the formation of a cabal, to the king's critics. Edward Hyde attributed the decision to a deeply troubled mind – the mind of a ruler caught 'between an enemy proud and insolent in success, an army corrupted or at best disheartened, a country mutinous and inclined to the rebels, at least not inclined to reduce them, and a Court infected with all three'.[3]

Twelve largely prosperous years had passed for Hyde since he shared his chambers in the Middle Temple with William Davenant, the thwarted saboteur. Since Davenant had offered the government his services to blow up the citadel at Calais, Hyde had sought out companions who 'enjoyed themselves with great delight and public reputation, for the innocence, and sharpness, and learning of their conversation', a more level-headed set of wits than those James Howell once termed the 'English roarers'.[4] He had married, and been bereaved, and felt the loss sorely. He sought comfort in his wide circle of friends and through absorption in business. As the thirties went on, his legal practice flourished, aided by the connections his late wife had brought him to the Villiers family. He had been entrusted with several delicate tasks, including the management of the Middle Temple's effort to distance itself from Prynne and *Histriomastix*, and the campaign to secure the banishment of Henry Jermyn. In the latter he failed, but was lifted into a new and higher set, and became known as a man who could be trusted with a secret.[5]

He could have taken as much work as he wished, but refused to let it govern his life, allotting a certain time each day (or 'borrowing' it from the night) 'to refresh himself with polite learning, in which he still made some progress'. He remarried, again combining social advantage with what seems to have been real fondness in his choice. When time permitted, he enjoyed the 'one continued *convivium philosophicum*' of his great friend Lucius Cary's relaxed academy at Great Tew.

Hyde was happy when Parliament was called in 1640, for personal as well as political reasons; it gave him the chance to see friends who rarely came to town. The chief of these was undoubtedly Cary, Viscount Falkland. 'His stature was low,' Hyde admitted, 'his motion was not graceful, and his aspect so far from inviting, that it had somewhat in it of simplicity.' As for his voice, that was 'the worst of the three'. Yet these unpromising attributes nevertheless held the greatest of souls: 'that little person and small stature was quickly found to contain a great heart, a courage so keen, and a nature so fearless, that no composition of the strongest limbs, and most harmonious and proportioned presence and strength, ever more disposed any man to the greatest enterprise.'[6] The two always sat together in the chamber at Westminster.

When the first 'short' Parliament of 1640 was summoned, Hyde was one of those who felt that a number of modest grievances required redress in order for the kingdom to remain as happy as he thought it was. He had, he claimed, no wish to tamper with fundamentals. He believed that in a conflict of the Crown and the Commons, both gained reciprocally from the limits history had placed upon them:

He had a most zealous esteem and reverence for the constitution of the government; and believed it so equally poised, that if the least branch of the prerogative was torn off, or parted with, the subject suffered by it, and that his right was impaired: and he was as much troubled when the crown exceeded its just limits, and thought its prerogative hurt by it.[7]

Decades later, he still firmly believed that the majority both in Parliament and the country at large were of a mind with him, and was positive that the 'spirits of the whole nation' could not have been more dampened than they were by the dissolution of Parliament in May. His memoirs and history of the civil wars are peppered with observations of lost opportunities; none of which seemed greater to him than the dismissal of that first assembly in 1640. It could not be hoped that another so reasonable and moderate would ever be elected. The party of 'ill purposes' would only grow.[8]

When Parliament met again in November, after the council at York proved a failure, Hyde's worst suspicions were confirmed by a conversation with John Pym in Westminster Hall. Hyde admired Pym as a 'man of good parts' – his standard phrase acknowledging natural ability and wit – and gave the dissident his due for his astute man-management and skill at sustaining a 'long, formed discourse'. But he now had no doubt as to Secretary Pym's intentions; or so at least he was sure he remembered, thirty years of war and exile later. Standing together in the panelled hall a few days before the first debate, Pym told Hyde that the House would need to bring another temper to its business this time. They could not risk the king dissolving Parliament again before their necessary business was complete. It would not be enough to sweep the floors, as he put it; they would need to take a broom to the cobwebs in the topmost corners of the house.[9] Every spider in the dusty palace had due cause to twitch. Hyde had already noticed that the men laid low by the dissolution in May – the followers of Pym in the Commons, and Warwick in the Lords – were full of cheer as they gathered once more in the autumn.

It made him gloomier still to see how the king managed the opening of this Parliament. Charles did not ride in full state to Westminster, but instead arrived by water and slipped in through the back entrance, as if Parliament had merely been adjourned, and was not beginning entirely anew.[10] Soon, to make matters worse, a delegation of Scots arrived to continue peace talks. With them they brought their spiritual leader, the co-author with Johnston of the National Covenant, Alexander Henderson. His preaching was soon thrilling London gatherings, while his writing continued assuring the public that the Scots meant no harm to the English. But they were looking now not only to preserve their religion at home, but also to have it extended across the British Isles. Their best legal mind, Johnston, was also in London, bringing his distinct blend of passion and calculation to the necessary details. His diaries fall silent at this time, yet of all the Scots voices calling for the trial of the king's 'evil councillors', his was both the most insistent and articulate.

As winter descended, Pym's allies in the Commons and their patrons in the Lords began to make their agenda clear. Moderates were purged, where possible, from the Commons. Strafford, who returned from Yorkshire sensing the end, was charged with high treason and his trial made a priority. Laud, suspended from office, soon joined him in the Tower.

There was also a delegation from the Irish Parliament. It arrived in November with inveterate grievances, which the lieutenancy of Strafford had only deepened and supplemented. Strafford's great achievement, as historians have ruefully joked, was a unique consensus in Ireland: the jarring groups of native Irish, 'Old English' and more recent settlers were united against him as they were by nothing else. The different shades of Catholic and Protestant in the visiting party sought varying forms of redress from the English Parliament. For the Catholic Old English, the restoration of the 'Graces' – exemptions from punitive legislation which Strafford had refused to observe – was high on the agenda.[11] Along with colonists of more recent extraction, many of whom sympathized with the cause of the Covenant, they wanted protection of their rights under English law. After a decade of contemptuous treatment, a heady mixture of Irish interests was thus forming against Strafford. The 'evidence' brought to London by their representatives was gratefully and carefully incorporated into the charges against him.

Suckling was back in London by December, and sketched his view of the situation in a long memorandum, apparently addressed to Henry Jermyn. When read alongside the accounts of this period in the great partisan chronicles – Hyde's or Thomas May's – or the specimens of active propaganda and debate collected in the Thomason Tracts, Suckling's 'Letter' is remarkable for its honesty. There was no doubt in Suckling's eyes that the equal poise and 'just limits' of Hyde's beloved constitution, and the factions it had suited best, were under attack – but an attack mounted in the form of a conceit. There was no direct assault on Charles himself, but on the 'evil councillors', the heirs of Buckingham, who had misled him for over a decade. By removing them, naturally, they knocked down the props of Charles's government. Suckling thus viewed the king's problem as a problem of wit: a problem of finding an apt riposte, and of timing it rightly. Unfortunately, the answer must not be sly and subtle, but huge and spectacular:

That it is fit for the Kinge to doe somethinge extraordinary att this present, is not onely the opinion of the wise, but their expectation. Men observe him more now than att other tymes, for Majestie in an Ecclypse, (like the Sun) drawes eies that would not soe much as have look'd towards it, if it had shin'd out, and appear'd like it selfe.

Now the scrutiny upon him was more unsparing than ever, what Charles did mattered less than how it seemed when he did it. The decisions to be made were as much rhetorical, theatrical even, as ideological. In practical terms, the course Charles followed in the winter of 1640–41 was entirely sensible. He maintained an aura of calm, negotiated with his critics and showed himself willing to compromise, accepting many of their demands. But the fashion of the time called for volume and grandeur:

To lie still now would att the best shewe but a calmnes of minde, not a magnanimitie: Since in matter of government, to thinke well (att any tyme, much lesse in a very Active) is little better than to dreame well.

The 'wise' in short wished Charles to behave more like the figure he had played so often in the royal masques. In the meantime, the king could not expect to receive active help, since most of his party 'have so much to doe for their owne preservation, that they cannot without breaking a lawe in Nature intend anothers'. He could not even hope for sound, disinterested advice, since his followers 'determine of his good by his desires, which is a kinde of Settinge the Sun by the Diall'.[12]

However just these words may have been, they were unlikely to lift morale in the king's 'partie'. The letter was an insult to the best efforts of Hyde and Cary to keep the king in control of the army and the English bishops in their palaces, however much they might have agreed with Suckling in essence. In their case, the risk to a united front lay not with self-preservation but with too much 'magnanimity' among the king's supporters. Hyde was upset, for example, when Cary changed his mind and supported a bill to exclude the bishops from Parliament, grumbling about a rare 'facetiousness' in his friend.[13] Giving thought to the question of what the king should do, however, Suckling urged that if he accepted change for the sake of reconciliation, it must appear vigorous and decisive.

Suckling laid bare the loyalists' position. If anything, his letter demonstrated how any option open to the king could lead to disaster. He concluded, with uncharacteristic hesitancy, with a prayer that the king 'bee neither too insensible, of what is without him, nor too resolv'd from what is within him'. Suckling thus argued *against* rashness of the sort with which his own name soon was fatally associated. Yet when it was published, first as 'A Letter Found in the Privy Lodgings at White-hall' in 1641, the careless document became one of numerous scraps of 'discovered' evidence which together supported the idea of a plot against Parliament. In fact Suckling argued that the king seize the initiative from Parliament with reforms of his own. A temporary solution, moreover, would end like a duel between equals, 'where the worsted Partie, the other having no opinion of him, hath his sword given him again without further hurt, after he is in the others power'. That would be all very well, very gentlemanlike:

But otherwise it is not safe to imagine what may followe: For the People are naturally not valiant, and not much cavalier.[14]

If things went unresolved, the king's Hydra-headed adversary might strike again when his back was turned or his sword returned to its sheath:

the country could be facing open war. Suckling had the sense that the movement against the king was not confined to a particular group of individuals, but spoke for a larger social energy: even if Charles could turn his enemies against one another, and remove them by degrees, others would simply appear to champion the same cause. For it was not the 'actors' in England or Scotland that mattered – opportunistic though they were – 'but the things they undertake'.[15] 'Nowe, it is the nature of Cowards to hurt, when they can receive none' – but supposing the king lost his duel, could a plebeian be trusted only to 'fetter royalty'? The people might not be content while the monarchy existed at all.[16] Such thoughts give ample evidence of how far Suckling's thinking on the rebellion had progressed since the jeers he first raised in 1638. As testimony, his letter to Jermyn goes against the tendency of recent historical interpretations to confine the rebellion of 1641–2 to a single group. Suckling detected a less definable but more ominous social pressure for change: 'There are two things in which the People expect to bee satisfied: Religion and Justice; Nor can this bee done by any little Arts, but by reall and Kingly resolutions.'[17] It was vital, though, that Charles make clear that he was author of such resolutions.

Hyde was taking a stroll in the churchyard beside Westminster Hall, one day later in the spring that year, the first time he heard anyone 'own himself a republican'. He was accosted by Henry Marten, a popular figure on all sides of the House, who asked him what he thought of Pym and his men. Hyde denounced them as knaves. Anticipating a familiar principle of modern revolution, he predicted 'that when they had done as much as they intended to do, they should be used as they had used others'. Remembering his manners, he asked for the other's point of view. There was a pause before Marten replied, saying, 'I do not think one man wise enough to govern us all.'[18] Though it was new to Hyde (or so he claimed), Suckling's letter to Jermyn confirms that the thought had been in the air for some time.

There was a rich and very public irony in Suckling denouncing the majority of people as 'not much cavalier', and suspecting foul play. While saying that only cowards strike without risking hurt themselves, this was precisely how he was generally suspected of behaving. One plan was to strike at once, before the rebels taking over Parliament could organize or arm themselves. This would be the approach favoured by Brennoralt:

> Who puts but on the face of punishing,
> And only gently cuts, but prunes rebellion:
> He makes that flourish which he would destroy.
> Who would not be a Rebell when the hopes
> Are vaste, the feares but small?[19]

Yet unlike his creation, Suckling in his letter saw the merits of conquering with a conciliatory strategy. In person, however, he reverted to his own tactic outside Blackfriars back in 1634: strike first, with greater numbers, on an unprepared opponent.

2

For in the early weeks of 1641 Suckling threw what weight he had behind a show of force. In January, or perhaps even earlier, he called for leadership and support from a 'gentleman of grandeur, generosity, loyalty, and steddy and forward courage', the Earl of Newcastle. He couched his appeal as an invitation to the earl, one of the most flamboyant members of the old aristocracy, to pay his friends in London a visit. Newcastle was the governor of young Charles, Prince of Wales. Having long sought prominence at court, he had withdrawn to an aloof position since a row over a point of honour during the first war against the Covenanters. In the summer of 1639 he had been hugely offended when his senior-in-command, the Earl of Holland, placed the prince's troop in the rear of the cavalry on the advance into Scotland. The king had ordered him to take back his gauntlet when he demanded satisfaction of Holland, but mollified him a few months afterwards with a place on the Privy Council. Since then Newcastle had kept his distance from the worsening situation at court. He could always content himself with his architectural projects in Nottinghamshire and Derbyshire, with his many obligations in the north, his love of the equestrian arts, and his writing. He had been the patron of Ben Jonson and, like Suckling, had in his time financed his own productions at Blackfriars. A later memoirist, although sympathetic, complained that 'his edge had too much of the razor in it; for he had a tincture of a Romantic spirit, and had the misfortune to have somewhat of the Poet in him.'[20] Such qualities could only magnify him as both kindred spirit and role model in the eyes of Suckling, who also knew that the earl despised puritans and put the emphasis on action.

Flattering Newcastle in the king and queen's name, Suckling tried coaxing him to make his presence felt at Whitehall. Using what Polonius would call a 'fetch of wit', he opened his epistle with an arch, circumspect conceit that bordered on the absurd. Was the earl so absorbed in tending his white and red rosebuds, the fusion of Lancaster and York, in the person of his ward the prince, that two full-blown roses, the king and queen themselves, could not entice him to visit? Or was he so satisfied with his own company – since as everyone knew, it was better than anyone else's – that he neglected the court? Though he realized that requesting the earl's presence in town was like asking the summer sun to roll round a month or two early, Suckling hoped the 'noblest Planett of our Orb' would be among his friends in London soon. Certainly at the end of May, Newcastle was one of those facing stiff questions from Parliament; and Suckling, having beckoned the sun too close, had fallen in flames.

As plans were laid in Parliament for the prosecution of Strafford, there were at least two groups, no doubt with overlapping personnel, fostering militant solutions to the king's predicament. They lacked Strafford's unwavering belief in his own power to prevail: for Strafford knew that he would face John Pym in an open court, and had no doubt who had the better mind, the greater force with words. He was sure he would undo the rebels' entire programme with the defence he had spent all winter devising at his table in the Tower. Once the move to impeach him failed, the rest of the plot would unravel. The mistake his rigidly logical mind made was, ironically, the mistake of a seasoned Parliamentarian, the Commons man who had once been Pym's comrade and one among the chief troublemakers of King Charles's first assemblies. Strafford put his faith in a cast-iron legal procedure, not fully appreciating that Pym, Hampden, St John and their supporters from above and below, including strong leaders in the Lords and an increasingly vocal committee man, Oliver Cromwell, were changing both law and convention wherever they blocked their path. These vigilantes were stripping the king of his powers and his props, moving to take away his right to choose his own councillors and dissolve Parliament, while pressing for a statutory guarantee that Parliament would re-gather at least every third year. This is not to say they saw themselves as revolutionaries: they were acting, so they thought, to uphold an ancient English constitution. In doing so they still took with them members with less dramatic ideas of how the proper balance of the state should be restored. Hyde, though he later downplayed his part in such measures, was the head of a committee preparing articles to prosecute the judges of the infamous ship money case.

As old council members – including the Secretary of State and the Lord Keeper – were forced to flee, the 'governing party', as Hyde called them now, began filling the vacated posts with their own personnel. While his fellow prisoner, Laud, was granted a last trip across the river to fetch a few books from Lambeth Palace, Strafford was kept under close guard. Despite regular visits and memoranda, his grasp on events was necessarily compromised by his relative isolation. Looking down through his window, he could not follow the situation on the ground; and as his trial in Westminster gathered pace he could not know that his enemy's son, Henry Vane the younger, cheated by Strafford of his title, had discovered a lethal slip of paper in his father's closet – the elder Vane's all but unreadable record of a council meeting the previous year. Among the other rough notes, the secretary had jotted down the promise made at the board by '*L.L.*' – 'Lord Lieutenant' Strafford – of an Irish army to subdue 'this kingdom'.

A week into the trial, a secret meeting was held in an apartment in Whitehall Palace. Present were Henry Percy, the brother of the Earl of Northumberland, and a group of fellow conspirators including Henry Wilmot and a number of others with whom Percy sat in Parliament and had served alongside in the army. This was the more elite set of plotters then active in the court. Representing another, raggier fellowship was Henry Jermyn, who had hardly ever half-unsheathed a sword in anger, and a man more dangerous than the others put together, Colonel George Goring.

Some thumbnail sketches of the great civil war personalities have been rightly moderated or rejected, but one verdict on Goring looks set to survive the test of time: he was 'a man born to be the ruin of any cause which availed itself of his services'.²¹ He would prove to be a champion on both sides in the civil war, and had long been renowned for his blind and stubborn courage. Davenant wrote a long elegy when Goring was supposed lost at the siege of Breda, where Protestant forces re-took a prize Spanish capture in 1637. The poem is a dialogue in which Jermyn (again as 'Arigo') and Porter ('Endymion') seek a ferryman who can take them to visit Goring, now drinking deep with the heroes of old in Hades. To those who lived to look back, Arigo's epitaph for Goring would seem a prophecy in negative:

> Thus he forsooke his glories being young:
> The warrior is unlucky who lives long.²²

In those years it rather seemed that Goring, who returned from the hellfire of Breda with a bullet in his ankle and a limp, and was rewarded with the governorship of Portsmouth, enjoyed the protection of Jupiter himself. He gave every indication that he would not go quietly when the time eventually came: 'the most dexterous in any emergency,' wrote one admirer, 'that I have ever seen . . . he had likewise his blind Side, for he strangely loved the Bottle, was much given to his Pleasures, and [was] a great Debauchee.'²³ On the Isle of Wight in late 1639, he was observed climbing up to the gibbet at Newport and orating to the gulls, before putting his head through the noose in demonic mimicry of the end he would keep on escaping.

In such company Suckling looked suddenly out of his depth. He was with Jermyn and Goring, it seems, the day they met Percy and his brother officers in Whitehall; but he was not permitted to enter. Standing in an antechamber, kicking shadows, mentally reconstituting his pride, his role in what ensued is best viewed at that moment. For despite the attention lavished on his works and papers by his outstanding modern editors, it has never really been stressed just how much of a puppet he was in the so-called 'army plots' of 1641. Edward Hyde, who clearly saw the letter Suckling wrote to Jermyn, was in little doubt that the 'Jermyn' conspiracy was anything more than a decoy.

Henry Percy's initiative was prompted by Parliament's decision in early March to start paying off the Scottish army with £10,000 which had been earmarked for English soldiers still waiting for their wages. His proposal was that all English officers should swear to support the king if the bishops were cast out of Parliament or the troops Strafford had mustered in Ireland were disbanded. The threat of direct action against Parliament, a re-mustering of men and a march on London, was thus put at several removes.

The first tentative stirring on the part of the army itself came towards the end of March. A council of officers at York drafted a polite letter of protest to their commander-in-chief, Northumberland. 'Wee com-playne as gentleman,' they wrote: they were tired of waiting for their pay, and sustaining their troops from their own pockets. They had had enough of opprobrium from the 'poor countre' in which their regi-ments were still stranded. They expressed a wish, too, to redeem their military reputation against the presumptuous Covenant army still occu-pying territory to the north.

This memorandum was drawn up very properly and respectfully, and addressed to the Lord General Northumberland: but its real destin-ation and import was not so transparent. Furthermore, if this was the first sign of political involvement from the English army, there was and is much doubt as to who would guide and liaise with it in London. For on reaching the capital the officer entrusted with delivering the letter, Captain John Chudleigh, did not seek out Northumberland. After his long ride down the northern road, the first person he met with, on 21 March, was William Davenant. They were possibly of old acquaint-ance; feasibly Davenant, tipped off by a former comrade at York, looked out for Chudleigh at Whitehall and took him aside. The letter was apparently unsealed, for when Davenant learned of its contents a look of wonder crossed his broken features. The words were haughty and formal, but carried powerful implications – this, he told Chudleigh, was a matter 'of greater consequence than he imagined'. Next Davenant took him to see Henry Jermyn and Suckling, who reacted as their friend had. Their instinct was that, if a show of force were to be made against Parliament, they might rely on a movement of troops from the north. Jermyn asked Chudleigh if he might take the letter to the queen. At this point Chudleigh seems to have drawn back. He refused to let anyone else see the letter before he delivered it to Northumberland.[24]

When Goring met Percy at the end of the month, he set forward a much more ambitious scheme. It would be better, he and Jermyn said, first to ensure total control of the army on the king's behalf. The Earl of Newcastle should forcibly replace Northumberland as commander-in-chief, with Goring taking over as lieutenant-general. The capital should then be occupied; and Parliament's courage in its convictions put to the test.

This was too 'sharpe and high' for Percy.[25] He dismissed the idea as madness, incompatible with either honour or law. The meeting broke up with no further plan to proceed, and Jermyn and Goring presumably rejoined their junior partner, Suckling, in the outskirts of the palace, cursing their counterparts' lack of resolve. In an audience he granted Percy and Jermyn soon afterwards, the king was thought to favour the more realistic plan – dismissing Jermyn's as foolery. Yet however more moderate – however more constitutional – Percy's thinking was, it excluded one detail crucial to the king's. The fate of Strafford did not enter into Percy's calculations.

The Goring plan, meanwhile, had filtered northwards. The army's messenger, Chudleigh, left London on or about 29 March, to report on the meeting between Goring and Percy. A few days later, at York, a council of officers considered sending a further letter, this time to the king, expressing their 'readiness' to do his bidding as needs arose. But they thought twice of doing so, a hesitation which the leading revisionist historian Conrad Russell interpreted as evidence of the innate constitutionalism of the English – even in such exceptional circumstances. With or without the constitution in mind, the hesitation was a hesitation. Some twenty miles away at Boroughbridge, however, a smaller group was ready to keep at least the talk of action alive. These men sent Chudleigh back to London with a letter for Goring himself, letting him know that if the king saw fit to appoint him lieutenant-general, they would accept him. When Chudleigh reached the city, however, on 4 April, Goring was nowhere to be found. With no alternative, he took the message to Suckling. Evidently pleased with this development, Suckling brought him to the king and queen to kiss hands. Suckling's own view, Chudleigh later said, was that the army ought not to show its teeth unless willing to bite. Yet by the time Goring – who had rejoined his garrison in Portsmouth – read of this new support for his idea and his promotion, the conspiracy had already been overtaken by events. Northumberland had fallen sick, and was replaced on 9 April by a much more ambiguous commander-in-chief, much more malleable to Parliament's 'governing' faction, the Earl of Holland.[26]

Yet as the year went on, as outbursts of violence continued in the city, and as the trial of his greatest councillor whipped the populace into ever greater frenzy, the king kept the Goring option in reserve. There were moments, however, when a rescue plan seemed wholly superfluous. Earlier that spring Charles had watched, like everyone else, a stooped, visibly emaciated and much hoarier Thomas Wentworth take his place before the court of Parliament; and like everyone else, though from a specially screened apartment, he had watched the Lord Strafford confound appearances. In one of the greatest self-defences in English history, the Lord Lieutenant bypassed the vapid rhetoric of Pym's opening address, and confronted the charges in his indictment on a factual basis, article by article. He used the very basic forensic tools his prosecutors should have brought to bear on him, exposing evidence as accusation not proof, highlighting inaccuracies, discrediting witnesses. On 5 April, he even survived the testimony of Sir Henry Vane. As to his alleged remark about bringing Irish troops to 'this kingdom', the prosecution found they could produce nothing more than a copy made by Pym of the original minutes obtained by Vane the younger. This Pym withheld for the time being, sensing that it would not be enough to bring about Strafford's impeachment, and the action crumbled.

It was the performance of a lifetime. In almost any other circumstances it should have been enough to save the defendant's life, if not, perhaps, to preserve him from banishment from future office – or deprivation of at least a portion of his vast estates – which most expected him to suffer. Yet while Strafford's self-defence took an effort he could not sustain much longer, the movement against him could not be expected to abate. The case for impeachment collapsed in the morning of 10 April; but in the afternoon, it was immediately succeeded by a motion for a bill of attainder against Strafford in the House of Commons. With the shift from the attempt to impeach to a push to attaint him, the trial became not so much legal as purely political. Impeachment meant that a majority of judges in the House of Lords decided Strafford was guilty of high treason. Attainder, determined by an Act of Parliament, meant that his death was essential for his country's good.

Now he was slowly overwhelmed. The contest was more thoroughly rhetorical, resting on eloquence and stamina more than mastery of detail. Pym's copy of Vane's notes was produced, this time to the required sensational effect; Vane senior, sensibly hedging his bets, made a display of horror, and publicly denounced his son. On 13 April Strafford made a long speech, again, defending both his record and the concept of royal prerogative, appealing to the same constitutional 'balance' and 'harmony' which Edward Hyde would long support. There were several outstanding speeches in his favour in both Houses. In particular, Falkland, no friend of Strafford, raised strong doubts as to the morality and legitimacy of the measure being debated. But these were insufficient, and on 19 April the Commons condemned the Lord Lieutenant of Ireland to death. A vote decided that he had intended to subvert the law, and that doing so was tantamount to treason.

Mad as the plots unfolded to him had seemed less than a month before, the king was now unsure that he could do without the help even of gamblers such as Goring and Suckling. As he set about his devotions for Easter Week, he began directing officers he could trust to fortify Whitehall. It was Good Friday, 23 April, when he promised Strafford that he would not suffer in life, honour or fortune. He still hoped he had enough support in the Lords to prevent the bill of attainder going through. The next day he received a stern request from Parliament, acting on a petition from the people of London, that he should immediately demobilize Strafford's army, which was still waiting in Ireland. This, in Henry Percy's original plan, was to be one of the triggers activating the first stage of the army plot. The Commons' additional demand for the removal of all Catholic officers from the English army was guaranteed to anger long-standing Roman allegiances in Percy's Northumberland. For the time being, Charles kept a stop on Percy by refusing to acquiesce to this new wave of pressure from Parliament.

Yet the following week saw an attempt by the king to install a garrison of his own men in the Tower. Hyde rose in alarm in the Commons to report a rumour that the Earl of Strafford was about to escape. A strike on Parliament itself seemed possible. It appeared that the king at the eleventh hour had hatched a plan of his own. Suckling, and one William Billingsley, an acquaintance with the rank of colonel who had formerly been a guest at Lord Cranfield's estate, had been given the task of recruiting and arming a hundred men to await further orders; not such a difficult job given the many dangerous characters hovering in the city, and being drawn into brawls on an almost daily basis. To complicate matters further, the official order they received as a cover for this action was a rash insult to Spain, whose representatives in London were still floundering with outrage from mass attack on their embassy the previous weekend.

On Monday 3 May, Suckling was ordered to appear before a Parliamentary committee. There he hoarsely declared that his commission in mustering his hundred was 'to get into Portiugall with armyes of horse'. Another comrade was to take three regiments of foot on the same expedition: their purpose, in other words, was to grant an appeal for an alliance against Spain which the Portuguese ambassador had, true enough, made to the king not long before. Yet Suckling, as his Parliamentary interrogators shortly pointed out, muddled his lines; for there was another troop of horse to be raised 'for what ends he knoweth not'. And he was unable to explain what he was doing the Friday before, 30 April, with sixty men 'in Cosse Coats, swords and pistoles' outside the White Horse Tavern in Bread Street, not far from St Paul's, and why they stayed there all night, giving 'great discontent to the citty'. The Lord Mayor himself, as the peace reached the brink of utter collapse, directly referred the matter to Parliament.[27]

By the time Suckling answered questions in the Painted Chamber at Westminster, before a gathering of both Lords and Commons, whatever threat his troops constituted had already been put to the test, and found inadequate. The idea of going to war in Portugal was exposed as a fraud when one of the men Suckling and Billingsley approached went and asked the Portuguese ambassador if any promise of military help had been made to him. Unsurprisingly, he replied that this was the first he had heard of it. Suckling himself, as a 'senior' conspirator, was probably not present when Billingsley marched the men they had gathered to the gates of the Tower. Met by the lieutenant in charge, Billingsley presented an order from the king to allow them to occupy the fortress. The lieutenant surveyed the small army of bandits, some, perhaps, still wearing the uniforms Suckling had given them two years before. They would still have been more than enough to overpower the guard of perhaps forty men on duty. John Adamson recently added the important detail of perhaps a thousand people gathering to protect the Tower; but such numbers seem not to have gathered until nightfall, by which time the crucial moment had passed.[28] On that spring afternoon, along both riverbanks, London was in turmoil; the embassies of Catholic powers were undergoing popular assault, and known English papists were being beaten in the streets. Behind the lieutenant, meanwhile, lay the one truly safe enclosure in the whole city, and the most wanted man in the land. The officer held his nerve and his ground. He turned Billingsley away and ordered the gates to be closed. This, it appeared, was the sum of the king's ploy to take the capital by force. A few days later the House of Lords took the extraordinary course of installing a man of their own to take command of the Tower – the Earl of Newport, a firm enemy of Strafford. 'Suckling and his desines are discovered,' Newport reported confidently, 'and I am assured he will pay for it if he stay by it.'[29]

In the eyes of apprentices and militant petitioners, Suckling was coming to typify the king's street-based support. The caricature of the cavalier was now being manufactured, by which an opposing 'round-head' depicted a debauched, alcoholic, ex-army bully, over-privileged yet desperate. The cavalier was a 'roaring boy' – one of London's oldest insults for a dissolute – and was willing to use whip, cane or blade on a protesting civilian. In truth there were moments in May when there was little choice but to counter blow with blow. On the ninth, pro-Parliament rioters breached the compound of Whitehall, scattering the servants and putting the queen to flight below stairs, seemingly for her life. Although Suckling himself had by then departed, the crowds were fought off by an unofficial bodyguard whom some now dubbed the 'Sucklingtons'.

In the Sucklington the honest Protestant subject could discover the wrongs of the age. A pamphlet of 1641 classified the Sucklingtons as 'prodigall children, the younger brothers (Luk.15.12) acting your parts of hotspur Cavaliers and disguised ding-thrifts'. 'Suckling': the name denoted one holding his estate by 'socage', by tenure of the plough; but it still carried the image of a fattened piglet, a fitting metaphor for an over-coddled child, one yet to be weaned. The pamphleteer some-what misses the point of his own parable – that the prodigal will and should always be forgiven if he returns – but the cavalier is unredeem-able: 'Now he acts his ryots, anon his revels, and forthwith ferries to a

Play-house, or Bawdy-house.' This is more than a response to a particular crisis. It is an indictment of a recurrent social pattern. In the Sucklington all the shortcomings of the free-spending tendencies of Stuart society are found in legion:

he sits by his liquor, and bloud of the Vine, and the spirits of the Celler . . . enraged into bloud, and most damnable resolutions and designes, terminated in the death and destruction of the next man he meets, that never did neither thought him harme. Or having a noyse of renegade Fidlers, Musicke-abusers, they with him, and he with them, sings and danceth, danceth and sings like a Nightingale, or Canarie bird. He is profuse and lavish.[30]

Suckling did answer this description, sitting by his liquor on May Eve: the portrait in miniature captures well the volatile melancholy of one who could equally collapse or explode.

May Days in London always rumbled with potential violence, with young men traditionally attacking en masse the brothels many of them frequented during the rest of the year. The spring set up opposite charges of puritanical and paganistic energy, and thunderbolts could be expected. It was no coincidence that the attack on Lambeth Palace the year before had fallen within this period. Charles could thus have chosen a better moment than Saturday 1 May to announce to Parliament that he could not in conscience sign the bill of attainder against Strafford. This refusal to bow to popular will gave extra passion to the rioting which broke out later in the day.

Yet the spectre of a co-ordinated martial counter-measure, to lock down the city, spring Strafford free and incapacitate the opposition, could never be much more than a dream. Pym, encouraging widespread anxiety, and no doubt glad to see even Edward Hyde sharing in it, knew all the salient details of the 'army plots' well in advance. Thus it is almost always recorded: and in all the tellings, it is Pym's prior knowledge that sucks any real danger out of the plot. In most versions of the conspiracy George Goring is reported as having an inexplicable crisis of doubt or frustration, and informing on his colleagues a month before the abortive 'attempt' was made. An interpretation of the plot which has been generally excluded from Suckling's biography, but with a vital bearing on it, is that reached by Edward Hyde. In Hyde's view, Goring was working on behalf of Pym and his men from the start. He merely used Suckling and company as a subterfuge, to maintain his credibility with the king's party at court and to win the confidence of a more dangerous political quantity, Henry Percy.[31] This he did not only by convincing Percy that he was in earnest but by alarming him with a scheme which had no detail in its planning, no resources, and no chance of success. It came down to Suckling and a few dozen of his cohorts gathering outside a tavern like latter-day hooligans, and carousing into the soft May night. Henry Jermyn was not even present: true to form, he was observed keeping a rendezvous with his laundress.

Conrad Russell, in a masterly though opinionated survey of the evidence, was sure that a real plot was there in the making, but fizzled out. In doing so, so far as the conspirators themselves were concerned, it served its purpose. For Russell, the army plot should be placed in the context of the escalating series of bluffs which both parties used to gain concessions from the other during 1641–2. Suckling and Davenant entered into the adventure with the gusto they bestowed on all their amateur dramatics, an enthusiasm Pym relied on and exploited for his own propagandistic ends. In Russell's account, which complements rather than contradicts Hyde's, the one conspirator in deadly earnest about going through with the business was the party who most denied all involvement – King Charles himself.[32]

None of Suckling's personal papers survive from this late time in his life; none, at least, which have reached the public demesne. His 'Letter' to Henry Jermyn is notable for going through all the options that remained to the king. Indeed his overall argument is that whatever the king chose to do he should do properly, and that its impact be 'extraordinary'. At one point he wonders whether the way for Charles to preserve his power might not be to 'do more than they [his enemies] desire' and to take control of the reform agenda itself: he might unbalance his critics, for example, 'by throwing away things they call not for, or giving things they expected not'.[33] He also urged that the queen be seen to join such a programme, to redeem her image in the public eye.[34]

Suckling imagined English history as a repeated tug-of-war between the monarch and a pack of 'wantons', the English people. In all 'the troublesome and unfortunate Raignes' of the past – he mentions as examples those of Henry III, King John, Edward II – the princes tugged and tugged stubbornly at their end of the rope; the lesson being that the people will 'pull and tugge as long as the Princes have pull'd with them'. By contrast, Suckling continued, the more masterly rulers, such as Elizabeth, knew when they were about to slip in the mud, and when to let the rope drop. Indeed, such governors generally found that when they let it go, their contestants came 'and putt it into their hands againe'. People at large, in Suckling's considered view, if not 'cavalier', were usually good sports.[35]

His actions were thus at variance with his words, though he was far from unique in that respect. He did not have the opportunity, as Edward Hyde did, of rationalizing his motives at a much later date. In going along with the noise and excitement of a plot, with his old weakness for a great show, while holding private reservations about the violent option, he mirrored the ambivalence of the king, who in the event followed simultaneous and equally ineffectual policies of appeasement and aggression. It is however strange that he should have become mixed up in a conspiracy to break the king's leading councillor out of gaol when, in his 'Letter', he very pointedly queried whether such councillors were worth saving, especially when the charges against them were reasonable. His consideration of this question forms the most systematic part of the essay. Firstly, the king had to think whether he should not, on utilitarian grounds, 'follow nature', and accept the sacrifice of Strafford, Laud and the others for the greater good. Secondly, there was the practical question of whether, once he had saved these ministers, 'they could bee of any use to him hereafter'. Thirdly, and more generally, Charles had to ask himself whether there were any other way of saving Strafford, or potentially any other member of his entourage, before he 'be first right with his people' – before, that is, amends had been made, a settlement reached, and the tug-of-war abandoned for cakes and ale.[36] The Suckling of this essay, in short, is very different from the one depicted as the brattish incendiary leading the prodigal Sucklingtons. The letter's argument suffers by his inescapable tendency to be flippant; but it is still one of the more intelligent assessments of the political situation written at the time. It shows him thinking hard about how the civic meltdown which followed in the spring could be avoided.

There was in fact one more attempt at a gaolbreak, and it was made by Strafford himself. He offered the Lieutenant of the Tower, Sir William

Balfour, £20,000 – a sum on which to found a dynasty – if he would only let him get as far as the river. From the wharf by rowboat he could reach a ship his brother, who had visited him in his cell, would make ready further down the Thames. Listening at the keyhole of Strafford's cell, one Elizabeth Nutt heard the two Wentworths plotting the escape. Mistress Nutt was one of the many citizens to slip into the Tower during those weeks for a glimpse of the prisoner. Strafford, conferring with his brother George, was obviously quite unaware of her – or the two friends who were with her, holding their breath outside the door. The women gathered that the break-out must take place in the dead of night, and there was no doubt of success if only the lieutenant could be brought to do a thing the eavesdroppers did not quite catch, as the earl and Sir George Wentworth moved to the far end of the room. Neither could they tell their Parliamentary questioners where exactly the ship would be, or where Strafford was so sure he could reach in just twelve hours. But they had no cause in the end to doubt the Lieutenant of the Tower. Balfour turned down the bribe, and was offended by Strafford's promise to help his son to a good marriage.[37]

3

Suckling's final word to his interrogators was that 'hee hadd undertaken the profession of a soldier and that his fortunes call'd him to itt': he was still, he claimed, destined for Portugal.[38] That was on Wednesday 5 May. On Thursday he fled the country, along with others who 'in their Jollityes' had spoken 'high words' the previous week.[39] As Suckling's uncle, Middlesex, was gravely informed by his brother-in-law, Suckling along with Henry Percy, Harry Jermyn and William Davenant had all made a dash for France. They evidently still trusted Goring, for they made their escape from Portsmouth, where their erstwhile colleague still commanded the garrison. Goring's motives, so far as they can be guessed at, were apparently not personal. He had agreed to sabotage a plot, not to betray the conspirators: a law unto himself, he recognized the hastily issued royal warrant which licensed Jermyn to travel overseas and rather handsomely overlooked Suckling's own lack of a passport. Together they boarded the *Roebuck*, the royal pinnace, and sailed for Dieppe.

Goring could not extend the same help to Davenant, who had tried making his escape across the North Kentish marshes only to be captured at Faversham. He was betrayed, the wits soon surmised, by his prominently compromised profile:

> Soon as in *Kent* they saw the Bard
> (As to say truth, it is not hard,
> For *Will* has in his face, the flawes
> Of wounds receiv'd in Countreys Cause:)
> They flew on him, like Lions passant,
> And tore his Nose, as much as was on't.

On the same day, the Earl of Northumberland, whom the plot had supposedly aimed at deposing as commander-in-chief, signed Parliamentary warrants for the arrest of all the suspects. There was little, it seems, that Davenant could tell his questioners, although he was examined several times. Both he and his manservant were kept under lock and key – in Covent Garden, thought the doggerel-writer quoted above, where Davenant spent much of his days in bed – as the news of the attempt on the Tower did its work in London and the country at large. The foiled plan was denounced widely as 'the greatest treason . . . that was in England since the powder plot'. Word got around that the schemers had even intended to co-ordinate with French, Spanish or Irish troops in an invasion of the entire kingdom. Davenant, along with Suckling and Jermyn, was placed at the head of a new 'Juntillio', even as professional military witnesses told Parliament that most officers, even those sympathetic to the king, would have had no truck with such leaders. Their flight, however, was popular proof of their guilt in the 'treacherous employment', and as the year drew on it became widely expected that Davenant would be executed on behalf of his friends, whose death sentences would be issued in absentia.[40]

To enormous jubilation, the Earl of Strafford was beheaded shortly after noon on 12 May, meeting his death with a 'composed undaunted courage'. Leaving the prison quietly and proudly, more like a commander inspecting his troops than a captive being led through a mob, he received a frail blessing from the Archbishop of Canterbury, who looked down from his window. On Tower Hill, the crowds stretched to the horizon, packing the wooden stands around the scaffold, filling every last gap on the ramparts of the old city walls. Horsemen and runners stood ready to carry the news to the ends of the kingdom. Strafford chided his friends for their tears with his usual briskness. He spoke measuredly, warning the expectant onlookers that they could expect little joy from a reformation 'begun in blood'. He felt more than a little sorry for them, for he knew there was a general faith that the troubles of the realm would all pass away once he, 'Black Tom Tyrant', was in his grave. He declined the offer of a blindfold.

Quite aside from the political magnitude of the moment, the twists of legal reasoning and peaks of empathic rhetoric which brought Strafford to the block form one of the most notable chapters in the history of the century's arts of wit. His fate, in the end, rested on the use of words. In his exceptionally eloquent summary of Strafford's career and character, Hyde praised especially 'a readiness of conception and sharpness of expression' – *sharpness* being a favoured term in this meticulous writer's vocabulary. This verbal and mental agility, admittedly, 'made his learning thought more in truth than it was',[41] but in the forensic debate over his record Strafford was unmastered. Only in the oratorical battle which ensued was he outnumbered and drowned out.

His execution marked one of many points of no return on the path to civil war, but the verbal means which condemned him were the sign for Hyde of a graver and more general decline in the English state. The death of Strafford was something to rejoice at or avenge; but the process by which he was convicted tainted everyone. In a key speech to Lords and Commons, Oliver St John – since November 1640 the Solicitor General – had argued that, regardless of solid legal evidence, 'private satisfaction' of the Earl of Strafford's guilt was quite sufficient to judge him guilty as charged. By way of illustration, St John argued that 'while we give law to hares and deer, because they be beasts of chase . . . it was never accounted either cruelty or foul play, to knock foxes and wolves on the head as they can be found, because they be beasts of prey.'[42] The lupine Earl of Strafford was thus made culpable by his very nature. Yet this gave prosecutors the right to play the part of the wolf themselves: they would all, as Jonson might well have reflected, turn into beasts.

King Charles, meanwhile, was proving unequal to the containing role required of him. He had given his word that the Lord Lieutenant could count on his protection, but succumbed to mass pressure, and dubious logic from his own advisers. Strafford could not die without the king's signature on the bill; and during his agony over whether or not to yield, Charles was bedevilled by a disquisition on the nature of conscience. Conscience, the Bishop of York assured him, was not a singular but a multiple entity. There were public, private and domestic consciences in a man – and the differences between them, in the case of a king, might force him to do as a ruler what he could never contemplate as an individual.[43]

Isolated further by the loss of Strafford, visibly enfeebled, Archbishop Laud had by now decided that the king was incapable of greatness, unworthy of the service he had received over the years.[44] For Strafford this would have been tantamount to admitting that he had made a mistake in his choice of a master: he made no such concession on his record. By early May, as his would-be rescuers bolted for safety abroad, he had accepted that escape was impossible, but set his sights, as Charles himself eventually would, on a posthumous struggle for the popular imagination. In a 'most pathetical' letter, as Edward Hyde judged it, soon widely distributed, Strafford urged Charles to let him die for the greater good. 'To say, Sir, that there hath not been strife in me, were to make me less man than God knows my infirmities make me' – and yet 'I do most humbly beseech Your Majesty (for preventing of evils which may happen by your refusal) to pass this bill.'[45] Charles gave way, and signed, and felt guilty for doing so to the end of his days. He bought himself no peace with the sacrifice, as Strafford was sure he would not, for the legislative assault on his kingship continued relentlessly.

This was not his only costly broken promise. With the destruction of Strafford, the unity of normally hostile Irish interests broke down. Only the more recent ultra-Protestant (or 'New English') colonists were welcome in the growing Anglo-Scottish puritan consensus. Indeed, only they would have wished to be part of it. But that excluded the more conservative Catholic faction of 'Old English' settlers whose roots in Ireland were older than the Reformation, and in many cases dated back to the original conquest, but who saw themselves as loyal British subjects. As for the 'Old Irish' ascendancy and the 'native' Catholic majority on the island, opposed to rule from London, they were seen as the spawn of the antichrist and ripe for extermination in any case. These excluded factions were to some extent accommodated, however, when the king promised in April to honour the long-defunct 'Graces', a set of selective concessions to the Old English from some of the punitive extremes of Protestant rule. In August, under more pressure from both his English Parliament and council in Dublin, Charles went back on his word. In a matter of weeks, the Old English would join with some misgivings in an attempt by the Old Irish to exploit the king's difficulties. And so the fuse was lit for an Irish revolution – albeit one driven by the hopes and fears of factions which could not coalesce for long.[46]

At the other end of the political hierarchy, the release of William Davenant in July was one of the few signs of public exhaustion with the inquisitional atmosphere. Appropriately, he saved himself with his pen. His *Humble Remonstrance* to the Commons provided light relief to the clashes which continued into the summer, until a new rebellion took the crisis to yet another level. Davenant was perfectly content to show himself with a 'befitting bashfulnesse', as he put it. He suspected that his case would be soon forgotten, since it was based on nothing more than 'suspicions and meere opinions' – the criteria which St John had urged, nonetheless, should have been sufficient to convict Lord Strafford – yet he still felt bound to apologize for having given offence. He generously put in a word for his absent co-defendants. He was friends with both Suckling and Jermyn, he confessed, and took no shame in the fact; for they would surely have both become 'strangely altered' from their true selves, had they ever harboured hostile intentions against the 'glorious proceedings' of the Parliament he addressed. Davenant admitted that he might have been guilty of 'mis-becoming words'; yet these were never concrete subversive plans, 'but loose Arguments, debated at Table perhaps, with too much fancy and heat'.[47]

4

Suckling may still have been alive on the day in early July when Davenant was freed by the Commons, the Members perhaps touched or amused by his 'Remonstrance', perhaps simply needing the bail they demanded of £4,000. While Davenant was able to find half this sum himself, and to find sureties to pay the other, Suckling in Paris was close to his last farthing. Offers of funds and support from his uncle Lionel, Lord Middlesex, who was keeping his head resolutely low, seem not to have been forthcoming.

Neither could men on the run expect a warm welcome from the English community. Their compatriots, some already in hiding from Parliament, understandably feared the consequences of aiding or harbouring fugitives. Henry Percy reached Paris on 22 July, 'very weak and indisposed', and called on the Countess of Leicester, wife of the ambassador, at her house in the Faubourg St-Germain. She received him kindly, and ordered treatment for his illness, but her husband, sending word on arrival at Dieppe the following day, instructed her to turn Percy away. He tottered on to seek other lodgings. Initially, however, Suckling enjoyed a warmer reception at the same residence. 'From Sukling we receave many visitts,' the countess reported early in the summer, 'who is good companie but much abaited in his mirth.'[48] It is likely however that he too suffered from the arrival of Leicester in July, and that a stop was put on his social calls. That may well have extinguished his mirth altogether.

In London, his critics had fun imagining his exploits in Paris and the company he kept. One puritan wit presented 'Four Fugitives Meeting', the transcript of a conversation between Suckling and three other notable exiles, including the former secretary of state Windebank. They initially show him little warmth. 'I wonder much, Sir John,' he is joshed, 'that you being a noble Gentleman, a Commander, and a Volunteere, that [you] would leave your poore souldiers without pay, and come away without taking leave of your Friends.' But as the banter proceeds it dawns on the company that Sir John is the man to help them have a better time of it overseas. He is encouraged to stick to his former vices: 'Sir John, 'tis charity to cheat the Monsieurs, you use your Quicksilverd die amongst them as securely as you could in England, and when you have got their money, wee'l spend it bravely.' Suckling himself concludes:

> Come, my brave boyes, money weel never lack,
> But drowne our sorrowes in a cup of Sack.[49]

Who Suckling's real intimates were in these last months is not on record, nor where he stayed. He could presumably turn to Jermyn, more at home in the city from his earlier spell of exile, and better placed to receive whatever royal favours found their way, long-distance, to the refugees swept into corners in the city's palaces. It happened that James Howell was also in Paris that spring and summer, avoiding the trouble at home, and seeking a publisher for the French version of a history he had written of the modern age – *Dendrologia: Dodona's Grove, or, The Vocall Forest* – and had translated by his own hand. Howell's plummy rectitude and Suckling's social snobbery made them mutually exclusive as companions in each other's eyes, the one used to pleasing his superiors, the other accustomed to pleasing himself. Yet certain passages in Howell's letters give the impression that there should have been greater hope in France for Suckling than he found. A 'roarer' could get mixed up in miracles. Howell mentions, for example, the story of two gamblers in a town in Languedoc, where an image of the Virgin Mary shows her carrying the infant Christ on her right arm, 'contrary to custom', as opposed to her left: 'the reason they told me,' wrote Howell, 'was this':

That two Gamesters being at play, and one having lost all his money, and bolted out many blasphemies, he gave a deep Oath, that that Whore upon the Wall, meaning the picture of the blessed Virgin, was the cause of his ill luck; hereupon the Child remov'd imperceptibly from the left arm to the right, and the Man fell stark dumb ever after: Thus went the Tradition there.[50]

There is a nice balance in this little fable between an oath producing an artistic idiosyncrasy, and the resulting wonder making a new – if speechless – man of the offender. No similar shock befell Suckling to make him change his ways, not even the good fortune of his escape from trial and possible execution. Although he professed admiration for flexible, shape-shifting souls adapting to circumstances and available means, artists like Shakespeare or Donne, or even a political pragmatist such as his uncle, Suckling's true influences were the immoveable egoists of the age, magnates who insisted the world fall into line around their shape – the likes, that is, of Buckingham, the king himself before his power was knocked from under him, Strafford, or even Laud, the perceived dictator of the Church, who 'did not sufficiently value what men said or thought about him'.[51] The example of Buckingham, mistaking confidence for wisdom, a constant show of fearlessness for courage, seems especially damaging, even though Suckling took a low view of the favourite himself. Thus it would always be difficult to imagine him contemplating any drastic alteration in his mode of life as he crossed the Channel aboard the *Roebuck*, or even coming to accept it as weeks of unaccustomed poverty and cool greetings went by in Paris. Even the idea of fighting a long war for his convictions might have been too much to bear.

The fictitious model Suckling always had in mind was one in which the truth of a hero's identity was always eventually brought to light; even if the occasion which triggered that restoral to rights was the tragic death of the protagonist or his love. Thus in *The Goblins*, a tribute to Shakespearean romance written in the late 1630s, Suckling has a prince's brother return from the dead, and brings to light the true nobility of a bandit chief, whose men, disguised as devils, play pranks on the surrounding countryside in Robin Goodfellow fashion. The action is supported by the same mixture of spirits that sustained Suckling himself, a blend of aristocratic disillusionment, tavern-based sport and sexual predation. He is recognizable in many of the characters – especially the melancholy nobles deflated by crossed honour and the libertines relishing the spectacle of a peasant bride, one protesting that he hates 'a woman dressed up to her height, worse then I doe Sugar with Muskadine: It leaves no roome for me to Imagine: I could improve her if she were mine.'[52] Yet he is also present among the simpler brigands, in sympathy with their approach to adversity:

> Some drinke, – what, Boy? – some drinke –
>> Fill it up, fill it up to the brinke.
>> When the Pots crie clinke,
>> And the pockets chinke,
>> Then 'tis a merry world![53]

The more dramatic version of Suckling's death illustrates the unspoken, unshown side of this merry world, in which a goblin's prank could end in manslaughter, a city gent's admiration for a 'country maid' in casual rape. One of the stories, which passed into the eighteenth century via a long chain of tellers, has Suckling killed by a grisly trap. On his flight from London, he arrives in Calais – rather than Dieppe, as the record shows – and falls into a dead sleep. During the night, his servant runs away. When Suckling wakes, to find his portmanteau gone and with it all his money, he immediately gives chase. Inquiring the way his servant took, he calls for his horses, pulls on his breeches and boots and rides so hard that he overtakes the thief at the second or third post along the road. Reclaiming his case, only then does he notice the pain in one of his feet. He collapses; and when bystanders pull off his boots, one is full of blood. The servant, 'who knew his master's temper well and was sure he would pursue him as soon as his villainy should be discovered', had driven a nail up through the heel. The underhand trap was not enough to stop Suckling, but the wound is mortal; he sinks into a lock-jawed fever, and dies a few days later.[54]

The tale has been discounted, for its magnification of Suckling, its flagrant inaccuracy over place, its omission of known fact, its convolution.[55] Yet the existence cannot be ruled out of a smashed kernel of truth, sprinkled through the anecdote. When Suckling arrived at the Countess of Leicester's house, his 'mirth much abaited', he might well have been limping. His portmanteau had very little money in it, of that there is no doubt, and the coins ran through his hands like the last few grains in an hourglass.

The shortage of ready money was fatal in Paris to a gentleman's sense of being a gentleman. It was around this time that Howell was drawing on his experiences abroad to write his *Instructions for Forreine Travell* (published in 1642), and he was explicit about the costs his reader could expect. In Paris, the Englishman would have to 'entertaine a Cook, a Laquay, and some young youth for his Page, to parley and chide withall'. Each servant in his employment would expect at least £50 a year; otherwise, the master should check his boots carefully before putting them on. And this was on top of the very basic expenses incurred through '*Riding, Dancing, Fencing,* the *Racket* [real tennis], with other casuall charges, together with his *Apparell*': for these the gentle traveller would need a minimum budget of £300.[56] Such figures had once meant very little to Suckling. Now the necessities they afforded were beyond him; and he had little credit to order up another glorious suit, as he used to after a bad night at cards.

He may, as John Aubrey was told, have taken poison, a dose of which he supposedly kept ready at a Parisian apothecary, reserving it for the worst and last possible moment, and 'which killed him miserably with vomiting'. This version is the most credible, since Aubrey's source was Davenant. He had the chance to investigate Suckling's disappearance during his own, slightly more comfortable exile in Paris during the war; but on the whole was silent as to any further details he obtained. Aubrey assumed that Davenant's friend was brought to despair at 'being come to the bottom of his fund, reflecting on the miserable and despicable condition he should be reduced to, having nothing left to sustain him'. He ended with one final antisocial action: antisocial, in that suicide was not only a crime against oneself and one's creator, but also against the community left behind. 'Nothing is more damnable, nothing more ungodly, then for a man to slay himself,' stormed a perfectly conventional essayist on this subject earlier in the century. 'For if an homicide be damned for killing another: so in like manner he that killeth himself, is guilty of murther, because he killeth a member of the commonwealth. Yea, this is a greater sinne.'[57]

Suckling had other ideals he had failed, or which had failed him. So too he had other codes to follow, and other authorities to cite in his defence. Montaigne, Donne, even Shakespeare, backed by a firm Stoic tradition and admiring the example of Seneca, had all suggested suicide could be the nobler course. However, any message Suckling tried sending with his death was unfortunately lost in the confusion surrounding it. Yet the verdict of any inquest into Suckling's fate would still be clear: whether intentional or not, it was a case of death by historical circumstance, induced by a culture of misadventure. Albeit with a keen sense of irony, he had tried following the recent leading examples of high cavaliering, from Philip Sidney's gallantry at Zutphen, to Charles on his ride to Madrid; from Buckingham in his headstrong assault on France and Spain, to the great Gustavus Adolphus on his grandiose charge through Germany. In his suicide a note of protest, more than faint if less than fully conscious, may be heard against them all.

10. Incivilities of War

He was of our contrarie faction, but forasmuch as he coun-
terfeited himself otherwise, I knew it not . . . your enemie
being neither by language nor by fashion, nor by any other
apparent marke distinguished from you; nay, which is more,
brought up under the same laws and customes, and breathing
the same ayre.

– Montaigne, *Essayes*, trans. Florio, II.V 'Of Conscience'

1

Suckling may have been gone, but events still followed a 'Sucklington'
plotline. In autumn 1641, as the Irish rebellion broke loose, Charles visited Scotland, attempting to win over his enemies with gifts, too late, of
powers and titles. There his mission was ruined by 'The Incident', a
bungled attempt to kidnap a number of leading Covenant nobles. Once
back in London for the winter, after the Commons had presented him
with a Great Remonstrance, the king finally lost patience when his
enemies spoke of impeaching the queen. Having already cowered in
fear of her life when rioters breached the precincts of Whitehall in May,
Henrietta Maria reportedly gave Charles a spirited ultimatum: 'Go, you
coward, and pull these rogues out by the ears; or never see my face
more.'[1] He acted accordingly, taking four hundred cavaliers with him
to Westminster to arrest the five chief plotters. The culprits, however,
had already slipped away by river. Looking about him in vain, confounded in full view of his subjects, Charles made a terse attempt at
levity. As the Speaker, on his knees, windily protested that he had no
eyes to see nor tongue to speak without the assent of the House, Charles
cut him short: although the birds were flown, he said, he expected the
Commons to send them to him when he returned. Yet these 'politic

birds' were not so obliging as those Davenant trained for his theatricals and communications.

The mood beyond the Chamber, meanwhile, was not so unanimously hostile as is sometimes thought. After the confrontation, shouts from the crowd of 'God save the king' were as voluble as those of 'Privilege of Parliament'.[2] But there was no denying the awkwardness of the moment. Had he been in London, had he still been alive, Suckling would surely have been among the swordsmen who trooped back sheepishly to Whitehall with their royal master. As it was, the departed gamester was undeniably present in spirit.

His influence could be felt, too, when a column of perhaps five hundred Kentish men marched from Blackheath into the capital at the end of April. London by then was a thoroughly frightened city, almost witless with reports of rebellion from Ireland, and torn as to which authority – king or Parliament – should be entrusted with repression and revenge. The protesters from Kent were carrying a petition which both Houses of Parliament had already ordered the hangman to burn. The Earl of Bristol, always politically unfortunate, had been imprisoned for reading an unofficial copy without informing the appropriate committee. The petition called for control of the county's militia to remain where it was, and for the Church's Book of Common Prayer to be preserved in Kent. Although ostensibly geared to local affairs, it touched on the two central questions of the moment: who or what in England had overall command of the armed forces, and what was the doctrine of the established Church? The author, Sir Edward Dering, claimed that forty thousand natives of Kent would gather in support of his demands. Those answering his call fell short of that number, but the document was revived shortly afterwards when a horde of young men supporting the king disrupted a meeting of Parliamentary sympathizers at Maidstone. It was decided then that they would rally before dawn at Blackheath the next day, and march with the petition to Westminster.

Oliver Cromwell had already passed word of the gathering to his colleagues and superiors. When the Kentish five hundred (at a generous count) reached London Bridge, they met soldiers blocking their way, and were ordered to disarm. Only a few were allowed to proceed across the river, past the closed shutters of the houses on the bridge, along streets where defences were already being improvised in expectancy of a struggle for the city. Crucially, at Westminster, these representatives were denied entry, both Houses having already concluded their business for the day. The worst of the tension passed. It was evident to a few private augurs that the enterprise was ill-fated in any case. One of the two young leaders of the excursion, Sir William Boteler (or Butler), was riding past the Royal Exchange, 'in a very fair plain place', when his mount stumbled without cause. Boteler tumbled over the horse's neck. One onlooker remarked, 'Take notice of this man, this is an ominous thing; mark what will betide him.'[3]

The next day, Boteler and his few companions looked to make their presence felt once more, resuming the idea of marching with their men up to Westminster Hall. Somewhat awkwardly for them, however, they found that all their followers had given up the plan and walked or ridden home. Less assertively than they had first intended, they were brought in hatless before the Commons. Their petition was taken, and read. A little while later, they were called back in to answer for themselves. Did they not know that the very same petition had already been publicly condemned – 'and that some Gentlemen were here for the Business'? They had indeed heard a 'general Rumour' to that effect. It was speedily resolved that they should consider their actions in prison. Boteler was committed to the Fleet, and one of his friends, Captain Richard Lovelace, in truth the ringleader who had revived the petition, to the Gatehouse at Westminster. In keeping the latter so near, the honourable members gave the impression that they might need more words with him.

Richard Lovelace was another veteran of the Scottish wars. He had served as ensign and then won promotion in George Goring's regiment. He was one of the many cavaliers disgusted by the Peace of Berwick, a peace 'made at the Foe's rate', as he described it in a popular song. In the same ballad he idolized his general, Goring, 'He whose Glories shine so brave and high'.[4] Lovelace himself was one of the heart-throbs of seventeenth-century literature. He turned twenty-five that year, and was all that Suckling failed to be, with much less effort. Beloved at court, at Oxford he had been 'accounted the most amiable and beautiful person that ever eye beheld'.[5] In his first year at the university he wrote a play performed by fellow undergraduates, and later shown privately in London. Even then, in his early teens, he was admired by at least one lady in the queen's court, whose influence was hazily connected with him receiving his degree in advance, in only his second year. Tall, fine-featured and customarily dressed in cloth of silver and gold, he did not look out of place alongside the university's foremost guest of the time, Prince Rupert, who was awarded his honorary MA on the same day as Lovelace in August 1636.

When he returned from Scotland, Lovelace could well have been drawn into the fraying network of military plots in which Goring and Suckling were enmeshed. There is however no evidence of Lovelace knowing Suckling well, and speculation as to their friendship is not well founded. Everything moreover that Suckling tended to deride, especially in the way of romantic devotion, Lovelace cherished. His father actually had been more of the raucous type, renowned for a 'moste lewd and wicked lyfe', often drunkenly drawing his 'outragious sword' and pursuing his wife with murderous threats.[6] But Lovelace was not to be found swearing oaths in arms and making threats at the White Hart Tavern on May Eve 1641. On leaving active service he retired instead to the family estate at Bethersden in Kent. A few years after his death the manor was celebrated as the 'Seminary or Seedplot from whence a Race of Gentlemen issued forth, who have in Military Affairs atchieved Reputation and Honour, with a prodigal Losse and Expence both of Blood and Life, and by their deep Judgement in the municipal Laws have deserved well of the Common-Wealth'.[7] Lovelace's grandfather, Sir William, had seen considerable service in Ireland. His father, Sir William the younger, died in an assault on Groll in 1627, 'rent with many wounds'.[8] In one account he was hit by a bullet, in another by a cannonball. Lovelace himself was possibly born in the Netherlands during one of Sir William's tours of duty. The eldest of five brothers and three sisters, he was expected, in any case, to follow his forefathers.

Lovelace was often praised for his chivalry, though no clear proof of it survives. Instead he was to inspire fellow royalists in his poems, and indeed say something for all political prisoners, by urging the captive to remain unconquered. Losing liberty, fortune or the trappings of civic identity should not bring despair, he argued – as it perhaps did in Suckling's case – but force you to reaffirm, in your own mind, who and what you really are. In one song, set by the court composer William Lawes, Lovelace made the almost Sartrean point that 'Care shackles you in Liberty.' You are never more free psychologically, that is, than when you are in prison.[9] The trick for Lovelace was to see the mental manacles on those depriving you of rights and justice: 'The Prison is thy Prisoner,' he admiringly told 'a Guiltlesse Lady imprisoned'.[10] Whether or not he wrote his most famous lyric on the subject after the failure of the Kentish petition, as has sometimes been claimed, his spell in the Gatehouse gave him his first opportunity to temper its principal idea:

> Stone Walls doe not a Prison make,
>> Nor Iron bars a Cage;
> Mindes innocent and quiet take
>> That for an Hermitage;
> If I have freedome in my Love,
>> And in my soule am free;
> Angels alone that soar above,
>> Injoy such Liberty.[11]

Regardless of very different opinions on angels and every other matter of faith, this stanza laid out the spiritual strategy adopted by many prisoners of conscience in the coming decades, from cavaliers to Quakers. Despite Lovelace's raptures on the 'glories of my KING' earlier in the poem, these lines from 'To Althea, from Prison' offer an anthem for all captives. Lovelace, however, discovered a more typically Caroline tangent to the thought in his poem to the 'Guiltlesse Lady'. By imprisoning the prison, becoming her gaoler's keeper, every other attribute of her cell is made to support, caress, and even depend upon her. Lovelace imagined the fetters binding the woman becoming enthralled, erotically fascinated by her. They enchain themselves:

> The Gyves to rase so smooth a skin,
> Are so unto themselves within,
> But blest to kisse so fayre an Arme
> Haste to be happy with that harme.

> And play about thy wanton wrist,
> As if in them thou so wert drest,
> But if too rough, too hard they presse,
> Oh they but Closely, closely kisse.[12]

The means of captivity become obsessed with the person of the prisoner, whose very pains are transformed into arousing sensations – at least for Lovelace, imagining his female friend. In the experience of reading the poem, the mental involution required to imagine the woman tying up the elements by which she is held ('thy very very bands/ Are bound to thee, to binde such Hands') provides a distraction – for all concerned – from the fact that she is being hurt.

Seven weeks later, after the members of the Commons had put him behind bars, Lovelace submitted another, this time personal petition for their consideration, 'beeinge verie sensible of the displeasure of this Great Assemblie'. He asked to be set free, 'in all humilitie', only to rejoin 'the Spring-tide of action' beyond the Irish Channel. He did so, however, in pointedly loyalist terms. The insurrection, he wrote, 'treads on the late peacefull bosome of his Maiesties Kingdome', and his grief was heightened by his internment preventing him 'from discharging parte of that duetie, which he owes unto his Kinge and Countrie by his service there'.[13] He was set free in June; but did not go to Ireland. It was thought instead that he spent the next few months living 'beyond the income of his Estate, either to keep up the credit and reputation of the Kings Cause by furnishing men in want'.[14] He seems to have travelled to Holland later in the year, done some service as a mercenary, and is not known to have returned until the English war was over.

2

Despite Lovelace's disappointment, the Kent petitions were indications of how the king's party managed to regain some support in the country at large. This recovery, which enabled him to begin mustering an army worth speaking of, was due less to any act or virtue on the part of Charles himself than to a radical faction of his enemies pushing their agenda too far in the Commons. A general collapse of state and Church was feared, driving back to the royal cause some who had been pleased to see the king's wings clipped. Many – including the famous example of his standard-bearer, Sir Edmund Verney – obeyed his call to arms from a sense of feudal obligation. As it was, Charles was able to scrape together a respectable if uninspiring show of support when he raised his standard on a dismal late-August day at Nottingham, on a bleak hill beyond the town. His campaign could only improve: already that summer he had been turned away not once but twice from the gates of Hull, where most of his munitions were stored, by the governor, Sir John Hotham. The king's greatest hope perhaps lay with the spirit and example of his nephew, Prince Rupert, who had readily accepted a cavalry command. He could rely, too, on 'the gentlemen's sons, younger sons and persons of quality', eager to make their names and if possible their fortunes, whom Cromwell later picked out as the chief threat to Parliament's troops before he took their training in hand.

Charles also had more esoteric, more surreptitious talents at his disposal. Henrietta Maria was co-ordinating an extensive fund-raising and arms-gathering operation in Amsterdam, having mortgaged some of her jewels there. This was no longer the fragile youngster who had arrived in Dover close to tears from a sickening passage and a proxy marriage to a heretic. As the years free of Buckingham went by, the queen became her husband's most demanding adviser: his opponents in Parliament were not fooling when they mooted the advantages of impeaching her. Henrietta Maria was a formidable campaigner. She was now a queen who ordered her spouse to grab their foes by the ears. She chided Charles unsparingly for 'waiting *till the Parliament declares war against you . . .* and thus you will be reduced to do *what the Parliament shall please,* and *I* shall be constrained to retire into a *convent,* or to beg alms'.[15] Charles took seriously her threat, one she often repeated, of withdrawing to a nunnery. After the war he implored those near her to prevent her from taking the veil.

With her in Holland was Davenant, for whom a spell of absence abroad was also expedient after his run-in with the new law-makers the year before. Along with other regulars from her court, he served the queen as an agent in urgent negotiations for ready cash in Amsterdam. The United Provinces, so long delayed from fulfilling their mercantile and imperialist potential by the war with Spain, were still buoyant from Tromp's destruction of the Spanish fleet off the English south coast in 1639. For decades English travellers had reacted nervously and enviously to Amsterdam's architectural demonstration of wealth. The parallels with the Venetian empire went beyond the city's construction on sunken timbers, a marvel in which, as Howell once observed, 'Whosoever could see Amsterdam underground should see a huge Winter-Forest.'[16] Holland, as Howell also remarked, through the vigour and invention of its people, was a land snatched from the jaws of the sea and military destruction; so different to its complacent island neighbour. In the spring and summer months of 1642, as English industry turned inwards on itself in preparation for war, there was a bitter paradox in both sides looking to sources in the Netherlands for remedy and rescue. The monarch's agents felt sympathy waning. 'The queen's entertainment at the Hague is, in my very soul, more royal than hearty,' it was reported. 'The Dutch liberality is at an end, and the queen's entertainment begins to slacken with them.'[17]

The task of pawning off the Crown Jewels would have been unsavoury to anyone but a person as practical as Davenant, who shared Queen Henrietta's realism. By the autumn, however, when civil war had been declared, she decided on another posting for the laureate. She wrote to the magnate in command of the king's northern army, the Earl of Newcastle, requesting him 'not to make any promise in the army that you are raising, for the place of master of the artillery, for I have it in my thoughts to propose you one whom I think very fit for it'.[18] This was the veteran pigeon-handling poet, who had already been liaising with Newcastle, and whose responsibilities as Lieutenant-General of the Ordnance in the north extended to wider logistics and supplies.

By the mid-1600s successful command lay as much with good organization and administration as with battlefield tactics and shows of personal bravery. In theory, Newcastle's eighteen-year-old son was Davenant's commanding officer, but effective control of supplies lay with the poet. Despite appearances, his talent for management – quite apart from his experience in the two Scottish campaigns – qualified him for the commission; just as much as his worldly but discriminating character as 'an eminent good Poet, and loyall Gentleman' recommended him to his flamboyant commander, Newcastle.[19] He was joined by George Goring, who had by now repented of his former dalliance with the rebels, as Newcastle's General of Horse; a veteran of the German wars, James King, as Lieutenant-General; and a clergyman, the Reverend Michael Hudson, as Scoutmaster General. Newcastle's own strengths lay with administration and man-management rather than presence in the field. His fame as a horseman rested on his skill at dressage. That he was 'a sweet general, lay in bed until eleven o'clock and combed until twelve' has always been debated, and is hard to reconcile with the record of his dedicated campaign;[20] but he was reliably depicted as enjoying a nice pipe in his coach before battle began.

Henrietta wrote asking Newcastle to reserve the artillery command for Davenant on 11 October, so it must have been around the time of the war's first major engagement, at Edgehill, on the twenty-third, that the new lieutenant-general took his place on Newcastle's staff. The northern army's first task was to secure Yorkshire from incipient squadrons sympathetic to Parliament, and since Parliament controlled Hull, the royalist grip on the other north-eastern ports was vital. Davenant's passage from Holland to the northern theatre in mid-October in all likelihood missed the shock and turmoil released by the great battle to the south. Yet the rebels controlled by far the greater part of the fleet, benefiting paradoxically from the ship money which Pym and his men had so fiercely opposed. An artful crossing in a disguised vessel, slipping past Parliamentary patrols, would become an accustomed mode of transport for Davenant. He docked quietly in a royalist-controlled harbour, and took the nervous ride cross-country to his new base of operations at York. The ancient northern road, so well known to him and always prone to accident, was already impassable without a run-in with the enemy.

Piecemeal over the last few months the land had been cut into a jigsaw of flashpoints for skirmishes, with the contest for conscripts and supplies still the priority for the local officers. Only with Edgehill did the scale of carnage the country could expect become terribly clear. Although the royalists claimed a narrow victory, with Essex's Parliamentary army scrambling to close the passage to the capital, it was apparent that it would take more than one big old-fashioned battle to settle things. The king himself was still trying to accept his predicament; but all generals were reluctant to give a killer instinct free rein against their fellow subjects. On the Sunday of the battle, from the brow of a steep slope – the 'edge' hill – overlooking a 'fair meadow land' between two Warwickshire villages, Kineton and Radway, Charles was struck with a thrill of fearful wonder at the sight of Essex's army beyond and below, an array of reds, purples and blues forming three lines in the uncertain autumn sunshine. 'I never saw the rebels *in a body* before,' he answered, when asked what so absorbed him.[21] His own supporters, perhaps some eleven thousand of them, were also still a somewhat foreign sight. In a sense, reluctant as he had been to go on progress, to have any great contact with labouring people, it was still a shock to see his ordinary subjects in such a number, even after his Scottish campaigns, let alone one massed against him. 'Your king is both your cause, your quarrel and your captain,' he told his men before they moved down to begin the slaughter.[22] By far the greater number of the dying had very little to do with him, but their fight and their deaths were about him, for him, because of him. It would take him some time to fall, quite literally, into step with them.

The king's predicament on Edgehill was strongly symptomatic of a much wider condition. He saw for the first time the rebels *in a body*: at the same time, his distraction suggests some difficulty in accepting, or processing, the agglomeration of factors, interests and individuals piling up against him. In this, however burdened he felt, he was not alone. People everywhere were struggling to come to terms with the magnitude of events. 'Cooper's Hill', a poem by a young squire, represented one such attempt. In it the desperate political situation prompts Sir John Denham's poetic speaker to look for a more coherent view of national circumstances through his local surroundings, from the vantage of a hill on his Surrey estate.

'Cooper's Hill' would be one of the most influential poems of the next hundred years. The poem's shifting focus respects the real bearing of things, but creates a complex symbolic landscape through them. Moving from the far distance to the foreground, the lush meadows on Denham's Egham property, it takes us from general to particular causes and immediate events. Far off on the horizon, the poet makes out in London the source of the present trouble, which he assigns to an innate restlessness and greed. He is disgusted by the spectacle of early modern capitalism:

> So rais'd above the tumult and the crowd
> I see the city, in a thicker cloud
> Of businesse, than of smoke, where men like ants
> Toil to prevent imaginarie wants;
> Yet all in vain, increasing with their store,
> Their vast desires, but make their wants the more.[23]

Although broadly a supporter of Charles, he by no means exonerates him from this empty desire of more, as he contemplates the battlements of Windsor. Denham was brought up in a tradition of free speech – or, put more accurately, the right to give honest counsel: his late father, a hugely respected jurist, had been one of the judges who gave his verdict against the king over ship money. The king's chief fault, Denham's poem later decides, was being poor, and thus having to intrude on private wealth to maintain his state: a diagnosis which Thomas Hobbes would also later reach. Denham finds some respite in a view closer to home, the Thames running through the nearby Egham meadows, though his eye moves with regret over signs of past destruction, including the remains of a shattered abbey. The river calls to mind larger processes of history and nature, and a cold sort of comfort is found in the reflection that harmony without discord is meaningless. But the picture of sufficiency and balance in the landscape only triggers further shame and anger at the state of the nation. Denham recalls a royal stag hunt he had witnessed, in which 'our Charles' enjoyed an afternoon of leisure: but even as he describes the king's success, he tacitly identifies him with the noble prey. It was the same place, Runnymede, where the barons surrounded King John in 1215 and forced Magna Carta upon him; and it distresses the poet that, four centuries on, neither monarch nor subjects have learned how to moderate their ambitions: 'Thus all to limit royalty conspire,/ While each forgets to limit their desire.'[24] The poem builds to an appeal for containment, for borders on the will to power as firm as the lines giving form to the countryside. In Denham's closing metaphor, if the river swells beyond its course, or if men try narrowing and diverting it, the result is the same: homes are swept away in the flood.

In person, Denham was described by a friend as the 'most dreamingst young fellow', a floating soul who, like Thomas Carew a generation earlier, caused his conservative father a fair deal of concern. Neither was he wholly free of Sucklington tendencies. He displayed his contempt for superfluous gain by pouring his money away at the bowling greens and card tables. To convince his father of his good intentions he had written a tract against gaming; but he wandered from its principles when his patronage was secure. By 1642, the lands about Cooper's Hill were not only being flooded by civil war; they were being eaten away, along with his other estates, as security for his rising gambling debts. Given his personal reputation, the maturity of the writing Denham suddenly produced took those about him by surprise. Besides 'Cooper's Hill' he had also penned a drama, *The Sophy*, which proved popular with the court. His companion and fellow poet Edmund Waller said that his literary powers '*broke out like the Irish Rebellion – threescore thousand strong* before anybody was aware'.[25]

The argument of 'Cooper's Hill' was unusual for 1642 in that it assigned blame and responsibility to both sides of the quarrel. Denham urged, in short, that the leaders amassing their forces at Edgehill could still escape the perspective Charles adopted on the prominence. Looking down, the king still had the option of classifying the enemy below not as a body of *rebels*, but as one part of a problem in which he too was at fault. Again, the name of Edgehill made the battlefield a symbolically apt location: the English governing classes were at the brink, but had yet to tumble down and break their heads.

Yet the results of moderation could be as damaging, albeit inadvertently, as the most subversive designs. The career of Denham's friend Waller illustrated the danger of such a course. Waller was a long-standing confidant of Lord Falkland, and had been schooled in the philosophies of tolerance developed over the years at Great Tew. As a member of the Commons before the war, he had spoken in support of dialogue and mutual respect between the factions. Like Denham, he too had urged his readers and listeners to reflect on their party's share of responsibility for the future. When military action began, Waller remained at Westminster as one of very few voices sympathetic to both the king's position and the moderate reforms of the Short Parliament. He sought, moreover, a wider audience for his views. Ever since he took his seat in the Commons in 1640, Waller had had his speeches printed for the general public. As the conflict widened he looked for some sort of action from the ordinary respectable citizenry. Their basic wish, he assumed, even if they did not support the king, was for peace: and although the evolution of what came to be known as 'Waller's Plot' is even murkier than Suckling's effort the previous spring, Waller clearly hoped for a display of protest against the war and the division of the state. What he may have imagined at first was a financial and mercantile strike, a cessation of the ant-like industry Denham observed in the city from Cooper's Hill.

This would cripple Parliament by cutting its sources of income. Yet Waller, a great speaker but an uncertain doer, was carried by events beyond such peaceful intentions. The predicament was all too common among the many would-be captains who tried taking affairs into their own hands. Just as Suckling was lifted and swept off, so was Waller, as his idea for civic action took on the character of an armed uprising. Like Sir Phelim O'Neill, the rebel captain in Ireland – though O'Neill was a more effective soldier than either of these English poets – he found himself preparing to use means that essentially appalled him. When Waller's group was, almost inevitably, infiltrated and exposed, Pym attributed to him the darkest of motives. Waller was put in the Tower and his plot for peace only hardened large sections of the London public to the need for war.

Waller later bought his life by a notorious show of repentance at his trial, turning his eloquence to the end of self-preservation. He was, as Hyde noted, 'a man in truth very powerful in language'. Captivating the lawyers, merchants and yeomen judging him presented little difficulty; as did bribing most of his accusers with large sums in return 'for their prayers and ghostly counsel'.[26] Yet the trust of Hyde, and other former fellows of the Great Tew company, was lost for ever, and Waller has been hounded through history as the lowest of turncoats. Gardiner's verdict is probably the hardest of all, classifying him as the worst of the 'rich, witty and licentious' sensualists who debased the Caroline court, 'preferring the dishonourable post of a spy on Charles's behalf to active service in the field'.[27] By this estimate his younger friend Denham made the nobler choice, descending from the higher ground of Cooper's Hill and taking a command for the king. From the Parliamentary and puritan view, Waller will probably always seem vaguely repellent; yet for those of his own persuasion, the paradox was that the ideas of Great Tew probably had no more consistent advocate than Waller. As Hyde and Falkland's other youthful friends closed ranks against nonconformity in the 1660s, Waller was still to be heard openly arguing for toleration and reconciliation in the Restoration parliaments.

For the present he was one of those forced to seek friends abroad. By the time his plot was discovered, the horrors of the long bleak slope at Edgehill had already made his duplicity irredeemable to all.

The battle of Edgehill lasted until nightfall, when the wounded lay freezing in their hundreds. Early the next day the king took a ride in his coach to survey the fields still carpeted with bodies. Although there was no great will to resume fighting, neither side was ready yet to withdraw, and it was evening before Essex decided that further action was pointless. Prince Rupert interpreted this as a retreat, and gave chase with his cavalry, capturing some equipment from the Parliamentary rearguard and taking possession of Kineton, a small town filled with little more than casualties. Back on the field of Edgehill, the dead were being sorted, and pits dug: the number of killed was put at around six thousand, a toll which increased in subsequent days as gangrene, fever and the cold of the nights did their work on the injured.

Clerics came from nearby parishes to help regimental chaplains bless the gathered bodies. Yet pagan as well as Christian mores directed the amateur humanists picking their way through the torn and the despoiled. Searching for corpses, for armour and regalia they could recognize, the words of the Sibyl hung over them along with the comforts of scripture. Those given burial would cross the river to the underworld; those left unburied would be stranded on the nearside.[28] This was where their education located the shade of Sir Edmund Verney, the bearer of the lost royal standard, whose body – save, it was said, for a severed arm – was never recovered. He had gone to his death, too, with the dedicated futility of an ancient hero, staying in the thick of the fight for nothing more than the reasons, familiar to all readers of civil war history, which he famously confided to Edward Hyde: 'my conscience is only concerned in honour and in gratitude to follow my master. I have eaten his bread, and served him near thirty years, and will not do so base a thing as to forsake him.' This was perhaps the most memorable, certainly the most poignant profession of squirely devotion in English history, but has an almost universal quality. It is similar in spirit to the sad, wise answer Sancho Panza gives when asked why he would not forsake his master, for all Quixote's 'wild Errantry': 'I have eaten his bread, I love him well, he is thankful.'[29] On the royalist side there was still, as many apart from Rupert saw, an advantage to be pressed, since the London road lay open, and there was much recrimination later for the king's failure to make at least an attempt on the capital. Yet on the ground, at the moment itself, the lack of heart and stamina for an advance seems more than understandable.

It was the familial aspect which moved sentimentalists of the eighteenth and nineteenth century: 'there,' as one historian described the aftermath of Edgehill, 'brother sought out brother, and sons their fathers, to snatch the remains of those they loved from an undistinguished grave; or it might be, to cherish and rekindle the yet lingering spark of life.'[30] The pain of seeing a relative or an old friend in the ranks of the enemy was of course a common theme in contemporary accounts: but there was an undercurrent of disgust to the sense of tragedy in one family member bearing arms against another crucial to the outrage felt against the mere idea of civil war. This war of Englishmen was more than fratricide; it was military incest. Yet the right to defy one's father or brother, to go over to the other side on principle, was a privilege that was in itself a marker of class. For tenants conscripted into a landlord's platoon and herded to a distant county, the choice of allegiance was not so free. For these loyalty often came from comradeship rather than abstract attachment to their 'cause, their quarrel and their captain'. Thus the grief that went with family drama, of brother seeking out brother in the fields of the dead, was a delayed emotion, one that came when those of 'knightly race' had been distinguished from ordinary troopers and given a separate bier.

It took a comparatively rare observer to comment on the universal annulling force of the war, the equality of the fallen. As the Parliamentarian George Wither, for example, observed in his 'field-musings', the grasslands where armies clashed held memories for all. The special horror of a civil war was further refined by its way of destroying such associations:

> In Meadowes, where our sports were wont to be,
> (And, where we playing wantonly have laine)
> Men sprawling in their blood, we now doe see;
> Grim postures, of the dying, and the slaine.[31]

The old arguments over sports and games are redundant for the dead lying in the pastures, along with distinctions of gentleman and commoner, royalist and roundhead: romantic assignations in the meadows, 'wanton' play, are not the property of cavaliers alone. Wither himself, now in later middle age, was a self-styled people's prophet with strong puritan leanings. Once a protégé of King James, he had spent most of his long career enduring official disfavour. When the war came he volunteered for Parliament's army, and was appointed commander of Farnborough Castle, the fort near his small Surrey estate of Wanborough. His wife and children were shortly turned out of their home when a squadron led by Sir John Denham seized Wither's property after claiming Farnborough for the king.

The emphasis in civil war literature on familial and interpersonal tragedy resembles an attempt to preserve old ties and distinctions amid bloodshed which by its very nature did away with such things; to distinguish the war itself from the indiscriminate massacres on the Continent of the past hundred years, or from the intertribal brutalities let loose in Scotland and north-east Ireland. The war in England by contrast was supposedly nobler, a 'war without an enemy', dignified by divisions of principle within great houses and institutions. There were also attempts to make light of it. Journalism on both sides seized on every chance of comedy. This usually involved crowing over a defeat or a misfortune, but the annals contain episodes which afforded mutual amusement.

In a much repeated jest, Denham asked the king to spare Wither's life – and thus save Sir John from being left the worst poet in England.[32] Not long passed, however, before Denham was in turn dislodged from Farnborough. Sir William Waller took an almost dangerously small unit to the castle walls, and Denham's men made a quick and indecently eager surrender. Denham himself showed little promise for a military career: he was a stringy, delicately constituted man, who belied his great height with a stoop and whose complexion had been 'unpolished' by smallpox. He would always attract greater renown for being 'much rooked by gamesters'; or for japes like the one during his time at Lincoln's Inn, when he took a friend and painted over all the signs between Temple Bar and Charing Cross, sending the district into chaos. (Aubrey had the anecdote on good authority from 'R. Estcott, esq., that carried the inke-pott'.[33])

Prominence was often given to stories of clemency, tales which suggested the antagonists fought, Verney-style, only to obey the constraints of honour or destiny, or which indicated that the decencies of a previous life had not died out. During the nine months Davenant spent as

Newcastle's Master of Ordnance, 'It was his hap,' as he reminisced to John Aubrey, 'to have two aldermen of York his prisoners.' Being 'something stubborn', these high-ranking captives refused to pay the ransom for their release; and being not only humane, but generous and hospitable, Davenant accommodated them in his own tent, 'and sat them at the upper end of his table à la mode de France'. Not long passed before Davenant's cupboards were bare. So, 'privately and friendly', he suggested they take the first opportunity to escape, with the unspoken offer of his turning a blind eye. But having made off from the royalist camp, they had not gone far before their consciences ached. So they stole back, past the same guards, running the risk of capture twice more in order to give their host and keeper proper thanks. They did, however, in Aubrey's summary, still then manage to reach York.[34]

Such stories were treasured by contemporary chroniclers since they supported the impression that the English had essentially fought a gentleman's war. Edward Hyde related a more elaborate and flamboyant adventure from early on in the hostilities, though with some reservations as to the hero. Early in the summer of 1642 an emissary from the queen visited the king, incognito, at York. This was Lord George Digby, a relative of Suckling's nemesis, Sir John, who had endeared himself to the king the previous year by speaking out in defence of Strafford. Lord George was the son of one of the leading rebels in the Lords, Buckingham's old enemy (and former host at Madrid) the Earl of Bristol, and initially a strong supporter of Pym's reforms, but had dramatically switched sides when Strafford was brought to bay. Thirty years old, blond, fine-featured, Digby was swiftly becoming one of the king's most trusted advisers, along with two other avowed converts to the royal camp, Hyde and Falkland. After secret discussions at York, maintaining a disguise, Digby set out once more for Holland, embarking in a little fly-boat. A short way off the coast he and his few companions rendezvoused by chance with the *Providence*, a ship carrying much-needed munitions to the king from Denmark. Three of his escort agreed to return with these supplies while Digby sailed on to the Netherlands. But they held conference too long, and though the cargo ship sailed on, Digby's barque was trapped by a flotilla of Parliament ships. He was taken into Hull. Although a well-known courtier, indeed an object of considerable contempt to the governor of the port, Sir John Hotham,

Digby's costume and false beard were apparently so effective that no one guessed his real identity. He further gulled his captors by pretending to be a Frenchman whose loyalties were entirely at their disposal. His fluency was sufficient to deceive Hotham and his men, but he knew that he could not sustain the act indefinitely. Hyde commented that Digby was always inclined to favour the audacious course of action, and that his 'noble stars' protected him in the 'perplexities' he regularly encountered by following that path.

After beguiling the guardroom with stories of his service in the French court, Digby asked for a private interview with the governor. Once they were alone, keeping up his French accent but speaking now in English, he asked Hotham if he knew him: Hotham shook his head. Digby went on to make it clear that *he* knew Hotham very well, and exploited the other's vanity by outlining his gaoler's character in highly gratifying terms. Having softened the governor with flattery, he then revealed his identity. Now Hotham in ordinary circumstances despised Digby as a flashy upstart, and when left to himself he was, at least in Hyde's opinion, 'a rough and a rude man; of great covetousness, of great pride, and great ambition; without any bowels of good nature, or the least sense or touch of generosity'. But since learning that we are esteemed by one we hate is frequently enough to change our feelings towards the person in question, Hotham mollified his former view of Digby in this surprising context: it is always a shame to execute an admirer if you have only a very few others to spare. Thus Hotham 'resolved to practise that virtue which the other had imputed to him'.[35] Another pressure, moreover, made his magnanimity sensible. Hotham had recently turned King Charles away from the gates of the city. Since then his courage on Parliament's behalf had been plaguing his dreams: he had learned that the king looked forward to seeing him hanged at the first opportunity.

Sitting down now with one who had the ear of Charles and Henrietta Maria, Hotham sighed out his regret and distress at things having reached such a pass. He groaned heavily to think of his extremist masters in London, and all those set on war. The relationship of prisoner and warden had by this point been inverted. Digby was adept at the delicate work such situations required of simultaneously reassuring while wreaking painful doubt. Over several conversations, for in Hyde's view Hotham could not take in too many thoughts at one time, Digby also bewailed their country's plight, and expressed much sympathy for Hotham's predicament. At the same time, holding the governor in thrall, he painted in words a crushing picture of the royals' military superiority. There was no doubt that, should it come to war, Charles would annihilate the rebels in the field. And in that event, Digby concluded gently – perhaps without even uttering the thought – Hotham should think of what his future held. Or rather, he should contemplate the glory and honour that would be his if he were to surrender Hull now, before it was too late, to the king, and thus gain the credit for stopping the war before it started. He, Digby, would take the message to Charles at York and see that all was set right.

A gentlemen's agreement was accordingly reached. Hotham was not, however, prepared simply to open the city to the royal troops. For fear of the town's continued support for Parliament, he insisted that the king fire his cannon at least once against the city walls. Then he could give in credibly. For the time being he allowed Digby to maintain his French disguise, and then to slip back to York, where he arrived before the arms from the *Providence* reached the king. Albeit with some misgiving, Charles accepted the plan, and marched his troops to Hull. There Hotham demonstrated the truism that while the weak-minded can easily enough be forced to make concessions, no great weight should be attached to their promises of positive action. With puritan suspicions high and observers from London reporting his every word and deed, he felt unable to let the king's force enter: unless, presumably, they preserved the governor's standing with his men by a show of adequate force. Charles returned fuming to York, angry above all that he had once more appeared publicly ridiculous, with his officers champing for vengeance.

Thus there was frequently more to shows of clemency than pure compassion. The combatants' enemies were their neighbours, or at least their fellow subjects, and some sort of civic coexistence would have to resume when the fighting stopped. Few could contemplate the dispossession or massacre of the losing side without considering the possibility that they might be on it themselves. It took a long time to stamp out the hope of a return to normality. Not even Edgehill could dispel it, nor a gruelling winter mixed with skirmishing and hollow talk of truce, with provisions in some places dwindling to a diet of dog and horse. The king's army fortified headquarters in Oxford, and Newcastle's struggled to stamp out Parliamentary forces in West Riding. Parliament made good its possessions in the south and east, while the war stirred into life in the West Country, with a contest imminent between the more conservative sympathies of Cornwall and the militant puritanism of Plymouth. In Scotland the Covenanters controlled the organs of state and the wider country, barring the wilder terrain to the far north. Only Ireland as yet was thoroughly steeped in blood. The rebellion there spread from Ulster far to the south and west, with perhaps four thousand Protestant planters dying in the first wave. Even that number seemed too small to express the outrage felt in England and Scotland, and incite an adequate revenge: the adjusted death toll reported in London ran into tens and occasionally hundreds of thousands.

A few English towns, such as Lancaster, stormed and burnt for the king by the Earl of Derby, had their first taste of scorched earth. The causes being fought for were as diverse as the areas involved: some upheld the Covenant, others the liberty of the subject and the status of the law; others the old Church, others still the Presbyterian system they wished to replace it; and some few the idea of dispensing with a monopoly on faith or power altogether. More still undoubtedly brought to mind some personal grudge or source of local gratitude when summoning their courage and accepting their fate. Yet people are rarely unanimous on what any war is being fought for.

It is vital to remember that in the minds of the couple at the centre and summit of the royalist cause, the king and queen, nothing whatsoever had changed. So far as Charles would ever be concerned, he remained God's chosen ruler. His wife, a de Medici on her mother's side, had no need even to elaborate a theory for her rights or justifying her supremacy. Early in 1643 she set off on a journey through England to rejoin her husband, in what began with a cannonade and became a grand tour which preoccupied her protector, Newcastle, for the first half of the year. In the last week of February, at the second attempt, she sailed from Holland with a Dutch escort, landing at the East Yorkshire port of Bridlington, a short way north of Hull, where she stopped for the night. Her ship was spotted, however, by a group of Parliamentary vessels, which entered the bay in the small hours and began bombarding the harbour. Sweeping the seafront, they pounded the house where Henrietta Maria was resting. Her party had no choice but to run for shelter further inland. Just as she had reassured her ladies-in-waiting during the rough crossing, the queen now showed remarkable composure under fire. After two hours the ships dropped their barrage, when the larger Dutch cruisers which had accompanied the queen threatened to move closer. By that point, however, Henrietta had already seen a sergeant blown to pieces a few yards ahead of her, dived for cover in a nearby ditch, and then run back to retrieve her dog, Mitte.

The escape occasioned lyrics from around the country, indignant, solicitous, scornful. Henrietta Maria herself described the ordeal in terms suggesting a royal entertainment gone wrong, an extreme form of antimasque. 'The balls were whistling upon me in such a style that you may easily believe I loved not such music,' she informed Charles, when there was peace for paper and pen.[36]

The civil war saw a predictable surge of poetic activities along factional lines. The rules of engagement, however, for complimenting and advising the great and clashing with hostile wits remained basically unchanged. The chief literary innovation of the war years would be journalistic, in an explosion of vying sectarian newspapers. In terms of poetic technique, however, the Jonsonian codes from earlier in the century still held. Since there was little development artistically, historians and critics would for some time look to the writing of the 1620s and '30s for their examples of 'cavalier' literature. As more recent scholars have argued at length, this was a mistake – since no distinct cavalier party existed before 1641–2. More accurately, the first half of Charles's reign saw the *making* of the cavaliers. Looking back, one sees the fashioning of values and literary attitudes which royalist poetasters and propagandists of the forties would take as their own. The remaking of the 1630s was aided as well by the efforts of some survivors from that time to meet the royal taste for insouciance, and write as if the old state of things still thrived.

When the queen reached York under Newcastle's guard, having avoided a plot to kidnap her as a hostage for Parliament, Davenant presented her a song which made no mention of the trying times. The old niceties were far from lost. Reviewing his 'old years crimes' as one seeking absolution – the tone is frankly Catholic – he found his greatest offences lay with the inadequacy of his former expressions of praise for the queen. He continued by putting that wrong right in ten easy stanzas.[37] The scene for the poem had been laid: Henrietta Maria had set up a miniature court in York, taking her time before rejoining the king at Oxford.

There was reason enough for Davenant making no attempt to keep up with events. Although histories often regard 1643 as the crucial year of royalist successes and opportunities – indeed it was felt as such in London, where a diversionary peace initiative gradually gave way to a drive for an alliance with Scotland – Newcastle's spring offensive reflected a wider failure to make solid progress. Drawn and redrawn week by week, the battle map of England would show the entire central body of the land coloured with gain and counter-gain. Taking the difficulty of efficient communication into account, it was impossible even at the time to know for sure where the overall advantage lay. Even the great published collections of contemporary documents and multi-tome chronicles of the war are unable to convey entirely the simultaneity and interdependence of actions across the regions.

Following the campaign in the north through the spring and early summer of 1643, one sees Goring triumph in madcap fashion at Seacroft Moor, and Newcastle take Rotherham to charges of plunder and pillage from his adversary, Fairfax; only for Goring to push his luck too far, and be defeated and captured at Wakeham. In the meantime, Parliament's vital garrison at Hull stays firmly in place. An overall trend was hard to make out, and there was a similar inconsistency in the nature and ferocity of the combat. Newcastle's gallantry towards Lady Ann Fairfax, captured riding pillion in the Parliament army's retreat from Adwalton Moor, a few miles from Bradford, kept up the war's gentlemanly appearance; having ordered that no mercy be shown to Sir John Savile, who forced a pointless siege at Howley House, he spared the prisoner the firing squad when his men brought him in. However, to be set against that is the fate at Gainsborough of Newcastle's cousin Sir Charles Cavendish, who having fallen and surrendered to the enemy was speared on the ground like a seal.

The world with which this book has mainly been concerned, the privileged world which had nourished John Suckling and Tom Carew, felt more intact the closer one was to the person of the queen. When she finally departed for Oxford, requiring Newcastle and a huge troop as escort, there was a blitheness to her progress which the earl's field officers found half maddening, half inspiring. Her transport took precious men away from the northern campaign, while at the same time failing to provide the relief which the southern armies keenly desired. Opinion in the army was split between whether Newcastle should unite his men with the king's and opt for an all-or-nothing push towards London, or continue with his efforts against Hull. Instead Newcastle did neither, leaving Henrietta Maria to proceed under heavy escort from Newark, while he turned back. Charles, expecting the roundheads to besiege him at Oxford, sent urgent letters commanding the earl to bring not only the seven thousand men he left at Newark with Henrietta Maria, but also the two thousand-odd with whom he returned. The queen, with a better knowledge than the king of the situation in Yorkshire, told Newcastle of the order but chose to suppress the letter which formally obliged him to obey it. She had a light certainty in action Charles never possessed, and it can be seen on her looping tour southwards to meet him. Her personal army naturally stabilized the situation wherever she stayed, and she arrived like a memory of Elizabeth, a young queen on horseback, quipping with her guards on the road, displaying a potential for the common touch which the Stuarts until recent times had never seen the need to master. Arriving at Stratford-upon-Avon on 22 June, she stayed the night at Shakespeare's house, New Place, where the second-best bed may have gone but much of his plate was still shelved and his granddaughter lived with her husband Nash. There were good tactical reasons for this choice of billet. The queen could not rely on a welcome in the grander setting of Charlecote Park a few miles away, where Elizabeth stayed on her progress in 1570, and where the young Shakespeare of legend poached deer: Charlecote backed Parliament, and the mistress of the estate, Lady Alice Lucy, ran one of the staunchest puritan households in Warwickshire.

Preoccupied as she was by military reality, it is not inconceivable that a touch of cultural tourism crept into the queen's itinerary. Shakespeare was still far from being the institution he became in the eighteenth and nineteenth centuries, but the queen, besides being fond of the theatre, presided over a court in which his works had vehement advocates, imitators and plagiarists. Davenant raided the plays with a godson's sense of

proprietorship, and was said to count among his most precious possessions a letter to the poet from King James. Suckling, portrayed by van
Dyck with the folio text of *Hamlet* draped open before him, was one of
countless others who plundered Shakespeare almost unthinkingly when
the need for a good line presented itself. He had also been among the
first to put the bard on a par with the classics. If a story which surfaced
some seventy years later has truth in it, he replied 'with some warmth'
during a meeting of wits, when Jonson held forth on Shakespeare's
'want of learning' and 'ignorance of the Antients'. Endymion Porter
and Davenant were also supposed to have been present at this debate,
along with Carew's supposed confessor John Hales, who challenged
that for every fine passage Jonson produced on a given topic by an
ancient author, he in turn 'would undertake to shew something upon
the same Subject at least as well written by Shakespeare'.[38] The anecdote
illuminates the manner in which the early moderns put their reading to
use, gathering and organizing material under topics (*loci*), and treating
Shakespeare's folio as a warehouse of resources for their own disquisitions and notebooks, a sort of giant commonplace book in its own right.
Given such debate among her entourage, the brief stop-over at New
Place may well have held some interest for Henrietta Maria. In any case she
marched into Stratford as a figure deeming herself well worthy of mention
in any Shakespearean history play, 'with 3000 foot, 1500 horse, 150 wagons
[she had left York with a hundred more] and a train of artillery'.

During her brief stay in the town the 'she-majesty generalissima', as
Henrietta Maria half-humorously styled herself, rendezvoused with
Prince Rupert, who conducted her to meet Charles at Edgehill. There
the royal couple fell out over the appointments and promotions the
queen had guaranteed her followers without consulting Charles. As
close to her as ever, now a peer and Master of Horse, was 'butcherly
Jermyn', as a Parliament pamphlet described the heavy-set courtier –
'contemptible Harry; the left leg of a lord . . . a featherbed traitor'.[39]

In and about the town, strong traces remained of the life Shakespeare
knew. Confusions of local memory, however, were unwittingly building up mythology rather than preserving fact. Small errors of name and
time then went into the notebooks of such interested parties as John
Aubrey. A short way down the London road, for example, there still
lived a village constable on whom Shakespeare was thought to have

based Dogberry in *Love's Labour's Lost*, a play Aubrey confused with *A Midsummer Night's Dream*. The townspeople remembered that another local butcher's son (for Shakespeare *was* a butcher's son, wasn't he?) had been as much a 'natural wit' as the poet, and was well known to him; but had died young.[40]

Perhaps the old constable could live through the conflict much as he had for his seventy years or more. It is often said that large numbers of people in the British Isles were unaffected by the wars. Yet a settled life was going up in flames along the wary route the queen's guides picked for her. This was not so much an old world giving way to an invasion from a new, as fuel and freedom being given to familiar and long-resented spirits of delinquency. The riotous energies with which Suckling's name had once been associated now swept across whole districts. While the roundhead armies boasted that they took nothing without paying for it, and refrained from plunder, the cavaliers gained a reputation for revelling in bad conduct – as, for example, in their descent on the chiefly puritan town of Birmingham at Easter, 1643:

Having thus possessed themselves of the town, they ran into every house cursing and damning, threatening and terrifying the poor women, setting naked swords and pistols to their breasts. They fell to plundering, as well malignants as others, picking purses and pockets, searching in holes and corners, tiles of houses, wells, pools, vaults, gardens, for money or goods; took much money to protect people's houses, and then betrayed them, and set them on fire. It is conceived they had 3000*l.* in money from the town. They outraged the women, broke windows, spoiled the goods they could not take away, leaving little to some but bare walls, some nothing but clothes on their backs, and some stripped to their very shirts and left naked. That night few of these ruffians went to bed, but spent it in revelling, robbing, and tyrannizing over poor affrighted women and prisoners, drinking healths upon their knees, yea, drinking healths to Prince Rupert's dog.[41]

Rupert was at pains to deny any involvement on his own part in such outrages, and published open letters in self-defence. But the image stuck, not least because it simply confirmed tendencies which a wide variety of sound citizens, puritan or not, from JPs to aggravated merchants, had been observing for decades in 'spirited' young men.

Horseplay escalating into arson and robbery was the other side of a gentleman's war.

3

Despite the back-history of his nose, and the stories he could tell of outings with Suckling and Young, nothing in Davenant's known war record connects him with such outrage. He was never the out-and-out cavalier, in war as in peace, concentrating instead on stores and supply lines and the maintenance of field pieces. The violence he witnessed glints only here and there in his writing. In the early battle scene in *Gondibert*, for example, we witness a Lombard skewered 'even till his heart did beat against his Hilt'.[42] Yet the same episode's remarkably concise descriptions of field manoeuvres, from a distance, are a better reflection of Davenant's view of the combat. He was a backstage worker and an overseer, and the dangers he met with came on the road, at sea and on the wharf rather than in the open field.

In August 1643 he left Newcastle's service to resume his place at the queen's side in Oxford, dodging a scattering of encircling forces en route. 'Davenant has arrived,' the queen reported on the thirteenth, monitoring arrivals and departures at her court; 'I have not yet spoken to him.'[43] To one raised in the city, there was a dream-like discrepancy to his well-known Oxford. The former college enclaves were now busy lodgings and storehouses, with soldiers billeted in the colleges. Artillery watched the deer in the eastern meadows. Twenty and more years earlier, Davenant had left his parents' tavern on Cornmarket for exhilaration and opportunity in London; now the cultural life of the capital had gathered to meet him in his home town. Even many of his theatrical acquaintance – most of the players having volunteered for the king – could be found in the city, while the court transposed its pleasures to the academic setting. Clearly needing relief from his duties in the field, Prince Rupert enjoyed a wild evening one Sunday in October, and 'accompanied with some Lords and other Cavaliers, danced through the streetes openly with musick before them'. Hearing that a play was being put on in one of the colleges, they suspended their street-party; and were last seen disappearing through the gatehouse 'followed by a pack of women, or Curtizans it may be supposed, for they were hooded and could not be knowne'.[44]

Rupert and his cohorts were carousing in the face of despondency and disappointment. A little more than a month before, the royal camp had been more hopeful than it would ever be again. Another chance had opened for a move on London. Newcastle's victory at Adwalton Moor at the end of June had eased some anxieties about the threat from the north; and Rupert's capture of Bristol, swiftly but with heavy losses to Cornish troops on the great port's Somersetshire side, felt like a signal victory. The court at Oxford exaggerated the meaning of these successes: it was out of touch with the score of deadlocked theatres of operations elsewhere in the country, and the pull they exerted in conflicting directions on troops and resources. This partial view of the overall situation made the queen in particular quite sure that the way back to Whitehall lay clear. Confidence alone is contagious: for in London, Parliament grew nervy. When Henry Marten said openly in the Commons that the royal family should be disposed of and monarchy abolished, he was barred from the House. Yet in Bristol, Prince Rupert, with a view to protecting recent gains, urged the king to concentrate on Gloucester instead of the capital, and to Henrietta Maria's disgust and mortification Charles agreed. The clash of strategy has attracted much attention in the standard chronicles, and the limitations of both perspectives subjected to lengthy analysis. Rupert, though never lacking boldness, was constricted by his experience of obstacles on the ground. Henrietta Maria, meanwhile, imagining the success from Oxford, was plotting an offensive too much from the air. The decision to take Gloucester marked a definite turning point, nevertheless, and brought about a bitter row between the king and queen. Two weeks into the siege which followed at Gloucester, he travelled back to Oxford to make peace with her.

When Charles returned to Gloucester, his poet-in-chief went with him, and was knighted for the part he played in the lengthy struggle that followed. Davenant's knighthood has always been seen as his reward for an unspecified show of resolve or heroism in the month-long siege. His specialization in ordnance would certainly have made him prominent in the organization of artillery about Gloucester, and the elaborate mining operation on the eastern gate of the city, from which the royalists were driven by a 'desperate sally'. Yet worthy though his service was of recognition, the knighthood may have been equally a conciliatory token for the queen, still keen to promote her favourites.

The quarrel with his wife and a series of further squabbles at court only set the king's mind more firmly on the task of Gloucester. This, he decided, was to be the crucial point of his campaign. In London, Parliament and the people sensed the same: although resources were sorely stretched, a special force of eight thousand was raised and dispatched for Gloucestershire under the command of the Earl of Essex. In Gloucester itself, the garrison and citizenry dug deep. So far as morale was concerned, every hopeful sign came to the royalist side: just before the end of August, for example, Suckling's old enemy John Digby, now a cavalier captain, won a small-scale yet resounding victory at Torrington. Yet at least one of Charles's inner council, Hyde's soul-mate Falkland, took no solace or encouragement from such news or the king's apparent advantage. He was heard to mutter – or, in Hyde's word, to 'ingeminate' – dejected prayers for 'peace, peace'.[45]

Early in September, the complex and dangerous engineering work to blow a breach in Gloucester's defences was washed out by 'a great glout of rain', as one of Davenant's fellow officers put it. Struggling to get out of their mine-chambers alive as the early-autumn 'land-flood' rose about them, they had no time to regroup and begin again before Essex, with greater speed and force than Charles or Rupert had anticipated, arrived at their backs. The royalists pulled out in the squall before Essex drew up, and he entered the city on 8 September. Neither army had the strength to give open battle, yet the Parliamentarians could not stay in Gloucester indefinitely. Having broken the royalists' grip on the city, they too pulled back. Despite the disappointment of the siege, and his loss of face to Henrietta Maria and her entourage, Charles was presented with another opportunity. Essex's large, tired army could be caught in the field, and its route back to London closed off.

In the energetic prose so typical of the period's military memoirs and reports, free with syntax but high in spirit, generous with detail and surprisingly sharp in focus, the officer quoted above described the chase over sodden terrain which resulted in the first battle of Newbury. The account reeks of the experience itself; of rain, exhaustion, and gritty eagerness:

And when we drew off, it proved to be a most miserable tempestuous, rainy weather, that few or more could have little or no rest on the hills where they were; and the searing winds next morning soon dried up our through-wet clothes we lay prickled in all night, (as a convenient washing of us at our coming from the trenches;) and we made such haste in pursuit of Essex's army, that there was an account of fifteen hundred men quite tired and spent, not possible to come up their colours before we engaged the enemy; and a night or two before, we lost two regiments of horse (Kentish men, and new raised regiments;) which were surprised and taken prisoners in their quarters; and what was worse, in most men's opinion, we were like to drop down every step we made with want of sleepe; yet, notwithstanding, we marcht on still, until the next evening we overtook the enemy at Newbury Towns end; then our quarter-masters, with their part, beat their quart-masters and their parties out of the town, and very early in the morning gave them battell.[46]

The king's army set up their camp and their ordnance on the most advantageous positions surrounding the town, where open heaths were interspersed with deep copses and hedgerows, and divided by blindly turning lanes. Skirting the higher ground, Essex's men were forced to take to these covered channels, which proved ideal for ambushing impatient cavaliers. More than two days' merciless fighting ensued, with huge losses on the king's side for every field and spinney.

The Parliament forces showed greater guile. Ever since royalist colours first mocked him for his cuckold's horns, Essex has been reputed a stodgy character and an unimaginative general – the mediocrity who gave way to Fairfax and Cromwell. It is true, admittedly, that he preferred to be cautious. Yet at Newbury his concern for getting his soldiers home stood in marked contrast to the royalist officers' poor regard for the lives of their men, and their own. Parliament's raw infantry acquitted themselves boldly, holding shape for the dangerous advances, and holding their nerve while lying in wait for Rupert's cavalry to fly out before their muskets. This the king's horsemen kept doing, falling into trap after trap and fighting their way forward with near-insane displays of courage and self-sacrifice. The profligacy with life seems to have been driven by a loss of patience with the war and the parvenus behind it; a desire to end things with a dashing individual stroke on the part of every officer.

An exception was Lucius Cary, the Viscount Falkland. In his case despair rather than frustration was the decisive passion, his recklessness purposeful and premeditated. That, at least, was how it seemed in retrospect. While for most participants, grimy and sleep-starved, the battle was a frantically improvised affair, with strength summoned up from moment to moment, there was a desolate calm and collectedness to Falkland's actions, from the early hour at which he surprised his servants by calling for a clean shirt. Despite his position as the king's secretary – and his responsibility as such to avoid capture – he placed himself at the forefront of the fighting, in the hedged fields skirting the commons by Newbury. While the royalists watched the road to Kintbury, they were surprised by a party sent by Essex through canopied lanes to their rear. A brigade of infantry, with a company of horse led by Sir John Byron, was sent to root them out, and Falkland attached himself to these. At a hotly contested rift in a hedgerow, Byron's horse was shot in the throat. While he called for another, and considered how the gap in the brambles might be widened to allow an effective advance, Falkland rode straight through. He was picked off immediately by Essex's riflemen in the field beyond: both man and horse were dead, Byron guessed, before they reached the other side of the opening.

Falkland's death has always been taken as a suicide prompted by dejection and weariness at war. He could see no end. His action accorded entirely with earlier descriptions of his character and conduct, from his preference for reasoned debate and consensus to his interest, in the celebrated discourses at Tew, in the more recondite tangents of philosophy and theology which could justify the extreme course he eventually took. His final act, however, struck his commanding officer as more impulsive than suicidal, not transparently different to many other deeds of self-destructive and less than helpful bravery in the environs of Newbury that day. Possibly annoyed, in the moment itself, at Falkland breaking the order to hold back, Byron could only note that the king's councillor spurred his horse and rode forwards 'more gallantly than advisedly'.[47] Yet his death was interpreted almost immediately as both the last resort of a delicate mind and a protest against the civil war: it was precisely the strong if desperate sacrifice which the same contemporary observers failed or refused to recognize in Suckling's miserable end. Falkland's companion, fellow councillor and devotee Hyde, was devastated by the loss. When, as Earl of Clarendon, he narrated the event decades later, he chose a wife's cry of bereavement to express his sorrow. He took as his epigram the outburst of Cornelia in Lucan's *Civil Wars* on hearing of the murder of her husband, Pompey: *Turpe mori, post te, solo non posse dolore*, Hyde intoned with the widow: 'It were base not to be able to die of grief for you.'[48]

Falkland was taken to be one who really was killed by grief, if his friends rightly understood the motives for his last charge at Newbury. His death came to occupy a special place in the book of the civil wars. As such, he achieved something many of his contemporaries would have sorely envied, including Hyde, whose career would be more chequered and his legacy, though greater, more ambiguous than his friend's. Falkland had furnished a commonplace exemplifying a particular topic, a principled death; and he himself become the *locus classicus* for it, the name with which it would be forever associated.

As for the battle in which he died, its symbolism was as ridden over and muddy as the fields around Newbury. Both sides claimed the victory. The end result could be construed as the repulsion of Parliament's army but also as its escape. Even the loss of Reading to the royalists, a town Essex judged indefensible, was a worthwhile concession from Parliament's point of view. In the king's camp, meanwhile, there was a nagging suspicion that a priceless initiative had been lost. At Oxford the populace was recovering from a near-pandemic bug: 'the ordinary raging disease of the army', noted the celebrated William Harvey, called in when Rupert's brother Prince Maurice succumbed to 'slow fever, with great dejection of strength'.[49] It was a debilitated crowd that turned out to greet the king on his return from Newbury, and raise a shallow cheer for the dubious victory. As autumn drew on, the praise dampened further amid family arguments at court, with the king and queen's favourites vying for power and regard. Big appointments were made to reward and show approval rather than direct the right gifts to the right task, as when Lord George Digby, the queen's secret agent and master of disguise, took the post vacated by Falkland as Secretary of State. In the meantime some of those most industrious on the king's behalf, notably Prince Rupert, suffered from a lack of firm friends at court.

Late in September 1643 triumphs could be witnessed both in London and Oxford; but whereas that in London was inspired by a genuine sense of collective relief, the one in Oxford sought to cloak a distinct ruefulness. Parliament's general and hero, Essex, had actually entered London in glory once before, as a boy of twelve, when James VI of Scotland made him his sword-bearer on his first arrival into the city, and again at his coronation.[50] Forty years and a loveless marriage later, having fallen out of favour with James and feeling mutual enmity with Charles, returning with his men in less pomp and ceremony – but genuine glory – Essex briefly tasted apotheosis. He had saved the capital and the rebellion, and was met in state by the city's dignitaries at his family house on the Strand. The avenue of mansions (and close-lying tenements) down which his father led a pack of rebels to St Paul's in 1601, in the last of the Elizabethan rebellions, was now lined with crowds to honour his name and his army's achievement. Essex was an unsure, long-embittered and introverted man with bad skin, and though he barely knew it this was his finest hour. His command would be undermined by disputes with Parliament's other generals, superseded by the creation of a 'New Model Army', and eliminated by new rules separating the military and political leadership.

Despite the bravery and skill shown at Newbury it was clear that a far-reaching reorganization would be necessary to defeat the king. Beyond London, small, decisive steps were taken towards the necessary overhaul. That autumn, Oliver Cromwell would dodge the Earl of Newcastle's ineffectual siege and bring Sir Thomas Fairfax, the new army's eventual commander-in-chief, back from Hull (where Sir John Hotham had long since been removed, and forfeited his life). In the eastern counties Cromwell had already perfected his new cavalry method, soon shown to great effect at the battle of Winceby, by drilling the horse to keep shape after a charge, and hit the enemy again on the turn. At Winceby, even though Cromwell himself – a fairly recent convert to arms – was brought to ground, his horsemen stuck to their orders and won the day. Yet more decisive still, in the long run, was Cromwell's realization that the war would not be won by gentlemen alone: he had begun a policy of promoting low-born talent over well-connected mediocrity.

Within the capital, meanwhile, the political leadership needed a shorter-term strategy to see them through the next year's campaign.

John Pym was ailing, 'eaten with worms', a royalist spy could report – and dying, in fact, of a cancer in his bowel – but using the last of his enormous energy and political talent to clinch an alliance with the Scottish Covenanters. The Scots were brought into the war by what they later claimed, and what still appears, a verbal sleight of hand, a feat of wit. In drawing up 'A Solemn League and Covenant' between the nations, to which every citizen of both would have to swear allegiance, it was agreed that the old episcopacy would have no place in the post-war Church or state. Yet the definite shape of Britain's future godly polity still defied universal acceptance, despite long clashes between the parties' theologians. From Edinburgh the Covenanters sent Archibald Johnston – now knighted, and appointed Lord Wariston of the Sessions – to take care of the fine print, and oversee the new 'Assembly of Divines'. When delegates also travelled from London requesting military aid, Wariston was among the most vocal in favour of sending it. He saw the full urgency of the situation confronting the puritan movement. His heart was full as ever for the cause, but he lost something of the legalistic care and political cunning he brought to drafting the Covenant. His anxiety to unify the cause was such that he missed – or dismissed – the danger of a loophole. The Scots were so confident that their Presbyterian society met the requirements of scripture that they eventually accepted the wording proposed by Parliament, which dictated that the future British Church should be established 'according to the Word of God'. This was no time, the English rebels urged, to recall that Europe's best minds and strongest armies had failed for centuries now to settle what the Word truly prescribed. In January 1644, another Scottish army was ready to invade England. Shortly afterwards, a group of Scotsmen travelled south to map out the future of the Church and state. Johnston, their principal legal adviser, saw the two as indistinguishable.

The autumn and winter after Newbury, as the Earl of Newcastle abandoned the siege of Hull, as Arundel was lost and then recovered by the rebels, Parliament tightened its policing of the capital. When Wat Montagu, a long-standing friend of Suckling and Davenant and a favourite of the queen, accompanied a French emissary to London, he was promptly plucked from Somerset House and shut up in the Tower. Another among the known and suspected fifth columnists still protesting their neutrality was James Howell. He had evidently tried maintaining his place in the old non-partisan society of wits, styling himself as one above the lamentable quarrel. Tucked up in his chambers and trying to keep as much of his former amiable life in place as he could, it was November 1643 when the authorities decided it was time to lock him up. He had 'divers times', he claimed, been to Westminster, 'where I convers'd with many Parliament-men of my Acquaintance', and thus thought himself free of suspicion. Then one morning his door was broken in by 'five armed Men with Swords, Pistols and Bills'. His attempt to debate the issue with them fell as flat as his appeal to protocol:

I desir'd to see their Warrant, they deny'd it: I desir'd to see the date of it, they deny'd it: I desir'd to see my name in the Warrant, they deny'd all. At last one of them pull'd a greasy Paper out of his Pocket, and shew'd me only three or four Names subscrib'd, and no more: So they rush'd presently into my Closet, and seiz'd on all my Papers and Letters, and anything that was Manuscript.

To his horror they laid their rough hands on his books as well – as objects of suspicion – 'and hurl'd all into a great hair Trunk, which they carry'd away with them'. They demanded he go with them forthwith to the Fleet, from where he was writing; but it happened that he had just taken some 'physick' – usually shorthand for a brisk purgative. The one decency he could grant the guards had shown him was to wait until the evening, when the laxative had worn off, before taking him to prison.[51]

Incarceration in the Fleet could hardly be pleasant, with the nearby river of hog-fat and dog-hides sending its aroma through the grating, but its walls at least removed the prisoner from the sight of distressing physical change to the city outside. There had been barricades and checkpoints on the major thoroughfares since early in the previous year, when an internal battle for control of Westminster seemed likely. Since then, Parliament having secured the capital, the great fear was a full-scale military assault from the north and west, rather than an insurgence from within. Thus, throughout 1643, enormous effort had been put into the fortification of the city. Veterans of the Dutch and German wars oversaw the creation of a ring of forts and earthworks. Old medieval bulwarks, even stretches of Roman wall, were also reincorporated into the defences. In the spring, engineers were fetched from Holland to assist seasoned officers such as Philip Skippon, the commander of the Westminster trained bands, to work from their memories of the old campaigns. It was also said that much of the work was done by the city's women:

> What have they done, or what left undone,
> That might advance the *Cause* at London?
> March'd, rank and file, with *Drum* and *Ensign*,
> T'entrench the *City*, for defence in;
> Rais'd *Rampiers*, with their own soft hands,
> To put the enemy to stands;
> From *Ladies* down to *Oyster-wenches*,
> Labour'd like *Pioners* in *Trenches*,
> Fell to their *Pick-axes*, and *Tools*,
> And help'd the men to dig like moles.[52]

Almost all of the labour was voluntary. Thousands of citizens and soldiers turned out each day to help with the new defences, and by the end of the year the basic circuit was in place. From outside, London was starting to look like a disputed central European town; the Continent had claimed the island.[53]

Deprived of his liberty, Howell welcomed the greater freedom to work on his writing. Until recently he had always looked for a post as a factor, a secretary, or a niche in the court. Indeed in the great purge of royal servants at Parliament's behest in the approach to the war, he had been disappointed not to win a clerkship to the council. Yet since his last trip to France in 1641 he had been considering a career as a professional writer – earning his living from his publications rather than from patronage. From prison, he began drawing in and reassembling material from more than two decades of industriously sociable letter-writing and note-making. At the same time, imprisonment brought greater introspection, or at least so he claimed in his ongoing correspondence. 'Surely God Almighty is angry with *England*,' he wrote, following a common diagnosis of the national problem. Since God was never angry without good reason, 'to know this cause, the best way is for every one to lay his hand on his breast, and examine himself thoroughly, to summon his thoughts, and winnow them':

When I ransack the three Cells of my Brain, I find that my imagination hath been vain and extravagant . . . When I descend to my Heart, the centre of all my affections, I find it hath swell'd often with tympanies of Vanity, and tumors of Wrath: when I take my whole self in a lump, I find that I am nought else but a Cargazon of malignant humours, a rabble of unruly Passions, among which my poor Soul is daily crucified as 'twixt so many Thieves.

Yet if this carried a flavour of puritan self-scrutiny and chastisement, it was puritanism of an inkhorn variety. Despite all these failings in his nature, Howell was sure God could not despise him or his well-bred correspondents. 'I thank you for your last visit,' he concluded to his friend, 'and for the Poem you sent me since.'[54]

II. Sulby Hedge

Let's all sink wi' th' King.

— *The Tempest* 1.1.63

1

The intervention of the Scots changed the shape of the war. A second front opened up for Newcastle (now a marquis), which effectively ended any hope of the king's northern and southern armies joining forces. Across England, the effect of the invasion was hugely demoralizing for the royalists: even among the Parliamentarians there were those whom the alliance made more nervous than grateful. There had been talk since the autumn that the king would reach a similar agreement with his loyal Irish subjects. A ceasefire in September 1643 had in theory freed Charles's main Irish representative, the Earl of Ormond – appointed Lord Lieutenant in January 1644 – to bring much-needed reinforcements to England. But the offer of assistance from Ireland proved more a headache than a help. The king's Protestant soldiers were outraged at the idea of serving alongside Catholics, let alone obeying Irish papist officers. In the court at Oxford, spirits were sinking. From London, a sprightly propagandist had already gloated that 'the Queen will not have so many Masks at Christmas and Shrovetide this yeare as she was wont to have other yeeres heretofore; because *Inigo Jones* cannot conveniently make such Heavens and Paradises at *Oxford* as he did at *White-hall*.'[1] In truth, such jeers also reflected considerable deflation in London, where despite general dedication to the war effort people still missed their old festivities, the bear-baiting, cock-fights and the theatres (it is peculiar how those three diversions were grouped together in the governing mentality, with the brothels completing a disreputable quartet) – except in the rare times when such entertainments enjoyed brief clandestine revivals. When Davenant wrote Henrietta Maria another of his offerings in verse, this year the pretence of normality was gone from his lines. Evidently set to music, the evening perform-ance of this year's song for her could only have borne the faintest resemblance to the old Whitehall spectacles. Davenant addressed the queen as 'unhappy excellency'.[2]

The poem for the queen, 'entertained by night', was probably pre-sented early that spring. At the end of March, Parliament won a significant victory at nearby Alresford, so in mid-April Henrietta Maria left Oxford, risking the journey to a place of greater safety in the West Country. She was pregnant, despite the recent tension with her hus-band over strategy, and Charles had misgivings about her leaving his side. In fact, they never saw each other again, and her removal to Exeter was the first stage of her evacuation to France. As the royalist campaign slowly unwound over the next eighteen months, many of the leading courtiers in Oxford were to take the same precarious path out of the country. By this time the various escape routes from England were well beaten by Davenant. Since his detachment from the northern army in the summer of 1643 he had been drawn back into the less well-documented offshore dimension of the war, returning to his former task of pawning jewels and plate in various marts, then smuggling con-signments of arms back into England. As infection and recrimination festered at Oxford in the aftermath of Newbury, Parliamentary report-ers had already passed word of individual merchants in Rotterdam each lending the royalists tens of thousands of pounds, and of 'whole ships full of plundered goods, and some very rich' being donated. In January another news sheet identified '_Davenet_ the Poet (now Knighted)' as the king's chief factor and gun-runner in the Netherlands.[3]

Among Davenant's supporters and superiors there were equal fears that Parliament was gaining the upper hand in the struggle for sup-plies. At Oxford, the royal council suspected, rightly, that the Dutch Republic had greater political sympathy for Parliament. In January 1644 Charles convened his own rival Parliament in his new capital, composed entirely – in theory, at least – of loyalists. One of the assembly's early disappointments came when ambassadors from Holland, received in state at Christ Church, did little more than 'harangue for peace'. The prospect of help for the king from abroad was bleak; Jermyn, pouring

scorn on the embassy, was cheered to hear of one ship reaching Wey-
mouth 'with some little quantity of arms'.[4] Across the water, despite his
reputation, and despite his best efforts with officials in Amsterdam and
the unpredictable shoals off Texel, Davenant had similar frustrations to
report. He was thwarted in particular by the skill with which the Parliamentary agent Walter Strickland anticipated and unpicked his plans.
Davenant's supply ships were frequently confiscated by the Dutch navy;
and when not caught out in the open seas they were often tied up in
harbour with red tape. At Rotterdam the Admiralty was happy to sell
him a frigate for £2,500, but could not find it in their hearts to let it
leave harbour. These were among the legal and administrative vex-
ations, slowing the war in the field, which he complained of in his lyric
of 1644 to the queen:

> Your patience, now our Drums are silent grown,
> We give to Souldiers, who in fury are,
> To find the profit of their Trade is gone,
> And Lawyers still grow rich by Civil War.[5]

By May, nevertheless, having lost a privateer fitted out at his own
expense, Davenant himself decided to make use of the lawyers. The lost
ship was named the *Newcastle*, after the peer who was still technically his
commanding officer, and had brought him at least two decent prizes.
When brought in by Parliament's navy its own value was put at some
£6,000. Later that spring Davenant became one of countless loyalists
applying to register and recover some of his financial losses from the
Crown.[6]

The war was still finely balanced. The final outcome, in the event of
victory on either side, was still anybody's guess: what place would the
king have, if Parliament brought him to bay; and what would Parliament be, if he defeated it completely? Those on active service fixed their
view upon winning the next engagement. The hero of Davenant's
imperialist poem *Madagascar*, Rupert, was still working wonders in
battle – and committing blunders in politics, mistakenly assuming that
the same cut and thrust would work at council boards. He had no talent
for compliment, or for soothing the egos of his fellow officers, and
though he saw the importance of administration, he was not suited to it.

As a general, his element was the vanguard, not the store wagon or the debating table. At Newark in March he was to be seen, as usual, plunging 'deep into the torrent of his opposing foes', in which:

three sturdy Roundheads at once assaulted him; one fell by his own sword, a second was pistolled by one of his own gentlemen, and a third, laying his hand on the Prince's collar, had it chopped off by [Daniel] O'Neal; his own troop now struggled up to him, with Sir Richard Crane, and set him free, with only one shot through his gauntlet.[7]

Through May and early June, the 'terrible Prince' led assaults on Stockport, Bolton and Liverpool. For all the wonders of the Rupert whirlwind, however, Newcastle was struggling in the north, as Parliament laid siege to York. Hopes of a push southwards by the Oxford army had ended with the important defeat at Alresford, and now Oxford itself was under threat. Yet another quandary presented itself: should Rupert march up to Yorkshire to aid the northern army, or stay close to Oxford to protect the king? The opinion of Newcastle was predictable. Masking his weariness and irritability – and some envy of the prince, who was stealing the show on the royalist side – Newcastle called for aid in one of the war's most famously insouciant cavalier letters. He congratulated Rupert on his 'huge and great victories, which indeed is fit for none but your Highness', but proceeded: 'if your Highness do not please to come hither, and that very soon too, the great game of your uncle's will be endangered, if not lost; and with your Highness being near, certainly won . . .' He ended by declaring himself the prince's 'most passionate creature'.[8]

In the meantime, at Oxford, against Rupert's advice, the king was planning a decisive push to the south-west, using the bases at Bristol and Exeter to secure the entire region. Knowing that such a move would leave Oxford open to an advance from Parliament, Rupert urged the council to consolidate their holdings around the city, in particular the garrison at Reading. For his own part, in May he began moving north, but remained unsure about going so far as the Marquis of Newcastle wished and needed. Pausing at Chester, he rehearsed his dilemma: to return south in support of the king, who had ignored his counsel and was fast being entrapped, would utterly demoralize the staunch defenders of York. To leave the king to his own devices, however, could mean the 'great game' was over. On the night of 3 June, with Oxford encircled, Charles was obliged to bring his forces out of the city on the northern side, and miraculously marched it in silence, between two resting Parliament armies, over the Cotswolds to Worcester. 'I confess the best had been to have followed your advice,' he admitted, writing to Rupert. Yet he had proved capable of the masterpiece which foresight should have made unnecessary. He proceeded to lead the Parliament generals, Essex and Waller, on a wild goose chase through the region. Feints ensued near Shrewsbury, Witney and Banbury, before the king won a close victory at Copredy Bridge at the end of the month.

By then Rupert was closing in on York. A fortnight before, even Davenant had thrown his pennyworth into the debate. On the very day Rupert set off to rescue the northern army, Davenant wrote to tell him he had made the right choice. Even if the king were driven to retreat northwards in his nephew's wake, the prince could do his work in York-shire with a clear mind. Essex could never give chase, since Davenant knew too well the Londoners he was leading: 'it was never heard that any force or inclination could leade them so farre from home.'[9] Dav-enant was writing from Halford in Shropshire, close enough to follow the news from Chester, and to join his old commander, Newcastle – Rupert having relieved York on 1 July – for the catastrophe at Marston Moor.

Rupert kept his faith with tornado tactics, and although both his army and Newcastle's garrison were exhausted, thought it best to press home the apparent advantage. They gave battle almost as soon as the siege was lifted, and were defeated in mist and twilight the following day. A few months on, as it still does centuries later, the battle of Marston Moor looked like a turning point; but it took some time for the result to become clear, and longer still to sink in. Early reports even gave victory to the royalists. Among those rejoicing prematurely, a roundhead pamphleteer noted, were 'our sottish and betwitched mole-eyed malig-nants of London' – the likes of Howell, that is, still scribbling away in the Fleet, preaching humility in his letters. The truth was that Parlia-ment's great enemy, 'Prince Robber [i.e. Rupert], the prince of blood and lies', had been defeated, and when he collapsed back in York after the fight he learned that the Marquis of Newcastle had already fled, gathering what dignity he could aboard a fishing boat which saw him to Hamburg. The London press alluded to Newcastle's patronage of the theatre, and his own small portfolio as a dramatist and poet, in summing up his chastened withdrawal: having 'played his part a while in the North', and having 'help't *Rupert* to a sound beating', he 'shew'd a paire of heels, and *exit* Newcastle'.[10]

It took a little while to clarify the smaller details: that '*Daunant* the Poet', for example, had not been killed, as one misinformed account claimed, and had possibly not even been present at Marston Moor. The larger significance of the battle was apparent to just a few minds, ready and eager to seize the victory as a sign of something greater. 'Truly England and the Church of God hath had a great favour from the Lord, in this great Victory given unto us,' wrote Oliver Cromwell, 'such as the like never was since this War began . . . God made them as stubble to our swords.' Billeted not far from York, Cromwell, whose fellow horsemen had overwhelmed the prince's cavalry, urged the friend he addressed, his brother-in-law Valentine Walton, to feel proud at the loss of his son:

Sir, God hath taken away your eldest Son by a cannon-shot. It brake his leg. We were necessitated to have it cut off, whereof he died.

. . . Truly he was exceedingly beloved in the Army, of all that knew him. But few knew him; for he was a precious young man, fit for God. You have cause to bless the Lord. He is a glorious Saint in Heaven; wherein you ought exceedingly to rejoice.

Comparatively few at this stage knew Colonel Cromwell, knew what they were speaking of when they met or mentioned him, even though many were already mesmerized by his leadership. Prince Rupert certainly admired what he could do with cavalry: at Marston he was eager to learn if 'Ironside', as he christened him, was present. His plan to ride directly opposite Cromwell, settling their contest head to head, was thwarted when Cromwell surprised him by moving his men forward first, in one of the war's most daring manoeuvres, charging through the twilight and over a steep ditch.[11] The Scottish general, Leven, whose abilities Cromwell was unafraid to say he doubted, was only one of the blunt eastern man's high-ranking admirers. The many rankling egos in

Parliament's hierarchy – the Earls of Manchester and Essex especially – were testimony in negative to the colonel's force and self-assurance. But nobody yet, including Cromwell himself, could guess quite what he was: he was discovering himself deed by deed.

It is telling how Cromwell admired the reticence of his friend's son Walton, even after the failed amputation, when the young man was 'so full of comfort that he could not express it, "it was so great above his pain."' For the wits in the king's camp, words were like playing cards; they were there to be shuffled, dealt, even marked, their real value kept close to the chest. For Cromwell words were nothing unless he tasted substance in them. 'Let this drink up your sorrow,' he continued: 'seeing these are not feigned words to comfort you, but the thing is so real and undoubted a truth.' There was something almost papistical in the bodily reality the great puritan found in his beliefs.[12]

Despite such conviction, the longer-term importance of Marston Moor remained open to debate. Later in the summer the king appeared to regain the initiative on a hard but rousing campaign through Devon and Cornwall. He was drawn to the West Country by hopes of rejoining the queen, who gave birth to a daughter, Henrietta, in June. Charles was too late: with Essex also moving towards her base at Exeter, leading London troops who were 'weary of well-doing' and whose refrain was 'Home, home!', she decided to quit the country altogether, and returned to France. The poet Herrick expressed his sympathy at the 'unhappy distances' separating the couple. 'Like Streams, you are divorced; but "twill come, when/ These eyes of mine shall see you mix agen.'[13] Deprived of a reunion with Henrietta Maria, Charles had to settle for pursuing Essex. Among his staff once more was Davenant, who in mid-August resumed his former brief of smuggling and message-bearing. Urgent orders were dispatched from Exeter to find a barque for him at the little harbour of Boconnoc in Cornwall, stressing the need for 'secrecy and speedy answer'. A delay prompted another memorandum, in a thinner tone: 'I am sure when you consider whose business he carries with him, you will need no quickening.' The letters came, nevertheless, in the midst of a tense operation to pin down Essex at Lostwithiel, when the royalists were preoccupied with the capture of houses along the River Fowey. Early in September, a few weeks before the anniversary of his great escape from Newbury, Essex accepted there was no hope of relief. To much unfair revilement, unable to contemplate imprisonment and ridicule by the king's dandies, Essex left his men and had himself rowed to Plymouth.

Robert Herrick was still – just – the vicar of Dean Prior, and in the privacy of manuscript he greeted the king to 'the drooping West' as an imperial conqueror. A region which had resembled a widow now blushed with pleasure like a bride, he declared, and:

> War, which before was horrid, now appears
> Lovely in you, brave Prince of Cavaliers![14]

The poem offered to 'fix' a conquest wherever Charles raised his standard. Yet the situation, as he knew, was more precarious than the poem suggested. Herrick's continued tenure of his benefice in the village indicated both the delicate mixture of factions in the region – indeed, in the English countryside generally – and some degree of continuity with the earlier ecclesiastical regime. It did not take the publication of his collected poems, *Hesperides*, to discredit him in the eyes of local moral powers. He was thought to be 'possest of a very good Living', but already in the last few years before the war it had been noticed that he was often absent, usually in London, without the excuse of being chaplain to a nobleman.[15] Canterbury had noted the nonresidence, words seem to have been spoken, and the matter had been left there. But in the parish and the wider county Herrick's record faced a sterner test: and before the royalists were finally defeated in Devon, he had been replaced. If the boisterous loyalties of his poems filtered through into his sermons – as seemed safe enough in Devon, by September 1644 – his reaction to Charles's western victories may have cost him his vicarage.

Yet he still clung on to his living for most of the war. He did so unwillingly, too, if his poems are to be believed (and unflinching criticisms of his Devon neighbours imply that the poems *are* to be believed on this point). When Charles – 'O you the best of kings!' – came to the south-west, Herrick was not a happy man. His old lifelines, back to London, and back to the country homes of Endymion Porter and other patrons, had of course been slit by the war. He was reduced to looking to each rural mishap, such as the loss of a finger, for a little *sententia*:

One of the five straight branches of my hand
Is lopt already; and the rest but stand
Expecting when to fall: which soon will be;
First dyes the Leafe, the Bough next, next the Tree.[16]

His writings – strangely, given his persisting rhythmic cheeriness –
give the impression of a man who felt he really was being frittered away,
a little at a time, by death's blade. Herrick's poems are full of pleasured
pastoral observations, but these recede as often to complaints against
rural tedium and vapidity. Even the 'warty incivility' of the rough-
flowing nearby river, Dean Burn, grated on him, and he took its
rock-studded and muddied waters as a metaphor for:

> *A Rockie Generation!*
> A people currish; churlish as the seas;
> And rude (almost) as rudest Salvages.[17]

In that metre-saving 'almost', as in the wider course of Herrick's
poetry, can be seen a mind trained hard to look on the bright side – and
having trouble finding it. The spluttering, redundant repetition of
'rude' suggests one falling short of words, in a recognizably English
manner, to describe what he found instead of comfort. Yet in the midst
of aggravation, he could still see that the years of social isolation in Dean
Prior had given him more time and matter for writing than he would
have had otherwise. ''Tis not every day,' naturally, 'that I/ Fitted am to
prophesie':

> No, but when the Spirit fils
> The fantastick Pannicles:
> Full of fier; then I write
> As the Godhead doth indite.[18]

There is more than a hint of scepticism here about the question of
inspiration: those of Herrick's political persuasion tended to blame such
spiritual influxes as a force of disorder. He may be posing here, sardonically, as one of the self-appointed visionaries currently rampant in the
countryside. The 'pannicles' were the lobes or fibres of the brain in

which imagination or 'fancy' resided (a sixteenth-century usage, already then rare). It occurred to Herrick that these tissues had been warmed by his long exile in Devon. The environment which bothered him so much, as well as the arrival of the divine fury, had a bearing on his prolificacy and made him willing to think of publishing:

> More discontents I never had
> Since I was born, then here;
> Where I have been, and still am sad,
> In this dull *Devon-shire*:
> Yet justly too I must confesse;
> I ne'er invented such
> Ennobled numbers for the Presse,
> Than where I loath'd so much.[19]

Herrick has always been thought of as a 'light' poet, and as a good Jonsonian he clearly worked hard to give the impression that he was. Yet perhaps nothing has been as detrimental to his reputation as his own levity on the subject of his dedication to his 'ennobled numbers'. Exile had given him space and concentration for poems, and for working seriously on them. The king's short-lived breakthrough in the region gave him cause to believe they might still have a readership when the war was over.

2

Those successes in Cornwall in 1644 cheered the royalists and made Parliament nervous: but the south-west was too isolated, geographically, to undermine the advantage Parliament had won in the north and still held in the east. The collapse of Essex's fundamentally ill-equipped and inexperienced force at Lostwithiel, meanwhile, only prompted greater efforts to re-structure and train a more professional New Model Army. The dozen or so peers who still took their seats at Westminster realized that a movement to split the military from the executive wing would create a popular army officered and even led by commoners and dissenters, the soldiers whose abilities and rights Oliver Cromwell rancorously defended. The increasingly desultory band of Scottish commissioners could not but see that this resurgent force would render their assistance unnecessary in the English war, and thus weaken their position in calling for a Presbyterian Church throughout Britain and Ireland. It was April 1645 when the decisive Self-Denying Ordinance, and the commissions for the reorganized, newly centralized army, were pushed through, giving Sir Thomas Fairfax overall command and making Cromwell his general of horse. Yet some time before then many among the original instigators of the war – puritan, but conventional, constitutionally minded gentlemen and peers – could envisage a victory for their own side which they found far from desirable. Despite overtures for a truce, the Parliamentary leadership made its intentions plain by completing a long-delayed piece of revolutionary business. In January 1645 Archbishop Laud was executed. William Prynne, who led the prosecution, crowed over Laud's fate in a pamphlet entitled 'Canterburies Doome': even in death the prelate was harried by his nemesis and former victim.

It was a trick of hindsight perhaps, but by the spring the sense of unendingness was lifting, even after another round of peace talks in the winter came to nothing. The loss of Shrewsbury, in the small hours of a February morning, was particularly bad for the royalists, instantly jeopardizing their Welsh supply lines and the route through which the long-expected Irish army would have to pass. But the king and his now ascendant councillor Lord Digby remained positive the war could still be won outright: and it was true that before the end of June 1645 they could justify their confidence with some powerful examples of success, notably the cut-throat pillage of Leicester in May. With a belated touch of demagogy the king was now often to be seen on foot, marching alongside and encouraging the ordinary men.

Above all, the English picture was distorted and the royalists' spirits buoyed by a spectacular royalist revival in the Highlands. James Graham, Earl – soon Marquis – of Montrose, was one of the minor Scottish chieftains, but probably the most inspired general Scotland has ever seen. With a handful of Highlanders and Irishmen, taking their wives in tow for much of the campaign, he embarked in September 1644 on a series of astonishing coups. In the best accounts of Montrose's campaign, John Buchan's still being the finest in literary terms, sheer wonderment is still the only adequate response to his daring zig-zag through the Grampians, ghosting down from the hills on one safe Covenant town after another, using tricks of light, fern and stone to give the sense that he had tenfold the number at his disposal.

Hobbes defined wit as the 'celerity' of mind: it consists in seeing and exploiting the extra turn, the potential inversion of a given set of terms or conditions, verbal, mathematical or spatial. On those terms Montrose's generalling was pure wit, from the provocations dropped to make the rival clansmen in his ranks compete for glory and spoils, to the wholly unexpected voltas, products of a breeze-light, blade-fine instinct, which caught his enemies unprepared on the offensive and threw them off the scent when they gave chase. Montrose was a poet, and in a more melancholy hour wrote one of the better known monarchist ballads:

> My dear and only Love, I pray
> This noble World of thee,
> Be govern'd by no other Sway
> But purest Monarchie.

But it was in the field, where he could catch the faintest trails and seemingly erase all trace of his own, that his wit found full expression, in forms the scribes will never tire of chronicling. So much so, in fact, that the almost unequalled horror of Montrose's year-long march – the famed *annus mirabilis* – is also easily forgotten.

He was the master of an unspeakably delicate alliance of normally hostile clans, united by a common enemy in the shape of Archibald Campbell, the Marquis of Argyll. After their astounding strikes on Perth and Aberdeen in the unusually bright and mild autumn of 1644, instead of pushing down towards the king's enemies in Glasgow and Edinburgh, they carried Montrose as much as he led them through their old enemy's northern fastnesses. His progress was uncanny, his attacks unsparing: 'He gois to Argile, burnis and slayis throw his hail countries, and left no houss nor hold, except impregnabill strenthis, on brynt [unburnt].'[20]

Crossing snow-covered ranges which for generations the Campbells had deemed impassable to strangers in winter, Montrose's troop of Gordons and MacDonalds circled in for an attack on Argyll's base at Inverlochy, at the neck of Loch Eil near Fort William. They surprised

Argyll by emerging from the very direction in which he assumed, at the time, they would be moving away, forcing him to look to his own safety. He had himself rowed to his galley on the loch, leaving a sizeable force of Lowlanders on the shore to hold off Montrose. For this, in contrast to Montrose's native courage, Argyll has always been criticized. The decision certainly highlights a contrast of character. Argyll was a silent, unreadable man, who left it to the last moment to declare his intent: he emerged only late in the day as the leader of the Covenant, by virtue of his unrivalled territorial power. As insistently as Montrose trusted to impulse, Argyll worked from rational checks of pros and contras. His retreat to the ship on Loch Eil, which he delayed from making sail only long enough to watch the onset of the ensuing massacre, captured the difference between the two men perfectly – the cavalier and the politician.

Hundreds of Argyll's men were killed at the lochside or drowned while trying to escape. Those who promptly dropped their weapons and ran were pursued into the hills, as far as eight miles, and were slaughtered where they were caught. Their commander was by then far away. But in Argyll's defence this was also the difference between a general improvising from one tribal region to the next, and one who truly was thinking in terms of three kingdoms: had Argyll stayed with those who were dismembered and left to float towards the wake of his disappearing vessel, the entire Covenanting cause might have collapsed. Argyll wrote off the defeat and looked at the war, not the battle.

Montrose's fire-trail blazed on through the spring and summer, and over-extended itself exactly as it presented a genuine threat to the ascendancy at Edinburgh and the rear of the Scottish army in the north of England. On 13 September his Irish foot were caught by a detachment of that army at Philiphaugh, not far from the border, while Montrose was at nearby Selkirk with his small band of cavalry. Riding up to assist, he was presented with a choice not unlike the one Argyll had faced and taken at the start of the year. Seeing his men trapped and routed, he spurred his horse to join them, Falkland-style, when a lieutenant urged him to escape. For once like Argyll, if less willingly and composedly, he accepted the demands of the larger picture and made for the Pentworth Hills, crossing the Forth to rethink and if possible regroup. The Presbyterian ministers of the victorious army urged that the Irish papist prisoners should not be considered for quarter. The women and children following the Montrose camp were killed in the fields along with the men.

The Presbyterian god was not a merciful one, and these chaplains could say they did nothing more than urge their general, Lord Leven, to follow official procedure. Parliament had after all recently ordered that Irish prisoners-of-war should no longer be treated as such, but were to be executed as a matter of course. As papists, they were scarcely Christian anyway, so the godly reasoned; scarcely human. To the south, a Parliamentarian, the governor of Nantwich, also showed he would take these instructions to the letter. He even indulged in some numerological symbolism, hanging thirteen suspected Catholics to make the point plain. Following his own 'soldier's law', Prince Rupert answered immediately in kind. Hearing of the atrocity, he sent an unopposable detachment of horsemen to the first small roundhead camp they could reach. Of fourteen prisoners taken he ordered thirteen to be killed on the instant, turning loose the one spared, as he often did, to bear a message of intent: henceforth he would execute two Parliamentarians for every Irish or Catholic denied rightful quarter.

It was a paradox that ruthlessness had to answer ruthlessness in the attempt to claw back the last vestiges of the idea that this was a war between brothers, between gentlemen, a war without an enemy. The death of that illusion was to be seen not only on the great glens, where Montrose's men as a rule 'hocked and slew' to the last man, but in most of the major engagements of the English war's terminal phase: in the death of an unarmed young woman, for example, run through when she tried to save her father, a clergyman, after the fall of Basing House in the autumn. A new loss of the restraint required after the heat of a charge, the breach of a wall or the dropping of arms was also to be seen on a larger scale, as in the treatment of female prisoners after the rout of the royalists on the grassy ridges near the village of Naseby in June 1645. After the king and the prince were put to flight, their cavalry vanquished and all their artillery captured, their carriages opened and their abandoned riches seized, the women and children in the army's train were also rounded up. Those who could pay for their freedom were given it, but the unmarried among them were branded whores and paid a sore price; and those whom the roundheads took to be Irish were murdered in a pack. The soldiers were subsequently excused for killing women who, they protested miserably, were 'of cruel countenances' and carried knives.[21]

It is an historian's cliché that the warfare in Britain and Ireland of the 1640s never reached the same pitch and scale of inhumanity to be found across the Continent during the Thirty Years' War. But that was only, perhaps, because the British and Irish wars did not last so long. There was every sign on the ground of conscience giving way; and Parliament's directive on the treatment of Irish prisoners indicated a growing readiness to countenance routine extermination. No one could be sure how much longer the conflict would go on, or what measures would prove acceptable or inevitable to force an ending. This was the prospect against which the irreconcilable last act of Lord Falkland, or before that the suicide of Suckling, should be interpreted: the three Stuart kingdoms had become at one in bloodshed with Europe.

The wars were saved from the last extreme of slaughter by the prospect of resolution, and by the continuing willingness of a few generals to make a compromise or authorize a withdrawal instead of licensing a massacre. After Naseby, Prince Rupert's last doubts about the king's real options gave way: the war could only be pursued to consolidate the weakened hand Charles would have in treating for peace. Rupert's own preferred strategy for 1645 had been ignored: in his view, the best course would have been to concentrate on Parliament's weak point, the Scottish army on which they still relied to hold the north. That way there was a chance of undoing the disaster of Marston and reducing the English war to one north–south front. In the meantime Montrose would occupy the Covenanters on the other side of the border – and perhaps even regain Scotland for the king. But despite promotion to effective commander-in-chief, Rupert had lost all influence with Charles: and when he conceded Bristol to Fairfax in September, he also lost all credit with him. Having watched from the battlements the defenders in one of the city's forts being killed to a man, he agreed to honourable terms, and for this supposed capitulation – or connivance, as the king suspected – he was deprived of his commission. His uncle had expected a greater sacrifice, perhaps even the ultimate one.

Besides decrying their country's fate, through their deaths, Falkland and Suckling also expressed inconsolable unhappiness at the life they had lost: in Falkland's case, the philosophical and social pleasures of Great Tew; in Suckling's, a free rein in London, his every whim covered by the family fortune. By the autumn of 1645 those halcyon days were emphatically over. Earlier in the summer, the Commons directed that the 'Boarded Masque House at *Whitehall*', the huge wooden theatre set up to spare Rubens's canvasses in the Banqueting House proper, was to be pulled down and its materials sold off; although another memorandum two years later indicates that the 'superstitious timber' from the hall was still mouldering in Scotland Yard. The author of the later document suggested that the wood be used for a towering bonfire – to welcome the defeated king and his nobles to their just deserts.[22]

The fate of Inigo Jones, one that even Jonson might have spared him, was another symbol of an era's extinction. As Cromwell wiped out the last cavalier bases in Wiltshire and Hampshire, Jones was among the few who took refuge with the Marquis of Winchester at Basing House. This 'house' was actually a complex of buildings blending old and modern tastes in architecture, and full of sumptuous things. When the holders' last stand was reduced unequivocally, the house bombarded and then stormed, the New Model soldiers could not believe the riches to be tipped out of sideboards and chests, the hangings and popish ornaments to be stripped from walls and mantelpieces. The survivors were divested even of their plastered and powder-burnt silks. Jones, now advanced in years, exhausted from the siege and shell-shocked, was turned out of the house in nothing but a blanket.

The following year, nevertheless, Jones set his symbolism aside. Submitting to the standard heavy fine and loss of property, he made his peace with Parliament in exchange for a pardon and the remains of his estate. Already, in Oxford, the players who had rallied to the royal side of the conflict in the earliest days of the war now tramped down the Thames Valley to ask pardon of Parliament. There was no hope of the ban on theatre being lifted, but they offered to take the Covenant and be of service as Westminster directed. They found that the 'new' Globe, just thirty years old, had been torn down to make room for housing. In any case, former members of the 'King's Men' could hardly go by that name any more.[23]

Yet the stoics among the royalists dug deep. One of Richard Lovelace's younger brothers, William, was killed when Parliament took the

Welsh town of Carmarthen in October. Another brother of the poet, Francis, was colonel of the same regiment, and was brought low by the loss. Hearing he was still 'immoderately mourning' an undefined time later, Lovelace tried coaxing Francis from his grief.

Whether Lovelace himself was back in England by this time is unknown. It seems unlikely. His courage was often celebrated, along with his come-liness, in his lifetime; Andrew Marvell praised the Lovelace:

> Whose hand so grasps the steely brand,
> Whose hand so melts the Ladies hand.[24]

But the historical record of Lovelace's service in arms is uncertain. He is often supposed to have been involved, and wounded, in the English contingent at the battle for Dunkirk in 1646. However, his verse-letters to beleaguered friends and relatives constitute very nearly the sum of his established wartime activity. Many of the court artists and writers lost in the wars were well known to him. His friend William Lawes, for example, who set a number of his songs, was killed in the siege of Ches-ter the previous year. Still Lovelace's advice in these circumstances was that crying would do little good. 'If Teares could wash the ill away/ A Pearle for each wet bead I'd pay,' he commented, persuasively: for as 'wet beads' tears suddenly seem pearl-like themselves, costly and newly unshelled from the deep, to be parted with sparingly.

Lovelace urged upon Francis the solution expressed so often in his writing – the strategy of making circumstance the close prisoner of a determined mind. His rhetoric in this regard reflected a signal difference between the responses of cavaliers and roundheads to defeat and bereave-ment. A godly campaigner in Lovelace's position might have felt obliged to observe a judgement of God in his brother's death. The cavaliers had a fatalism of their own, but they in general refused to give up a sense of entitlement to the victory whatever the result. Lovelace's younger brother was to keep the upper lip stiff:

> Then from thy firme selfe never swerve;
> Teares fat the Griefe that they should sterve;
> Iron decrees of Destinie
> Are ne'er wipe't out with a Wet Eye.[25]

The peculiarity of Lovelace's language indicates both the difficulty of following his advice, and the futility of doing otherwise: it is not the weeping eye which is wiped, but which tries wiping out reality – shut tight as it seems with tears. The poem may well have been written by the time defeat was final, but this in any case was the sort of talk the king welcomed. He was impatient with all those he dubbed the 'melancholy men', a group which now included Prince Rupert.

Pursing his lips at any talk of compromise, supported in his display of blindness by his secretary, Lord Digby, Charles carried on as if his reign were still in full swing, the kingfisher's nest still intact on the waters. Withdrawing to south Wales in the aftermath of Naseby, confident another army could be raised, he hunted with his life-guards, debated with his divines, played bowls and went to church. Yet it was not long before he was forced back on to the road, and was presently driven through his crumbling southern refuges. He nevertheless remained inflexible on the core issues, even as the last of his power disappeared in the dregs of 1645. His detailed, loving though often vexed correspondence with Queen Henrietta shows that he was not as blinkered as his conduct made him seem to royalists risking and losing their lives for him in the field. Yet his principles gave him a duty to denial. If he did not hold to them, with the almost fantastic but unbreakable consistency he sustained to his death, they would be rendered invalid for ever.

The king's person had for the first time been made a legal target by Parliamentary ordinance. When the commissions for the New Model Army were issued in the spring before Naseby, the standard order for Charles's person to be protected and preserved was dropped from the rubric. To save him – to save, perhaps, the Crown itself – from elements of the army and populace who were willing to take that technicality to its logical conclusion, anxious moderates in Westminster needed him to make the concessions they had demanded five years earlier: to accept their proposed changes to the Church, and reassign powers of appointment in state affairs and command of the armed forces. But that would mean ceasing to be the sort of king Charles held himself to be. His letters show how irritated he could become with those among his supporters who could not see that simple fact or appreciate the subsequent reality that, if they supported his view of monarchy, their position in fact required him to go on saying the same thing right to the bitter end. If he flinched, it would never be a case of 'restoring' the monarchy but moving on to another system, another polity, because everyone would know that monarchy was no longer what it was. It would mutate, and diminish, by concession.

Only the orthodox constitutionalists in Parliament saw the ideological strength, the perverse cunning of this stance. In real terms, down to the perception people had of their physical environment, the countryside in which they would be expected to return to work, nothing was the same. It was patently wishful thinking on the part of Hugh Peter, the puritan divine who offered thanks for:

. . . the blessed change we see, that can travel now from Edinburgh to the lands end in Cornwall, who not long since were blockt up at our doors. To see the highways occupied again; to heare the Carter whistling to his toiling team; to see the weekly Carrier attend his constant mart; to see the hills rejoycing, the valleys laughing.[26]

This was the hope, expressed from London, not the reality. The singing hills were still the scene of ambushes; the roads still saw the movement of troops and were regulated by checkpoints. The village where a carrier found a market one week could the next bear marks of local reprisal, or an unauthorized cavalier raid. In the fields, the ploughshare was prone to strike on debris from combat. Parochial landmarks were changed by the alien roles they had acquired in the course of military action, and the hundreds now divided war zones. On the left flank of Parliament's army at Naseby, General Henry Ireton faced Rupert's cavalry across a high, thick hedgerow known as Sulby Hedge. The hedge and the thorny track running through it marked the end of one manor and the beginning of another.[27] After Naseby – after the word 'Naseby' came to denote an event more than the place, an obscure scattering of homesteads – the function and nature of that shattered demarcation was altered indelibly. In history Sulby Hedge will always be something other than one of the great hedgerows currently disappearing from the landscape. In the records it will stand instead as both a battle-line and a quietus. After 1645 the victors looked for ways to make that landmark return to being a mere hedge again, a good fence keeping neighbours on good terms in the run of practical life. The conciliators among them needed the king to accept that the land itself had been changed, deeply and permanently, by what had happened. They needed that alteration to be recognized inside the king's head. As soon as that happened, the king's supporters could then only accept the new Commonwealth, the new future.

Late in April 1646, with his forces whittled virtually to nothing and his garrison pressed to breaking point at Oxford, the king distracted Parliament with a false offer of compliance. Then he disappeared: for a week his movements were unknown. Having cut his hair short and wearing a plain black suit, accompanied by two of his best scouts and just a single servant, he left his wartime capital and dipped out of sight. Escaping notice on each road he assayed, Charles conceivably might have got as far as Land's End or Edinburgh. He had struck southwards first, with the idea of simply going to London. One plan he had also considered was of making for King's Lynn and then escaping to Europe. But instead, flabbergasting Parliament and the rest of Europe, he succeeded in riding north, in a similar fashion to his trip on horseback to Spain two decades earlier, and surrendered himself to the Scots at Southwell.

3

The Covenanters were almost as confounded by his arrival as their erstwhile English partners. Over the previous bitter winter they had proudly declined every overture the king made towards them, sensing trickery. They were right to be suspicious, since it was soon revealed that Charles had been chasing simultaneously a pact with the Vatican, offering even to return to the old Church all the land it had lost in the Reformation. But once he had turned up at their door, like the Earl of Bristol in 1623 they had little choice but to let him in. Having taken Charles into somewhat embarrassed custody, with the English Parliament demanding that they hand him over, the Covenanters did all they could to find some advantage in an extremely awkward situation. They brought their guest to Newcastle, which Lord Leven's men still held, where Wariston and his divines harangued him relentlessly with disquisitions on the righteous claims of Presbyterianism and their Covenant. Yet with all his old amused, faintly offended haughtiness, Charles held fast. Whenever he wavered, his infuriated captors were slow to spot that he was bluffing them once more, playing for time.

The tenor of his thinking, in short, was entirely in key with Richard Lovelace's model of the stoic political prisoner. The idea was to imprison the prison in one's frame of mind. King Charles was one of the very few individuals currently detained for whom that was not only a last resort, but one which still carried huge political consequences. So long as he refused to conform, he held both London and Edinburgh to ransom – even if his enemies in those cities raised the stakes.

It chanced that Sir William Davenant was given the firmest demonstration, in person, of the king's resolve. Nerves were wearing thin; schemes in Scotland and Ireland alike were proving fruitless. Despite the troubling precedent of imprisoning a lawful sovereign, there was no great show of support from foreign rulers. Thus in addition to his daily dose of puritanic sermons, Charles was still being harried to compromise by his own supporters. There was a strong case for making some sort of detente with the Scots, even though they were his original enemies in the saga of the wars. By accepting the Covenant, he would have an army once more. Troops could be raised in Wales, support in England given fresh inspiration. By the autumn of 1646, Charles could conceivably press down on Parliament from the north, advancing for the first time with no enemy in the rear. It made good sense: and Charles would have none of it. Before his flight from Oxford, the queen had been the strongest advocate of his seeking refuge with the Scots. He had not borne their homilies very long before he rebuked her bitterly.

Davenant was an obvious choice as her emissary when Henrietta Maria made one last effort to urge Charles to give ground. The poet was one of the most experienced of her trusted servants at crossing the Channel or the North Sea undetected. After his part (or otherwise) at Marston Moor he had returned to the seas, now abandoning his frustrating work as procurer and smuggler for outright buccaneering. Since Parliament controlled the king's precious navy, Charles and his council were forced to turn for assistance to the traditional maritime enemies of the Crown. These were the 'Dunkirkers', brigands working from harbours on the Cornish coast and the French Atlantic seaboard, and terrorizing all waters from the North Sea to the Irish Channel. For

longer than any could remember, they had played havoc with the shipping of all nations, although Strafford managed to subdue their presence
in the western seas during his deputyship and lieutenancy of Ireland.
Yet by taking advantage of the Dunkirkers' guile for intelligence and
supplies – and a share of their spoils in return for letters of marque –
Charles had only lowered his stock further with the other European
naval powers. In the first full year of the war, the Dutch admiral Tromp
was willing to escort Henrietta Maria to England, and threaten the Parliamentary ships which fired on her. By the end he was to be found
co-operating with his Parliamentary counterparts in policing the mutual
threat to trade and transport.

Yet even this loss of standing and support proved worthwhile, for the
sake of rescuing the heir. To get their ward safely off the mainland, the
Prince of Wales's minders had no choice but to rely on piratical expert-
ise. Aboard *The Proud Black Eagle*, taking a turn at the helm, the
sixteen-year-old prince dodged a fleet of twenty Parliamentary sail in
bad weather to harbour in Jersey. With him was the Chancellor of the
Exchequer, Sir Edward Hyde. They were welcomed by the acting governor, Sir George Carteret, and other 'persons of quality'. The island
was still a stronghold, and with the terror of the chase suddenly over,
for perhaps the first time in seven years Hyde was left with time on his
hands. His arrival on Jersey in spring 1646 was the opening of a two-
year stay, marooned from the hubs of political life and military danger:
accordingly, 'he presently betook himself to his study; and enjoyed, as
he was wont to say, the greatest tranquillity of mind imaginable.'[28] He
had already begun sketching a history of the civil wars. Now he continued it in deepening earnest, still with no sure idea of how it would
end. Word of the project reached the king, sunk in captivity, and he
welcomed it.

Hyde's peace was in fact disturbed much sooner than he mentioned
in his memoirs or his history. The prince and his attendants had not
been settled long at St Helier before Lord Digby blew in with several
hundred Irish soldiers. Digby had long since become the king's favoured
adviser for his indestructible optimism: elegant, indefatigable, eternally
unflustered, 'he was a person of so rare a composition by nature and art'
that the realist Hyde now almost welcomed his complacency.[29] Digby
gave the impression of believing that the cause he backed could escape

from any predicament; and it was undeniable that he had always escaped any personally dangerous situation in which he found himself – such as the one in Hull, at the very dawn of the war. With his usual coolness Digby thus proposed that the younger Charles should go with him to Ireland and provide the resistance there with a figurehead. Should the prince refuse to go, he suggested that his councillors should lure him aboard ship on some pretence, and cast off before he knew what was happening. The prince would easily fall for it: the swarthy teenager, who was learning to sail a little yacht in St Aubin's Bay, was always diverted by a fair sail.[30] But Hyde declined to co-operate, and Digby proceeded to France, leaving his troops behind for the chancellor to billet and feed.

Davenant was among Digby's train on the return trip, along with butcherly Lord Jermyn. By this time the laureate knew the Channel Islands well, and had evidently distinguished himself among the region's disreputable mariners. London had received a report that the well-known poet and theatre man was 'now the great pirott . . . No man hath don you more hurt, and hath been a greater enemy to the parliament.'[31] Yet by the time the royalist campaign collapsed on land and sank at sea, Davenant had taken himself to join the queen's court in exile near Paris, at St-Germain-en-Laye. There the depressed and dispossessed entourage briefly caught the glow of Digby's blithe thinking. He had a fantastic plan for an alliance between an Irish Catholic army and the Scottish Covenanters. Only Digby, working on his listeners as he had on dull-witted John Hotham four years earlier, could sell such a proposal. After a short stay the queen dispatched him to Jersey once more, to send the prince back to her. Again Hyde's calm for study was disturbed, and again he advised against the prince leaving. It was a mistake, in his view, one shared by the prince's other companions, to lodge the king's heir with a foreign power whose loyalties and intentions were at best uncertain. Digby and his followers were outraged at Hyde's defying the queen; but conscious also that the chancellor stood high in the king's confidence and esteem. Davenant, who had been in touch with Hyde before with the news that had reached Paris of London, clearly irritated his old room-mate by supporting the queen's directions.

For three days over a mid-June weekend the argument was fought out at Castle Elizabeth, the tidy renovated fortress on the islet standing off the bay. Hyde and his fellow courtiers were in the habit of taking a rowboat out to his friend the governor, Carteret, or walking across the flats at low tide. On his last trip back before the prince's departure, to complete writing up a long and detailed account of the debate – in his customary meticulous way – he could reflect that the matter was out of his hands. The prince put an end to the discussion by deciding on his own account to go to his mother.

Davenant too returned to Paris – or rather, to the little manor to the west of the old city where the queen now held court. There Henrietta Maria had a special task for him, perhaps the most difficult assignment that any royalist agent could be given. In the autumn he, of all people, was to change the king's mind. He was to carry a letter from the queen and urge Charles in the strongest terms to make his peace with the Covenant. The queen had general assurances from Cardinal Mazarin, the late Richelieu's protégé, that France could then provide assistance. Her choice of emissary was a surprise to many; certainly, when he heard of it, to Chancellor Hyde, who thought Davenant 'an honest man and a witty, but in all respects inferior to such a trust'.[32] But there was considerable sense behind Henrietta Maria's choice of Davenant. The number of self-declared master strategists in the field, each pursuing their own military and diplomatic fantasies, was already quite sufficient. Davenant's will on such matters, by contrast, was all hers. He could be relied upon to reach the king at Newcastle-upon-Tyne, deliver his papers and say what she told him to say. That was enough. With him went a relative of the two leading Covenant generals, Alexander (Lord Leven) and David Leslie, to provide a plausible introduction, along with another dependable minion to assist. Access to the king was to be arranged by the special French ambassador, Jean de Bellièvre (or 'Belliever', as the English punningly called him).

They reached the north-east through the familiar turbulence as the year was turning, and their arrival was reported in London. From his service in the region Davenant must have known the city well, 'a spacious, extended, infinitely populous place', as Defoe later described it; 'seated upon the River Tyne, which is here a noble, large and deep river, and ships of any reasonable burthen may come safely up to the very town'.[33] Such ships berthed in view of the ancient Tyne Bridge, a long stone span of seven stately arches, on which – as on London Bridge –

shops and houses were built. By October 1646 Tyneside had suffered siege and occupation by an army low on both provisions and morale. The one commodity that was not running short was argument in favour of the king signing the Covenant. Yet here were three more missionaries on something like the proverbial fool's errand – bringing coal to Newcastle.

As promised, they gained 'easy admission' to the king. He was being kept at guarded lodgings on Grey Street, in the old market district of the town, a short ride up from the bridge. 'They have bin with his Majesty,' a Parliamentarian journalist noted twitchily, 'and had severall discourses.'[34] The monarch's hosts were also increasingly nervous. They were afraid of keeping the king in England, where the prospect of a military attack to recapture Charles for Parliament was still a possibility, and where there was considerable local support in the predominantly royalist town. Yet they also feared the consequences of taking him over the border, where the Covenant had never been less popular. They were less than entirely sure, either, of their army's lasting obedience. The invading soldiery had gone a long time unpaid, although an agreement with London on their outstanding pay was close; so close that elsewhere it looked like a bribe to the Covenanters for giving up Charles.

When Davenant reached him the king was exhausted from long dispute and coercion. He was at capacity with scheming and hoping, with looking for signs of cracks in his enemies' alliance. He was worn out, too, from bearing the weight of his castles in the air, and from fighting a war in an entirely hypothetical future. His letters to his supporters in Ireland, the Earls of Glamorgan and Ormond, or his instructions to Sir Kenelm Digby, his agent in the Vatican, comprise some of the age's purest works of imagination. In the meantime he endured the daily storms of preaching. Quite possibly, however, it was he who was the first in these debates to score a conversion: Alexander Henderson, the foremost theologian of the Scottish Kirk, seemingly went to his grave that autumn suspecting that the king might be right about God's wishes after all. Charles's wits, in short, were at full stretch; and he was not grateful to Davenant for testing them further.

It would be another couple of months, after a failed escape, before Charles would be explicitly classed a prisoner: although under guard, he could go and play golf down at Shields, and has always been said to

have drunk and dined at a tavern just off Bigg Market. He had, however, already acquired the almost insensate patience of one accustomed
to detention, and went through the details his visitors wished to discuss
somewhat testily but thoroughly. Davenant's assignment was to spell
out the options: both the English Parliament and the Covenanting
Scottish Estates demanded Charles sign the Covenant. But whereas the
English required he accept terms of absolute defeat, the Scots – once
they had his oath – might be willing to march with him south. The king
should therefore yield, urged Davenant, adding that 'amongst other
things . . . it was the advice and opinion of all his friends.'[35] When
Charles tiredly demanded to know which of his friends thought this
way, in Hyde's account, Davenant gave Lord Jermyn as an example.
Remembering old scandals with laundresses and ladies-in-waiting,
Hyde had Charles reply that Jermyn knew nothing about the Church.
But this was the monarch being used as mouthpiece for the historian's
personal views. In a forbearing but expansive letter to Henrietta Maria,
Charles simply begged her, on marital grounds, to let the matter rest:

As I know thou canst not doubt of my perfect, real and unchangeable love to
thee, and that there is no earthly thing I study more (indeed none so much)
than thy contentment (for it must always return to me with interest), so it
would infinitely add to my afflictions if thou shouldst not be satisfied with that
account which Davenant and this inclosed copy will give thee.

One of the key skills conveyed by the standard literary education was
'variation', the ability to say the same thing in any number of ways and
tones at any length required. In writing and speech, Charles had proved
himself a master of this Erasmian virtue. He had little freedom left
except to repeat himself, so he made himself clear yet again. Accepting
the Covenant, he explained, from the Scots side or the English, would
leave him at best a 'titular king', for:

They intend to take away all the ecclesiastical power of government from the
crown, and place it in the two houses of parliament (and of this there is no
question). Moreover they will introduce that doctrine which teaches rebellion
to be lawful, and that the supreme power is in the people, to whom kings (as
they say) ought to give account, and be corrected when they do amiss.[36]

In asserting the exact opposite of what even his most moderate opponents insisted four years of civil war had established – that the monarch 'ought to give account' – Charles refused to concede the victory. His point was that his politics, and all the art which had extolled it for twenty years, could only be discredited as fiction if he too accepted it as such. With stronger feeling yet, though not with anger, he wrote to the 'friends' who, so Hyde claimed, thought he was wrong. Yet in fact he only asked that they prevent the queen from 'retyring from all businesses into a monastery', as she had threatened. 'This if it all fall out (which God forbid) is so distructif to all my affaires: I say no more of it; my hart is too bigg.'[37]

He still believed that his old tools would work. But attempts at straightforward, old-fashioned political bribery also let him down. It is easy to forget that despite defeat, despite imprisonment, the king still technically controlled appointments and ennoblements. He thus persisted in the almost poignantly stubborn assumption that the gifts of honour and office brought obedience, or lip-service at the very least. Davenant, having accepted defeat, may still have been in Newcastle when the Covenanters' chief lawyer arrived in the city. Archibald Johnston, Lord Wariston, had spent the past three years in tireless argument and travel between the two kingdoms. Throwing off his cloak, he too now set to work on the king. It was a surprise when Charles made him his Lord Advocate in Scotland, hoping to purchase some respite, if not an ally. Yet Wariston took the promotion unsmilingly and eased none of the pressure on his benefactor.

In Hyde's engaging and mostly hypothetical reconstruction, Davenant left Newcastle much abashed. He is cast as a minor figure dwarfed by the issues at stake, and redeemed by his ignorance of their magnitude. He appears, in short, as a lightweight, a cavalier poet, a 'poor man who had in truth very good affections', flitting into vapidity.[38] But this was a hard-liner's verdict on a pragmatist. The closing stages of the war saw a dialogue of monomaniacs in which one of 'good affections' – as Hyde confessed Davenant was – could no longer hope to be heard. Unsurprisingly, Wariston and Charles failed to find a patch of common ground. Davenant was seeking further diversion in Paris that December when the king, for what looked like blood money, was handed over to his English Parliament.

4

It would be superfluous here to tell at length the story of Charles's cir-
cuitous path back to London and the trial which led to his death on a
cold morning in 1649. As his biographers tend to agree, nevertheless, it
is the part of his story which does the greatest credit to his fortitude and
presence of mind. In this final phase, we see the wit shown in his manoeuvre out of Oxford in 1644 displayed both more variedly and
consistently. He was at his most striking when fighting this last losing
battle, when he was almost free of his God-given crown. Yet, as with
the daring nocturnal march to Worcester, the shows of ingenuity rarely
brought a decisive advance or much more than a short-term victory. He
managed at best to sustain a state of confusion and prolong matters, not
to gain ground.

Occasionally he was the beneficiary of chance, as in the summer of
1647, when the split between the army and Parliament worked in his
favour. He was taken from close quarters at Holdenby House in North-
amptonshire by Cornet George Joyce. Charles went quietly: now in the
custody of the army, he was given back his chaplains and the use of his
prayer book. Transferred to Hampton Court, he was visited by Sir John
Denham, whose now limping figure Parliament had wished to exclude
from royal counsels.[39] At Hampton he acquainted himself with Denham's
poetry, and while admiring it advised him to write no more. He meant
kindly. Verse was a diversion for young men, for venting 'the overflow-
ings of their Fancy'. If Denham persisted it would only disqualify him
from 'serious Employments'. This was a standard objection: it had been
raised when Donne continued issuing new poems after becoming Dean
of St Paul's. But it did not prevent Charles making use of Denham.
He ordered him to London, and used him as a means of sending and
receiving secret correspondence. The times, Denham recalled, were in
any case 'too hot and busie' to let him vent much fancy; but he returned
to verse-making during the 'evil hours of our banishment'.[40]

After much internal debate, the army offered him a more generous
peace settlement than the one tabled by Parliament; he refused to take it
seriously. The proffered deal, summarized in the New Model Army's
Heads of Proposals, was relatively lenient to Charles himself, but too mean

with pardons for his subordinates. The fate of Strafford still burdened him: he had sacrificed enough councillors. He trusted instead to caprice, and when the moment to escape presented itself, he seized it: creeping out in his doublet, he left his keepers to find 'his Majesties cloake there and foure letters lying on the table' in his chamber. It was the work of a grave-faced japer, to leave his guards calling out in confusion, torn between anger and the respect still officially required of them. 'It was supposed he might be in the garden; downe the back stares; but it seems his Majesty was gone through the garden and parke, and so away, some think for *Scotland*.'[41]

Instead he made for the Isle of Wight. A stalwart there, Sir John Oglander, was representative in counting this a waste of freedom and committed his sighs to his diary. Oglander, whom we encountered long ago through his comments on the Duke of Buckingham, was one of those the king could count on to the end, and who yet almost by definition could do nothing for him. Oglander was the classic 'delinquent' of defeated royalist affiliation. He had spent time in prison during the war. Although he still held his house at Nunwell on the island, he had lost most of his income and estates. The hardest blow he suffered, however, was the death of his wife, Frances – Ann Donne's sister – in 1644. He had no doubt that the effort of petitioning for his liberty had cost Lady Oglander her life: the distress 'overheated' her blood, and she succumbed to smallpox. At a gathering soon after his arrival on Wight, Charles recognized Oglander's son by name, and gave an audience shortly afterwards to the corpulent squire himself. They would converse regularly during the king's time on the island. With a whitening beard and 'somewhat large mustachios', Oglander simmered constantly with melancholy anger at the tailors and tradesmen now running the parishes, and still wore mourning clothes. He took to waiting on the king at least once a week.[42]

There was no raising an army on Wight, no accomplishing anything of purpose, and the king was quickly prisoner again. But he had succeeded in creating a shock and, more importantly, in escaping the army's clutches. The more radical among its ranks already had plans for the future. The New Model Army had not only defeated the cavaliers; it had given hope and purpose to the idea of a Godly Commonwealth in which liberty of conscience was guaranteed and Church and king might be things of the past. As the army's captive, Charles was merely an obstacle. As Parliament's, he was still the head of state. In safe custody at Carisbrooke Castle, where he played bowls on the green within the walls and took exercise on the downs nearby, Charles could send the various factions of his enemy spinning and turning against one another, army against Parliament, Scots against both. As he did so, the long ensuing rounds of negotiations bought his supporters time to regroup and reopen hostilities. Yet when the English cavaliers rose again, aided by 'engaging' Scots, they were crushed, emphatically, in all regions: the Scottish 'engagers' fell to Cromwell at Preston in 1648. For some time still Prince Rupert – improbably, for a self-acknowledged land-lubber – tried continuing the fight by sea; but the 'second' civil war was hardly a war at all. It was a coda.

Yet even as the arena of possibility diminished, Charles grew ever more ingenious within it. For centuries the consensus has been that he touched greatness only at the last, when he was brought back to London and put on trial. He conducted his defence by declining to defend himself. Controlling his stutter, he was able to demonstrate that no English state could have any legal foundation without him; that the court judging him, indeed, had no authority to do so. After his execution in January 1649, the sovereignty of the English Commonwealth which emerged to face the world was highly questionable at best.

With characteristic profligacy these last small moral victories by the king, resonant if ineffective, cost more than they were worth. His misplaced belief in a military solution wasted the lives thrown away in the cavalier rising of 1648. His duplicity in negotiations ensured harsh treatment for the royal armies in the field. He could then hardly expect clemency from the court that was trying him for his life by refusing to recognize it. Yet the popular majority of his support did not, however, hold him accountable for such consequences. His final years and months yielded the last parts to a canon of noble acts and gestures which his followers endowed with all but religious significance. Anecdotes of the Stuart years and defenders of the collapsed regime, dead and alive, were already being compiled into an extensive loyalist literature. From this emerged Fuller's *Worthies*, Izaak Walton's lives of Wotton and Donne; even volumes such as Carew's scandalous collected poems were incorporated into a genre of relics. Gatherings of Suckling's poems, dramas and letters to 'Aglaura' were issued between 1646 and 1659. The title page of an early edition of his *Poems*, 'printed by his owne copy', stressed the old connection to the court: 'The Lyrick Poems were set in Musick by Mr. *Henry Lawes*, Gent. of the Kings Chappel, and one of His Majesties Private Musick.' The concept of another anthology, *The Last Remains of Sir John Suckling* (1659), could be taken to describe the entire memorial genre. The booklist would grow throughout the decades – far into the eighteenth century – with biographies of Caroline grandees and memoirs by attentive subordinates such as Sir Philip Warwick, and the eventual publication of Clarendon's *History of the Rebellion*.

By far the most venerated collection of such last remains, however, was the little volume purportedly written by the king himself: published shortly after his death as *Eikon Basilike*, but known immediately as 'the king's book', this was a litany of Charles's experiences from the outset of the rebellion, which reached its climax at the verge of martyrdom. To a large extent the king's troubles began with the issue of one religious text, the Scottish Book of Common Prayer; now they closed with a furious dispute over another, in which Charles himself was the focus of worship and revilement. The response it moved in a nation evidently insecure over what it had allowed to pass was so powerful that John Milton took on the role of image-smasher, challenging the *Eikon*'s version of events and seeking to expose it as a moral fraud.

Milton's *Eikonoklastes* pointed out that there was more cunning than purity in the king's book: one of the prayers interspersing the prose meditations had been pasted in from no more sacred a work than Sir Philip Sidney's *Arcadia*. Milton smelt the presence of a ghost-writer: and at least two candidates emerged after the Restoration. Yet the brunt of Milton's argument was not in fact driven against Charles himself. His quarrel was with the idolatry with which people were treating the *Eikon*, and their superstitious reverence for kings. They were going beyond papism, looking for the real presence of Charles in the pages of his book. Milton defended the sentence which had been passed on the king, and the court's right to reach the verdict which required it. Yet by repeating the charges against Charles, and repudiating those made against the new Commonwealth, Milton was forced on to the defensive; and he could not, by force of decency, strike at the person of the late king himself. The royal icon, as the blast smoke of *Eikonoklastes* cleared, remained strangely intact and immune: Milton could only attempt to destroy the soppiness and stupidity of the popular reaction to it. It is worth remembering that before the publication of the *Eikon*, Charles's image was associated with a very different boot-leg volume. If you referred to something as 'the king's book' even a year or so earlier, you called to mind *The Kings Cabinet Opened*, a hastily printed selection of Charles's papers acquired after Naseby. The documents covered almost the entire span of the war. As Parliamentary editors pointed out in detail, the stolen letters revealed the king courting friendship with all and sundry, including Irish Catholics and foreign powers, who might conceivably lend him a hand. With *Eikon Basilike*, that picture of the king was all but sealed away with him in his grave. Even a Milton could no longer take Charles himself to task for the results of his reign, but only castigate his neophytes.

Printing the king's private letters had been another irreversible step towards depriving him of royal status, criminalizing his actions and, ultimately, putting him on trial. Yet the illicit documents in *The Kings Cabinet* put Charles in a much more human light than the purple prose of the *Eikon*. 'It is plaine here,' wrote the Parliamentary annotators, 'that the Kings Counsels are wholly managed by the Queen; though she be of the weaker sexe, borne an Alien, bred up in a contrary Religion, yet nothing great or small is transacted without her privity & consent.' This was, in fact, the chief crime they detected in the letters. But there is always a danger, in letting the public come closer to a person they are taught to fear, that they might make up their own minds about the supposed villain. The letters show Charles trickily seeking aid from almost any quarter; but they also show him speaking frankly and warmly to the woman he loved, trusted and missed. They personalize him: he shows a wit and quickness that few of his subjects could have known he possessed. He emerges, too, as a better writer than Bishop John Gauden or the other suspected hands at work in *Eikon Basilike*. 'Deare heart,' Charles writes, after Henrietta Maria's fraught landing on the north coast in 1643, 'I never till now knew the good of ignorance, for I did not know the danger that thou wert in by the storme, till I had certaine assurance of thy happy escape.' The ardour of another sentence from the same letter might have caught a Parliamentary officer – or his wife – off guard: 'thou hast expressed so much love to mee that I confesse it is impossible to repay, by any thing I can doe, much lesse by words; but my heart being full of affection for thee, admiration of thee, and impatient passion of gratitude to thee, I could not but say some thing, leaving the rest to be read by thee, out of thine owne noble heart.'[43] His editors clearly expected such sentiments to raise a scoff from a war-exhausted readership, and no doubt they did from a great number of readers; yet they were capable of stirring sympathy as well, of softening the ground for the *Eikon Basilike*, and contributing to the public uncertainty which followed the king's death.

Images abound of Charles in his last weeks and days. A defining last glimpse might show the plainly dressed, legalistic Scotsman, seated before his judges like a fellow bencher in Westminster Hall. He speaks evenly and ably, the one suggestion of nerves given out by the tight clutch he maintains on his walking stick. Then there is the little figure on the scaffold specially built outside the Banqueting House, wearing two shirts in case a shiver should betray a sign of fear to the crowd amassed before Whitehall. They are pictures of a quixotic character who tried governing reality by rules that were only truly apparent to his own mind; yet besides being more than faintly adulatory, such portraits show the inner conviction that governed him at exceptional moments of performance, rather than regular, private maintenance. For our last sight of Charles alive it would be better to look at the man still uncertain of the outcome, sustaining what he could of his essentials. At his prayers, for example, in his room high up in the governor's mansion behind the walls of Carisbrooke, he moves with the greatest concentration through a cycle of devotions, still sure of his own central place – and burden – in the divine scheme.

The measure of an external view is always a help, and here it is provided by the unhappy Thomas Herbert, a watcher appointed by Parliament to act as the king's official amanuensis. It was part of Herbert's fate to chronicle afflicted missions. His previous adventure had come two decades earlier, on an embassy to Shah Abbas of Persia, which saw the swift death of both leading emissaries, Sir Dodmore Cotton and Sir Robert Shirley. Herbert returned home through the expanses of Persia, via Mauritius and the Cape of Good Hope; but intellectually revisited those places in successive expanding editions of his memoir of the journey. Back in England, from 1630 on he had resumed a provincial gentleman's pursuit of small honours and advances. The appointment as royal secretary he accepted in 1647 was by those standards a major boon; although he could be forgiven for missing the simpler trickiness of Persian etiquette. Like the fine travel writer he was, Herbert noted how Charles passed time at his various stations, the quality of his conversation and his choice of reading. At Carisbrooke, Herbert's memoir preserves Charles returning to *The Faerie Queene* and Harington's translation of Ariosto, a favourite of his elder brother Henry's, or touching local people for the King's Evil on the castle barbican. The secretary then powerfully depicts the king's arrival at Hurst Castle, the coastal fortress connected to the mainland by a narrow spit of sand, 'a poor receptacle for so great a Monarch', and his confinement to a room 'neither lightsome nor large' above the booming tides.[44]

Herbert is unreliable, however, as a spectator: he was not long in appreciating the difficulty of his position. When the Stuarts returned to power, he was anxious to show that he too was converted by Charles's zeal and dignity, and to pass himself off as a cavalier. As a recent biographer mentions, he was given to making first-hand observations of places he had never visited in the later editions of his *Some Yeares Travels into Divers Parts of Asia and Afrique*. In a similar spirit, he placed himself somewhat closer to the king's side and confidence than in truth he had been.[45]

Despite the abundance of other materials, from the prose-portraits to the faintly absurd imitation of Christ on the title page of *Eikon Basilike*, the king is better perceived at a moment recorded through a set of drawings he commissioned from the apprentice of Inigo Jones, John Webb; at the moment at which, in his mind's eye, he moves through the corridors of a new home for his reasserted post-war kingship. At some point during his captivity Charles instructed Webb to continue Jones's plans for a vast new palace at Whitehall. The complex would be executed in the high classical idiom of the Banqueting House, and in scale equal anything he had seen years earlier in Spain. A great historian of architecture has detected a certain horizontal monotony in Webb's designs, wanting the flourish of his master, but with a purposeful focus on immensity, overwhelming the real landscape of the present day. Contemplating these sheets, Charles superimposes a London of his own future making over the one awaiting him for trial and offering at best the smallest portion of his former power. It would be simple to dismiss Webb's fastidious schematics as the product of the most arrogant delusion; but more accurate to file them with the pages Charles once possessed from the notebooks of Leonardo – as a set, that is, of structures and machines which the gazer knew in the end would never be built, and in reality were probably unbuildable. The plans served their true function not as a diagram of things to come, but as a crib, a crutch, an aid to surviving the present and sustaining the persona Charles presented to the world.[46]

Charles would become the first and only saint of the Restored Church of England, to the dismay of orthodox Protestants: but it was a time of strange divinities. And despite all the life lost through his faults, the king could not be blamed for the purging of the New Model Army's dissident sectarians. By 1647, a group dubbed 'the Levellers' (possibly by Cromwell himself), led by the veteran and pamphleteer John Lilburne, was urging a much more radical settlement of the state than all but a few had so far contemplated. The Levellers represented the most politically developed of a multitude of new creeds, born under the open air during the itinerant war years, which proclaimed freedom of worship and government by the people. The commonplace book of Sir John Oglander testifies to the fears they raised: when Charles tried justifying his strange choice of refuge on the Isle of Wight, Oglander fully believed in the imminence of a bloody revolution on the mainland. By their very nature, however, the Levellers and other, still more spontaneous groups had no unified programme. Lilburne took exception, for example, to the convenient judicial murder of the king and the coup d'état it perfected. The one thing which did unite the sects, speaking largely, was the future free of political violence they imagined in their different ways. They could not be suffered to continue unchecked.

However much an iconoclast he was, Oliver Cromwell's opinions on suffrage were orthodox, and he was moving towards a conventional position on the question of conscience. Christians were free to believe as they wished, he upheld – even Catholics, it seemed – but what they did with those beliefs, outwardly and publicly, was another matter. Conformity was essential for any state to function, making a religion based on personal inspiration rather than instructed truth especially dangerous. Hobbes would shortly assert that 'if men were at liberty, to take for Gods Commandements, their own dreams and fancies, or the dreams and fancies of private men; scarce two men would agree upon what is Gods Commandement; and yet in respect of them, every man would despise the Commandements of the Common-wealth.'[47] In his suppression of the sects within and beyond the army's ranks in the late 1640s, Cromwell recognized this principle; even though he remained supremely sensitive to the Almighty's commands through what some might still have called his 'fancy'.

The key, as Cromwell knew, was authority. The religious side of the civil war lay not so much with a fight over freedom of Christian belief, as one over which form of Christianity was to have official status. The views of affable James Howell give a measure of the toleration which could be expected, at best, in early modern society at large. As long ago as 1635 he had insisted that he would never hold a grudge on account of another's beliefs or allegiances: 'difference in opinion may work a dis-affection in me, but not a detestation.' At the same time, he loved 'the sweet peace of our Church, so that I could be content to see an *Anabap-tist* go to Hell on a *Brownist's* back'.[48] 'Toleration' actually describes such an attitude rather well, as it does a policy of merely wishing Brownists in hell instead of sending them there; for toleration always implies an inequality of rights, a controlling party relaxing the rules against a less emancipated group. As soon as that inequality appears surmountable, something more than tolerance, something much less tolerable to the interest in power, has come into force.

Howell was still in prison when the king was executed. The poisons of the River Fleet, as immortalized decades earlier by Jonson in his *On the Famous Voyage*, stayed rich all the while with animal debris, and the fumes from its spidery undercurrents rose through the prison. Object-ively debilitating though such conditions were, their psychological effect was all the greater on one accustomed to 'a rambling life': Howell was 'as the *Dutchman* saith, a *Landloper*'. He stayed sane, as many of those who shared his instincts did, by roving with his thoughts across paper, and venting a little self-pity to his many correspondents. 'Methinks I have travell'd more since I have been immur'd and martyr'd' 'twixt these walls than ever I did before,' he informed Sir Kenelm Digby; 'for I have travell'd the *Isle of Man*, I mean this little World, which I have carried about me and within me so many years.'[49] More positively, he distilled much of his learning and wandering into pedagogic epistles. Reflecting on the causes of the war from his corner in the prison, he had put the quarrel in the context of a larger historical process. England, he judged, had caught the Continental disease of religious war: the conflict in Britain and Ireland had resulted from a Reformation which had, long before, been taken too far. He imagined it as a corrupt Pentecostal spirit visiting all the territories he knew by heart; a bird which from Geneva flew to France:

and hatched the *Huguenots*, which make about the tenth part of that People: it took wing also to *Bohemia* and *Germany* high and low, as the *Palatinate*, the Land of *Hesse*, and the Confederate Provinces of the State of *Holland*, whence it took flight to *Scotland* and *England*. It took first footing in *Scotland* when K. James was a child in his Cradle; but when he came to understand himself . . . and being come to *England*, he utterly disclaimed it, terming it . . . a *Sect* rather than *a Religion*. To this Sect may be imputed all the Scissures that have happen'd in *Christianity*, with most of the Wars that have lacerated poor *Europe* since; and it may be called the Source of the Civil distractions that now afflict this poor Island.[50]

Howell overlooked the side of Parliament's quarrel which spoke of defending the rights and liberties of the subject through the law. Or rather he rejected it altogether; for it was instrumental to the royalist position that those freedoms were guaranteed by the king. At his trial Charles argued that the rights of the common people had no safeguard without him. So this could by definition be no war for liberty: it was a puritan revolt, pure and simple.

Howell could accept that the religious motives behind that revolt might be sincere. At the root of it all for a more typical cavalier, a Sucklington, however, there would never be little more than a crude bid for power, a case of mass disobedience. In such circumstances it was not only the king's image that was transformed. He had an army of martyrs to satisfy a yearning for saints which was still strong among his followers. Now even Suckling seemed a model of propriety, the very archetype of the courtier, and to some was just the poet to mourn the nation's crimes. The misdemeanours of the 1630s were laid to rest; the man, meanwhile, was summoned from his grave. 'Call Suckling from his

Ashes, reinspired/ With an Elizian Trance,' implored one elegist for Charles; 'to Sing/ Royal Distresses and lament a King.'[51]

Where would Suckling have cropped up now, had he lived – assuming, of course, that he had not tipped the balance of the war? He would have been at home among the redundant cavaliers fighting each other for want of active service, as the late king's rival lieutenants – Digby, Rupert, Percy, et al. – fell into open vendetta. Pointless scraps were a means of avoiding deeper consideration. The destiny it is hard to see Suckling dealing with is Howell's, 'immur'd and martyr'd', coping day upon day with prison walls and little distraction but the inkpot. Yet for want of the diversion on which a Suckling thrived, Howell was better able to put Europe's shock into words, in his twittery, theatrical manner. This was the first destruction of a monarch by criminal proceedings, 'a black tragedy', as he put it, which had not only 'fill'd most hearts among us with consternation and horror', but was 'no less resented abroad. For my own particular, the more I ruminate upon it, the more it astonisheth my imagination, and shaketh all the cells of my brain.'[52]

Recovering from this astonishment would be the work of many decades. It would be beyond old Elizabethans such as Oglander, riding the Brading Downs in 'sad-coloured clothes'; although some, including Howell, adapted sooner than might have been expected.

12. Angling for Quiet

Did ever War so cease
That all might Olive weare?
All sleepy grow with Peace,
And none be wak'd with fear?

– Davenant, song from '*The First Dayes* Entertainment'

1

Sir Edward Hyde was happy enough living in St Helier in 1647, working on his history in the mornings, then meeting his fellow fugitives for prayers at church and then dinner at one or another's house. Skipping supper, they then 'met always upon the sands in the evening' to stroll and talk.[1] As the others left Jersey, Hyde continued these walks alone. Parliament's navy was already driving out royalist resistance in the Channel Islands, but Jersey would hold on for the king for some time. The commander of the island, Carteret, invited Hyde to stay as his guest, across the bay in Castle Elizabeth. Hyde welcomed both the company of the family and the shelter they offered him:

He built a lodging in the castle, of two or three convenient rooms, to the wall of the church, which sir George Carteret had repaired and beautified; and over the door of his lodging he set up his arms, with this inscription, *Bene vixit, qui bene latuit* [Ovid: 'He has lived well, who has escaped notice']: and he always took pleasure in relating, with what great tranquillity of spirit (though deprived of the joy he took in his wife and children) he spent his time here, amongst his books (which he got from Paris) and his papers; between which he seldom spent less than ten hours in the day.[2]

Since antiquity, the literature of male, enfranchised citizens (or subjects) had expressed a tension between public duty and desire for private peace. The philosophical gentleman or noble's heart supposedly pushed him to the country, to his estates, his family and (often above all) his library. But his duty drew him to the capital, the centre of power, where a contribution to the nation's civic and political life was demanded of him. The resulting dilemma preoccupied writers in a multitude of genres through the later Middle Ages and on into the early modern period. It was a source of bucolic idyll, escape to Arcadia; it was a central theme of debate in numerous philosophical dialogues. It preoccupied Montaigne, Castiglione; and Shakespeare dramatized it obsessively, from the reluctant kingship of Henry VI to Lear's abdication and Prospero's neglect of his dukedom.

Yet as one might expect, the weariness and the quandary behind it concealed at least two white lies. Firstly, gentlemen and noblemen clamouring for preferment and power showed at least as much eagerness to cling to the city as they did to catch up on their reading and oversee their lands in the country. Repeated statutes were deemed necessary, from the sixteenth through the seventeenth century, to set limits on the amount of time the gentry and nobility could spend each year at court. Secondly, moreover, the debate constructed a dilemma where there was frequently no real choice to be made. Retirement was all too often the gentleman's only option, the result of failed prospects or banishment.

Such was the case for the exiled royalists of the interregnum. Those among the vanquished who paid their fines and yielded up the requisite fifth-and-twentieth part of their property returned grimly to the remains of their manors. For the indicted officers and politicians whom Parliament could not pardon – with Sir Edward Hyde near the top of the list – there was no longer a *domus* to which they could retire. A copious literature developed with the aim of expressing, and trying to accept this lot, the fate which Suckling very early on seems unable to have borne. Countless poems of the mid-century, however, strove to embrace the comforts it did afford – 'a few friends, and many books', as Abraham Cowley expressed it. Cowley, a poetic prodigy, had stayed with the court throughout the wars, and continued as Henry Jermyn's much-esteemed secretary after it. A period back in England as a spy during Cromwell's rule, and a frightening stay in prison, convinced him that loyalists would do best by lying low for the time being, awaiting 'better occasions'.[3]

Predictably, that philosophy rankled with the royalist champion Prince Rupert. The prince had always believed in making the opportunity rather than waiting for it, and he upheld that conviction to the last. Having remained at sea after the failure of his efforts with the royalist navy in 1648, his ambit widened rapidly and his activities degenerated into outright piracy. Fighting seasickness and cajoling his pay-famished crews, he terrorized Spanish and English republican merchantmen in all imaginable waters, tore down the coast of West Africa and eventually preyed on the Atlantic shipping lanes. By the time he reached Barbados he had only a handful of ships left from the dozen of his original flotilla, and more of these were lost in a four-day hurricane, in which his younger brother Maurice was swept away. Chastened at last – for the time being – Rupert brought his last two limping vessels back to France. He arrived in Paris bronzed and blasted in 1653, sick in health and heart, and was soon caught up in the ill winds of the exiled court.

Rupert's nautical sabre-rattling agitated the new English Commonwealth's trade and distracted its navy. There were few concrete gains to show, however, for all the storming energy and self-discipline he put into his new metier. Although that was hardly the point: a kind of seaborne George Mallory, a puritan of venture, heedless of comfort or safety, Rupert belonged with later explorers, running up mountains because they were there. Yet his exploits during the interregnum set more than a pattern for the efforts of his former comrades who fought on, raided, laid plots or looked for ways of raising troops; they worked almost like a fatal charm. Rupert himself may have been touched with the Sucklington jinx.

George Villiers, Second Duke of Buckingham, exhibited a more mercurial strain of restlessness. Villiers was seven months old when his father was assassinated in 1628, and he inherited the First Duke's lust for greatness. He had a lifelong urge to be a hero, which generally failed him at the moment a chance to do so came along. Other teenagers – indeed, countless boys – served in the civil wars, but the young duke accepted his wardens' view that he was too young to bear arms. The injunction served him well as a cause for sullenness. He grew up with the king's children, with the Earl of Rutland and Marquis of Newcastle his guardians, and much of his adolescence passed abroad. His twenty-first birthday fell on the same day Charles was executed, 30 January 1649: he was by then the endlessly excitable, mutable, fiendishly intelligent character the English would know for decades, unpredictable in public and given to sadistic contemplations in private. The week after the execution, when the king's body was taken by water for a small snowy funeral at Windsor, saw Buckingham disguise himself as a balladeer and perform with a group of musicians outside Whitehall. He avoided recognition, as he sold his song-sheets, with a mask of floury paste and a suit of rags decorated with feathers; a foxtail in his hat gave his costume its finishing touch. He even deceived his sister, a prisoner on her way to Windsor, when he danced up to her carriage with his sheaf of music. A wink through the window, and she knew him; and having given her some ballads he was gone, back to his busking post and his fiddlers. This was the earliest of his many sorties from the Continent, attired as clown or troubadour. Buckingham later called these journeys spying missions; yet they also allowed him to foster tacit connections in the new Commonwealth, and to explore the likelihood of regaining his estates, which were among the richest in the country. He set something of a trend. His younger companion John Wilmot, the Second Earl of Rochester, would also be given to escapades in disguise, and inhabit his chosen character for weeks on end (so it was said), posing as an Italian mountebank in Tower Street, or dressing as a vagabond 'to follow some mean Amours, which, for the variety of them, he affected'.[4]

While Buckingham conducted his adventures at his own discretion, and at his own chosen level of risk, many in the various royal retinues were presented with fanciful or downright impossible tasks. The one given to Davenant, typically, ended in a living burlesque of the sort of grand expedition he had envisaged for Rupert, years ago, in his poem about the Madagascar scheme.

In February 1650 Davenant arrived on Jersey with a shipload of convicts, bound for the New World. By that time Edward Hyde's pleasant den in Castle Elizabeth stood empty: Hyde had forfeited his quiet for an adventure of his own. Davenant was welcomed, however, by Carteret, to whom the king had recently granted the eastern American province to be renamed 'New Jersey'. For the moment such royal grants were largely theoretical: yet with the war lost on the British and Irish islands, the fight was still alive for the Crown's old network of international holdings. The last, Barbados, would fall to Commonwealth supporters a cruelly short time before Rupert could reach it. In the north, there was no hope of gaining staunchly puritan New England. Yet Virginia, governed by a playwright, Sir William Berkeley, still declared for the king, while the contest for Maryland hung in the balance. Both colonies, unlike New England, were short of skilled labour, and it was ostensibly Davenant's task, under the title of treasurer to Berkeley, to bring in fresh artisans. These he had picked arbitrarily from various prisons in Paris. When he asked through the bars for craftsmen to go to America, the inmates of one gaol shouted, to a man, 'We are all weavers!'[5] Yet Davenant's masters also clearly had heavier graft in mind for the transportees. His final instructions mentioned a formidable if optimistic programme of fortification for Virginia, the building to be done by slaves – including Davenant's weavers – at the planters' expense.

It seems that many of these volunteers – Aubrey put the original number at thirty-six – had escaped Davenant's custody by the time he reached Normandy. There was little surprise on that score: the episode with the two aldermen of York, who still remembered his kindness, had shown he lacked the care or ruthlessness of a good gaoler. The stranded English wits in Paris, some no doubt envious of his commission, had bidden him '*Bon voyage*' in their usual caustic fashion. The author of the following is thought to have been Denham:

> . . . *America* must breed up the Brat,
> From whence 'twill return a *West-Indy* Rat.
> For *Will* to *Virginia* is gone from among us,
> With thirty two Slaves, to plant *Mundungus* [tobacco].[6]

Davenant stopped off in Jersey to lay in supplies and recruit more colonists. The Jersey Protestants who joined him, mostly bondsmen of Carteret, murmured against his convicts – who were in effect slaves – and even more so against two French friars who were also taken aboard. Yet by spring their ship had been overhauled and stocked. At nightfall on Friday 24 April (3 May by the French calendar) they set sail.[7]

Jersey's reefs and red cliffs were quickly behind, and by dawn the five-gunner had made it past Guernsey, sailing westward, when it was sighted by a privateer. The swift frigate, allied to Parliament, immediately gave chase to Davenant's vessel. Land's End and the Scillies lay in reach, and the open ocean was close beyond. Yet the twenty-gun *Fortune* was soon alongside, and its prize surrendered without resistance.

John Green, the *Fortune*'s captain, was soon aware that he had found a gem. Aboard Davenant's little ship, a Danish sloop captured by royalist pirates during the war, Green found cargo for a long voyage and equipment for settlement in America: rich stores of oil and Spanish wine, vine stock for plantation, precious weapons and munitions, and a large array of little novelties to be used as gifts and trades with Native Americans. When opened, the ship's papers revealed that Davenant's orders were more ambitious than his original commission allowed. It transpired that he was now to head to Maryland, where dissidents from Virginia, 'all kinde of Schimaticks, and Sectaries, and other ill-affected persons', had taken refuge under the governance of Cecil Calvert, Lord Baltimore. Baltimore was a papist: and using an argument which fellow Catholics in England would use during the Restoration, he promoted emancipation for his own Church through a policy of 'toleration' for members of the radical sects. In America these still adhered to the side of the English Parliament, full of hope for a new, cross-Atlantic Christian fellowship. The young King Charles complained that Baltimore 'doth visibly adhere to the Rebells of England', and thus licensed Davenant to take over the administration of the Maryland plantations. Without depriving Baltimore of his property rights, Davenant was to be the lieutenant-governor of the colony, and to bring it into line with royal dictates. His patent was notably vague on how this transfer should be enforced. From the distance of Breda, the king's hope was that Baltimore would be sufficiently impressed with Davenant's letters of patent.[8]

It was a tall order for the dispirited company brought up on deck an ocean away from the Americas. Captain Green's men commanded them all to strip, commoners and gentlemen alike. Along with the experienced Jersey crew were the thirty or more civilian colonists and a small clutch of obviously richer prisoners, including one bizarrely irrepressible character with a ruddy face and a strange protruding crater where his nose should have been. Some time seems to have elapsed before the pirates learned the name of this person. Besides these were an altogether more ravaged set: the fifteen or so remaining, convicts. As the search went on, individual identities became clearer. After moving from the piles of clothes the prisoners dropped on deck to rifle through the chests below, Green's men discovered the robes of the two Capuchins in the group. Once identified, the priests were promptly subjected to more particular ridicule and discomfort. They had changed their cassocks for more practical clothing back in Jersey. On discovering the hidden vestments, crosses and chalices, the sailors held a mock Mass on the bridge, forced confessions from the clerics and demanded impossible acts of repentance in exchange for absolution. The rest of the moneyed captives, Green was satisfied, were obviously papists too. He was well pleased with his catch. Besides the proceeds that would come from the prize itself, the prisoners would be valuable hostages to exchange for men from his last ship – including his brothers – who were still being held in Rennes. With Parliament's blessing, Green had terrorized hostile Channel shipping in the closing stages of the war, and had been concentrating on the torture of a Jersey merchant below deck when two French battleships bore down on his previous frigate, the perversely named *Welcome*. The incident had cost him his liberty, and he had only won it back the previous year, in 1649.[9]

Some of the captives were deposited at Falmouth; the friars, persons of some importance in France, were traded for Green's brothers. As for the French prisoners, 'The Slaves I suppose they sold,' was Aubrey's best guess. Yet on learning that his disfigured prisoner, evidently the chief of the company, was none other than the dead king's general, poet laureate and 'great pirott', Green retained Davenant for higher bargaining. He was kept close prisoner for several weeks aboard the *Fortune*, until Green deposited him profitably at Cowes Castle on the Isle of Wight.

'We have not heard one word from Sir W. Davenant since he left us,' wrote Cowley from Paris early in May. Two months later, amid his own trials, Hyde wrote to him asking for news. His letter reveals a very different feeling to that indicated by his treatment of 'poor Will Davenant' in the *History*. 'I am exceedingly afflicted,' he told Cowley. 'I beseech you let me know what is become of him.' As historian, Hyde felt obliged to take the hardest view of persons and events. In personal correspondence, now his former lodger faced a traitor's death, he could express his fondness for Davenant. 'We are strangely pursu'd in all things, and all places,' reflected Cowley to another correspondent, 'even [in] our retreats to the other world.'[10]

2

When in 1648 a royal order came to join the younger Charles, Hyde instantly abandoned his sanctuary on Jersey. He took ship, rendezvousing with fellow servants on the first stage of what proved an exacting journey. Yet returning to the fray brought with it experience of value and novelty. In normal circumstances Hyde was unlikely to have met Marshal Ranzaw, the German governor of Dunkirk, a rugged veteran with surprising good manners. The marshal's front-line post demanded a thick hide. Dunkirk, always a prized North Sea naval base, had been wrenched from the Spanish in 1646. Now, as the French were overtaken by more civil wars of their own, the Habsburgs were moving to regain the port and other lost possessions. The Peace of Westphalia concluded later in 1648 would technically end the Thirty Years' War, and was of immense future significance for the premises of its treaty – but the Continent would never go long without military arguments. For all his cares, Ranzaw received Hyde's party 'with great civility, being a very proper man, of a most extraordinary presence and aspect, and might well be reckoned a very handsome man, though he had but one leg, one hand, one eye, and one ear'. Wit and eloquence truly were to be found in unexpected quarters. In Ranzaw Hyde found 'a very graceful motion, a clear voice, and a charming delivery'. Yet he commented that the marshal's fondness for his bottle had prevented him from becoming a great navigator.[11]

Since even the most peaceful crossing made him sea-sick, Hyde claimed that a dose of heavy seas, no place to rest on board but the open deck, a brush with pirates or pursuit by the enemy could not have made the voyage any worse for him. Before eventually catching up with Prince Charles at The Hague, his little company was pursued and captured by freebooters off Ostend, 'who boarded the vessel with their swords drawn and pistols cocked'. Hyde was coldly indignant that the pirates made no distinction of rank, plundering all 'with equal rudeness' – failing to see, perhaps, that the nobler prisoners were likely to yield greater booty – although he admitted they at least left the gentlemen with their coats. Yet he was less offended by the pirates' conduct than the treatment he and his friends received in Ostend. The municipal authorities made very detailed inquiries as to the possessions stolen from the broken trunks and valises. They only did so, it transpired, to be sure of getting their due share of the loot.[12] In the end Hyde viewed the affair resignedly. He had, he felt, no moral right to give up when it was still possible to fight on; and no right to do otherwise when that chance disappeared. The art consisted in judging where a possibility existed.

Hyde's practice of that art over the decades provoked a mixture of exasperation – at his caution, his lawyerly calculation, his priggishness and paternalism – and envy. In time he was identified by friend and foe alike as the royalists' chief of intelligence, often working independently of the new king and his brother, since he 'had managed most of the secret correspondence in England, and all dispatches of importance had passed through his hands'.[13] He might have secretly thought that matters would be made much easier had he been the undisputed master of policy, but he never achieved that role and outwardly rejected all pretensions to it. As if the war itself had not been enough, the years gave him ample training in accepting elements beyond his control, from the sharp blows of fortune to the hostility of the queen mother – who never quite accepted him as an ally – the headstrong inclinations of the young king and his brothers, and the outright decadence of the king's boyhood friend, the Second Duke of Buckingham.

Soon after reaching the king Hyde agreed to go on a pauper's embassy to Spain, to canvass support against the Commonwealth. With some doubts, he now agreed with the idea of an alliance with a foreign power, assisted by the former Parliamentarians ousted by Cromwell, to reinstate the monarchy. But he knew there was little prospect of Spain or France's direct intervention – they were too preoccupied with fighting one another – and had misgivings about even requesting it. He travelled with one of the dead king's first companions to Spain in 1623, Francis (now Lord) Cottington. Despite Cottington's enthusiasm they met with the courteous reluctance to help that he expected; and despite this disappointment, Spain beguiled him. The gravity and decorum which James Howell took lightly, attracted more by the energy and colour of the land, Hyde deeply admired. Spain was always the home of the exact formality and distinction of which the first Charles dreamed to the very end of his life. The nation's polity rested on a scheme of things burnt into place by a climate suffering no resistance. It held the ideal of what a Stuart monarchy should have been, and during his stay Hyde also fell under its spell. The essence of this order was apparent in the bull-fight, 'a spectacle very wonderful'; from the toreadors trotting into the ring 'in grave order' to the rapt public attending in strict yet passionate echelons.

The marketplace was converted to a bullring with temporary scaf-folding in front of 'handsome brick houses'. Each house had a balcony 'adorned with tapestry and very beautiful ladies'. The scaffolds reached as high as the first storey, and it impressed Hyde how the citizens all knew their places according to rank on the stands. He was struck too by the severity of a form which was spoilt by the slightest lapse or trans-gression, the disgrace to the rider if his cloak so much as brushed the ground, the often-fatal consequences ensuing if he mistimed his dance or misjudged his thrust. The 'fatal stroke can never be struck,' Hyde noted, 'but when the bull comes so near upon the turn of the horse, that his horn even touches the rider's leg', allowing the toreador to find the mortal vein with the 'full strength of his arm'. A miss, and the resulting wound would only enrage the bull further. Hyde seems tempted to suggest that the event required an all but impossible fixity from all concerned, not only the bull and the rider but the onlookers as well. Those who leapt into the ring when the bulls were released paid dearly for their impetuosity. The animals were brought in from the mountains the night before the bullfight and rustled through the empty streets by 'people used to that work'. All knew the custom: revellers wandering too late in town had only themselves to blame if they heard the ring of hooves too late. In some respects, certainly, the *toros* called for regula-tion of unimaginable rigour. Yet Hyde realized that the event owed its immense power – at once ritualistic and theatrical – to the undertow of something beyond all control. For that reason, perhaps, he refused in his memoirs to claim that the bullfight offered an image of ideal order. He admired the figures of the fighters, 'all persons of quality richly clad, and upon the best horses in Spain; every one attended by eight, or ten, or more lackeys, all clinquant with gold and silver lace'. But what impressed him most was the moment when the toreador extinguished the potential for chaos and rage with a flash of applied, long-practised judgement – 'and they who are most skilful in the exercise, do frequently kill the beast with such an exact stroke.' A master gave the unpredictable event an air of inevitability, so much that two or three animals would die in that fashion on a single day of fighting.[14]

If only years of training and experience could yield such a strike in affairs of state. Instead Hyde was forever obliged to contend with the weather of events, the policies of lesser intellects – the Digbys and Jermyns of the world – and the actions of hotheads. During his absence in Spain, the over-impressionable king was persuaded to accept the Scottish National Covenant in return for a throne at Edinburgh, a concession Hyde had tirelessly opposed. Meanwhile, in Madrid his work was ruined when royalist bruisers murdered the English republic's agent, Anthony Ascham. It was another in the long series of Sucklington moments that had wrecked the efforts of Hyde's patience and cunning since 1641. With increasing insistence, Spanish courtiers suggested Hyde and Cottington leave the country. Both ambassadors were uncertain where they should go. Cottington asked permission to remain as a private resident, and ended his days on the peninsula. But in March 1651 Hyde departed for France, crossing the Pyrenees by mule. He was convulsed along the way by a recurrent attack of gout. At Bayonne, at Bordeaux, finally at Paris, 'he was forced to keep his bed, and to bleed, for many days,' but was driven on by his wish to save the king from disaster.[15]

He was consoled by the example of other dispossessed grandees. Briefly reunited with his family at Antwerp, he also met William Cavendish, the Marquis of Newcastle, still recovering from his much-publicized 'exit' from the northern theatre of operations; 'who having married a young lady, confined himself most to her company; and lived as retired as his ruined condition in England obliged him to'.[16] That lady, some thirty years his junior, was Margaret Cavendish, née Lucas, one of the few survivors of a dynasty ruined by the civil wars: two years previously Fairfax had ordered the shooting of her brother Charles after the grinding siege of Colchester. Cavendish was a royal lady-in-waiting when Newcastle met her in Paris, and their marriage quickly followed. A reluctant figure at court, she was an uncomfortable cross of introvert and extrovert, who seems often to have felt pressured to laugh off the seriousness of her literary and philosophical pursuits. In those years Cavendish was taken up with philosophical poems, producing an atomistic theory of the cosmos in verse which she published in 1653, recanted in another work brought out the same year, but seemingly returned to and developed in her *Philosophical and Physical Opinions* in 1655. Like another female Lucretian of opposing political sympathies, Lucy Hutchinson, Cavendish found it difficult to assert her intellect before a wider audience: whereas Hutchinson avoided the issue altogether, confining her poetic speculations to manuscript, Cavendish, a more public figure, and one evidently tempted by performance, used lavish displays of eccentricity to distract from the controversies her books stirred. She was noted for her wild attire, her freedom with obscenity and for insisting on making a bow instead of a curtsey, but a letter-writer of 1653 observed that her poetry was 'ten times more Extravagant then her dresse'.[17] There was clearly an element of subterfuge in her costume and conduct, a demonstrative admission that she had breached the rules of femininity with her writing. She made a show of daffiness while continuing to work intently, and to participate in the fascinating intellectual circle surrounding her husband's brother. In Sir Charles Cavendish, the patron of Hobbes, Hyde regained something of the atmosphere of Great Tew. Even physically, Sir Charles reminded the chancellor of his great lost friend: like Falkland, 'he had all the disadvantages imaginable in his person' – a small, ungainly figure and an odd countenance, in which nevertheless 'there was a mind and soul lodged that was very lovely and beautiful.'[18]

The respite of such company was always short-lived. Across the Channel, Cromwell was undefeatable. The previous autumn he had routed the Scots at Dunbar, finally bringing the Covenant to heel and the Scottish revolution to an end. It was an unlikely victory against superior odds on unfamiliar ground. Cromwell, along with the defeated Presbyterians at Edinburgh, attributed the outcome to God's judgement. As so frequently in those years, the general had been made the instrument of divine will. Instrumental too, as so often, was his own instinct for the time to strike, as the Scots hazarded a sortie from their defences on Dunbar's higher ground. It was also thought that there were times when Cromwell simply knew he could not be beaten. John Aubrey set this down as a leading instance of preternatural 'impulse':

One that I knew, that was at the Battle of Dunbar, told me that Oliver was carried on with a Divine Impulse; he did Laugh so excessively as if he had been drunk; his Eyes sparkled with Spirits. He obtained a great Victory; but the Action was said to be contrary to Human Prudence.

Aubrey had it from another source that the same afflatus seized Cromwell in the build-up to Naseby. He had many other examples of people with some gift of divination. An alumnus of his from Trinity at Oxford was given to regular predictions – anticipating robbery on a stage-coach and the death of a brother.[19] Yet Cromwell seemed less to intimate a happening than catch a scent, time a pounce, and when he did he had the instinct of a matchless bullfighter. Among the victims of his 'impulse' were the thousands massacred at Drogheda in 1649, and the prisoners marched to death on the long road south from Dunbar.

To Hyde that power could not be opposed in the field on uncertain terms. In his view, the new king's best course was merely to stand firm in constitutional principles, be constant, and wait for potential allies to drop their preconditions for supporting him. If mortifications such as Dunbar continued, united by opposition to Cromwell, all opponents of the English Commonwealth would have no other choice but to lend Charles their help.

But Charles wanted and needed a kingdom, and the Scots offered him theirs – if, that is, he would take their Covenant, and accept in doing so all that his father had resisted to the end. The Covenanters set about him with their trusted doctrinal bludgeons. The king later complained of the Scots' 'barbarous behaviour' towards him, 'their insupportable pride and pedantry in their manners'.[20] As Hyde recuperated in Antwerp, his former ward took the Scottish crown at Edinburgh. The subsequent moral compromise led to the king taking a patched-up army on a long, lonely expedition to the south, as far as Worcester, expecting all the way a voluntary burst of militancy from supporters in the country. They did not, however, flock to join him, and he experienced the exact opposite of a Cromwellian impulse. His adversary, racing to catch him, looped eastwards to block off the approach to London. Once again, Cromwell's leadership appeared well beyond 'human prudence', stealing victory by refusing defeat. Charles, admittedly, was hindered by divisions within his command, a surplus of chiefs and too few warriors. Buckingham had gone into a mighty sulk when Charles refused to let him lead; and his umbrage deepened when he learned that Lord Leven would outrank him. Resentments carried by the generals from Scotland broke whatever unity of purpose the army might have had. The battle around the Severn degenerated into terrible skirmishing within Worcester itself, with the republicans eventually turning the royalists' own guns on the city. As the king stole away to the south, laid-out corpses made a morbidly appropriate last salute to the most prurient of British monarchs. 'The *penes* of the dead stript bodies,' Aubrey heard, '2 or 3 dayes were all erect.'[21]

'Yet much remains to conquer still,' Milton advised Cromwell in a laudatory sonnet; 'peace hath her victories/ No less renowned than war.'[22] As Cromwell turned his attention back to internal politics, he delegated the reduction of Scotland to a proven subordinate, General Monk. By coincidence, the general had been the one English officer to distinguish himself against the Scots at Newburn a decade earlier: and ten years later, he would determine the future of both kingdoms by inviting Charles to return. For the present time, from John O'Groats to Land's End, there was little here to encourage future uprisings for the king, and for the remainder of the decade Hyde had some greater success in directing his master's strategy. When the two met again at Paris, Charles a changed man and Hyde weaker than ever with his gout, they agreed that 'the King had nothing at this time to do but to be quiet.'[23]

3

Charles led from the front at Worcester, and escaped in rags. His romantic journey to the south coast, avoiding capture in the branches of Boscobel Oak, could not have been in greater contrast to the progress home of a calm loyalist who saved one of the throneless king's most precious possessions.

Charles was not an easy figure to disguise: he was an exceptionally tall man with atypically dark features – a complexion which had distressed his fair-haired mother since his nonage. In the hours after Worcester he did what he could with his appearance by ditching his jewellery and making a drastic change of clothes. Donning peasant clothing, the treasure he found hardest to abandon was his father's Garter medal, the 'lesser George'. He passed it to an attendant, who managed to hide it in a Staffordshire farm. There another confidant, a local lawyer, recovered it, and passed it to another native of Stafford, a draper in his late fifties with a business in London. As militia scoured all ends of the country for the skulking youthful six-footer, Izaak Walton took the George back to London. His directions were to return it to Colonel Thomas Blagge, or Blague, the officer who had first hidden it. The colonel had since then been caught and locked up in the Tower, but presently found means of escaping.

The story of the king's flight became the prologue to the Jacobite legend, a saga consisting largely of dramatic getaways. It was a story to raise false expectations, hopes of a kind Walton strove to set at peace in a book he published two years after Worcester. With his biographies of Donne, Herbert, Wotton, and other departed worthies, he contributed to the stock of literary *reliquiae*, fragments of the vanished past. But with *The Compleat Angler*, he offered like-minded readers a guide to living through the difficult present. He rewrote the book almost entirely during the next thirty years, but throughout its subsequent editions it remained both a detailed and authoritative fishing manual and a work of practical philosophy. Written in the form of a narrative dialogue, it drew on the classical conventions of didactic writing. Though obviously humbler in execution, it has something of the scope of Hesiod's *Works and Days* or Virgil's *Georgics*, covering the run and return of the seasons, and the line of life itself within its chosen field. Walton's teacher and principal speaker, Piscator, offers modest lessons on how to live as well as how to angle. Where he needs back-up on fact and opinion, he turns to ancient poets and historians; where he needs illustration of a thought or feeling, he quotes his favourite recent authors, often reciting a poem entire. His character, like Walton's, is grounded on respect for an older world. During their rest at the hearth in the evenings, he tells the company that he prefers Elizabethan lyrics, 'choicely good', to the 'strong lines' of the current age.[24] Piscator finds his host unpleasant company because:

his conceits were either scripture jests, or lascivious jests; for which I count no man witty: for the devil will help a man, that way inclined, to the first; and his own corrupt nature, which he always carries with him, to the latter.[25]

The Compleat Angler might not, then, seem like a book for cavaliers or Sucklington 'roaring boys'. Indeed one can almost see Suckling's ghostly lip curling at its first appearance in 1653. Yet one of Walton's closest friendships was with a man who in many respects resembled the dead gamester. Charles Cotton the younger was forty years Walton's junior and was possessed by a much less settled personality. There was little to appeal to Walton in Cotton's versions of profane burlesques of Virgil, but the common values of the old man and the young could be seen in the latter's translation of a work of French Stoic philosophy, another book for royalists in need of consolation. The affinity was evident above all in their shared passion for the river. Ben Jonson once said that a good poet must necessarily be a good man:[26] Izaak Walton thought much the same of an accomplished angler. So there is no saying what he might have found to love in an older, mellower Suckling, who always loved his retreats to Suffolk and Middlesex.

Walton discounted cynicism, nevertheless. To move through the pages of the *Angler* is to enter the countryside of the seventeenth century, and Walton takes for granted a strong sympathy with his affection for it. There are many passages of rapt contemplation, where natural detail gives rise to allegory and moral speculation. But elsewhere, when the speaker dips his hand, so to speak, in the water, the environment comes alive. When it comes to catching a frog or a grasshopper, slitting the belly of a snail, or explaining how to cook chub well – in clumsy hands 'the worst of fish' – then the slight creak to the rapture vanishes in a practitioner's enthusiasm. When Piscator describes at length a certain caterpillar, 'his lips and mouth somewhat yellow; his eyes black as jet; his forehead purple; his feet and hinder parts green; his tail two-forked and black', concreteness profits where elegance, perhaps, loses out. The vividness becomes wholly functional, because the little beast is good for catching trout, and Walton wants to teach his reader how to spot him; 'and you shall find him punctually to answer this very description.'[27]

Piscator is an instinctive ecologist. He has harsh words for 'unnatural fishermen' preying on fry and spawn with unlawful nets and gins, and for the over-exploiting of rivers which shall lead, he has no doubt, to their destruction. He dislikes the idea of hunting for mere sport. 'I am not of a cruel nature,' he insists; 'I love to kill nothing but fish.'[28] That requires some qualification, since many other creatures must die in order for the angler to catch his fish. First there are those animals which prey on fish, the otters and water-rats of the world; then there are those who must conspire in the catch. Piscator offers meticulous instructions for preparing bait. He advises, for example, that his pupil pull out the black gut of a yellow case-worm and snip off its head before putting it on a small-sized hook, 'as little bruised as possible'. But that is by the by, a little practice as necessary as knowing what kind of twig to choose, ideally 'a little hazel, or willow, cleft', to catch such worms 'that nick out of the water'.[29] Know-how is the angler's greatest tool and patience his chief virtue. You should be prepared to spend the best part of a year readying your frog for bait. Only the warmest months, April to August, are right for putting the hook through his mouth and stitching his leg to the wire; 'and in so doing, use him as though you loved him, that is, harm him as little as you possibly may, that he may live the longer.'[30]

The sentences about frogs encapsulate Walton's attitude to fishing, to the environment, and much of his straightforward moral philosophy. 'Have but a love to it, and I'll warrant you,' he encourages his avid pupil, Venator, when teaching him how to catch grasshoppers.[31] That love annuls for Piscator any thought of callousness in the piercing and eviscerating required for successful angling. The tenderness and dexterity of the angler is a dim reflection of the continuing benevolence of the Almighty, 'He Whose Name Is Wonderful' and whose wit enables frogs to live for six months without eating a thing. But the desire for skill is not sufficient. Piscator demands the total devotion of his apprentice in obtaining it. The man for Walton who becomes a fisher of men is the one who brings his concentration to bear on his own soul. Through this he achieves the ancient goal of ordering his passions. The key lay with the imperative from 1 Thessalonians which became the *Angler*'s epigram: 'Study to be quiet.'

The philosopher Pascal said that to avoid doing harm men should never leave their rooms; Walton put them instead by the riverbank. Large numbers of the fieldsmen Walton wrote for had spent the best part of a decade using their knowledge of the land against one another. *The Compleat Angler* was a book to counteract that alienation, to help the terrain recover some normality. More particularly still, it accorded with the stoicism thoughtful royalists now put to the fore of their reading. In a nutshell, its argument was that cavaliers should leave their cavalier ways until the right moment. This was exactly Hyde's advice to the king.

The philosophy was by no means confined to royalists. The most famous servant of the Commonwealth to take cover in the 1650s was none other than Lord Thomas Fairfax (who succeeded to his father's title in 1648), the commander-in-chief of the New Model Army. Unlike his deputy, Cromwell, Fairfax had no taste for politics, no programme to implement, and was appalled by the turn events took in January 1649. The general first indicated a wish to withdraw from public life by absenting himself from the old king's trial. 'He had more wit than to be here,' cried a voice from above when Fairfax's name was called, in an awkward start to the proceedings. After another interruption, soldiers were sent into the recess of the hall where the voice was heard; only to find that it belonged to Fairfax's wife, Lady Ann. Clarendon sensed that Fairfax had stayed away largely at her bidding.[32] The general was a huge loss to the legitimacy of both the trial and the political order which succeeded it, although he did not resign from active service immediately. He suffered no internal conflict in brutally cutting short a series of mutinies inspired by Leveller ideas in 1649. But he could not endorse, let alone lead, the invasion of Scotland in 1650: he gave up his commission and seat in the Council of State, and retired to his vast properties in Yorkshire. In a fashion Hyde admired, he devoted himself to study and translation at his birthplace above the River Wharfe, his fine townhouse in York, and his favourite home, the converted rural convent of Nun Appleton.

Around the time that Fairfax shed his powers, he employed a young intellectual as tutor to his daughter, Mary. Andrew Marvell, then in his early thirties, was also a northerner, a native of the East Riding, and a Cambridge graduate who had passed much of the war in travel on the Continent. When Cromwell returned from Ireland in 1650, Marvell composed his celebrated 'Horatian Ode' in honour of the Commonwealth's effective ruler. This opens with the poet dispelling the urge to which Fairfax was just about to yield, celebrating instead the spirit of full-blooded outward endeavour embodied by Cromwell: ''Tis time to leave the Books in dust,/ And oyl th'unused Armours rust.'[33] The future

Lord Protector, Marvell notes, had left behind his 'private gardens' as soon as the call to action came.

Superficially, the argument of the ode was the definitive vote of confidence in the new regime. Marvell's poem is full of praise for Cromwell's achievement and the power of his character: he gives the impression that the Irish (for whom he has no sympathy) were quelled by Cromwell alone. Very subtly, however, his succinct lines quietly insist that the great general's overwhelming energies lie at the disposal of the new state, and that much more would be expected of him. Like Milton, Marvell saw that Cromwell would still have to win the peace: 'The same *Arts* that did *gain*/ A *Pow'r* must it maintain,' the poem concludes, ominously, with the only awkward couplet in its crisp imitation of the Horatian manner. Marvell urges everyone to get behind the new leader, but at the same time illustrates the danger of the new republic becoming a one-man show. The ode gives a famous portrait of Charles on the scaffold, trying the axe's edge with his eye and laying his head upon the block as if it were a pillow. A spirit of historical fairness is not Marvell's only concern in this passage; he is making a political point. Through Charles's dignity in death – which almost all conceded – Marvell vividly demonstrates the lasting emotional (and political) power of the alternative to the kingless Commonwealth. Very gently, he tightens the vice of expectation upon Cromwell.

In other circumstances, Marvell might have extolled Fairfax's 'active Star' in similar terms; as indeed Milton had in a martial sonnet after the siege of Colchester. Instead, as he took up his teaching post in the north, enchanted by his young student and evidently fascinated by both the wild and cultivated landscapes surrounding him, he developed another poetic register for his patron. If Marvell's Horatian ode spells out the demands of active and public life, the greatest of his poems for Fairfax is a survey of private distractions and preoccupations. 'Upon Appleton House' falls into the long tradition, exemplified by Carew and Jonson, of using a country residence to praise its owner but also to comment on the world beyond. In a novel tetrametric stanza, Marvell also brought a wholly new strangeness to the English lyric. His attitude to Nun Appleton is ostensibly conventional; but the house and especially its environs, as they offer up allegories, grow immeasurably odd. At times the effect results from a paradox created by nature, as eels squirm amid cattle and fish swim through stables in the aftermath of a flood. At others, the observer seems myopically at fault:

> But now the *Salmon-Fishers* moist
> Their *Leathern Boats* begin to hoist;
> And like *Antipodes* in Shoes,
> Have shod their *Heads* in their *Canoos*.[34]

The poet praises Nun Appleton as a retreat, but he is ambivalent towards the act of retreating. He has mixed feelings on the cloistered life of the nuns who once occupied the site, before an earlier Fairfax forcibly extracted his bride from the convent and claimed the property after the dissolution. In another, more manifestly dramatic poem, 'The Garden' – possibly though not certainly contemporary with 'Appleton' – Marvell associated retirement to nature with solitary, almost onanistic pleasures: eventually, the speaker sinks into the depths of the mind, 'Annihilating all that's made/ To a green Thought in a green shade.'[35] The poet's attitude, then, to the course his lord Fairfax had chosen was not entirely encouraging. 'Upon Appleton House' picks out the retired general in his garden. There Fairfax resembles Tristram Shandy's Uncle Toby, tending the five 'imaginary Forts' created through topiary rather than the Cinque Ports which had been among his cares on the Council of State.[36] Marvell praises highly his decision to put conscience before ambition, yet in contrast to more vigorous ancestors and lusty mowers, the great general is the most inert presence in Marvell's poem.

The work strongly suggests, too, that although one might resign a post in the government, there was no escaping memory. When the mowers come to subdue the meadows, the outcome is described as nothing short of a massacre, as the young birds die under the scythes. And in evoking that animal carnage, the poet unmistakeably recalls the 'Camp of Battail' and the soldier-strewn grasslands of the civil wars, 'Where, as the Meads with Hay, the Plain/ Lyes quilted ore with Bodies slain'.[37] Fairfax had presided over countless scenes of this nature with unbounded vitality, although he had also been prone throughout the wars to strange lapses of health – attacks of rheumatism, the stone and the gout. 'Upon Appleton House' does much to play upon any lurking psychosomatic sensitivities. Fairfax's appearance is also exactly the point where the poem launches into its extreme descriptive fantasia, with the 'unfathomable Grass' of the meadows making men seem like grass-hoppers while nourishing up real grasshoppers into giants. The fields themselves become a sea, a chasm, into which all disappear except those wielding scythes.

In 'Upon Appleton House' Marvell called into question the benefits of studying to be quiet. The mind becomes a prey not only to symbolic distortions but also to disturbing upsurges of memory. Those nobles and gentlemen seeking to put the wars behind them in their stately sanctuaries were defied, Marvell suggests, by what their lands had seen. The peace Walton found in angling and Elizabethan lyrics was only possible, perhaps, to a soul as complacent as Walton. Significantly, Mar-vell decided that retirement was not the life for him; although he did not view leaving it as choosing ambition over conscience. Instead he embarked on a career from which a desire for high office was distinctly absent. Late in 1652 he left Fairfax's northern estates to take up a post in the Commonwealth administration as one of Milton's assistants. He soon proved an able bureaucrat and in time a dedicated Member of Par-liament for Hull. He remained a supremely accomplished verbal artist; but found his gifts increasingly suited to satire rather than panegyric.

Fairfax was still forced occasionally to surface from his religious and scholarly habits in the deeps of Nun Appleton. While his mind was else-where, his daughter Mary fell prey to the attentions of the Duke of Buckingham, and broke off another engagement in order to marry him. By that time Buckingham had been estranged from the king for years, following their spat before Worcester, and by 1657, when the wedding took place, he was reportedly a double agent. His marriage to Mary Fair-fax spelled unhappiness for her; and for him, so royalists supposed, it entailed a sordid alliance to the Commonwealth establishment. Allied to Fairfax, the duke could now canvass more effectively to regain his seques-tered estates. It suited Cromwell, however, that Buckingham remain under Fairfax's supervision; for he rightly suspected the duke of con-tinuing to spy for the enemy. It was later claimed that only Cromwell's death saved Buckingham from execution. Yet for the time being, despite his protests, the duke was placed under house arrest, and confined with his in-laws to the abyss of memory and hallucination at Nun Appleton.

★

A retired existence, Marvell suggested, could go poorly with inner dis-
quiet. Some, including Charles, were always going to tire of keeping
still. A somewhat amateur secret society, the Sealed Knot, agitated for
the overthrow of Protector Cromwell and the Commonwealth. The
group's leadership, however, consisted of comparatively minor royalist
aristocrats and veterans: lacking either a major backer or a true figurehead to excite old loyalties, it proved too weak a knot to snare or choke
Cromwell's new order. The revolutionary government had a tightly
organized and well-funded secret police, run with passionate commitment and innovative efficiency by John Thurloe. The squires and
cavalrymen of the Sealed Knot were no match for Thurloe's intelligence
network, and their fraternity was riddled with his agents. An attempt to
kidnap Cromwell in May 1654 by a royalist working independently,
Colonel John Gerard, became little more than a trap devised by Thurloe. The French crown was later implicated in the plan to snatch
Cromwell from his carriage on the way to Hampton Court, but there
seems to have been no serious danger to the Protector's life. Suspicions
of involvement from France were not, at least, serious enough to arrest
the movement towards an entente between Cromwell and Mazarin,
which soon enough obliged Charles to quit Paris. As for Gerard and his
thirty fellow riders, they were rounded up with little difficulty. The
colonel was left with the consolation of facing the death penalty with a
coolness admired on all sides.

Such martyrs made their point, but failed to rouse the nation: the
mood 'King' Charles encountered on his race to Worcester still predominated. A move on a grander military scale, at the planning stage at
least, met with failure the following year. In March 1655, royalists hoped
for a rising on a national scale, with muster points assigned across the
country. Yet his comrade Viscount Henry Wilmot, subsequently the
First Earl of Rochester, was forced to emulate Charles and flee in disguise from his ill-omened rendezvous on Marston Moor. Only one
party, far to the south, managed a show of force. Colonel John Penruddock took a band of cavaliers into Salisbury, enlisted inmates from the
gaol and imprisoned the mayor and sheriff. Marching on to the plain,
Penruddock and his lieutenants were confronted by the question of
what to do next – and found no answer. The limited hopes of this and
the other conspiracies were reflected in the scant sense of what should

follow the initial attempt. Penruddock and his friends took their troops into the West Country, where the inhabitants wanted nothing to do with them, and where the inevitable rout ensued near Tiverton.

Charles vetted the conspiracies in the hope that they might achieve something, often too careless of the spies Thurloe had planted in his rootless court. The cold reaction Penruddock met at Exeter, Taunton and the other towns he called on for help was an index of the antipathy to cavalier actions. Cromwell's government responded to the Penruddock Rising by cracking down further on suspected and proven royalists, with a 'Decimation Tax' confiscating 10 per cent of their income. England and Wales were parcelled out into a set of mini-protectorates, to be governed unsparingly by trusted deputies, styled 'major-generals'. The governors of the new cantons were given a relatively free hand in suppressing diversions such as race-meetings, sports, dances and cockfighting. These old pastimes had begun re-emerging as the decade progressed and the Commonwealth administration grew in confidence, depending on the threat each event posed to public order. But while such measures lessened the government's popularity, it hardly boosted affection for the cause which had brought them about.

As the impetuous continued their efforts, Hyde diligently continued casting his lines in England and abroad. He hoped for a bite from 'the amity of Christian princes', and put more hopeless years into working for an alliance with Spain. He was equally angry with those who bolted into action and those who sat and did nothing. In political as much as angling terms, the 'study', the work of the dissident, was as important as the stoic 'quiet'. Indeed Walton's epigram could be spliced on perfectly to the Ovidian motto Hyde put above his door at Castle Elizabeth back in 1647: *Bene vixit, qui bene latuit* . . . He who has lived well has escaped notice, has studied to be quiet.

4

Davenant studied, but the quiet rarely came; nor did it ever really suit him. At Paris in the late 1640s he worked on an epic poem to be called *Gondibert*. The finished romance – or 'heroicall poem', as Davenant styled it – would be told in five books, corresponding to the five acts of a tragedy. The story was dominated by the love and ambition of a Lombardian knight, the eponymous Gondibert, and Davenant's hope was that it would offer models of virtue to cultivated readers. 'Princes and Nobles being reform'd and made Angelicall by the Heroick,' as he confidently expected, 'will be predominant lights, which the people cannot chuse but use for direction; as Gloworms take in, and keep the Suns beams till they shine, and make day to themselves.'[38]

Davenant had grand hopes for his heroic poem: his earlier works he now dismissed 'as papers unworthy of light'.[39] *Gondibert* would win him his laurels. It went against his nature, however, to toil on in isolation. As writing progressed, many fellow exiles offered their comments on 'parcels' of the text. His readers included both admirers such as Abraham Cowley, and the contributors to a later poetic miscellany making cruel fun of his ambitions. Another supportive critic was the long-term exile Edmund Waller, who had fled for France upon his pardon for conspiracy in 1644. A common literary agenda is suggested by the group's varying efforts and researches: Cowley sought to sustain the more intellectually elaborate mode of Donne, while Waller looked to the tradition of Elizabethan song and Davenant still followed Jonson as his model. Yet all exemplified a move to greater 'smoothness' in their writing, polishing out what Gardiner called the 'chastened irregularity of the Elizabethan poets'.[40] Waller in particular would be considered, deemed Aubrey, 'one of the first refiners of our English language and poetery [sic]'; and he had had, unlike the majority of his fellow wits, the leisure and comfort to develop his art in peace.

Money was never a problem to Waller, in spite of the enormous £10,000 fine with which he bought his liberty after trial by Parliament. During the lean years for the cavaliers, Waller was said to be the only Englishman overseas who kept a decent table: supper, as we saw, was a rarity for Hyde and the other refugees on Jersey.[41] Some found that the image of his melodramatic and much-publicized contrition before Parliament, close to tears and dressed in mourning, still stuck in the throat. He had betrayed comrades, prostituted his gifts – and it was long said that any panegyric he offered should not be treated seriously. Over the years, Waller would praise whoever held power, Cromwell and Charles II equally. Yet his offence was not great enough to keep most of those he invited from eating and drinking with him. Davenant clearly thought he no longer had a charge to answer; and even Hyde, while never placing faith in him, was satisfied that his conscience had suffered enough. After his disgrace, Hyde conceded, Waller lived 'in the good affection and esteem of many, the pity of most, and the reproach and scorn of none': there were few, after all, whose record of loyalty was entirely untainted.[42]

The chief of the intellectuals Davenant consulted was Thomas Hobbes, then in his sixties and preparing his masterpiece, *Leviathan*, for the press. Davenant was so pleased with the great thinker's comments on his work that he could not forbear from thanking him publicly even before the first instalments of his poem were published.

The tranquillity such labour required was hard to come by in Paris, nevertheless, and there is evidence that Davenant did not seek it out as zealously as he might have done. He was too easily moved to passion, to pity, to mischief. When the Lords Jermyn and Digby came to fight a duel, Davenant was at the centre of the affair, spreading the necessary gossip, delivering Jermyn's challenge and standing as his second. The quarrel came to nothing, with Digby declining Jermyn's gauntlet and retiring to his chamber, but it kept the exiles talking for months, with Davenant in demand for the inside story. Nor was he free from domestic obligations, however adeptly he had sidestepped them over the years. 'I understand I have 2 Children newly arrived at Paris,' he wrote from St-Germain in 1646, 'which a servant of my wives hath stolne from an obscure Country education.' His oft-forgotten family appears to have lived as quietly as they could through the wars in a suburb near London. His first wife had died by the time he was free again in England, but he took some steps towards the children's care, asking the Resident at Paris, Richard Browne, to give them clothes while he searched for someone to place them with.[43] A twenty-two-year-old man and a four-year-old girl, the two 'children' were evidently in poor attire. 'Such necessarie things as shall refine their bodies' were not, however, so easy for exiles to come by as Davenant assumed. At around the same time, his old friend and fellow courtier Endymion Porter complained that 'I want clothes for a Court, having but that poor riding suit I came out of England in.'

Porter had enjoyed long, fat years and endured hard journeys under Charles. No doubt expecting a peaceful old age, he could not have anticipated that his exhausting caper to Spain with the prince in 1623 would prefigure and define his eventual condition in life. Porter's great wealth – much of it less than legitimately gained – the houses, the art collection, his friends in foreign palaces, the attributes, in other words, for which he had been envied and vilified, all proved ephemeral. The state to which he would always return was that of a rider with no escort and a single suit of suffering clothes, searching for a place to sleep and eat some soup. On making his last escape from England, he declared that 'I am in so much necessity, that were it not for an Irish barber that was once my servant, I might have starved for want of bread.' The kindly Irishman had spared him a few coins which might see him through a fortnight. As time passed, he saw his place as belonging with the inner retinue in Paris, but complained at being 'so retired into the streets of a suburb that I scarce know what they do at the Louvre'. He appealed to Henrietta Maria for sustenance; she blamed the low in his fortunes on his own 'want of wit'.[44] He fell sick, and Davenant was pained to watch him fail. He composed a poem to encourage a whip-round for Endymion:

> Arise! Bring out your Wealth! perhaps some Twigge
> Of Bay, and a few Mirtle Sprigs
> Is all you have: but these ought to suffice
> Where spacious hearts make up the Sacrifice.
> Be these your Off'ring as your utmost Wealth,
> To show your joy for lov'd Endymions Health.[45]

Yet Porter faded, and died in August 1649. The drawback even with 'spacious hearts' is that they may ring hollow in times of adversity; they too can run empty.

Davenant's writings carry a sense that conditions in Paris, while as glamorous as ever for those with ready money, lacked something the wits missed more – a certain homeliness. The emigrants shuffled about for charity and company in draughty, unaccommodating spaces. The centre of the city was dominated by a set of grandiose yet unaccomplished architectural dreams. Davenant joked that someone who did not point in wonder at the sight of the Louvre could be thought to have gout in their finger; but so too they might be left a little cold, even sad, at the ever-expanding complex:

The fame of the Palace consisting more in the vast design of what it was meant to be, then in the largenesse of what it is: the structure being likewise a little remarkable for what is old, but more even for the antiquity of what is new; having been begun some Ages past, and is to be finished many hence.

At Pont Rouge, a 'heavy Londoner' could only stop short 'at a broken Arch', lacking the 'French vivacity to frisk o'er so wide a gap to the Fauxbourgs'. One had to stare past the physical interruptions to picture instead the great scheme they indicated, the idea which had been abandoned. A similar mental leap was required, after a while, to appreciate the celebrated cuisine. Davenant's description of the palace kitchens could be a scene from Swift. The French cooks, 'Embroiderers of Meat':

(though by education cholerick and loud) are ever in profound contemplation; that is, they are considering how to reform the mistakes of Nature in the original composition of Flesh and Fish; she having not known, it seems, the sufficient Mysterie of *Hautgouts* [gourmets, connoisseurs]: and the production of their deep studies are sometimes so full of delicious fancy, and witty seasoning, that at [their] Feasts when I uncover a Dish, I think I feed on a very *Epigram.* Who can comprehend the diversity of your *Pottages, Carbonnades, Grillades, Ragouts, Haches, Saupiquets, Demi-Bisques, Bisques, Capilotades,* and *Entre-mets*?[46]

One could have a surfeit of invention. The demands of Davenant's epic were quite enough to occupy his intellects.

He was testing a quatrain, rather than the more familiar couplet, as his basic form, and found it supple to his purposes; in fact, almost too flexible. Despite the tightness of the plan he explained in his long preface to the poem, he found his material wandering away from him. He sympathized with the builders of the Louvre. He hoped his readers would enjoy, however, the poem's 'underwalks' and that its 'meanders' would appear to them 'as pleasant as a summer passage on a crooked River, where going about, and turning back is as delightful as the delays of parting Lovers'.[47]

The poem contained the fruit of much reading of history, political philosophy and the scientific works of Francis Bacon. It is a work full, too, of delightful moments, particularly in discussing and describing the effects of love – always the first law of nature for Davenant. Yet in following his hero his mind by times coiled back to scenes he knew better and missed. When he evoked a city at dawn, for example, he ceased to be a literary tourist, and called up instead the sights of home ground; the 'early Lawyer' crossing town to court, where the 'earlier Client' has already waited long for him; and in the great bourses, 'greedy Creditors' closing in on their frightened debtors, who make a getaway by 'herding in th'indebted Throng' – escaping to a crowd in which every person owes money to someone. A practised eye falls on other guilty parties nervously sniffing the air:

> Here through a secret Posterne issues out
> The skar'd adulterer, who out-slept his time;
> Day, and the Husbands spie alike does doubt,
> And with a half-hid face would hide his crime.[48]

As so often, Davenant improved when able to write of what he knew. He claimed to be prey to a common weakness for belittling the objects of his own land in comparison to those abroad.[49] A lengthy and well-researched account of Veronese architecture comes before the passage above, laying out the city and its environs before taking us through the gates; but it suffers from the veneration Davenant pays his sources. Once he is within the city walls, however, he can portray constants of urban life from memory, and draw on a deeper level of acquaintance with his subjects. As for Jonson, it was the native character of London and the nearby English countryside that nourished Davenant's imagination; and for all his best efforts, *Gondibert* suffered for his distance from it.

The decisive interruption to his study and writing came when he was sent to America. Again, despite his devotion to the project, this new adventure better suited his temper. In his preface to what he had so far composed of *Gondibert*, he declared his preference for an active life. Echoing the teaching of Donne, he had harsh words for 'such retir'd men, as evaporate their strength of mind by close and long thinking; and would every where separate the soul from the body, e're we are dead'. Davenant thus rejected the Stoic arguments to be found in other royalist literature. Indeed he claimed that the world would be a better place if fewer talents hid away in their rooms or stared into space by a riverbank:

If these severe Masters (who though obscure in Cells, take it ill if their very opinions rule not all abroad) did give good men leave to be industrious in getting a Share of governing the world, the Multitudes (which are but Tennants to a few Monarchs) would enjoy that subjection which God hath decreed them.

Davenant, accepting his commission for Virginia and Maryland, eagerly took up his share of government, 'for the world is onely ill govern'd, because the wicked take more pains to get authority, then the vertuous, for the vertuous are often preach'd into retirement.'[50]

Hobbes, to whom Davenant dedicated his endeavours, might forgivably have taken offence at this upstart criticism of isolated work. From his long seclusion in France, the philosopher was about to send out his opinion on how the world should be governed – indeed his theory on how it *was* ruled.

Aubrey knew Hobbes well and admired him greatly, observing from his astrological chart that he was destined for eminence in his field: his stars gave him a '*satellitium* of 5 of the 7 planets', the same arrangement that marked out Cromwell. Hobbes was a tall, stringy man with an unhealthy complexion lingering from earlier years and a 'quick eye' he kept sharp to the last. He liked music, and was comfortable in banter – 'marvellous happy and ready in his replies, and that without rancor (except provoked)'. Quick though he was at repartee, Hobbes always refused to give an instant answer to a serious question.[51] Thus when Davenant requested thoughts on his poem, Hobbes took the matter seriously and offered a meditation on the provenance and nature of poetry itself.

His charisma clearly impressed Davenant, who declared himself his pupil. 'The Preface to *Gondibert*', however, reveals that the poet took exception to important aspects of Hobbes's teaching – or had failed to appreciate them. To the dismay of active royalists, *Leviathan* offered perhaps the last word on the philosophy of keeping quiet. Hobbes's central point, reiterated with patient lucidity, was that subjects owed peaceful obedience to their sovereign, whoever he was and whatever he did. Any tyranny was preferable to what the philosopher famously defined as the 'natural' condition of humanity without a ruler; a state of perpetual war in which life is 'nasty, brutish and short'. His theory offered harsh counsel to those who had undermined the rule of Charles I, but it was notably short on comfort to the dead king's supporters. A sovereign, the 'artificial man' or 'Leviathan' given supreme power by unwritten covenant, could come in the form of a monarch or an assembly, in the person of a Charles or a Cromwell – it was simply all-important that his subjects abided by his rule. Hobbes went so far as to say that if the Turk ever established sovereignty over England, the bishops, along with everyone else, would be obliged to accept his power as legitimate.[52]

Hobbes's idea of a Commonwealth thus rested on the outcome of a simple choice between a stable polity and outright civil war. The latter could only be avoided by an unbreakable covenant between sovereign and subjects. As a result of this agreement, a sovereign was not only the ruler but the representative of his people. Anything he did, he did by their licence and consent. It was therefore futile to complain about the actions or policies of a sovereign: they were all authorized by those he ruled and protected. If that seemed harsh, Hobbes also deemed it irrelevant to ask *when* or *how* such a covenant was ever made: for a state to work, one had no choice but to believe such a contract existed. It was the precondition of any lasting civil peace, and could be assumed to have held in any kingdom or commonwealth which had not collapsed into civil war.

Before leaving with his troop of weavers for Jersey and on to America, Davenant published his 'Preface'. His little book, explaining the 'edifice' of his epic, was accompanied by Hobbes's incisive and cordial answer but by no material from the actual poem. Some of Davenant's other acquaintance had great sport with this masterpiece of pretension, bouncing the language of the 'Preface' back against him:

> A Preface to no Book, a Porch to no house:
> Here is the Mountain, but where is the Mouse?[53]

Davenant was no longer a young man, but Hobbes treated his work with paternal leniency. He advised him to beware and ignore 'the clamour of the multitude, that hide their Envy of the present, under a Reverence of Antiquity'.[54]

Despite the jests at its expense, Davenant's 'Preface' did a great deal to spell out the cavalier attitude to questions ranging from the function of literature to the challenge of the political situation. He could not overcome the rancour of defeat, and gave way to bad humour and bigotry. Thus there are standard slights in his treatise against the avarice of Jews and the simplicity of Native Americans, along with galled comments on the morality of the labouring classes. Part draconian, part libertarian, the 'Preface' contains many supercilious passages which could easily have come from the pen of Suckling, and do much to expound the shock and disenchantment his friend suffered almost a decade earlier, when their world collapsed.

Much of Davenant's essay is taken up with a problem which had preoccupied Hobbes for years and now seemed more urgent than ever. How are the energies of people to be contained and directed when they group into large numbers; when, that is to say, they become 'the people' and come to comprise a nation? For Davenant, as for Hobbes, the desired result of government is 'obedience'. Only when the people do as they are told is civic order possible. Like Suckling, Davenant put much of the blame for the present state of things on turbulent priests – cloaking political ambition in godliness. He saw the Reformation as having given greater power to a greater number of people in Europe, fostering rebellion. This was largely the work of 'divines' who failed to see what they were unleashing. The result had been civil war across the Continent, spreading finally to Britain and Ireland. 'We have observed that the People since the latter time of Christian Religion, are more unquiet then in former Ages; so disobedient and fierce, as if they would shake off the ancient imputation of being Beasts by shewing their Masters they know their own strength.'[55]

Like Suckling, Davenant was cynical about 'statesmen' and 'makers of lawes', who differ only in their means. The former, he says, 'make new Lawes presumptuously without the consent of the People': this, he implies, being the error of Kings James and Charles and grandees such as Buckingham and Strafford. Law-makers, meanwhile, 'more civilly seem to whistle to the Beast, and stroak him into the Yoke: and in the Yoke of State, the People (with too much Pampering) grow soon unruly and draw awry'.[56] In these upstarts one can identify the Parliamentary rebels of the early 1640s, Pym and his circle. Though he takes it that statesmen and law-makers must co-operate, it is evident which type of ruler Davenant prefers should it come to a choice. Better a benign dictatorship, for him, than consensual tyranny: and although his own political motives are clearly reactionary, he offers one of the most piercing critiques of the 'bourgeois revolution' taking place in England.

Still more predictably, Davenant is scathing towards 'the people' en masse. He refers to the multitude in traditional and entirely derogatory terms: it is a Hydra, a monster and, at best, a beast which may be tamed and yoked. He has no doubt whatsoever about the necessity of armed force, both within a state and against others. 'If any man can yet doubt of the necessary use of Armies,' he argues, 'let him study that which was anciently call'd a Monster, the multitude.'[57] The pursuit of empire, as he had accepted years earlier in *Madagascar*, is also inevitable: part of being human is an inescapable expansive urge for greater space and dominion over it. For 'the Mindes of Men are more monstrous, and require more space for agitation and the hunting of others, then the Bodies of Whales.'[58]

Davenant's cetacean image almost certainly alludes to Hobbes's *Leviathan*. He reflects the philosopher's view of the human mind and its irrepressible – and, for Hobbes, entirely natural and rightful – will to power. In Hobbes's philosophy, individuals give up absolute rights over one another, following the natural law of self-preservation, in exchange for the protection of the greater, 'artificial man' they created together, the Leviathan. Yet Davenant's otherwise authoritarian tract takes another approach to the multitude. He argues that the riotous spirits of the people can best be quelled by keeping them happy, entertaining them, and improving their mood and their conduct through shows of beauty: and the people best qualified for this task are poets. Anticipating the charge that poets are mere titillators, spreaders of light or even lewd emotion, he is indignant at any who might counter him on religious or moralistic grounds. The enemies of poets will be cloistered thinkers of the kind he disparages, and divines who have failed in their charge to urge the people to peace; and their arguments are ultimately unholy and unnatural:

They who accuse Poets as provokers of Love, are Enemies to Nature; and all affronts to Nature are offences to God, as insolencies to all subordinate officers of the Crown are rudeness to the King. *Love* (in the most obnoxious interpretation) is Natur's Preparative to her greatest work, which is the making of *Life*.[59]

Love remained Davenant's central theme; while his defence of poetry was based on the example of Orpheus. The people remain beasts when considered as 'the people', a homogeneously riotous mass. Their obedience can be won by charming them, with the gift of sophisticated pleasures, luxury circuses, engaging their minds individually, and activating their higher sensibilities.

In the 1630s the wits around Henrietta Maria aimed at the refinement of the court. Now, it seemed, Davenant intended to export that ethos to a wider public. He would be unable to implement the agenda his preface outlines, however, for many years. As such his immediate intention with *Gondibert* was to offer models of virtue for those with education and power. Whether Davenant read *Leviathan* in manuscript, or absorbed the book's ideas through Hobbes himself, his thoughts on poetry make an indirect answer to a point about the halcyon days of the last king's reign. Hobbes held that part of Charles's failure as sovereign had been his inability to convince and remind the people that he was indeed their sovereign, their representative. Instead the public were allowed to believe that sovereignty actually lay with a Parliament which, in Hobbes's view, was merely 'sent up by the people to carry their Petitions' and offer the king advice 'if he permitted it'.[60] The old king himself had anticipated and ruefully accepted this idea.[61] The failure to instruct the people in the nature of the king's office was, by implication, partly the fault of the writers and poets on whom the sovereign relied to get his message across. In his 'Preface to *Gondibert*' Davenant took up the challenge of this criticism – and used it to raise the dignity of his vocation.

Work on *Gondibert* itself was interrupted yet again when Davenant was ordered to depart for Virginia and Maryland. He was in prison on the Isle of Wight when his 'Preface' was published, with commendatory verses by Cowley and Waller. The first two books of the poem itself had travelled with him in manuscript on his journey, and in his cell in Cowes Castle he continued with a third. His trial was pending, and the chances of acquittal were poor. Cavaliers had not only murdered the Commonwealth's agent in Madrid but also the new government's representative at

The Hague, Isaac Dorislaus. Parliamentary prosecutors thus looked for retributive justice against their more prominent prisoners. Davenant's name was entered on a list of six suitable victims.

With his neck tingling, his concentration cracked and he abandoned his heroic poem. ''Tis high time to strike Sail, and cast Anchor (though I have run but halfe my Course),' he apologized, in his 'Postscript to the Reader'. The malicious among his public, he expected, would note that he would not get to enjoy the fame he had sought from his great project. Yet fame, he reflected, 'like Time, only gets a reverence by long running; and that like a River, 'tis narrowest where 'tis bred, and broadest afar off'. But he expected the majority of his readers to understand and excuse him for leaving them with a substantial fragment rather than a finished work: 'even in so worthy a Designe I shall ask leave to desist, when I am interrupted by so great an experiment as Dying.'[62]

The fame of Hobbes's *Leviathan* would broaden to a much larger extent than that of *Gondibert*, although at first the latter work may have caused a greater sensation. The two books were published in the same year, 1651, by which time Davenant had been transferred to the Tower. The dominant response to the first two parts of his poem was one of continuing mirth at his pretensions to grandeur, although in some quarters there was serious admiration: no less a judge than Andrew Marvell paid a sincere compliment to Davenant's descriptive powers. In others, there was genuine offence. James Usher, the one-time Primate of Armagh, famous for calculating the date of the Creation, was particularly upset by Davenant's survey of his greater precursors. 'Out upon him, with his vaunting Preface,' the elderly archbishop shortly told John Denham; 'he speakes against my old friend, Edmund Spenser.'[63] Hobbes's great, bleak work, by contrast, would receive widespread reverence much later, when Davenant's *Gondibert* was all but forgotten.

Awaiting trial in the Tower, where he was still close prisoner, Davenant had few illusions of the processes deciding his fate. 'He expected no mercy from the Parliament,' Aubrey recorded, 'and had no hopes of escaping [with] his life.'[64] In the summer of 1650, before he left Cowes, he was almost saved by an outburst of humour and compassion in the Commons. Voting on whether or not to proceed against him, 'some *Gentlemen*, out of pitty, were pleased to let him have the *Noes* of the House, because he had none of his own.' The following day the Members repented of their joke, and resolved to press on with the case against him.[65] A year later Davenant did his utmost, as he had after the plot of 1641, to scrape himself free with his pen and sent a 'humble petition' to the Council of State. The letter was a masterpiece of revisionism. Writing with his usual happy trust in his readers' sympathy, he told his judges how he had left the country long before the end of the wars; and how, determined to do nothing to undermine the new government, he had then set out for a new life in America. This version of the facts was put in jeopardy a few years later when a copy of Davenant's bellicose commission turned up in the possession of a puritan who had formerly served the governor of Virginia. Yet by that time Davenant had already been granted the liberty of the Tower, and an unofficial consensus was forming in favour of granting him pardon.

The slow, bureaucratic rescue of Sir William Davenant from a traitor's death was a sign in itself of wider social repair. There were notes of support in the occasional verses praising his poem. James Howell, newly at liberty himself, wrote lines against 'Some, Who Blending Their Brains Together, Plotted How to Bespatter . . . Sir Will. Davenant, Knight and Poet'. Yet even these detractors, led by Denham, had no wish to see Davenant on the scaffold: they were clearly fellow loyalists whose criticisms were entirely literary. Their derision of *Gondibert* only served to raise Davenant's (famously blighted) pre-war profile as a public figure of fun. Importantly, though, his case had support in the camp of his former enemies. Davenant was sure that the two aldermen of York, his captives during the war, had petitioned for his release. There is an old story too that Milton, now Parliament's Latin Secretary, spoke up for his fellow poet, laying aside his differences in religion, politics and private morals: how long and how vociferously he did so would seem to be the moot point. The two poets shared friends, notably the composer Henry Lawes, who were more than willing to canvass Milton's fellow officials on the prisoner's behalf. Bulstrode Whitelocke, one of the original Parliamentary rebels and now a member of the council, certainly did intervene in Davenant's favour, and received a fervent letter of thanks shortly afterwards.[66] Most quaintly of all, Henry Marten is supposed to have asked the Commons why they were thinking of making a scapegoat of 'an old rotten Rascall', when they all knew that a true sacrificial victim should be 'pure, & without blemish'. The same joke was used to save Marten's own neck a few years later when the tables were turned.[67]

The exact truth of these anecdotes is less important than the spirit they reflect, a movement to avoid unnecessary bloodshed without betraying the cause of Parliamentary freedom. It was a mood which met with tentative conciliatory noises from erstwhile foes. Settling back in England in the mid-1650s, while continuing to work as a royalist agent, Abraham Cowley wrote in favour of burying the past: 'we must lay down our *Pens* as well as our *Arms*, we must *march* out of our *Cause* it self,' he argued, 'and *dismantle* . . . the *Works* and *Fortifications* of *Wit* and *Reason* by which we defended it.' In words that recalled Thomas Carew – and which might well have earned his approval – he insisted that a poet's calling demanded 'serenity and chearfulness of *Spirit* . . . it must like the *Halcyon* have *fair weather* to breed in.'[68]

Cowley could later insist that these views allowed him to maintain his cover as an agent for the exiled king; but in the context of their moment they breathe a genuine weariness of dissent – and would have stood without comment had the succession to Cromwell turned out differently. As it was, having spent two years in prison and another two confined to the precincts of the Tower, Davenant applied in much the same spirit to Cromwell himself in 1654. With his usual clemency to those who acknowledged defeat and accepted his 'engagement', the Lord Protector, now universally addressed as 'His Highness', granted Davenant his general pardon.

Charles II was greeted by impressive numbers in May 1660 when he arrived in London to take up his throne. There were tapestries decking the streets, fountains running with wine, the bell of every church along his path ringing loud. The young king – Charles had just turned thirty – was greeted with his brothers at the outskirts of the city by the Lord Mayor and the aldermen, and the cavalcade which moved towards Whitehall, where nobles and commoners alike had converged, was said to be some twenty thousand-strong. Long-impoverished churchmen had unpacked and donned their old, forbidden vestments, and stood to offer Charles their blessing. As quite often before in recent history, the festivities were driven by relief at a safe transfer of power – the reincarnation of Leviathan – as much as joy at the sight of the monarch himself.

With this particular succession, there was still a great deal to be worked out in practice. The palaces lay open to him; but the people had little more to give Charles than a few 'twigges of bay'. There was not much disguising the fact that he entered London by consent rather than by conquest.

Davenant, now fifty-four and somewhat heavy-jowled, was prominent among those offering their felicitations. In some circles, nevertheless, his allegiances were considered suspect. He was overheard protesting at the king's treatment of Abraham Cowley – who had been branded a turncoat. Even when Cowley prostrated himself, Charles refused to let him kiss the royal hand. Davenant was upset by the king's 'irreconcileableness', and spoke too freely of it in company. Charles's secretary, old Sir Edward Nicholas, received word of 'an imprudent discourse . . . from one that pretends to witt, but might very well have more discretion or loyalty, viz. *Sir Wm. Davenant*'.[69] He had shown impressive cunning and discretion over the years, but Davenant remained at heart a man of the theatre, quickly moved, open and demonstrative with his emotions.

Yet in its outcome the incident above demonstrated how Davenant had served too long and too well, in spite of the mishaps, for the king to ignore him. He was granted a controlling interest over London's theatre, and a few months after the king's entry into London he penned a new prologue for an old Jonson play, *Epicoene, or the Silent Woman*, which was the first to be officially performed for the Restoration court. In smart couplets he played up the old link between the monarchy and the theatre:

> This truth we can to our advantage say,
> They that would have no KING, would have no *Play*:
> The *Laurel* and the *Crown* together went,
> Had the same *Foes*, and the same *Banishment*.[70]

It could be said, however, that Davenant's Restoration began some four years earlier, on a Friday afternoon in May 1656.

13. Twigs of Bay

Fond City, its Rubbish and Ruines, that builds,
Like vain Chymists, a flower from its ashes.

— Marvell, 'Clarendon's House-Warming'

And to be rich, be diligent! Move on
Like Heavens great Movers that inrich the Earth;
Whose Moments sloth would shew the world undone,
And make the Spring strait bury all her birth.

— Davenant, *Gondibert* (III.VI)

1

The scene that spring of 1656 was Davenant's own home, Rutland House, a rather splendid residence for one of his slender income and proliferating debts, situated off Charterhouse Square in Upper Aldersgate. He had already filled the mansion with the children born and acquired through two marriages, having just embarked on his third.

Shortly after his release on bail from the Tower he had married Ann Cademan, the widow of the physician who had treated him for syphilis in the early 1630s. At first they set up home together in a small house on Tothill Street in Westminster. She brought with her four boys, three from her first-deceased husband, aged twenty-two, sixteen and eleven, and a nine-year-old from the late Dr Cademan. Davenant took only one of his children, Mary, then in her mid-teens, into their bustling little home. He had another daughter, however, and possibly two more sons were alive somewhere in England, probably stowed away with relatives in Oxford and elsewhere in London. But the son he had fathered as an adolescent in his early days in London, the first William the younger, had died in 1651. Davenant's first wife had gone to her grave at some point in the middle years of the war.[1] In *Gondibert* Davenant asserts that 'wedlock, to the wilde, is the State's net,' and that marriage 'is too oft but civil warre'.[2] Yet it seemed that his wild days were behind him, his energy for civil war spent, and that he married his second bride in a moment of mutual pragmatism, both spouses grateful for the other's company and protection. Though penniless and technically still a delinquent, Sir William brought a wide and secure social network to support his wife, who was a Roman Catholic. More substantially, Dame Ann could finance the household with some diamonds and pearls, which Davenant pawned for £600. She brought another £800 which was, strictly, her sons' inheritance. Thomas Crosse, her eldest boy, had already had a taste of life with Davenant by serving as secretary on the ill-fated American mission. On returning from a spell in Barbados he was displeased to find his new stepfather spending his estate. Yet Davenant met Crosse's anger with open arms, a frank countenance, and support he trusted would repay his new ward in kind: another offer of work as his amanuensis.

The wits, like the young secretary, took a dim view of the marriage. The lover of beauty had not married for love. But there was a nugget of respect for the character of his bride:

> Her beauty, though 'twas not exceeding,
> Yet what in Face and shape was needing,
> She made it up in Parts and Breeding.[3]

And in her jewellery and pin-money, her son Thomas could comment bitterly, as he toiled for nothing more than bread and board at the packed house on Tothill Street.

The mid-1650s, Cromwell's supremacy, was a dispiriting time for most of the figures who have featured in this story. We find them eking out an existence. Robert Herrick, his priesthood seemingly lapsed, lives off relatives in and around the city, happy enough to be back on home ground, penning perhaps a few last epigrams, but falling into silence from old age and hardship. Richard Lovelace is one of many diehards kept under surveillance by the government's men on the street, until his death in poverty in 1657. His songs to Lucasta, a more elusive beauty than Suckling's Aglaura, have become fixtures of the repertoire. For music in the home is not suppressed in Commonwealth London; Cromwell, like Milton, is an avid private listener. Meanwhile Endymion's widow, Olivia Porter, holds the fort at their now near-derelict mansion on the Strand, a home where a duet written for the couple by Davenant might still sometimes be sung:

> Before we shall again behold
> In his diurnal race the Worlds great Eye,
> We may as silent be and cold
> As are the shades where buried Lovers ly.[4]

The best sought by most is a truce: John Cleveland, a polemical writer of doggerel and long-term political prisoner, petitions for his liberty by telling Cromwell that they should simply respect their differences, and call off hostility. Others, the Duke of Buckingham a powerful example, are willing to go further. Some, with unconscious irony, look for 'halcyon days' in Cromwell's reign.[5]

Davenant's old urban public keep seeking their former pleasures, and the Commonwealth authorities keep snuffing them out. Efforts to put on plays at old venues invariably end in government raids. In September 1655, when soldiers storm the Red Bull Tavern Theatre in Clerkenwell, they confiscate not only the players' costumes and properties, but also the cloaks of those in the audience who cannot pay the fine. In the same year the theatre at Blackfriars is finally demolished, for the construction of tenements in its place. London could be the Vienna of Shakespeare's *Measure for Measure*: the old festivities are banned, adultery is punishable by death and illicit fornication gets you three months in gaol. Prostitutes are to be flogged and branded with 'B' – for bawd. With black plumes rising from its chimneys, the city itself, to Davenant, has the appearance of one bereaved:

> London is smother'd with sulph'rous fires;
> Still she wears a black Hood and Cloak,
> Of Sea-coal Smoak,
> As if she mourn'd for Brewers and Dyers.[6]

It is an ugly, overcrowded, over-homely metropolis. The close-set houses huddle like indigents; the boatmen are noisy and churlish, the children are ill-bred; the bread is too heavy, the drink too thick, and the only beds which fit the rooms are as narrow as coffins. The place seems ripe, as some sects believe, for purgation.

Many of the king's old guard were wasting away. It would, though, be a mistake to think that the country's governors were living in complacency. Even if their religion, in the stricter cases, forbade such contentment, Cromwell's violent expulsion of the Rump Parliament, the embarrassment of its short-lived successor, the 'Barebones' assembly, and the essentially temporary and provisional nature of the Protectorate, gave little grounds for confidence. Their greatest success, the naval campaign led by Admiral Robert Blake against the Dutch, was much needed to steady the republic's nerves before the world.

By the summer of 1655, when Davenant left his veiled city on a trip to France, he was by rights still in mourning, his wife Ann having died in March. Yet despite his recent ordeals, despite the mounting but familiar suits against his debts, and for all his faults – to the point perhaps of domestic villainy – he remained one of London's few true optimists. He was not at all shy of asking favours of the suspicious authorities at Westminster: he made his request for a passport with all his customary assuredness, which did not desert him on his arrival in France. A stopoff in Paris to wait on his old mistress the queen mother, who would outlive him by a year, seems to have been more than likely: but his destination was Anjou, the home of a much younger woman 'of an ancient family' – who would outlive him by decades.[7] Her name was Henrietta-Maria du Tremblay, a widow whom Davenant had surely known years earlier, and when he brought her to England, he introduced her proudly as his wife.

They moved with his daughter and brood of stepsons and set up home. Rutland House, in its fashionable neighbourhood, was the city residence of the late Earl of Rutland, for whom Davenant had written an elegy. When the old man's Catholic wife also died, the property was seized by the Commonwealth and was subsequently bought for a song by two Parliamentarians. These yielded to the pressure of old acquaintance, and leased the place to Davenant at a friendly rate. From there

Davenant began his personal Restoration. Disregarding the ban on theatrical performances, he and one William Cutler persuaded a number of wealthy friends to finance 'a structure for representations and shows'.[8] The plan was to build or adapt a location near Charterhouse Square, but when a site could not be found or the money ran out, Davenant made his family clear a space and arranged to put on a show at home.

The 'entertainment', Davenant was at pains to make clear, was semi-public and entirely non-dramatic: he could not be charged with reviving the public theatre – although that was exactly what he aimed at in the longer term. What he had in mind, and what a select audience sat down to watch in a rather cramped hall at the back of his house, was a set of comic speeches with songs and intermezzi. There was a mock debate between Diogenes and Aristophanes on the virtue of public shows, and another between a Londoner and a Parisian, who clashed amiably in defence of their native cities. That may not sound altogether scintillating, and Davenant apologized for the modesty of the fare, but the performance was a daring resumption. It offered a mixture of pleasures novel and familiar, blunt and refined. The disquisitions, naturally written by Davenant, were of the kind traditionally put on in the Inns of Court and colleges at the end of terms. The contest between Paris and London no doubt contained a number of private jokes between the newly married couple. There were touches of real sophistication too: the lyrics were by Davenant – showing all his old feeling for a line which could be sung well – and the 'consort of Instrumental Musick, after the French composition', was by Henry Lawes, the finest living English composer. Some of the singers were rusty, others were unused to performing in public, and the government spy who checked in on the opening night commented sneeringly on the harmonies. Yet there was at least one voice to be heard of true character and brilliance: it belonged to 'Captain' Henry Cooke, an old army friend, who had been a chorister in the king's chapel and would eventually run the royal choir in the 1660s. Pepys later adored him, and John Evelyn accounted him the country's greatest singer in the Italian style. Among the musicians, meanwhile, were two other dignified composers of the extinguished court, George Hudson and Charles Coleman.[9]

Davenant could offer nothing in the way of spectacle to call back the vanished masques; his efforts were in any case moving towards another Continental genre, the opera. Yet the scene put on for his public, who made do with hard seats on closely ordered wooden benches, was not entirely bare. A small stage was set before them, with two side platforms railed and adorned with purple cloth and gilt, with a curtain embroidered with cloth of gold veiling the entire assembly. The band played above in a curtained gallery. *The First Days Entertainment at Rutland House* pleased those who were disposed to be pleased; passed the scrutiny of the authorities; and openly announced itself as the first of many days to be spent in entertainment.

Thus Davenant was not being wholly truthful four years later when, in his prologue to the revived Jonson comedy, he spoke of the dramatist's laurel sharing the banishment of the Crown. A few leaves of bay sprouted at the height of Cromwell's reign; sheltered by a few upstanding citizens whom Davenant took care to charm and persuaded to vouch for him. These included such pillars of the community as the sergeant-at-law John Maynard.[10] The fact that *The First Days Entertainment* could take place – that Davenant could advertise it openly on placards and handbills in Commonwealth London – was a strong sign in itself of a latent will to recover a life more recognizable; even, that is, if the residents of Blackfriars were unready yet for a return to the days when they or their parents saw:

men and women of debaucht consciences and conversations, impudent, impenitent, jearing, mocking and scoffing at all means of recovery, wasting their precious times in Plays, Pastimes, Masks and such fooleries, spending their wits and parts in complements and Courtships, rising up in the morning wreaking from their beds of lusts.[11]

Suckling's former haunts were no longer what they were. However, it was impossible to banish or convert everyone in London 'of debaucht consciences and conversations': by no means all of them had even fought against Parliament. In the fathomless puritan literature of the period, which in print and manuscript can represent but a fraction of the sermons and prayers poured out and over listeners of the time, the rapt and the resistant, there is even a sense that the godly *needed* these irredeemable characters. Rather than being real people, flesh-and-blood

Sucklingtons, the 'late wanton courtiers' imagined by the writer quoted above represented what the faithful were scared of being or becoming. This was the condition of all who lacked the grace of God or the help of their brethren. It was as though the figure of the cavalier, embodied now by the Second Duke of Buckingham on his clandestine cross-Channel visits, represented man in his state of nature; a state not of war, as Hobbes thought, but of perpetual debauchery. Paradoxically, amid the often lurid verbal performances being given from the city's pulpits, Davenant's congenial and low-key theatrical struck a discordantly moderate note.

The First Days Entertainment was merely the start of his revival, as he had hoped and planned – along with his wife and business partner Henrietta-Maria ('Dame Mary' as she was known), who soon became his in-house manager and gave birth to the first of their nine sons. They followed up the *Entertainment*, more miraculously still, with arguably the first opera in English, *The Siege of Rhodes*, 'the story sung in Recitative Musick'. This production too, which Davenant mischievously termed a 'maske' when he printed it the same year, was staged just a few months after his debut on the same 'cup-board stage' at the back of his house. Yet this time he bared a little more of his ambition; the piece was sung, and this was still no play, but he used designs by John Webb for the proscenium and one or two theatrical machines in something of the old style. An elegant backdrop showed a Turkish fleet bearing down on the island of Rhodes, a use of painted scenery which Davenant would soon enough transfer, with huge success, to the public theatre. Music was once again provided by Lawes (with additions by Matthew Locke), performed by Coleman and Hudson, with Captain Cooke in a prominent role. It may have been at this stage of their relationship that the company's perfectionism began reasserting itself. Cooke was unafraid to give advice on how a change to the verse might better suit the melody, while the writer-director would beat the libretto and cajole him to perfect the notes themselves before commenting on the words. Cooke would then break out roaring and swearing at Davenant; 'a vain coxcomb he is,' Pepys later decided, 'though he sings and composes so well.'[12]

Davenant achieved his next great coup in 1658, when he began staging his shows at the old Cockpit Theatre in Drury Lane. How he was allowed to do so was a mystery to his admirers and enemies alike, although the answer was simple enough. He now enjoyed enough support within the government from moderates such as Whitelocke, and by the late 1650s was in any case a fully fledged collaborator. He had useful and friendly connections to John Thurloe on the Council of State. He wrote in praise of the Cromwellian general Lord Broghill, and composed an epithalamion for the Protector's daughter, Mary, when she married Viscount Falconbridge. According to one of his oldest foes, the former Master of the Revels, Davenant even wrote 'a poem in vindication and justification of Oliuers actions and government' – probably meaning the long and extensive panegyric for Broghill.[13] But such attacks misjudged the often provisional and circumstantial nature of loyalty at the time. Broghill, one of Cromwell's brutal and efficient Irish enforcers, later became a Stuart hero for imposing the Restoration settlement in Ireland. Charles II made him Earl of Orrery for services rendered; and thus Davenant's poem for the general, published posthumously, looked like a work of rare political prophecy. He had, it could be said, identified virtues in a servant of 'Oliver Tyrant' which would only flower when the Stuarts returned. Both ways, he won.

With his safety net in place, Davenant was able to stage more elaborate entertainments at the Cockpit. These were also calculated to gratify the ruling powers and also catch the national mood, buoyed by naval victories against the Dutch and Spanish. The first, with extensive masque-derived machinery, was *The Cruelty of the Spaniards in Peru* in late 1658, another set of speeches with musical and visual support. With jingoistic fervour and dubious geography, the backdrops behind the proscenium arch illustrated Peruvian landscapes and scenes of Spanish atrocity – at one point featuring two inquisitors turning an 'Indian Prince' on a spit. *Peru* was a flagrant work of pro-Protectorate correctness. Some years earlier Cromwell had reopened the historic naval conflict with Spain, afire with the Elizabethan zeal of his generation. The Protector's great 'Western Design' had the time-honoured goal of severing Spain's treasure supply and overturning its foreign possessions, now officially incorporating a puritan agenda. The Spanish colonies were to be liberated and made Protestant. An additional political purpose was served: when England's revolutionary government entered into closer relations with France, the young king and his entourage were obliged to leave Paris and seek help instead from Spain. This defined the

Anglo-Hispanic battle lines still more sharply. Initially, however, the project revived memories of the first Buckingham rather than Queen Bess. A failed assault on Hispaniola in 1655 combined the deprivations of the Île de Ré mission with a blistering climate of staggering hostility. Yet by the time Davenant staged his *Peru*, which was based on a book dedicated to the late Protector, amends had been made for the wobbly start. Between the autumn of 1656 and the following spring, Spain's treasure fleets were comprehensively destroyed and Admiral Blake was confirmed as a national hero.

The death of Cromwell in 1658 and the strained shift of power to his son Richard jeopardized Davenant's next production, probably *The History of Sir Francis Drake*. As in 1642, the authorities were minded to order a clamp-down, viewing the theatre as a threat to the peace. Voices in the Council of State and in Parliament protested at how, despite the laws against such things, Davenant's performances took place each day 'to the scandal of Religion and the Government'. Even when Richard Cromwell's interim rule collapsed, and thousands of hitherto dormant cavaliers arrived or emerged with threat of force in London, the exist-ence of Davenant's playhouse continued to preoccupy the council. Davenant himself was caught up in the hubbub, more by association than because of any active sabre-rattling on his own part, and spent a few days in prison until something like quiet returned.[14]

If anything, the eighteen-month crisis which led to the Restoration spurred Davenant to greater daring – and, some complained, to lower aesthetic standards in the interests of populism. *Drake* was richer in spe-cial effects than any public show yet. It featured ships with working sails, miracles of puppetry and ventriloquism, and most controversially of all, something at last in the way of plot. This was, to all intents and purposes, drama, vamped up at the end with a choral closing number. Despite the best efforts of the godly, Davenant was untouchable; and if they could not stop him now, they never would.

And so the comeback began, with the old showman's striking balance of cunning, collusion and cheek. He had readied not only his people and properties, but also gone some way to warming up his public, when the Crown once more rejoined the laurel in London. Davenant had clearly prepared his strategy well in advance for the time when the theatres were brought back to life. There was, he had resolved, to be no return to the celebrated Elizabethan rivalries between the great playhouses, nor to his own clashes with Thomas May and other challengers in the 1630s. As Whitehall welcomed back the king, who knew he must reward his trusty servants, Davenant aimed at nothing less than complete control of the city's theatre business.

Neither did he achieve much less. His partner in the venture was Thomas Killigrew, a younger playwright of moderate talent and a gentleman of higher birth than Davenant, whose closer personal connections to the uppermost levels of the new court proved vital to obtaining their monopoly. Killigrew saw some action during the wars, and Charles sent him to Venice as the royalists' resident in 1651. Just a year later he was back, trailing charges of 'corruption and general debauchery', although his friend Denham, a touch cynically, held him up as a plain-dealing 'good fellow'. Denham credited Killigrew with blunt advice on how sufferers of syphilis could avoid the injuries incurred by Davenant:

> Nor shall you need your Silver quick Sir,
> Take *Mungo Murry's Black Elixir*,
> And in a week it Cures your P —, Sir.[15]

Among his other boons upon the Restoration, Killigrew was appointed Gentleman of the Bedchamber and Chamberlain to the Queen, making him an ideally placed associate for Davenant. Their patent was finalized as early as August 1660, and approved a new artistic dictatorship. Together Killigrew and Davenant annulled the outburst of unlicensed theatre which ensued in the early months of the year, when the days of the Interregnum Commonwealth seemed numbered. Every bit as effectively as the Commonwealth's censors, using red tape rather than troopers, they put a stop to the unauthorized performances which had been staged in old and near-decrepit theatres. Players emerging from retirement or, like the celebrated George Jolly, returning from the Continent, swept and lit up ruinous venues – the Red Bull, Salisbury Court, and also Davenant's trusty refuge, the Cockpit – and began acting from old copies and often, it would seem, from memory. Many, such as Major Michael Mohun, were veterans of the troubles. Other actors had found a living in alternative trades, as craftsmen, shop-hands, booksellers. Had this vagabond seizure of the stages been permitted to continue, there might have been a true return to the old pioneer days of the public theatre. As it was, the king's officials were anxious to appease the still-powerful puritan sections of the citizenry. The Restoration offered little freedom, in truth, for romantic ventures: the contest for place and profit was harsher than ever, and no enterprise could proceed unpatented.

The Davenant–Killigrew partnership did not mean that the talent which resurfaced in 1660 was lost, merely that it was treated as capital: the two managers absorbed the pick of the players into their respective companies. In other respects they also divided the spoils, of which Killigrew by contract seemed at first to take the lion's share. While he gained the sponsorship of the king himself, Davenant's patron was the Duke of York. He took his time preparing his permanent theatre, on the site of a disused tennis court near Lincoln's Inn Fields. Unlike Killigrew, who got on promptly with business at his old-fashioned playhouse on Vere Street through the winter and spring months of 1661, Davenant customized his premises with precision and foresight. He was still following the intention stated in the 'Preface to *Gondibert*' of bringing patterns of virtue to the public: and the best way of doing that, he reckoned shrewdly, was to use something of the theatrical technology and musical accompaniment perfected at court in the 1630s. Thus the plan for his Duke's Theatre incorporated large and secure storage areas for his expensive scenery, properties and instruments: this, it was true, made the auditorium itself rather small. But with the expanse of the fields to the east of the building's main entrance, Davenant at least eliminated one of the perennial problems at Blackfriars. The wealthier punters would have space to draw up their coaches.

Davenant put public success above material return. The expense of readying the Duke's Theatre quickly burnt up any early profits he might have hoped for from the award of his patent. He was forced to sell seven and a half of his valuable shares in the company, and would spend his remaining years in a cloud of lawsuits. His stepsons, led by his administrator Thomas Crosse, were also beginning to growl in earnest for their lost inheritance. But although he ran his theatre at a loss, maintaining what extravagance the petty cash allowed, Davenant's approach to the work itself was entirely professional. He made his person a near-permanent fixture at the Duke's, putting himself at the heart of the concern by converting part of the building into lodgings. In that nerve centre, along with Henrietta-Maria, his resentful stepson secretary and a rapidly growing family, he could be found outside the hours of performance, rehearsal or revelry. Like a modern restaurateur whose life passes on site, he was perfectly placed to handle deliveries, cast squabbles, or calm the more than occasional scandal – such as when one leading lady, Hester Davenport, announced she was pregnant with the Earl of Oxford's child. After a close start, his musicals were soon outselling the offerings of his competitor and sometime collaborator on Vere Street. He submerged himself in his art and trade as the tumults of the next era rumbled alongside and overhead.

2

In the distribution of offices and perks, and even the return of estates, many old cavaliers were disappointed of the bounty they had counted on. But there were keen-sighted entrepreneurs such as Davenant who were glad enough to be re-lodged in their former niches. More modestly, Robert Herrick returned to his vicarage in Devon in 1660, without leaving a line of complaint to the record, and nothing further was heard of him during his final years. The elderly poet died in 1674, aged eighty-three.[16]

Considerably greater in number were those who had to scratch and dig for a place in the new regime. James Howell had spent the years of republican rule seeking favour with Cromwell, albeit with his accustomed lack of success. When Charles II arrived in London he began courting his old masters once more. In his *Cordial for Cavaliers* (1661) he urged that long-suffering loyalties be rewarded; an argument rebutted by Sir Roger L'Estrange, formerly a king's cavalryman and now a disillusioned journalist, in a tract pointing out Howell's efforts to ingratiate himself with the king's enemies. But finally the decades of canvassing met with success, and Howell won his court appointment. Clarendon turned him down as tutor to the new queen, Catherine of Braganza, but agreed to create for him (at Howell's suggestion) the post of historiographer royal. It was debatable whether Howell merited his trust as the government's official interpreter of the archives, or whether he was qualified to make the difficult choice between tact and truth that the post demanded. The questionable authenticity of many of the letters he had 'gathered' (substantially rewritten or simply composed from scratch) for publication in the 1640s gave a strong savour of irony to his new public role. Howell's *Epistolae Ho-elianae: Familiar Letters* were by no means pure imagination but consisted of much reworking of fact in the light of experience. Howell supplied missing originals where they were wanting, and brought later refinement to bear on the papers returned to him from his old correspondents. The fruit of his efforts contributed to the ever-growing body of royalist literature which gave a cavalier slant to the pre-war decades.[17]

But as he had been telling all who might employ him for many years, he was a loyal pen for hire. His last full-length work, *Proedria Basilikē*, argued that the English monarchy's roots went as deep as those of any in Europe. That was not, on reflection, a thesis to give great comfort to the other European monarchs; but Howell had yet to shirk from it by the time he died in 1666.

Others were granted their quiet. If he never quite regained the love of the king, Abraham Cowley had other powerful friends. Settling on a 'good farm' bought for him by the Duke of Buckingham, he spent his last years 'conceal'd in his beloved obscurity, and possess'd that Solitude, which from his very childhood he had always most passionately desir'd'.[18] There he spent most of his time until his death in 1667.

Some, with Edward Earl of Clarendon at their head, took on the task of deciding how to proceed. Of all the leading figures of the 1660s, few seem more lost in the gaudy new world than the ennobled Edward Hyde, despite all he could command. Hyde belonged to a class and generation that believed in something Hobbes and others now claimed had never existed: namely, an ancient constitution balancing Church and state which, if only Englishmen would conform, could bring national harmony and prosperity like a process of nature. The idea that what mattered was power rather than principle, legitimizing government and propping up the law, never ceased to distress him. He presently found himself the most unpopular of the vibrant king's politicians, and it suited Charles that he should attract the bulk of the blame for the new administration's failings and compromises.

It was now the time for the zealots of the Commonwealth, in particular republicans and proponents of the 'good old cause', to undergo the experience of defeat, consulting the Stoics for comfort and in many cases seeking cover for fear of their lives. One distinguished victim of the reversal was Milton, now blind from his service to liberty, but still believing that a republic of emancipated citizens could be made a reality: that the way to such a state, in fact, was 'ready and easy'. In later years it was said that Davenant returned Milton's supposed favour of 1651 by putting in a word for him. Some voices suggested Davenant should join the other poet in hiding.

The more thoughtful of the long-term fugitives and émigrés returning hungrily in 1660 realized that there were few in any of the kingdoms whose record of service was entirely unambivalent. There were some, nevertheless, inveterate enemies and unrepentant regicides, who were excluded from mercy. Since the soul of Cromwell was beyond earthly torment, the royalists had to content themselves with desecrating his corpse. Yet the civilities deemed necessary for reconciled Englishmen were not extended so generously in Scotland and Ireland. The life of Montrose's old opponent Argyll, for example, who for a time was all but king of Scotland, was a necessary forfeit. Symbolically, the surviving author of the Covenant, Sir Archibald Johnston, was also irredeemable. Johnston, whose intensities had left him friendless, 'flitting from place to place for safety', was tracked down to his hiding place in a puritan chapel at Bolbec, near Le Havre. Even in his dreams he protested his innocence. In one, recorded in the last volume of his diary, '[I] saw the King lying in his bedd in the room, and I fell doun befor the bedsyde and took the Lord to witnesse that I had not layde any desseigne for the ruyne of his father or himself or their Crown.'[19] Royalists held him responsible for doing exactly that; while former comrades despised him for compromising with Cromwell and betraying the Covenant he had brought into being.

Anyone reading his diaries could have seen that his actions by no means reflected a straightforward 'design'. Told in full length, a life of Johnston of Wariston would reveal a person of near-deranged sensitivity, fighting to detect the will of God in all phenomena and reconcile it with his own. That was where, as he knew, his human impurities lurked; in his wishes. His eldest son, Archibald, had inherited the need to set down his struggles in writing. But whereas Johnston did so in the slim, pocket-sized notebooks which hold his journals, prayers and meditations, the younger Archibald inscribed his covenant on his body, taking his blood for ink. When Johnston returned from his last assignment in London, attending the Parliament summoned by Cromwell's son Richard, he found the boy raving and rolling in filth. A few months later, as a hunted man in France, the strain of rationalizing his convictions began taking the last of his sanity. He was eventually captured in 1663, brought back to Edinburgh and hanged at the Mercat Cross. By the end, he could barely recognize his own children. He made a sad spectacle at his trial. 'My lord Warriston was once in case to have reasoned before the greatest assembly in Europe, yea to have presided in it,' wrote one commentator; 'but now he could scarce speak to any purpose in his own case.' He was held until execution in the Tolbooth, where visitors remarked on his serenity: he seemed to have no doubt, at last, in his salvation. 'I have so often seen God's face in the house of prayer,' he is reported to have said. His mantra on his final morning was 'Abba, Abba,' and as he was taken to the Mercat Cross, a short way from his prison, his powers of memory and reasoning returned to him, enabling him to give a long speech in self-defence from the huge gallows erected in the open square.[20]

The hangings and eviscerations which the new regime could not forego were a far cry — as far as London from Edinburgh — from the heady milieu of the new court, or the stereotyped excesses of the era. There all Waltonesque thoughts of studying to be quiet could surely be thrown out of the carriage window: the imperative instead was to make one's views known, one's presence felt, and one's figure observed in a good seat at the theatre. Samuel Pepys was always upset when a place of honour was unavailable at the Duke's or the Royal, and consoled, with his characteristic honesty, to see other dignitaries pushed to the back. It appalled him, towards the end of the sixties, to see increasing numbers of commoners filling the opera.

Davenant remained immersed in work. For much of the decade that involved reviving and adapting old material — comedies from the thirties, entertainments from the fifties: his revamp of *The Siege of Rhodes* proved a major hit in 1661 upon the opening of the Duke's Theatre. The first few performances were graced by royal audience, and marred here and there by mishap. The fixtures were not quite ready; nor were the greener members of his cast. His leading countertenor froze under the king's gaze, and a rail or plank gave way on one of the balconies, plastering wigs and bosoms below with dust.[21] But there was no losing or suppressing the excitement of the liberated medium, or the chatty and salacious culture of which it was a focal point. Wits crowded the coffee houses in the mornings, the theatres in the afternoons and evenings. The slightest sign of a return to Commonwealth mores put Davenant on the defensive. Dedicating a new edition of *The Siege* to Clarendon, he complained that 'Dramatic Poetry meets with the same persecution now . . . as it ever did from the Barbarous.' With more than a touch of melodrama, he asserted his faith in eventual victory. The puritans undid themselves: in condemning 'heroic poetry', claimed Davenant, 'they entertain the People with a Seditious *Farce* of their own counterfeit Gravity.'[22]

The puritan lobby was still both powerful and wealthy – Charles could not rule without it – yet Davenant had more to fear from other quarters. His popular ascendancy over his business partner slipped somewhat when Killigrew opened a larger, plusher playhouse, the Theatre Royal, on Drury Lane in 1663. From then on Killigrew too could offer optical treats through scenery and devices; and more importantly still, he could profit from a substantially larger auditorium. Thus Davenant also began to contemplate moving. Chief though among his 'vertuous Enemies', as he styled them, was Sir Henry Herbert. The Master of the Revels had never liked Davenant, and was outraged at the old laureate's rebirth, given his record from the last years of the Commonwealth. Faced with Davenant's new sway, Herbert denounced him for serving as 'Master of the Reuels to Oliuer the Tyrant'.[23] Yet as reliable – and often similarly compromised – witnesses knew, this was a tetchy elderly man overstating the case. Davenant's position at the heart of London theatre was unassailable.

Theatre itself, for the first time, was becoming an institution rather than a dubious side-interest, a vagabond profession. Much was lost by the change, but much gained: Davenant and Killigrew were not the first in English history to direct a woman on the public stage, but they were the first to make it a professional norm. The greatest problem posed by female actors was their vulnerability to male attention; and not vice versa, as Prynne and others had feared back in the thirties. Hester

Davenport, Davenant's foremost soprano, was tricked into a fake wedding by the Earl of Oxford, and later pacified with an allowance which let her leave the stage behind. Another, Moll Davis, caught the fancy of the king himself – displaced though she was in time by the more celebrated Nell Gwyn. The atmosphere surrounding such liberties with scenery, music and the presence of women was thus newly urbane, newly initiate, even though the era quickly defined itself by a supposed return to a bygone era. Rather than 'restored', the first Caroline period looked both callow and past it by comparison.

Were the two great scourges, the Great Plague and the Fire, God's judgement upon the new age? Certainly they exposed its fragility. Instead of looking again at the familiar imagery of the plague, the empty streets and branded doors, the lime-pits, the dead-carts and the inspectors in their frightening rodentine masks, we should perhaps reconsider what the disease could claim, and view its victims as they were before the public spaces were closed. Taking in poor weary Thomas Crosse's sphere of activity at the Duke's, as he runs Davenant's office near the Fields, orders and arranges 'Properties, Candles, Oil, and other things', one sees a host of customers and colleagues of all backgrounds, from the 'hireling Players both men and Women, Music Masters, Dancing Masters, Scene men, Barbers, Wardrobekeepers, Doorkeepers and Soldiers'.[24] They pass in and out, along with the better-off spectators, powdered and pampered, among whom we find the Pepyses, and John Evelyn. A performance would begin in the later afternoon; by the time it ended, darkness would be drawing in on a metropolis alive with 'Common Whores, Wanderers, Pick-Pockets and Night-walkers'.[25] There are still darker characters at large: on an August night in 1662, Walter Clun, renowned for his Iago, leaves Killigrew's playhouse and is 'most cruelly butchered and bound' on his ride home to Kentish Town.[26] The assassins are the type to haunt Pepys's dreams, but they are parts of a mass which, in all its variety, is merely seeking to live; and they will all receive their share of the great pestilence.

There were human maladies, nevertheless, which neither plague nor fire could exterminate. Driven by universal hypocrisy, the entire populace was play-acting, and the city itself one great decaying theatre: Sir Roger L'Estrange, the scourge of James Howell, transferred the judgements of the Spanish wit Quevedo to an English setting:

The page styles himself the child of honour; and the lackey calls himself my lady's page; and every pickthank names himself a courtier. The cuckold-maker passes for a fine gentleman; and the cuckold himself for the best-natured husband in the world; and a very ass commences [as] a master-doctor. Hocuspocus tricks are called sleight of hand; lust, friendship; usury, thrift; cheating is but gallantry; lying wears the name of invention; cowardice, weakness of nature; and rashness carries the countenance of valour . . . Every little whore takes upon her to be a great lady; every gownman to be a counsellor; every bully to be a soldier; every gay thing a cavalier . . . So that the whole world, take it where you will, is but a mere juggle.[27]

Jonson would have recognized such characters. Knowing the end they met – or, at the best, feared – in 1665, gives one the eyes of a tragedian's pupil, seeing bone through skin and a *memento mori* in the slightest habitual action. Iconic though the Great Plague might be, the disease itself was at least a constant, a hangover of times past. The epidemic was harrowing in duration and extent, and crushingly predictable in its operation. Most adults in the city could recall the plagues of the thirties, and many also remembered the outbreak of 1625, hitherto unequalled.

Another cause for national soul-searching, the fleet's poor showing in the wars against the Dutch, was also depressingly familiar. Despite Blake's victories in the 1650s, the English were long accustomed to bad news from the seas. Yet whereas the Commonwealth navy owed its success, New Model-style, to investment, collective organization and proficient leadership, the Restoration sea-campaigns still yielded brilliant instances of heroic service and cavalier individualism. A popular example is the dash shown by the poet Rochester in taking a rowboat, 'through all the shot', to convey orders from the flagship, *Dreadnought*, to a captain who was straggling – purely in order to pass 'the greatest trial of clear and undaunted valour'.

It hardly counted that almost all of Rochester's fellow voluntary shipmates were slaughtered at the terrible Four Days' Battle in 1666, one dying in his arms, and that the young earl leapt into the little cock-boat in, at best, a state of extreme disorientation. Neither was it widely reported that Rochester was struggling with the guilt brought by an attack of fear in a battle the previous year. Aboard the *Revenge* in 1665, having served bravely throughout the appalling assault, 'he fell on a

sudden into such a trembling that he could scarce stand.' His friend
Edward Bergen ran and climbed to support him, only to be struck directly by a cannonball as he took him in his arms. He and Bergen had
made a pact that if either man should die, his ghost would seek out the
other, to reveal the mysteries of death. A year later, performing his mad
feat, Rochester still had the half-fearful, half-longing expectation that
his dead comrade would visit him from beyond the grave.[28] So long as
such displays still featured in dispatches, the public could feel, as it had
after the Île de Ré, that its men had been undone by poor planning and
resources, and had, in a sense, been defeated by their own commanders.

Military disasters were depressingly regular; plague was part of urban
life. The fire of 1666, however, felt like a special visitation. The blaze
exposed the impermanence not only of life but of place, of culture
itself. It demonstrated how the frames and channels of a civilization
could quite simply be annihilated. Again, to grasp something of the
impact of the fire, it helps to look at the habitats it destroyed. The city
had gone fundamentally unchanged in character for many generations,
despite the 'fantastical looks' of recent buildings, which had 'more
Ovals, Niches and Angles, than are in your Custards [i.e. pastries]'.
When Davenant had his Parisian describe London for '*The First Dayes
Entertainment*', the ugly yet amiable river-city still seemed as stubborn
as a wart. The Frenchman complained of 'misshapen streets' with
'umbrellas of Tiles to intercept the sun', and where neighbours in garrets
on opposite sides 'may shake hands without stirring from home'.[29]

Here was a view of urban solidity if nothing else. Yet the very concreteness of those ranks of houses, charming for neighbourly conferences,
maddening for cart-drivers, contained the secret of their transience. As
everyone knows, those clogging lanes were kindling in waiting. Once the
drama of the inferno itself had passed, the change it had worked on the
once 'goodly Landscape' of old London took a generation to accept and
forget. From Puddle Lane to St Paul's, it made the earthiest of the earth's
cities seem ephemeral, the inhabitants like flecks at the wrong end of a
telescope. It called to mind Prospero's words on the dissolving globe:

> We are such stuff
> As dreams are made on, and our little life
> Is rounded with a sleep.

Or at least it would have done, had Davenant not excised the passage from his reworking of *The Tempest* in 1667.[30] He collaborated with an aspiring poet, yet another convert from the Protectorate bureaucracy, who had impressed in the right places by praising the government at the very height of disaster. John Dryden, then aged thirty-six, formerly an assistant to Milton, would subsequently reconsider some of the finer points of Davenant's theories of poetry; but he would never lose his affection for his master at the Duke's, nor his enthusiasm for 'tagging' modern classics of English literature for the musical stage. He would take on to new levels what was in effect Davenant's nascent neo-classicism, his belief in clear and comprehensible verse as opposed to the 'strong lines' he found in Donne, Shakespeare and other Elizabethans. Davenant had owned the rights to large portions of Shakespeare's canon since early in the reign, and he set about refreshing them for his audience. He did so, however, by expunging knotty bits, words and phrases he assumed the play-goers would not understand: these he swept away as unapologetically as the fire which consumed the heart of London. His instinct for popular taste was confirmed by the reception of *The Tempest, or The Enchanted Island* in early November.

This, in his straightforward enterprise, was how Davenant treated most of his godfather's plays; only *Lear*, oddly enough, went on stage relatively unscathed. Yet he claimed to exercise more than purely professional judgement in his doctoring of the texts. If he had not floated the idea that he was really Shakespeare's son long before, it was in any case during these later years that he confided it to Aubrey, who had gravitated towards him, as he did to most expansive personalities. The spirit of Shakespeare might not have been guiding Davenant's hand, yet by implication he would have inherited his godfather's natural parts. How else could his pre-eminence in the realm of theatre be explained? He could even claim that his revisions of the old folios and quartos made changes that his great precursor, given hindsight, would have wished. It was a preoccupation with mixed benefits. His affectionate plundering of Shakespeare may have corrupted the texts, but kept the plays alive in the repertoire: his fancy as to his origins, transmitted via Aubrey, would send a number of scholars on a hapless quest to identify his mother as the fatal woman of the *Sonnets*.

Yet when it came to sheer prolificacy, there *was* a likeness. Davenant worked ceaselessly, toiling to preserve his cloud-capped towers. In this he resembled not only his symbolic father, Shakespeare, but also his real one, John Davenant. He ran his theatre with the adept industry the sometime mayor of Oxford brought to the tavern on Cornmarket. Yet he still protested weariness, on occasion, with the vagaries of his public, his aversion to the 'multitude' was strong and well, and he suggested in 1667 that he was nearing 'the danger of his Climacterick year'. He was two years short of this astrological crisis-point; yet he may also have meant a critical moment, a decisive step towards yet greater things – a larger, more comfortable theatre, and still more spectacular wonders. Cromwell, as it happened, had also said he felt 'climacterick' a decade earlier, in urging the colonists of his Western Design on to greater, godlier exploits.[31] The danger lay in missing opportunities.

Richard Flecknoe, no friend of Davenant's, admitted that he had 'chiefly civiliz'd the Stage':[32] under his stewardship, that is, the theatre had been brought in from the cold, and made part of respectable society – although respectable society had met it halfway. Many of Davenant's actors and collaborators testified to his professionalism; even Captain Cooke's curses are a backhanded compliment to his high artistic demands. In 1669, Dryden described him as 'a Man of quick imagination', who was clearly exciting to work with: 'nothing was propos'd to him, on which he could not suddenly produce a thought extreamly pleasant and surprizing.' Quickness of imagination and swiftness of thought were Shakespearean gifts (but also, to the eighteenth century, vices: Dr Johnson felt that Shakespeare's mind was often *too* quick for his writing's good). Still, Dryden's record of their partnership also shows the older master upholding Jonsonian principles of hard work and self-criticism: 'he corrected his own Writings much more severely than those of another man, bestowing twice the time and labour in polishing, which he us'd in invention.'[33]

He continued his pursuit of fame, preferably but still not always at a profit, up until the spring evening in 1668 when word spread around London that he had collapsed and died at his theatre. Across town, Pepys had seen a play at the Theatre Royal, and was chatting backstage with one of Killigrew's leading ladies when he heard 'Sir W Davenant is just now dead.' A second before, Mrs Knepp had been telling him how she feared her maid was too beautiful to last long backstage without being undone by some admirer. It was an appropriate moment to learn of Davenant's passing.[34]

The laureate was now beyond the pain of love, or problems with the staff. He died intestate, but left a thriving business for his wife, their nine sons and his resentful stepchildren to dispute. Death came to him, another admirer imagined, in the shape of a 'thin Poet', his escort to Elysium. The elegist envisaged a fond greeting for Davenant in the other world:

> Now *Davenant* is arriv'd, the Fields and Plains
> Resound unto his Welcome, Lofty Strains.
> For every Poet there it shall be free
> To raise his Joy into an Extasie.

All the greats embrace him, from Shakespeare and Jonson, Beaumont and Fletcher, to the recently departed Cowley, demanding 'a share in him': that is, a portion of the credit for influencing his life's writing, but also, one suspects, a financial stake in his first venture in heaven. Somewhere in the throng, presumably, was Carew, diverted from his raptures elsewhere by the arrival. But the last to welcome Davenant claimed the strongest bond with him. Suckling, standing back from the crowd in order to surpass it, insisted on priority since they were both knights, and both (a bold boast, in his case) 'writ concise'.[35]

Back on earth, Davenant's remains were buried in Westminster Abbey. Imitating the inscription on Jonson's stone, someone had ordered that 'O Rare *Sir Will. Davenant*' be carved on the grave. His religion at the end, like much of England's, was indeterminate: some counted him a Catholic. He told Aubrey that all religions would eventually resolve themselves into 'a kind of ingeniose Quakerisme'. Those who suspected him of atheism or, worse, indifference to such questions, would be set right by a dialogue of poems between a Christian and a dying philosopher, published in his posthumous folio of *Works* and possibly meant for inclusion in the never-completed *Gondibert*. At any rate, his walnut coffin was borne from the Duke's Theatre down to the Abbey, where 'at the great west dore, he was received by the singing men and choristers.' Like his casket, the service it seems was one of some splendour. Yet Aubrey, who attended the funeral, was saddened to note that no laurel was put upon the coffin, although 'me thought it had been proper.'[36]

Perhaps prophetically, Davenant was in the end deprived of his twigs of bay. Greater works would dwarf his efforts: *Paradise Lost*, telling the story of a civil war in heaven and its consequences, was published in 1667 to gradual but widespread awe. More immediately, Davenant's efforts in the heroic direction were eclipsed (and lightly derided) by a burlesque. He had hoped that *Gondibert* might shape a new public sensibility; instead Samuel Butler's *Hudibras*, the doggerel epic of a western squire who goes 'a-colonelling' when 'civil dudgeon' erupts, took a much stronger hold on popular taste.

A near-contemporary of Davenant's and, almost inevitably, a friend of Aubrey's, Butler preferred to keep most of his writing out of circulation. Even *Hudibras* was slow to appear, coming out in separate parts between 1662 and 1678. Each instalment gave roasting comment on current events by reference back to the conflict of the mid-century. Hudibras, a Presbyterian, takes up Parliament's cause, but an entire class is implicated in the satire of his quixotic progress. He is the archetypal landed gentleman, a land-owning JP, from his outlook on affairs of the day to his grammar-school rhetoric and smattering of law. Hudibras's wartime loyalties could exempt cavalier readers from implication in the satire, but his vices could quite clearly belong to a gentleman colonel on either side. Butler set out to scorch the conventions and presumptions – legal, social, cultural and educational – which made possible the hypocrisy and poltroonery of a Hudibras. In consequence there is very little in the England of the seventeenth century which escapes his satirical scrutiny, from the sectaries of the revolution to the new cult of the Royal Society. Even Aubrey catches a faint lick of the whip for an idea he brought before the learned fellowship. He had been impressed by the notion of a cart which ran on legs rather than wheels.[37]

The public preferred Milton's sublime, and Butler's ridiculous, to the pattern of virtue set forth in *Gondibert*. Davenant's stage, meanwhile, was soon the property of wits not, as he put it, of 'the former age'.[38] Prominent among these, taking her cue from Margaret Cavendish, was Aphra Behn. A poet and previously a royalist spy, Behn became one of the chief contributors to the theatre now run by Dame Mary, and took over Davenant's mantle as loyal propagandist: no chauvinist when it came to sound business, Davenant had set the scene for the career of England's first avowedly professional woman writer.

He was soon enough joined in the afterlife by his one-time gadfly Sir John Denham, now 'ancient and limping', and the court's unlikely chief engineer. When the Surveyorship of the King's Works was restored, along with the other old offices, in 1660, the logical choice to succeed Inigo Jones – who died in 1652 – was his nephew and devoted pupil, John Webb. But Charles had a large surplus of followers with a stronger claim to a favour: and he appointed Denham to honour a promise made long before. The Surveyor General's days would not end happily, however. In 1665 Denham married Margaret Brooke, a woman of great beauty who was younger than he by almost three decades. When the Denhams returned to the capital after avoiding the plague, she and the Duke of York fell in love. The ensuing affair drove Denham out of his mind. The king, as if to make amends, sent for an Irish healer, Valentine Greatrakes, to help the poet's lameness. In the meantime Denham continued numbly with his duties as Surveyor. But on the way back to London from inspecting quarries in Dorset, he collapsed into derangement at the prospect of home. 'Sir John Denham, that great master of wit and reason, is fallen quite mad,' was the news in many letters from London in April 1666. Some attributed the 'fit' to Lady Margaret's infidelity; others to the mercury-based cure which Greatrakes had given him to rub into his shins.[39]

Months passed before he regained his lucidity; and as he recovered, the king's brother tired of his lover and their very public passion. In 1667, conveniently for all related parties, Lady Denham sickened and died – dispatched, it was thought, by a poisoned cup of cocoa. A dubious post-mortem ruled against the suspicion of murder, but could not dispel it, and the dark business clouded Denham's name for ever. An equally popular suspect, however, and a likelier one than the raddled poet, was the Duchess of York. Prince James's much-harried wife was better placed than Denham to appoint the Countess of Rochester, who supposedly delivered the fatal cup, as the agent of revenge. Suicide was also a possible cause of death, as was an order given by the duke himself.

Yet Denham appeared the sprightlier for his widowhood. With his reputation tainted, he cast decorum to the winds. Along with his old friend Edmund Waller (who would live until 1687), he seized on every opportunity to socialize and flirt, dominating the talk at balls and dinner parties, and delighting the malignest of the city's gossips. Yet at the same time he prepared his collected *Poems and Translations*. The volume appeared in 1668 and displayed, light comrade-songs aside, his full excellence as a maker; from the subtlety of the last refinements made to 'Cooper's Hill', to the economy and control of his influential translations from Virgil. Almost inevitably, some poems carry a personal tint in the light of his tragic marriage: one new lyric, for example, took up Suckling's old cause of arguing for 'Friendship and Single Life against Love and Marriage':

> How happy he that loves not, lives!
> Him neither Hope nor Fear deceives,
> To Fortune who no Hostage gives.[40]

Yet Denham seems to have issued the collection with a view to facing down the predictable inferences. Pieces which must read as works of brazen hypocrisy, if Denham really was involved in foul play, protest the integrity of the author's character. There is an austere rendering of two Latin poems on the virtues of Prudence and Justice, and a resounding late achievement in a version of the Ciceronian dialogue 'Cato Major'. Resigned to old age, glad for relief from the torments of youth's pleasures, Denham's elderly consul is at peace with death and enchanted by nature's cycles of decline and renewal. Cato is ready to depart yet happy to remain:

> For never any man was yet so old,
> But hoped his life one Winter more might hold.[41]

The *Poems and Translations* unfold a lifetime's accomplishment. Denham's wider oeuvre is unjustly overshadowed by 'Cooper's Hill', important though that early poem would be for its hymn to the Thames and its local Parnassus: without Denham, eighteenth-century poetry would have read very differently. Instead, thanks to him, in more than a hundred years the *Gentleman's Magazine* would note wearily how 'some gentle Bard' might be found 'reclining on almost every mole-hill'.[42]

He continued his public career to the end, nominating Wren as his successor to the Surveyorship, and voicing strong opinions on matters of moment. In Parliament he spoke with energetic praise for *Paradise Lost*, and argued cogently for religious toleration. He finally gave in to old ailments in March 1669.[43]

Aubrey found a 'strange piercingness' in Denham's small, goose-grey eyes, so that it seemed 'when he conversed with you he look't into your very thoughts.'[44] There was no gazing into his, it seemed; yet guilty or innocent, if a 'Sessions of the Poets' was awaiting him in the next life, Denham knew better than to expect an easy time from it.

14. Aubrey

Truth, the discovery made by travelling mindes.

– Davenant, *Gondibert* (II.V)

1

What worthy thing came of it, passing time like this?

John Aubrey put the question (in Latin) in the sketch of a memoir he left to Anthony 'à' Wood, his fellow antiquarian and one-time friend. 'Truly nothing,' he decided; 'only umbrages' – shadows.[1] Yet his chief virtue, so he claimed, was gratitude, and he was generous enough not to ask the same question of the 'persons of honour' who fill the folios of manuscript which came to comprise his classic, the *Brief Lives*.

Aubrey confessed a fascination from childhood with old things, old structures, old people and the departed. Or one should perhaps say his fascination lay with *elders*. He was impressed by forms which pre-dated him, and which thus held more knowledge than he did. As a boy he had little patience for other children, but loved listening to his grandfather speak of 'the old time, the rood-loft, etc., ceremonies, of the priory, etc.'. In some respects his life from the age of eight or nine, progressing from his grandfather's tuition to grammar school and Oxford, was a search for a master authority. Yet he could never dwell on one subject for long, or content himself with one guide. He was about twenty-eight – it was 1654, deep in Cromwell's Protectorate – when he began noting down 'philosophicall and antiquarian remarques' in the first of countless pocket-books.

He was relentlessly curious not only about how things were, but also how they worked. He was enchanted by clockwork, machinery, and by the age of eight, he claimed, 'I was a kind of engineer.' He practised drawing obsessively, and felt he could have been a painter, since he could 'fancy a thing so strongly and had so cleare an idea of it'. His mind was acutely impressionable, 'like a mirror, pure chrystal water which the least wind does disorder and unsmooth'. The same delicacy left him vulnerable to illness and distress.[2]

He later presented a number of scientific observations to the Royal Society – not only the cart on legs – the institution for 'Physico-Mathematicall Experimentall Learning' given official form after the Restoration and housed for the time being at Gresham College. Yet although Aubrey's world was made of the infinitesimal, he lacked the engineer's patience with springs, nuts and bolts, or the painter's absorption in a single canvas. He was an observer, and a recorder of observations, rather than a fashioner. The machine he kept incessantly in motion and development was his intellect – his 'natural parts'. 'My head was alwaies working,' he wrote, was 'never idle, and even travelling (which from 1649 till 1670 was never off my horseback)'. His autobiographical notes suggest that this compulsive movement of mind and body was connected, symptomatically, to financial anxieties and poor health. With his father's estate he also inherited his debts, and in the time it took him to lose almost everything he never had a moment's calm. When all was gone, and he could only appeal for the charity and hospitality of colleagues and patrons, he found peace for the first time, oddly enough, since the outbreak of civil war in 1642, the year he matriculated at Oxford.

Aubrey was a slight, sensitive-looking man with eyes at a suggestively bird-like distance from his thin, ridged nose. He made friends almost as easily as breathing. Despite the difference in character – Aubrey could only take claret with sugar, and even then was prone to throw up his wine – he became quite an intimate of Sir William Davenant. The relationship was not difficult to understand: Aubrey was a supporter and sympathizer of Davenant's preferred myths. He had been a royalist, although a non-active partisan, and that allegiance determined his interpretation of 'the old time'. But that did not extend to decrying the king's – or Davenant's – enemies. Thomas May, for example, had not only been Parliament's official historian during the civil war, but had been Davenant's opponent in a 'war of the theatres' and his rival for the laureateship a decade earlier. He was thought to have died quite wretchedly: an obese man in the end, the story was that he unwittingly strangled himself by tying his nightcap-strings too tight. Aubrey saw the origins of May's republicanism in his translation of Lucan. In his youth, May had been 'debaucht *ad omnia*: but doe not by any means take notice of it,' warned Aubrey, 'for we have all been young.'[3]

Aubrey was a natural conciliator, and such sympathy for all sides was rare. Andrew Marvell was far less generous with regard to May, or any who failed to meet his exacting standards. He signed May off as a 'most servile wit, and Mercenary Pen . . . / Malignant Poet and Historian both'.[4] His belligerence is significant, since Marvell had formerly been one who lamented the rise of bitterness in letters which followed the wars, complaining to Richard Lovelace that 'our wits have drawne th'infection of our times,' and that 'Word-peckers, Paper-rats, Book-scorpions' had infested the land.[5] A popular target and dispenser of such creatures' venom, the Earl of Rochester, even insisted that malice was essential to the aesthetic of satire, and accuracy an obstacle:

A man could not write with life [he told his confessor, Bishop Burnet], unless he were heated by Revenge: For to make a *Satyre* without Resentments, upon the cold Notions of Phylosophy, was as if a man in cold blood, would cut mens throats who had never offended him: And he said, The Lyes in these Libels came often in as Ornaments that could not be spared without spoiling the beauty of the *Poem*.[6]

Some things had not changed. Satire required excoriation, and libels, between friends, were implicitly accepted. Yet John Aubrey's constitution was tender to bites from book-scorpions. He took care to be on good terms with all; and his mildness made him a hard man to slander. He was, however, prepared to be brave when the time came to record his contemporaries and the experiences of their century. Aubrey asserted to Wood that *Brief Lives* contained the 'naked and plaine trueth, which is here exposed so bare that the very *pudenda* are not covered'.[7] His accounts would therefore show such 'shameful parts'. However horrified – or not – Wood was by this statement of intent, he was nevertheless the first who encouraged Aubrey to organize his biographical notebooks into a 'book of lives' for eventual publication. Aubrey had been helping Wood with his work for many years by the time this suggestion was made.

Wood was a famously cantankerous person, but they shared an obvious affinity in their intellectual preoccupations. Wood, too, the historian of Oxford University, was a gatherer of minutiae, anecdotal and topographical, though unlike Aubrey a jealous one. With veiled eagerness he quickly accepted Aubrey – all but penniless and technically homeless – as his research assistant. Then when he published his crowning work, the *Athenae Oxonienses*, in 1691–2, he made no acknowledgement of Aubrey's help. He was quick to pass him the blame, however, when some of his acquired material proved costly.

Together they embodied a tendency of thought which had developed through more than a century but which intensified in both scale and precision in the decades following the Restoration. Like so many of their compatriots, Aubrey and Wood were all but possessed with producing a description of their world. They were compilers rather than synthesizers. Their researches reflected the relentless gathering instincts of late-sixteenth-century antiquarianism, which treated the whole universe as a source of recondite knowledge. Yet their methodology reflected the developing 'scientific' approach championed by the Royal Society. In recent times Aubrey in particular has been credited with discovering basic principles of modern archaeology through his approach to the monuments of Britain.

The expansive, perfectionistic and rather compulsive tendency shown by Wood and Aubrey could be observed in many different fields of activity. Cartography is a good example. 1676 saw the publication of John Ogilby's *Britannia*, mapping and measuring the country with hitherto unrivalled exactitude. It would be wrong, however, to suggest that Ogilby's skills were confined to geography. By the time *Britannia* appeared he had already translated Homer's two epics, and much of Virgil. Davenant had praised him for making 'grave Aesop warm in deaths detested shade' in a translation of the *Fables*.[8] Ogilby was a publisher, cosmographer and masque-maker, the author of an *Entertainment of His Most Excellent Majestie Charles II*, staged in 1661 to celebrate the return of the monarchy. His experience with masque stretched back into old times: Ogilby was said to owe his lameness to an injury he suffered performing for King James I, in a similar entertainment, forty years earlier.

Before *Britannia*, Ogilby had already printed maps of Japan, China

and the Americas in revolutionary detail. Yet *Britannia* did something strange in its representation of the land. It illustrated the country
one road at a time, showing the centres on each major thoroughfare:
2,519 miles of road were shown through 100 'strip maps', a format which
remained highly influential throughout the following century. Each
strand of highway bears a picture of each town and landmark on its
way. The endeavour also washed the places on its separate strips free and
clean again of their wartime associations. Yet although one has no sense,
for example, of the forestland destroyed by the wartime desperation for
building materials and fuel, the format still gives the impression of a
land cut to ribbons, hanging in shreds.

A project such as Ogilby's was manifestly driven by a wish for both
fixity and renewal (as well, of course, as profit and patronage). Producing a definitive map of 'Britain' – politically indefinite though that
entity remained – screwed each place into place. Aubrey and Wood
were driven by the same urge to catalogue and describe; but their vast
projects were wrought with intrinsic despair. Aubrey's restless eye and
brain made it apparent to him that his endeavours were by nature beyond
completion. His mind would always be prodding him onward, spurring
his horse. This and a natural modesty made him reluctant to give his
findings final form. Wood was more stubborn, more prosaic and more
shameless. Both worked on multi-volume works they could not end:
Aubrey left behind his *Monumenta Britannica*, a vast miscellany of ruins
which would in time change the consensus of thought on Stonehenge
and suggest a new method for understanding sites of historical interest.
His loving natural history of Wiltshire was also left in rough draft for
the Bodleian Library to shelter. Wood, whose efforts concentrated on
his immediate surroundings, produced an unfinished word-map of
Oxford.

No work seemed less finishable than the 'Brief Lives' Aubrey began
compiling and writing in earnest through the 1680s. His own miniature
'Life', which he said should be used only as an end-paper, and the outline it gave of his unceasingly whirring, 'inventive and philosophical
head' could tell him as much. There is no concluding the life of a person, no gathering in all the possible facets and accidents. There was
certainly no hope of writing up biographies of all the names he had in
mind. It was impossible too, despite his perceptiveness, that he capture

every subtlety of character in his subjects. He can only sketch, for example, the motives and causes behind Suckling's suicide. A 'Life' is thus by definition brief, a narrative in shorthand. The outcome of a project such as Aubrey's would inevitably be 'umbrages', as he admitted, an encyclopaedia articulated by lacunae, by instructions for the next draft, by hesitations and points of query. He was at best a rescuer of shadows, '[that] which was neglected and quite forgot'. 'Name them,' he directed himself, referring to the things he had managed to salvage in his race against the decay of living memory.

In his own judgement he left no monument to his work. Although he lacked the egotism to regret this failure excessively, the end result, the finished thing, still mattered greatly to him. His colleague Wood was given to fiercer bitterness on that subject, and directed much of it against Aubrey. Unconsciously, however, the pair typified the lifestyle – of quiet devotion to a private pastime – which their more politically preoccupied contemporaries often claimed to covet.

Aubrey had first met Wood at Oxford in August 1667. Wood was grieving for his mother at the time, and was more open to Aubrey's frank and warm character than he might normally have been. Aubrey, meanwhile, was enchanted and excited by their comradeship. Recent events gave their work an urgency unusual to antiquarian studies. The previous three years had seen the English defeated at sea by the Dutch (only two months earlier), London eaten to the bones by plague, and the old city consumed by fire. Such events felt to many like the overture to apocalypse. That feeling drove different people to different extremes. It gave extra abandon to the hedonists at the court of Charles II, yet raised puritans to new pitches of fearful expectancy. Its effect on men such as Aubrey and Wood was to make them work all the harder at putting their age on record.

A few months after they met, another watershed came with the swift and brutal end to a long life in politics. The career of Edward Hyde, Earl of Clarendon, Charles II's mentor and Lord Chancellor, was over. It had stretched and widened through the decades to the point where his name was all but synonymous with government and even the continuity of the royal line: his daughter was the Duchess of York – the neglected and jealous wife of the future James II. In some quarters, his reputation was assured. Clarendon retained the respect of countless intellectuals and officials: Pepys was awestruck by his learning and rhetorical command. Yet in considerable numbers his enemies saw him combining the ruthlessness of both the First Duke of Buckingham and the Earl of Strafford – with Strafford's indisputable intellect to boot.

Clarendon had already weathered much envy and hatred before it proved convenient to blame him for the catastrophic war with Holland in the mid-1660s. Buckingham's campaign at sea was an unqualified disaster; yet when the Dutch sailed up the Medway all but unopposed in June 1667, the choice of scapegoat was obvious. This numbered Clarendon's days in power, and the great seal was taken from him shortly afterwards. Even then, he might have escaped further persecution had he retained the king's personal support. That he finally lost, so they said, when he cheated Charles of a mistress, arranging for the beautiful Frances Stewart to marry the Duke of Richmond. In the autumn of 1667 he was driven from office and then from the country, avoiding formal impeachment only by accepting, once again, a sentence of exile.

A kindred spirit of Aubrey and Wood, the diarist John Evelyn, another antiquary, polymath and scientist, visited Hyde shortly before his departure. Evelyn waited on the ousted chancellor at his huge though incomplete mansion near Piccadilly, close to the site of the green where Suckling once played bowls and squandered fortunes. The house, in the classical style, with two wings projecting at right angles into a large, long forecourt, was the work of Roger Pratt, one of the period's lesser known and less prolific but most gifted architects.

When he paid his last respectful call at the Piccadilly building site, Evelyn found the corpulent grandee sitting outside in a wheelchair, dejectedly watching the builders erect gates in the fields to the north of the house. Lord Clarendon would never make much use of them himself – except to leave. To the south, towards the sullen river, the city was still an ashen wasteland from the fire of the previous year. Yet Hyde was raising his huge home, in defiance of his baiting and by now over-powering critics, at a cost of £50,000. Most assumed the funds had been gathered by dishonest means. Many took satisfaction in knowing that at least the blocks of fine Portland stone, allegedly diverted from a project to restore the gutted wreck of St Paul's, were being set upon the ruins of Hyde's political career. Shortly after Evelyn's visit, Clarendon was gone from public life for good, back to France, to work on his memoirs and his chronicle of the rebellion.

So it was that Hyde returned to his old regime of wandering and writing, moving over the years from Rouen to Avignon, Montpellier to Moulins. With it came the jarring combination of study and hazard. Clarendon's writing was disturbed by near-expulsion from France, and a brutal beating at Évreux, where a pack of English sailors accosted him with their grudges. In time he hoped for another return to England, for peace with the king, but died abroad, aged sixty-five, in December 1674.

2

The former age was passing; but its memorials would take many years to bring to perfection. Aubrey worked avidly on the biographical project his colleague Wood suggested. 'This morning being up by 10,' records a letter to Wood of 27 March 1680, 'I writ two [lives]: one was Sir John Suckling, of whom I wrote a leafe and ½ in folio.'[9] Suckling was still accorded the status of a modern classic in cavalier circles, treasured for his loyalty and what was now construed as martyrdom. His sister still had van Dyck's portrait of him 'all at length, leaning against a rock, with a play-booke, contemplating', on prominent display in her house at Bishop's Gate. In strictly literary terms, he (like most of his contemporaries) had fallen behind Cowley, but was now upheld, rather shockingly, as a model of gentility. The poet and playwright Edward Howard (who styled himself proudly as a 'Gentleman of Quality') praised Suckling as a writer 'whose wit was every way at his command, proper and useful in Verse and Prose, equally gentile and pleasant'. The literary historian Gerard Langbaine, writing in 1691, paid the usual compliments to Suckling's 'Fragrant and Sparking' invention, but observed that readers should look more closely at his ideas – for 'his Thoughts were not so loose as his Expression, witness his excellent Discourse to my Lord *Dorset*, about religion.'[10]

Had they scraped away the veneer, they would have discovered thoughts less gentile and pleasant, and more interesting, and a more complex personality. Yet it was the complacent courtier, repulsive to some, a pattern of elegance and integrity to others, that lodged in the cultural memory. The real Suckling, the overstretched figure who struggled to reconcile the expectations of his age with the limitations of his talents and the realities of Caroline politics, was one best forgotten.

'Roaring boys' and prodigals still abounded in London. Andrew Marvell reportedly said that 'he would not play the good-fellow in any man's company in whose hands he would not trust his life.' In consequence Marvell was teetotal unless alone in his lodgings, where he kept a large stock of wines 'to refresh his spirits'.[11] When Clarendon was finally forced from office, it might even be said that the nation lay at the mercy of an arch-Sucklington. With the old chancellor gone, the influence of the second Buckingham seemed paramount. A few months before Davenant collapsed at work, Buckingham had Thomas Killigrew's brother Harry assaulted outside the theatre. Killigrew's crime was to have confirmed the common knowledge of a love affair between the duke and the Countess of Shrewsbury. After an ugly duel in which the cuckold was fatally wounded, Buckingham ordered the murder of Harry Killigrew. In the assault of the courtier by a gang in the street there is a flash of Suckling and his men assaying Sir John Digby in Blackfriars more than three decades earlier. The difference may have been the ruthless precision of the attack, in which Buckingam's hirelings ran their swords through Killigrew nine times and left him to die. Or the discrepancy may have lain with the victim, this time no Digby but a braggardly yet fragile man. It seemed for a while that the duke's whim, like his father's, would be law.

Suckling could be imagined as a spiritual father-figure to Buckingham and his fellow celebrated libertine and poet Rochester, running their legendary inn on the Newmarket Road. In kidnapping his eventual bride, the northern heiress Elizabeth Mallet, Rochester was also acting to type. The pair again conformed to their symbolic forebear in arranging to have John Dryden sorely beaten up in Rose Alley in November 1679.[12] Yet both, in truth, were far above Suckling's league, whether in vice, virtue or talent. However much he may have been their literary prototype, Suckling lacked both the introspection of the duke and his genuine deadliness, and did not possess the puritan streak, inherited from his mother, that gave additional depth and intellectual complication to Rochester and his work. He wanted too the earl's philosophic extension of mind; Rochester was a collapsing star, living in a drunken blur outside his own edges, possessed with a critically unstable vivacity. Suckling's love of pleasure, unlike Rochester's, was steady rather than violent; he was a wit, but not, like Rochester, with 'a disposition to *extravagant* mirth'.[13] Unlike the Restoration libertine, Suckling did not willingly assume the role of clown. He took himself more seriously while missing, however, Rochester's almost unthinking courage as a soldier and duellist.

In the last decades of the seventeenth century, 'odorous', 'sweet' Suckling's verse still conjured up the mythical well-being of the years before the war. He was spoken of as an equal of Shakespeare, Jonson, Dryden and Donne. In 1712, a poem for the Earl of Oxford could declare that 'What *Suckling* writes, the Gentleman displays,/And gay *Ideas* gives of former days'; but the same writer felt obliged to ask for charity on the part of Suckling's readers:

> Let then familiar Lines of hasty Birth,
> Produc'd by Accidents of wine or mirth,
> Uncensur'd pass; nor Pedants there pretend
> To find those Faults which they want wit to mend.[14]

Suckling himself could really only belong to a world of pre-war expectations, a setting more naive and in retrospect more homely. He would take his place at the vanguard of the poetasters whom Alexander Pope defined as a 'mob of gentlemen who wrote with ease', flippant spirits knocking off thoughtless stanzas and couplets, writing between romps and recovery, as it were.[15]

Suckling was brought up short in 1641; he would have been entirely out of his depth amid the shrewd political managers who ousted James II in 1688–90. The cavaliers, a heterogeneous and shifting body even in their heyday, were split for good by the political crisis of the late 1680s, and the 'Glorious Revolution' that ensued. Their instinct was to support Charles's brother – who with Buckingham was in a strong sense the leader of their party. But James's insistence on supporting the Catholic interest drove his high Anglican supporters away from his papist and more permissive Protestant following. The replacement of James with William of Orange sealed the victory of Parliament. The heirs of some cavaliers remained to play their part in the new political settlement. Others scattered to join the Jacobite romance of rebellion and regret.

More time, therefore, would be needed before the Stuarts' sense of kingship by divine right became moribund. Their doctrine had been supported by a Kentish gentlemanly thinker, Sir Robert Filmer, who claimed that all kings were the rightful heirs of Adam. Filmer's works caught the popular imagination late in the day, when they were reprinted in the 1680s to uphold the case for James's kingship and that of his heirs. Their influence was such that they demanded a reply from John Locke, who established himself as the leading political philosopher of the day by doing so. Although in life he had been a private family man, and in his writing a meticulous introvert, Filmer was depicted by posthumous enemies as an idle blusterer, a cavalier Hudibras. In consequence he would never escape his reputation as a rustic philosopher, a writer of 'glib nonsense', but his unyielding monarchism still posed awkward questions. It called for a thinker of Locke's ability to counter the real problems it raised – which is no small compliment.[16]

A physical change in London was taking place as slowly but surely as the shift in ideas. Aubrey, who died in 1696, would not live to see the dome of the new St Paul's solidify in the space left by the storm-blunted spire of the ancient cathedral. Yet in keeping with Wren's centrepiece, the capital's buildings were already becoming more neo-classical, in a spreading elaboration of Inigo Jones's Banqueting House. Simultaneously, the goods on sale in the bourses, the fabrics on the burghers' backs, the plate on their tables and the hangings on their walls became richer and more exotic still. As the century and an exchange of monarchic dynasties passed, the country drifted towards power and profit beyond the dreams of the early Stuarts.

As always, the cost of such affluence and power was borne elsewhere. There were limits to the rewards that England alone could offer each generation of winners. Within the British and Irish islands the most harrowing consequences of the century's successive coups d'état were borne by the Catholics of Ireland, in particular the groups once commonly known as the Old Irish and Old English. The Cromwellian conquest resulted in mass dispossessions, giving huge numbers of 'unauthorized' Irish the infamous and remediless choice of Hell or Connacht. These expropriations were of course out of keeping with the cavalier side of the English story: yet the confiscations of the 1650s were ratified upon the Restoration.[17] The programme would be taken further after the 'glorious' deposition of James, finishing the Catholic aristocracy as a political power.

Overall, it was a time we are rightly schooled to view as an epoch of violent upheaval, even revolution, but its chief outcome was still greater opportunity for the limited circle of gentlemen and noblemen we have followed here. From Elysium, Davenant must have regretted having to leave it so soon. Not tasting it at all must have pained Suckling.

3

Decades had passed since civil war ended in England, but the expulsion of the Stuarts made it seem closer. The country was for the first time openly divided into two political camps, Tory and Whig, and the past was still a bitterly contested territory. One casualty of a particularly fierce and unequal battle over a matter of historical record was John Aubrey's collaboration with Anthony à Wood. The point at issue was the integrity of the First Earl of Clarendon.

That Clarendon worked corruptly in office seemed so obvious a fact that it hardly seemed worth checking. Besides the unofficial benefits of his position in the state, he was supposed to have made a huge private profit when he arranged the sale of Dunkirk – acquired in 1658 – to the French in 1662. How else could he build his mansion on Piccadilly, esteemed 'the best contriv'd, the most usefull, gracefull and magnificent house in England'?[18] Marvell had skewered the Lord Chancellor, along with the court 'cabal', in a sequence of satires on a government he regarded as nothing less than criminal. He devoted an entire poem to Clarendon's 'house-warming', with extensive comment on his ministry; elsewhere he branded the 'troop of Clarendon' as 'gross Bodies, grosser Minds, and grossest Cheats'. He decried the notion of Clarendon as a great Parliamentarian: to Hyde, Marvell said, the House was no more than a means of dispatching his enemies – it was to him what a cup of 'mortal chocolate' had been to Denham.[19]

Thus in his entry on Hyde in *Athenae Oxonienses*, Wood felt little uncertainty, indeed was moderate by contemporary standards, in mentioning that Hyde had taken bribes in return for appointments in the early 1660s. He used information supplied, as so often, by Aubrey. The *Athenae* was published in 1691–2, three years after James II was driven from the throne. The two-volume work was tepidly received by gentlemen who were displeased to have their – or their fathers' – 'pudenda' bared by Wood and Aubrey's researches. And Hyde's son Henry, the Second Earl of Clarendon, decided to sue.

Wood's health and reputation were brought low by the action. He was thrown out of his beloved university, and the pages his judges found libellous were burned by the hangman. One of his few remaining consolations lay in work, which still stretched endlessly in all mental directions. Another was in blaming his ruin on Aubrey, whom he now denounced as 'a shiftless person, roving and magotie-headed'. Most woundingly of all, he labelled his collaborator 'a pretender to Antiquities'.[20] Aubrey, characteristically humble, but also mortified and baffled, was hurt to the core when Wood returned a set of his manuscripts in mutilated state. Wood's motives, in fairness, were precautionary, in destroying material which could – and did – prove incriminating. Yet Aubrey was inconsolable. Then in his late sixties, he was appalled that Wood could destroy truthful work. 'Was ever any body so unkind?' protested Aubrey, in a stricken letter. 'I thought you so deare a friend that I might have entrusted my life in your hands and now your unkindnes doth almost break my heart.'[21]

Aubrey grieved bitterly for his lost friend and his lost pages – even though, on sending Wood his first brief 'minutes of lives' some twelve or more years earlier, he had in fact licensed him to censor passages that might be tetchily received: 'after your perusall,' he directed floridly, 'I must desire you to make a castration . . . and sowe on some figge-leaves – i.e., to be my *Index expurgatorius.*' The task of the antiquary was in short thankless: subjects would resent their 'castration' as much as they would having their 'shameful parts' exposed to public view:

What uncertainty doe we find in printed histories? they either treading too neer on the heeles of trueth that they dare not speake plaine, or els for want of intelligence (things being antiquated) become too obscure and darke![22]

Having already lost all he owned through the courts, Aubrey was in favour of leaving the lives he wrote un-neutered, and cleaving to the truth. He was not always capable, admittedly, of honouring his intentions: the waywardness of memory, lack of reliable sources, a strong imagination and a preference for a positive, forgiving slant on things interfered with strict accuracy. Yet we have his persistence to thank for preserving much of what we know about many of the people assembled in this book, and for presenting them free of their metaphorical fig-leaves.

Cavaliers and roundheads alike were being remade, and some were acquiring monumental bulk in the process. In separate party mythologies, the royalists would be cherished by the Tories as protectors of the monarchy and the old constitution; the rebels by the Whigs as defenders of Parliament and the rights of the common subject. Later generations sought to maintain the air of respectability, and in some cases heal the breach. The fictitious gentleman of Defoe's *Memoirs of a Cavalier* (1720) actually combines the virtues of a staunch royalist with those of a godly warrior, fighting for the Protestants in Europe before returning to defend his king. He is also, interestingly, a model son, 'extraordinarily caressed' by a fine upstanding father. On travelling abroad to pursue a career in arms, he is caught up and wounded in a duel in Paris, but only enters the fray to rescue his captain. Defoe's rendering of history ignored the profoundly depressing sense of shame, failure and uncertainty which followed the war, and doctored the associations of the cavalier. He catered to wishes like those of adolescents who wish their parents might behave a little more properly. For initially the cavaliers were reprobates and delinquents, prodigals: and if the term had a wider symbolism, it encompassed a generation of straying children who had squandered the Elizabethan and Jacobean inheritance of supposed peace and plenty which they still idealized so keenly.

The Whig and Tory versions of the wars are vital to an ongoing argument over what British history is really about – tradition or reform. Yet the original cavalier gallants, the courtiers often wrongly classified as roaring boys, offer a different lesson. Like Aubrey's *Lives*, the books of Carew, Suckling, Davenant and Herrick are more concerned with the idiosyncrasy and censored dimensions of human life from that time. The supporters of both Charles I and II needed 'cavalier' writing, poetry celebrating a many-pleasured lifestyle, merry and refined, aristocratic yet earthy. They needed confirmation that the old days were better. But their real legacy consisted in not quite conforming to type. On closer inspection, they were both more and less than real cavaliers. They offer a lasting suggestion of how, when a society cleaves into warring parties, people remain more complex than their partisan labels allow. Impure as puritans, often lacking as cavaliers, Aubrey's contemporaries retained human depths and edges in common; and it was these which allowed them to keep their scarred world running.

Notes

Place of publication is London unless otherwise specified.

List of abbreviations

Aubrey	*Brief Lives, Chiefly of Contemporaries, Set Down by John Aubrey, between the Years 1669 and 1696*, ed. A. Clark, 2 vols. (1898)
Beaurline	*The Works of Sir John Suckling*, 2 vols. (Oxford, 1971), II: *The Plays*, ed. L.A. Beaurline
Clayton	*The Works of Sir John Suckling*, 2 vols. (Oxford, 1971), I: *The Non-Dramatic Works*, ed. Thomas Clayton
CSPD	Calendar of State Papers, Public Record Office
Davenant, *Works*	*The Works of Sr William D'avenant K^t* [1673], 2 vols., in facsimile (1966). This edition, which may be taken to reflect Davenant's final intentions for his works, was clearly intended for issue in *three* volumes. Pagination starts over in vol. II after 486, with 'Newes from Plimouth'. The remaining III pages may then have been deemed too little to comprise a separate tome: however, for convenience, if somewhat unorthodoxly, I refer to text within this final section as forming vol. 'III' of the set.]
DNB	Oxford Dictionary of National Biography (new edn)
Dunlap	*The Poems of Thomas Carew*, ed. Rhodes Dunlap (Oxford, 1949)
Edmond	*Rare Sir William Davenant*, by Mary Edmond (Manchester, 1987)
Gibbs	*Sir William Davenant: The Shorter Poems, and Songs from the Plays and Masques*, ed. A.M. Gibbs (Oxford, 1972)
Herrick, *Poetical Works*	*The Poetical Works of Robert Herrick*, ed. F.W. Moorman (Oxford, 1921)
HMC	Historical Manuscripts Commission

Howell	*Epistolae Ho-elianae: The Familiar Letters of James Howell*, ed. J. Jacobs (1890)
Hyde, *History*	*The History of the Rebellion and Civil Wars in England* by Edward Hyde, Earl of Clarendon, ed. W. Dunn Macray, 6 vols. (repr. Oxford, 1958)
Hyde, *Life*	*The Life of Edward Earl of Clarendon*, 3 vols. (Oxford, 1827)
Jonson, *Complete Poems*	Ben Jonson, *Complete Poems*, ed. George Parfitt (Harmondsworth, 1975)
Knowler	*The Earl of Strafforde's Letters and Dispatches*, ed. William Knowler, 2 vols. (1739–40)
Lovelace, *Poems*	*The Poems of Richard Lovelace*, ed. C.H. Wilkinson (Oxford, 1930)
Nethercot	*Sir William D'Avenant: Poet Laureate and Playwright-Manager*, by Arthur H. Nethercot (Chicago, 1938)
Wariston, *Diary*	*The Diary of Sir Archibald Johnston of Wariston*, ed. G.M. Paul and others, 3 vols., Scottish History Society, 61, 2nd ser., 18, 3rd ser., 34 (1911–40)

Introduction

1. See Conrad Russell, 'The First Army Plot of 1641', in *Unrevolutionary England, 1603–1642* (1990), 281–302.

2. Hyde, *History*, I, 456.

3. Sir Philip Warwick, *Memoires of the Reigne of Charles I with a Continuation to the Happy Restoration of King Charles II* (1701), 64.

4. John Adamson, *The Noble Revolt: The Overthrow of Charles I* (2007), 279.

5. The key book on Caroline writers of the 1630s who were formerly described as cavaliers is Kevin Sharpe, *Criticism and Compliment: The Politics of Literature in the England of Charles I* (1987). For an idea of the heterogeneity of Charles's court see, for example, the multidisciplinary collection edited by Sharpe and Peter Lake, *Culture and Politics in Early Stuart England* (1994).

6. Davenant, 'Song ("The Lark")', Gibbs, 173.

7. Kevin Sharpe, *The Personal Rule of Charles I* (1992), 233.

8. Irwin Smith, *Shakespeare's Blackfriars Playhouse: Its History and Design* (1966), 491.

9. Davenant, *Newes from Plymouth*, *Works*, 'III', 2. The tavern bush was a garland of ivy (in honour of Bacchus) hung upon the door of a private house serving drinks during a fair.

10. Smith, *Shakespeare's Blackfriars Playhouse*, 493.

11. Smith, *Shakespeare's Blackfriars Playhouse*, 283, 264.

1. Fathers and Sons

1. On the character of St Giles-in-the-Fields, see Peter Ackroyd, *London: The Biography* (2000), 131–43.

2. Stow, *A Survey of London* [1603 text] (Sparkford, Somerset, 2005), 366.

3. Carew, 'The Spring', Dunlap, 3.

4. Howell, 69, 70.

5. Francisco de Quevedo, *Visions* [*Sueños*], trans. Sir Roger L'Estrange (Illinois, 1963), 39.

6. *The Prose Works of Sir Philip Sidney*, Albert Feuillerat (ed.), 4 vols. (Cambridge, 1962–3), III, 124–5.

7. See Dunlap, xix, and the letter by Carew printed on 202–3.

8. Dunlap, xiv.

9. Alfred Inigo Suckling, *History and Antiquities of the County of Suffolk*, 2 vols. (1846), I, 35–46; Clayton, xxvii–xxviii.

10. Dunlap, xxii–xxiii.

11. Dunlap, 202.

12. Dunlap, xxv.

13. Dunlap, xxvi.

14. John Chamberlain, writing in fact to Carew's former master, Carleton, on 26 October; cited in Dunlap, xxix–xxx.

15. Dunlap, xxvii–xxviii.

16. Howell, 43–50.

17. On Davenant's parents and early life, see Edmond, 10–26; Nethercot, 21–37.

18. Edmond, 27; Nethercot, 39.

19. Edmond, 29: virtually any conjecture by this meticulous researcher and eminently sensible writer is worth heeding.

20. Aubrey, I, 205.

21. Odell Shepherd, *The Lore of the Unicorn* (1930; repr. 1968), 113–18; John Webster, *The White Devil*, 2.1.14–16.

22. Davenant, '*The First Dayes* Entertainment *at* Rutland-House, *by* Declamations *and* Musick', *Works*, I, 351–2.

23. Stow, *Survey of London*, 36.

24. Aubrey, I, 204; Edmond, 14; Nethercot, 16.

25. Aubrey, II, 204.

26. Davenant, 'Preface to *Gondibert*', *Works*, I, 11–12.

27. Suckling, 'Whether These Lines Do Find You Out' [variously titled 'A Summons to Town' and 'An Epistle'], Clayton, 70.

28. Jonson, 'On the Famous Voyage' (*Epigrams*, 133) (ll. 146–9), *Complete Poems*, 90.

29. Jonson, *Underwoods*, no. 88, in *Complete Poems*, 62.

30. Ian Donaldson, 'Benjamin Jonson' ('Early Life'), *DNB*.

31. Jonson, *Discoveries* (ll. 1872–5), in *Complete Poems*, 419. But on Jonson's mixed feelings towards the visual arts – and the visual side of theatre – see Stephen Orgel and Roy Strong, *Inigo Jones: The Theatre of the Royal Court*, 2 vols. (1973), I, 2–6.

32. Jonson, *Discoveries* (ll. 714–18), in *Complete Poems*, 392.

33. See Arthur Terry, 'Theory and Practice' in *Seventeenth-Century Spanish Poetry: The Power of Artifice* (1993), 56.

34. John Donne, 'Obsequies to the Lord Harington' (ll. 133–9).

35. Donne mentions 'that Strykinge clocke which I ordinarilye weare' in his will, bequeathing it to Sir Thomas Grymes (see the transcript in R.C. Bald, *John Donne: A Life* [1970], 563). Such watches (on the model of the *Taschenuhr* developed by Peter Henlein) had been available in London since the early sixteenth century.

36. Jonson, *Conversations* (ll. 119–22, 109–11), in *Complete Poems*, 464.

37. Jonson, *Conversations* (ll. 187–8), in *Complete Poems*, 466.

38. Hyde, *Life*, I, 34.

39. Jonson, 'To the Memory of My Beloved, the Author William Shakespeare' (ll. 59–61), *Complete Poems*, 264.

40. Jonson, *Discoveries* (ll. 1137–8), in *Complete Poems*, 392.

41. See Ian Donaldson's marvellous *DNB* entry, 'Ben Jonson' ('The Middle Years').

42. The 'Conversations with William Drummond' can be found in *Complete Poems*, 459–80.

43. Jonson, *Conversations* (ll. 681–90), *Complete Poems*, 479.

44. Jonson, 'An Expostulation with Inigo Jones' (ll. 69–70), *Complete Poems*, 346.

45. Jonson, *Discoveries* (l. 1), *Complete Poems*, 375.

46. Jonson, 'An Epistle, Answering to One that Asked to be Sealed of the Tribe of Ben' (ll. 9–10), *Complete Poems*, 191.

47. Jonson, *Conversations* (ll. 294–302), *Complete Poems*, 469.

48. Jonson, 'An Epistle to One that Asked to be Sealed of the Tribe of Ben' (ll. 59–61), *Complete Poems*, 193.

49. Jonson, *Sejanus*, I, 376–7.

50. Jonson, *Sejanus*, V, 820–22.

51. Hyde, *Life*, I, 41.

52. Jonson, *Discoveries* (ll. 68–73), *Complete Poems*, 376.

2. *The Quixotic Prince*

1. Howell, 151.

2. Howell, 73.

3. Howell, 17–18.

4. Howell, 154.

5. Howell, 164.

6. Anonymous, *The Spanish Pilgrime: Or an Admirable Discovery of a Romish Catholicke* (1625), title page.

7. H. Hexam, *An Experimentall Discoverie of Spanish Practises or The Counsell of a Well-Wishing Souldier* (1623), I, 32.

8. See R.C. Bald, *Donne and the Drurys* (1959), 153.

9. Hyde, *History*, I, 16–21; the king's words, of course, are largely hearsay and Hyde's invention.

10. Hyde, *History*, I, 22.

11. Comments by Orazio Busoni, chaplain to the Venetian ambassador, quoted by Stephen Orgel in *The Jonsonian Masque* (1965), 70–71.

12. James I and VI, 'A Meditation upon the 27. 28. 29 Verses of the XXII. Chapter of Saint Matthew', *Political Writings*, ed. Johann P. Somerville (1994; repr. 2001), 229–30.

13. James I and VI, *Basilikon Doron*, *Political Writings*, I.

14. Such episodes were a standard of Spanish romance: some readers may recall Don Quixote's rueful appeal to the example of Diego Pérez de Vargos in Part I, chapter 8, after his encounter with the windmills.

15. Howell, 166.

16. Howell, 57.

17. Howell, 95–6.

18. Howell, 57.

19. Howell, 166.

20. Howell, 175.

21. Howell, 291–2.

22. J. Wadsworth, *The Present Estate of Spayne*, 2nd edn (1630), 61–5.

23. Howell, 183.

24. Howell, 155; Wadsworth, *The Present Estate of Spayne*, 74.

25. Michel de Montaigne, *Essayes*, trans. John Florio, 3 vols. (Everyman edn, 1910), 'Of Cruelty', II, 114.

26. Wadsworth, *The Present Estate of Spayne*, 73–4.

27. Howell, 59.

28. Dorothea Townshend, *The Life and Letters of Endymion Porter* (1897), 44, 47.

29. Townshend, *Endymion Porter*, 50, 48.

30. Townshend, *Endymion Porter*, 47.

31. Howell, 120.

32. On Quevedo's presence in Madrid during the prince's courtship see Glynn Redworth, *The Prince and the Infanta: The Cultural Politics of the Spanish Match* (2003), 114–15.

33. Terry, *Seventeenth-Century Spanish Poetry*, 4. See too Terry's discussion of the underlying interdependence between the 'high' mode of *culteranismo* and the more conceited, irony-laden tendencies of *conceptismo* (the style associated, often wrongly, with Quevedo in Spanish and the followers of Donne in English), 53–7; his chapter on 'Theory and Practice' (and more largely the book as a whole) offers one of the best recent synopses of critical thought on the seventeenth-century conceit.

34. Townshend, *Endymion Porter*, 48–9.

35. Howell, 170–71.

36. Francisco de Quevedo, *Historia de la vída del Buscón* (1.10), published in 1626 although written over twenty years before: for a lively if problematic translation see Francisco Villamiquel y Hardin, *Don Pablos the Sharper* (1928) (for the 'decree', see 90–95).

37. Howell, 171.

38. See Simon Barton, *A History of Spain*, 2nd edn (2009), 72. For a summary of the wider European context of such grants of privilege, see J.C. Holt, *Magna Carta*, 2nd edn (1992), 25–6.

39. *Every Man in His Humour*, 2.2.26. For a sense of the fairly standard sort of character the word invoked, compare *2 Henry IV* 5.3.57–8.
40. Edmund Verney, eventually the king's standard-bearer.
41. Howell, 187.
42. Howell, 183.
43. Sir John Summerson, *Architecture in Britain 1530–1830* (1953), 107.
44. Howell, 178–9.
45. Howell, 192–3.
46. Howell, 233.
47. Howell, 239.

3. The End of Steenie

1. Sharpe, *Personal Rule*, 14 (citing *CSPD 1627–8*, 409).
2. *CSPD 1627–8*, 182; see Clayton, xxx.
3. Sir John Oglander, *A Royalist's Notebook*, ed. Francis Bamford (1932), 41.
4. Howell, 54.
5. Howell, 251.
6. Oglander, *Royalist's Notebook*, 28.
7. Howell, 251.
8. Edward, Lord Herbert of Cherbury, *The Expedition to the Ile of Rhe* (1860), 241.
9. From Denzil Holles's description of the trouble caused by the mission, printed in Knowler, I, 41–2.
10. Herbert, *Expedition to the Ile of Rhe*, 284–5.
11. Suckling, 'A Dreame', Clayton, 13.
12. Aubrey, II, 241.
13. Oglander, *Royalist's Notebook*, 75.
14. Oglander, *Royalist's Notebook*, 49; see also 192.
15. Oglander, *Royalist's Notebook*, 89–90.
16. Herrick, 'Corinna's Going a Maying' (ll. 43–50), *Poetical Works*, 69.
17. Jonson, *Explorata* (ll. 2570–72), *Complete Poems*, 436.
18. Herrick, 'Corinna's Going a Maying' (ll. 5–9), *Poetical Works*, 68.
19. Alfred Pollard, 'Life of Herrick', in *Hesperides and Noble Numbers*, 2 vols. (Aberdeen, 1891–2), I, xv–xxvi; Tom Cain, 'Robert Herrick', *DNB*.
20. Herrick, 'An Ode for Him [Jonson]'('Ah Ben!'), *Poetical Works*, 282.

21. Herrick, 'To the Virgins, to Make Much of Time', *Poetical Works*, 84.

22. Herrick, 'To the High and Noble Prince, GEORGE, Duke, Marquesse and Earle of Buckingham', *Poetical Works*, 99.

23. Herrick, 'Duty to Tyrants', *Poetical Works*, 33.

24. Herrick, 'The Difference Betwixt Kings and Subjects', *Poetical Works*, 12.

25. Herrick, 'Pollicie in Princes', *Poetical Works*, 162.

26. Hyde, *History*, I, 51–3.

27. Hyde, *History*, I, 30.

28. Hyde, *History*, I, 28.

29. Hyde, *History*, I, 29.

30. Howell, 217.

31. Howell, 232.

32. Hyde, *History*, I, 55.

33. See Roger Lockyer, 'George Villiers, First Duke of Buckingham', a timely retrospective on his biography, *Buckingham: The Life and Career of George Villiers* (1981), *DNB* (in particular with reference to Buckingham's approach to the Admiralty, see 359–68).

34. J. Rushworth, *Historical Collections* (1721 edn), I, 618; quoted by Roger Lockyer in his *DNB* article on the duke. See also Alastair Bellany, 'John Felton', *DNB*.

35. Oglander, 'Murder of the Duke of Buckingham', *Royalist's Notebook*, 34–42.

36. For the contemporary sense that this was so, see Sharpe, *Personal Rule*, 49–50.

37. Sir Charles Petrie, ed., *Letters, Speeches and Proclamations of Charles I* (1935), 40–41.

38. Petrie, *Letters, Speeches and Proclamations*, 40.

39. Townshend, *Endymion Porter*, 82.

40. Howell, 238.

41. Mary Anne Everett Green, ed., *Letters of Queen Henrietta Maria* (1857), 9–10.

42. Townshend, *Endymion Porter*, 83.

43. Edmond, 30.

44. Jonson, *Conversations* (ll. 223–4) in *Complete Poems*, 467.

45. Aubrey, I, 205.

46. Oglander, *Royalist's Notebook*, 230.

47. Hyde, *Life*, I, 75–6.

48. A line from Jonson's *Every Man in His Humour* [1616 version] 3.5.9. The *reformados* had been stock characters in London life for a generation.

49. *CSPD 1628–9*, 435, dated 'abt 1628': quoted by Alfred Harbage, *Sir William Davenant: Poet Venturer 1606–1668* (Philadelphia, 1935), 38. It was assumed at one time that Davenant *had* (along with his friend Sir John Suckling) gone on the island mission; this is shrewdly and succinctly cleared up by Edmond, 35–6.

50. James Heath, *Flagellum, or the Life and Death, Birth and Burial of Oliver Cromwell, the Late Usurper* (2nd edn, 1663), 8; quoted by Amanda Frasier, *Cromwell: Our Chief of Men* (1993 edn), 28.

51. Hyde, *Life*, 75–6.

52. Oglander, *Royalist's Notebook*, 26, 43, 46.

53. Petrie, *Letters, Speeches and Proclamations*, 75.

54. Herrick, 'An Ode to Master Endymion Porter, upon his Brothers Death', *Poetical Works*, 72.

55. Herrick, 'To His Dying Brother, Master William Herrick', *Poetical Works*, 72–3.

56. Davenant, 'To Endimion Porter, Passing to Court to Him, by Water', Gibbs, 59.

57. Oglander, *Royalist's Notebook*, 61.

58. *CSPD, 1628–9*, 393, 412; quoted by Sharpe, *Personal Rule*, 171.

59. Davenant, *The Tragedy of Albovine, King of Lombardy, Works*, II, 425.

60. Sharpe, '"A Rule of Order in His Own House": The Reformation of the Court and Administration', *Personal Rule*, 209–74; especially 209–22, 242–9.

61. Townshend, *Endymion Porter*, 98.

62. Green, *Letters of Henrietta Maria*, 18.

4. Dancing to the Drum

1. Fulke Greville, *The Life of the Renowned Sr Philip Sidney*, in *Prose Works*, ed. John Gouws (1986), 77.

2. Jonson, 'An Epistle to a Friend, to Persuade Him to the Wars', *Complete Poems*, 150.

3. John Donne, *Letters to Severall Personnages of Honour* (1651), 211.

4. Jonson, 'An Epistle to a Friend, to Persuade Him to the Wars,' *Complete Poems*, 151.

5. H. Hexham, *A Historicall Relation of the Famous Siege of the Busse* (1630), 8.

6. Hexham, *Historicall Relation*, A3^r.

7. Hexham, *Historicall Relation*, 9.

8. Hexham, *Historicall Relation*, 20.

9. Hexham, *Historicall Relation*, 14.

10. Hexham, *Historicall Relation*, 17–18.

11. Hexham, *Historicall Relation*, 31.

12. On the somewhat puzzling sequence of Suckling's travels see Herbert Berry, *Sir John Suckling's Poems and Letters from Manuscript* (Ontario, 1960), 50, and Clayton, xxxi, and 'Sir John Suckling', *DNB* ('Education, Military Service and Travel Abroad, 1623–1632').

13. Suckling, 'To Mary Cranfield, 30 October 1629', Clayton, 107, and *Times Literary Supplement*, 29 January 1960, 68.

14. Suckling, 'A Candle', Clayton, 19.

15. Suckling, 'To Mary Cranfield', Clayton, 109.

16. Howell, 32, 127.

17. Suckling to 'Will' [Davenant or Wallis], from Leiden ('Leydon', erroneously printed as 'London' in early editions of Suckling's 'Fragments'), 18 November 1629; Clayton, 112–13.

18. Thomas Clayton, *DNB* entry on Suckling, 'Education, Military Service and Travel Abroad, 1623–1632'. See also K. van Strien, 'Sir John Suckling in Holland', *English Studies*, 78 (1995), 443–54.

19. Suckling to 'Will', Brussels, 5 May 1630, Clayton, 116–18: also printed in Berry, *Poems and Letters from Manuscript*, 60–62. Clayton and Berry observe that the holograph of this letter (in the Sackville mss) shows the recipient was one William Wallis, a gentleman in the service of Suckling's uncle the Earl of Middlesex, whom Clayton and Berry deduced to be the 'Will' addressed in the earlier letter from Leiden. In the nineteenth century, however, W.C. Hazlitt (*Works of Sir John Suckling*, 2 vols. [1892]) suggested that in November 1629 Suckling had in fact been writing to William Davenant. Clayton (310) and Berry (*Poems and Letters from Manuscript*, 51) rejected this conjecture on the grounds of stylistic parallels, in particular the recurring joke about Judas. That recurrence, however, suggests in itself that the first letter was addressed to a William other than Wallis (if not necessarily Davenant); since, unless Suckling simply forgot he had already used that witticism on Wallis, it looks like the negligent recycling of material.

20. Jonson, 'An Epistle to a Friend, to Persuade Him to the Wars', *Complete Poems*, 151.

21. Brussels, 3 May 1630, letter 10 in Clayton, ed., *Works*, 114–16; Berry, *Poems and Letters from Manuscript*, 56–9.

22. Davenant, *Gondibert*, 3.6.31–3, *Works*, I, 191.

23. Davenant, *Gondibert*, 3.6.41, *Works*, I, 192.

24. Davenant, *Gondibert*, 3.6.34, *Works*, I, 191.

25. John Denham et al., *Certain Verses Written by Severall of the Authors Friends, To be Re-printed with the Second Edition of Gondibert* (1653), 24.

26. Baldassare Castiglione, *The Book of the Courtier, Done into English by Sir Thomas Hoby* [1569] (Everyman edn, 1920), 150.

27. Davenant, *The Cruel Brother*, 5.1, in James Maidment and W.H. Logan, eds, *The Dramatic Works of Sir William D'Avenant, with Prefatory Memoirs and Notes*, 5 vols. (1872–4), 181–2.

28. Even Davenant seems to have found the scene too horrible. For the revised prose version of the play eventually printed in his *Works* (II, 482), the image of lute-strings in the fireplace was cut: 'The torture's past. Thy wrist Veins are cut. Here in this Bason bleed away thy soul.'

29. Davenant, *Albovine*, *Works*, II, 430.

30. Davenant, 'To the Duchess of Buckingham', *Works*, I, 320.

31. Davenant, 'To the King on Newyeares Day, 1630'; 'To Him who Prophecy'd a Successes End of the Parliament, in the year 1630': *Works*, I, 220, 287–8.

32. William Clowers, *A Short and Profitable Treatise Touching the Cure of the Disease Called (Morbus Gallicus)* quoted by Gibbs, Commentary, 375–6; see also Nethercot, 92.

33. Nethercot, 94.

34. Quoted by Gibbs, 376.

35. Davenant, 'To Doctor Cademan, Physitian to the Queen', *Works*, I, 234–5.

36. Quoted in Jonathan Burton's excellent study *Traffic and Turning: Islam and English Drama 1579–1624* (Delaware, 2005), 34.

37. Edmond, 45.

38. Davenant, 'To I.C. Robbed by His Man Andrew', *Works*, I, 229.

39. Davenant, 'To Endimion Porter', *Works*, I, 217.

40. Quoted by Nethercot, 90.

41. Berry felt the 'eventual association' dated only from '1637 and after' (*Poems and Letters from Manuscript*, 51), but to most of the other authorities this seems too late. Nethercot surmised that Davenant and Suckling met at the

Inns of Court in 1627 or 1628 (68–9), and (much more reliably) Edmond also seems to support an earlier date for the beginnings of the friendship (37). My own guess would be that the two got to know each other properly when Davenant's first real success on the stage, *The Wits*, brought him fame in 1633.

42. Letter 15, Clayton, 122. No holograph of this letter survives, and its date is uncertain. Clayton tentatively ascribes it to 'November 1631', but suggests it could have been written as late as 1637 (see his commentary, 314).

43. Howell, 301; his account of the 'thirty-five healths' with Leicester, in which the earl 'bore up stoutly all the while', at 295.

44. Suckling to Mary Cranfield, 5–10 October 1631, Clayton, 110.

45. Hyde, *History*, II, 548–9.

46. The first quotation is from Letter 15 in Clayton, 121, printed without date and addressee in *Fragmenta Aurea*; Clayton's guess that the letter was for Middlesex and written in the autumn of 1631 is borne out by the second quotation, from a letter addressed and dated 9 November (Letter 14 in Clayton, 120; also printed in Berry, *Poems and Letters from Manuscript*, 68–72).

47. Howell, 301.

48. Suckling to the Earl of Middlesex, 9 November 1631, Clayton, 119–20; Berry, *Poems and Letters from Manuscript*, 68–72.

49. Suckling to an unidentified nobleman, October 1631, Clayton, 119.

50. Quoted in Michael Roberts, *Gustavus Adolphus: A History of Sweden 1611–1631*, 2 vols. (1953), I, 787.

51. Suckling to Middlesex, Clayton, 120; Berry, *Poems and Letters from Manuscript*, 70.

52. Suckling to the Earl of Middlesex, 29 November 1631, Clayton, 123; Berry, *Poems and Letters from Manuscript*, 74–6.

53. Roberts, *Gustavus Adolphus*, I, 611.

54. Suckling to an unidentified nobleman, Clayton, 119.

55. Suckling to 'Mr Gifford', December 1631, Clayton, 125–6.

56. Suckling to Sir Henry Vane, 2 May 1632, Clayton, 126–9.

57. Roberts, *Gustavus Adolphus*, II, 614.

58. Howell, 305–6.

59. Howell, 305.

60. Davenant, 'To the Lady Bridget Kingsmill', *Works*, I, 219–20.

61. Suckling to Mary Cranfield, '1629–1635 (?)', Clayton, 109.

62. Davenant, 'To Endymion Porter', *Works*, I, 233.

63. Edmond, 47; Nethercot, 99.

64. Davenant, 'A Journey into Worcestershire', *Works*, I, 215.

65. Davenant, 'To Endymion Porter', *Works*, I, 223.

66. *The Life of Edward, First Lord Herbert of Cherbury, Written by Himself*, ed. J.M. Shuttleworth (1976), 41–2, 47.

67. E.K. Chambers, ed., *Aurelian Townshend's Poems and Masks* (1912), 38.

68. Chambers, *Aurelian Townshend's Poems and Masks*, xxiv; Peter Beal, 'Aurelian Townshend', *DNB*.

69. Appendix D: 'Poems and Letters Addressed to Carew', Dunlap, 207–8.

70. See Kevin Sharpe's excellent chapter on Townshend 'and the poetry of natural innocence' in *Criticism and Compliment*, 152–78.

71. Carew, 'In Answer of an Elegiacall Letter . . .' (ll. 16–25), Dunlap, 77.

72. Davenant, 'The Wits', *Works*, II, 168–9.

73. Suckling, 'Upon T.C. Having the P.', Clayton, 32; see commentary, 239.

5. Backslidings

1. Wariston, *Diary*, I, 4.

2. Wariston, *Diary*, I, 61.

3. Wariston, *Diary*, I, 6.

4. Wariston, *Diary*, I, 8.

5. Sir William Brereton, 'Travels', in *Early Travellers in Scotland*, ed. P. Hume Brown (Edinburgh, 1978), 143–4.

6. Wariston, *Diary*, I, 11–12.

7. Wariston, *Diary*, I, 12–13.

8. Brereton, 'Travels', *Early Travellers in Scotland*, 134.

9. On this moment see Sharpe, *Personal Rule*, 779.

10. Hyde, *Life*, I, 19.

11. Sir Anthony Weldon [?], 'A Perfect Description of the People and Country of Scotland', Brereton, *Early Travellers in Scotland*, 97.

12. Brereton, 'Travels', *Early Travellers in Scotland*, 140, 142.

13. Hyde, *History*, I, 69–70.

14. Geoffrey Trease, *Portrait of a Cavalier: William Cavendish, First Duke of Newcastle* (1979), 66.

15. Sharpe, *Personal Rule*, 779.

16. 'In this house the king lodged three nights': Brereton, 'Travels', *Early Travellers in Scotland*, 136.

17. John Spalding, *The History of the Troubles and Memorable Transactions in Scotland and England*, 2 vols. (Edinburgh, 1828), I, 15–16.

18. Spalding, *The History of the Troubles*, I, 20–22.

19. Wariston, *Diary*, I, 15, 16.

20. Wariston, *Diary*, I, 35.

21. Wariston, *Diary*, I, 31.

22. Wariston, *Diary*, I, 45.

23. I'm most grateful to David Colclough for his thoughts and assistance on this passage, which inevitably generalizes a vast range of responses across Europe to Calvin and his followers. An excellent starting place for those interested in pursuing the detail of these beliefs is Diarmaid MacCulloch's majestic *Reformation: Europe's House Divided 1490–1700* (2003). On the first fracture lines between attitudes to salvation and the sacraments see especially 106–57.

24. Wariston, *Diary*, I, 31.

25. Blaise Pascal, *Thoughts on Religion* [*Pensées*], trans. Basil Kennett, ed. Sir John Lubbock (1893), 67.

26. Wariston, *Diary*, I, 17.

27. Knowler, I, 207; quoted in Dunlap, 274.

28. Aurelian Townshend, *Tempe Restored*, 'The Description of the Scene' (ll. 49–50); Orgel and Strong, *Inigo Jones*, II, 480.

29. Jonson, 'To a Friend, an Epigram of Him' ('Sir Inigo Doth Fear It as I Hear'), *Complete Poems*, 348–9.

30. Carew, *Coelum Britannicum*, 'The Description of the Scæne', Dunlap, 153–4.

31. On the importance of the king and queen's position at the masque see Stephen Orgel, *The Illusion of Power: Political Theater in the English Renaissance* (Berkeley, 1975), 14–16.

32. Carew, *Coelum Britannicum* (ll. 70–71; 84–5; 90–100), Dunlap, 155.

33. Howell, 317–18.

34. Davenant, 'The Platonick Lovers', *Works*, II, 393.

35. Hyde, *Life*, I, 14–16.

36. Carew, *Coelum Britannicum* (ll. 56–60), 154.

37. Carew, 'A Rapture' (ll. 119–20, 108–9), Dunlap, 52.

38. Carew, 'A Rapture' (ll. 49–50), Dunlap, 50.

39. J.E. Ruoff, 'Thomas Carew's Early Reputation', *Notes and Queries*, 202 (1957), 61–2.

40. William Prynne, *Histriomastix, The Players Scourge or Actors Tragedie* (1633), 2.

41. Prynne, *Histriomastix*, 962.

42. Prynne, *Histriomastix*, 858.

43. Prynne, *Histriomastix*, 410.

44. Prynne, *Histriomastix*, 193.

45. Suckling, 'Loves World', Clayton, 24.

46. William Lamont, 'William Prynne', *DNB*.

47. J.Q. Adams, ed., *The Dramatic Records of Sir Henry Herbert 1623–1673* (New Haven, 1917), 22.

48. Sharpe, *Personal Rule*, 190, 192.

49. Adams, *Dramatic Records of Sir Henry Herbert*, 54.

50. Sharpe, *Criticism and Compliment*, 215.

51. Sharpe, *Personal Rule*, 233.

52. Carew, *Coelum Britannicum* (ll. 175, 227), Dunlap, 156, 159.

53. Carew, *Coelum Britannicum* (ll. 228–87), Dunlap, 159–60.

54. Carew, *Coelum Britannicum* (ll. 188–94), Dunlap, 158.

55. Carew, *Coelum Britannicum* (ll. 892–6), Dunlap, 176.

56. Carew, *Coelum Britannicum* (ll. 951–6, 972–3), Dunlap, 179.

57. Carew, *Coelum Britannicum* (ll. 1011–20, 1049–50), Dunlap, 181, 182.

58. Carew, *Coelum Britannicum* (ll. 1049–50), Dunlap, 182–3.

59. Adams, *Dramatic Records of Sir Henry Herbert*, 55.

60. Knowler, I, 177.

61. Lucy Hutchinson, *Memoirs of the Life of John Hutchinson*, ed. N.H. Keeble (1995), 63.

62. Aubrey, II, 241.

63. Petrie, *Letters, Speeches and Proclamations*, 82.

64. Howell, 280.

65. Suckling to Sir Kenelm Digby, '18–30 November 1634', Clayton, 130.

66. Clayton, introduction, xxxvii; *HMC, Various Collections*, VII, 406–7. For Garrard's account of the affair, see Knowler, I, 336–7.

67. Aubrey, II, 241.

68. Samuel Butler, *Hudibras* (2.1.230–34), ed. John Wilders (1967), 107.

69. Aubrey, II, 244.

70. Petrie, *Letters, Speeches and Proclamations*, 82.

71. 'To Charles I from Sir Henry Willoughby, 31 October 1634'; in Clayton, Appendix A, 195.

72. Suckling, 'Loves Sanctuary', Clayton, 50–51.

73. Suckling, 'Against Fruition [I]', Clayton, 37.
74. Clayton, xxxv; Berry, *Poems and Letters in Manuscript*, 94.
75. Aubrey, II, 241.
76. Suckling to Anne Willoughby, 'Autumn 1633', Clayton, 129.
77. Printed in Clayton, Appendix A, 194.
78. Hutchinson, *Memoirs*, 70.
79. Suckling, 'A Session of the Poets' (l. 66), Clayton, 74.
80. Suckling [and Carew?], 'Upon My Lady Carliles Walking in Hampton-Court Garden: Dialogue/ T.C. [and] J.S.', Clayton, 31–2.
81. Suckling [and Carew?], 'A Letter to a Friend to Diswade Him from Marrying a Widow' and 'An Answer to the Letter', Dunlap, 211–12. Dunlap follows the format in Suckling's *Fragmenta Aurea*, printing the letters in adjacent columns.
82. Carew, 'The Second Rapture', Dunlap, 103.
83. Carew, 'The Second Rapture', Dunlap, 104.
84. Hyde, *History*, I, 318.
85. Aubrey, II, 241.
86. Charles Cotton, *The Compleat Gambler*, in J. Isaacs, ed., *Games and Gamesters of the Restoration* (1930), 1.
87. Cotton, *The Compleat Gambler*, 11.
88. Aubrey, 294.
89. Aubrey, II, 245.
90. Linda Levy Peck, *Consuming Splendour: Society and Culture in Seventeenth-Century England* (Cambridge, 2005), citing Bodleian ms, Bankes 14, 2.
91. On the solution advanced by Luther to this antinomian problem see MacCulloch, *Reformation*, 130.
92. Aubrey, II, 241.
93. Hutchinson, *Memoirs*, 69.
94. Knowler, I, 111.

6. Blind Mouths

1. Thomas Fuller, *The Worthies of England*, ed. John Freeman (1952), 346.
2. Howell, 403–4.
3. Davenant, 'The Long Vacation in London, in Verse Burlesque, or Mock-Verse', in Gibbs, 125–30 (quotation from 129). Gibbs prints both the 1673

and 1656 versions of the poem, which by Nethercot's reckoning dates from 1635 (see Nethercot, 125–8 and Gibbs's commentary, 403).

4. Fuller, *Worthies*, 603.

5. Joan Parkes, *Travel in England in the Seventeenth Century* (1925), 65–6.

6. Davenant, 'The Wits' (2.1), *Works*, II, 179, in a passage reworked, embellished by times and contracted at others, with every revival and reprinting of the play; quoted here from Davenant's final revision. Mary Edmond compellingly suggests that Davenant's scorn for the rustic dates from his enforced exile in the country during his illness and convalescence (Edmond, 48). Luce's speech and similar passages also voice a standard urban attitude, anticipating that of much Restoration comedy. It is interesting, though, that the lines quoted hardly have an *urbane* polish; the three successive caesurae give them a rougher lilt, splitting each line into a lop-sided lyric. When one listens closely, they have the rhythm of a metrically uneven country ballad.

7. A.B. Grossart, ed., *Annalia Dubrensia, or A Celebration of Captain Robert Dover's Cotswold Games* (1877), ix–x.

8. Davenant, Gibbs, 53–4. The poem was first printed anonymously (see Grossart, ed., *Annalia Dubrensia*, 71–2) but although 'Sung by a Poet that Conceals His Name' (l. 33) was included in Davenant's *Madagascar* and later collections.

9. Jonson, 'An Epigram to My Jovial Good Friend Mr Robert Dover . . .', *Collected Poems*, 277–8.

10. Grossart, *Annalia Dubrensia*, ix.

11. 'The King's Majesty's Declaration to His Subjects Concerning Lawful Sports to be Used' (1633).

12. See Aubrey, II, 243.

13. The marble bust, based on van Dyck's famous 'triple portrait' of Charles, arrived at Oatlands on 17 July (see Sir Oliver Millar, *Van Dyck in England* (1982), 65–6, and 94; Jeremy Wood, 'Sir Anthony van Dyck', *DNB*).

14. Knowler, II, 114.

15. Suckling, '[The Wits] A Sessions of the Poets' (ll. 17–24), Clayton, 72.

16. Suckling, '[The Wits] A Sessions of the Poets' (ll. 33–8), Clayton, 72–3.

17. Suckling, '[The Wits] A Sessions of the Poets' (ll. 44–8), Clayton, 73.

18. Thomas Clayton's reading of the ballad (71–6), the text followed here, is the strongest attempt to systematize its stanzas. See his commentary, 266–78.

19. Suckling, '[The Wits] A Sessions of the Poets' (l. 57), Clayton, 73.

20. Aubrey, I, 262.

21. See Aubrey, I, 262; Gordon Campbell, 'Alexander Gill the Younger', *DNB*.

22. Suckling, '[The Wits] A Sessions of the Poets' (ll. 101–2), Clayton, 75.

23. Suckling, 'Epistle' to Edward Sackville, Earl of Dorset, in *Account of Religion by Reason: A Discourse upon Occasion Presented to the Earl of Dorset*, in Clayton, 169.

24. Aubrey, I, 150.

25. Suckling, '[The Wits] A Sessions of the Poets' (l. 108), Clayton, 76.

26. Knowler, II, 99; Peter Heylyn, *Cyprianus Anglicus or the History of the Life and Death of William Laud* (1668), 313. See Sharpe's discussion of these and other reactions in Sharpe, *Personal Rule*, 763–5.

27. The charge of humourlessness was Anthony à Wood's; see Edmond, 64.

28. Edmond, 35.

29. Clayton, xl–xli.

30. Suckling to Mary and Lady Anne Bulkeley, Winter 1635?, 'For the Two Excellent Sisters', Clayton, 134.

31. Suckling to Mary Bulkeley, 1636–39, Clayton, 136.

32. Suckling to Mary Bulkeley, 1636–39, Clayton, 138.

33. Suckling, 'To T.C.', Dunlap, 213 (see also introduction, xxxviii). Carew was evidently staying at the home of his distant relative, Carew Raleigh, at West Horsley. Suckling's references to love ebbing and flowing recall or allude to one of his songs, 'No No Faire Heretique' (Clayton, 63; see commentary, 331).

34. Suckling to Mary Bulkeley, 1636–39, Clayton, 135.

35. Suckling to Mary and Lady Anne Bulkeley, Winter 1635?, 'For the Two Excellent Sisters', Clayton, 133–4.

36. Suckling to Martha Lady Carey, Spring 1635, Clayton, 130.

37. Aubrey, II, 244. Although the *Account* certainly does have an air of haste, it may not have been written from scratch in West Kington, and was apparently not completed there: the text is dated at Bath. In the opening 'Epistle' to Lord Sackville, Suckling says the work has been 'enlarged' from an earlier essay, drafted or at least discussed, which had upset his wife the countess (Clayton, 169).

38. Suckling, *An Account of Religion by Reason* (ll. 7–9), Clayton, 170.

39. Suckling, *An Account of Religion* (ll. 51–3, 67–9), Clayton, 171–2.

40. Suckling, *An Account of Religion* (ll. 164–6), Clayton, 174.

41. Suckling, *An Account of Religion* (ll. 159–63), Clayton, 174.

42. Suckling, *An Account of Religion* (ll. 178–82), Clayton, 175.

43. Suckling, *An Account of Religion* (ll. 287–300), Clayton, 178.

44. Suckling, *An Account of Religion* (l. 321), Clayton, 179.

45. Suckling, *An Account of Religion* (ll. 378–84), Clayton, 180.

46. Knowler, I, 365.

47. For material relating to King and poems not included in *Justa Edouardo King* see Norman Postlethwaite and Gordon Campbell, 'Edward King, Milton's "Lycidas": Poems and Documents', *Milton Quarterly* 28.4 (1994).

48. Sharpe, *Personal Rule*, 384.

49. Milton, 'Lycidas', ll. 119–21.

50. Milton, 'Lycidas', ll. 190–93.

51. William Riley Parker, *Milton: A Biography*, ed. Gordon Campbell, 2 vols. (1996), I, 584.

52. Parker, *Milton*, I, 577–8.

53. Clayton, 186; for attribution see commentary, 340.

54. Suckling, 'A Prologue of the Author's to a Masque at Wiston', Clayton, 28. The lines 'answer' the song by Suckling, 'Why So Pale and Wan, Fond Lover?' (Clayton, 64).

55. See David Norbrook, 'The Reformation of the Masque', in *The Court Masque*, ed. David Lindley (Manchester, 1984), 94–110; the argument is taken further by Barbara K. Lewalski, 'Milton's Comus and the Politics of Masquing', in *The Politics of the Stuart Court Masque* (1999), ed. David Bevington, 296–320.

56. Although it needs pointing out that when we read of 'blind mouths' we enter another verbal universe from that run on Jonsonian laws of clarity and aptitude. Properly or even metaphorically speaking, it can never be said that mouths are blind. In rhetoric, the expression falls under the domain of *catachresis*, or *abusio*, the deliberate misuse of a word; and also that of a more complex figure, *metalepsis* (expressing something via another thing to which it bears only slight relation). The phrase works by what Jorge Luis Borges identified as a typically Miltonic trick with adjectives, applying to 'mouths' a term proper only to 'eyes'. Even then Milton is not speaking of the literal blindness of eyes but the figurative blindness of minds and souls.

57. Ian Green, 'Brian Duppa', *DNB*.

58. Pollard, *Hesperides and Noble Numbers*, I, xxii.

59. Herrick, 'The Argument of His Book', *Poetical Works*, 5.

60. Herrick, 'On Himselfe', *Poetical Works*, 17.

61. George Herbert, 'The Affliction'.

62. Samuel Rawson Gardiner, *The First Two Stuarts and the Puritan Revolution* (1908), 79–80.

63. Herbert, 'The Pearl'.

64. Gardiner, *The First Two Stuarts*, 79.

65. Wariston, *Diary*, I, 258, xxv, 265.

7. *The Court and the Covenant*

1. Sharpe, *Personal Rule*, 145; Millar, *Van Dyck in England*, 22.

2. Millar, *Van Dyck in England*, 22.

3. Millar, *Van Dyck in England*, 23.

4. Millar, *Van Dyck in England*, 50; Jeremy Wood, 'Anthony Van Dyck' ('Second Visit to London, 1632–4'), *DNB*.

5. See Timothy Raylor, *Cavaliers, Clubs and Literary Culture: Sir John Mennes, James Smith, and the Order of the Fancy* (1994), 74; Charles Nicholl, *Leonardo da Vinci: The Flights of the Mind* (repr. 2007), 98–9.

6. Suckling to the Earl of Middlesex, 'A Character', Clayton, 121. Clayton supports dating the letter to November 1631 but leaves open the possibility of it belonging to 1637–8, when Suckling's portrait was painted. It remains possible, too, that the portrait itself belongs to one of van Dyck's earlier periods in England – although Suckling's apparent maturity and the symbolic language of the study argue against such a dating.

7. Lovelace, 'To My Worthy Friend Mr Peter Lilly . . .', *Poems*, 58.

8. For an elaborated discussion see 'The Meaning of Van Dyck's Portrait of Sir John Suckling', *Burlington Magazine* 120 (1978), 741; meanwhile Thomas Clayton's comments are typically assured and astute in 'An Historical Study of the Portraits of Sir John Suckling', *Journal of the Warburg and Courtauld Institutes*, 23 (1960), 105–26.

9. Francis Bacon, *Advancement of Learning*, I, in B. Vickers, ed., *Major Works* (Oxford, 1996), 140; see note on 596.

10. Sharpe, *Personal Rule*, 233.

11. Beaurline, Commentary to *Aglaura*, 253.

12. Knowler, II, 150; Clayton, xliv–xlv.

13. Joel Elias Spingarn, ed., *Critical Essays of the Seventeenth Century*, 2 vols. (1908–9), II, 92.

14. Suckling, *Aglaura* (1.4), Beaurline, 44.

15. Suckling, *Aglaura* (2.5), Beaurline, 62.

16. Suckling, *Aglaura* (3.2), Beaurline, 67.

17. Suckling, *Aglaura*, 'Prologue to the Court', Beaurline, 96.

18. Richard Brome (?), 'By This Large Margent Did the Poet Meane' [upon Aglaura in Folio], Clayton, 202.

19. Quoted by Clayton, Commentary, 235.

20. Suckling, 'A Prologue of the Author's to a Masque at Wiston', Clayton, 28.

21. William Sainsbury Noel, ed., *Original Unpublished Papers Illustrative of the Life of Sir Peter Paul Rubens* (1858), 37.

22. Davenant, 'Galatea's Song', from *Britannia Triumphans*, Gibbs, 225.

23. Howell, 319.

24. Sharpe, *Personal Rule*, 553.

25. William Cobbett et al., ed., *Complete Collection of State Trials and Proceedings for High Treason and Other Crimes and Misdemeanors* (1809), 33 vols., III, 1098.

26. Bulstrode Whitelocke, *Memorials of the English Affairs* (1709), 24; Sharpe, *Personal Rule*, 726.

27. Thomas Hobbes, *Leviathan, or The Matter, Forme, & Power of a Commonwealth, Ecclesiasticall and Civil* (1651), ch. 24 (in the section on 'The Distribution of Land'), 129.

28. Hobbes, *Leviathan*, 129.

29. Davenant, 'The Queene, Returning to London after a Long Absence' (ll. 1–16), Gibbs, 47.

30. 'For the Lady, Olivia Porter. A Present, upon a New-Yeares Day' (ll. 1–8), Gibbs, 43.

31. Endymion Porter, 'To My Worthy Friend Mr. William Davenant; upon his Poem of *Madagascar*', Gibbs, 5.

32. Andrew Marvell, 'Last Instructions to a Painter' (ll. 29–34), *Poems and Letters*, ed. H.M. Margoliouth, rev. Pierre Legouis, 2 vols. (3rd edn, 1971), 148.

33. Dunlap, xxxv; Scott Nixon, 'Thomas Carew', *DNB*.

34. Thomas Carew, 'To Will Davenant My Friend', Gibbs, 8.

35. Knowler, I, 488; Howell, 656.

36. Patrick Morrah, *Prince Rupert of the Rhine* (1976), 33.

37. Princess Elizabeth to Sir Thomas Roe, 4 April 1636; quoted in Gibbs, Commentary, 343.

38. Davenant, 'Madagascar: A Poem Written to Prince Rupert' (ll. 37–62), Gibbs, 10.

39. Davenant, 'Madagascar' (ll. 110–14), Gibbs, 13.

40. Davenant, 'Madagascar' (l. 244), Gibbs, 16.

41. Davenant, 'Madagascar' (ll. 283–300), Gibbs, 17.

42. Davenant, 'Madagascar' (ll. 311–16), Gibbs, 18.

43. See Christopher G.A. Clay, *Economic Expansion and Social Change, England 1500–1700*, 2 vols. (1984), II, 30–31; Linda Levy Peck, 'New Wants, New Wares', in *Consuming Splendour*, 346–59.

44. Milton, 'A Masque Presented at Ludlow Castle' (ll. 715–17).

45. Milton, 'A Masque' (ll. 729–30).

46. Milton, 'A Masque' (ll. 768–73), *Major Works*, 64.

47. Davenant, 'Madagascar' (l. 322), Gibbs, 18.

48. Davenant, 'Madagascar' (ll. 443–4), Gibbs, 21.

49. Carew, 'To Will. Davenant', and Suckling, 'To My Friend Will. Davenant', Gibbs, 7–8.

50. Davenant, 'Song', Gibbs, 173. Gibbs prints the setting by Lawes on 290.

51. Davenant, 'O Thou that Sleep'st like *Pigg* in Straw', Gibbs, 215; Davenant, *Works*, II, 14b. See Douglas Bush's volume in the old *Oxford History of English Literature* series, *English Literature in the Earlier Seventeenth Century, 1600–1660* (rev. edn, 1962), 127.

52. Hutchinson, *Memoirs*, 45–6.

53. Hutchinson, *Memoirs*, 47.

54. Suckling, 'A Ballade upon a Wedding' (st. 1), Clayton, 79.

55. Suckling's ballad has traditionally been associated, though far from conclusively, to the marriage of Lady Ann Wentworth, a daughter of the Lord Deputy of Ireland, and John Lord Lovelace in July 1638, though scholars have also identified other candidates among the high social weddings of the period. On the textual and historical issues surrounding the poem see Clayton, 279–84 and Berry, 11–18. Berry prints what he takes to be an early draft of the poem at 19–25. See also Lovelace, *Poems*, Introduction, xxiv.

56. Suckling, 'A Ballade' (st. 2–3), Clayton, 80.

57. Hyde, *History*, I, 145–6.

58. David Stevenson, *The Scottish Revolution, 1637–1644* (2nd edn, Edinburgh, 2003), 100.

59. Stevenson, *Scottish Revolution*, 130.
60. Wariston, *Diary*, I, 275.
61. Wariston, *Diary*, I, 306, xxx, 280.
62. Wariston, *Diary*, I, 330–31.
63. Wariston, *Diary*, I, 385.

8. Northern Discoveries

1. Letter from Anne Merrick to one 'Mrs Lydall', 21 January 1639, *CSPD 1638–1639*, 342: Clayton, xlvi, Dunlap, xxxviii. Merrick was staying at Wrest, the seat of Thomas Carew's friends and patrons the Earl and Countess of Kent. See Michael P. Parker, 'To My Friend G.N. from Wrest': Carew's Secular Masque', in *Essays on Jonson and the Sons of Ben*, ed. Claude J. Summers and Ted-Larry Pebsworth (1982), 171–91, 172.
2. Suckling, 'An Exchange of Purported Letters between a London Alderman and a Scottish Lord, Summer–Autumn 1638', Clayton, 140–42.
3. Clayton, xlvii.
4. Aubrey, II, 242.
5. John Vernon, *The Young Horse-man or The Honest Plain-Dealing Cavalier* (1644), B2^v.
6. Vernon, *The Young Horse-man*, A3^r.
7. Cruso, *Military Instructions for the Cavallrie, or Rules and Directions for the Service of Horse* (1644), 2.
8. Sir John Mennes [?], 'Upon Sir John Suckling's Hundred Horse', Clayton, 204–5.
9. Heylyn, *Cyprianus Anglicus*, 360; quoted by Sharpe, *Personal Rule*, 803.
10. Sharpe, *Personal Rule*, 799, 803.
11. William Barriff, *Military Discipline, or The Young Artillerieman* (1635), 2.
12. Sharpe, *Personal Rule*, 233, warning specifically against the idea of a 'uniform courtly style and aesthetic'; this is largely the argument of his *Criticism and Compliment* (see especially chapter 1).
13. Herrick, 'His Cavalier', *Poetical Works*, 31.
14. Montaigne, *Essayes*, 'Of Experience', III, 361.
15. Suckling, *Brennoralt* (3.2.151–4), Beaurline, 213.
16. Suckling, 'An Exchange', Clayton, 140.
17. Carew, 'To My Friend G.N. from Wrest' [Autumn 1639?], Dunlap, 86.

18. Suckling, 'Epistolary Tract, April 1639: An Answer to a Gentleman in Norfolk that Sent to Enquire after the Scotish Business', Clayton, 142–4.

19. From Fynes Morison's account of his journey to Scotland in 1598, printed in *Early Travellers in Scotland*, 81.

20. Edward Norgate to Secretary Windebank, 28–9 May, *CSPD 1639*, 249.

21. Edmond, 77.

22. Aubrey, II, 245.

23. Sir John Mennes [?], '[Upon Sir John Sucklings Northern Discoverie]', Clayton, 207.

24. Hamilton to King Charles, 7 & 21 May 1639, *The Hamilton Papers*, ed. Samuel R. Gardiner (1880), 79, 84.

25. Suckling, 'To an Unknown Correspondent, late May or 1–2 June 1639', Clayton, 145.

26. Mennes [?], 'Upon Sir John Suckling's Hundred Horse', Clayton, 205.

27. Suckling, *Brennoralt*, Beaurline, 189.

28. Cruso, *Military Instructions for Cavalry*, 42, 50.

29. Suckling to the Earl of Middlesex, 6 June 1639, Clayton, 145–6.

30. Suckling to the Earl of Middlesex [?], 7–17 June 1639, 146–7.

31. Izaak Walton, *The Compleat Angler* (Everyman edn, 1906), 16. Pigeons had been famed as carriers since antiquity; Noah's dove, of course, being the first 'faithful and comfortable messenger' (Walton, 17).

32. Suckling, 'To an Unknown Correspondent [Before 18 June 1639]', Clayton, 147–8.

33. Mennes [?], '[Upon Sir John Suckling's Northern Discoverie]', Clayton, 207–8.

34. See E.G.R. Taylor, *Tudor Geography 1485–1583* (1930), 46.

35. On Mennes' supposed authorship of the 'Hundred Horse', see Clayton, 348–9 and Hazlitt, *Works of Sir John Suckling*, I, xli.

36. Raylor, *Cavaliers, Clubs and Literary Culture*, 32–5; C.S. Knighton, 'Sir John Mennes', *DNB*.

37. Raylor, *Cavaliers, Clubs and Literary Culture*, 76–7.

38. Suckling, *Brennoralt* (2.3.95–100), Beaurline, 206.

39. Suckling, *Brennoralt* (1.1.54), Beaurline, 188.

40. Suckling, *Brennoralt* (3.2.38–40), Beaurline, 210.

41. Richard Brome, *The Court Beggar*, in *Five New Playes* (1653; but probably composed *c.* 1640), P6; Beaurline, commentary on *Brennoralt*, 288.

42. Suckling, *Brennoralt* (3.2.99–103), Beaurline, 211.

43. Suckling to the Earl of Middlesex, 30 September 1639, Clayton, 148–9.

44. Suckling to Mary Bulkeley, Summer 1639, Clayton, 139.

45. Suckling to the Earl of Middlesex, 30 September 1639, Clayton, 149.

46. Suckling, 'A Disswasion from Love', Clayton, 158.

47. Suckling to Mary Bulkeley, Winter 1639/40 [?], Clayton, 139.

48. Suckling, 'A Disswasion from Love', Clayton, 159.

49. 'To the Earl of Middlesex from Sir George Southcot, 18 November 1635', Clayton, 200.

50. Suckling to Martha Lady Southcot, October 1639, Clayton, 149–50.

51. Mary Frederica Sophia Hervey, *The Life, Correspondence and Collections of Thomas Howard, Earl of Arundel* (1921), 418.

52. Suckling, *Brennoralt*, Beaurline, 209.

53. Suckling, *Brennoralt*, Beaurline, 210–11.

54. Carew, 'To My Friend G.N. from Wrest' (ll. 2–5), Dunlap, 86.

55. Carew, 'To My Friend G.N. from Wrest' (ll. 31–6), Dunlap, 87.

56. Aubrey, II, 220: the lines making the nature of Talbot and Selden's relationship explicit were censored in Andrew Clark's Victorian *Brief Lives*, but are restored in more recent collections.

57. On the identity of 'G.N.' see Dunlap, commentary, 256–7.

58. Carew, 'To My Friend G.N. from Wrest' (ll. 106–10), Dunlap, 89.

59. Carew, 'To Saxham' (l. 38), Dunlap, 28.

60. Parker, 'Carew's Secular Masque', 171.

61. Davenant, *Salmacida Spolia. A Masque. Presented by the King and Queenes Majesties . . .* (1640).

62. Suckling, 'On New-Years Day 1640. To the King', Clayton, 85.

63. Clayton, introduction, l.

64. *HMC, House of Lords Calendar*, 25.

65. Hyde, *Life*, I, 81.

66. Hyde, *History*, I, 342.

67. Hyde, *History*, I, 342.

68. Suckling to Edward Viscount Conway, April/May 1640, Clayton, 151.

69. Hyde, *Life*, I, 83–4.

70. Hyde, *Life*, I, 41.

71. Suckling, 'A Sessions of the Poets' (l. 96), Clayton, 75.

72. Hyde, *Life*, I, 59–60.

73. Dunlap, Introduction, liii.

74. Carew, 'An Elegie upon the Death of the Deane of Paules, Dr John Donne', Dunlap, 71. Carew's perhaps subtlest and most effective Donnean moment comes in the manuscript poem 'To a Friend' (Dunlap, 130–31). Rather than recycling a familiar figure from Donne's oeuvre – as Carew often did – it appropriates a Donnean technique, developing a complex observation (the muscular familiarity of a pianist's hand with a certain exercise) which is then applied metaphorically to illustrate another (the mind's custom of following a certain run of thoughts), and furnishes a reflection true to both (a loss of spontaneity, a sense of passion becoming over-rehearsed).

75. [George Wither?], *The Great Assises Holden in Parnassus by Apollo and his Assessours* (1645), 19.

76. [Wither?], *The Great Assises*, 25–7.

77. Carew, 'To My Worthy Friend *Master Geo. Sands*, on His Translation of the Psalmes.' (ll. 1–4, 23–8), Dunlap, 95–6.

78. Spalding, *History of the Troubles*, I, 335–6.

79. Hyde, *History*, I, 189–91.

80. Suckling, *Brennoralt* (5.2.283), Beaurline, 235.

9. *Plots and Prodigals*

1. Fuller, *Worthies*, 634.

2. Fuller, *Worthies*, 667.

3. Hyde, *History*, I, 192–3.

4. Hyde, *Life*, I, 31; Howell, 260.

5. Hyde, *Life*, I, 14–16.

6. Hyde, *Life*, I, 44.

7. Hyde, *Life*, I, 109.

8. Hyde, *History*, I, 183.

9. Hyde, *History*, I, 222.

10. Hyde, *History*, I, 220.

11. On the chief alienated faction, see Aidan Clarke, *The Old English in Ireland 1625–42* (1966); for the crux of their 'campaign for legislative independence', see 148–9.

12. Suckling, 'To Mr. Henry German, In the Beginning of Parliament 1640' (ll. 1–10, 25–8), Clayton, 163.

13. Hyde, *History*, I, 311.

14. Suckling, 'To Mr. Henry German' (ll. 78–84), Clayton, 165.

15. Suckling, 'To Mr. Henry German' (ll. 52–66), Clayton, 164–5. 'Of those now that lead those parties, if you could take off the major number, the lesser would governe, and doe the same things still; Nay if you could take off all, they would sett up one and follow him.'

16. Suckling, 'To Mr. Henry German' (ll. 85–8), Clayton, 165.

17. Suckling, 'To Mr. Henry German' (ll. 49–51), Clayton, 164.

18. Hyde, *Life*, I, 91–2.

19. Suckling, *Brennoralt* (1.3.73–7), Beaurline, 193.

20. Warwick, *Memoires of the Reigne of Charles I*, 235–6.

21. Quoted in Clayton, Introduction, liv. See the account of the conspiracy in Samuel Gardiner, *History of England from the Accession of James I to the Outbreak of the Civil War, 1603–42*, 10 vols. (1884–90), IX, 309–60.

22. Davenant, 'Written, When Collonell Goring Was Beleev'd to be Slaine, at the Siege of Breda', Gibbs, 72.

23. Sir Richard Bulstrode, *Memoirs and Reflections upon the Reign and Government of King Charles the 1ˢᵗ . . .* (1721), 134.

24. Russell, 'The First Army Plot of 1641', in *Unrevolutionary England, 1603–1642*, 281–302, 284–5.

25. Russell, 'The First Army Plot of 1641', 287.

26. Russell, 'The First Army Plot of 1641', 288–90.

27. Diary account of the Parliamentary committee's questioning of Suckling; Clayton, lv.

28. Russell, 'The First Army Plot of 1641', 292.

29. Russell, 'The First Army Plot of 1641', 292. Adamson, *The Noble Revolt*, 283.

30. 'The Sucklington Faction, or (Sucklings) Roaring Boyes' (1641); helpfully reprinted in Hazlitt, ed., *Works*, II (a folded insert between pp. 274 and 275).

31. Hyde, *History*, I, 326–7.

32. Russell, 'The First Army Plot of 1641', 296. Russell's specific deductions from the papers, many of which he brought to light for the first time, seem unassailable. It is his overall – and in this instance, lightly stressed – conclusion that the conduct of ordinary officers reflected an instinctive English 'constitutionalism' which begs further argument. First printed in 1988, his paper on the army plot shows this controversial historian doing what he did best – directing other scholars back to relevant sources.

33. Suckling, 'To Mr. Henry German' (ll. 71–3), Clayton, 165.

34. Suckling, 'To Mr. Henry German' (ll. 89–93), Clayton, 165.

35. Suckling, 'To Mr. Henry German' (ll. 122–9), Clayton, 166.

36. Suckling, 'Letter to Henry German', Clayton, 166.

37. Russell, 'The First Army Plot of 1641', 291.

38. Arthur Brett to the Earl of Middlesex [probably 6 or 7 May 1641], quoted in Clayton, lvi.

39. Lady Monmouth [Suckling's cousin] to the Earl of Middlesex, 5 May 1641, quoted in Clayton, lvi.

40. Edmond, 87–9, mustering a considerable array of sources on Davenant's arrest.

41. Hyde, *History*, I, 341–2.

42. Hyde, *History*, I, 307.

43. Hyde, *History*, I, 338.

44. William Scott and James Bliss, eds., *The Works of the Most Reverend Father in God, William Laud, D.D. Sometime Lord Archbishop of Canterbury*, 7 vols. (Oxford, 1847–60), III, 443.

45. John Rushworth, *The Tryal of Thomas Earl of Strafford* (1680), 743–4.

46. For two foundational discussions in the modern historiographical debate see Clarke, *The Old English in Ireland*, 220–34, and Russell, 'The British Background to the Irish Rebellion of 1641', *Unrevolutionary England*, 263–79. Clarke advanced the idea that foolish political trickery by the king during the summer of 1641 was integral in bringing the Old English over to the side of revolt.

47. The *Remonstrance* is printed in full in Harbage, *Sir William Davenant*, 84–5; Edmond gives a lovely reading of it, 89.

48. Michael P. Parker, 'Suckling in Paris', *Notes and Queries*, n.s., 232 (1987), 316–18; Clayton, *DNB*.

49. 'Four Fugitives Meeting, or, The Discourse amongst my Lord Finch, Sir Francis Windebank, Sir Iohn Sucklin, and Doctor Roane ...' (1641), printed in Hazlitt, ed., *Works*, II, 267–71.

50. Howell, 260.

51. Hyde, *History*, I, 196.

52. Suckling, *The Goblins* (4.3.10–12), Beaurline, 156.

53. Suckling, *The Goblins* (3.2.28–34), Beaurline, 142–3.

54. Joseph Spence, *Observations, Anecdotes, and Characters of Books and Men Collected from Conversation*, ed. James M. Osborn, 2 vols. (1966), I, 190–91.

55. Clayton, lx.

56. Howell, *Instructions for Forreine Travell*, ed. Edward Arber (1895), 26.

57. Sir William Vaughan, *The Golden Groue, Moralized in Three Bookes* (1608), E1ʳ.

10. Incivilities of War

1. Quoted by Godfrey Davies, *The Oxford History of England*, 9: *The Early Stuarts 1603–1660*, 120.

2. Conrad Russell, *The Causes of the English Civil War* (1990), 3.

3. *Strange Newes from Kent. Concerning the Passages of the Kentish Men which Came to Westminster, April 29* (1642), quoted in Lovelace, *Poems*, xxix.

4. Lovelace, 'Sonnet. To Generall Goring', *Poems*, 81.

5. Anthony à Wood, *Athenae Oxonienses*, III, 460.

6. *HMC, De L'Isle and Dudley*, IV, 286; quoted by Raymond A. Anselment, 'Richard Lovelace', *DNB*.

7. Philipott, *Villare Cantianum* (1659), 72; quoted in Lovelace, *Poems*, xiv.

8. 'De Domino *Richardo Lovelacio* . . .', in Lovelace, *Poems*, 14.

9. Lovelace, 'The Vintage to the Dungeon. A Song', *Poems*, 46.

10. Lovelace, 'A Guiltlesse Lady Imprison'd; after Penanc'd', *Poems*, 84.

11. Lovelace, 'To Althea, from Prison', *Poems*, 79.

12. Lovelace, 'A Guiltlesse Lady', *Poems*, 84.

13. Lovelace, Petition to the House of Commons, June 1642; *Poems,* xxxviii–xxxix.

14. Wood, *Athenae Oxonienses*, III, 460.

15. Green, *Letters of Henrietta Maria,* 61.

16. Howell, 126.

17. Green, *Letters of Henrietta Maria,* 51.

18. Green, *Letters of Henrietta Maria,* 134.

19. Warwick, *Memoires of the Reigne of Charles I*, 235–6.

20. From a letter from Newcastle's enemy Hotham the younger, quoted in Geoffrey Trease, *Portrait of a Cavalier,* 109.

21. Eliot Warburton, *Memoirs of Prince Rupert and the Cavaliers: Including Their Private Correspondence, Now First Published from the Original Manuscripts*, 3 vols. (1849), II, 13.

22. Warburton, *Memoirs of Prince Rupert*, II, 20.

23. Sir John Denham, 'Cooper's Hill', in *The Poetical Works of Sir John Denham*, ed. T.H. Banks, 2nd edn (Connecticut, 1969), 64. Denham revised his 1642 version of the poem, quoted here, and dulled much of its radicalism for a Restoration readership. Banks prints the earlier and later texts along with manuscript variants.

24. Denham, 'Cooper's Hill' (1642 version), *Poetical Works*, 86.

25. Aubrey, I, 217.

26. Hyde, *History*, III, 352.

27. Samuel R. Gardiner, *History of the Great Civil War*, 4 vols. (1893; repr. 1987), I, 7–9.

28. *Aeneid* VI, as the priestess escorts Aeneas to Hades.

29. Hyde, *Life*, I, 160; Miguel de Cervantes, *Don Quixote*, trans. Thomas Shelton [1612–20], 4 vols. (1896), III, 252.

30. From Richard Cattermole's account of the battle, quoted by Warburton, *Memoirs of Prince Rupert*, II, 33.

31. George Wither, *Campo-Musae: or the Field-Musings of Captain George Wither* (1643); quoted in a brilliant discussion of Wither and his work by David Norbrook, *Writing the English Republic: Poetry, Rhetoric and Politics 1627–1660* (1999), 88.

32. Aubrey, I, 221.

33. Aubrey, I, 219–20.

34. Aubrey, I, 206.

35. Hyde, *History*, II, 259–63.

36. Green, *Letters of Henrietta Maria*, 167.

37. Davenant, 'A New-Years-Gift to the Queen, in the year 1643', Gibbs, 134–6.

38. Nicholas Rowe, 'Account of the Life, &c, of Mr. *William Shakespear*', in *The Works of Mr. William Shakespear*, 6 vols. (1709), I.

39. Warburton, *Memoirs of Prince Rupert*, II, 227–30.

40. Aubrey, II, 226.

41. Warburton, *Memoirs of Prince Rupert*, II, 153.

42. Davenant, *Gondibert*, 1.5.37, *Works*, I, 65.

43. Green, *Letters of Henrietta Maria*, 225.

44. Leslie Hotson, *The Commonwealth and Restoration Stage* (Massachusetts, 1928), 9.

45. Hyde, *History*, III, 189.

46. John Gwynne, *Military Memoirs of the Great Civil War* (Edinburgh, 1822), 34–7.

47. Accounts of Falkland's death by Byron and Bulstrode Whitelocke are gathered by Gardiner in his *History of the Great Civil War*, I, 212–13.

48. Hyde, *History*, II, 178–9; Lucan, *Civil Wars*, IX.108.

49. Warburton, *Memoirs of Prince Rupert*, II, 307.

50. John Morrill, 'Robert Devereux, Third Earl of Essex', *DNB*.

51. Howell, 355.

52. Butler, *Hudibras* (2.2.799–808), 149. There is an echo in the last three lines of *Hamlet* 1.5.170–71 ('Well said, old mole . . . a worthy pioneer'), a subliminal indicator, perhaps, of something 'rotten' or amiss in nature and the state.

53. On the fortification of London and other physical and economic changes to the city, see two excellent recent volumes: David Flintham, *London in the Civil War* (2008) and Stephen Porter, ed., *London and the Civil War* (1996).

54. Howell, 360–61. Hooke observed the 'honeycomb' subdivisions of cork in the 1660s, coining the term 'cell' in his *Micrographia* (1665), and Van Leeuwenhoek studied 'animicules' under his microscope a decade later. By 'cells' Howell obviously did not refer to the microscopic structure of the brain as it is understood today; but to the broader 'compartments', usually responsible for various faculties, into which contemporary medicine divided the mind. He is being self-deprecatory, but being modest about his abilities rather than the size of his brain itself.

11. *Sulby Hedge*

1. Hotson, *Commonwealth and Restoration Stage*, 9: the author is George Wither, on whom see also Norbrook, *Writing the English Republic*, 87.

2. Davenant, 'To the Queen; Entertain'd at Night. In the Year 1644', Gibbs, 136.

3. *The Parliament Scout*, 24 November 1643 and *The True Informer*, 13 January 1644; quoted by Nethercot, 210, working from an unpublished dissertation by Leslie Hotson.

4. Warburton, *Memoirs of Prince Rupert*, II, 374–5.

5. Davenant, 'To the Queen . . . 1644', Gibbs, 138.

6. Nethercot, 212.

7. Warburton, quoting Richard Baker's *Chronicle*, *Memoirs of Prince Rupert*, II, 397.

8. Warburton, *Memoirs of Prince Rupert*, II, 395–6.

9. See Edmond, 94; Nethercot, 214–15; Harbage, *Sir William Davenant*, 93. The letter itself, written on 13 June from 'Haleford' (see Edmond's astute comment on the location, 232, note 41), is in British Library Addl. MS 20723, f.20.

10. A conflation of two reports quoted by Hotson, *Commonwealth and Restoration Stage*, 20.

11. C.V. Wedgwood, *The King's War* (1958), 315: Rupert interrogated a prisoner on the road to Long Marston, and set him free to deliver his challenge. 'By God's grace, he shall have fighting enough,' remarked Cromwell.

12. Cromwell, 'To My Loving Brother, Colonel Valentine Walton: These', in Thomas Carlyle, *Oliver Cromwell's Letters and Speeches, with Elucidations*, 3 vols. (Everyman edn, 1926), I, 152–3.

13. Herrick, 'To the King and Queene, upon Their Unhappy Distances', *Poetical Works*, 26.

14. Herrick, 'To the King, upon his Comming with his Army into the West', *Poetical Works*, 25.

15. Tom Cain, 'Robert Herrick', *DNB*, quoting a letter from one of Archbishop Laud's secretaries.

16. Herrick, 'Upon the Losse of His Finger', *Poetic Works*, 201.

17. Herrick, 'Dean-Bourn, a Rude River in Devon, by which He Sometimes Lived', *Poetic Works*, 29.

18. Herrick, 'Not Every Day Fit for Verse', *Poetic Works*, 238.

19. Herrick, 'Discontents in Devon', *Poetic Works*, 19.

20. Spalding, *History of the Troubles*, II, 443.

21. 'A More Exact Relation of the Great Victory . . . in Naisby Field' (1645).

22. Hotson, *Commonwealth and Restoration Stage*, 13.

23. Hotson, *Commonwealth and Restoration Stage*, 74; Edmond, 94, 96.

24. Marvell, 'To His Noble Friend Mr. Richard Lovelace, upon His Poems', *Poems and Letters*, I, 3.

25. Lovelace, 'To His Deare Brother Colonel F.L. . . . .', *Poems*, 86.

26. Hugh Peter, *Gods Doing, and Mans Duty* (1646), 24; quoted by Wedgwood, *The King's War*, 516.

27. Gardiner, *History of the Great Civil War*, II, 244–5.

28. Hyde, *Life*, I, 239–40.

29. Hyde, *History*, IV, 174.

30. Hyde, *History*, IV, 178.

31. Letter to Oliver St John, quoted in Edmond, 96.

32. Hyde, *History*, IV, 205.
33. Daniel Defoe, *A Tour through the Whole Island of Great Britain* (1971), 535.
34. *The Perfect Diurnall*, 19 October 1646: quoted by Nethercot, 228.
35. Nethercot suggests that Hyde decided to ignore letters from the king which indicate he took a much milder tone with the poet (229–30); Edmond agrees the *History*'s version 'is grossly exaggerated, and in part untrue' (99).
36. John Bruce, ed., *Charles I in 1646: Letters of King Charles the First to Queen Henrietta Maria* (Edinburgh, 1856), 71.
37. Edward Hyde, *State Papers Collected by Edward, Earl of Clarendon*, 3 vols. (1767–86), 277–8.
38. Hyde, *History*, IV, 206.
39. Banks, Introduction, *Poetical Works of Sir John Denham*, 11.
40. Denham, 'Epistle Dedicatory', *Poetical Works*, Banks, 59–60.
41. Edmund Whalley [?], 'A Letter from *Hampton-Court*, of the Manner of His Majesties Departure' (1647), A2.
42. Oglander, *Royalist's Notebook*, 107; arrival of Charles on Wight, 112–17.
43. *The Kings Cabinet Opened* (1645), 'Annotations', 43; 38–9.
44. Sir Thomas Herbert, *Memoirs of the Two Last Years of the Reign of King Charles I*, abridged in *The Trial of Charles I*, ed. Roger Lockyer (1960), 35, 52–3.
45. Ronald H. Fritze, 'Sir Thomas Herbert', *DNB*.
46. Summerson, *Architecture in Britain 1530–1830*, 90–91.
47. Hobbes, *Leviathan*, 149.
48. Howell, 337.
49. Howell, 507.
50. Howell, 516–17.
51. George Daniel, 'An Eclogue: Spoken by Hilas and Strephon', in *Poems*, ed. Alexander Grosart, 2 vols. (1878), II, 195; quoted by Clayton, lxvii–lxviii.
52. Howell, 552.

12. Angling for Quiet

1. Hyde, *Life*, I, 240.
2. Hyde, *Life*, I, 242–3.
3. Thomas Sprat, 'Account of the Life and Writing of Mr. Abraham Cowley',

in Abraham Cowley, *Poetry and Prose* [selections] (1949), ed. L.C. Martin, xx. A new edition of Cowley's works is in progress, ed. Thomas Calhoun et al. (New Jersey, 1989–); otherwise see A.R. Waller, ed., *The English Writings of Abraham Cowley*, 2 vols. (Cambridge, 1905–6).

4. Gilbert Burnet, *Some Passages of the Life and Death of the Right Honourable John, Earl of Rochester* (1680; in facsimile, 1875), 27–8.

5. Aubrey, I, 207.

6. Sir John Denham [?] et al., *Certain Verses Written by Severall of the Authors Friends* (1653), 3–4.

7. See Nethercot's entertaining account of Davenant's preparations, 258–60, working largely from a rich contemporary source, Jean Chevalier's *Journal*, 7 vols. (1906–14), I, 799.

8. See Clayton Colman Hall, *Narratives of Early Maryland* (New York, 1910), 179–80 and Nethercot, 256–8. Problems obviously exist with the transcription of the documents and the evolving orders they communicated; compare Edmond, 103 and Harbage, *Sir William Davenant,* 110–11.

9. Chevalier, *Journal*, I, 412; II, 473–6.

10. Abraham Cowley to Henry Bennet (later Earl of Arlington), in May 1650; letters printed in Thomas Brown, ed., *Miscellanea Aulica* (1702), 133–7. Hyde to Cowley, 12 July, Bodleian manuscript summarized in *Calendar of Clarendon State Papers*, II, 67–8. See also Harbage, *Sir William Davenant,* 112–13. Nethercot is unduly harsh to Hyde, 267; as Edmond points out (104), dealing expertly as ever with the same sources, news travelled with painful slowness between the exiles. Davenant's orders were only given final shape in a document drafted at Breda in June, over a month after his capture.

11. Hyde, *Life*, I, 248.

12. Hyde, *Life*, I, 250–51.

13. Hyde, *Life*, I, 317.

14. Hyde, *Life*, I, 266–7.

15. Hyde, *Life*, I, 278.

16. Hyde, *Life*, I, 292.

17. James Fitzmaurice, 'Margaret Cavendish, Duchess of Newcastle', *DNB*.

18. Hyde, *Life*, I, 292.

19. From Aubrey's 'Miscellanies', in *Three Prose Works*, ed. John Buchanan-Brown (1972), 70–71.

20. Hyde, *History*, V, 237.

21. Aubrey, *Three Prose Works*, 349.

22. Milton, 'To the Lord General Cromwell'.

23. Hyde, *History*, V, 240.

24. Walton, *Compleat Angler*, Third Day, 68.

25. Walton, *Compleat Angler*, Third Day, 50. See J.B. Leishmann's comment on the frequent seventeenth-century complaint against 'strong lines', in *The Monarch of Wit* (6th edn, 1962), 19. Insofar as Piscator's views may be identified with Walton's, the remark indicates the archaic rather than modern features he sought in the 'strong-lined' poets he obviously admired: Donne, Herbert and their imitators. No less a judge than Hobbes agreed with Walton: 'Which Expressions, though they have had the honour to be called strong lines, are indeed no better then Riddles, and not onely to the Reader, but also (after a little time) to the Writer himself dark and troublesome' ('The Answer of Mr Hobbes . . .', in Davenant, *Works*, I, 26).

26. In the preface to *Volpone*, dedicating the play to the 'two most equal sisters', the universities of Oxford and Cambridge.

27. Walton, *Compleat Angler*, Fourth Day, 87.

28. Walton, *Compleat Angler*, Third Day, 49–50.

29. Walton, *Compleat Angler*, Fifth Day, 189.

30. Walton, *Compleat Angler*, Fourth Day, 128.

31. Walton, *Compleat Angler*, Third Day, 57.

32. Hyde, *History*, IV, 486–7.

33. Marvell, 'An Horatian Ode upon Cromwell's Return from Ireland' (5–6), *Poems and Letters*, I, 91.

34. Marvell, 'Upon Appleton House' (769–72), *Poems and Letters*, I, 86.

35. Marvell, 'The Garden' (47–8), *Poems and Letters*, II, 52.

36. Marvell, 'Upon Appleton House' (349–52): see Commentary, *Poems and Letters*, I, 285.

37. Marvell, 'Upon Appleton House' (421–4).

38. Davenant, 'Preface to *Gondibert*', *Works*, I, 18.

39. Davenant, 'Preface to *Gondibert*', 9.

40. Gardiner, *History of the Great Civil War*, I, 8.

41. Elijah Fenton, 'Life' of Waller, in *The Works of Edmund Waller, Esq., in Verse and Prose* (1711), xxviii; Warren Chernaik, 'Edmund Waller', *DNB*.

42. Hyde, *History*, III, 53.

43. Edmond, 98; Nethercot, 224–6; Harbage, *Sir William Davenant*, 104.

44. Townshend, *Endymion Porter*, 209; 227–30.

45. Davenant, 'To All Poets upon the Recovery of Endimion Porter from a Long Sickness', Gibbs, 430. Commentators generally agree the poem dates from this period: see Edmond, 97.

46. Davenant, '*The First Dayes* Entertainment *at Rutland-House*', *Works*, I, 354–5.

47. Davenant, 'Preface to *Gondibert*', 7–8.

48. Davenant, *Gondibert* (II.i), 79–80.

49. Davenant, 'Preface to *Gondibert*', 5.g

50. Davenant, 'Preface to *Gondibert*', 6–7.

51. Aubrey, I, 347, 340.

52. Hobbes, *Leviathan*, chapter 43, 330–31.

53. Denham [?] et al., *Certain Verses Written by Severall of the Authors Friends*, 3–4.

54. Hobbes, 'The Answer', Davenant, *Works*, I, 27.

55. Davenant, 'Preface to *Gondibert*', 17.

56. Davenant, 'Preface to *Gondibert*', 15.

57. Davenant, 'Preface to *Gondibert*', 6.

58. Davenant, 'Preface to *Gondibert*', 14.

59. Davenant, 'Preface to *Gondibert*', 19.

60. Hobbes, *Leviathan*, chapter 19, 95.

61. Charles I/ John Gauden et al., *Eikon Basilike*, ed. Philip A. Knachel (Ithaca, 1966), 12: 'The sum of that business was this: those men and their adherents were then looked upon by the affrighted vulgar as greater protectors of their laws and liberties than myself, and so worthier of their protection.'

62. Davenant, 'Postscript to the Reader', *Works*, I, 196–7.

63. Aubrey, II, 233.

64. Aubrey, I, 207.

65. Nethercot, 268.

66. Edmond, 119.

67. Aubrey, I, 207–8; the authenticity of this anecdote has often been doubted (see Edmond, 117–18), but Marten was undoubtedly one of Davenant's chief sponsors – 'I had rather owe my libertie to you than to any man,' Davenant wrote to him shortly after the gag in question was made (Nethercot, 284–5).

68. Cowley, Preface to *Poems* (1656), in Martin, *Poetry and Prose*, 67.

69. Letter from Robert Whitley to Sir Edward Nicholas, quoted in Nethercot, 342.

70. T.H. Banks, following Wood, makes a case for Denham as the author of the lines (see *Poetical Works*, 94–5); but the verses are delivered by someone with an emphatically greater presence in London's theatrical community, someone speaking, in fact, *for* the profession. The light handling of historical matter ('Our Harries and our Edwards') is more in keeping with Davenant's court manner than Denham's, while the argument for the positive educational force of the popular theatre (though of course not original to Davenant), echoing the thought in the 'Preface to *Gondibert*', is also one the more classically minded Denham would have hestitated to make. The prologue, printed anonymously in 1660, is not included in any of Davenant's later gatherings (nor is it in Denham's), but the attribution is generally thought sound; the entire poem is reprinted in Hotson, *Commonwealth and Restoration Stage*, 208–9.

13. Twigs of Bay

1. Edmond, 98, 119–20; Nethercot, 285–7.
2. Davenant, *Gondibert*, 3.1.41–2, *Works*, I, 147.
3. Denham [?] et al., *Certain Verses*, 5–7; the poet clearly sets up Gondibert as a dummy Davenant – and alludes to his involvement in a street fight which is not on record elsewhere.
4. Davenant, 'Song. Endimion Porter, and Olivia', Gibbs, 173.
5. Henry Fletcher, *The Perfect Politician or a Full View of the Life and Actions . . . of O. Cromwell* (1660); quoted in Antonia Fraser, *Cromwell: Our Chief of Men* (2nd impression, 2004), 569.
6. Davenant, '*The First Dayes* Entertainment', 358.
7. Edmond, 120.
8. Nethercot, 300.
9. Edmond, 123–4; Nethercot, 301–4.
10. Aubrey, I, 208.
11. 'J.P.', *Tyrants and Protectors Set Forth in Their Colours* (1654); quoted in Hotson, *Commonwealth and Restoration Stage*, 10.
12. From Pepys's entry for 13 February 1667, quoted by Nethercot, 314.
13. Adams, *Dramatic Records of Sir Henry Herbert*, 123.
14. Nethercot, 330–31.
15. Denham, 'A Dialogue between Sir *John Pooley* and Mr. *Thomas Killigrew*'

and note; 'On Mr *Tho. Killigrew's* Return from his Embassie', *Poetical Works*, 103, 105, 111.

16. Cain, 'Robert Herrick', *DNB*.

17. For a preliminary survey of the evidence see V.M. Hirst, 'The Authenticity of James Howell's *Familiar Letters*', *Modern Language Review*, 54 (1959), 558–61.

18. Sprat, 'Account', xxii.

19. Wariston, *Diary*, III, 185.

20. Robert Wodrow, *History of the Sufferings of the Church of Scotland, from the Restoration to the Revolution*, ed. Robert Burns, 4 vols. (1838–9), I, 355–62; John Nicholl, *A Diary of Public Transactions and Other Occurrences, Chiefly in Scotland, from January 1650 to June 1667*, ed. D. Laing, Bannatyne Club, 52 (1836), 393–5; John Coffey, 'Sir Archibald Johnston', *DNB*.

21. Nethercot, 371.

22. Davenant, 'Epistle Dedicatory' to *The Siege of Rhodes*, *Works*, II, π^v.

23. Adams, *The Dramatic Records of Sir Henry Herbert*, 122.

24. Hotson, *Commonwealth and Restoration Stage*, 222.

25. Hotson, *Commonwealth and Restoration Stage*, 92.

26. Edmond, 181.

27. Quevedo, *Visions*, 72.

28. Burnet, *Passages*, 11, 18.

29. Davenant, *Works*, I, 351.

30. Nethercot, 399.

31. Fraser, *Cromwell*, 670.

32. Richard Flecknoe, *Sir William D'avenant's Voyage to the Other World* (1668), 6–7.

33. Dryden's preface to the 1670 edition of *The Tempest, or The Enchanted Island*, quoted by Edmond, 199.

34. Edmond, 202–3.

35. Anonymous, 'An Elegy upon the Death of Sr William Davenant', printed in Hotson, *Commonwealth and Restoration Stage*, 224–6.

36. Aubrey, I, 209.

37. Butler, *Hudibras* (3.1.1564), ed. Wilders, 232, and commentary, 420.

38. Davenant, 'Prologue [to 'The Wits'] Spoken at the Duke's Theatre', *Works*, II, 167.

39. Banks, Introduction, *Poetical Works of Sir John Denham*, 22; Aubrey, I, 219.

40. Denham, 'Friendship and Single Life against Love and Marriage', *Poetical Works*, 96.

41. Denham, 'Cato Major' (ll. 135–6), *Poetical Works*, 211.

42. Banks, Introduction, *Poetical Works of Sir John Denham*, 57.

43. Banks, Introduction, *Poetical Works of Sir John Denham*, 23–4; W.H. Keliher, 'Sir John Denham', *DNB*.

44. Aubrey, I, 220.

14. Aubrey

1. Aubrey, I, 39: '*Quid digni feci, hic processus viam?*'

2. Aubrey, I, 36–7.

3. Aubrey, II, 56.

4. Marvell, 'Tom May's Death' (40–42), *Poems and Letters*, I, 95.

5. Marvell, 'To His Noble Friend Mr. Richard Lovelace'(4, 19), *Poems and Letters*, I, 3.

6. Burnet, *Passages,* 26.

7. Aubrey, I, 11.

8. Davenant, 'To My Friend Mr. Ogilby, upon the Fables of Æsop Paraphrased in Verse', Gibbs, 155.

9. Aubrey, I, 2–3.

10. Edward Howard, *Poems and Essays, with a Paraphrase in Verse on Cicero's Lælius . . . Written in Heroic Verse by a Gentleman of Quality* (1674), 48–9; Gerard Langbaine, *An Account of the English Dramatick Poets* (1691), 498–9; these sources and other late-seventeenth-century criticism of Suckling discussed by Clayton, lxxi–lxxii.

11. Aubrey, II, 53–4.

12. Rochester's part in ordering this assault has been persuasively questioned by Frank H. Ellis, whose two-volume edition of the *Works* is now the standard, in his entry on the poet for the *DNB*; but suspicion will always linger. There is a touch of the 'who will rid me of this turbulent satirist' about Rochester's role in the affair, 'encrusted with misinformation' though it surely is.

13. Burnet, *Passages*, 13.

14. *A Miscellaneous Poem, Inscribed to the Earl of Oxford* (1712), 86; Clayton, lxxiii.

15. Alexander Pope, *Satires and Epistles of Horace Imitated*, II.I, l. 108 in *The Poems*, ed. John Butt (New Haven, 1963), 639; obviously referring as well to later, more haphazard versifiers such as Cleveland. See the thoughtful

review by Scott Nixon of David Norbrook's *Writing the English Republic* in *Early Modern Literary Studies* 5.2 (September 1999), which touches on how Pope's comment reflected and encouraged a habit of 'lumping' royalist writers together. In passing it should be noted that, privately, Pope himself was both apologetic and proud for often writing with ease: those familiar with Joseph Spence's *Anecdotes* may recall Pope stressing that a number of his major works were composed 'fast' (in Osborn's edition see, for example, I, 45).

16. See Peter Laslett's introduction to his edition of *Patriarcha and Other Political Works of Sir Robert Filmer* (Oxford, 1948), 1–46.

17. For a detailed analysis of the expropriations see Aidan Clarke, *Prelude to Restoration in Ireland: The End of the Commonwealth 1659–60* (Cambridge, 2006).

18. Summerson, *Architecture in Britain 1530–1830*, 95: the assessment of Clarendon House is John Evelyn's.

19. Marvell, 'Last Instructions to a Painter' (179, 342), *Poems and Letters*, I, 151, 156.

20. *The Life and Times of Anthony Wood, Antiquary, of Oxford*, ed. A. Clark, 5 vols. (1895), II, 117.

21. Aubrey, I, 13.

22. Aubrey, I, 11.

Further Reading

The following is a list of starting points for readers interested in pursuing some of the literary and historical topics approached in this book. It is selective in the extreme and does not duplicate items already given in the 'List of Abbreviations' prefixed to the notes above. Place of publication is London unless otherwise specified.

General Literary and Historical Sources

Bacon, Francis, *Works*, J. Spedding, R.L. Ellis and D.D. Heath, eds., 14 vols. (1857–74) [to be ventured upon with Brian Vickers's compact yet superbly annotated Oxford anthology of *Major Works* (1996) close to hand]

Beaumont, Francis and Fletcher, John, *Dramatic Works in the Canon of*, F. Bowers et al., ed., 10 vols. (1966–96)

Burnet, Bishop Gilbert, *Bishop Burnet's History of His Own Time*, 2 vols. (1838)

Davenant, Sir William, *Dramatic Works*, ed. James Maidment and W.H. Logan, 5 vols. (Edinburgh, 1872–4)

Evelyn, John, *Diary*, E.S. de Beer, ed., 6 vols. (repr. 2000)

Ford, John, *Dramatic Works*, W. Gifford and A. Dyce, eds., 3 vols. (1895)

Fuller, Thomas, *The Worthies of England*, John Freeman, ed. (1952)

Herbert, Sir Henry [Master of the Revels], *Dramatic Records . . . 1623–1673*, J.Q. Adams, ed. (New Haven, 1917) [see also Bawcutt's critical edn, below]

Hyde, Edward, Earl of Clarendon, *Calendar of the Clarendon State Papers Preserved in the Bodleian Library*, 5 vols. (Oxford, 1869–1970)

—*State Papers Collected by Edward, Earl of Clarendon*, 3 vols. (Oxford, 1767–86)

Jonson, Ben, *Works*, C.H. Herford and P. Simpson, eds., 11 vols. (Oxford, 1925–52)

May, Thomas, *A Breviary of the History of the Parliament of England: Expressed in Three Parts* (1680)

Orgel, Stephen and Strong, R., *Inigo Jones: The Theatre of the Stuart Court*, 2 vols. (1973)

Pepys, Samuel, *Diary*, R. Latham and W. Matthews, eds., 11 vols. (1970–83)

Spence, J., *Observations, Anecdotes, and Characters, of Books and Men*, J.M. Osborn, ed., 2 vols. (2nd edn, 1966)

Warburton, Eliot, *Memoirs of Prince Rupert and the Cavaliers: Including Their Private Correspondence, Now First Published from the Original Manuscripts*, 3 vols. (1849)

Whitelocke, Bulstrode, *Diary* . . . Ruth Spalding, ed. (Oxford, 1990)

Wood, Anthony à, *Athenae Oxonienses 1500–1690*, 2 vols. (1691–2)

Works on Seventeenth-Century Literature, History and Court Culture

Barton, Anne, *Ben Jonson, Dramatist* (Cambridge, 1984) [Still the standard modern introduction to the poet]

Bawcutt, N.W., ed., *The Control and Censorship of Caroline Drama: The Records of Sir Henry Herbert, Master of the Revels, 1623–73* (1996)

Bentley, G.E., *The Jacobean and Caroline Stage*, 2 vols. (Oxford, 1941)

Bevington, David, and Peter Holbrook, eds., *The Politics of the Stuart Court Masque* (Cambridge, 1999)

Butler, Martin, *Theatre and Crisis 1632–1642* (Cambridge, 1984)

Cowan, E.J., *Montrose for Covenant and King* (1977)

Harris, John, Orgel, Stephen and Strong, Roy, *The King's Arcadia: Inigo Jones and the Stuart Court* (1973)

Lindley, David, ed., *The Court Masque* (Manchester, 1984)

—*Court Masques: Jacobean and Caroline Entertainments 1605–1640* (Oxford, 1998)

Millar, Oliver, *The Tudor, Stuart and Early Georgian Pictures in the Royal Collection*, 2 vols. (1963)

Nicholl, Allardyce, *A History of English Drama 1660–1900*, 6 vols. (4th edn, 1967), I: *Restoration Drama 1660–1700*

Norbrook, David, *Writing the English Republic: Poetry, Rhetoric and Politics 1627–1660* (Cambridge, 1999)

Orgel, Stephen, *The Illusion of Power: Political Theater in the English Renaissance* (Berkeley, 1975)

—*The Jonsonian Masque* (Cambridge, Mass., 1965)

Orrell, John, *The Theatres of Inigo Jones and John Webb* (1985)

Parry, Graham, *The Golden Age Restor'd: The Culture of the Stuart Court, 1603–42* (Manchester, 1983)

Powell, Jocelyn, *Restoration Theatre Production* (1984)

Sharpe, Kevin, *Criticism and Compliment: The Politics of Literature in the England of Charles I* (Cambridge, 1987)

—and Peter Lake, eds., *Culture and Politics in Early Stuart England* (Stanford, 1994)

'Cavalier' Poetry: Critical Works

Some of the older works listed here conflate the pre-war and post-war senses of 'cavalier', a problem inherent in the use of the label as a critical term: they should thus be read alongside the volumes written and edited by Sharpe, Lake, Lindley and others mentioned above. However, all of those below are rich in critical insight and historical knowledge, and should not be neglected.

Chalmers, Hero, *Royalist Women Writers 1650–1689* (2004)

Clayton, Thomas, introduction to *Cavalier Poets: Selected Poems* (Oxford, 1978)

Hartmann, C.H., *The Cavalier Spirit: And Its Influence on the Life and Work of Richard Lovelace* (1925)

McEuen, K.A., *The Classical Influence upon the Tribe of Ben* (2nd edn, 1968)

Miles, Josephine, *The Primary Language of Poetry in the 1640s* (Berkeley, 1948)

Raylor, Timothy, *Cavalier Clubs and Literary Culture: Sir John Mennes, James Smith, and the Order of the Fancy* (1994)

Selig, Edward I., *The Flourishing Wreath: A Study of Thomas Carew's Poetry* (repr., Connecticut, 1970)

Skelton, Robin, *Cavalier Poets* (1960)

Summers, C.J., and T.-L. Pebworth, eds., *Classic and Cavalier: Essays on Jonson and the Sons of Ben* (1982)

Walton, G., *Metaphysical to Augustan* (Cambridge, 1935)

Intellectual and Religious Background

Cogswell, Thomas, *Blessed Revolution: English Politics and the Coming of War 1621–1624* (Cambridge, 1989)

Colclough, David, *Freedom of Speech in Early Stuart England* (Cambridge, 2005)

Collinson, Patrick, *The Elizabethan Puritan Movement* (repr., Oxford, 1990)

Hill, Christopher, *The Origins of the English Revolution Revisited* (revised edn, Oxford, 1997)

—*The World Turned Upside Down: Radical Ideas during the English Revolution* (1973)

Hobbes, Thomas, *Correspondence*, Noel Malcolm, ed., 2 vols. (Oxford, 1994) [The letters and Malcolm's excellent notes offer a superb way of gaining a sense of the intellectual activity of the period]

Kerrigan, John, *Archipelagic English: Literature, History, and Politics, 1603–1707* (Oxford, 2008)

MacCulloch, Diarmaid, *Reformation: Europe's House Divided 1490–1700* (2003)

Mack, Peter, *Elizabethan Rhetoric: Theory and Practice* (Cambridge, 2002)

Masson, David, *The Life of John Milton*, 7 vols. (1859–94)

Milton, Anthony, *Catholic and Reformed: Roman and Protestant Churches in English Protestant Thought, 1600–40* (Cambridge, 1995)

—*Laudian and Royalist Polemic in Seventeenth-Century England: The Career and Writings of Peter Heylyn* (Manchester, 2007)

Moss, Ann, *Printed Commonplace-Books and the Structuring of Renaissance Thought* (Cambridge, 1996)

Skinner, Quentin, *Liberty before Liberalism* (Cambridge, 1998)

—*Visions of Politics*, 3 vols. (Cambridge, 2002), III: *Hobbes and Civil Sciences*

Smith, David L., *Constitutional Royalism and the Search for Settlement, c. 1640–1649* (Cambridge, 1994)

Civil War, Republic and Restoration

Adair, B., *By the Sword Divided: Eyewitness Accounts of the English Civil War* (1983)

Adamson, John, *The Noble Revolt: The Overthrow of Charles I* (2007)

Atkin, M. and Laughlin, W., *Gloucester and the Civil War* (1992)

Barnard, T.C., *Cromwellian Ireland* (Oxford, 1975)

Bennett, Martyn, *The Civil Wars in Britain and Ireland 1638–1651* (Oxford, 1957)

Dow, Frances, *Cromwellian Scotland* (Edinburgh, 1979)

Fissell, Mark Charles, *The Bishops' Wars: Charles I's Campaigns against Scotland 1639–1640* (Cambridge, 1994)

Gardiner, Samuel R., *The Commonwealth and Protectorate*, 4 vols. (1892)

—*The History of the Great Civil War 1642-1649*, 4 vols. (1893)

Gentles, Ian, *The New Model Army in England, Ireland and Scotland, 1645–1653* (Oxford, 1992)

Harris, Tim, *Restoration: King Charles and His Kingdoms* (2005)

Hutton, R., *The Royalist War Effort 1642–1660* (New York, 1982)

Kearney, Hugh, *Strafford in Ireland 1633–1641: A Study in Absolutism* (2nd edn, Cambridge, 1989)

Kenyan, J.P., *The Civil Wars of England* (1988)

Morrill, John, *The Revolt of the Provinces* (1976)

—(ed.), *The Scottish National Covenant in Its British Context 1638–1651* (Edinburgh, 1990)

Newman, P.R., *Royalist Officers in England and Wales 1641–1660: A Biographical Dictionary* (New York, 1981)

Perceval-Maxwell, M., *The Outbreak of the Irish Rebellion of 1641* (Dublin, 1994)

Royle, Trevor, *Civil War: The War of the Three Kingdoms 1638–1660* (2004)

Russell, Conrad, *The Causes of the English Civil War* (Oxford, 1990)

—*The Fall of the British Monarchies* (Oxford, 1991)

Stevenson, David, *Revolution and Counter-Revolution in Scotland, 1644–51* (2nd edn, Edinburgh, 2003)

—*The Scottish Revolution 1637–44* (2nd edn, Edinburgh, 2003)

Varley, F.J., *The Siege of Oxford* (1932)

Young, P., and Emberton, W., *Sieges of the Great Civil War* (1978)

Social and Political History

Carlton, C., *Going to the Wars: The Experience of the British Civil Wars, 1638–1651* (1994)

Clarke, Aidan, *The Old English in Ireland* (1966)

Durston, C., *The Family and the English Civil War* (Oxford, 1988)

Gardiner, Samuel R., *The History of England: From the Accession of James I to the Outbreak of the Civil War, 1603–1642*, 10 vols. (1883–4) [Standard reading, but see also his earlier, cheekier]

—*A History of England under the Duke of Buckingham and Charles I* (1875)

Heal, Felicity, and Holmes, Clive, *The Gentry in England and Wales, 1500–1700* (1994)

Lockyer, Roger, *Buckingham: The Life and Political Career of George Villiers, First Duke of Buckingham, 1592–1628* (1981)

Peck, Linda Levy, *Consuming Splendour: Society and Culture in Seventeenth-Century England* (Cambridge, 2005)

—*Court Patronage and Corruption in Early Stuart England* (1993)

—(ed.), *The Mental World of the Jacobean Court* (1991)

Peltonen, Markku, *The Duel in Early Modern England: Civility, Politeness and Honour* (Cambridge, 2003)

Russell, Conrad, *Unrevolutionary England, 1603–1642* (1990)

Sharpe, Kevin, *The Personal Rule of Charles I* (1992)

Smith, Geoffrey, *The Cavaliers in Exile, 1640–1660* (2003)

Spurr, John, *The Restoration Church of England 1646–1689* (1991)

Stone, Lawrence, *The Crisis of the Aristocracy 1558–1641* (1967)

Stoye, John Walter, *English Travellers Abroad, 1604–1667: Their Influence in English Society and Politics* (1952)

Acknowledgements

This book grew out of some work on a group of poets of the 1630s, mostly admirers of Ben Jonson and John Donne. I was interested in recovering and exploring some of the contexts and personalities invoked in, for example, the old *Oxford Book of Seventeenth-Century Verse*, and finding out how so many of the latter came to be cavaliers. In doing so I learned how the various writings of these 'gallants' might allow one to navigate and narrate the immensely complicated period – surely the Bermuda Triangle of British and Irish historiography – in which they were formed. What began as quite a localized investigation thus turned into a somewhat larger task, and I'm consequently indebted to many people for their help and encouragement. Some taught me to understand the subject-matter better, some to communicate my sense of it more clearly, while others simply made it possible to get on with the work; and a great many of those I can only mention below lent their aid in all these respects.

Toby Eady, literary agent and a vital mentor, challenged me to enlarge the initial historical scope, and take the story through the civil wars and into the Restoration. He along with Jamie Coleman and Laetitia Rutherford helped me draw the material out into more concrete form and give the work direction as a project. Susan Hitch and David Norbrook discussed some ideas with me at an early stage; indeed Susan first suggested the literary and philosophical milieu of Lucius Cary as a subject. The writing took me into less refined company, but the idea for following a generation was hers. I would also like to say thank you to Nicholas Seddon for our talks, years ago now at Cambridge, on Jonson, Donne and the Great Tew circle. Robert Macfarlane, as ever a great friend and an inspiration, talked through many versions of this book, in conversation and correspondence, and offered crucial thoughts on both approach and execution.

For helping me bring the thing from an outline to a narrative I am lucky to have such a clear-sighted editor in Mary Mount. I would also like to thank Keith Taylor and the whole team at Viking and in particular Will Hammond for his comments during the process. In the final stages Sarah Day copy-edited the text with extraordinary care and attention: I'm very thankful indeed to her. The index was prepared by Janet Dudley.

It goes without saying that responsibility for the book's remaining errors and shortcomings is entirely mine. But there would be many more had I not received a lot of help along the way. In approaching the writing, I owe a great deal to thoughts offered by biographers, historians and other writers and researchers, on sometimes unrelated topics but often common pursuits: in various contexts, Peter Ackroyd, Anna Beer, Maggie Fergusson, Hazel Forsyth, John Fuller, Jonathan Heawood, Dominic Hibberd, Thomas A. Green, Hisham Matar, Andrew McConnell Stott, William Ian Miller, Ruth Padel, Simon Schama, Miranda Seymour and John Worthen all helped me make progress. For their interest in my work I would also like to thank Paula Johnson and Thomas Ponsonby, my friends at the Jerwood Trust, David Grylls of the Continuing Education programme at Oxford, Alan Morrison at the University of Westminster, David Ryland and all at the Suffolk Book League, Jonathan Beckman, Brendan Barrington at Penguin Ireland, the directors and staff of the Irish Writers' Centre in Dublin and the judges of the 2007 Glen Dimplex/Irish Writers' Centre New Writers' Award.

In places the book draws on research I carried out for my MPhil (2002) and doctorate (2005). I would like to thank Gavin Alexander, Colin Burrow and John Kerrigan, my supervisors and advisers at Cambridge, for their guidance and instruction during my graduate and postgraduate studies, and for deepening my enjoyment and interest in early modern literature. This is a welcome opportunity as well to thank Raphael Lyne for an ongoing dialogue on Renaissance rhetoric.

Although I hope the notes on the text go at least some way to meeting my scholarly obligations, I must express a more general sense of indebtedness here to the research community, present and past. Anyone working in British and much Irish history, indeed most with an abiding interest in it, will know what a fabulous resource the new *Oxford Dictionary of National Biography* is, and many will share my wonder and gratitude for the online edition. My thanks go to the editors of the project and the authors of all the entries I have used. In addition I would particularly like to acknowledge the scholarship of Thomas Clayton and Herbert Berry on Suckling and that of Mary Edmond on Davenant. In my own research I owe thanks especially to the staff of the University Library, Cambridge.

I must pay special tribute to two wonderful friends and teachers. I am extremely grateful to Christopher Burlinson and David Colclough for each reading large portions of an evolving manuscript. In their writing and in our conversations both have taught me a huge amount, and profoundly affected my approach to literature and history. It was a privilege to receive these scholars' notes. Both suggested a great many improvements to content, style and structure, and were unfailingly generous – as always – with their time and their learning.

Patricia Boulhosa and Noah Charney also read parts of the book for clarity and coherence: I'm very appreciative of their acuity as readers and critics as well as their personal support. Many other friends gave specialist direction on points relating to the text: at the University here in Ljubljana I would like to thank Matej Accetto, Matjaž Jager, Miha Pintarič, Renata Salecl, Jure Smole, Katja Škrubej and Aleš Završnik for their help with problems of philosophy, art history and literary and legal theory. Aleš Novak and I have generally used our walks and discussions over the years to escape the confines of our own work, on literary history in my case and the philosophy of law in his: but they have always brought new light and fresh air to whatever topic I was tackling at the time, and I cannot but acknowledge his influence here.

Also for their moral and in some cases material support I would like to send the warmest of thanks to Bernadette Aubert, Patrice Braconnier, Jožica Demšar, David Dunton, Ciara and Paul Ferrier, my brothers Conal and Daniel, Denise and Robin Gallagher, Irena Ivelja, Richard Lodge, Michel Massé, Zoran Milivojevič, Iggy McGovern, Alan Monger, Helen and Richard Mountford, Boštjan Novak, Philip and Sylvia O'Doherty, John and Kriszti na Pheby, Nicky and Christopher Padfield, Tanja Gostinčar Smole, Christopher and Mary Stubbs, Betka and Rajko Šugman, Jernej and Andreja Šugman, Lea Šugman Bohinc and Metod Bohinc, Ann and Steve White, Dean Zagorac, Barbara Vrečko and

Borut Šantej. Borut found me a room to do my writing across the corridor from his office. I might have lost my sense of humour altogether without his practical help, the benefit of his thoughts and reading, and our essential coffees.

Above all my thanks go to my wife Katja, for listening, reading, responding, keeping me going and putting up with me. The book is dedicated to her and our children Lana and Martin, but many volumes would be needed to do justice to the joy they bring me.

Ljubljana, July 2010

Index